ROMAN STATE &

CHRISTIAN CHURCH

ROMAN STATE
&
CHRISTIAN CHURCH

A Collection of Legal Documents
to A.D. 535

P. R. COLEMAN-NORTON

VOLUME ONE

WIPF & STOCK · Eugene, Oregon

Wipf and Stock Publishers
199 W 8th Ave, Suite 3
Eugene, OR 97401

Roman State & Christian Church Volume 1
A Collection of Legal Documents to A.D. 535
By Coleman-Norton, P. R.
Copyright©1966 SPCK
ISBN 13: 978-1-5326-6615-5
Publication date 8/23/2018
Previously published by SPCK, 1966

AD MAIOREM DEI GLORIAM

PER QVEM REGES REGNANT ET LEGVM CONDITORES

IVSTA DECERNVNT

ATQVE

IN MEMORIAM

IMPERATORVM CAESARVM

CONSTANTINI THEODOSII IVSTINIANI

AVGVSTORVM NOMINATORVM MAGNORVM

QVI PROVIDENTIA DEI FIDEI DEFENSORES

ECCLESIAM CHRISTIANAM ENIXISSIME CONFIRMAVERVNT

CONTENTS

VOLUME ONE

Preface	vii
Abbreviations	ix
Table of Documents	xi
Introduction	xxxvii
Names and Dates of Emperors	lxxiii
Documents Nos. 1–177	1

VOLUME TWO

Documents Nos. 178–486	371

VOLUME THREE

Documents Nos. 487–652	845
Appendix on Persecutions	1179
Titles of Address	1197
Glossary	1199
INDEXES	
Sources	1249
Persons	1254
Places	1279
Subjects	1288
Biblical Quotations and Allusions	1344
Classical Quotations and Allusions	1348
Legal Quotations and Allusions	1350
Patristic Quotations and Allusions	1355

PREFACE

My obligations to scholars who have written on Roman law and on Christian patrology are perhaps obvious and, I hope, are acknowledged adequately. But I wish to thank Mrs Elizabeth Craddock Casale for lending to me her unpublished dissertation, *A Study in Roman Ecclesiastical Legislation: An Annotated Translation of the Sixteenth Book of the Theodosian Code*, which was submitted successfully to Vanderbilt University for her doctorate in 1946. And I owe particular thanks to Professor Clyde Pharr, of the University of Texas, for most generous permission to use his monumental translation of *The Theodosian Code and Novels and the Sirmondian Constitutions* (Princeton, 1952). To Doctor Kenneth Sperber Gapp, Librarian of the Princeton Theological Seminary, I am grateful for the courteous privilege of borrowing books from the seminary's library for extended periods.

The late Professor Allan Chester Johnson and Professor Frank Card Bourne, both of Princeton University, read portions of the typescript (particularly documents anterior to A.D. 364) and suggested improvements in it.

To the University Research Committee of Princeton University, which not only subsidized the conversion of manuscript into typescript, but also contributed to the cost of typesetting, and to my departmental colleagues, who authorized from the William Kelly Prentice Publishing Fund a liberal subvention for printing, I express my appreciation.

Thanks are also due to the following for permission to use extracts from copyright sources: The Clarendon Press (B. J. Kidd's *History of the Church*), Professor François Graffin (*Patrologia Orientalis*), the Society of Authors and Mr Christopher Dawson (*The Making of Europe*), and the University of Chicago Press (an article by F. C. Conybeare in the *American Journal of Theology*, Vol. 9, 1905).

I am indebted also to the Society for Promoting Christian Knowledge for their interest and assistance in the production of this sylloge.

Princeton University　　　　　　　　　　　　　　　　　P.R.C.-N.
10 May 1961

ABBREVIATIONS

A superior figure after a book's title indicates the edition used.

AJT	*American Journal of Theology* (Chicago, 1897–1920)
Bury	J. B. Bury, *History of the Later Roman Empire* (2 vols., London, 1923)
CA	*Constitutiones Apostolorum*
CAH	S. A. Cook et al., *The Cambridge Ancient History* (vols. 10–12, Cambridge, 1934–9)
CG	*Codex Gregorianus* (see *FIRA*)
CH	*Codex Hermogenianus* (see *FIRA*)
CI	P. Krueger, *Codex Iustinianus*[11] (Berlin, 1954)
CMH	J. B. Bury et al., *The Cambridge Medieval History* (vols. 1–2, Cambridge, 1911–13)
CS	*Constitutiones Sirmondianae* (see *CT*)
CSEL	*Corpus Scriptorum Ecclesiasticorum Latinorum* (Wien, 1866–)
CT	T. Mommsen and P. M. Meyer, *Theodosiani Libri XVI cum Constitutionibus Sirmondianis et Leges Novellae ad Theodosianum Pertinentes*[2] (2 vols. in 3 parts, Berlin, 1954)
Coleman	C. B. Coleman, *Constantine the Great and Christianity* (New York, 1914)
Coll.	*Mosaicarum et Romanarum Legum Collatio* (see *FIRA*)
D	T. Mommsen and P. Krueger, *[Iustiniani] Digesta*[16] (Berlin, 1954)
Denny	E. Denny, *Papalism* (London, 1912)
FIRA	S. Riccobono et al., *Fontes Iuris Romani Antejustiniani*[2] (3 vols., Firenze, 1940–43)
GI	F. de Zulueta, *The Institutes of Gaius* (2 vols., Oxford, 1946–53)
Gibbon	E. Gibbon, *The History of the Decline and Fall of the Roman Empire* (6 vols., London, 1776–88; ed. by J. B. Bury, 7 vols., London, 1896–1900)
H	G. Haenel, *Corpus Legum ab Imperatoribus Romanis ante Iustinianum Latarum* (2 parts in 1 vol., Leipzig, 1857–60)
HE	*Historia Ecclesiastica*
HTR	*Harvard Theological Review* (New York: Cambridge, 1908–)
Huttmann	M. A. Huttmann, *The Establishment of Christianity and the Proscription of Paganism* (New York, 1914)

ABBREVIATIONS

II	J. B. Moyle, *Imperatoris Iustiniani Institutionum Libri Quattuor* [5] (Oxford, 1912)
ILCV	E. Diehl, *Inscriptiones Latinae Christianae Veteres* (3 vols., Berlin, 1925–31)
Introd.	Introduction to this Sylloge
introd.	Introduction to a document in this Sylloge
JRS	*Journal of Roman Studies* (London, 1911–)
JTS	*Journal of Theological Studies* (London, 1899–)
Jalland	T. G. Jalland, *The Church and the Papacy* (London, 1944)
Kidd	B. J. Kidd, *A History of the Church to A.D. 461* (3 vols., Oxford, 1922)
LNMaior.	*Leges Novellae Maioriani* (see *CT*)
LNMarc.	*Leges Novellae Marciani* (see *CT*)
LNS	*Leges Novellae Severi* (see *CT*)
LNT	*Leges Novellae Theodosii II* (see *CT*)
LNV	*Leges Novellae Valentiniani III* (see *CT*)
M	G. D. Mansi, *Sacrorum Conciliorum Nova et Amplissima Collectio* (vols. 3–9, Firenze, 1759–63)
MAMA	W. M. Calder *et al.*, *Monumenta Asiae Minoris Antiqua* (Manchester, 1928–)
MARE	F. F. Abbott and A. C. Johnson, *Municipal Administration in the Roman Empire* (Princeton, 1926)
N	R. Schoell and G. Kroll, *[Iustiniani] Novellae* [6] (Berlin, 1954)
P	S. G. F. Perry, *The Second Synod of Ephesus* (Dartford, 1881)
PG	J. P. Migne, *Patrologia Graeca* (Paris, 1857–66)
PL	J. P. Migne, *Patrologia Latina* (Paris, 1844–66)
PO	R. Graffin *et al.*, *Patrologia Orientalis* (Paris, 1907–)
Palanque	J. R. Palanque *et al.*, *The Church in the Christian Roman Empire* (vols. 1–, London, 1949–)
Pitra	J. B. Pitra, *Iuris Ecclesiastici Graecorum Historia et Monumenta* (vol. 2, Roma, 1868)
SEG	J. J. E. Hondius *et al.*, *Supplementum Epigraphicum Graecum* (Leiden, 1923–)
TT	P. R. Coleman-Norton, *The Twelve Tables* [5] (Princeton, 1960)
Toynbee	A. J. Toynbee, *A Study of History* [1-2] (10 vols., London, 1934–54)
VC	*Vita Constantini*
Vasiliev	A. A. Vasiliev, *History of the Byzantine Empire* (Madison, 1952)

TABLE OF DOCUMENTS

VOLUME ONE

1. Rescript of Trajan on Trials of Christians, c. 113	1
2. Rescript of Hadrian on Trials of Christians, c. 121	5
3. Letter of Aurelius on Trials of Christians, c. 161	8
4. Rescript of Gallien on Restoration of Christians' Property, 260	13
5. Mandate of Aurelian on Persecution of Christians, 273 or 274	16
6. Letter of Maximian I on Persecution of Christians, c. 301	17
7. Edict of Galerius on Toleration of Christians, 311	18
8. Letter of Sabinus on Maximin II's Orders about Christians, 311	22
9. Rescript of Maximin II on Anti-Christian Petitions, 311 or 312	24
10. Letter of Constantine I on Restitution of Property to the Church, 313	27
11. Edict of Licinius on Military Prayer, 313	29
12. Letter of Constantine I and Licinius on Restoration of the Church, 313	30
13. Letter of Maximin II on Behalf of Christians, 313	35
14. Edict of Maximin II on Behalf of Christians, 313	38
15. Letter of Constantine I on State Subsidies to Churches and on Seducers of Christians, 313	41
16. Letter of Constantine I on Clerical Exemption from Public Duties, 313	43
17. Letter of Constantine I on the Donatist Schism, 313	46
18. Letter of Constantine I on the Donatist Schism, 313	51
19. Letter of Constantine I on the Donatist Schism, 313	53
20. Letter of Constantine I on a Donatist Appeal from Catholic Bishops, 314	59
21. Rescript of Constantine I, Maximin II, and Licinius on a Donatist Forger, 315	62
22. Letter of Constantine I on Personal Cognition of Donatist Bishops' Appeal, 315	65
23. Mandate of Constantine I on Jewish Molestation of Christians, 315	66
24. Letter of Constantine I on Personal Cognition of the Donatist Schism, 315	68
25. Letter of Annian and Julian on Transportation for Donatist Clergy, 316	71
26. Mandate of Constantine I on Manumission in Church, 316	72
27. Letter of Constantine I on Caecilian's Innocence, 316	73

TABLE OF DOCUMENTS

28. Edict of Constantine I on Episcopal Jurisdiction, 318 — 74
29. Mandate of Constantine I on Clerical Exemption from Public Duties, 319 — 76
30. Mandate of Constantine I on Clerical Exemption from Public Duties, (?)319 — 77
31. Edict of Constantine I on Rescission of Penalties for Celibacy and for Childlessness, 320 — 77
32. Edict of Constantine I on Clerical Exemption from Taxation, 320 — 79
33. Mandate of Constantine I on Admission of Poor Persons to the Clericate, 320 — 81
34. Mandate of Constantine I on Recognition of Sunday, 321 — 82
35. Mandate of Constantine I on Manumission in Church, 321 — 84
36. Edict of Constantine I on Legacies to the Church, 321 — 85
37. Mandate of Constantine I on Emancipation and Manumission on Sunday, 321 — 86
38. Edict of Constantine I on Military Prayer, (?)321 — 87
39. Letter of Constantine I on Toleration of Donatists, 321 or 322 — 88
40. Letter of Constantine I on Transfer of Heretics' Oratories to the Church, 322 or 332 — 90
41. Mandate of Constantine I on Clerical Immunity from Pagan Sacrifices, 323 — 92
42. Rescript of Licinius on Punishment of Christians, c. 323 — 93
43. Letter and Rescript of Constantine I, Constantine II, and Constantius II on Status of Orcistus, 323–31 — 95
44. Letter of Constantine I on Condemnation of Idolatry and on Behalf of Peace, 324 — 98
45. Letter of Constantine I on Repair and Construction of Churches, 324 — 103
46. Edict of Constantine I on Behalf of Christians, 324 — 106
47. Letter of Constantine I on the Arian Controversy, 324 — 114
48. Letters of Constantine I on Convocation of the Nicene Council, 324–5 — 122
49. Decree and Orations of Constantine I on Conciliar Procedure, 325 — 127
50. Letter of Constantine I on Exile of Eusebius, 325 — 135
51. Letter of Constantine I on Conformity with Orthodoxy, 325 — 142
52. Letter of Constantine I on the Paschal Question, 325 — 143
53. Letter of Constantine I on Conformity with Orthodoxy, 325 — 150
54. Letter of Constantine I on Erection of the Church of the Holy Sepulchre, 326 — 153
55. Mandate of Constantine I on Exclusion of Rich Persons from the Clericate, 326 — 156
56. Mandate of Constantine I on Clerical Privileges, 326 — 157
57. Mandate of Constantine I on Privileges for Novatians, 326 — 158
58. Letter of Constantine I on Recall of Arius, 327–34 — 158

TABLE OF DOCUMENTS xiii

59. Letter of Constantine I on Clerical Exemption from Public Duties and on Construction of a Basilica in Numidia, 330 — 159
60. Mandate of Constantine I on Clerical Exemption from Senatorial Service, 330 — 163
61. Letters of Constantine I on Episcopal Election, 330 — 164
62. Law of Unknown Emperor on Clerical Defendants in Lawsuits, 330–534 — 169
63. Letter of Constantine I on Suppression of Idolatry and on Erection of a Basilica at Mambre, 332 — 172
64. Letter of Constantine I on Preparation of Copies of the Bible, 333 — 174
65. Rescript of Constantine I on Confirmation of Episcopal Jurisdiction, 333 — 177
66. Letter of Constantine I on Arianism, c. 333 — 182
67. Rescript of Constantine I on Arianism, c. 333 — 185
68. Letter of Constantine I on Accusations against Athanasius and on Punishment of Rioters, 334 — 194
69. Letter of Constantine I on Adherence to Athanasius, 334 — 198
70. Rescript of Constantine I on John Archaph's Conformity with Orthodoxy, 334 — 201
71. Letter of Constantine I on Readmission of Heretics, 334 or 335 — 201
72. Letter of Constantine I on Readmission of Heretics, 335 — 203
73. Letter of Constantine I on Conciliar Unity, 335 — 204
74. Letter of Dionysius on Conciliar Procedure, 335 — 206
75. Letter of Constantine I on Transfer of the Tyrian Council to Constantinople, 335 — 208
76. Letter of Constantine I on Jewish Molestation of Christians, 335–6 — 213
77. Letter of Constantine II on Recall of Athanasius, 337 — 215
78. Letter of Hemerius on Erection of a Church in Egypt, c. 337 — 218
79. Mandate of Constantius II on Jewish Ownership of Christian Slaves, 339 — 219
80. Mandate of Constantius II on Jewish Proselytism among Christian Women, 339 — 220
81. Mandate of Constantius II and Constans I on Exemption of Clergymen's Sons from Civic Duties, (?)342 — 220
82. Mandate of Constantius II on Redemption of Christian Prostitutes, 343 — 221
83. Letter of Constantius II on Clerical Exemption from Taxation, 343 — 222
84. Letters of Constantius II on Recall of Athanasius, 345–6 — 222
85. Letter of Constantius II on Recall of Athanasius, 346 — 225
86. Letter of Constantius II on Recall of Athanasius and on Enforcement of Laws against Riot, 346 — 227
87. Mandate of Constantius II on Rescission of Statutes against Athanasius and on Clerical Exemption from Public Duties, 346 — 229

xiv TABLE OF DOCUMENTS

88. Mandate of Constantius II on Dispatch of Documents about Athanasius, 346 — 231
89. Mandate of Constantius II on Clerical Exemption from Civic Duties, 349 — 231
90. Letter of Constantius II on Episcopal Duties, 350 — 232
91. Mandate of Constantius II and Julian II on Christian Converts to Judaism, 352 or 357 — 233
92. Mandate of Constantius II on Rape of Religious Women, 354 — 234
93. Letter of Constantius II on Ecclesiastical Unity, 355 — 235
94. Edict of Constantius II on Episcopal Obedience, 355 — 237
95. Colloquy between Constantius II and Pope Liberius on Adherence to the Milanese Council, 355 — 238
96. Letter of Constantius II and Constans I on Episcopal Defendants in Lawsuits, 355 — 245
97. Mandate of Constantius II and Julian II on Clerical Exemption from Taxation, 356 — 246
98. Letter of Constantius II on Disparagement of Athanasius, 357 — 247
99. Letter of Constantius II on Return of Frumentius, 357 — 250
100. Letter of Constantius II on Condemnation of Athanasius, 357 — 252
101. Mandate of Constantius II and Julian II on Privileges of the Roman Church, 357 — 253
102. Letter of Constantius II and Julian II on Clerical Exemption from Taxation and Public Duties, 357 — 254
103. Letter of Constantius II on Expulsion of Anomoeans from Antioch, 358 — 255
104. Letter of Constantius II on Conciliar Faith and Unity, 359 — 257
105. Rescript of Constantius II on Detention of the Riminese Council, 359 — 259
106. Mandate of Constantius II on Ecclesiastical Exemption from Taxation, (?)360 — 261
107. Letter of Constantius II and Julian II on Clerical Exemption from Taxation and Public Duties, 360 — 263
108. Edict of Constantius II and Julian II on Clerical Exemption from Public Duties, 361 — 265
109. Mandate of Constantius II on Clergymen's Property, 361 — 266
110. Mandate of Constantius II on Admission of Imperial Officials to the Clericate, 361 — 268
111. Letter of Julian II on Pagan Riots in Alexandria, 362 — 270
112. Letter of Julian II on Recall of Aetius, 362 — 273
113. Mandate of Julian II on Christian Writings, 362 — 274
114. Mandate of Julian II on Recall of Decurions from the Clericate, 362 — 275
115. Edict of Julian II on Exile of Athanasius, 362 — 276
116. Letter of Julian II on Christian Teachers, 362 — 277
117. Edict of Julian II on Christian Riots in Bostra, 362 — 281

TABLE OF DOCUMENTS xv

118. Edict of Julian II on Clerical Exemption from Public Duties, 362 284
119. Letter of Julian II on Preference of Pagans over Christians, 362 285
120. Rescript of Julian II on Recall of Donatists, 362 287
121. Mandate of Julian II on Exile of Athanasius, 362 288
122. Rescript of Julian II on Recall of Athanasius, 362 289
123. Edict of Julian II on Christian Riots in Edessa, 362 or 363 292
124. Petitions of Arians to Jovian and Jovian's Answers, 363 294
125. Letter of Jovian on Recall of Athanasius, 363 or 364 298
126. Mandate of Jovian on Proposals to Religious Women, 364 299
127. Mandate of Valentinian I and Valens on Taxation of Christian Merchants, 364 300
128. Mandate of Valentinian I and Valens on Merchants' Charity to Christian Paupers, 364 303
129. Edict of Valentinian I and Valens on Exclusion of Rich Plebeians from the Clericate, 364 304
130. Edict of Valentinian I and Valens on Admission of Curials to the Clericate, 364 304
131. Subscription of Valentinian I on Laic Interference with Clerical Concerns, 364 305
132. Mandate of Valentinian I and Valens on Condemnation of Christians to the Arena, 365 305
133. Mandate of Valentinian I and Valens on Exclusion of Bakers from the Clericate, 365 306
134. Mandate of Valentinian I and Valens on Christian Custodians for Pagan Temples, 365 309
135. Mandate of Valentinian I, Valens, and Gratian on Amnesty for Prisoners at Eastertide, 367 309
136. Rescript of Valentinian I on Laic Judgement in Clerical Cases, 367 311
137. Letter of Valentinian I, Valens, and Gratian on Recall of Ursinians, 367 311
138. Letter of Valentinian I, Valens, and Gratian on Restoration of a Roman Basilica, 367 313
139. Letter of Valentinian I, Valens, and Gratian on Protection of Graves, (?)367–75 314
140. Mandate of Valentinian I, Valens, and Gratian on Expulsion of Ursinians from Rome, 368 315
141. Rescript of Valentinian I, Valens, and Gratian on Ecclesiastical Disturbances, 368 316
142. Rescript of Valentinian I, Valens, and Gratian on Schismatical Assemblies, 368 318
143. Rescript of Valentinian I, Valens, and Gratian on Schismatical Assemblies, 368 319
144. Mandate of Valentinian I and Valens on Judicial Process against Christians on Sunday, 368–73 320

xvi   TABLE OF DOCUMENTS

145. Mandate of Valentinian I, Valens, and Gratian on Amnesty for Prisoners at Eastertide, 368 — 320
146. Mandate of Valentinian I, Valens, and Gratian on Ecclesiastical Appeals, 369 — 321
147. Mandate of Valentinian I and Valens on Admission to Ascetic Life, 370 or 373 — 322
148. Mandate of Valentinian I and Valens on Confirmation of Constantius II's Pro-Christian Legislation, 370 — 323
149. Mandate of Valentinian I, Valens, and Gratian on Exemption from Capitation, 370 — 325
150. Letter of Valentinian I, Valens, and Gratian on Donations and Legacies to Clergymen at their Solicitation, 370 — 326
151. Mandate of Valentinian I and Valens on Recall of Curials from the Clericate, 370 — 327
152. Letter of Valentinian I, Valens, and Gratian on Measures against Ursinians, 370–2 — 328
153. Letter of Valentinian I, Valens, and Gratian on Measures against Ursinians, 370–2 — 329
154. Mandate of Valentinian I, Valens, and Gratian on Release of Christian Players from the Theatre, 371 — 331
155. Mandate of Valentinian I, Valens, and Gratian on Clerical Exemption from Senatorial Service, 371 — 332
156. Mandate of Valentinian I and Valens on Manichaeism, 372 — 333
157. Mandate of Valentinian I, Valens, and Gratian on Donations and Legacies to Bishops and Virgins at their Solicitation, 372 — 334
158. Mandate of Valentinian I and Valens on Rebaptism, 373 — 335
159. Letter of Valentinian I, Valens, and Gratian on Consubstantiality, 375 — 336
160. Mandate of Valens, Gratian, and Valentinian II on Confiscation of Heretics' Churches, 376 or 380 — 342
161. Letter of Valens, Gratian, and Valentinian II on Episcopal Jurisdiction in Ecclesiastical Interests, 376 — 342
162. Mandate of Valens, Gratian, and Valentinian II on Clerical Exemption from Public Duties, 377 — 343
163. Mandate of Valens, Gratian, and Valentinian II on Rebaptism, 377 — 344
164. Rescript of Gratian and Valentinian II on Papal Jurisdiction, 378 or 379 — 345
165. Mandate of Gratian, Valentinian II, and Theodosius I on Clerical Exemption from Taxation, 379 — 351
166. Mandate of Gratian, Valentinian II, and Theodosius I on Prohibition of Heresies, 379 — 351
167. Edict of Gratian, Valentinian II, and Theodosius I on Establishment of the Catholic Religion, 380 — 353
168. Edict of Gratian, Valentinian II, and Theodosius I on Sacrilege, 380 — 356

TABLE OF DOCUMENTS   xvii

169. Mandate of Gratian, Valentinian II, and Theodosius I on Suspension of Criminal Cases during Lent, 380   359
170. Mandate of Gratian, Valentinian II, and Theodosius I on Exemption of Christian Actresses from the Theatre, 380   360
171. Letter of Valentinian II, Theodosius I, and Arcadius on Amnesty for Prisoners at Eastertide, 380 or 381   361
172. Mandate of Gratian on Convocation of the Aquileian Council, 380 or 381   362
173. Mandate of Gratian, Valentinian II, and Theodosius I on Heretical Assemblies and on Adherence to the Nicene Creed, 381   364
174. Mandate of Gratian, Valentinian II, and Theodosius I on Clerical Exemption from Capitation, 381   366
175. Mandate of Gratian, Valentinian II, and Theodosius I on Apostate Christians' Wills, 381   367
176. Mandate of Gratian, Valentinian II, and Theodosius I on Testamentary Restrictions for Manichaeans, 381   367
177. Mandate of Gratian, Valentinian II, and Theodosius I on Return of Apostate Actresses to the Theatre, 381   370

VOLUME TWO

178. Edict of Theodosius I on Exemption of Bishops as Witnesses in Lawsuits, 381   371
179. Mandate of Gratian, Valentinian II, and Theodosius I on Heretics' Incapacity to Build Churches, 381   371
180. Mandate of Gratian, Valentinian II, and Theodosius I on Amnesty for Prisoners at Eastertide, 381   372
181. Mandate of Gratian, Valentinian II, and Theodosius I on Interment in Constantinople, 381   373
182. Mandate of Gratian, Valentinian II, and Theodosius I on Transfer of Churches to Orthodox Bishops, 381   375
183. Mandate of Gratian, Valentinian II, and Theodosius I on Exemption of Christian Actresses from the Theatre, 381   377
184. Mandate of Gratian, Valentinian II, and Theodosius I on True Worship of God, 381   377
185. Mandate of Gratian, Valentinian II, and Theodosius I on Special Courts for Prosecution of Heretics, 382   378
186. Mandate of Gratian, Valentinian II, and Theodosius I on Ecclesiastical Exemption from Public Duties, 382   380
187. Mandate of Gratian, Valentinian II, and Theodosius I on Disposition of Remarried Persons' Property, 382   382
188. Mandate of Gratian, Valentinian II, and Theodosius I on Clergymen's Prior Discharge of Public Duties, 383   383

xviii   TABLE OF DOCUMENTS

189. Mandate of Gratian, Valentinian II, and Theodosius I on Apostate Christians' Wills, 383 — 384
190. Mandate of Gratian, Valentinian II, and Theodosius I on Apostate Christians' Wills and on Penalties for Manichaeans, 383 — 385
191. Mandate of Gratian, Valentinian II, and Theodosius I on Heretics' Use of Churches, 383 — 387
192. Mandate of Gratian, Valentinian II, and Theodosius I on Suppression of Heretics, 383 — 387
193. Mandate of Gratian, Valentinian II, and Theodosius I on Curials' Surrender of Property before Admission to the Clericate, 383 — 388
194. Mandate of Gratian, Valentinian II, and Theodosius I on Heretical Assemblies, 383 — 389
195. Rescript of Valentinian II, Theodosius I, and Arcadius on Luciferians, 383 or 384 — 390
196. Mandate of Gratian, Valentinian II, and Theodosius I on Expulsion of Heretical Clergymen from Constantinople, 384 — 392
197. Letter of Valentinian II, Theodosius I, and Arcadius on Clerical Immunity from Secular Courts, (?)384 — 393
198. Mandate of Gratian, Valentinian II, and Theodosius I on Amnesty for Prisoners at Eastertide, 384 — 394
199. Mandate of Gratian, Valentinian II, and Theodosius I on Jewish Ownership of Christian Slaves, 384 — 395
200. Letter of Valentinian II, Theodosius I, and Arcadius on Papal Election, 385 — 396
201. Mandate of Gratian, Valentinian II, and Theodosius I on Amnesty for Prisoners at Eastertide, 385 — 397
202. Mandate of Valentinian II, Theodosius I, and Arcadius on Clerical Exemption from the Public Post, 385 — 398
203. Rescript of Maximus on Support of Orthodoxy, 385 — 399
204. Mandate of Gratian, Valentinian II, and Theodosius I on Exemption of Priests from Torture, (?)385 — 402
205. Mandate of Valentinian II, Theodosius I, and Arcadius on Indulgences to Arians, 386 — 404
206. Mandate of Gratian, Valentinian II, and Theodosius I on Veneration for Martyrs, 386 — 405
207. Letter of Valentinian II, Theodosius I, and Arcadius on Amnesty for Prisoners at Eastertide, 386 — 407
208. Mandate of Gratian, Valentinian II, and Theodosius I on Prohibition of Christians as Chief Priests, 386 — 409
209. Mandate of Gratian, Valentinian II, and Theodosius I on Suspension of Litigation on Sunday, 386 — 410
210. Mandate of Gratian, Valentinian II, and Theodosius I on Substitutes for Decurions before Admission to the Clericate, 386 — 411

TABLE OF DOCUMENTS   xix

211. Rescript of Valentinian II, Theodosius I, and Arcadius on Construction of St Paul's Basilica, 386 — 412
212. Mandate of Valentinian II, Theodosius I, and Arcadius on Illegal Detention of Ecclesiastical Land, 387 — 414
213. Mandate of Gratian, Valentinian II, and Theodosius I on Suppression of Apollinarians, 388 — 415
214. Mandate of Valentinian II, Theodosius I, and Arcadius on Prohibition of Jewish–Christian Marriage, 388 — 416
215. Mandate of Gratian, Valentinian II, and Theodosius I on Oppression of Heretics, 388 — 418
216. Mandate of Valentinian II, Theodosius I, and Arcadius on Public Discussion of Religion, 388 — 419
217. Mandate of Gratian, Valentinian II, and Theodosius I on Arian Pretensions, (?)388 — 419
218. Rescript of Valentinian II, Theodosius I, and Arcadius on Testamentary Restrictions for Eunomians, 389 — 420
219. Mandate of Valentinian II, Theodosius I, and Arcadius on Penalties for Manichaeans, 389 — 422
220. Mandate of Valentinian II, Theodosius I, and Arcadius on Paschal Days and Sundays as Legal Holidays, 389 — 423
221. Mandate of Valentinian II, Theodosius I, and Arcadius on Prohibition of Corporal Punishment during Lent, 389 — 426
222. Mandate of Valentinian II, Theodosius I, and Arcadius on Expulsion of Clerical Heretics from Their Religious Assemblies, 389 — 426
223. Mandate of Valentinian II, Theodosius I, and Arcadius on Treasure-Trove, 390 — 427
224. Mandate of Valentinian II, Theodosius I, and Arcadius on Exemption of Clerical Property from Municipal Levy, 390 — 428
225. Mandate of Valentinian II, Theodosius I, and Arcadius on Deaconesses' Legacies, 390 — 429
226. Mandate of Valentinian II, Theodosius I, and Arcadius on Ecclesiastical Exemption from Public Duties, 390 — 432
227. Mandate of Valentinian II, Theodosius I, and Arcadius on Rescission of Law on Deaconesses' Legacies, 390 — 433
228. Mandate of Valentinian II, Theodosius I, and Arcadius on Sequestration of Monks, 390 — 434
229. Mandate of Valentinian II, Theodosius I, and Arcadius on Religious Significance of the Decurionate, 390 — 435
230. Mandate of Valentinian II, Theodosius I, and Arcadius on Profaners of Baptism, 391 — 436
231. Mandate of Valentinian II, Theodosius I, and Arcadius on Dishonour for Apostate Nobles, 391 — 437
232. Letter of Valentinian II, Theodosius I, and Arcadius on Expulsion of Heretics from Communities, 391 — 438

TABLE OF DOCUMENTS

233. Mandate of Valentinian II, Theodosius I, and Arcadius on Admission of Curials to the Clericate, 391 — 439
234. Mandate of Valentinian II, Theodosius I, and Arcadius on Clerical Interference in Criminal Cases, 392 — 440
235. Mandate of Theodosius I, Arcadius, and Honorius on Clerical Interest in Appeals, 392 — 441
236. Mandate of Valentinian II, Theodosius I, and Arcadius on Suppression of Circensian Contests on Sunday, 392 — 442
237. Mandate of Valentinian II, Theodosius I, and Arcadius on Restoration of Monks, 392 — 444
238. Mandate of Valentinian II, Theodosius I, and Arcadius on Suspension of Litigation at Eastertide, 392 — 444
239. Mandate of Valentinian II, Theodosius I, and Arcadius on Heretical Ordination and Worship, 392 — 445
240. Mandate of Valentinian II, Theodosius I, and Arcadius on Disturbers of Religion, 392 — 446
241. Mandate of Theodosius I, Arcadius, and Honorius on Sanctuary, 392 — 447
242. Mandate of Theodosius I, Arcadius, and Honorius on Pagan Rites Offensive to Christianity, 392 — 448
243. Mandate of Gratian, Valentinian II, and Theodosius I on Prohibition of Spectacles on Sunday, 392–5 — 451
244. Mandate of Theodosius I, Arcadius, and Honorius on Christian Acts of Anti-Semitism, 393 — 452
245. Mandate of Theodosius I, Arcadius, and Honorius on Heretical Consecration of Bishops, 394 — 452
246. Mandate of Theodosius I, Arcadius, and Honorius on Testamentary Rights of Eunomians, 394 — 453
247. Mandate of Theodosius I, Arcadius, and Honorius on Association of Christians with Players, 394 — 454
248. Mandate of Theodosius I, Arcadius, and Honorius on Heretical Instruction, 394 — 455
249. Mandate of Arcadius and Honorius on Confirmation of Theodosius I's Legislation on Heresy, 395 — 456
250. Mandate of Arcadius and Honorius on Confirmation of Ecclesiastical Privileges, 395 — 457
251. Mandate of Arcadius and Honorius on Heretical Assemblies, 395 — 457
252. Mandate of Arcadius and Honorius on Testamentary Rights of Eunomians, 395 — 458
253. Mandate of Arcadius and Honorius on Penalties for Deviation from Christianity, 395 — 459
254. Mandate of Arcadius and Honorius on Definition of Heretics, 395 — 460
255. Mandate of Arcadius and Honorius on Divine Oaths in Pacts and in Transactions, 395 — 461

TABLE OF DOCUMENTS   xxi

256. Mandate of Arcadius and Honorius on Heretics in Governmental Service, 395   463
257. Mandate of Arcadius and Honorius on Christian Officials in Egypt, 396   464
258. Mandate of Arcadius and Honorius on Expulsion of Heretics from Constantinople, 396   465
259. Mandate of Arcadius and Honorius on Apostate Christians' Wills, 396   466
260. Mandate of Arcadius and Honorius on Expulsion of Eunomians from Municipalities, 396   467
261. Mandate of Arcadius and Honorius on Confirmation of Ecclesiastical Privileges, 397   467
262. Mandate of Arcadius and Honorius on Confirmation of Papal Privileges, 397   468
263. Mandate of Arcadius and Honorius on Religious Significance of the Decurionate, 397   469
264. Mandate of Arcadius and Honorius on Expulsion of Apollinarians from Constantinople, 397   469
265. Mandate of Arcadius and Honorius on Confirmation of Ecclesiastical Privileges, 397   470
266. Mandate of Arcadius and Honorius on Sanctuary, 397   471
267. Mandate of Arcadius and Honorius on Clerical Privileges, 397   471
268. Mandate of Arcadius and Honorius on Penalties for Eunomians and Montanists, 398   472
269. Mandate of Arcadius and Honorius on Ordination of Monks in a Shortage of Secular Clergymen, 398   473
270. Mandate of Arcadius and Honorius on Recruitment of Clergymen from Local Districts, 398   474
271. Mandate of Arcadius and Honorius on Restriction of Episcopal Jurisdiction, 398   475
272. Mandate of Arcadius and Honorius on Clerical Interference in Criminal Cases, 398   476
273. Mandate of Arcadius and Honorius on Sanctuary, 398   478
274. Mandate of Arcadius and Honorius on Clerical Exemption for Guildsmen, 399   479
275. Mandate of Arcadius and Honorius on Punishment of Manichaeans, 399   480
276. Mandate of Arcadius and Honorius on Penalties for Impairment of Ecclesiastical Privileges, 399   480
277. Mandate of Arcadius and Honorius on Rescission of Disabilities for Eunomians, 399   481
278. Mandate of Arcadius and Honorius on Episcopal Jurisdiction in Ecclesiastical Interests, 399   482
279. Mandate of Arcadius and Honorius on Suppression of Shows on Sunday, 399   483

TABLE OF DOCUMENTS

280. Mandate of Arcadius and Honorius on Clerical Exemption from Senatorial Service, 399   483
281. Mandate of Arcadius and Honorius on Suppression of Spectacles on Certain Holy Days, 400   484
282. Mandate of Arcadius and Honorius on Clerical Exemption from Taxation and Public Labour, 401   485
283. Mandate of Arcadius, Honorius, and Theodosius II on Tumultuous Assemblies, 404   485
284. Edict of Arcadius on Chrysostom's Adherents, 404   486
285. Mandate of Arcadius and Honorius on Expulsion of Foreign Clergymen from Constantinople, 404   488
286. Mandate of Arcadius, Honorius, and Theodosius II on Tumultuous Assemblies, 404   489
287. Mandate of Arcadius, Honorius, and Theodosius II on Illicit Assemblies, 404   490
288. Letter of Arcadius, Honorius, and Theodosius II on Episcopal Deposition of Bishops, 405   491
289. Mandate of Arcadius, Honorius, and Theodosius II on Rebaptism, 405   493
290. Mandate of Arcadius, Honorius, and Theodosius II on Rebaptism, 405   495
291. Edict of Arcadius, Honorius, and Theodosius II on Rebaptism, 405   496
292. Edict of Arcadius, Honorius, and Theodosius II on Manichaeans and Donatists, 405   496
293. Mandate of Arcadius and Honorius on Rescission of Julian II's Rescript on Behalf of Donatists, 405   497
294. Mandate of Arcadius, Honorius, and Theodosius II on Christian Unity, 405   498
295. Letter of Honorius on Convocation of a Thessalonican Council, 405   499
296. Letter of Arcadius, Honorius, and Theodosius II on Swift Justice for Donatists, 405   500
297. Rescript of Arcadius on Chrysostom's Adherents, 406   501
298. Mandate of Arcadius, Honorius, and Theodosius II on Juristic Restrictions for Manichaeans, Phrygians, and Priscillians, 407   501
299. Mandate of Arcadius, Honorius, and Theodosius II on Confession of Catholicism as a Test of Orthodoxy, 407   504
300. Mandate of Arcadius, Honorius, and Theodosius II on Advocates as Representatives of the Church, 407   505
301. Letter of Honorius and Theodosius II on Suppression of Heretics and Pagans, 407-8   506
302. Mandate of Honorius and Theodosius II on Trial of Bandits during Lent or at Eastertide, 408   509
303. Mandate of Honorius and Theodosius II on Jewish Sacrilege Offensive to Christians, 408   510

304. Mandate of Honorius and Theodosius II on Employment of Christians at Court, 408 ... 511
305. Letter of Honorius and Theodosius II on Disturbance of Sacraments, 408 ... 511
306. Mandate of Honorius and Theodosius II on Schismatical Assemblies, 408 ... 512
307. Letter of Arcadius and Honorius on Return of Ex-Clergymen to Civil Duties, 408 ... 513
308. Letter of Honorius on Christian Supervision of Restoration of Captives, 408 ... 514
309. Mandate of Arcadius, Honorius, and Theodosius II on Confirmation of Episcopal Jurisdiction, 408 ... 519
310. Letter of Honorius and Theodosius II on Sacrilege and on Enforcement of Laws on Heretics, Schismatics, and Non-Christians, 409 ... 520
311. Mandate of Honorius and Theodosius II on Selection of Christians as Civic Defenders, 409 ... 524
312. Mandate of Honorius and Theodosius II on Episcopal Interest in Prisoners, 409 ... 525
313. Mandate of Honorius and Theodosius II on Conversion of Astrologers, 409 ... 526
314. Mandate of Honorius and Theodosius II on Capitation for Rural Clergymen, 409 ... 528
315. Mandate of Honorius and Theodosius II on Penalties for Caelicolans and Christian Converts to Judaism, 409 ... 529
316. Mandate of Honorius and Theodosius II on Suppression of Amusements on Sunday, 409 ... 531
317. Mandate of Honorius and Theodosius II on Petitions from Heretics or Pro-heretical Persons, 409 ... 531
318. Mandate of Honorius and Theodosius II on Speedy Trial of Lawsuits involving the Church, 409 ... 532
319. Mandate of Honorius and Theodosius II on Limitation of Corpse-Carriers in Constantinople, 409 ... 533
320. Mandate of Honorius and Theodosius II on Heretics in Governmental Service, 410 ... 533
321. Mandate of Honorius and Theodosius II on Disabilities for Eunomians, 410 ... 534
322. Mandate of Honorius and Theodosius II on Return of Clergymen to Civic Status, 410 ... 536
323. Mandate of Honorius and Theodosius II on Heretical Assemblies, 410 ... 537
324. Letter of Honorius and Theodosius II on the Carthaginian Conference between Catholics and Donatists, 410 ... 537
325. Edict of Marcelline on the Carthaginian Conference between Catholics and Donatists, 411 ... 541

326. Edict of Marcelline on Procedure at the Carthaginian Conference between Catholics and Donatists, 411 — 544
327. Letter of Honorius and Theodosius II on Ecclesiastical Exemption from Public Duties, (?)411 — 549
328. Edict of Marcelline on Donatism, 411 — 551
329. Mandate of Honorius and Theodosius II on Penalties for Donatists, 412 — 554
330. Mandate of Honorius and Theodosius II on Exile of Jovinian, (?)412 — 556
331. Mandate of Honorius and Theodosius II on Recovery of Exposed Children, 412 — 557
332. Mandate of Honorius and Theodosius II on Christian Immunity from Jewish Prosecutions, (?)412 — 558
333. Mandate of Honorius and Theodosius II on Jewish Reverence for Christianity, 412 or 418 — 559
334. Mandate of Honorius and Theodosius II on Confirmation of Episcopal Jurisdiction, 412 — 560
335. Mandate of Honorius and Theodosius II on Rebaptism and on Celebration of Easter, 413 — 563
336. Mandate of Honorius and Theodosius II on Rebaptism, 413 — 564
337. Mandate of Honorius and Theodosius II on Penalties for Donatists and Heretics, 414 — 565
338. Mandate of Honorius and Theodosius II on Validity of Proceedings at the Carthaginian Conference between Catholics and Donatists, 414 — 567
339. Mandate of Honorius and Theodosius II on Heretical Assemblies, 415 — 568
340. Edict of Honorius and Theodosius II on Allocation of Pagan Religious Property to the Church, 415 — 569
341. Mandate of Honorius and Theodosius II on Punishment of Jewish Proselytizers of Christians, 415 — 569
342. Mandate of Honorius and Theodosius II on Penalties for Montanists, 415 — 571
343. Mandate of Honorius and Theodosius II on Penalties for Eunomians, 415 — 572
344. Mandate of Honorius and Theodosius II on Jewish Ownership of Christian Slaves, 415 — 574
345. Mandate of Honorius and Theodosius II on Ecclesiastical Liability to Public Duties, 415 — 575
346. Mandate of Honorius and Theodosius II on Return of Lukewarm Jewish Christians to Judaism, 416 — 576
347. Mandate of Honorius and Theodosius II on Ecclesiastical Sick-Nurses, 416 — 577
348. Mandate of Honorius and Theodosius II on Jewish Ownership of Christian Slaves, 417 — 579

TABLE OF DOCUMENTS   XXV

349. Mandate of Honorius and Theodosius II on Ecclesiastical Sick-
     Nurses, 418   579
350. Rescript of Honorius and Theodosius II on Condemnation of
     Pelagius and Caelestius, 418   581
351. Edict of Palladius, Monaxius, and Agricola on Condemnation of
     Pelagianism, 418   585
352. Rescript of Honorius on Papal Election, 419   586
353. Rescript of Honorius on a Priestly Petition, 419   588
354. Letter of Honorius on the Eulalian-Bonifacian Schism, 419 590
355. Mandate of Honorius on Roman Celebration of Easter, 419 591
356. Letter of Honorius on Roman Celebration of Easter, 419   592
357. Oration of Honorius on Roman Celebration of Easter, 419 593
358. Edict of Honorius on Roman Celebration of Easter, 419   594
359. Letter of Honorius on Convocation of the Spoletan Council, 419 596
360. Letter of Honorius on Convocation of the Spoletan Council, 419 597
361. Letter of Placidia on Convocation of the Spoletan Council, 419 598
362. Letter of Placidia on Convocation of the Spoletan Council, 419 599
363. Letter of Constantius on Execution of Imperial Orders about
     Eulalians, 419   600
364. Letter of Honorius on Penalties for Eulalians, 419   600
365. Rescript of Honorius on Confirmation of Papal Election, 419 603
366. Mandate of Honorius on Cancellation of a Conciliar Convocation,
     419   604
367. Letter of Largus on Cancellation of a Conciliar Convocation, 419 606
368. Letter of Honorius and Theodosius II on Condemnation of
     Pelagianism, 419   606
369. Mandate of Honorius and Theodosius II on Episcopal Intercession
     for Shipwrights, 419   608
370. Edict of Honorius and Theodosius II on Sanctuary and on Episcopal
     Visitation of Prisons, 419   609
371. Rescript of Honorius on Papal Election, 420   611
372. Letter of Honorius and Theodosius II on Clerical Cohabitation and
     on Delation about Rapists of Consecrated Virgins, 420   612
373. Letter of Constantius III on Expulsion of Pelagians from Rome, 421 615
374. Edict of Volusian on Expulsion of Pelagians from Rome, 421 616
375. Mandate, Letter, Rescript of Honorius and Theodosius II on
     Ecclesiastical Jurisdiction in Illyricum, 421–3   617
376. Mandate of Honorius and Theodosius II on Christian Restitution to
     Jews, 423   622
377. Mandate of Honorius and Theodosius II on Ecclesiastical Exemption
     from Public Duties, 423   623
378. Mandate of Honorius and Theodosius II on Jewish Circumcision of
     Christians, 423   624

TABLE OF DOCUMENTS

379. Mandate of Honorius and Theodosius II on Jewish Ownership of Christian Slaves, 423   625
380. Mandate of Honorius and Theodosius II on Confirmation of Laws on Heretics, 423   625
381. Mandate of Honorius and Theodosius II on Enforcement of Laws on Heretics, 423   626
382. Mandate of Honorius and Theodosius II on Penalties for Heretics and for Christian Plunderers of Non-Christians, 423   627
383. Mandate of Honorius and Theodosius II on Heretics in Governmental Service, 423   629
384. Rescript of Theodosius II on Ecclesiastical Exemption from Capitation, 424   629
385. Mandate of Theodosius II and Valentinian III on Prohibition of Amusements on Certain Holy Days, 425   630
386. Mandate of Theodosius II and Valentinian III on Restraint of Reverence to Imperial Images, 425   632
387. Mandate of Theodosius II and Valentinian III on Confirmation of Episcopal Jurisdiction, on Heresy, and on Christian Slaves, 425   632
388. Mandate of Theodosius II and Valentinian III on Expulsion of Heretics from Rome, 425   635
389. Mandate of Theodosius II and Valentinian III on Punishment of Heresy, Perfidy, Schism, Pagan Superstition, and Religious Error, 425   636
390. Mandate of Theodosius II and Valentinian III on Confirmation of Ecclesiastical Privileges, 425   636
391. Mandate of Theodosius II and Valentinian III on Apostate Christians' Wills, 426   637
392. Mandate of Theodosius II and Valentinian III on Testamentary Benefits for Christian Converts, 426   638
393. Mandate of Theodosius II and Valentinian III on the Sign of the Cross, 427 or 447   640
394. Mandate of Theodosius II and Valentinian III on Episcopal Interest in Freedom of Prostitutes, 428   641
395. Mandate of Theodosius II and Valentinian III on Penalties and Disabilities for Heretics and Schismatics, 428   642
396. Law of Theodosius II and Valentinian III on Seduction from Orthodoxy, c. 429   645
397. Letter of Theodosius II and Valentinian III on Convocation of the Ephesian Council, 430   646
398. Letter of Theodosius II and Valentinian III on Conciliar Attendance, 430   649
399. Mandate of Theodosius II and Valentinian III on Procedure in Lawsuits against Clergymen and on Sanctuary, 430   652
400. Mandate of Theodosius II and Valentinian III on Sanctuary, 431   654

TABLE OF DOCUMENTS xxvii

401. Letter of Theodosius II and Valentinian III on Conciliar Procedure, 431 ... 662
402. Edict of Candidian on Conciliar Procedure, 431 ... 664
403. Letter of Candidian on Conciliar Procedure, 431 ... 667
404. Edict of Candidian on Conciliar Procedure, 431 ... 668
405. Letter of Theodosius II and Valentinian III on Conciliar Procedure, 431 ... 669
406. Letter of Theodosius II and Valentinian III on Conciliar Depositions, 431 ... 672
407. Colloquy between Theodosius II and Bishop Theodoret on Conciliar Decisions, 431 ... 674
408. Letter of Theodosius II and Valentinian III on Dissolution of the Ephesian Council, 431 ... 675
409. Letter of Theodosius II on Dissolution of the Ephesian Council, 431 ... 677
410. Letter of Isidore on Commitment of Nestorius to a Monastery, 431 ... 678
411. Letters of Theodosius II on Ecclesiastical Peace and Unity, 432 ... 679
412. Letter of Theodosius II and Valentinian III on Ecclesiastical Peace and Unity, 432 ... 684
413. Mandate of Theodosius II and Valentinian III on Sanctuary, 432 ... 686
414. Letter of Domitian on Ecclesiastical Peace and Unity, c. 434 ... 688
415. Letters of Dionysius on Ecclesiastical Peace and Unity, c. 434 ... 690
416. Letter of Titus on Ecclesiastical Peace and Unity, c. 434 ... 692
417. Interpretation of Mandate on Exile of Meletius, c. 434 ... 694
418. Letter of Titus on Ecclesiastical Peace and Unity, c. 434 ... 695
419. Letter of Dionysius on Ecclesiastical Peace and Unity, c. 434 ... 696
420. Letter of Titus on Exile of Alexander, c. 434 ... 697
421. Mandate of Theodosius II and Valentinian III on Clerics' and Monks' Inheritances, 434 ... 698
422. General Law of Theodosius II and Valentinian III on Nestorianism, 435 ... 700
423. Edict of Isidore, Bassus, and Reginus on Destruction of Nestorius' Writings, 435 ... 703
424. Mandate of Theodosius II and Valentinian III on Erection of the Cross on Sites of Heathen Shrines, 435 ... 705
425. Interpretation of Mandate on Exile of Nestorius, 436 ... 706
426. Letter of Theodosius II on Exile of Irenaeus and Photius, 436 ... 707
427. Letter of Theodosius II and Valentinian III on Ecclesiastical Peace and Unity, 436 ... 708
428. Mandate of Theodosius II and Valentinian III on Episcopal Exemption from Taxation, 436 ... 710
429. Letter of Theodosius II and Valentinian III on Disabilities for Jews, Samaritans, Heretics, and Pagans, 438 ... 711
430. Mandate of Theodosius II and Valentinian III on Corpse-Carriers' Service to the Church, 439 ... 716

TABLE OF DOCUMENTS

431. Letter of Theodosius II and Valentinian III on Retention of Certain Ships for Public Service, 439 — 717
432. Mandate of Theodosius II and Valentinian III on Clerical Misuse of Imperial Insignia, 439 — 719
433. Letter of Theodosius II and Valentinian III on Successions to Clerical Estates, 439 — 720
434. Mandate of Theodosius II and Valentinian III on Ecclesiastical Levies for Imperial Tours, 440–1 — 723
435. Letter of Theodosius II and Valentinian III on Cancellation of Clerical Exemption from Public Duties, 441 — 723
436. Mandate of Theodosius II and Valentinian III on Privilege for the Nobility, 442 — 726
437. Mandate of Theodosius II and Valentinian III on Ecclesiastical Privileges, 445 — 726
438. Mandate of Theodosius II and Valentinian III on Ecclesiastical Levies for Imperial Tours, 445 — 727
439. Rescript of Theodosius II and Valentinian III on Recall of Roman Guildsmen from the Clericate, 445 — 728
440. Letter of Theodosius II and Valentinian III on Penalties for Manichaeans, 445 — 729
441. Rescript of Theodosius II and Valentinian III on Privilege of Clergy for Tenant Farmers, 445 — 731
442. Rescript of Theodosius II and Valentinian III on Papal Jurisdiction, 445 — 732
443. Letter of Theodosius II and Valentinian III on Clerical Violators of Sepulchres, 447 — 736
444. Letter of Theodosius II and Valentinian III on Exclusion of Palatines from the Clericate, 447 — 740
445. Mandate of Theodosius II on Condemnation of Porphyry, Nestorius, and Irenaeus, 448 — 741
446. Edict of Hormisdas and Albinus on Condemnation of Porphyry, Nestorius, and Irenaeus, 448 — 743
447. Mandate of Theodosius II on Trial of Three Bishops by an Episcopal Commission, 448 — 744
448. Mandate of Theodosius II on Admission of a Layman to a Synod, 448 — 746
449. Letter of Theodosius II and Valentinian III on Convocation of the Ephesian Council, 449 — 747
450. Letter of Theodosius II on Conciliar Attendance, 449 — 749
451. Letter of Theodosius II on Conciliar Attendance, 449 — 750
452. Letter of Theodosius II and Valentinian III on Conciliar Attendance, 449 — 751
453. Mandate of Theodosius II on Conciliar Discipline, 449 — 752
454. Mandate of Theodosius II on Conciliar Discipline, 449 — 754

455. Letter of Theodosius II on Conciliar Maintenance of Orthodoxy, 449 — 755
456. Mandate of Theodosius II and Valentinian III on Conciliar Action about Ibas, 449 — 756
457. Mandate of Elpidius on Conciliar Procedure, 449 — 758
458. Letter of Theodosius II on Presidency of the Ephesian Council, 449 — 760
459. Edict of Theodosius II on Confirmation of the Ephesian Council, 449 or 450 — 761
460. Letter of Theodosius II on Orthodoxy, 449 or 450 — 766
461. Letter of Valentinian III and Marcian on Convocation of a Council, 450 — 767
462. Letter of Marcian on Convocation of a Council, 450 — 768
463. Rescript of Pulcheria on Convocation of a Council, 450 — 769
464. Letter of Valentinian III and Marcian on Convocation of the Chalcedonian Council, 451 — 771
465. Edict of Marcian on Decorum in Churches, 451 — 772
466. Letter of Pulcheria on Conciliar Attendance, 451 — 773
467. Letter of Valentinian III and Marcian on Conciliar Procedure, 451 — 774
468. Rescript of Valentinian III and Marcian on Transfer of the Council from Nicaea to Chalcedon, 451 — 775
469. Letter of Valentinian III and Marcian on Transfer of the Council from Nicaea to Chalcedon, 451 — 777
470. Decrees of Imperial Commissioners on Conciliar Procedure, 451 — 778
471. Mandate of Marcian on Conciliar Procedure, 451 — 791
472. Oration and Decrees of Marcian on Conciliar Procedure, 451 — 792
473. Mandate of Valentinian III and Marcian on Conciliar Procedure, 451 — 799
474. Mandate of Valentinian III and Marcian on Confirmation of Ecclesiastical Privileges, 451 — 800
475. Letter of Valentinian III and Marcian on Confirmation of the Chalcedonian Council, 451 — 801
476. Edict of Valentinian III and Marcian on Confirmation of the Chalcedonian Council, 452 — 804
477. Constitution of Marcian on Confirmation of the Chalcedonian Council, 452 — 808
478. Letter of Valentinian III on Episcopal Judgement and on Various Matters, 452 — 811
479. Mandate of Valentinian III and Marcian on Confirmation of the Chalcedonian Council, 452 — 817
480. Letter of Valentinian III and Marcian on Confirmation of the Chalcedonian Council and on Penalties for Eutychians, 452 — 820
481. Letter of Marcian on Conformity with Orthodoxy, 452 — 826
482. Letter of Valentinian III and Marcian on Confirmation of the Chalcedonian Council, 453 — 829

TABLE OF DOCUMENTS

483. Letter of Marcian on Lawlessness of Theodosius, 453   830
484. Rescript of Marcian on Lawlessness of Palestinian Monks, 453   835
485. Letter of Pulcheria on Anathematization of Heretics, 453   840
486. Rescript of Pulcheria on Anathematization of Heretics, 453   842

VOLUME THREE

487. Letter of Marcian on Lawlessness of Theodosius and on Condemnation of Heretics, 453   845
488. Letter of Marcian on Religious Women's Legacies, 455   849
489. Letter of Marcian on Penalties for Eutychians and Apollinarians, 455   852
490. Mandate of Marcian on Patriarchal Jurisdiction in Ecclesiastical Interests, 456   858
491. Mandate of Marcian on Clerical Defendants in Lawsuits, (?)456   859
492. Edict of Leo I on Burial of Heretics, 457   861
493. Edict of Leo I on Episcopal Interest in Manumission and in Restraint of Actresses, 457–67   862
494. Edict of Leo I on Clerical Manumission of Prostitutes, 457–67   862
495. Letter of Leo I on an Alexandrian Dispute, 458   863
496. Letter of Leo I and Majorian on Regulations for Nuns, 458   866
497. Letter of Leo I and Majorian on Admission of Curials to the Clericate, 458   870
498. Mandate of Leo I on Respect for the Cross and Relics, 459   872
499. Law of Majorian on Ecclesiastical Privilege, (?)459–60   873
500. Mandate of Leo I and Majorian on Forced Ordination to the Clericate, 460   873
501. Mandate of Leo I on Sanctuary, 466   875
502. Mandate of Leo I on Ex-Officials in the Clericate, 466   878
503. Mandate of Leo I on Alienation of Ecclesiastical Property to Heretics, (?)466–72   879
504. Law of Unknown Emperor on Disturbance of Churches, 466–534   880
505. Law of Unknown Emperor on Decorum in Church, 466–534   881
506. Mandate of Leo I and Anthemius on Restriction of the Legal Profession to Christians, 468   882
507. Mandate of Leo I on Episcopal Interest in Legacies for Ransom of Captives, 468   883
508. Mandate of Leo I and Anthemius on Episcopal Election, 469   884
509. Mandate of Leo I and Anthemius on Observance of Sunday, 469   887
510. Mandate of Leo I and Anthemius on Alienation of Ecclesiastical Property, 470   888
511. Mandate of Leo I on Orthodoxy for Civil Officials, (?)470   892
512. Mandate of Leo I and Anthemius on Restriction of Monks to Monasteries, 471   893

TABLE OF DOCUMENTS   xxxi

513. Mandate of Leo I on Biblical Oaths in Sales, 472   893
514. Mandate of Leo I and Anthemius on Clerical Wills, 472   895
515. Mandate of Leo I and Anthemius on Clerical Defendants in Lawsuits, 472   896
516. Mandate of Leo I and Anthemius on Foster-Fathers' Management of Wards' Property, 472   900
517. Mandate of Leo I and Anthemius on Prenuptial Gifts in Mixed Betrothals, 472   902
518. Mandate of Leo I and Anthemius on Privileges for Ecclesiastical Institutions, 472   903
519. Edict of Glycerius on Simoniacal Ordination, 473   904
520. Edict of Himelco, Dioscore, Aurelian, and Protadius on Simoniacal Ordination, 473   907
521. Mandate of Leo I and Zeno on Treasure-Trove, 474   909
522. Law of Zeno on Promises about Shrines and Charitable Institutions, 474–7   910
523. Edict of Zeno on Retention of the Urban Episcopate, (?)474–84   912
524. Letter and Edict of Basiliscus and Mark on the Christian Faith, 475   915
525. Mandate of Zeno on Concubines' Marriages and on Legitimation of Children, 477   920
526. Mandate of Zeno on Rescission of Basiliscus' Ecclesiastical Legislation, 477   922
527. Letter of Zeno on Ecclesiastical Unity, 482   924
528. Mandate of Zeno on Admission of Tenant Farmers to Ascetic Life and of Slaves to the Clericate, 484   933
529. Mandate of Zeno on Admission of Slaves to Ascetic Life, 484   936
530. Law of Unknown Emperor on Ecclesiastical Exaction of Offerings, 484–524   937
531. Law of Unknown Emperor on Monastic Discipline, 484–524   939
532. Law of Unknown Emperor on the Bible's Use in Official Investigation, 485–534   939
533. Law of Zeno or of Anastasius I on Right of Residence for Manichaeans, 487 or 510   940
534. Law of Anastasius I on Episcopal Interest in Purchase of Grain, 491–505   941
535. Law of Anastasius I on Episcopal Interest in Military Payment, 491–505   942
536. Mandate of Anastasius I on Soldiers as Guards for Churches, 491–518   942
537. Law of Anastasius I on Alienation of Ecclesiastical Property, 491–518   944
538. Law of Anastasius I on Christian Funerals in Constantinople, 491–518   947
539. Law of Unknown Emperor on Episcopal Interest in Purchase of Grain, 491–534   948

xxxii TABLE OF DOCUMENTS

540. Mandate of Anastasius I on Selection of Civic Defenders, 503 or 504 948
541. Mandate of Anastasius I on Selection of Christians as Civic Defenders, 505 949
542. Letter of Anastasius I on Anathematization of Heretics, 505 950
543. Letters of Anastasius I on Summoning Severus to Court, 507 or 508 953
544. Letter of Anastasius I on Convocation of the Heraclean Council, 514 955
545. Letter of Anastasius I on Ecclesiastical Unity, 515 956
546. Letter of Anastasius I on Ecclesiastical Unity, 515–16 957
547. Letter of Anastasius I on Ecclesiastical Unity, 516 961
548. Letter of Anastasius I on Ecclesiastical Unity, 516 962
549. Letter of Justin I on Ecclesiastical Unity, 518 964
550. Letter of Justinian I on Ecclesiastical Unity, 518 966
551. Letter of Justinian I on Expulsion of Monks from Rome, 519 968
552. Letter of Justinian I on Theopaschism, 519 970
553. Letter of Justinian I on Theopaschism, 519 972
554. Letter of Justin I on Ecclesiastical Unity, 519 973
555. Edict of Justin I on Orthodoxy for Soldiers, 519 or 520 975
556. Letter of Justin I on Ecclesiastical Unity, 520 976
557. Letter of Justin I on Episcopal Appointments, 520 978
558. Letter of Justin I on Diptychs of Eastern Churches, 520 979
559. Mandate of Justin I on a Religious Celebration at Cyrus, 520 981
560. Letter of Justin I on Diptychs of Eastern Churches, 520 983
561. Letter of Justinian I on Diptychs of Eastern Churches, 520 987
562. Letter of Justinian I on Theopaschism, 520 989
563. Letter of Justinian I on Diptychs of Eastern Churches, 520 991
564. Letter of Justinian I on Ecclesiastical Unity, 520 993
565. Mandate of Justin I on Clerical Intervention in Probate, 524 993
566. Law of Unknown Emperor on Monastic Rights, (?)525 994
567. Law of Justin I and Justinian I on Penalties for Heretics, 527 995
568. Rescript of Justin I and Justinian I on an Oratory's Estates, 527 999
569. Edict of Justinian I on Penalties for Heretics, (?)527 1001
570. Law of Justinian I on Orthodox Children as Heirs of Heretical Parents, 527–9 1003
571. Law of Justinian I on Disabilities for Heretics, 527–9 1004
572. Mandate of Justinian I on Manichaeans' Wills, 527–9 1005
573. Law of Justinian I on Disabilities for Manichaeans, 527–9 1006
574. Law of Justinian I on Disabilities for Samaritans, 527–9 1007
575. Law of Justinian I on Disabilities for Heretics, 527–9 1008
576. Mandate of Justinian I on Sanctuary, 527–34 1012
577. Constitution of Justinian I on Status of the Smyrnan Church, 527–65 1014
578. Edict of Justinian I on Composition of the Code, 528 1016
579. Mandate of Justinian I on Selection of Bishops, on Management of Ecclesiastical Property, on Clerical Duties, 528 1017

TABLE OF DOCUMENTS xxxiii

580. Letter of Justinian I on Episcopal Journeys to Constantinople, 528 1022
581. Mandate of Justinian I on Donations for Pious Purposes, 528 1024
582. Mandate of Justinian I on Episcopal Interest in Disputed Loans, 528 1025
583. Law of Justinian I on Episcopal Information about Pagans, (?)528 1026
584. Law of Justinian I on Ecclesiastical Exclusion from Military Provisioning, c. 528 1027
585. Law of Justinian I on Legacies to Clergymen or Churches or Charities, 528–9 1028
586. Mandate of Justinian I on Episcopal Interest in Prisoners, 529 1029
587. Mandate of Justinian I on Episcopal Interest in Exiles, 529 1031
588. Mandate of Justinian I on Segregation of Monks and Nuns, 529 1032
589. Mandate of Justinian I on Episcopal Interest in Private Prisoners, 529 1034
590. Mandate of Justinian I on Confirmation of the Code, 529 1035
591. Mandate of Justinian I on Episcopal Interest in Foundlings' Rights, 529 1036
592. Mandate of Justinian I on Biblical Oaths before Judicial Torture of Slaves, 529 1037
593. Mandate of Justinian I on Episcopal Interest in Gambling, 529 1038
594. Mandate of Justinian I on Oaths in Lawsuits, 529 1039
595. Mandate of Justinian I on Donations and Legacies to Ecclesiastical Institutions, 529 1040
596. Mandate of Justinian I on Donations for Pious Purposes, 529 1041
597. Mandate of Justinian I on the Church as Depository of Disputed Revenue, 529 1043
598. Mandate of Justinian I on Alienation of Ecclesiastical Property, 529 1044
599. Mandate of Justinian I on Orthodox Children's Rights in Heretical Parents' Property, 529 1047
600. Law of Justinian I on Conversion of Pagans to Christianity, (?)529 1048
601. Mandate of Justinian I on Donations for Pious Purposes or to Religious Persons, 530 1050
602. Mandate of Justinian I on Manumission in Church, 530 1051
603. Mandate of Justinian I on the Bible's Significance in Lawsuits, 530 1053
604. Mandate of Justinian I on Prescription affecting the Church, 530 1053
605. Mandate of Justinian I on Biblical Oaths in Lawsuits, 530 1055
606. Mandate of Justinian I on Episcopal Interest in Municipal Matters, 530 1058
607. Mandate of Justinian I on Manumission in Church, 530 1064
608. Mandate of Justinian I on Episcopal Interest in Guardianship, 530 1065
609. Mandate of Justinian I on Foster-Daughters' Marriages, 530 1067
610. Mandate of Justinian I on Episcopal Interest in Prenuptial Settlements by Lunatics' Children, 530 1068
611. Mandate of Justinian I on Episcopal Jurisdiction in Clerical Lawsuits, 530 1069

TABLE OF DOCUMENTS

612. Mandate of Justinian I on Legacies to the Church, 530 — 1072
613. Mandate of Justinian I on Clerical Celibacy, 530 — 1078
614. Mandate of Justinian I on Abbatial Election, 530 — 1080
615. Mandate of Justinian I on Legacies to the Church, 530 — 1082
616. Mandate of Justinian I on Disabilities for Heretics, 530 — 1084
617. Letter of Justinian I on Composition of the Digest, 530 — 1086
618. Edict of Justinian I on Contractual Usage of Ecclesiastical Property, 530 — 1088
619. Mandate of Justinian I on Biblical Oaths in Lawsuits, 531 — 1092
620. Mandate of Justinian I on Episcopal Celibacy, 531 — 1096
621. Mandate of Justinian I on Episcopal Interest in Guardianship, 531 — 1097
622. Mandate of Justinian I on Heretics' Evidence in Court, 531 — 1099
623. Mandate of Justinian I on Clerical Interest in Property left to Prisoners and Paupers as Heirs, 531 — 1100
624. Mandate of Justinian I on Clerical Wills, 531 — 1103
625. Mandate of Justinian I on Clerical Lawsuits, 531 — 1105
626. Mandate of Justinian I on Heretics as Soldiers' Heirs, 531 — 1107
627. Mandate of Justinian I on Episcopal Interest in Detention and in Debt, 531 — 1107
628. Mandate of Justinian I on Clerical Exemption from Guardianship, 531 — 1109
629. Mandate of Justinian I on Clerical Candidates, on Ex-Clergymen, and on Admission to Ascetic Life, 531 — 1110
630. Mandate of Justinian I on Imperial Property for Ecclesiastical Purposes, 531 — 1115
631. Mandate of Justinian I on Rescission of the Claudian Senatusconsult, 531-4 — 1117
632. Law of Justinian I on Episcopal Interest in Payment of Rent, 531-4 — 1119
633. Rescript of Justinian I on Governors' Grant of Sanctuary and on Extortion from Heretics, 531-5 — 1121
634. Mandate of Justinian I on Ecclesiastical Interest in Creditors' Possession of Debtors' Property, 532 — 1122
635. Rescript of Justinian I on Episcopal Interest in Guardianship, 533 — 1124
636. Edict of Justinian I on Theopaschism, 533 — 1125
637. Letter of Justinian I on Condemnation of Heretics, 533 — 1128
638. Mandate of Justinian I on Rapists of Religious Women, 533 — 1132
639. Edict of Justinian I on Use of His Institutes, 533 — 1134
640. Statutes of Justinian I on Legacies to the Church, 533 — 1136
641. Statutes of Justinian I on Sacred and Religious Things, 533 — 1138
642. Edict of Justinian I on Confirmation of the Digest, 533 — 1145
643. Statute of Justinian I on Invalidity of Heretics' Oaths, 533 — 1147
644. Statute of Justinian I on Vows, 533 — 1148
645. Letters of Pope John II and Justinian I on Theopaschism, 533-4 — 1149

646. Mandates of Justinian I on the Office Staff of the Praetorian Prefect of Africa and on the said Diocese's Entire Status, 534   1157
647. Edict of Justinian I on Non-Catholic Ownership of Christian Slaves, 534   1162
648. Mandate of Justinian I on Legacies to Ecclesiastical Institutions, 534   1162
649. Rescript of Justinian I on Episcopal Interest in Actresses, 534   1165
650. Mandate of Justinian I on Episcopal Interest in Actresses and Danseuses, 534   1167
651. Mandate of Justinian I on Episcopal Jurisdiction in Clerical Misconduct, 534   1169
652. Mandate of Justinian I on Admission to Religious Life, (?)534   1176

INTRODUCTION

1. This collection of legal documents affecting the Christian Church in the Roman Empire is the first of its kind in any language.[1]

In time the monuments here translated cover the period from the foundation of the Church to the deposition of Romulus Augustulus,[2] the last emperor in the West (476), and to the publication of the second (and only extant) edition of the Code of Justinian I,[3] the most conspicuous champion of Caesaropapism in the East (534)—each *terminus ad quem* being an arbitrary, but a natural, limit.[4]

The character of the originals, which are mostly in either Greek or Latin, is strictly secular,[5] that is, the documents emanate from the State's officials, ordinarily the emperors,[6] and thus expose the State's attitude toward the Church.

Most of the documents are drawn from the *Codex Theodosianus* and from the *Codex Iustinianus*. The former is the first official compilation of imperial laws and was constructed at the command of Theodosius II (408–50), who instructed (435) a commission to collect all imperial constitutions issued in and after Constantine I's reign (306–37). The *Codex* (approved on 15 February 438) contains sixteen books, of which ample portions are preserved. The latter is another collection of imperial laws, also collected by a commission instituted (528) by Justinian I (527–65), but including constitutions issued from Hadrian's reign (117–38) onward and often repeating, though occasionally with changes (addition or omission or alteration) the enactments contained in the earlier code. This *Codex* (accepted in a second edition[3] on 16 November 534) comprises twelve books, which are still mostly complete. The remaining constitutions are chosen chiefly from writings of ecclesiastical writers (especially historians), who incorporate these instruments into their works, from the so-called Avellan Collection,[7] which *inter alia* preserves emperors' epistles to popes, from conciliar *acta*, wherein occur imperial ordinances, and from inscriptions containing constitutions concerning the Church.[8]

2. The type of instrument or constitution varies. Since the imperial will must prevail,[9] the emperor was not restricted to any single form of

expression. Consequently several kinds have been distinguished: (1) *edict* (proclamation, whether oral or written, but generally the latter), (2) *epistle* (whether rescript, reply to a subordinate official's letter, or subscription, answer to a subject's petition,) (3) *decree* (judicial decision), (4) *mandate* (administrative instruction to an official), (5) *edictal law* (law emanating from an edict), (6) *general law* (law of general character), (7) *formulary* (enactment establishing a legal norm), (8) *pragmatic sanction* (important ordinance concerning either general administration or privileges conferred upon large groups of persons or orders given to juristic persons), (9) *sanction* (ordinance).

The first four are called generically *constitutiones principum* or *principum placita*; the last five are generally late synonyms for the first and perhaps the fourth of the first group, for the nomenclature seems not to have been too nice in a period wherein emperors were empowered to enact laws—what and how and when they willed. Quite constant are the Latin terms to distinguish the first four forms: (1) *edictum*, (2) *epistula* or *rescriptum* or *subscriptio*, (3) *decretum*, (4) *mandatum*. While *epistula* embraces both *rescriptum* and *subscriptio*, *rescriptum* is found rather frequently for *epistula* and occasionally even refers—inconsistently, it is thought—to a letter sent *motu proprio* without previous request for reply. Sometimes *oraculum* or *responsum* is used for *rescriptum*. The Latin terms for the last five are: (5) *lex edictalis*, (6) *lex generalis*, (7) *forma*, (8) *pragmatica sanctio* or *pragmatica forma*, (9) *sanctio*. Accurate distinction among the plethora of Greek words assigned to these documents still awaits solution; synonyms abound and the situation that the same word sometimes is applied to more than one category simply confounds the confusion.[10]

Some civilians consider that during the Dominate the commonest forms of the constitutions were edicts and rescripts, while other authors accept general (edictal) laws for general enactments and rescripts for particular legislation as the more usual vehicles, into which were merged the several types. But what some writers, loosely using the word as a class name for any imperial expression on legal matters, call edicts—especially when Justinian's so-called edicts are meant—read rather like mandates. In this sylloge an attempt at precise distinction is made.

While for generations the imperial legislation was emitted ordinarily in Latin, yet provision early was made for translation of documents into Greek, when applicable to a Greek-speaking district, either at the source or at the destination.[11]

3. None now holds that the sovereigns customarily composed holographic constitutions.[12] Evidence that they had and used their secretariat is too common to demand demonstration.[13] And if some of the legislation of the early emperors after official and final recognition of Christianity as a tolerated religion (*religio licita*) seems to the sceptical reader to reflect too much Christian sentiment, it may be said that there also is evidence that Christian clerks then were employed in the imperial bureaux.[14] When he signed, the sovereign used a particular purple ink, restricted (on pain of death) for his sole use.[15]

In drafting legislation the emperor could look for aid to his council (*consilium*), later called consistory (*consistorium*), composed of eminent jurists, whose advice he was free to accept. By the mid-fifth century (446) an elaborate procedure for such preparation was established by Theodosius II, but it is not known how great was the devotion to its details ere imperial confirmation was signified.[16] It is reasonable to suppose that legislation treating theological niceties was drafted—at least partly—by courtier-clerics, who at times, of course, were not averse from partisanship in the service of their sovereign, who might, and occasionally did, prefer heterodox (especially in the East) to orthodox opinions.

The permanent division of the Empire, when Theodosius I the Great at his death in 395 divided it between his sons, Arcadius in the East and Honorius in the West, created a permanent situation which called for solution: what to do about the validity of legislation enacted by one of the two emperors?[17] This problem presented difficulties, especially when the emperors did not see eye to eye on theological tenets,[18] and was decided in 438 by Theodosius II, who declared that one emperor's enactments would be invalid in his colleague's realm, unless these first should have been submitted to him and then should have secured his sanction.[19] But, as the event proved, the theory of the law's unity occasionally failed in practice.[20]

4. Although it is true that in all ancient monarchies known to us religion and sacerdotalism, where the latter is present, appear both as a political and as a social power, yet the emergence first and then the establishment of the Christian Church in the Roman Empire—a veritable *imperium in imperio*—was unprecedented,[21] in that it created problems of a character which were so new and yet so necessary that a prince might well have asked himself the question which Mordecai put to Queen Esther: "Who knoweth whether thou art come to the

kingdom for such a time as this?"[22] As soon as Christians had become sufficiently strong to attract governmental attention, the imperial administration proscribed Christianity as a religion and the Church as a society. Intermittent persecution in civic and provincial units characterized the emperors' attitude until the mid-third century, when Decius (249-51) inaugurated the initial effort to crush Christianity throughout the Empire. It is not difficult to discern the pagan Romans' reasons for these pogroms. The Christian religion was contrary to the spirit of the Roman civilization, in that the Christians were charged rightly with refusal to discharge a subject's duties toward the State, with obstinate opposition to law, and with organization in outlawed and seditious societies.[23] Such charges were not only sufficiently serious when imputed against individuals, but also even more momentous when cast collectively against the Church, whose constitution of compact and coherent character, clergymen and communicants and converts, common possession of corporate property, pervasive presence in community after community, constant communication with its cellular congregations, conspired to create an *imperium in imperio* and to establish an ecclesiastical enclave amid and against the Empire.[24] Moreover, the Church, as a divine and supernatural society, a living organism as well as a mystical union of souls, claimed to possess the necessary and exclusive means of salvation, to be visible and recognizable, to exercise authority in its office of instruction (*potestas magisterii*) and of government (*potestas iurisdictionis*), to be indefectible, to be universal in its notes of unity, sanctity, catholicity, apostolicity, and to have the conditions requisite for a perfect society.[25]

Though in theory the emperors were completely competent to legislate in all matters, yet the exercise of the right to rule on religious questions [26] was dictated in practice by considerations of policy, which could and did vary from prince to prince. Scarcity of sources for the Principate suggests that the pagan emperors (taken as a group), despite their occasional passion for persecution, which seldom was world-wide, often reflected the oft-quoted attitude of Lucius Junius Annaeus Gallio (*c.* 52 proconsul of Achaea), who "cared for none of those things".[27] But with the constitutional recognition of Christianity (313)—which, evolving from the faith of the oppressed, the hope of the repressed, the comfort of the suppressed, by the Dominate had established a community without nationality and a catholic league of humanity, excluding neither barbarian nor bondman—[28] the emperor's legislative activity in religious affairs became enormous, as is seen, for instance, in the documents emanating from Constantine I (306-37), the first Christian emperor, who even considered himself as a kind of lay bishop [29] and, as a bishop is supposed to be the shepherd of his sheep, so busied himself with often careful, but occasionally careless, cultivation of spiritual matters on an ecumenical basis.

While it is perhaps true that Christianity owed more to Constantine than to anyone since St Paul (its second founder, so to speak)—no matter whether in recognizing its mission the emperor was executing a grand idea or merely introducing an energetic priesthood into power for the purpose of confirming his own position—it was very easy for him,[30] as well as for some of his successors, to mistake the Church's aggrandizement for the advance of Christianity. And it may be added that, though Christianity's progress was independent of the careers of crowned personages, yet the fortunes of Christianity frequently were hindered or were helped by them, for "the theory, which was afterwards to prevail in western Europe, of a trenchant separation between the spiritual and temporal powers was still unborn".[31] And it eventually appeared that authoritarian emperors' interfering appetite increased with eating. So matters of religion, whether pagan or Christian, in the Empire were managed as part and parcel of imperial legislation,[26] which saw first in its gemmate and then in its ripened absolutism the need to control the thoughts of men's minds even in religious beliefs, with the result that, after imperially inspired persecution had ceased during the fourth century's second decade,[32] State and Church moved ever closer to each other, each affecting and altering the other (because the citizen was often a Christian and the Christian was usually a citizen),[33] until the collapse of the former in the West gave the latter its autonomy first and then its supremacy, while in the East ecclesiastical affairs continued to be more and more under governmental control, so characteristic of oriental organization.[34]

That there were controversies between Church and State is true, but such strife seems to have assumed chiefly the aspect of disputes between emperors (and bureaucracy) and prelates (and clergy), since Christians were beginning to believe that both Church and State should collaborate in promotion of the kingdom of God: the clerical authorities, functioning in matters spiritual, to guide men to everlasting life; the laical powers, operating in secular affairs, to manage men in their mutual dealings—that thus by the peaceful pursuit of the spiritual life mankind might achieve the common goal of eternal felicity.

Of course, an understanding between Church and State, a friendship between Peter and Caesar, was desirable for Christendom's peace and prosperity. When this amity was subjected not seldom to attacks, their violence was allayed by soothing applications in the shape of concessions—sometimes from each side, occasionally from Peter's, oftener from Caesar's. As early as the mid-second century this interaction could inspire the celebrated confession of St Melito (*ob. c.* 190), bishop of Sardis, who in an apology addressed to Aurelius (161–80), the philosopher-emperor, suggested, in attracting attention to the coevality of Christianity with the Empire, that the State had secured more from the Church's spiritual support than the Church had profited from the State's intermittent patronage during the imperial peace.[35] But time made true a contrary expression (equally classic), that imperial services had subserved ecclesiastical interests at least by the mid-fifth century, set in a sermon by Pope St Leo I (440–61), who saw God's providence providing through the single polity of the Empire a field for the Church's propagation of the faith.[36]

But this is an idealized picture of the period; the realistic portrait is not so pleasant or serene, for in the fourth century were sown the sinister seeds of the fifth century's doctrinal controversies, which were far fiercer than any that the Church had known and which do not constitute a happy chapter in the history of the Church.[37] Ecclesiastical partisanship, jealousy of rival patriarchates, political issues, rabid intolerance, religious enthusiasm of recently converted clergy and laity, monastic fanaticism, imperial interference, confused cogitation, exaggerated emphasis on one or other element of the Lord's person, racial antipathy—all these factors played their part in prostituting the fair name of Christianity. It was a period wherein men, while they thought much of discipline and of order, yet did not perceive that religious tolerance is needful for catholic concord. The equipoise between order and freedom—so hard at all times to adjust—was especially difficult to maintain when men—then as now—had little use for the golden mean (*aurea mediocritas*) preached by the pagan poet Horace.[38]

Perhaps the confusion came partly from the Church's lack of preparation for the so-called Constantinian peace, which promoted the Church, the State's principal internal rival, from the position of a social pariah to that of the State's patronized favourite. That the Church failed to previsualize this fatal fortune is patent from the circumstances of the fourth and the fifth centuries. And one may well wonder whether Constantine's conversion, in which Christians then rejoiced as their deliverance from persecution, did not perpetrate the worst disaster to descend upon them, for in reality it fastened more firmly the chains of the State's control over the Church, since it was Constantine who admitted the Christian Church into the Roman State with the result that the Church accepted the State and the Roman law regnant in the State. The concessions conferred on the Church were such as scarcely could have been denied much longer during the fourth century, but the State in exchange gained an enormous measure of control in religious matters, especially in endeavouring to enforce spiritual concord among its Christian subjects—Christianity ever has been the most quarrelsome of religions—by legislation,[39] which led inevitably to civil disabilities and to penal laws. For if the principal purpose of an absolute government, which the Empire had become in the Dominate, is to preserve peace by protecting its subjects' life and property, then the Roman State could not remain indifferent either to their religion, which always has been a chief cause of human strife, or to a religious organization owning property (acquired chiefly by purchase or donation or legacy), since property ranks second only to religion in its power to cause dispute and discord.

5. There seem to be only six statutes (nos. 1–6), presenting the *veritable* words of the State's legislation concerning the Church before persecution of Christians ceased in 311. Only one law (no. 4) favours Christianity; the other five constitutions concern punishment of Christians. It is not necessary here to dwell upon the State's attitude toward the Church during the period of persecution and it appears preferable to postpone such an account to the Appendix on Persecutions, where are collected all references to *reported* imperial legislation on this subject.[40]

But after persecution had ended in 311, the State's influence upon the Church was expressed through the medium of law in various ways, of which the following means (illustrated in nos. 7–652) are the more important:[41]

(*a*) The emperors recognized the ecclesiastical organization as observed in dioceses (which patriarchs or exarchs ruled), provinces (over which metropolitans or archbishops or primates presided), and cities (where bishops supervised the lower clergy).[42] Legislation pertaining to ordination and to consecration as well as to the hierarchy's jurisdiction and to relative rank within it was enacted, with the result that the episcopate not only was strengthened at the expense of the inferior clergy, but also was subjected to the mercy of the State.

(b) The State interfered with the Church's internal affairs chiefly to preserve civic peace, which was flouted by heretical and schismatical factionalism (occasionally founded on nationalistic separatist tendencies), and sometimes to compel orthodoxy, for it was unconscious that heresy is the perpetual horizon of progress.[43] Emperors convoked ecclesiastical councils, at which they assisted either personally or by proxy, and published conciliar canons under imperial sanction and imposed civil and criminal penalties against persons who contemned synodal sentences.[44] Even without conciliar inspiration various emperors, whether orthodox or heterodox, issued constitutions to confirm or to condemn this or that tenet and to penalize those individuals or groups who refused to conform with past or current regulations by extruding them from clerical office or by excluding them from membership within the Church. Sometimes the sovereigns even intervened in episcopal elections.

(c) The dynasts in varying degrees conferred on the clergy both immunity from taxation and exemption from compulsory public services (liturgies), which privileges had been granted to pagan professors, priests, and physicians on the score of professional utility to the Empire. The considerable effect of this boon was shown by the measures taken by the government to limit the extent of this operation, when flight from the oppressive and unequal burdens laid upon all who were possessed of real property tended to become more frequent.

(d) The State recognized the Church as a juristic person capable of proprietary rights in receiving and administering gifts and bequests. When much of such property was devoted to "pious causes", that is, not only to churches, oratories, monasteries, nunneries, asceteries, but also to ecclesiastically directed charitable institutions (such as almshouses, asylums, gerontocomiums, hospitals, hostels, nurseries, orphanages) and funds (such as for relief of the non-domiciled poor and for ransom of prisoners of war), the emperors established rules for its management.

(e) The emperors empowered bishops to conduct episcopal courts, whose sentences in civil causes were final.

(f) The government, as time elapsed, increasingly impressed bishops into its civil and social administration as checks upon magistrates (particularly provincial governors), as overseers of the execution of public works, as intercessors against maladministration of criminal

INTRODUCTION xlv

justice, as enforcers of laws against gambling, as protectors of fugitives, who fled for sanctuary to the churches, which received the right of asylum once enjoyed by pagan temples.

(g) The sovereigns, whether through personal conviction or from clerical persuasion, legislated on numerous matters—beyond those already mentioned—affecting the life of their Christian subjects. Among these enactments—to name only a few—may be listed: proper observance of Sunday, manumission of slaves in church, inheritance involving heretical testators or heirs, juridical oaths taken on the Bible, rape of nuns, sacerdotal misconduct, monastic discipline, simony, funeral customs, pagan or Jewish ownership of Christian slaves, marriage and divorce, rebaptism, disturbances in church, recruitment to the clericate, amusements, amnesty for criminals at Eastertide, construction of churches, redemption of captives, apostasy, interdiction of idolatry and of pagan practices, service of non-Christians and of heretics in civil or military capacities, evidence of Jews and of pagans and of heretics in lawsuits.[45]

6. This sylloge contains only such documents as seem to be in a legislator's words and to be legislative or mandatory in purpose—no matter whether such directives are for universal or local or individual application. Known forgeries and documents whose authenticity is accepted generally as dubious are excluded.[46] To have included all notices of and references to *reported* legislation, of which sometimes summaries are found in the reporter's words, would have enlarged the volume to an unwieldy size and would have caused some duplication. Such allusions, scattered throughout the writings of the Fathers of the Church, are concentrated especially in the works of the early ecclesiastical historians. In the commentary attention is attracted to important allusions.[47] While there is no doubt that in the Christianized Empire legislation assumed a Christian coloration[48] without definite reference to Christianity or to the Church always being inserted in the laws and while Christian influence has been claimed as responsible for the altered Roman attitude toward many of the matters mentioned in the preceding paragraph,[49] yet only such legislation as clearly and indubitably indicates Christian influence is included in this collection.

7. Since many statutes touch several subjects and since some laws are like what is colloquially called "omnibus legislation", in the Table of Documents is listed, when a constitution contains more than one topic,

that subject which seems the most important—but in several instances, indeed, the document includes a second important subject. Readers who may regret the brevity of the Table of Documents should resort to the Index of Subjects, which collects complete references and many cross-references to all topics treated in the documents. In a sylloge of this sort, though a table of contents is usual, yet an index of subjects is more useful, because the latter, amid the complexity of the legislation, which is listed chronologically, leads the reader more rapidly to such relations of State and Church as relate to his special interests.

In respect to the instruments' introductions and annotations an inequality of treatment will be noticed. Since many documents discuss the same subject, there would be rather much repetition, if fullness in preface as well as in commentary should have been furnished for each constitution. Consequently, as a general rule, the more important laws on any topic, whereon it has been thought that the reader would welcome some fuller exposition, receive a fullness which is not extended to every occurrence of ordinances on that topic.

8. While legal language is perhaps difficult to read in any native tongue and ordinarily tends to develop a technical terminology resulting in jargon (in both its good and its bad meaning),[50] yet to turn such diction and syntax from one language into another and still to create sense is a gift from the gods, who—we are assured on ancient authority—have not given all their gifts to one and the same person.[51] The task is complicated by the added hazard of having to treat not seldom at the same time theological and ecclesiastical words and phrases, of which some in our period have not achieved universally accepted meanings.[52] So the present translator, striving to steer his stylistic ship in such stormy seas between the Scylla of literalness and the Charybdis of looseness,[53] nevertheless hopes that he has escaped the one without encountering the other: but the benevolent reader, if such shall have remained after reading the result, will be the judge.[54]

9. During the twentieth century the decline of instruction in both Greek and Latin has deprived the rising generation of lawyers [55] and of clergymen [56] and of historians [57] of a first-hand acquaintance with such documents of Roman Law as affected the Christian Church in a critical period during the development of occidental civilization, when the old order of paganism was passing and was yielding place to the new dispensation of Christianity. In the belief that such a sylloge

INTRODUCTION xlvii

as this, wherein many documents appear for the first time in English, will be of both assistance and interest to these and to others this collection has been compiled.

10. Among aids to the reader are: a *Table of Names and Dates of Emperors* represented by their legislative documents; a *Glossary* describing sects of heretics and of schismatics, technical terms (both legal and ecclesiastical), and magistracies and offices; an *Index of Subjects* listing all laws on a particular subject; an *Index of Persons* with their dates when known; an *Index of Places;* an *Index of Titles of Address* recording complimentary titles appearing in the constitutions; and Indexes of *Sources, Quotations, and Allusions.*

As ancillary assistance for readers of English may be mentioned two religious histories (the one Roman Catholic and the other Anglo-Catholic), which traverse most of the period treated: (1) J. Lebreton and J. Zeiller, *The History of the Primitive Church* (4 vols., London, 1942–8), and their continuators, J. R. Palanque *et al., The Church in the Christian Roman Empire* (4 vols., London, 1949—); (2) B. J. Kidd, *A History of the Church to A.D. 461* (3 vols., Oxford, 1922). On the secular side special attention is attracted to (1) J. B. Bury, *History of the Later Roman Empire* (2 vols., London, 1923), which portrays the period 395–565 and which, despite the advance in our science since its appearance, still is dateless, especially for the description of the monarchy and of the bureaucracy contained in its first two chapters; (2) A. A. Vasiliev, *History of the Byzantine Empire* [2] (Madison, Wis., 1952), whose first chapter surveys critically the principal products of European scholarship in Byzantine studies and whose story starts with the year 324 and thus treats two generations before Bury's history begins.[58] Much useful material on both ecclesiastical and secular matters is scattered *passim* in A. J. Toynbee's magnificent masterpiece, *A Study of History* [1-2] (10 vols., London, 1934–54).[59]

Besides these books more particular information will be found in the following specialized works of encyclopaedic character:

W. Smith, ed., *A Dictionary of Greek and Roman Geography* (2 vols., London, 1854–7)
O. Shipley, ed., *A Glossary of Ecclesiastical Terms* (London, 1872)
S. Baring-Gould, *The Lives of the Saints* (15 vols., London, 1872–7)
J. H. Blunt, ed., *A Dictionary of Sects, Heresies, Ecclesiastical Parties, and Schools of Religious Thought* (London, 1874)

W. Smith and H. Wace, eds., *A Dictionary of Christian Biography* (4 vols., London, 1880)
W. Smith, ed., *A Dictionary of Greek and Roman Biography and Mythology* (3 vols., London, 1880)
W. Smith et al., eds., *A Dictionary of Greek and Roman Antiquities* ³ (2 vols., London, 1890-1)
H. Nettleship and J. E. Sandys, eds., *A Dictionary of Classical Antiquities, Mythology, Religion, Literature and Art* ³ (London, 1895)
H. T. Peck, ed., *Harper's Dictionary of Classical Literature and Antiquities* ² (New York, 1897)
C. S. Hebermann et al., eds., *The Catholic Encyclopedia* (18 vols., New York, 1907-58)
S. M. Jackson, ed., *The New Schaff-Herzog Encyclopedia of Religious Knowledge* (13 vols., New York, 1908-14)
J. Hastings, ed., *Encyclopaedia of Religion and Ethics* (13 vols., New York, 1908-27)
H. Wace and W. C. Piercy, eds., *A Dictionary of Christian Biography and Literature* (London, 1911)
L. R. Loomis, *The Book of the Popes (Liber Pontificalis)* (New York, 1916)
H. B. Walters, *A Classical Dictionary of Greek and Roman Antiquities, Biography, Geography, and Mythology* (Cambridge, 1916)
J. E. Sandys, ed., *A Companion to Latin Studies* ³ (Cambridge, 1921)
F. G. Holweck, *A Biographical Dictionary of the Saints* (London, 1924)
H. Thurston et al., eds., *Butler's The Lives of the Saints* (12 vols., London, 1926-38)
C. B. Pallen et al., eds., *The New Catholic Dictionary* (New York, 1929)
L. Whibley, ed., *A Companion to Greek Studies* ⁴ (Cambridge, 1931)
C. S. Carter and G. E. A. Weeks, eds., *The Protestant Dictionary* ² (London, 1933)
D. Attwater, *A Dictionary of the Popes from Peter to Pius XII* (London, 1939)
M. Cary et al., eds., *The Oxford Classical Dictionary* (Oxford, 1949)
F. A. Wright, ed., *Lemprière's Classical Dictionary* (London, 1949)
P. Harvey, *The Oxford Companion to Classical Literature* ⁴ (Oxford, 1951)
E. H. Blakeney and J. Warrington, eds., *Everyman's Smaller Classical Dictionary* rev. (London, 1952)
J. Warrington, ed., *Everyman's Atlas of Ancient and Classical Geography* rev. (London, 1952)
A. Berger, *Encyclopedic Dictionary of Roman Law* (Philadelphia, 1953)
P. G. Woodcock, ed., *Concise Dictionary of Ancient History* (New York, 1955)
F. L. Cross, ed., *The Oxford Dictionary of the Christian Church* (London, 1957)
W. E. Addis et al., eds., *A Catholic Dictionary* ¹⁶ (St Louis, 1957)
D. Attwater, ed., *A Catholic Dictionary* ³ (New York, 1958)
D. Attwater, *A Dictionary of Saints* (New York, 1958)
H. Kühner, *Encyclopedia of the Papacy* (New York, 1958)
C. B. Avery, ed., *The New Century Classical Handbook* (New York, 1962)

INTRODUCTION   xlix

NOTES

1. The only five recent comparable collections in English are: B. J. Kidd, *Documents Illustrative of the History of the Church* (3 vols., London, 1920–41), J. C. Ayer, Jr., *A Source Book for Ancient Church History* (New York, 1922), H. Bettenson, *Documents of the Christian Church* (Oxford, 1943), S. Z. Ehler and J. B. Morrall, *Church and State through the Centuries* (Westminster, Md., 1954), J. Stevenson, *A New Eusebius* (London, 1957). Although all, of course, contain legal documents and some reprint also ancient authors' reports of such legislation (a classification excluded from the present compilation for reasons stated later) and some do not supply comments to clarify their contents, yet these sylloges emphasize doctrine rather than legislation and, because they traverse far more space in time (Ehler and Morrall to 1949; Bettenson to 1922; Kidd to 1522; Ayer to 787; Stevenson, to 337, is based upon Kidd), do not pretend to be complete in the legal phase—nor, indeed, do their compilers claim completeness in any category.

The timely significance of this sylloge may be seen in the acuteness of the problem of the interrelation of Church and State in the United States since World War II—witness the organization (1947) of Protestants and Other Americans United for Separation of Church and State as well as the spate of literature on this subject. For, if it is true, as Cicero asked, "What is the worth of man's life, unless it is linked with our ancestors' life by the record of past events?" (*Orat.* 34. 120), then it is useful for students of history (both secular and ecclesiastical) and of politics to see how an earlier and ecumenical society, wherein man was simultaneously both a member of the Church and a citizen of the State, concerned itself with jurisdiction over the individual in this double capacity, since religion—now as then—cannot be divorced from citizenship.

2. This incompetent ruler ironically combines in his name those of Rome's first king (Romulus, who traditionally reigned 753–716 B.C.) and first emperor (Augustus, whose principate was 27 B.C.–A.D. 14).

As Bury and Vasiliev and others (see text of Introd. before n. 59 *infra*) have shown (Bury, 1. 408; Vasiliev, 22), "the resignation of Romulus Augustulus did not even shake the Roman Empire; far less did it cause an empire to fall. It is unfortunate, therefore, that Gibbon spoke of the 'fall of the Western Empire', and that many modern writers have given their sanction to the phrase." (See also n. 5 to the Table of Names and Dates of Emperors and Vasiliev, 265–9.) But the writ of the emperors of the East no longer ran in the West, where their erstwhile subjects were lost by them to the barbarian suzerains, who emitted their own laws (modelled indeed upon Roman law) notably in the three following codes (written in Latin), through which the administration of Roman law survived in Western Europe during the Dark Ages: (1) the *Lex Romana Burgundionum* of c. 500, published by Gundobad, king of the Burgundians (475–506), for his Roman subjects' use; (2) the *Lex Romana*

INTRODUCTION

Visigothorum of *c.* 506, promulgated by Alaric II, king of the Visigoths (484–507), for the use of his Roman subjects and derived mostly from the *Codex Theodosianus* (cf. text *infra* after n. 6) by abridgement (whence it also is called the *Breviarium Alaricianum*) and the chief document through which knowledge of Roman law was disseminated widely in the West until the twelfth century, when real study of the *Corpus Iuris Civilis* (cf. *infra* n. 3) in Italy began at the infant University of Bologna under the inspiration of Irnerius (1050?–?1130), who, though perhaps not the first of the glossators in time, in rank was *facile princeps* and was called by his pupils "the Lamp of the Law" (*lucerna iuris*) (3) the *Lex Romana Ostrogothorum* of *c.* 513, proposed by Theodoric the Great king of the Ostrogoths (474–526), for both his barbarian and his Roman subjects and known also as the *Edictum Theodorici*.

3. The issuance of the two other principal parts of the *Corpus Iuris Civilis* (as the complete codification of Justinian I's legislation is called), the *Institutiones* and the *Digesta* (or *Pandectae*), the one on 21 November 533 and the other on 16 December 533, involved so many alterations in the law that a new compilation of the *Codex* was necessitated. Therefore, the first edition, the so-called *Codex Vetus*, issued on 7 April 529, was recalled when the second edition, the *Codex Repetitae Praelectionis*, superseded it on 16 November 534. Since the fourth and last part of the *Corpus*, the *Novellae*, Justinian I's original legislation (promulgated 535–65) and some constitutions of his immediate successors, Justin II (568–78) and Tiberius II (578–82), was not added, of course, until afterward, the practicable date for the close of the collection coincides with the republication of the *Codex*, which can be regarded as the virtual end of ancient Roman law.

The title *Corpus Iuris Civilis* is taken from the edition (2 vols., Lyon, 1583) of Denys Godefroy (*al.* Dionysius Gothofredus [1549–1621]), since Justinian, though he speaks of the *omne corpus iuris* ("the entire body of the law") in *CI* 5. 13. 1. pr. (dated 530), seems never to have designed for his collection a collective designation.

4. Cf. *supra* nn. 2 and 3.

5. For apparent exceptions see nos. 95, 124, 407.

6. Occasionally imperial officials arranged for republication of the emperors' legislation, that this might be brought to the information and the guidance of all concerned. In such instances sometimes only these republished constitutions have survived. Also the occasional implementations of imperial ordinances have been included.

7. Thus called from the fact that in the Fonte-Avellana Valley amid the Apennines of the Marche in east-central Italy was from 977 to 1570 the Hermitage (after 989 the Priory and after 1325 the Abbey) of Santa Croce di Fonte-Avellana, whose library owned one of the two oldest codices of the collection. This manuscript was bought by the Vatican Library between 1585 and 1591.

8. None knows why so few imperial laws concerning the Church are found among the thousands of Christian inscriptions, which, besides being frag-

mentary for the most part, are mostly sepulchral epitaphs, dedications of churches and of altars, pious formulas, quotations from the Bible or from liturgies or from patristic writings, invocations, doxologies, hymns, prayers, petitions to prelates or to potentates, hierarchic decisions, conciliar canons, eulogies of martyrs and of saints, memorials, testimonials, names and titles, salutations, records of pilgrimages, verses, monograms, devices.

So far papyri also have proved a scanty source of legislation concerning the Church. Search through the volumes of published papyri pertaining to the period of this sylloge has revealed none emanating from governmental offices on ecclesiastical legislation, although, of course, many papyri of theological tenor have been printed. But to be noted as illustrative of the State's relation to the Church are the papyri mentioned in no. 28, n. 1 *ad med.*, and the *libelli* from the Decian persecution noticed in the Appendix on Persecutions, n. 12.

9. Ulpian (*ob.* 228), who, as a jurisconsult and a praetorian prefect, contributed about one third (2,462 extracts) of Justinian's *Digest*, established the doctrine that whatever has pleased the emperor has the force of law, since by the royal law (*lex regia*), which has been passed concerning his supreme power (*imperium*), the people confer on him and to him all their power and authority (*D* 1. 4. 1).

Our earliest example of the bestowal of this power on the emperor exists in the so-called Law of Vespasian's Power (*Lex de imperio Vespasiani*), promulgated in 70 and discovered (on a bronze tablet set in the structure of a Christian altar) *c.* 1347 in time for Cola di Rienzi to use it as anti-papal propaganda (in that the powers conferred by it came from the people), when he harangued the Roman populace on the rights which the Senate and the People of Rome (SPQR) had surrendered to the Papacy. The inscription is in *FIRA* 1. 154–6.

In the Empire popular legislation soon vanished: first the Assemblies ceded their rights to the Senate and the emperor; then the Senate surrendered its right to the emperor. The last law known to have issued from a Roman Assembly was enacted in Nerva's reign (96–8), and the Senate passed its last recorded senatusconsult of legislative character in the principate of Probus (276–82).

H. J. Wolff in discussing imperial legislation rightly remarks that "from Constantine on . . . The emperors were the masters of the law as they were masters of the Empire . . . The law had lost its quality of being an integral part of the life of the nation and had become a mere tool in the hands of authoritarian government . . . completely dependent on the absolute will of the ruler" (*Roman Law: An Historical Introduction* [Norman, Okla., 1951], 90–1).

In short, by the end of Constantine I's reign (306–37) the Roman Empire was transformed into what surely may be termed a totalitarian state. But, since totalitarianism hardly appears without a cause, what had caused this transformation? Doubtless it was the imperial desire of Diocletian (284–305) to inhibit the decay which, having begun after the death of Alexander Severus (222–35), he inherited at his accession. In an abnormal dance of death, within almost fifty years of anarchy (235–84), appeared about thirty legitimate and illegitimate emperors, of whom only one escaped a violent end. It was a period wherein barbarian battles and military mutinies, growing authority of the greedy army in government, brigandage and piracy, pestilence and famine, debasement of coinage and departure of currency through booty or ransom or tribute, economic depression and devastation of natural resources and deterioration of soil, desolation of countryside and depredation of communities, disruption of industry and commerce, decrease of population and destruction of property, confiscatory taxation and administrative corruption, biological degeneration and moral decay and social disintegration, upper-class disregard and middle-class despair and lower-class discontent, crisis after crisis causing constant confusion and spreading lowered standards of living—to mention merely a few factors—in troublous times tried men's souls. The conclusion of the third century's age of anarchy can be declared to be the proper division in imperial history between the Principate and the Dominate: between the ending of the old order and the beginning of the new order, when the emperor ceased to be the *princeps* (first of the citizens) and came to be the *dominus* (master of his subjects). Then a centralized autocracy, aided by sacred sanctions and courtly ceremonial, through its burdensome bureaucracy—expensive and extensive as well as corrupted and corrupting (Tacitus, *Ann.* 3. 54. 2)—began to consume, like cancer, its own cells, which from decades of decay already were rotten at their roots, and soon achieved a melancholy array of maladies, which often have been observed in totalitarian states and to which testify the Theodosian Code's (see text of Introd. after n. 6 *supra*) constitutions (312–438) and its suppended statutes (438–68). For the administrative alterations, devised by Diocletian and by Constantine confirmed, and sundry other schemes, started or substituted by succeeding sovereigns, controlled men's modes of livelihood through hereditary corporations in occupations, expanded the system of enforced public services, tightened taxation for the poor in favour of the rich, assisted agriculture to the injury of industry, so that investment of wealth in plantations increased the large landed estates manned by slaves or by serf-like tenants, who were scarcely superior in status to slaves, and induced a less urban and a more rural social structure, and eventually disorganized the public economy in almost all its departments (most markedly in communications, defence, finance, interior, welfare). All this amounted to an abortive attempt to save the slowly sinking Ship of State, which, being buffeted by billows of economic distress, political confusion, religious discord, social collapse, and being battered by swells of barbarians dashing upon its sloping decks, soon resembled a ruin in repair. And while the ship was being shivered, the officers, who alone possessed life-preservers, bickered on its bridge about their prerogatives and protected their plank of safety in a shipwrecked society. Thus again was proved that perhaps the only thing that is learned from history is that from history is learned nothing.

On Rome's decay see M. Rostovtzeff, *The Social & Economic History of the*

INTRODUCTION   liii

Roman Empire (Oxford, 1926), 478-87; R. F. Arragon, *The Transition from the Ancient to the Medieval World* (New York, 1936), 1-23, 28-31, 42-4, 51-89; W. Durant's rhetorical summary in his *Caesar and Christ* (New York, 1944), 665-70; S. Katz, *The Decline of Rome and the Rise of Mediaeval Europe* (Ithaca, 1955), 70-84, where historians' and philosophers' and theologians' hypotheses are presented and treated; and, most recently, R. M. Haywood, *The Myth of Rome's Fall* (New York, 1958).

Perhaps one of the imperial motives for confirming Christianity was the emperors' hope of having the Church's help in conserving what of civilization could be salvaged amid the economic, military, political, and social difficulties and disasters confronting the State during the Dominate. On this see E. Troeltsch, *The Social Teaching of the Christian Churches* (New York, 1949), I. 126-7.

10. On these classes consult W. W. Buckland, *A Text-Book of Roman Law from Augustus to Justinian* (Cambridge, 1921), 16-21; id., *A Manual of Roman Private Law* [2] (Cambridge, 1939), 12-13; *MARE* 235-40 (esp. 236, n. 1); H. F. Jolowicz, *Historical Introduction to the Study of Roman Private Law* [2] (Cambridge, 1952), 374-83, 478-82; J. W. C. Turner, *Introduction to the Study of Roman Private Law* (Cambridge, 1953), 95-6, 102-3; R. W. Lee, *The Elements of Roman Law* [4] (London, 1956), 17-18.

11. But from the context of the documents in the collection are noted many instances where the preserver of the constitution obviously has had access to it in only one language, for he writes that he has turned it either from Greek (rarely) or from Latin (generally).

The language used for teaching in the law schools, even in the East, was solely Latin until *c*. 400, when Greek was allowed in the institutions not located in Rome and in Carthage, viz. Alexandria, Antioch, Athens, Beirut, Caesarea in Palestine, Constantinople, of which the most celebrated was that in Beirut (Berytus), called "the Nurse of the Laws" (*legum nutrix*).

On translation in the imperial bureaux see the reference to Abbott in n. 13 *infra*.

On publication of imperial laws the latest comprehensive study seems to be in German by Fritz Freiherr von Schwind, "Die Veröffentlichung der Kaiserkonstitutionen" in his *Zur Frage der Publikation im römischen Recht* (München, 1940), 128-84 (esp. 157-74); L. Wenger, W. Otto, M. San Nicolò, eds., *Münchener Beiträge zur Papyrusforschung und antiken Rechtsgeschichte*, 31.

12. Occasionally, however, an emperor wrote a legal document by his own hand (Eusebius, *VC* 2. 47). Such, e.g., is no. 52.

13. But see convenient summaries by F. F. Abbott, *A History and Description of Roman Political Institutions* [3] (Boston, 1911), 362, and by M. P. Charlesworth, "Claudius as Re-Organizer and Legislator" in *CAH* 10. 685-8.

14. None disputes that Christian soldiers served in the army long before Constantine I is said to have seen the Cross in the sky en route to battle at the Milvian Bridge outside Rome on 27 October 312 (on which vision see A.

Alföldi, *The Conversion of Constantine and Pagan Rome* [Oxford, 1948], 16–24). For, apart from the early conversions of certain centurions on evangelical and apostolical authority (Matt. 8. 5–13, 27. 54; Luke 7. 2–10, 23. 47; esp. Acts 10. 1–8, 17–48—and there is no indication that they then ceased to be soldiers (but see no. 555, n. 4), it is accepted that under Aurelius the composition of the celebrated Thundering Twelfth Legion (*Legio XII Fulminata*), which (c. 174) had been stationed for almost a century at Melitene in eastern Cappadocia, was considerably Christian (Eusebius, *HE* 5. 5. 1–6).

If so, why would it be a matter for marvel that legislation designed to affect ecclesiastical affairs should have been prepared for imperial signature by Christian secretaries after 311 (when the last general persecution of the Church had ended) and that these scribes should have incorporated Christianlike statements into the constitutions which they either composed or copied? (Cf. *infra* n. 49.) Add also that there had been "saints . . . of Caesar's household" as early as c. 61 according to St Paul's testimony (Phil. 4. 22); that Hosius, the centenarian bishop of Córdoba, was between 313 and 326 the chief ecclesiastical adviser to Constantine I (cf. Socrates, *HE* 1. 7 with Eusebius, *HE* 10. 6. 2 and *VC* 1. 32, 42; 2. 63, 73), who caused him to preside over the First General Council of the Church at Nicaea in 325; that Lactantius, the Latin Christian apologist, tutored Constantine I's oldest son Crispus (Jerome, *De Vir. Illus.* 80).

15. This custom cannot be traced higher than 470 under Leo I (it is noted in *CI* 1. 23. 6), but it well may be older.

16. So Jolowicz, op. cit., 481.

17. Previously, of course, there had been joint rulers, but ordinarily there had been no great difficulty in this regard, for usually one was sufficiently ascendant to enforce his will on his colleague and customarily the constitutions issued by one carried the names of all. As a record, we can count as many as six emperors exercising their *imperium* at one time in 308: Maximian I, Maxentius, Maximin II, Galerius, Licinius, Constantine I (*CAH* 12. 347), of whom the last survived to be the sole sovereign from 324 to 337, when at his death he left the Empire to his three sons, Constantine II, Constans I, and Constantius II.

18. This contemporary difference, while eventually lessened somewhat (see text before next note), was accompanied by inter-successions of orthodox, semi-heretical, heterodox sovereigns (not to mention even one apostate autocrat, Julian II, whose reign, fortunately for the Church, was brief) and explains to some extent the vacillation characteristic of legislation from Constantine I to Justinian I, as the imperial interest was attracted toward or turned from contentions of clamant Christian clerics, of whom some, either representatives of "spiritual wickedness in high places" (Eph. 6. 12) or adventurers with sundry sacerdotal accretions, employed the emperors as agents to advance what they asserted to be the Church's claims, which ranged from the right to harass heretics and schismatics to the embodiment of Christian ethics in both civil and criminal law. See also introd. to no. 159 and n. 16 thereon.

19. *LNT* 1. 5.

20. See Huttmann, 133–5.

21. Perhaps this is what St Optatus (*flor.* 385), bishop of Milevis in Numidia, meant, when he asserted that "the State is not in the Church, but the Church is in the State, that is, in the Roman Empire" (*Non enim respublica est in ecclesia, sed ecclesia in republica, id est, in imperio Romano* [*De Schis. Donat.* 3. 3 = *CSEL* 26. 74]). But St Ambrose (340?–97), bishop of Milan, reversed this *dictum* when he declared that "the emperor is within the Church, not over the Church" (*Imperator enim intra ecclesiam, non supra ecclesiam est* [*Serm. cont. Aux.* 36 = *PL* 16. 1061]). As late as the early nineteenth century St Optatus' opinion was repeated by Count Maximilian Joseph von Montgelas (1759–1838), a Bavarian statesman, who maintained that "the church is in the state and not the state in the church" (quoted by R. A. Graham, s. J., *Vatican Diplomacy* [Princeton, 1959], 278). On the patristic opinions see C. H. McIlwain, *The Growth of Political Thought in the West* (New York, 1932), 151–3, 163–4.

One must differentiate, of course, between Christianity and the Church: the former is the spirit inherent in the Christian religion, the latter is the society incorporating that spirit; Chrisitianity and the Church seem seldom to have coincided to a conspicuous extent ever since the sacerdotal seal had been stamped upon the ecclesiastical establishment, for "the idea creates the institution, and the institution crushes the idea" (E. Caird, *The Evolution of Religion* [New York, 1893], 2. 248). Moreover, the Church is a divine institution in the sense that it, instituted by Christ (Matt. 16. 18, on which see no. 442, n. 7), exists for a divine purpose: to subject man into conformity with the divine will (e.g. Rom. 12. 1–5, 1 Thess. 4. 1–8, Heb. 13. 20–1, 1 John 2. 15–17); but in another sense the Church is a human society and it is left to human wisdom to adapt its forms from time to time so as to make the institution fitter for its work. As the form is always less than the purpose (cf. 2 Cor. 3. 6), so the errant spirit, which changes existing forms for the sake of change, is as reprehensible as the inflexible spirit, which adheres to existing forms for the sake of age. While divine wisdom declares "Jesus Christ the same yesterday, and today, and forever" (Heb. 13. 8), yet human wisdom holds that "All things change, and we change with them" (Borbonius: *Omnia* [al. *tempora*] *mutantur, nos et mutamur in illis*).

22. Esther 4. 14. The Septuagint and the Revised Version and the Revised Standard Version correctly read a negative, which the Vulgate and the Authorized Version omit, but the quotation as given will be perhaps more familiar to those into whose hands my work shall have come (Tacitus, *Ann.* 4. 11. 5).

23. Despite St Paul's and St Peter's authoritative advice in Rom. 13. 1–7 and 1 Pet. 2. 13–17—not to exclude the example set by Jesus himself, who saw no inevitable conflict between Caesar's and God's claims in concluding that Caesar's "image and superscription" on coins implied that one should pay imperial taxes (Matt. 22. 15–22; Mark 12. 13–17; Luke 20. 20–6). But behind the Pauline and Petrine precepts probably appear, *inter alia*, Ps. 2. 10–11 and

Wisd. 6. 1–3 (see also John 19. 11), where is developed the doctrine that their thrones were owed to God not only by Jehovah-worshipping Jewish kings, such as Hezekiah, who "trusted in the Lord God of Israel, so that after him was none like him among all the kings of Judah nor any that were before him" (2 Kings 18. 5), but also by pagan sovereigns, such as Nebuchadnezzar II, to whom "the most high God . . . gave a kingdom" (Dan. 5. 18; cf. 2. 37) and who warred against Jehovah's worshippers, as well as by pagan monarchs, such as Cyrus I the Great, to whom "all the kingdoms of the earth hath the Lord God of heaven given" (2 Chron. 36. 23; Ezra 1. 2) and who aided Jehovah's adherents.

24. See McIlwain, op. cit., 144–7.

For the sociological aspect of the relation of Church and State in this period consult L. Sturzo, *Church and State* (New York, 1939), 21–50. Add now R. M. Haywood, *The Myth of Rome's Fall* (New York, 1958), 48–50.

25. In more than one way the Church may be said to have fulfilled two prophecies, one Roman and one Christian: Vergil, *Aen.* 1. 278–9 and Matt. 16. 18 (second half).

26. Evidence for the close relation of pagan religion to the Roman State appears in the assignment of religious matters with a political significance to the magistracy. It abounds therefore throughout Roman history, and this applies even under the early Christian emperors. Though this testimony is perhaps too notorious to need proof, yet attention may be attracted in passing to several selected points, such as (1) the sacral law, (2) solemn sacrifices made by magistrates, (3) auspices taken in connection with important business of the State (especially in respect to election of magistrates, their entrance into office and their departure for campaigns, and to meetings of the popular Assemblies for legislative purposes), (4) sessions of the Senate by preference in sacred precincts, (5) construction of and care for deities' edifices and statues at the State's expense, (6) deposit of spoils of war in shrines, (7) governmentally sponsored religious festivals (including games and processions), (8) election or selection of pontiffs, augurs, flamens, quindecimvirs, vestals, and minor sacerdotal officials, (9) the imperial cult, (10) deification of emperors.

But above all the emperors assumed both the title and the functions of the pontifex maximus. The fact that republican Rome had been familiar with decrees of the college of pontiffs, of whom the pontifex maximus was the chief, no doubt assisted the early emperors, who were so careful to consider republican institutions, in arrogating to themselves first consultation on and then legislation in religious affairs. The title continued to be borne by the Christian emperors, until Gratian rejected it in 379 (previously proposed dates are 367, 375, 382) according to A. Alföldi, "A Festival of Isis in Rome under the Christian Emperors of the IVth Century" in *Dissertationes Pannonicae*, 2. 7 (1937) 336–7. But, though the title thus was discarded, yet the spirit survived and the tradition, inherited from paganism, inspired imperial interference, then and thereafter, in the Church's dogma and discipline.

INTRODUCTION   lvii

As a papal appellation, *pontifex maximus* appears to have been applied first and ironically by Tertullian (*De Pud*. 1. 6) to St Callistus I (217–22), after whom is called the Roman catacomb whereof, as archdeacon, he had been the custodian, but wherein he, as pope, was not buried (see Jalland, 125, 127, n. 1, 133, n. 2), though some scholars suppose that Tertullian thus called a contemporary bishop of Carthage: for the controversy consult Jalland, 144–5; J. Quasten, *Patrology* (Westminster, Md., 1953), 2. 234–5; O. Cullmann, *Peter: Disciple—Apostle—Martyr* (London, 1953), 160, n. 5; H. Burn-Murdoch, *The Development of the Papacy* (London, 1954), 77, 119. After intermittent use the title was adopted permanently in Paul II's pontificate (1464–71). R. Graves recently has remarked that "the Chief Pontiff, in Republican and early Imperial times, was personally responsible to the Capitoline Trinity (Juppiter, Juno and Minerva), for the chaste behaviour of the Vestals, as his successor now is to the Christian Trinity for that of Roman Catholic nuns" (*The White Goddess* ³ [London, 1952], 347–8).

27. Acts 18. 12–17.

28. Cf. Gal. 3. 28; Col. 3. 11.

29. Eusebius, *VC* 4. 24; cf. 1. 44, where Eusebius characterizes Constantine as "a general bishop constituted by God". If it could occur to this unbaptized fautor of Christianity to call himself "a bishop of those without" (4. 24), the emperor equally well could present himself as a Christian preacher, occasionally preaching in the presence of his courtiers and of a multitude of auditors (4. 29).

For a recent discussion of Constantine as a bishop (a claim of his which has caused heated comment) see W. Seston's article of the same title in *JRS* 37 (1947) 127–31.

Accepting the accomplished fact that monarchy had succeeded the city-state, after Alexander the Great's (336–323 B.C.) ecumenical empire had dissolved into successor-states and after kings had appeared elsewhere in the Mediterranean milieu, Hellenistic philosophy rationalized the phenomenon by proposing that a monarch should mirror God, should organize his kingdom so that it would imitate the order of the universe and thus be a copy of the cosmos, and, assisted by the Logos, that immanent principle of order which pervades the universe, should be the human agent of the Divine Power controlling the cosmos.

Christian philosophy, as propounded in the conception of Eusebius of Caesarea, Constantine's confidant, with slight adaptation transformed this thought so that the monarch from being a god-king should become God's vicegerent, should imitate the Christians' God, and, counselled by the Logos, the Divine Word, should establish on earth a City of God as a copy of the "heavenly Jerusalem" (Heb. 12. 22), "a city which hath foundations, whose builder and maker is God'" (Heb. 11. 10), who "hath prepared for them a city" (Heb. 11. 16), wherein is "a building of God, an house not made with hands, eternal in the heavens" (2 Cor. 5. 1).

Consult N. H. Baynes, *Byzantine Studies and Other Essays* (London, 1955), 8, 18, 48, esp. 168–72, and see no. 127, n. 7.

30. Indeed Constantine is still called by the Greek Church Ἰσαπόστολος ("Peer of the Apostles") and was interred in Constantinople in his Church of the Holy Twelve Apostles (on which see no. 463, n. 5). And in this connection one is reminded of William Drummond's (1585-1649) later eulogy of King James I of England (1603-25), whom King Henry IV of France (1589-1610) called "the wisest fool in Christendom":

> "Great King, but better far than thou art great,
> Whom State not honours, but who honours State!"

It is certain that, when Constantine decided to deal with Christianity, the emperor encountered a confirmed ecumenical organization as an established tradition. Without that he probably would not have shown Christianity any consideration. Constantine's search for the Christian Church's support and his acceptance of its assistance perhaps initially meant scarcely more than the imperial attempt (inaugurated by Augustus [cf. Suetonius, *Aug.* 7. 2]) to buttress the imperial authority by reliance upon religion (for the imperial use of *divus* and of various religious forms of address see no. 127, n. 7). But whether or not Constantine considered that he should join an enemy whom he could not conquer, in effect that was what the emperor did. His profession of Christianity made it possible to replace Roman political unity with Christian religious unity—at least in theory.

31. Bury, 2. 360. On this subject see also Toynbee, 4. 346-53, and C. D. Burns, *The First Europe* (London, 1947), 186-8, 625-43.

The medieval conception of the one Church-State, shattered by the Reformation, had not yet been created completely in this sylloge's period, though the doctrine of "the two swords"—spiritual authority and temporal power (see Luke 22. 38: so interpreted by Pope Boniface VIII in his bull *Unam sanctam* of 1302)—of which, while each acts in its own sphere of action, yet the former is so superior to the latter that one may conceive of one jurisdiction under one head (see Jer. 1. 10; Matt. 28. 18-20; Acts 5. 29; Rom. 13. 1: texts often cited to confirm this thesis)—apparently was formulated papally first in 494 (cf. *supra* n. 21 *ad init.* for St Ambrose's earlier episcopal assertion in 386) for Emperor Anastasius I by Pope St Gelasius I (*PL* 56. 634-5; 59. 42-3; 128. 436-7; 129. 1216; 130. 958-9; 148. 597), who famously displayed both a fine disregard for his Lord's words (John 18. 36) and a finer regard for the Vergilian view of Rome's mission to mankind (*Aen.* 6. 581-3) and on whose dogma see R. W. and A. J. Carlyle, *A History of Medieval Political Theory in the West*[3] (London, 1930), 1. 191-2; McIlwain, op. cit., 164-7; W. E. Brown, "Relations of Church and State from Constantine to Charlemagne" in *Church and State* (op. cit. in n. 32 *infra*), 44-6; Toynbee, 4. 346-53; Jalland, 326-8; and F. Dvornik, "Pope Gelasius and Emperor Anastasius I" in *Byzantinische Zeitschrift*, 44 (1951) 111-6.

Gelasius' letter to Anastasius revealed no new thought on the former's part, since, employed as a drafter of ecclesiastical documents for and in the name of

Pope St Felix III (or II), his papal predecessor, he had written to Emperor Zeno in 484 as follows: "I think that without any doubt it would be advantageous for you, if in the period of your principate you should allow the Catholic Church to use its own laws and should not permit anyone to oppose its liberty, which to you has restored the power of reign. For it is certain that this is beneficial for your affairs: that, when it concerns the just causes of God—and according to his ordinance—you should desire to subject, not to exhibit, the royal will to Christ's bishops [*sacerdotes,* on which see no. 16, n. 4] and to learn through their presidents [*praesules*] rather than to teach most holy matters; to follow the Church's decision, not to prescribe, after the manner of men, laws to be followed by it; and not to wish to dominate its sanctions, to which [the Church] God has willed your Clemency to submit the neck of pious devotion" (*PL* 58. 935). And about 489, while still a secretary, in another epistle (perhaps to the same emperor) the future pope had found that " . . . the emperor is a son, not a president [*praesul*] of the Church: it befits him to learn, not to teach, what belongs to religion. He has the privileges of his power, which [privileges] he has acquired by Divine Providence for administering public affairs; and, not being ungrateful for its benefits, he should usurp nothing contrary to the celestial order's authority. For God has willed the things which must be administered by the Church to pertain to bishops, not to the world's powers; and, if these are faithful [i.e. loyally Christian], he has willed these to be subject to his Church and to the bishops" (*PL* 58. 950).

The medieval papal position meant that the civil power should be subordinate to the religious authority in the sense that the priesthood is superior to the laic status. Hence the authority of sovereignty depends on the authority of priesthood, as human things depend on divine things and temporal things depend on spiritual things. Moreover, if temporal felicity, which professedly is the end of civil power, is subordinate to eternal felicity, which assumedly is the end of sacerdotal authority, it must appear not only that, to achieve the ends whither God would have this power and that authority proceed, the former power is subordinate to the latter authority, but also that, as between these, as there exists a subordination of ends, so there exists a subordination of functions.

Probably the Papacy saw its political programme as a struggle to perfect the prophecy that "the kingdoms of this world are become the kingdoms of our Lord and of his Christ" (Rev. 11. 15), particularly since a pope—for instance, Innocent III (1198–1216)—sometimes imagined himself to be both "the King of kings and Lord of lords" (1 Tim. 6. 15) and "a priest for ever after the order of Melchizedek" (Ps. 110. 4; Heb. 5. 6, 6. 20, 7. 17, 21; cf. Heb. 5. 10, 7. 11, 15), who was "king of Salem [i.e. Jerusalem], priest of the most high God" (Heb. 7. 1).

In more modern times this deduction that the Church should be superior to the State was drawn again by Pius IX (1846–78), who on 8 December 1864 promulgated his *Syllabus* of errors to be eschewed by all Catholics in communion with the Sacred See. Of errors 39–55 concerning Civil Society, considered both in itself and its relation to the Church, the condemnation of errors 42, 54, 55 especially reasserts this theory. But Pio Nono's successor, Leo XIII (1878–1903), surpassed him on 20 June 1894 in his encyclical *Praeclara gratulationis,* when he supported such sole sovereignty by saying *ex cathedra*: "We hold upon this earth the place of God Almighty" (cited from G. O. Nations, *The Canon Law of the Papal Throne* [New York, 1926], 22). Moreover, the papal coronation service still contains the statement: "Receive the tiara with the three crowns, and know that thou art the Father of kings and princes, the Pastor of the universe, and the Vicar on earth of Our Lord Jesus Christ, to whom be honour and glory, world without end. Amen" (so P. Pfister, *Pius XII: The Life and Work of a Great Pope* [New York, 1955], 142).

Although doubtless no universally accepted formula for the ideal relation between Church and State can be devised, yet on this problem much has been printed. Among most recent publications may be noted J. Lecler's study, *The Two Sovereignties* (New York, 1952); L. Pfeffer's tome, *Church, State, and Freedom* (Boston, 1953); J. C. Murray's essay, "On the Structure of the Church-State Problem", in W. Gurian and M. A. Fitzsimons, eds., *The Catholic Church in World Affairs* (Notre Dame, Ind., 1954), 11–32; and T. M. Parker's lectures, *Christianity and the State in the Light of History* (London, 1955).

32. Cessation of persecution by the State, however, produced no permanent surcease, so far as the Church was concerned, for now Christians sued to secure the State's support to persecute one another—a practice which both orthodox and heterodox pursued and of which some evidence still exists on earth. And, of course, both the hundred-headed hydra of heresy and the subtle serpent of schism—while couchant occasionally in infancy, yet in maturity often rampant (cf. *infra* n. 43)—were reptiles which voided their venom scandalously upon the Church and calamitously upon the State.

P. N. Ure later remarks in his *Justinian and His Age* (Harmondsworth, 1951), 167: "Heresy hunting and savage suppression of deviationists are sure signs of something radically wrong either with the gospel on whose behalf they are invoked or with those who use such methods to propagate it".

It was this century that saw persecution superseded by patronage and by the State's protection of the Church, for, now that the Church had found at long last a home in a world no longer hopelessly hostile to it, the emperors helped its episcopal heads in their efforts to control that world in the name of him whom the world once had crucified. The privileges accorded by the State to the Church were furnished for a price which religion always has paid for governmental favours: political interference in religious affairs. And history shows that then disappears the distinction between Caesar and God (cf. Matt. 22. 21; Mark 12. 17; Luke 20. 25—on the varied interpretations of which texts in the apostolic age see C. Lattey, "The New Testament and the Pagan Emperors" in *Church and State: Papers Read at the Summer School of Catholic Studies, Held at Cambridge* [England], *July 27th to August 6th, 1935* [London, 1936], 21–4, and F. Gavin, *Seven Centuries of the Problem of Church and State*

INTRODUCTION   lxi

[Princeton, 1938], 8-10) as well as between Caesar's laws and Christ's laws (cf. St Jerome's statement, *Ep.* 77. 3 *ad med.* = PL. 22. 691)—a disaster deplored by the admirable Americanism of Charles Joseph Bonaparte (1851-1921) of Baltimore, who was attorney general of the United States (1906-9), when in 1889 he said: "Caesar does not work for nothing; he must be paid for his protection; if he makes heresy treason, he asks that she [the Church] make treason heresy, and this is little less than a ruinous price for a less than doubtful service" (quoted by J. T. Ellis, *The Life of James Cardinal Gibbons, Archbishop of Baltimore, 1834-1921*, [Milwaukee, 1952], 2. 353, n. 99).

33. While Constantine I's conversion to Christianity in 312 and the Edict of Milan in 313 (no. 12) made profession of the hitherto ignored or tolerated or persecuted religion popular, it was not until 380 that Christianity became the established religion of the Empire, when Theodosius I emitted his celebrated edict *Cunctos populos* (no. 167), which made the Catholic Church in the Empire the Christian Church of the Empire and on which latter legislation see Gavin, op. cit., 13-14.

The tendency to identify Church and State in the post-Nicene period had two chief results: (1) Confusion between the secular power's and the ecclesiastical authority's principles. Though the State could use physical penalties to coerce all its subjects, yet ideally the Church could apply only spiritual penalties to its members. Confusion of these methods carried into the Church thousands of nominal Christians. (2) Confusion between civil and ecclesiastical legislation, which produced lower Christian standards. Though the State's laws seldom could precede public opinion professed by its Christian and non-Christian subjects, yet often the Church's rules set higher standards than non-Christians could be expected to observe. Thus the State's attempt to enforce ideal Christian morality on all its subjects ended not only in conspicuous failure—as repeated legislation on the same matters testifies—but also in a double standard of morality: superior for clergy and inferior for laity.

34. The appellation accorded to this exhibition of Caesaropapism—for a recent review of which in antiquity see Lecler, op. cit., 88-93—is Erastianism, coined from the surname of Thomas Erastus (1524-83), a German theologian and physician, who is supposed to have taught the Church's subordination to the State—a doctrine, however, not discoverable explicitly in his extant works. See no. 127, n. 7.

In time the Byzantine dynasts reduced the Constantinopolitan patriarchate, whose primacy in the East was proclaimed by the Second General Council at Constantinople in 381 and was confirmed by the Fourth General Council at Chalcedon in 451 (see no. 375, n. 7), to little more than the chaplaincy at the imperial court and often appointed as well as expelled patriarchs.

35. Eusebius, *HE* 4. 26. 7-11.
36. PL 54. 423.

While the political constitution of the Roman Empire undoubtedly favoured the diffusion of the Christian idea over the then known world, yet that idea was universal in form from its very birth, for its founder had commanded his disciples to "go . . . into all the world and preach the gospel to every creature" (Mark 16. 15; cf. Matt. 28. 19; Luke 24. 47; Acts 1. 8, 13. 47).

K. S. Latourette in *A History of the Expansion of Christianity: The First Five Centuries* [8] (New York, 1937), while seeing the substantial cause for Christianity's success in the unique personality of Jesus Christ (1. 167–9), yet finds several other factors for the Christian conquest (1. 163–7): (1) Constantine I's endorsement, (2) disintegration of Graeco-Roman society, (3) ecclesiastical organization, (4) Christianity's inclusiveness, (5) Christianity's intransigence as well as flexibility, (6) Christianity's superior offering in religion and in philosophy, (7) assistance of its Jewish origin in Christianity's growth, (8) miracles attributed to Christianity, (9) Christianity's moral standards.

37. Regarding difference in doctrine it should be realized that the catechumens, coming into the Church from many origins, had received too diverse educations and had embraced Christianity for too various reasons for complete uniformity of doctrine to be achieved. Doubtless most converts were attracted by the absolution of sins which was stressed, by the immortality of the soul which was promised, by the mystery which surrounded the sacraments, which for many was only a parallel to the pagan mysteries. Add also the considerable mass of underprivileged persons, "whether bond or free" (1 Cor. 12. 13), for whom Christian freedom and fraternal love and economic assistance—"rice Christians" existed even then—were added attractions.

38. *Carm.* 2. 10. 5.

39. The concordats made in later times between Church and State are likewise to be regarded as legislation, according to the legalist theory advanced by regalists. In this view concordats are neither bilateral contracts between the State and the Papacy nor privileges conceded by the Papacy and obligations owed by the State, but are civil laws concerning the Church passed by the State and may be revoked by the State but not by the Papacy, since the State's authority over all affairs falling within its sphere is omnipotent and the Church existing within the State's territory is subject to the State in the same way as are private corporations. In modern times the principal proponent of this view was Paul Hinschius (1835–98), the German jurist and canonist.

40. A satisfactory synopsis of the period of persecution is in Latourette, op. cit., 1. 135–62. In conclusion the author apologizes for his assignment of so many pages to his presentation of a tale told so many times, but notes its necessity, since his summary shows (1) "some indication of the opposition against which the faith made its way" (160), (2) "the light which the story sheds on the revolution which Christianity proposed making in the structure of the Graeco-Roman world" (160), (3) "the effect of the persecutions upon the Church" (161).

41. These are adapted from those arranged by H. F. Stewart in *CMH* 1. 590–2.

42. Care must be taken to distinguish between ancient and modern uses of

these terms. While the classical meanings of these words are explained in the Glossary, it is not inappropriate to note here that among the Diocletiano-Constantinian (284-337) administrative reforms was a coalescence of provinces into a larger territorial unit called a diocese: thus the civil diocese of Hispania (Spain) contained seven provinces (listed in no. 19, n. 27). But in modern times an ecclesiastical province contains several dioceses: thus the Roman Catholic province of Newark includes the State of New Jersey apportioned as follows: archdiocese of Newark and dioceses of Camden, Paterson, and Trenton. On the other hand, the archdiocese of Washington, D.C., comprises only the District of Columbia and five circumjacent counties of the State of Maryland, has no suffragan dioceses, and, though nominally included in the province of Baltimore, since 1947 has been subject immediately to the Holy See.

The fact that cities and dioceses often have the same name in the United States does not mean that they have the same areas. Thus, e.g. the diocese of Trenton comprises eight counties in the State of New Jersey. In some cases the population of a diocese is greater than that of the city of the same name because of its greater area, such as Trenton, where the population of the diocese (1960) was 435,731, but the city's population (1960) was 114,167; but in other cases the contrary is true, such as Brooklyn, where the estimated population (1956) of the borough was 2,772,000, but the estimated population (1956) of the diocese (the largest—populationwise—bishopric under a mere bishop, though its penultimate bishop was created an archbishop *honoris causa* and *pro hac vice* in 1951, and surpassing all archdioceses save Chicago in population) was 1,497,598 (distributed throughout the four counties of Long Island, N.Y., whose borders are conterminous with the diocesan boundaries, until 18 April 1957, when the creation of the new diocese of Rockville Center on Long Island took from the old diocese of Brooklyn two of that island's counties and about 400,000 adherents).

Again, modern bishops are not always necessarily the chief pastors in cities. In 1957 the Roman Catholic archbishop of New York, N.Y., who is, of course, in orders simply a bishop, had as his assistants in the cure of souls and without territorial jurisdiction ten auxiliary bishops, of whom two were military delegates concerned with supervision of chaplains in the armed forces of the United States and one was national director of a society for the propagation of the faith. Such suffragan bishops have no dioceses of their own, but take their titles from titular sees, i.e., dioceses where the Church formerly flourished but which were overrun by infidels and now have not residential bishops. Such a bishop was said to be a bishop of such and such a bishopric *in partibus infidelium* until 1882, by which time the renewed presence of a considerable population of Christians in such districts made a change in title desirable.

43. To take only two typical examples: Constantine and Justinian. The former intervened in the Donatist schism and in the Arian heresy, not, it is believed, because of any profound conviction in theological principles, but because in a centrifugal commonwealth (as the Empire by its enormous size

had become) the sovereign's primary duty was that of consolidation. The latter, believing ecclesiastical order to be the prop of empire, beheld in the religious differences among his eastern subjects in Asia Minor, Syria, and Egypt separatist tendencies threatening his sovereignty; and so, when affairs of dogma and of discipline arose, he, regarding himself as an imperial pope, was ever ready to legislate—on the theory that religious intolerance was a public virtue. Above all other emperors—with the possible exception of Julian II and Theodosius I—both Constantine and Justinian often were eager to shift their pronouncements, so to speak, from the politician's platform to the pastor's pulpit. Especially on Justinian's energies and efforts, which eventually found fruit in the West as well as in the East and for mankind proved more potent than Constantine's, consult Gavin, op. cit., 14-23.

In the struggle for security the Church failed the State in two chief respects. First, in the process of elaborating an intellectual expression of the Christian faith which would satisfy both its old members and its new converts and would oppose antagonistic pagans and philosophers, who, worshipping powers which transcended nature and disbelieving that divinity was immanent in natural processes, eventually expressed their opposition to the orthodox Christian doctrine that Jesus Christ represented the union of humanity and divinity in one person, the Church presented to the world a usually unharmonious household, "by schisms rent asunder, by heresies distressed" until the Fourth Ecumenical Council at Chalcedon in 451 evolved a final statement in its famous Definition of Faith. But even this conclusion failed to finish controversy, for the attempt to impose the Chalcedonian formula created independent Monophysite churches in Armenia, Syria (the Jacobites), and Egypt (the Copts, with their daughter communion in Ethiopia). And since the clergy as leaders of the laity led the way into schism and heresy, in a sense it seems that the Church both nationalized the pastorate and de-Christianized the populace! Thus started permanently what some scholars consider the pernicious separation into national churches—a fission which certain fautors of Christianity's catholicity find at utter variance with its universal character, since they connect the Saviour's words that there should be "one fold and one shepherd" (John 10. 16) with his similarly celebrated promise to St Peter about the construction of his Church (Matt. 16. 18, on which see no. 442, n. 7). And the day was not far distant, though beyond our period, when the fatal alienation of Monophysite Christians from Orthodox Christendom, and their nationalistic antagonism, found its fruit in their failure during the seventh century to render timely and effectual aid against the encroaching tide of Islam, for which their perversion paved a political path. They thus assisted in the dismemberment of what of the Empire remained in the East, after the northern barbarians had established themselves amid the ruins of the West in the fifth century. Second, the proud patriarchal sees of Christendom—Rome, Constantinople, Alexandria, Antioch, Jerusalem (see no. 53, n. 3), to which much was given and from which much was required (cf. Luke 12. 48)—were a disruptive force and an effective factor

INTRODUCTION lxv

against the imperial effort to achieve concord and unity. Their incumbents' internal and scandalous rivalry and external and ambitious aggrandizement against one another were echoed in smaller sees throughout the Empire. At times it seems that these prelates too frequently forgot the Pauline preachments of peace, particularly that "ye all speak the same thing and that there be no divisions among you; but that ye be perfectly joined together in the same mind and in the same judgment" (1 Cor. 1. 10; cf. also Rom. 12. 5, 15. 5; 1 Cor. 12. 12-27, esp. 25; 2 Cor. 13. 11; Eph. 1. 10, 4. 3-6; Phil. 1. 27, 2. 2; Col. 3. 14-15), and Tertullian's teaching that "emulation of the episcopate is the mother of schisms" (*De Bapt.* 17 *ad med.*). Internally the record is held perhaps by Rome, the otherwise conspicuous champion of order, which within this sylloge's period provided seven egregious examples of papal schism: St Hippolytus (217), Novatian (251), Felix II (355), Ursinus (366), Eulalius (418), Laurence (498), Dioscore (530). Of these the Hippolytan was the longest, ending *c.* 235, when this saint was reconciled soon before his death in Sardinian exile, and the Dioscorean was the shortest, lasting only 22 days; but it is difficult to determine the Novatianist, which (in the end a puritanical party) caused the most confusion in the Church at large, since, though Novatian perished in Valerian's persecution of 257-60, his followers flourished throughout the Empire, were expelled (perhaps finally) from Rome between 422 and 432—which may serve as the terminal date for the local schism—by Pope St Celestine I, and were active in Alexandria as late as 600. Externally perhaps the most notable—as a foreshadowing of the future—is the schism between Rome and Constantinople (484-519), whose solution brought union with the Latin West bought by disunion of the Greek East. Add also the linguistic fact that Greek was Greek and Latin was Latin, thus supplying a common source of theological suspicion, the political fact of the permanent division of the Empire in 395, and the ecclesiastical facts that the Roman patriarchate resented the rise of Constantinople (see no. 375, n. 7)—the only great see not of apostolic origin—to patriarchal rank and that the patriarchates of Alexandria, Antioch, and Jerusalem in the East were jealous rivals of that of Constantinople in the eastern capital.

On separatism consult E. L. Woodward, *Christianity and Nationalism in the Later Roman Empire* (London, 1916), whose observations deserve more notice than they have received, and the learned lectures of S. L. Greenslade, *Schism in the Early Church* (London, 1953), which has several sections on the causes of schism (personal, national, social, economic, patriarchatical, liturgical, disciplinary, puritanical).

Mutatis mutandis, the Church's role in nationalistic separatism is seen notably in modern Ireland, where both clerical and laical Roman Catholics long have cultivated a boisterous and bloody impetus not only to divorce the whole island from British domination (partly won in 1921), but also (since then) to force the fifth fragment (six northern against 26 southern counties) of Ulster into union with Eire and to reduce the entire isle to their ecclesiastically inspired rule (see P. Blanshard, *The Irish and Catholic Power* [Boston, 1953], *passim*).

44. The character of the Church as an institution of the State is clear especially from the control exercised by the emperor over the ecumenical councils, which were convoked by him (e.g. nos. 48, 397, 409, 464), over which he (e.g. nos. 49, 472) or his laic deputy (e.g. nos. 401–6) or deputies (e.g. no. 470) presided, whose agenda was conducted by imperial authority (e.g. nos. 48, 49, 397, 398, 401–6, 408, 409, 461–4, 466–73), and whose canons became law only when confirmed by imperial constitutions (e.g. nos. 52, 375, 410–12, 414–20, 422–6, 475–7, 479–87). (On the emperors and ecumenical councils see no. 48, n. 2.) But independently of general councils the emperor intervened in matters ecclesiastical (most of this sylloge's documents demonstrate this interference) and theological (e.g. esp. no. 527, an imperial instruction reading like a theological treatise defining doctrine and by almost all the eastern episcopate accepted for a generation as the competent description of Christological dogma). And he even controlled occasionally election to (e.g. no. 61) and deposition from (e.g. no. 50) the episcopate as well as the selection of Roman popes (e.g. no. 365).

Apropos the last interference: the last direct intervention of a Roman Catholic sovereign in a papal election occurred in 1903, when His Apostolic Majesty, Emperor Francis Joseph I of Austria (1848–1916), exercised the so-called right of exclusion (*ius exclusivae*) to prevent the preferment of Mariano Cardinal Rampolla del Tindaro (1843–1913), whose Francophile policy as secretary of state to Pope Leo XIII (1878–1903) had made him *persona minus grata* to Vienna (and Berlin) and whose promotion to the Papacy had been anticipated by almost all and apparently was assured from the result of the first ballot. But one of the initial acts of Pope St Pius X (1903–14), the successful candidate, was to interdict forever interference of this character by his constitution *Commissum nobis* (20 January 1904).

Christian emperors could look, of course, to Jewish kings, whose spiritual successors they were in regard to religion, when they wished to find precedents in appointing (1 Kings 2. 35) and deposing (1 Kings 2. 27) prelates as well as in regulating worship (2 Kings 16. 10–16; 1 Chron. 16. 4–6, 37–41, 23. 24—26. 12; 2 Chron. 8. 14–15) and in constructing or reconstructing churches (1 Kings 5–6; 2 Kings 12. 4–16, 22. 3–6; 1 Chron. 28. 11—29. 5; 2 Chron. 2. 1—5. 1; Josephus, *Ant. Iud.* 15. 11. 1. 380–7, 425; id., *Bell. Iud.* 1. 21. 1).

45. Just as from the establishment of the Empire the emperors catered to the soldiers, on whom their rule rested, (e.g. the conduct of the soldiers in the crises of 68–9, 193–7, 235–84 and the testimony of Tacitus [*Hist.* 1. 4] that the secret of sovereignty had been divulged, that a prince could be created elsewhere than in Rome), and conferred such privileges upon them that their position with regard to civilians resembled the older relation of Romans to peregrines, so from the recognition of the Church, with which the sovereigns soon had to reckon as a political power, elevation of orthodox Christians and depression of other religionists appeared in imperial legislation against heretics, schismatics, apostates, pagans, Jews, and Samaritans, who, considered as underprivileged

INTRODUCTION   lxvii

classes, were subjects of discrimination and thus were subjected to incapacities and to disabilities.

46. The three most famous fabrications in the former category perhaps are: (1) the Letter of Aurelius to the Senate and the Roman People on toleration of Christians and on punishment of accusers of Christians, which, known to Tertullian (*Apol*. 5. 6) and to Eusebius (*HE* 5. 5. 1–6) among the earlier fathers and found in manuscripts of St Justin Martyr's *Apologies*, is printed with an English translation by C. R. Haines, *The Correspondence of Marcus Cornelius Fronto* (London, 1920), 2. 300–5; (2) the Letter of Constantine I on the constitution of the Feast of St Peter's Chains (1 August), which, preserved amid St Jerome's *Letters*, is edited in *PL* 30. 235; (3) the so-called Donation of Constantine, which, fabricated between 750 and 850, confers great privileges and rich possessions on the popes and on the Roman Church and appears in Latin in *PL* 8. 567–78 and 130. 245–52 and is translated completely—except for an extensive excursus explaining the Christian creed—by S. Z. Ehler and J. B. Morrall, *Church and State through the Centuries* (Westminster, Md., 1954), 15–22.

In Sir Hermann Gollancz's *Julian the Apostate* (Oxford, 1928)—a legendary history of Julian II translated from the Syriac of a certain Apolloris, a Christian confidant of Jovian (Julian's successor)—appear many edicts and epistles (e.g. 19–22, 26–7, 44–5, 46–7, 69, 76–7, 82–6, 136–7, 149, 150–1, 239) ascribed either to Julian or to Jovian, but none of these constitutions is considered authentic.

47. See especially the Appendix on Persecutions for some of this material.

48. Indeed, according to A. Toso, the influence began at least as early as the early third century and before the recognition of Christianity as a lawful religion: see his "Emilio Papiniano e influenze cristiane nell' evoluzione del diritto romano classico" in *Acta Congressus Iuridici Internationalis* (Roma, 1935), 2. 21–35.

49. An egregious illustration of how ecclesiastics influenced emperors in legislation is seen in the public penance—reported by Theodoret (*HE* 5. 16. 6—18. 23) and by Cassiodorus (*HE* 9. 30. 3–22, 25–9)—imposed in 390 by St Ambrose, bishop of Milan, upon Theodosius the Great, who ordered the terrible massacre at Thessalonica. As a result, the saint secured from the penitent a law permitting thirty days' interval between sentence and execution in crimes for which a rather severe punishment was constituted. The constitution is in *CT* 9. 40. 13 and *CI* 9. 47. 20 and is given also by Cassiodorus (*HE* 9. 30. 23–4). See also nos. 148, 242, 313, 382, n. 1. Cf. *supra* n. 14.

For a bibliography of studies in various languages (overwhelmingly foreign) on Christian penetration into Roman law see the 22 items in B. Biondi's *Guide bibliografiche*, 3: *Discipline giuridiche* 1: *Diritto romano* (Milano, 1944), 55–7, to which should be added at least C. P. Sherman, "The Influence of Christianity on Roman Law", in his *Roman Law in the Modern World* [2] (New York, 1924), 1. 126–234; J. Vogt, "Zur Frage des christlichen Einflusses auf die Gesetzgebung Konstantins des Grossen" in L. Wenger, W. Otto, M. San Nicolò, eds., *Münchener Beiträge zur Papyrusforschung und antiken Rechtsgeschichte*,

35 (1945) 118–48; and which should be supplemented by works listed under "Droit romain et romano-byzantin" in J. Marouzeau's *L'année philologique* (Paris, 1946), vols. 16 et seq. Consult also L. Caes et al., *Collectio Bibliographica ad Ius Romanum Pertinentium* (Bruxelles, 1949–), vols. 1 et seq. Add now the bibliography "Christianity and Roman Law" in A. Berger, *Encyclopedic Dictionary of Roman Law* (Philadelphia, 1953), 796–7.

50. While according to F. Schulz, *Principles of Roman Law* (Oxford, 1936), 82, it seems that the language of the imperial constitutions still needs investigation, there is no doubt that this language from Constantine I to Justinian I departed from the classical tradition and delivered itself to bombastic rhetoric, wherein often it is difficult to discover the forest amid the trees.

51. Livy, *Ab Urbe Cond.* 22. 51. 4.

52. This problem was canvassed recently by R. A. Knox, *On Englishing the Bible* (London, 1949), esp. 66–72. His was a harder task, for he was handling matter hallowed to millions.

But the problem is older, for over two generations ago E. Hatch in *The Organization of the Early Christian Churches* [3] (London, 1888), 6, explained that "the words are for the most part familiar enough to a Greek or Latin student; but the meaning which attaches to those words is often very remote from that which seems to lie on the surface". And in a carefully reasoned argument Hatch shows that one must take cognizance of distinction of both time and space, for what is true, say, of Alexandria in the fourth century is not necessarily valid for Rome in the fifth century or for Constantinople in the sixth century. More recently this subject has been re-examined by B. F. C. Atkinson, *The Greek Language* [2] (London, 1933), 291–303, who apologizes for the brevity of his treatment, and by L. R. Palmer, *The Latin Language* (London, 1954), 183–205, who presents an excellent exposition. And see also Toynbee, 7. 527–33, who supplies a "brief, casual, and nothing like exhaustive"—but interesting—"survey of the etherialization of the Greek and Latin vocabulary, in the course of its transference from pagan to Christian use".

And still older is a witness of the fifth century, when amid the confused welter of words was heard "the voice of one crying in the wilderness" (Isa. 40. 3; Matt. 3. 3; Mark 1. 3; Luke 3. 4; John 1. 23)—that of St Vincent of Lérins, whose threefold test for acceptance of articles of faith could be applied also to the technical terms then tossed from faction to faction: "Also in the Catholic Church itself care must be taken especially that we should hold that which everywhere (*ubique*), always (*semper*), by all (*ab omnibus*) has been believed" (*Comm. Prim.* 2 = *PL* 50. 640).

To Clement of Alexandria (*c.* 150–*c.* 215) and to Tertullian of Carthage (*c.* 160–*c.* 235) we owe the creation of Christian Greek and Christian Latin technical terminology respectively—each an African and each denied the honours of the altar by the Roman Catholic Church (see no. 98, n. 15 *ad fin.*), which, however, had venerated the former as a saint until Gregory XIII's pontificate (1572–85), when in 1584 he was uncanonized (so to speak) because

INTRODUCTION lxix

both his excellencies and his defects placed him out of sympathy with the prevailing spirit of Latin Christianity. Apropos of Gregory XIII's action: it is regrettable that E. W. Kemp in his *Canonization and Authority in the Western Church* (Oxford, 1948) pretermits this pontiff, who won not only renown for reform of the calendar but also reproach for subtraction from the catalogue of saints.

53. Since classical allusions seldom appear in American prose subsequent to the subsidence of classical studies in the United States, it may save some reader's time to explain that these characters were personified by the ancients as female monsters, although the one, a rock on the Italian coast, was opposite to the other, a whirlpool off the Sicilian shore, and symbolized two dangers, either of which was hard to avoid without approaching the other. The figure is as old as Homer, *Od*. 12. 73-126, 234-59.

On the trials of translation one may turn to the still classic *Essay on the Principles of Translation* of A. F. Tytler (Lord Woodhouselee) (Edinburgh, 1813; reprinted London, 1907); A. J. Toynbee's *Greek Historical Thought*[2] (New York, 1952) xiv-xxv; and R. A. Brewer, ed., *On Translation* (Cambridge, Mass., 1959), esp. 271-93.

54. That the tortuosities of translation were comprehended by Cicero, both a lawyer and a philosopher, who was *facile princeps* in turning Greek into Latin (as his long list of versions vouches), may be gathered from his complaint that he sometimes considers his translation a failure, because in telling us that obscurity may be due to abstruseness of subject, but not of style, he proffers in testimony Plato's *Timaeus* (*De Fin*. 2. 5. 15): there is no doubt that, while he knew what Plato wrote, Cicero yet fails to give his readers a clear idea of what Plato meant. And Cicero's judgement is justified by St Jerome, who calls the *Timaeus* "a most obscure book, ... which by not even Cicero's golden mouth is made clearer" (*Comm. in Amos*, 2. 5. 283 = *PL* 25. 1088). It must be observed that at least on this occasion Jerome, whose admiration for Cicero, he confides (*Ep*. 22. 30=*CSEL* 54. 189-91), was ardent, does not allow his manifest virtue of diction to be overshadowed by his disastrous vice of malignity (cf. Palladius, *Hist. Laus*. 36 *ad fin*. And Macrobius, who also marks a Ciceronian crux (Cicero's adaptation of his "Dream of Scipio" [*De Rep*. 6. 18. 18-19] from Plato's "Myth of Er" [*Pol*. 10. 614B-621D]), may have had in mind too the *Timaeus*, when he writes that "in a matter naturally obscure, he who explains more than is necessary in his exposition deepens the darkness and dissolves not the density" (*Comm. in Somn. Scip*. 2. 4. 12).

As any translator may appreciate, the process of translation has been attended with problems. Between servile adherence to a literal version and liberal indulgence in a free paraphrase the present translator has tried to pursue a middle path, although it is admitted that this procedure will not command the commendation of all persons and although it cannot be supposed that the compromise is completely satisfactory, especially since the translator, who for almost fifty years has been reading and writing and teaching the classical languages, sometimes seems to be more literal than liberal. The Greekless and the Latinless readers, on the one hand, are assured that the translator neither has tampered with what he has taken to be the sense of the original texts nor has imported inane or insidious interpretations into the translation. The classicist and the medievalist, on the other hand, if they shall have compared the translation with the original, doubtless will detect that occasionally a deliberate attempt to represent the structure and the style of the original documents has been made, particularly with respect to the reproduction of various figures of speech, which, it is allowed, are more prevalent both in Greek and in Latin than in English. This convention, though it should not dismay the strict constructionists, who may favour and so forgive such fidelity, yet may displease the advanced persons who assert that artistry and aestheticism have no longer a place in any kind of composition, despite copious evidence of their contemporary presence in inspiring prose as well as in intelligible poetry. In any event, it is hoped, sense has not been sacrificed to style.

55. In preparation for an article "Why Study Roman Law?" in the *Journal of Legal Education*, 2 (1950) 473–7, I conducted in 1949 a survey of the status of Roman Law in the 112 schools on the "Approved List" of the American Bar Association (1948) and in the 58 law schools not on that list. There were 139 replies to the 170 questionnaires, i.e. almost 82% (96% for the approved institutions).

Only ten schools offered courses in Roman Law: optional in nine, required in one. The required course was at the graduate level, as were the optional courses in four schools; the other five elective courses seemed to be of undergraduate status.

56. Many western clergymen, whether Catholic or Protestant, acquire only enough Greek to read parts of the New Testament in their theological seminaries; but a superior record in Latin characterizes Roman Catholic clergy.

57. So Ehler and Morrall (op. cit., ix; cited *supra* in n. 1): "In English-speaking countries the lack of knowledge of classical . . . languages is often a serious handicap to historical studies . . . Nowhere is this lack likely to lead to more fundamental misapprehensions than in the study of the history of the Christian Church."

58. Since Vasiliev's long-awaited and thoroughly revised second edition of his two-volume work was received when this sylloge was ready for the printer, cognizance of this newest contribution has been taken as far as has been operationally practicable.

59. Nor should be overlooked the appropriate chapters in another and earlier Englishman's monumental history—that of Edward Gibbon, *The History of the Decline and Fall of the Roman Empire* (6 vols., London 1776–88), which, despite its date, still is superb for this sylloge's period, when perused with J. B. Bury's corrective commentary (7 vols., London, 1896–1900), which itself in the light of the twentieth century's advance in Byzantine studies can admit some correction.

But, since many historians pay hardly any heed to philosophy and—what is worse—some philosophers try their hand at history, few works written on this period and its problems can be studied safely, unless the student simultaneously swallows strong doses of doubt. Certainly no popular histories are worth anything to the researcher and not many are worth anything to anyone else. For the better the historian is, the harder is it to detect his delinquency. It is a commonplace to hold that all historians, who obviously are conditioned by their climate of contemporary opinion, both choose and omit as well as overestimate and underestimate certain data and deliberations. Any historian must be read with caution, because the bounds of historical knowledge are circumscribed by the chance survival of all kinds of sources.

TABLE OF NAMES AND DATES OF EMPERORS

Trajan
98–117
Hadrian
117–138
Aurelius[1]
161–180
Gallien[2]
253–268
Aurelian
270–275
Maximian I
286–305 (West), 306–310 (West)
Galerius
305–311 (East)
Constantine I
306–337 (West, 306–324)
Maximin II
307–313 (East)
Licinius
307–324 (East)
Constantine II
337–340 (West)
Constans I
337–350 (West)
Constantius II
337–361 (East, 337–350)
Julian II
361–363
Jovian
363–364

Valentinian I
364–375 (West)
Valens
364–378 (East)
Gratian
367–383 (West)
Valentinian II
375–392 (West)
Theodosius I[3]
379–395 (East)
Maximus I[4]
383–388 (West)
Arcadius[3]
383–408 (East)
Honorius[3]
393–423 (West)
Theodosius II
408–450 (East)
Constantius III[4]
421 (West)
Valentinian III
425–455 (West)
Marcian
450–457 (East)
Majorian
457–461 (West)
Leo I
457–474 (East)
Anthemius
467–472 (West)

NAMES AND DATES OF EMPERORS

Glycerius
473–474 (West)
Zeno[5]
474–491 (East, 474–476)
Basiliscus[4] and Mark[4]
475–476 (East)

Anastasius I
491–518
Justin I
518–527
Justinian I
527–565

Notes

1. Aurelius shared the sovereignty with his adopted brother Verus as Augustus from 161 to 169 and with his son Commodus as Augustus from 177 to 180, but from 161 to 180 Aurelius was the dominant emperor.

2. Gallien was associated with his father Valerian in the government of the Empire from 253 to 260.

3. Although Theodosius I created as Augustus at Constantinople his six-year-old son Arcadius in 383 and at either Milan or Rome his nine-year-old son Honorius in 393, the real power remained always in Theodosius I's hands. Valentinian II's death in 392 thus left Theodosius I, though not nominally, yet virtually, sole emperor. On Theodosius I's death in 395 the Empire was divided between his sons.

4. This emperor was a usurper.

5. The western half of the Empire fell at the deposition of Romulus Augustulus (combining in his name those of the first king and of the first emperor) by the German Odoacer, king of the Heruls, who dispatched to Constantinople the useless insignia of imperial power and declared that as Zeno's viceroy he would govern Italy, which he ruled from 476 to 493 rather as a Germanic king than as a Roman magistrate. But the end proved to be a beginning, for the nations of medieval Europe were being born in the barbarian kingdoms already established in the western provinces.

Since Romulus Augustulus was not recognized as the constitutional emperor of the West by Zeno, emperor of the East in Constantinople, who considered Nepos (proclaimed emperor in Rome on 24 June 474) still, though in exile, the rightful emperor, those who lived then apparently did not accept Romulus' short reign as ending any such momentous era as some modern scholars have supposed (see Introd., n. 2 *ad init.*). This statement may be supported by at least three reasons.

First, within the last 21 years, after Valentinian III's long reign of 32 years (423–55), the West had seen nine sovereigns (Maximus II, Avitus, Majorian, Severus, Anthemius, Olybrius, Glycerius, Nepos, Augustulus) as its emperors, of whom four (Avitus, Majorian, Anthemius, Nepos) had been acknowledged as Augustal colleagues by the emperor of the East, five (Avitus, Severus, Olybrius, Glycerius, Augustulus) had been created by barbarians, eight (Maximus, Avitus, Majorian, Severus, Anthemius, Glycerius, Nepos, Augustu-

NAMES AND DATES OF EMPERORS   lxxv

lus) either had fled from or had succumbed to or had been deposed by barbarians. In this kaleidoscopic change the suppression of a Roman sovereign reigning in the West seemed of scant significance on the surface of the western scene in 476.

Second, earlier in the fifth century Rome's western subjects had seen their weak rulers' frequent failures to protect the provinces from the barbarian hordes, which hastened through the northern borders to overrun and/or to occupy the principal parts of many provinces. Recruitment of Roman subjects virtually had stopped, because not only the populace became too pacific, but also the shortage of man-power was made worse by exemption of both secular and regular clergy and of the senatorial order from military service and in the practice of not conscripting men from the vocational castes, wherein so many served in agricultural, commercial, industrial, transportational duties and performed compulsory public services. The emperors, making a virtue of necessity and adopting a policy of appeasement, accepted the first invaders as federates (*foederati*) and, finding in the barbarians the best recruits, incorporated these bands into so-called Roman armies to buttress the frontiers against future barbarian invaders (who wanted to become federates themselves), but could not prevent their armed allies' power to create kingdoms for themselves after 418 (starting with Wallia's Visigothic state in south-western France) as well as to elect puppet emperors after 455 (Avitus *et al.*). Thus after 401 Africa had been invaded by Vandals; Britain by Angles, Jutes, Saxons; Belgium and France by Franks, Alans, Alamans, Burgundians, Sueves, Vandals, Visigoths, Huns; Spain and Portugal by Alans, Sueves, Vandals, Visigoths; Austria by Visigoths, Rugians, Alamans, Thuringians, Heruls; Switzerland by Vandals, Alamans, Burgundians, Ostrogoths, Huns; Italy itself by Visigoths, Ostrogoths, Alans, Quadians, Huns, Vandals, Heruls—to mention only the chief modern areas and the more important invaders—and by 476 the barbarians' independent régimes had been recognized throughout Africa west of Libya, eastern Britain (the rest of the island had reverted to native rulers), Belgium, France, Portugal, Spain, Austria, Switzerland, while in Italy the barbarians after 455 had controlled the government, whose power was bounded practically by the peninsula. Consequently Romans and Romanized provincials had been so battered by the progressive process of barbarization that the abdication of Augustulus created little comment in a continued time of troubles. And already, c. 415, Rutilius Claudius Namatianus had remarked that Rome was a captive before it was captured (*De Reditu Suo*, 2. 50). S. Dill, *Roman Society in the Last Century of the Western Empire* [2] (London, 1899), discusses the general character of the invasions and, although allowing that the invasions were complex in character and inspired very different impressions on different minds, yet decides that the Romans were not so much startled by the invasions as we should expect (pp. 285–302) and details the views of persons, representing various localities and differences of circumstances and character, concerning the Empire's condition and future in the face of its invaders (pp. 303–45). On the barbarian

lxxvi   NAMES AND DATES OF EMPERORS

settlements in the West see the summary by F. Lot, *The End of the Ancient World and the Beginnings of the Middle Ages* (New York, 1931), 201-15, esp. 209-15.

Third, the extinction of a western Roman emperor in 476 resulted constitutionally in reunion of the West with the East, where a Roman sovereign still reigned, because some of the barbarian western kings (notably Euric in Spain and Odoacer in Italy) nominally admitted allegiance to and acted as viceroys of the eastern emperors, who cast the shrinking shadow of their suzerainty over such sections of the West as they could control until Charlemagne's coronation as western emperor in 800. It is beside the point that practically the western kings conceded only cheilotherapy to the eastern emperors, who ordinarily were too impotent to insist on obedience overseas. The idea of a Roman Empire still existed in the West among most Christian churchmen and many political philosophers and some barbarian kings; thus the Roman tradition, recognized, if not always respected, remained in some successor-states of the West. On the idea's persistence in the West see C. Oman, *The Dark Ages, 476-918* [6] (London, 1914), 369-72.

Since in 476 the cessation of an emperor in the West did not destroy (though it debilitated) in idea the Empire, which lasted without a serious lapse in the East until the capture of Constantinople on 29 May 1453, legally there was no extinction of the Western Empire, but only a reunion of the West with the East under the eastern emperors. Therefore, Zeno and his successors, while actually ruling in the East and exerting nominally an oft-dormant suzerainty over the barbarian kings in the West, may be believed to have been the sole rulers of the Roman Empire, until on Christmas day in 800 Pope St Leo III—seemingly catching Charles, the Frankish king, by surprise in St Peter's Basilica in Rome—suddenly crowned Charlemagne to revive on the ruins of Roman rule the Roman Empire by evoking in Western Christendom the Roman ghost of an extinct Hellenic ecumenical state—as Toynbee shows (4. 322-3, 337-8, 378-9; 9. 8-9, 12, 15-18, 20-1, 122, 125-6, 162, 164, 650; cf. 1. 343; 2. 276; 4. 593). And according to the philosopher Hobbes this apparition was not the only phantom present to share the situation, if one subscribes to his statement that "the Papacy is no other than the *ghost* of the deceased *Roman empire*, sitting crowned upon the grave thereof" (*Leviathan,* 4. 47 *ad fin.* = W. Molesworth, ed., *The English Works of Thomas Hobbes* [London, 1839], 3. 697-8).

But, although the faithful in the basilica acclaimed Charles as *Augustus,* the additional phrase that he was crowned by God (*a Deo coronatus*) showed that the Roman emperor (*imperator* also was included in the salutation) whom Charlemagne was to copy was not Augustus, the first pagan prince, but Constantine I, the first Christian sovereign, for Pope Hadrian I (772-95) earlier also had apostrophized Charles as "a new Constantine, that most Christian of God's emperors" (M. Deanesly, *A History of Medieval Europe 476 to 911* [London, 1956], 379). And in the contemporary climate of opinion this new empire was conceived as Christian (*Imperium Christianum*), and its emperor as holding an apostolic office, even as Constantine through his conversion was accepted as a peer of the apostles (ἰσαπόστολος) and was buried in his Church of the Holy Twelve Apostles in Constantinople.

Though it commonly is considered that Charlemagne created the Holy Roman Empire, yet in reality he established what may be called merely the Carolingian Empire, whose last emperor was Charles III the Fat (867–87), his great-grandson. After the latter's death the Empire split into separate kingdoms: one in Italy, one in France, one in Germany, two in Burgundy. Otto I the Great, duke of Saxony (936–73), was elected king of Germany in 936 and in 962 was crowned emperor of Germany by Pope John XII. In this coronation may be seen the creation of the Holy Roman Empire, by its contemporaries conceived to be the revival of the Carolingian Empire, just as the latter had been regarded by its coevals as the resuscitation of the Roman Empire in the West.

The title of Holy Roman Empire apparently appears first in a letter of Emperor Frederick I Barbarossa dated in 1157 and is rendered memorable by Voltaire's remark that eventually the Holy Roman Empire was neither Holy nor Roman nor Empire (J. Bryce, *The Holy Roman Empire* [7] [New York, 1909], 199–200, 216).

One of history's ironies, as Toynbee demonstrates (7. 28), is that in 1952— almost 150 years after the Napoleonic liquidation of the Holy Roman Empire, whose last legitimate ruler, Francis II, renounced his title to it on 6 August 1806 —the sovereign pontiff (Pius XII, then *gloriosamente regnante*) of the Vatican Church-State was still awarding the title "Count of the Holy Roman Empire" with a fine disregard for the fact that his papal predecessors had wrought so well to weaken this imperial institution in the conflict between the Papacy and the Empire during the western Middle Ages. Toynbee thinks that perhaps the pope thus "pled a victor's right to dispose of the sole remaining spoils".

1. RESCRIPT OF TRAJAN ON TRIALS OF CHRISTIANS, c. 113
(Pliny, *Ep.* 10. 97)

The letter of Gaius Plinius Caecilius Secundus Minor, governor of Bithynia and Pontus, on the Christians (*Ep.* 10. 96) long has attracted learned attention, for it presents the first pagan account of Christian worship known to us and it shows how widely through his province Christianity prevailed among persons of all ages and ranks and of both sexes.[1]

Pliny writes to Trajan that, since he never has attended trials of Christians, he is ignorant both of the thoroughness of the investigation and of the customary penalties for conviction. After describing his procedure [2] and after mentioning that information about Christians has been received anonymously and by informers, the governor asks the emperor's advice. In response to Pliny's queries Trajan's rescript establishes certain rules for the conduct of cases in which Christians are tried on the charge that they are Christians.

Trajan to Pliny, greeting.

In investigating the cases of those who had been accused as Christians to you, my Secundus, you have pursued the procedure which you ought to have pursued. For there cannot be established as a general rule any method which can have—as it were—a fixed standard.

Search for them must not be made; but if they should be accused and should be charged, they must be punished,[3] in such a way, however, that he who shall have denied that he is a Christian and shall have made this clear in reality, that is, by praying to our gods,[4] may gain pardon as a result of his penitence, although suspected in the past.

Moreover indictments presented without an author ought not to have a place in any accusation.[5] For it both is of very bad precedent and is not in accord with our time.[6]

1. While considering Christianity only as "a depraved and extravagant superstition" (10. 96. 8) and while complaining at its prevalence in his province (10. 96. 9), yet the governor could not grasp the "underlying connexion between the two phenomena in Bithynia that caused Pliny the greatest concern—the decay of civic institutions and the spread of Christianity—" in that "a vitality which was no longer finding a satisfactory outlet in secular civic life was flowing into the self-government of the local Christian com-

munities in the municipal cells comprising the Roman body politic" (Toynbee, 7. 406).

Pliny's characterization of Christianity as "a depraved and extravagant superstition" (*superstitio prava* <*et*> *immodica*) is corroborated by two of his contemporaries and friends: Tacitus (*Ann.* 15. 44. 4) calls it "a destructive superstition" (*exitiabilis superstitio*) and Suetonius (*Nero,* 16. 2) considers it "a new and nefarious superstition" (*superstitio nova ac malefica*).

2. Pliny thus describes his interim (pending imperial instructions) procedure (10. 96. 3–8):

"I have asked them whether they are Christians. If they confess, I have asked them again and thrice, threatening punishment; if they persist, I have ordered them to be led to punishment. For I did not doubt that, whatever might be the character of the crime which they admitted, at least their pertinacity and inflexible obstinacy ought to be punished. There have been others of similar madness, whom, because they are Roman citizens, I have designated to be returned to the city [Rome] for punishment.

"Then—as usually happens—by the very handling of the matter, since accusation thus becomes widespread, more cases have occurred. An anonymous indictment, containing many persons' names, was presented. Whoever denied that they were or had been Christians, when they called upon the gods—repeating the words after me—and when they worshipped with incense and with wine your image, which I had ordered to be introduced for this purpose with the deities' statues, and when especially they cursed Christ—none of which things they who really are Christians are said to be able to be compelled to do—those persons I have thought ought to be dismissed. Others, named by an informer, have said that they were Christians and then have denied it, saying that they have been but have ceased to be so—some many years ago and at least one even twenty years ago. All these have worshipped your image and the gods' statues and have cursed Christ.

"Moreover they declared that . . . this very deed [assembling for worship] they had ceased to do after my edict, whereby, pursuant to your mandates, I had forbidden assemblies to exist. And therefore I have believed it to be the more necessary to seek by tortures what is the truth from two female slaves, who are called deaconesses. I have discovered nothing other than a depraved and extravagant superstition. Therefore, after I had postponed the examination, I have hastened to consult you."

3. On the charge that they are Christians, for the crimes which cling to their name (*flagitia cohaerentia nomini*: 10. 96. 2) are ignored in the injunction not to search for Christians. See no. 12, n. 33.

Both Tertullian (*Apol.* 2. 7) and Eusebius (*HE* 3. 33. 3) emphasize this part of the rescript. The former eloquently finds fault with the emperor's reply, when he writes (§ 8): "What a necessarily confused decision! He says that search for them must not be made, as if they are innocent, and he orders that they must be punished, as if they are guilty. He spares and he rages; he ignores and he notices. Why cheat yourself with your judgement? If you condemn, why do you not also search? If you search not, why do you not also acquit?"

From the emperor's words it is evident that it is erroneous to consider this persecution a continuing process. Frequently governors avoided going to extremes—as appears in the earlier *Acts of the Martyrs*. But popular clamour (see no. 2 at n. 16) or natural disaster (see no. 3 at n. 21 and also nn. 24, 25), whereby people could persuade themselves that divine wrath was displayed, often was another incentive to institute persecution. Again Tertullian testifies to this (*Apol.* 40. 2): "If the Tiber has risen to the walls [of Rome], if the Nile has not risen to the fields, if the sky has stood still [viz. a drought], if the earth has moved [viz. an earthquake], if there has been famine, if there has been pestilence, at once is raised the cry: 'The Christians to the lion!' [*Christianos ad leonem*]". Even over two centuries later and on the same continent St Augustine preserves a current proverb: "Rain falls; Christians are the cause" (*De Civ. Dei*, 2. 3 *ad init.*).

For the pagan and then the persistent Judaeo-Christian view (proceeding from sundry Scriptural passages) that tempests, thunder and lightning, hailstorms, snow and ice, floods, droughts, earthquakes, and almost every sort of atmospheric and elemental disturbance producing destruction for man were either of divine provenience to punish mankind for its impiety and its sins or of diabolic perpetration through "the prince of the power of the air" (Eph. 2. 2; cf. 6. 12), permitted by God for the same purpose, see A. D. White, *A History of the Warfare of Science with Theology in Christendom* (New York, 1932), 1. 323–50, 364–72.

Recently A. N. Sherwin-White in his admirable article, "The Early Persecutions and Roman Law Again" in *JTS*, N. S., 3 (1952) 199–213, in canvassing the three chief theories (concocted since 1890, when serious study of the subject started) about the imperial administration's attitude toward Christian communities during the period before the major persecutions of the Church began in the third century, has concluded that "the limitation of the early persecutions is . . . partly the result of official policy, a determination not to take the matter too seriously, as evinced in Trajan's [no. 1] and Hadrian's [no. 2] rescripts, and to confine the issues to real offences (*flagitia, contumacia*). But it results also from the Roman system of jurisdiction, the wide latitude allowed to the provincial governor [who could use his judgement in cognition of crimes and in determination of sentences *extra ordinem*], and partly again from the checks imposed by the Roman system of private delation" (212).

4. It was the secession from the State's religion which was punished, because the administration believed that those who refused at least lip service to the traditional gods and to the emperor's image (cf. *supra* n. 2 *ad med.* and no. 127, n. 7) were concealing some political conspiracy against the State. That Christians already prayed for, not to, the emperor is shown by a Christian document dated in Trajan's times: see the Greek prayer for emperors in St Clement of

Rome, *1 Cor.* 61 (composed 75–110; more narrowly, perhaps, 90–100). For later (197–8) Latin, but still ante-Nicene, evidence see Tertullian, *Apol.* 30–3. And, above all, anterior to these add the apostolic injunction in 1 Tim. 2. 1–3. See also no. 255, n. 3.

That refusal to reverence the imperial image could be taken as treason need not be a matter for marvel. Control of men's minds by the State—not to mention the Church—was a familiar phenomenon before contemporary exposure to it in such dictator-controlled countries as were Fascist Italy, Kemalist Turkey, Pilsudskian Poland, Metaxan Greece, Nazi Germany, Peronist Argentina and as are Soviet Russia, Falangist Spain, Salazaran Portugal, Titoist Yugoslavia, Communist China, and many Latin-American nominal republics. The conflict of religions in the early Roman Empire resulted not seldom in persecution, when the claims of Caesar clashed with the Christian conscience.

However, taken with Pliny's report (*supra* n. 2 *ad med.*), Tertullian's testimony (*Apol.* 10. 1) that the Christians, because they neither worship the gods nor sacrifice for the emperors, are accused of sacrilege and treason (*sacrilegii et maiestatis rei convenimur*), shows that no new legislation was needed to serve as a basis for prosecution of Christians. For if an edict of Augustus to the Cyrenenses (6 B.C.) commanded a man to be held on the charge of stealing a statue on which the emperor's name had been inscribed (*FIRA* 1. 408), if in Tiberius' principate a master was guilty of impiety for striking his slave who had on his person a silver coin stamped with that emperor's image (Philostratus, *Vita Apol. Tyan.* 1. 15), if in the same reign a charge of treason was the complement of all accusations (Tacitus, *Ann.* 3. 38. 1), then Christians could be convicted conveniently under extant enactments such as the *Lex Iulia de maiestate* of 46 B.C.—so close was the connection of sacrilege (on which see no. 168, n. 1) and treason even in the early Empire. Add also Tertullian's testimony that the *institutum Neronianum,* Nero's constitution against Christians (on which see Appendix on Persecutions, n. 3 *ad med.*),was still in force in Trajan's reign.

Moreover Trajan, for whose attitude toward Christianity consult B. W. Henderson, *Five Roman Emperors* (Cambridge, 1927), 53–8, required no new policy for persecution, so long as Christianity could be regarded as an unlicensed religion (*religio illicita*) and consequently was considered without the law, since it could not qualify as coming within the lauded concept of legality: "if indeed by 'lawful' we mean what is allowed by the laws and by our ancestors' customs and institutions" (Cicero, *Phil.* 13. 6. 14). And although the early emperors never appear to have constituted a fact-finding commission about the Christian sect, which at first had sheltered itself "under a very famous, at least a licensed, religion's shade" (Tertullian, *Apol.* 21. 1), viz. Judaism, yet the Jews early attracted governmental attention to the new cult's illegal status (e.g. Acts 18. 12–17). And even apart from Jewish aid, Christianity's nature made a conflict with the secular power inevitable—a conclusion well canvassed recently by A. E. R. Boak, *A History of Rome to 565 A.D.*[4] (New York, 1955), 394–7.

2. TRIALS OF CHRISTIANS, C. 121

5. In ordinary cases the principle of Roman law was that there must be an acknowledged accuser to initiate a trial.

Herein is seen the application of the Roman virtue *humanitas,* for in the forms of accusatorial procedure Cicero condemns Gaius Verres' scandalous administration of the law as unrepresentative of Roman justice, when during 73–70 B.C. that greedy governor of Sicily permitted for a price prosecution without an accuser and pronounced condemnation without a defence (*In Verr.* 2. 5. 9. 23). Nearer to Trajan's day Cicero's complaint is confirmed by the practice to which Porcius Festus, procurator of Judaea (55–6 or 59–60), refers in the proceedings against St Paul, when he says: "It is not the custom of the Romans to surrender [to unjust condemnation] any man, before the accused may have the accusers face to face and may have had an opportunity for defence concerning the charge" (Acts 25. 16).

But, while Trajan conferred some real relief for Christians by this ruling against anonymous accusation, yet by his rescript's evidence he must be considered as personally responsible for persecution of the Bithynian Christians in the third pagan pogrom (as the Church later counted it), although by contrast he has been hailed as not having "the wanton cruelty of a Nero and the malignant caprice of a Domitian" (quoted by Kidd, 1. 238), who respectively in 64 and in 96 perpetrated the first and the second persecutions.

Later Christian emperors, who call anonymous accusations defamatory indictments (*famosi libelli*), pursued the policy here taken by Trajan, who characterizes these documents as *sine auctore libelli*. Their legislation is preserved in *CT* 9. 34, whose ten laws are dated from 319 to 406. Of this group *CI* 9. 36. 2 preserves only part of *CT* 9. 34. 7 and 9. The only other constitution in *CI* 9. 36 (9. 36. 1) is in Greek and is undated, but from its precedence apparently is anterior to 365 (the date of *CI* 9. 36. 2) and is the only new legislation on this subject added by Justinian.

6. The phrase *nec nostri saeculi est* perhaps points to "the plenitude of the time", one of history's periods wherein thinkers think that a long-entertained hope has been obtained, a definite height has been achieved, and the end of a journey has been attained. On this consult J. Ortega y Gasset, *The Revolt of the Masses* (New York, 1932), 33–4.

2. RESCRIPT OF HADRIAN ON TRIALS OF CHRISTIANS, *c.* 121

(Rufinus, *HE* 4. 9)

After much controversy in the last century scarcely any scholar in patristic studies doubts the genuineness of this document, which seems to have been known within a decade of the death (*c.* 165) of St Justin Martyr, its first preserver, and independently of Justin's preservation of it (*Apol. pro Christ.* 1. 68. 6–10).[1]

Eusebius says (*HE* 4. 8. 6) that Serennius [2] Granianus, governor of Asia, requested from Hadrian instruction about the Christians, because he had considered it unjust to condemn them to death without accusation or trial, merely to satisfy popular clamour. It seems that Granianus demitted his post before a reply had been received and that the rescript, therefore, was addressed to Gaius Minucius Fundanus, his successor.

Hadrian's rescript to Fundanus surpasses Trajan's more famous rescript to Pliny (no. 1) in several respects: [3] (1) it proposes to protect public peace and to check calumniators; (2) it permits provincials to prosecute Christians, if they have evidence; (3) it requires proof of illegal acts; (4) it orders that the penalty must be proportionate to the nature of the offence; (5) it demands punishment of those whose prosecution is based on false charges.

Eusebius (*HE* 4. 9) and Nicephorus (*HE* 3. 27) give the rescript in Greek, but Rufinus, who translates Eusebius' *Ecclesiastical History,* has it in what most scholars suppose is the original Latin, from which the English version is made. That in some phrases the Latin seems to be stronger than the Greek may be charged to Eusebian carelessness,[4] for it is scarcely likely that Eusebius deliberately would have debilitated his version, which has supplanted Justin's text of this letter.[5]

Copy of Emperor Hadrian's letter to Minucius Fundanus, proconsul of Asia.[6]

I have received a letter written to me by the most distinguished Serennius [7] Granianus, your predecessor,[8] and [9] it does not please me [10] to pass by the report silently,[11] lest both innocent persons [12] should be disturbed and opportunity for outrage [13] should be furnished to calumniators.[14]

Therefore, if the provincials are able to rely manifestly on this their [9] claim against the Christians, that they may accuse them in any point [15] before a tribunal, I do not prohibit them from prosecuting this matter. But I do not permit them to use in this matter mere entreaties and outcries.[16] For it is much more just, if anyone shall wish [17] to accuse, for you to investigate about the charges.[18]

Therefore, if anyone accuses and proves that the said persons [19] do anything contrary to the laws,[20] you shall decide [21] also [9] punishments [9] in accord with the importance of the offences.[22] By Hercules,[23] you shall take particular care that if anyone shall have accused any of these persons as a defendant for the purpose of calumny,[14] you should exact vengeance on him by rather severe punishments in proportion to his villainy.[24]

2. TRIALS OF CHRISTIANS, C. 121 7

1. For the arguments see A. W. F. Blunt, *The Apologies of Justin Martyr* (Cambridge, 1911), 135–6. Cf. *infra* n. 5.

2. Cf. *infra* n. 7.

3. W. Schmid holds that "Hadrian's rescript does not essentially vary from the spirit of Trajan's rescript" ("The Christian Re-interpretation of the Rescript of Hadrian" in *Maia*, 7 [1955] 9).

4. Cf. e.g. *infra* nn. 12, 13, 22.

5. Though Eusebius writes that Justin appended a Latin copy of the epistle to this *Apology* and that he turns it into Greek as best he can (*HE* 4. 8. 6–8), yet no extant manuscript of Justin's *Apology* contains the Latin text, which some copyist has replaced with the Eusebian version. Most critics believe that Rufinus had access to Hadrian's rescript in Latin and then inserted it into his version rather than retranslated the Eusebian translation.

6. Eusebius and Nicephorus substitute respectively "To Minucius Fundanus" and "Hadrian Caesar to Minucius Fundanus". His name is properly Gaius Minicius Fundanus (D. Magie, *Roman Rule in Asia Minor* [Princeton, 1950], 2. 1583).

7. "Silvanus" is the true lection, since Quintus Licinius Silvanus Granianus Quadronius Proculus was proconsul of Asia 120–1 (Magie, loc. cit.). The reading "Serennius" is either a Eusebian emendation (copied by Nicephorus, who throughout his copy faithfully follows Eusebius) or a scribal error.

8. The Greeks substitute "whom you have succeeded".

9. Omitted in Greek.

10. In Greek "therefore" is inserted.

11. The Greek reads "to leave the matter unexamined".

12. Here we should expect ἀθῷοι in Greek, but, if Eusebius wrote it for *innoxii* (innocent persons), it has been corrupted into ἄνθρωποι (persons).

13. The Rufinian *occasio latrocinandi* (occasion for committing banditry) is softened into the Eusebian χορηγία κακουργίας (provision for doing wrong).

14. See no. 334, n. 3.

15. The Greek looks rather to the defendants, when it reads "that they also may answer charges".

16. *I do not prohibit . . . outcries* is reduced in Greek to "let them turn to this matter merely, but not by demands or by mere outcries". See no. 1, n. 3 *ad med.*

17. The Greek verb is present subjunctive.

18. This phrase is simply "this" in Greek.

19. For *the said persons* the Greek has "they".

20. Tertullian (*Apol.* 5. 7) claims that Hadrian, though that emperor—so he says—was an explorer of all curiosities, never enforced the laws which the impious, the unjust, the foul, the fierce, the vain, the demented used only against Christians.

It was Hadrian to whom Quadratus and Aristides addressed their apologies for Christianity (Eusebius, *HE* 4. 3). These treatises, the earliest-known examples of this *genre*, were presented after this rescript's issuance. Of the former we have only the fragment found in Eusebius (4. 3. 2); of the latter we have a complete version in Syriac, an Armenian fragment, and several large portions in Greek (see J. Quasten, *Patrology* [Westminster, Md., 1950], 1. 190–5).

On Hadrian's attitude toward Christians consult B. W. Henderson, *The Life and Principate of the Emperor Hadrian* (London, 1923), 221–31.

21. Present imperative in Greek.

22. Singular in Greek.

23. The most famous of the Greek heroic demigods and after death admitted to the celestial company of the deities as the god of strength. The interjection (*hercules*, more frequently *hercule* or *hercle,* also with a prefixed *me* and with *me* written separately) was common as an oath or an asseveration among the Romans, who got it from the Greeks.

24. For this sentence the Greek has "By Hercules, if anyone should offer this for the purpose of calumny, determine with skill and consider [thus—inserts Nicephorus] that you should exact vengeance".

3. LETTER OF AURELIUS ON TRIALS OF CHRISTIANS, c. 161

(Eusebius, *HE* 4. 13. 1–7)

The authenticity of this document is still debatable, although in 1895 Harnack [1] asserted his belief that in the main it is a genuine letter with the exception of a few interpolated or reworded clauses.[2]

The epistle exists in two variant forms: (1) as an appendix to St Justin Martyr's *First Apology for Christians* (1. 68. 10, immediately after Hadrian's rescript [no. 2]), where it is ascribed to Antoninus Pius (138–61), and (2) in Eusebius' *Ecclesiastical History* (4. 13. 1–7; copied by Nicephorus, *HE* 3. 28), where it is assigned to Marcus Aurelius (161–80). Most critics have seen in the Justinian version signs of an "improved" text and therefore think that it has been adapted from the Eusebian version. For this reason the latter version has been taken as the text for translation. The dilemma of the dual authorship has caused various conjectures,[3] but in itself it is insufficient to condemn the epistle as counterfeit.[4]

The epistle, which Eusebius erroneously calls an edict [5] and which from its penultimate sentence before the subscription probably should be regarded rather as another rescript, prohibits prosecution of Christians, unless they have seemed to be conspiring against the State, and commands not only acquittal for Christians accused in court merely because of being Christians [6] but even action against or condemnation of their accusants.

Emperor Caesar Marcus Aurelius Antoninus Augustus Armenius,[7]

3. TRIALS OF CHRISTIANS, C. 161

Pontifex Maximus, with the Tribunician Power for the fifteenth time, Consul for the third time, to the Assembly of Asia,[8] greeting.[9]

I know [10] that to the gods it is a care [11] that such persons [12] escape not detection. For they, far more than you,[13] would punish the [14] persons unwilling to worship them.[15] And you cast them into disorder,[16] confirming them in their opinion, which they hold,[17] by accusing them as atheists. But to them also, when accused, it would be preferable to be reputed to die on behalf of their own god rather than to live;[18] consequently [19] they even win, surrendering their own lives rather than complying with what you demand them to do.[20]

Concerning the past and the present earthquakes:[21] it is not out of place [22] to remind you that, whenever these occur, you are disheartened and you compare our [23] condition with theirs.[24] They indeed become more boldly outspoken toward their god,[25] but you during the entire time, in which you appear to be ignorant, neglect both the other gods and the worship of the Immortal;[26] and you accordingly harass and persecute to death the Christians worshipping him.[27]

On behalf of such persons many [28] also of the provincial governors formerly [19] wrote to our [29] most divine father,[30] to whom he also replied that they should not molest such persons, unless they should appear to be making some attempt against the government of the Romans.[31] And to me also many,[32] whom I also answered, adhering to my father's opinion, gave information about such persons. But if anyone should persist in bringing to charges [33] any one of such persons for being such, let that one who is accused be acquitted of the complaint, even if he should appear to be such, but the accuser shall be liable to a penalty.[34]

Published at Ephesus in the Assembly of Asia.[35]

1. A. Harnack, *Texte und Untersuchungen zur Geschichte der altchristlichen Literatur* (Leipzig, 1895), 13. 4.

2. Its genuineness is capable of defence and in certain quarters it has found not a few defenders.

3. The situation caused by the variant superscriptions is complicated by the fact that in his introduction to the document Eusebius attributes it to Antoninus and then in its title accepts Aurelius as its author. But even if Eusebius may have had the Justinian version, it is quite possible that he, as is his wont, simply has confused the names of the two emperors, since elsewhere in this work it is evident that the web of the Antonine emperors' names has enmeshed Eusebius (e.g. Aurelius he calls Antoninus in 4. 14. 10, 4. 18. 2, 4. 26. 2, 5. praef. 1, 5. 4. 3 [or 5. 5. 1], 5. 9. 1).

To account for the alteration in the authorship some scholars have suggested that this letter was issued jointly late in the principate of Antoninus, when

Aurelius was associated with him in the administration of the Empire. But if so, both names should have been in the superscription.

4. Common charges against its authenticity are: (1) it is a concoction without conviction; (2) it reveals a frivolous view of the pagan gods (but cf. *infra* n. 15), a view, moreover, not in keeping with the character of both Antoninus and Aurelius; (3) it unhistorically insists that Christians are innocent exemplars of religious fidelity; (4) it is too favourable toward the Christians in its last sentence for even Aurelius—not to mention any other emperor of the second century—to have enunciated it.

On Aurelius' considerate attitude toward Christians consult C. R. Haines, *The Communings with Himself of Marcus Aurelius Antoninus* (London, 1916), 381-5. Haines says, "that there was in any sense a general persecution of the Christians at this time is contrary to all the facts" and doubts whether many Christians perished in his principate, particularly in Gaul at Lyon and Vienne in 177, where they are said to have died amid scenes of refined torture more expected of a savage chieftain than of a civilized sovereign. Certainly such considered and contemptuous cruelty was not consistent with the philosopher-emperor's character as revealed by the rest of his domestic policy and as portrayed by the inspired principles of his *Meditations*.

W. Schmid, the latest investigator, thinks that the rescript is fictitious and a Christian concoction framed *c*. 180: (The Christian Re-interpretation of the Rescript of Hadrian" in *Maia*, 7 [1955] 10-13).

5. The word is διάταξις, which equals the Latin *edictum*, one of the several forms of imperial legislation. The use of χαίρειν (greeting) is characteristic of epistles, not of edicts.

6. This statement about pagans prosecuting Christians merely because they were Christians is reminiscent of the common charge of the Christians that at times these were persecuted simply because of the "name" of Christian (see no. 12, n. 33).

7. *Armenius* is an unusual adjectival form for *Armeniacus*, an anachronistic *agnomen* marking Roman victories over Parthians in Armenia: the title was not assumed by Aurelius until 164 and his father Antoninus never had it at all.

8. This organization, whose president was a chief priest called the asiarch, comprised representatives from the principal communities of the province of Asia (western part of Asia Minor). Its sessions shifted from city to city. Among its duties was supervision of religious cults and of such festivals and games as were associated with those.

According to Eusebius (*HE* 4. 12. 1) Asiatic Christians had petitioned Antoninus Pius about their injurious treatment and he sent this "edict" to the Assembly of Asia as his answer. While it was quite possible for a Roman emperor even in the mid-second century to address anyone whom he chose, it certainly seems strange that Antoninus or Aurelius (cf. *supra* n. 3) sent his reply not to the petitioners or to the provincial governor, but to the κοινὸν τῆς 'Ασίας,

3. TRIALS OF CHRISTIANS, C. 161

which, so far as our information apart from this document goes, had no *jurisdiction* whatever in legal matters of this character.

9. Justin's superscription is "Emperor Caesar Titus Aelius Hadrian Antoninus, Augustus, Pious, Pontifex Maximus, with the Tribunician Power for the twenty-first time, Consul for the fourth time, Father of the Fatherland, to the Assembly of Asia, greeting", to which is prefixed the caption "Letter of Antoninus to the Assembly of Asia".

10. Justin uses the epistolary imperfect of a weaker verb meaning "I think".

11. Justin, using an infinitive for the Eusebian indicative, reads "the gods will be careful".

12. This is such an abrupt statement that it appears that some introductory words have been lost. If not, the phrasing is extraordinary. Would the Assembly of Asia know who are the *such persons* (οἱ τοιοῦτοι), who seem to be Christians, although, as such, they are not named till the latter half of the letter? If this sentence had not appeared with an informative introduction in an ecclesiastical document, it would be completely meaningless, as it probably was to the assembly, unless an explanatory epistle had accompanied it.

13. For *far more than you* Justin substitutes "if they could".

14. Justin reads "those".

15. If it be claimed that this clause slyly impugns the inability of the pagan gods to punish and that no emperor could or would have written it, one should remember the epigram fathered upon the earlier emperor Tiberius by Tacitus (*Ann.* I. 73. 5): *Deorum iniurias dis curae*.

16. Or "disturbance", "tumult", even, perhaps, "rebellion". The word is ταραχή. Justin reads "And you cast upon them disorder", and for the rest of the sentence reads "and you accuse their opinion, which they hold, as that of atheists and you cast certain other charges, which we cannot prove".

17. Nicephorus, who faithfully follows Eusebius save at this point, inserts "about you".

18. Justin reads "But to them also it would be advantageous to be reputed to die for that of which they are accused".

Though Harnack holds that the Greek represented by the words *on . . . live*" (Μᾶλλον ἢ ζῆν ὑπὲρ τοῦ οἰκείου θεοῦ) is a portion of the original document, Justin omits these seven words.

A preference to have the reputation of dying for their belief in their god seems a distinctly Christian idea, especially when coupled (in the next clause) with the notion of conquering by sacrificing their lives rather than comply with pagan commands. But as this doctrine is ascribed to the Christians by the emperor, naturally such ascription does not gainsay the genuineness of the passage, if we can presume that by this time a Roman emperor had heard of non-Roman ideas held by his Christian subjects.

19. Justin omits this word.

20. That is, to sacrifice to the pagan gods and thus to show that they are not atheists. A common charge against Christians in this century was that they

were atheists, because the casual pagan observer saw no idol in the Christian cult (cf. Eusebius, *HE* 4. 15. 6).

21. It is impossible to assign an exact date to any earthquake in Asia Minor during the principates of these emperors, although we know that the peninsula was subject to these and that some were reported from that region between 138 and 180. Doubtlessly these catastrophes, not unlike other natural calamities, were ascribed to the practice of Christianity and afforded convenient pretexts to persecute Christians. See no. 1, n. 3 *ad fin*.

22. Justin has "not seemly".

23. Justin reads "your", which is preferable, though the Eusebian *our* is intelligible.

24. It seems rather brutal on the emperor's part to remind the provincials of their calamities suffered from earthquakes. Probably this sentence is a Christian addition (cf. next note). And in the following sentence the imperial rebuke to the assembly for neglecting the worship of the Christian God adds insult to injury.

25. This may mean that the earthquakes served a triple purpose: (1) the Christians spoke more freely about their belief in God, because they were convinced that the earthquakes evinced God's displeasure with the heathen; (2) the Christians resorted to more fervent and more frequent supplication for God's protection against these phenomena; (3) the pagans considered that there were no longer any gods, just as earlier at the eruption of Mt Vesuvius and in the consequent destruction of Pompeii (79) Pliny records (*Ep*. 6. 20. 15) the opinions of most of the Misenians, who concluded that there were no gods anywhere.

26. The Greek text is muddled, but the present translation perhaps interprets what was meant. It may be that καθ' ὃν ἀγνοεῖν δοκεῖτε has been advanced ahead of περὶ τὸν ἀθάνατον and *in which you appear to be ignorant* should be appended to *the Immortal* and then should be read "about whom you appear to be ignorant".

Moreover, unless the emperor quotes the Christians, it seems strange for him to refer to the Christian God as the Immortal.

Justin reads "and you during that time seem to be ignorant of the gods and neglect the temples and recognize not the worship concerning God".

27. Justin has more simply "and accordingly you are jealous of the worshippers and persecute them to death".

28. Justin reads "certain others".

29. Singular number in Justin.

30. Hadrian, if Antoninus wrote this, or Antoninus, if Aurelius is the author.

Hadrian's rescript (no. 2) makes no such statement about conspiracy or rebellion as the rest of the sentence reveals. Similarly also is silent the letter of Antoninus, to which alludes St Melito, bishop of Sardis, whose apology to Aurelius (written *c*. 176) is quoted partly by Eusebius (*HE* 4. 26. 5-11). According to it Antoninus, after Aurelius had become associated with him in

147 in the imperial administration, "wrote to the cities that no new measures concerning us [Christians] should be introduced; among which [letters are those] both to Larissans and to Thessalonicans and Athenians and to all Greeks" (4. 26. 10).

31. In Trajan's rescript (no. 1) the imperial view is that the Christians should be punished if they refuse to worship the pagan gods. Hadrian's rescript (no. 2) permits condemnation of Christians if they act contrary to the laws. In the present letter it is implied that Christians should have religious freedom and it is ordered that prosecution should be permitted only if a subversive attempt against the State has been alleged.

32. It is possible, though not probable, that soon after his accession Aurelius received many complaints about the Christians, if 161 must stand for this rescript's date, for he became emperor on 7 March of that year.

33. Justin reads "But if anyone has a charge to accuse against".

34. This sentence seems to make Christianity a lawful religion (*religio licita*)— a situation which is anachronistic by almost a century in some scholars' view (see no. 4, n. 2) or by even more lapse of time in others' opinion (see no. 5, n. 1)—although Christianity had to wait from this document's date for one and one-half centuries longer for full and final recognition by the Caesars (see no. 7, n. 21). It also creates other difficulties. Does ἔνοχος δίκης or τῇ δίκῃ (so Justin) mean "liable to a penalty" or "liable to an action"? What was the penalty and what was the action? See no. 334, n. 3.

Later, probably between 169 and 176, Aurelius seems not to have been so tender toward Christians, for in *D* 48. 19. 30 is summarised his rescript directing that anyone who has done anything whereby men's fickle minds may be terrified by superstitious belief in divine power should be subject to insular relegation. Though it is true that this rescript apparently was not aimed directly at Christians, for Aurelius could take a liberal view toward rites which others would view as superstitious (see J. B. Lightfoot, *The Apostolic Fathers* [London, 1885], 2. 1. 449–50), yet this constitution could be manipulated so as to apply to Christians. In its Justinianian context, some 350 years later, this constitution was aimed at non-Christians.

On this emperor's other letter (a Christian forgery), favouring Christians and addressed to the Roman Senate, see Introd., n. 46 *ad init.*

35. Justin omits the sentence.

4. RESCRIPT OF GALLIEN ON RESTORATION OF CHRISTIANS' PROPERTY, 260

(Eusebius, *HE* 7. 13. 2)

Eusebius translates from Latin into Greek this rescript, which Gallien issued, Eusebius explains, immediately after his accession as sole emperor in succession

4. RESTORATION OF CHRISTIANS' PROPERTY, 260

to his father Valerian, with whom he had been associated in rule.[1] This constitution, while it does not make Christianity an authorized religion (*religio licita*),[2] evidently ends the current persecution of Christians [3] and restores their public property to Christian congregations. The rescript regards Christianity as neither outside nor against the law, when it, in effect, recognizes the churches as juristic persons capable of proprietary rights.

Though Eusebius calls this epistle, which Nicephorus also preserves (*HE* 6. 12), a rescript, yet no evidence exists that it replied to any problem presented to the emperor. It may be conjectured that Gallien gave this constitution to gain Christian aid against his revolting rivals.[1]

Emperor Caesar Publius Licinius Gallien, Pious, Fortunate, Augustus to Dionysius and Pinnas and Demetrius [5] and the other [6] bishops.

I have ordered the benefit of my bounty to be enforced throughout all the world, that they [7] may depart from the places of religious worship,[8] and therefore you also can use the ordinance of my rescript, so that none may molest you. And this thing, which it is in your power to be able to perform, already [6] for a long time [9] has been conceded by me.

And therefore Aurelius Quirinius, the administrator of the supreme treasury,[10] will observe the ordinance given by me.

1. Valerian was captured by the Persians in June 260. If Gallien wrote this epistle in 260, it is unknown what effect it had in Egypt, whither it was addressed, for the revolt of Macrian and Quietus, who were recognized as Augusti in Egypt as early as September 260, was continued after their deaths in the spring and the autumn, respectively, of 261 by Aemilian, prefect of Egypt, and still was dividing Alexandria as late as Easter 262. But, while its execution may have been delayed in Egypt, there is no ground to deny that the writ of Gallien ran elsewhere in the Empire.

2. However, it seems that as early as the reign of Alexander Severus (222–35), who included Christ in his pantheon of minor deities, the right of the Church to possess property, which it could use as a place of religious assembly, was recognized by an imperial rescript (Scriptores Historiae Augustae: *Sev. Alex.* 49. 6).

Severus' general interest in Christianity (on which see op. cit., 22. 4, 29. 2, 43. 6–7, 45. 7, 51. 7) finds an ironical echo in the epigram of his contemporary Tertullian, the African advocate converted to Christianity, who asserts that "the Caesars too would have believed on Christ, either if Caesars had not been necessary for the world or if Christians too could have been Caesars" (*Apol.* 21. 24). See no. 498, n. 2.

But Tertullian (op. cit., 5. 2; cf. 21. 24) also tells that Tiberius, the second emperor (14–37), earlier than Severus, likewise recognized Christians. Tiberius received from Palestine a report concerning Christ and requested the Senate to

4. RESTORATION OF CHRISTIANS' PROPERTY, 260

favour Christianity, but the senators, because they had not approved the doctrine, rejected his request. Tiberius, however, persisted in his opinion and threatened danger to accusers of Christians. Eusebius (*HE* 2. 2. 6) quotes this tale from Tertullian, but emends Tertullian's "danger" (*periculum*) to "death" (θάνατος). Orosius later (*Adv. Pag.* 7. 4. 6-7) carries the story a step farther and says that Tiberius wanted Christ to be considered a god, but that the Senate refused through pique that the Palestinian report had not been presented to it prior to the emperor's reception of it. But if the report had come from official sources, it should have been submitted only to the emperor, under whose jurisdiction then lay Judae, a minor imperial province governed by a procurator, who in this case apparently was Pontius Pilate, answerable during his tenure (26-36) only to Tiberius.

It was in this emperor's reign, however, that Ulpian (Domitius Ulpianus), his chief juriconsult and his praetorian prefect, collected in the seventh book of his treatise *On the Proconsul's Office* (*De Officio Proconsulis*) anti-Christian imperial rescripts, that he might show with what punishments it was proper for persons who confessed themselves worshippers of God to be punished (Lactantius, *Inst. Div.* 5. 11. 19). Such a collection, however, would not prove Ulpian's hostility toward Christianity, because the author of such a work normally could not omit constitutions, no matter what their tenor, affecting the regulation of the proconsular magistracy. Although thirteen fragments of this part of Ulpian's treatise are preserved in Justinian's *Digesta*, none of these—as may be surmised after Justinian's compilers had done their work—seems to pertain particularly to Christianity, save possibly *D* 1. 18. 13, 48. 2. 7. 5, 48. 13. 7 (6), which refer to sacrilege (on which see no. 168, n. 1), and *D* 48. 4. 1, which ranks treason (on which see no. 1, n. 4) next to sacrilege. In these four instances Christians, as well as others, were likely candidates for prosecution before pagan proconsuls in the provinces.

Earlier, St Melito, bishop of Sardis, with a fine disregard for the fact that Augustus, the first Roman emperor, had died (in 14) before the foundation of the Church, maintained that the Empire and the Church were contemporaneous and that the emperors should protect the Christian philosophy, even as Augustus had patronized it and as Hadrian and Antoninus Pius had protected the Christians (Eusebius, *HE* 4. 26. 7-10).

3. Valerian's ordinance against Christians has not reached us in legal form, but its contents are summarized in the Appendix on Persecutions.

4. Already almost two generations before this document's date, Tertullian calls the Christians a corporation (*corpus*) and tells of their treasury (*arca*) and of the common property (*rei communicatio*) of the congregation in Carthage (*Apol.* 39. 1, 5, 11). See also no. 133, n. 1.

5. It is assumed generally that these prelates were Egyptian, because the Dionysius mentioned so frequently in the earlier part of this book of Eusebius' *Ecclesiastical History* was the bishop of Alexandria *c.* 247–*c.* 265. No satisfactory identification of either Pinnas or Demetrius, however, has been made.

6. Nicephorus omits this word.

7. The non-Christians.

8. After recording this rescript Eusebius states that the same emperor sent to other bishops another ordinance, allowing them to recover the sites of the Christian cemeteries.

9. This probably means that Gallien had been favourable toward the Christians ere he became sole emperor in 258 after already five years of collegiate rule.

10. Nicephorus reads "legion" (τάγματος) for *treasury* (πράγματος)—clearly a literal confusion.

Since the Christians' property—and indeed confiscated property of all kinds and from any previous owner—had come into the control of the treasury (nos. 6, 12, 14), which sometimes then sold or gave it to citizens (nos. 10, 12, 14), Quirinius as the prefect of the treasury (ὁ τοῦ μεγίστου πράγματος προστατεύων = *rationalis summae rei*: so D. Magie, *De Romanorum Iuris Publici Sacrique Vocabulis Sollemnibus in Graecum Sermonem Conversis* [Leipzig, 1905], 107) was charged with the return of their property to the Christians. Some fifty years later, however, provincial governors (nos. 10 and 12) were ordered to effect—or at least supervised—such restitution.

5. MANDATE OF AURELIAN ON PERSECUTION OF CHRISTIANS, 273 or 274

(H 170)

This mandate is supposed to have been the signal for the penultimate persecution of the Church, but it seems that the emperor died ere the constitution could be carried into effect.[1]

Emperor Aurelian to the assistants, governors of provinces.[2]

We learn [3] from those persons who in our times say that they are Christians that the laws' commands are violated.

Therefore subject to different punishments these persons, after they have been arrested, unless they shall have sacrificed to our gods, that both prolonged torture [4] may render [5] justice and vengeance, when terminated in curtailing crimes, already may have [5] an end.

1. So Eusebius (*HE* 7. 30. 20–1), who also reports that earlier the emperor in effect recognized Christianity as a lawful religion (*religio licita*). The historian records that Paul of Samosata, bishop of Antioch, who was the last and the ablest exponent of Dynamistic Monarchianism as well as perhaps the earliest exemplar of the secular type of prelate (soon to become only too common

among the incumbents of the greater sees), relying upon the patronage of Queen Zenobia of Palmyra, had refused after excommunication and deposition (269) to surrender possession of the Antiochene church to Domnus, his successor. When the case had been referred by petition to Aurelian, the emperor ordered (272) the edifice to be transferred to those to whom the bishops of the doctrine (ἐπίσκοποι τοῦ δόγματος—probably Eusebius' translation of Aurelian's words) throughout Italy and the Romans' city should send letters; and, apparently ascertaining that the Italian prelates decided for Domnus, drove Paul from his position (*HE* 7. 30. 18–19).

It is interesting to observe that this was the first occasion that a petition was carried to an emperor by ecclesiastics on an ecclesiastical point, if we except— as is proper—St Paul's appeal from Festus to Nero and Festus' chiastic answer (Acts 25. 9–12), and that the imperial "test is that of recognition by the bishops of the religion in Italy and Rome, not communion with the bishop of Rome only, for papalism was unknown in Aurelian's day" (Kidd, 1. 500). But two generations earlier than Aurelian exists evidence of papalism, when Pope St Victor I (189–99) attempted to excommunicate from the common unity the Asiatic churches, which celebrated Easter according to their ancient custom (Eusebius, *HE* 5. 24. 9; see no. 52, n. 3).

2. The denomination of provincial governors as aides (*administri*) is rare in superscriptions. See no. 234, n. 3.

Or "have learned", for the present and the perfect tenses have the same form in the plural number of the first person.

4. The word is *districtio*, literally "a stretching out" and may indicate punishment on the rack. Later it means "punishment", "severity", "investigation".

5. The verb (*habeat*) is zeugmatic with two objects and must be translated differently in each case.

6. LETTER OF MAXIMIAN I ON PERSECUTION OF CHRISTIANS, c. 301

(H 182)

This directive, which is defective, but apparently is addressed to Venustian, Augustal of Tuscia,[1] orders Christians, unless they shall sacrifice to the gods, to be put to death and their property to be confiscated to the fisc. If the date is correct, this constitution preceded the final persecution of the Church by almost a biennium.

From the report of our father [2] Hermogenian,[3] praetorian prefect,[4] know that it has become clear, etc. . . .[5]

18   7. TOLERATION OF CHRISTIANS, 311

Therefore we advise that, wherever Christians shall have bee
found worshipping superstition, they either should be compelled t
sacrifice to the gods or certainly should perish by punishments an
should be stripped of their property. The said property should t
joined to the fisc with the public tributes.

Farewell, dearest cousin.²

Given on 30 April.

1. From Diocletian's reorganization of Italy *c.* 300 into regions until *c.* 3'
it seems that Tuscia (Tuscany) and Umbria formed one provincial distri
and were governed by an imperial official whose title was *corrector Tusciae
Umbriae*; thereafter he was called *consularis Tusciae et Umbriae*. There is no oth
evidence that an Augustal, who with five other Augustals (the college of *sev.
Augustales*) was ordinarily a freedman, in his maintenance of the emperor's cu
in Italy exercised such power as is conferred upon him by this constitution.

F. Lanzoni, who has examined the *Passio Sancti Sabini*, whence comes tl
letter, in *Römische Quartalschrift*, 17 (1903) 1–26, adopts an earlier suggestic
that the anonymous author called Venustian an Augustal because during tl
fifth and the sixth centuries—the work was written between 450 and 700,]
thinks (11)—it was customary to call the lawyers, who were judges' assessor
Augustals (18).

2. A complimentary title, for no relation by blood or by adoption is inferre

3. Unidentified otherwise than by the following title and, though often
jurist was a praetorian prefect, probably not the compiler of the unofficial co
of imperial constitutions called by this name.

4. On the first occasion of this official title it is proper to remark tha
though the first syllable of each word is *prae* in the Latin words whence ea
word is derived, Webster's preferred spelling, which prefers *praetorian
pretorian* and *prefect* to *praefect*, is followed—an indication of the inconsisten
which is so offensive in Anglo-American orthography of the twentieth centur

5. The lacuna is in the text.

7. EDICT OF GALERIUS ON TOLERATION OF CHRISTIANS, 311

(Lactantius, *De Mort. Pers.* 34)

This famous document, extant both in its Latin original and in its Gre
translation, was issued 30 April 311 at Nicomedia jointly by four emperor
Constantine, Galerius, Licinius, Maximin, although it is called commonly t
Edict of Galerius after its actual author, who published it in the name of al
Galerius, who is represented as suffering from a loathsome disease [3] and

conscience-stricken for his cruelty against the Christians, shortly ere his death voluntarily surrendered by seeking to placate the God of the persecuted and endeavoured to secure the Christians' loyalty to the Empire by an edict stopping the persecution, urged the Christians to assemble in their congregational meetings, entreated them to perform their accustomed worship, and asked Christian prayers for his and their and the State's welfare. This palinode, in putting a term to the last persecution, which lasted for ten years,[4] showed that the supreme effort of the pagan State to extirpate Christianity had been confounded.

Eusebius (*HE* 8. 17. 3-10) and Nicephorus (*HE* 7. 23) give the edict in Greek, but the present translation is from Lactantius' Latin, prefaced by a superscription from Eusebius' Greek, an effect which erroneously converts the edict into an epistle.

Emperor Caesar Galerius Valerius Maximian,[5] Unconquered, Augustus, Pontifex Maximus, Germanicus Maximus, Aegyptiacus Maximus,[6] Thebaicus Maximus, Sarmaticus Maximus five times, Persicus [7] Maximus twice, Carpicus [7] Maximus six times, Armeniacus [7] Maximus, Medicus [7] Maximus, Adiabenicus [7] Maximus, with the Tribunician Power for the twentieth time, Imperator for the nineteenth time, Consul for the eighth time, Father of the Fatherland, Proconsul; and Emperor Caesar Flavius Valerius Constantine, Pious, Fortunate, Unconquered,[8] Augustus,[8] Pontifex [8] Maximus,[8] with the Tribunician Power,[9] Imperator for the fifth time, Consul, Father of the Fatherland, Proconsul; and Emperor Caesar Valerius Licinian [8] Licinius, Pious, Fortunate,[8] Unconquered,[8] Augustus,[8] Pontifex [8] Maximus,[8] with the Tribunician Power for the fourth time, Imperator thrice, Consul, Father of the Fatherland, Proconsul: to their provincials greeting.

Among all other measures, which we arrange always [10] for the State's advantages [11] and profit, we indeed hitherto had wished [12] to correct all things in accordance with the ancient laws and the public order of the Romans and to provide for this: that also the Christians, who had abandoned [12] the way of life [13] of their fathers, should return to their right minds.[11] For indeed, through some reasoning, such wilfulness had seized and such folly had possessed the said Christians [14] that they followed not their ancestors' well-known institutions, which perchance their own forefathers formerly had established, but they, through their own decision [15] and as it had pleased them, made for themselves laws, which they were observing,[16] and in various places assembled various peoples. Therefore, when our command had ensued to the following effect, that they should betake themselves to the ancient institutions, many [17] have been subjected to danger and many [17] also [10] have been dispossessed.[18] And since very many[19] still persevered in their determined[20] course[20] and because we perceived that the said persons neither were showing veneration and[10] reverence[10] due to the gods nor were worshipping the Christians' god,[21] we, in view of our most[10] kindly[10] Clemency, having[10] regard[10] also for our continual custom, by which we are wont to bestow pardon upon all men, have believed that we ought to extend our promptest indulgence also in these matters,[11] that Christians may exist again[22] and may arrange their own conventicles,[23] yet so as that they do nothing contrary to public order.[24]

Moreover in another letter[25] we shall show the governors what they ought to observe.

Wherefore in accordance with this our indulgence they shall be bound[26] to beseech their own god for our[27] and the State's and their own welfare, that in every way the State may be preserved safely and they may be able to live securely in their own homes.

1. Perhaps one reason why Eusebius omitted the name of Maximin (see next note) is that Galerius refused to recognize his Italian rival as among the real Augusti (cf. Lactantius, op. cit., 32. 5).

2. So Lactantius, who says (36. 3) that the *indulgentia*, by which he characterizes the proclamation's chief purport, was conferred *communi titulo*. His omission of the four imperial names is supplied partly by Eusebius, who, however, gives at most only the names of Galerius, Constantine, Licinius. Maximin is mentioned not at all and Licinius is lacking in some MSS. Because both Licinius and Maximin later persecuted Christians, this circumstance may have caused omission of their mention.

3. Of this disease—phthiriasis (φθειρίασις) or pediculosis (*morbus pedicularis*)— some other sanguinary-minded persecutors of Christians in antiquity are said to have died: Herod Agrippa I, king of Judaea, in 44 and Huneric, Vandal king in Africa, in 484. Earlier had died of it both Antiochus IV Epiphanes, the Seleucid king, who persecuted Jews, in 163 B.C. and Lucius Cornelius Sulla Felix, the Roman dictator, who instituted proscriptions in Rome, in 78 B.C.

4. Diocletian's five edicts against the Christians have not descended to us in legal form, but their provisions are recorded in the Appendix on Persecutions.

5. Nicephorus reads "Maximinus", incorrectly.

6. Nicephorus inserts "Germanicus Maximus, Aegyptiacus Maximus", to which he adds "twice", after *Persicus Maximus*, from which he removes *twice*.

7. The Greeks give this word as a genitive plural noun, but the usual style is the nominative singular of the adjective (as earlier in the superscription).

8. Nicephorus omits this word.

9. Nicephorus adds "for the fifth time" erroneously and omits the rest of Constantine's characterization.

10. Eusebius omits this word. Nicephorus's evidence will be cited only when he differs from that of Eusebius.

7. TOLERATION OF CHRISTIANS, 311

11. Singular in Eusebius.
12. Perfect tense in Eusebius.
13. Eusebius translates *secta* (the way of life) by αἵρεσις (whence "heresy"). Each word is used in a favourable sense, obviously, for it would be absurd for us to think that the pagan Galerius in a state paper was belittling the traditional religious beliefs of the great majority of his subjects. It is true that some commentators have thought that Galerius meant either Christianity or Judaism, but the prevailing opinion is that he had paganism in mind.

Secta means properly a trodden path and then tropically a prescribed way of conduct or principles of living and particularly a school or sect of thought, whether legal or philosophical or scientific or religious. Perhaps Galerius used it to characterize the Christian community united in thought taught by Christ, their teacher.

St Jerome uses *secta* for αἵρεσις in Acts 24. 5, 26. 5; Gal. 5. 20; 2 Pet. 2. 1; but shows *heresis* for αἵρεσις in 1 Cor. 11. 19. However, he has both *secta* and *heresis* for ὁδός and αἵρεσις in Acts 24. 14, where "the way which they call heresy" is mentioned by St Paul.

The traditional meaning of the word *heresy* already occurs in the New Testament and denotes a doctrine which is erroneous, temerarious, injurious, calumnious, scandalous, or offensive to pious ears (*piarum aurium offensivum*). Here, for example, beginning with the words of Jesus, that "many shall come in my name ... and shall deceive many" (Matt. 24. 5; Mark 13. 6; cf. Luke 21. 8), we read about persons who superstitiously worship angels (Col. 2. 18); incipient Gnostics with their "fables and endless genealogies" (1 Tim. 1. 4) and "profane and vain babblings and oppositions of science [*gnosis*] falsely so called" (1 Tim. 6. 20); deniers of the resurrection of the flesh (2 Tim. 2. 18; cf. 1 Cor. 15. 12); Nicolaitanes, who have some kind of immoral worship (Rev. 2. 6, 15); Docetists, who "confess not that Jesus Christ is come in the flesh" (1 John 4. 3). Heretical doctrines are described as "doctrines of devils" (1 Tim. 4. 1), "profane and old wives' fables" (1 Tim. 4. 7), "profane and vain babblings" (2 Tim. 2. 16), "cunningly devised fables" (2 Pet. 1. 16), "damnable heresies" (2 Pet. 2. 1). Preachers of heresies are portrayed as "false prophets" (Matt. 7. 15, 24. 11, 24. 24; Mark 13. 22; 2 Pet. 2. 1; 1 John 4. 1), "false teachers" (2 Pet. 2. 1), "men of corrupt mind and destitute of the truth" (1 Tim. 6. 5), "speaking lies in hypocrisy and having their conscience seared with a hot iron" (1 Tim. 4. 2), "deceivers" (2 John 7), and "antichrists" (1 John 2. 18, 2. 22, 4. 3; 2 John 7).

14. For *the said Christians* Eusebius substitutes "them".
15. Eusebius has "proposal".
16. Eusebius transforms the relative clause into a verb correlative with and joined to the preceding verb.
17. Eusebius has the superlative degree.
18. Eusebius evidently regards the Lactantian *deturbati sunt* as a euphemism, for he translates it as if it means "endured all kinds of deaths" (παντοίους

θανάτους ὑπέφερον). He precedes it with a participle meaning "having been harassed".

19. Eusebius has the positive degree.
20. Eusebius substitutes "loss of sense".
21. This need not be a matter for marvel, since only courageous Christians ordinarily would assemble for worship in a period of persecution, and the ranks of such were being reduced rapidly.

For this much of the sentence Eusebius reads "And since, when many were persevering in the said madness, we perceived that they neither brought due worship to the celestial gods nor offered it to the Christians' god".

22. Here fully and finally (see no. 3, n. 34 *ad init.*) Christianity is recognized as a *religio licita*.

Doubtless the emperors capitulated to the Christians, because they had come at long last to realize that Christianity could not be exterminated and that they had been fighting "not against flesh and blood" (Eph. 6. 12; cf. Matt. 16. 17; 1 Cor. 15. 50; Gal. 1. 16; Heb. 2. 14), but against the apocalyptic and invisible army of 144,000 (Rev. 7. 4, 14. 1, 3), which increased both quantitatively and qualitatively with every confessor who had sealed his confession with his blood (cf. Matt. 10. 32; Luke, 12. 8; Rev. 3. 5, 7. 9-17).

23. Some interpret this clause to mean "may build their own churches". The noun is *conventiculum* and οἶκος. Eusebius adds "in which they used to assemble".
24. This elastic proviso is most important, for on it could be put various interpretations, which might nullify the preceding concessions.
25. This letter is lost, but in the Edict of Milan (no. 12) two references to it imply that it contained some serious modifications of what was conceded to the Christians by the Galerian edict.
26. Present tense in Eusebius.
27. See no. 1, n. 3 *ad init.*

8. LETTER OF SABINUS ON MAXIMIN II'S ORDERS ABOUT CHRISTIANS, 311

(Eusebius, *HE* 9. 1. 3-6)

This letter from Sabinus, Maximin's praetorian prefect, implements the Galerian Edict of Toleration issued 30 April 311 (no. 7). But the instructions contained in the letter constitute a faint shadow of the operative clauses of the edict, doubtless because of the tepidity evinced toward the edict by Maximin, whom Eusebius excoriates with the epithet "Tyrant of the East". According to Eusebius this emperor reluctantly consented to the edict and carried his reluctance to such a stage that he refused to give written effect to it, contenting

8. MAXIMIN II'S ORDERS ABOUT CHRISTIANS, 311

himself only with commanding orally his chief officials to send written instructions to the provincial governors in his part of the Empire that they should stop the persecution against the Christians (HE 9. 1. 1).

The document, which Eusebius translates from Latin into Greek, thus is an imperial directive from Maximin's prefect to the governors under his jurisdiction in the East. Since all the subordinate officials mentioned in the letter's last paragraph are found in the administration of Egypt, it may be that this epistle was directed especially thither.

With most splendid and devoted zeal the Divinity of our most divine lords, the emperors,[1] for quite a long time determined to direct all men's thoughts toward the holy and correct course of life, that also those seeming to follow a custom foreign to the Romans should render acts of worship due to the immortal gods. But the opposition and the harshest determination of some were carried to such a degree that neither they could retreat from their own purpose by just reasoning contained in the command nor the impending punishment could frighten them.

Since therefore it transpired that by such conduct many involved themselves in peril, in consonance with their innate nobility of piety the Divinity of our lords, the mightiest emperors, considering it alien to their most divine policy that they should involve men in such great peril for such cause, ordered through my Devotion to write to your Sagacity that, if any of the Christians would be discovered engaging in the worship of his own nation, you should free him from molestation aimed against him and from danger and you should not suppose that anyone ought to be afflicted with punishment on this charge, since by the experience of so long a period it has been proved that in no way they can be induced to desist from such obstinacy.

Therefore your Carefulness ought to write to the curators[2] and the governors[3] and the provosts[4] of each city's district, that they may know that it is not befitting for them to heed any longer that letter.[5]

1. This letter thus purports to be based on the Galerian edict emitted by the four emperors (no. 7), although from Eusebius' introductory account it appears that Maximin alone authorized its composition.

2. In Egypt these officials were attached to and supervised the financial administration of the nomes (districts) into which the province was divided.

3. In Egypt the governors of nomes (on which cf. *supra* n. 2), not the provincial governors (which is what the word [στρατηγός] usually means elsewhere in imperial administration), for the governor of Egypt was a prefect (ἔπαρχος, on which see no. 489, n. 12).

4. In Egypt these officers commanded troops billeted in a municipal area.

5. This must refer to an earlier and written order (not preserved) commanding the persecution of Christians, perhaps the so-called sixth edict of the autumn of 308 (Eusebius, *De Mart. Pal.* 9. 2), which orders the same officials named in nn. 2 and 3 *supra* to enforce it. See its summary in the Appendix on Persecutions.

9. RESCRIPT OF MAXIMIN II ON ANTI-CHRISTIAN PETITIONS, 311 or 312

(Eusebius, *HE* 9. 7. 3–14)

Eusebius translates from Latin into Greek this rescript of anti-Christian propaganda, wherein Maximin II authorizes a renewal of persecution against Christians. Because even the most important imperial constitutions seem to have been publicized usually on ordinary writing material, although occasionally (as here) more permanent media were used, this rescript assumes some significance from its display on a stele erected at Tyre.

Eusebius' claim that other cities received the rescript is confirmed by the discovery, in 1892 at Arycanda (Aruf) in Lycia, of the Lycians' and the Pamphylians' Greek petition [1] with Maximin's Latin reply, of which the latter (so far as we have it in fragmentary form) corresponds quite closely with what—to judge from the Eusebian Greek—was the original Latin of the Tyrian inscription.[2]

But before Constantine and Licinius had met at Milan and had published their famous Edict of Toleration in 313 (no. 12), Maximin was compelled to suspend his persecution and he soon afterward issued instructions to enforce the edict (no. 14).

Copy of a translation of Maximin's rescript, translated from the stele at Tyre, to the acts [3] against us.

Now at length the weak overboldness of the human intelligence, after having discarded and dispersed all obscurity and mist of error, which hitherto was besieging the senses of men, not so much unholy as unhappy, when enveloped by the destructive darkness of ignorance, has had the strength to recognize that it is controlled and steadied by the immortal gods' benevolent providence. Wherefore it is an incredible thing to tell how acceptable, how very pleasant and agreeable it has been for us that you have given an exceedingly great evidence [4] of your god-loving policy, since even ere this none could not know what kind of observance and piety you happened to have toward the immortal gods, in whom is demonstrated a faith, not of mere and hollow phrases, but continuous and admirable in respect to distinguished deeds. Wherefore worthily your city may be called both a temple and a habitation of the immortal gods; at least by many proofs it is clear that it flourishes by the residence of the celestial gods there.

Behold, therefore, your city, after having no care for all its own interests and after having disregard for former petitions concerning its own affairs, when again it perceived that those engaged in the accursed folly were beginning to spread, even as an unwatched and quiescent funeral pyre, when its fires are rekindled, providing a vast conflagration, straightway and without any delay, demanding some healing and help, had recourse to our Piety, just as to a metropolis of all godly fears. And it is clear that the gods have implanted in you this salutary thought on account of the confidence in your religiousness.[5] Accordingly that one, that highest and mightiest Zeus,[6] he who presides over your most illustrious city, he who protects your hereditary gods and women and children and hearth and homes from all deadly destruction, infused into your souls the saving purpose, showing and indicating how special and splendid and salutary it is to approach the worship and the divine rites of the immortal gods with due reverence. For who can be found so senseless or foreign to all intelligence who does not perceive that by the gods' benevolent exertion it comes to pass neither that the earth rejects the seeds bestowed upon it, balking the farmers' hope with vain expectation, nor again that the aspect of impious war sets itself on the earth without hindrance and drags down to death squalid bodies, while the mildness of the sky is corrupted, nor indeed that the sea, when tossed by blasts of immoderate winds, swells with crests, nor at any rate that hurricanes burst unexpectedly and excite destructive tempest,[7] nor, moreover, that the earth, the nurse and mother of all, sinking from its deepest hollows in terrible tremor, and the mountains hanging over the resultant chasms are dissolved?[8] And none is ignorant that all these things and things even more cruel than these occurred often before this time. And all these things happened together on account of the destructive error of the hollow folly of those lawless men, when it prevailed over their souls and—one might almost say—everywhere weighed upon the world with shameful deeds. . . .[9]

Let them behold in the wide plains the standing crops, already blooming and waving with ears of grain, and the meadows, gleaming with plants and flowers because of abundant rain, and the state of the weather, which has been given to us well-tempered and quite mild; furthermore, let all together rejoice that through our piety and sacrifice and veneration the most mighty and most obstinate air has been propitiated [10] and let them be glad in enjoying therefore securely and with quiet the most sheltered peace. And let as many as have been rescued entirely from that blind wandering and circuit [11] and have returned to correct and noblest thought rejoice indeed the more, as if they have been reclaimed from an unexpected tempest or a grave disease and will be reaping life's sweet enjoyment for the future. But if they should remain in their accursed folly, let them be separated and extruded very far from your city and vicinity, according as you have asked, that thus, in pursuance of your praiseworthy zeal in this respect, your city, separated from all defilement and impiety, may obey its innate purpose with due reverence to the sacred worship of the immortal gods.

And that you may know how agreeable to us has been your petition on this subject and how our soul has been most eager for benevolence by its voluntary will, without proposals and without entreaty, we permit your Devotion to [12] ask whatever great gift you may wish in return for this your god-loving purpose. And now resolve to do this and to receive this, for you will obtain it without any postponement. And this, granted to your city, will present for all time the testimony of god-loving piety toward the immortal gods and will demonstrate to your sons and descendants that on account of this your course of conduct you have obtained from our Goodness worthy rewards.

1. Both Lactantius (*De Mort. Pers.* 36. 3) and Eusebius (*HE* 9. 2; 9. 4. 2; 9. 7. 1; 9. 9a. 4–6) mention that Maximin encouraged communities to send to him embassies with petitions against the Christians' presence amid them.

2. Petition and rescript have been edited at least seventeen times within 52 years with the result that various restorations, grounded on the Eusebian Greek, have been made by many epigraphists. The latest edition appears to be E. Kalinka's in *Tituli Asiae Minoris* (Wien, 1944), 2. 3. 785.

3. A ψήφισμα (the word here) is a proposal passed by an assembly. In this case it is the petition to the emperor enacted by the municipal senate of Tyre.

4. The Tyrians' petition against the Christians is meant.

That a Christian community existed as early as the mid-first century at Tyre is shown by the statement that there St Paul discovered disciples and spent seven days (Acts 21. 3).

5. Or, perhaps, "on account of the guarantee of your godly fear" or "on account of the faith coming from your godly fear" or "on account of the gods' belief in your righteousness".

6. While Heracles (Hercules), identified with the Phoenician divinity Melkart, was the tutelary god of Tyre, yet it is possible the Zeus (Jupiter), the father of Heracles and equated with Baal, the supreme Phoenician deity, enjoyed especial esteem at Tyre, where excavation has revealed evidence of a temple to Zeus, and therefore mention of Zeus here may have had some singular significance.

7. This would be of special concern to a seaside city, whose main interests were traditionally maritime. As far distant as the days of Isaiah we hear the

prophet characterize this "crowning city" as one "whose merchants are princes, whose traffickers are the honourable of the earth" (Isa. 23. 8).

8. The Greek is awkward: the word for *earth* is without predicate. The idea seems to be that earthquakes, to which Tyre was subject, cause the earth to part and to sink in some places and then the mountains, lying on its surface and perched—as it were—at the edges of chasms thus created, fall into the abysses. Cf. Seneca, *Nat. Quaest.* 6. 26. 5. See also no. 1, n. 3 *ad fin*.

Doubtless earthquakes as well as enemies contributed in time to the collapse of Tyre, whose ruins inspired not a little *Ruinensehnsucht* in travellers—so R. Macaulay, *Pleasure of Ruins* (London, 1953), 49–54.

It is obvious that the points to which attention has been attracted in nn. 5–7 *supra* would not be suitable for mention in rescripts to other petitioning cities. Doubtless some modification to conform with local circumstances was made in this part of the emperor's answer.

9. Eusebius himself makes a break here, when he writes "After other remarks he adds to these:" and then resumes his translation.

That the proposition that the Christians were considered responsible for the natural—not to mention other—disasters which debilitated the Empire played a prominent part in pagan polemics is proved by the extensive efforts of the Christian apologists to controvert the accusation (cf. e.g. Arnobius, *Adv. Gent.* 1. 1–24; see no. 1, n. 3 *ad med.*).

10. This seems to be the sense of this corrupted clause.

11. The expression *wandering and circuit* seems to signify simply "error" in the literal sense and then "error" in the metaphorical meaning.

12. The Arycandan fragment starts here. Cf. *supra* n. 2 for the futility of attempting to translate the emended Latin versions of it and see also the second paragraph of this document's introduction. In it are only twelve complete words, from which and from twelve incomplete words editors have conjectured enough text to fill six lines. One of the larger reconstructions runs to 55 words.

10. LETTER OF CONSTANTINE I ON RESTITUTION OF PROPERTY TO THE CHURCH, 313

(Eusebius, *HE* 10. 5. 15–17)

Eusebius translates from the Latin into Greek this imperial constitution, which Constantine wrote to Anuline, his proconsul of Africa, after he had added that province to his share of the Empire as a result of his victorious battle at the Milvian Bridge outside Rome (312).

From the superscription which the historian has supplied it is evident that Eusebius understood that this epistle excluded the schismatic Donatists in

Africa from sharing the emperor's generosity with the ecclesiastically loyal Catholics in that province. But from other sources it seems quite clear that Constantine had not yet heard about the Donatist schism in the African Church and that the phrase [1] misinterpreted by Eusebius refers simply to the Church in Africa as it existed before the persecution ended by the Galerian Edict of Toleration (no. 7) and before the schism subsequent to the cessation of that persecution.[2]

While it seems evident from the Eusebian superscription that the emperor sent this epistle after the emission of the Edict of Milan (no. 12), the epistle probably preceded the edict, on the reasoning that, since the former provides no compensation for purchasers and possessors of property confiscated from the Christians and the latter permits such compensation, the epistle presents a less matured programme for meeting this problem than that proposed in the edict.

Nicephorus (*HE* 7. 42) also has this letter.

Copy of another imperial ordinance, which he next made, indicating that the bounty had been given to only the Catholic Church.[3]

Greeting, our most honoured Anuline.

This is the custom of our Goodness,[4] that we desire that those things which belong to another's legal right not only should not be molested, but even should be restored, most honoured Anuline.

Wherefore we desire that whenever you will receive this letter, if any of those things belonging to the Christians' Catholic Church [1] in each several city or even in other places should be possessed now either by citizens or by any others, you shall cause these to be restored immediately to the said churches, inasmuch as we have chosen deliberately that these [5] things [5] which the said [5] churches previously possessed should be restored to their legal right.

Therefore, since your Devotion perceives that this our command's ordinance is quite clear, hasten that all things, whether gardens or buildings or whatsoever belonged to the legal right of the said churches, should be restored to them as speedily as possible, that we may learn that you have exhibited the most careful obedience to this our ordinance.

Farewell, our most honoured and [5] most [5] cherished [5] Anuline.

1. This phrase *the Christians' Catholic Church* Eusebius takes to denote only those Christians in communion with Caecilian, bishop of Carthage, whose consecration the Donatists considered invalid (no. 17). But if Constantine had heard about the schism (see nos. 15, n. 11, and 16, n. 8), it was important that Anuline should know which faction in Carthage constituted the Catholic Church.

2. If the Eusebian explanation (cf. *supra* n. 1) should be accepted, then it

simply attests to the State's interference in the Church's quarrel—not only an early indication (but see no. 5, n. 1) of eventual intervention in ecclesiastical affairs of all kinds, but also an evidence for the then current Christian conception of the propriety of such imperial participation.

3. Nicephorus omits the caption.
4. "Gentility" is read by Nicephorus.
5. Nicephorus omits this word.

11. EDICT OF LICINIUS ON MILITARY PRAYER, 313
(Lactantius, *De Mort. Pers.* 46. 6)

On the eve of the battle near Perinthus [1] in 313, when Licinius, joint-sovereign with Constantine I, defeated Maximin II, their fellow-emperor, an angel, according to Lactantius, appeared to Licinius while he slept and admonished him with his army to pray to God, assured him that by so doing he would conquer Maximin, and directed him how and in what words he should pray. Licinius awoke, summoned a secretary, dictated the following prayer,[2] and commanded copies of it to be distributed among the prefects and the tribunes with instructions that they should teach it to their soldiers.[3]

Supreme God, we beseech thee; Holy God, we beseech thee; all righteousness to thee we commend; our safety to thee we commend; our Empire to thee we commend. By thee we live; by thee we are victorious and fortunate. Supreme, Holy God, hear our prayers; our arms to thee we extend; hear, Holy, Supreme God.

1. See no. 544, n. 2.
2. See no. 38 for a similar imperial prayer.
3. Lactantius concludes that the soldiers' courage increased because of their belief that victory had been announced to them from heaven.

See no. 42, n. 1 for Licinius' later attitude toward Christianity.

Despite the Lactantian declaration, J. Burckhardt believed that "it is very questionable whether the fighting armies were in any sense aware . . . [that] what was involved was patently a struggle between Christianity and paganism" (*The Age of Constantine the Great* [New York, 1949], 276).

12. LETTER OF CONSTANTINE I AND LICINIUS ON RESTORATION OF THE CHURCH, 313

(Lactantius, *De Mort. Pers.* 48. 2-12)

This document is the so-called Edict of Milan, a landmark not only in the history of Christianity, since it recognizes the Church as a corporate body,[1] but also in the religious history of mankind, because it declares for the first time the doctrine that full freedom in the realm of religion belongs as of right to everyone.[2] Both Lactantius and Eusebius (*HE* 10. 5. 1-14), of whom the latter is followed closely by Nicephorus (*HE* 7. 41), have this ordinance; but Eusebius and Nicephorus preserve a part of the preamble not found in Lactantius' transcription and prefix to it a different superscription. The Latin redaction of Lactantius is taken as the text of the letter.[3]

Though usually called an edict, this constitution is really an epistle, for it is addressed to an individual—in fact to a provincial governor, as Lactantius in his introduction to it states [4]—as each version demonstrates in the not infrequent use of the second person singular number. Much controversy over whether this letter was based on an edict of toleration now lost still continues.[5] But surely, if there had been such a constitution which presumably would have been accessible to them, both Lactantius and Eusebius would have preferred to have inserted it into their works rather than to have relied upon copying the epistle which implemented the edict. What Constantine and Licinius probably did was to compose a canon of instructions for their provincial governors' information and guidance. That this set of regulations could be copied with some variation seems probable, since the Lactantian and the Eusebian versions differ in some details.

Some modern scholars also dispute the document's authenticity, but most critics accept it as authentic, because in it is no indication of any special pro-Christian sentiment and its authors attempt to ensure an equitable compromise for both Christians and pagans. Although the document purports to have been a double production, yet traditionally and by its late superscription it is credited by his Christian panegyrists to Constantine. It is perhaps paradoxical that he, who lived longer in the West than in the East, should have initiated the recognition of Christianity, which originated in the East and was observed widely only in the East—despite the rapid expansion of this religion during the first three centuries of its existence.

The document not only refers to some provisions of the Galerian Edict of Toleration (no. 7; see nn. 8, 10, 29 *infra*), but also declares that the Church must receive such property as the State has confiscated from it during the last persecution—the imperial fisc furnishing financial compensation to the present proprietors, after they have carried their claims to the diocesan vicar (Lactantian version) or to the provincial governor (Eusebian version).

Copy of imperial ordinances translated from the Roman tongue.[6]

12. RESTORATION OF THE CHURCH, 313

Ordinance of Emperor Constantine the Great, written concerning matters pertaining to Christians.[7]

Already long ago, when we were watching that liberty of religion should not be denied, but that to each one's thought and desire should be given authority to practise divine things according to each individual preference, we had ordered [8] that both to Christians . . . and to non-Christians should be conceded the freedom [9] to maintain the faith of their own sect and religion; but since many and various conditions in that rescript,[10] wherein such authority was granted to the same persons, clearly appeared to have been added, perhaps some of them from such maintenance soon afterward were repelled.[11]

When I, Constantine Augustus, and also I, Licinius Augustus,[12] had met happily at Milan and were conferring about all matters which concerned advantages and public security,[13] among these other matters which we saw would benefit most men—or indeed first and foremost—we have believed[14] that there should be ordained those matters by which [15] reverence for the Divinity was contained,[16] that we should concede both to Christians and to all an unrestricted possibility [17] of following which religion each one [18] had wished, whereby whatever Divinity exists in its celestial abode [19] can be placated and [20] propitious to us and to all who are placed under our authority.

Accordingly we have believed [14] with sound and most correct reasoning that we ought to enter into [21] this plan: that facility [22] ought to be denied to no one at all, who had given his mind either to the Christians' observance or to that religion [23] which he himself thought [24] most suitable to himself, in order that the Supreme [25] Divinity, whose worship with free conscience we follow, may vouchsafe to us in all things his wonted favour and benevolence.[26]

Wherefore it is proper that your Excellence should know [27] that it has pleased us that when all [28] the conditions altogether had been abolished, which conditions were contained in letters [29] previously [32] sent to your Devotion [31] concerning the name of [32] Christians,[33] also those things which seemed truly unfavourable and alien from our Clemency may be removed and that now freely and simply each one of those who shows [34] the said purpose to observe the Christians' religion may exert himself to observe [35] this very thing without any inquietude and molestation to himself.[36] And these things we have believed [14] ought to be made known in the fullest manner to your Diligence, that you may know that we have granted [37] to the said Christians free and unconditional facility [22] to practise their own religion. And when you perceive that this has been given [38] by us to the said persons, your Excellence [39] understands that also has been granted similarly open and free [40] authority to others [41] for their own religion or [42] observance in keeping [43] with the peacefulness of our time, so that each one may have free facility [22] in practising what he has chosen.[44] And this we have done, that neither from any rite nor from any religion we may appear to have detracted anything.

And this, moreover, with regard to the persons [45] of the Christians we have resolved [46] ought to be ordained: that, if any appear to have purchased at an earlier period,[47] whether from our fisc or from any other source whatever, the same places at which they formerly had been accustomed to assemble and about which also a definite [48] formulary had been established formerly [49] in a letter [50] sent to your Devotion,[31] they should restore the said places to the [51] Christians without money and without any demand for payment, disregarding all deception [52] and doubtfulness; that also they who [53] have obtained these by gift should restore the said places to the said Christians as quickly as possible; that also those who either have bought or have acquired [54] by gift should apply to the vicar,[55] if they have had any claim from our Benevolence,[56] in order that thought may be taken also for them through our Clemency. And all these things must be delivered to the corporation of the Christians through your intervention [57] immediately and without delay.

And since the said Christians are known to have had [58] not only those places at which they have been accustomed to assemble, but also other places belonging to the legal right of their corporation, that is, of the churches,[59] not of individual persons, you shall command under the law, which we have expressed above, all these to be restored without absolutely any doubt or [60] dispute to the said Christians, that is, to their corporation and assemblies:[61] preserving the aforesaid condition, of course, that those who return the said places without compensation, as we have said, may hope for [62] indemnification from our Benevolence.

In all these things you shall be bound to exercise your most effective intervention [57] for the abovementioned corporation of Christians, that our order may be fulfilled as speedily as possible, so that also in this matter thought may be taken for the [63] public tranquillity through our Clemency. So far it shall result then that,[64] as has been expressed above, the divine favour [57] toward us, which in so many matters we have experienced, for all time may attend steadfastly [65] and prosperously our successes together with the happiness of the State.

Moreover, that the form of this our Benevolence's [66] ordinance may be able to come to the knowledge of all, it shall be fitting for you by your own edict both to publish everywhere what has been written [67] and to bring it to the knowledge of all, in order that this our Benevolence's ordinance cannot escape [68] notice.[69]

1. It is accepted commonly, but erroneously, that by this constitution the emperors established Christianity as the State's religion. But such establishment lay later in this century, for not until the time of Theodosius the Great was this advance achieved—when in his edict *Cunctos populos* of 380 he recognized the Church in the Empire as the Church of the Empire (no. 167).

2. That this part of the epistle, as the event proved, was premature casts no censure upon the emperors. Many centuries and much persecution had to pass before liberty of conscience could be said to have won the day, if indeed today it so can be claimed. As late as 1941 the president of the United States was pleased to emit an edict (in the Roman sense), when in addressing the Congress he looked forward "for a world founded upon four essential human freedoms", of which "the second is freedom of every person to worship God in his own way—everywhere in the world".

3. The Lactantian text used is that edited by S. Brandt (Prague, 1897), who occasionally incorporates into it Eusebian lections. Only when Nicephorus fails to follow Eusebius will be entered in the notes his evidence.

4. *De Mort. Pers.* 48. 1: "Licinius ... ordered a letter (*litterae*) of this tenor, directed to the provincial governor (*ad praesidem*), to be promulgated." On the other hand, Eusebius calls it (10. 5. 1) a διάταξις, which is sufficiently close to διάταγμα, a Greek equivalent of the Latin *edictum*.

5. On the conflicting views about the Edict of Milan consult the evidence collected by Coleman, 26–31, and by Huttmann, 44–58. Add also N. H. Baynes, *Constantine the Great and the Christian Church* (London, 1930), 69–74 (n. 42), and more recently Palanque, 1. 7–12, and most recently Vasiliev, 50–2.

6. From Eusebius.

7. From Nicephorus.

8. Apparently a reference to the edict of Galerius (no. 7).

9. Some words have disappeared from the text. The translator has supplied conjecturally *and . . . freedom*.

10. This rescript may have been that which Galerius promised to send to the provincial governors for their instruction in procedure (no. 7, n. 25), but which has not survived. The repulsion, of course, would have been due to the conditions added.

11. From Eusebius and Nicephorus.

12. According to Lactantius (48. 1) Licinius alone issued the document at Nicomedia and on 13 June, but here both he and Eusebius, who is silent about the purely Licinian authorship, prefix Constantine's name.

13. Eusebius has "advantage and usefulness to the State".

14. Eusebius reads "resolved".

15. Eusebius inserts "respect and".

16. Eusebius inserts "that is".

17. Eusebius reads "preference".

18. This subject is not expressed by Eusebius, who pluralizes the verb.

19. Eusebius reads "whatever Divinity and celestial reality exists". For *Divinity* Nicephorus substitutes "most divine" in following Eusebius.
20. Eusebius omits *placated and*.
21. Eusebius omits *that . . . into*.
22. Eusebius substitutes "authority".
23. For this much of the relative clause Eusebius has "to follow and to choose the Christians' observance and religion and that to each one should be given authority to give his mind to that religion".
24. Eusebius has the present tense.
25. Eusebius omits the adjective and the following relative clause.
26. Eusebius substitutes "esteem and goodness".

Thus far the letter puts Christians on a par with pagans, but in what follows it makes concessions to the former.

27. Eusebius has "It thus was consistent for us to reply".
28. The adjective Eusebius omits.
29. This refers to the Galerian edict and to the letter of instructions for its implementation to the provincial governors (cf. *supra* n. 10).
30. Eusebius reads "in our previous letters".
31. The Eusebian καθοσίωσις is translated instead of the Lactantian *officium*, which means "office staff" ordinarily (see no. 34, n. 3), but can be understood in the sense of "diligence in office".
32. Eusebius omits *name of*.
33. Perhaps a reference to the common charge of the Christians that at times they were persecuted simply because of the name of Christian. The first pagan cognizance of this count is as old as Pliny, who writes c. 113 (*Ep.* 10. 96. 2) that he has hesitated whether the name itself (*nomen ipsum*), even though it be free from crimes, should be punished. Certainly the early Christians' evidence shows that the *nomen ipsum*, apart from any crimes associated with it (as Pliny puts it, the *flagitia cohaerentia nomini*, on which see no. 1, n. 3 *ad init.*), was a sufficient cause for condemnation starting in the second century. Of course, the Christians were prepared for such persecution, if they recalled (as they did) Jesus' words (Matt. 10. 22, 24. 9; Mark 13. 13; Luke 21. 12, 17).
34. Eusebius has "had".
35. Eusebius reads "may observe" for *may . . . observe*.
36. Eusebius has simply "without any molestation".
37. Nicephorus substitutes "signified".
38. Eusebius inserts "unrestrictedly".
39. Eusebius substitutes "Devotion".
40. Eusebius omits *similarly . . . free*.
41. For *for* Eusebius substitutes "wishing to follow". Nicephorus follows Eusebius thus far but more briefly in writing "And when your Devotion perceives that this has been given unrestrictedly by us to the said persons and authority to others wishing to follow".
42. Eusebius reads "and".

43. For the prepositional phrase Eusebius has a parenthetical clause "which, it is clear, is consistent".

44. Eusebius substitutes for the last eight words "authority to choose and to practise whatever he may wish in respect to the Divinity".

45. Singular in Eusebius.

46. Eusebius has the present tense and omits the next four words.

47. Eusebius omits the temporal phrase.

48. Eusebius has "another" for *definite*, as if he misread the Latin *certa* as *cetera*, and is supported by Nicephorus, as usual.

49. Eusebius has "at a former time", but Nicephorus has "at another time".

50. Eusebius inserts "formerly".

51. Eusebius inserts "said".

52. Eusebius substitutes "negligence".

53. For *they who* Eusebius reads "if any persons".

54. Eusebius inserts "the said places".

55. Eusebius substitutes "judicial governor in the places".

56. For *that also those . . . Benevolence* Nicephorus reads "and if any persons have obtained by gift the said places or by gift have obtained them thus from our Benevolence, they should apply to the judicial governor in the places".

57. Eusebius reads "zeal".

58. For *are . . . had* Eusebius reads simply "have had", but inserts these words below after *but also*.

59. Eusebius alters *churches* to "Christians".

60. Eusebius omits *doubt or*.

61. Eusebius substitutes "synod".

62. Eusebius inserts "their own".

63. Eusebius inserts "common and".

64. For the opening words Eusebius has "For by this reasoning".

65. Eusebius omits the rest of the sentence.

66. Eusebius inserts a connective here.

67. Eusebius adds "by us".

68. Eusebius inserts "anyone's".

69. It was usual for provincial governors to arrange for publication of such imperial constitutions as affected provincials.

13. LETTER OF MAXIMIN II ON BEHALF OF CHRISTIANS, 313

(Eusebius, *HE* 9. 9a. 1–9)

Eusebius translates from Latin into Greek this letter from Maximin, the emperor in the East, to Sabinus, his praetorian prefect. The historian tells us that the emperor, after he had been informed of the Edict of Milan (no. 12),[1] which he deplored privately, wrote to his provincial governors that they should placate the Christians by suspending the persecution which Maximin had renewed after Galerius' death in 311.

Eusebius, who never has a good word for Maximin, asserts that in this letter, which is the only one preserved, the emperor belied himself and pretended that he had done things for the Christians which he never had done. According to Eusebius none of the Christians was deceived by this letter, for they no longer thought that Maximin was truthful or even trustworthy and they considered that this command came from his colleagues' compulsion. Moreover the Christians construed the absence of any provision about public assembly or for erection of churches as a prohibition against such activity.

For Maximin's final edict of toleration see no. 14.

Nicephorus (*HE* 7. 31) also has this letter.

Copy of a translation of the tyrant's epistle.[2]

Jovius Maximin Augustus to Sabinus.

I have been persuaded that it is evident both to your Gravity and to all men that our Lords Diocletian and Maximian, our fathers, when they perceived that almost all men,[3] after they had abandoned the worship of the gods, had associated themselves with the nation of Christians, rightly commanded all men who had withdrawn from the worship of their immortal gods to be recalled by manifest chastisement and punishment to the worship of the gods.

But when I came with happy auspices for the first time [4] to the East and found that very many persons, able to serve the public interests, were being banished to certain places by the governors on account of the abovementioned reason, to each of the governors I gave orders [5] that none of them in the future should apply harsh treatment to the provincials, but rather by persuasion [6] and by exhortations should recall them to the worship of the gods. At that time, therefore, when, pursuant to my order, what had been commanded was observed by the governors, it resulted that none from the eastern regions either was exiled or was insulted, but rather from no severe treatment against them they were recalled to the worship of the gods;[7] but later, when in the past year with happy auspices I went to Nicomedia [8] and there was staying, to me came citizens of the same city along with images of the gods, rather strongly begging that by all means such a nation [9] ought not at all to be allowed to dwell in their native city. But when I learned that very many men of the same religion lived in those very regions, to them I thus rendered the reply: "That I had excessive gratitude for their petition, but I discerned that this had not been petitioned by all; if, then, there should be some continuing in this same superstition, each one should have thus his desire pursuant to his

13. ON BEHALF OF CHRISTIANS, 313

individual choice and, if they should so desire, should recognize the worship of the gods." However, to the Nicomedians of the same city and to the rest of the cities, which also themselves so very eagerly have made to me a similar petition, namely, that none of the Christians should dwell in their cities, I was constrained to answer kindly, because this very thing [10] all the ancient emperors had maintained and because it pleased the gods, through whom all men and the very government of the State subsist, that I should confirm such a petition as they present on behalf of the worship of their divinity.[11]

Therefore, although especially to your Devotion it had been commanded in letters before this time and likewise through ordinances it has been ordered [12] that one should treat not harshly, but forbearingly and moderately, the provincials who have made it their care to maintain such a custom, nevertheless, that they may not submit to insults or to extortions [13] either by the beneficiarians [14] or by any other persons, I have considered it consequent upon these letters also to remind your Firmness that you should cause our provincials to acknowledge the attention due by them to the gods rather by persuasion [15] and by exhortations.

Wherefore, if any by his choice should assume that the worship of the gods ought to be recognized, it is proper to welcome them;[16] but if some should wish to follow their own worship, you should leave it in their own power.

Accordingly your Devotion ought to observe carefully what has been ordered you and authority should be granted to none that [17] he may afflict our provincials by insults and by extortions, since—as has been written above [17]—it is proper to recall rather by exhortations and by persuasion [15] our provincials to worship of the gods.

And that this our order may come to the knowledge of all [18] our provincials, you ought to reveal what has been enjoined by an edict emitted by yourself.

1. Huttmann, 38-44, reviews scholarly arguments *pro* and *con* that Maximin's action was impelled rather by an edict (not preserved) issued by Constantine (and Licinius) at Rome late in 312 after the Battle of the Milvian Bridge. More recently the earlier date has found favour: see Palanque, 1. 4-5.

2. Nicephorus omits the caption.

3. This claim is not exaggerated, for, unless a pagan who had forsaken both the traditional Graeco-Roman gods and the deities of the Oriental mystery-religions adopted atheism, he had little other choice except to embrace either Judaism or Christianity.

4. In 305.

5. This is probably true, for no persecution in the East has been recorded for several months after Maximin's accession.

6. Literally "flattery", "fawning"; but perhaps even in Greek this meaning is too strong for characterizing the activity expected from a provincial governor.

7. A palpable lie, for he ignores the persecution begun in 306.

8. In 311.

9. The Christians are meant.

10. It is not clear what is meant by *this very thing* (αὐτὸ τοῦτο). Maximin may have meant that his imperial predecessors answered petitions in kindly manner and that so tradition compelled him to reply thus, or that the previous emperors took especial pains to approve requests on religious activities from non-Christian subjects. Probably the latter is intended.

11. This sentence seems to contradict the previous sentence in that a petition is denied first and then confirmed. Each statement is true: the first petition came too soon after the Galerian Edict of Toleration (no. 7) for Maximin to dare to disregard the edict; but, when the Nicomedians and others (Antiochenes, Tyrians, Arycandans) had perceived both that Maximin's adherence to it had been compelled and that he would welcome an excuse for a change of policy, then they presented to him a similar (the second) petition, which the emperor granted, taking refuge (in this letter) in the reason that their request was pleasing to the gods.

12. Eusebius earlier asserts that Maximin issued only verbal orders to Sabinus (9. 1. 1; see no. 8).

13. Possibly "harassments", i.e. persecutions, another meaning for this word (σεισμός), which is repeated. By *they* are meant Christians.

14. On these see no. 14, n. 6.

15. Here in the plural: cf. *supra* n. 6 for its literal meaning.

16. Nicephorus reads "him".

17. Either Nicephorus or his editor omits all between these numbers, thus illustrating homoeography (a common omission by scribes and typists), for what has been omitted fits between the two occurrences of ἐπαρχιώτας (provincials).

18. Nicephorus omits the word.

14. EDICT OF MAXIMIN II ON BEHALF OF CHRISTIANS, 313

(Eusebius, *HE* 9. 10. 7–11)

Maximin's record consistently had been anti-Christian till the Galerian Edict of Toleration (no. 7) compelled him to co-operate with his imperial colleagues. But this co-operation was given grudgingly, it seems (no. 8), since Maximin, becoming master of the entire East after Galerius' death, resumed his persecutory attitude. Eventually his civil warfare with Constantine and Licinius

14. ON BEHALF OF CHRISTIANS, 313

led Maximin to make a bid for Christian support by instructing Sabinus, his praetorian prefect, to suspend the renewed persecution (no. 13) and by issuing this final constitution of toleration, after the Edict of Milan (no. 12) had forced his hand. This edict, which Eusebius translates from Latin into Greek, is Maximin's personal palinode and grants the Christians their liberty in the most complete and fullest manner.

Nicephorus (*HE* 7. 38) also copies this edict.

Copy of a translation of the tyrant's ordinance, translated from the Roman language into the Greek, about the Christians.[1]

Emperor Caesar Gaius Valerius Maximin, Germanicus, Sarmaticus, Pious,[2] Fortunate,[2] Unconquered, Augustus.

We believe that none is ignorant, but that each person has recourse to the fact itself and that each person both knows and understands[3] that it is evident that in every way we provide unceasingly for the advantage of our provincials and wish to furnish them with those things which are intended to be especially profitable for all, and such as are of advantage and useful for their common good, and whatever are suitable for the public utility and happen to be agreeable to the thoughts of every person.

Therefore, since ere this it has been clear to our knowledge that from this excuse, whereby it had been commanded by the most divine Diocletian and Maximian, our fathers, that the Christians' assemblies should be abolished,[4] many extortions[5] and despoliations have been perpetrated by the officials[6] and that this was proceeding for some time against our provincials, for whom we particularly are eager that there should be proper provision, since their own possessions were being destroyed: when letters had been given in the past year to each province's governors,[7] we legislated that, if anyone should desire to follow such a custom or the same[8] observance of worship, this person should cling unhinderedly to his own course and by none should be impeded or should be prevented, and they should have licence without any fear and suspicion to do whatsoever pleases each one.[9] Not even now it has been able to escape our notice that some of the governors disregarded our orders and caused our people to be in doubt about our ordinances and made them rather reluctant to attend those worships which were pleasing to them.

Therefore, that for the future every suspicion or uncertainty from fear[10] may be dismissed, we have legislated that this edict should be promulgated, that to all it may be evident that whoever wish to follow this sect[11] and worship are allowed, in pursuance of this our bounty, according as each person wishes or as it pleases him, so to attend that worship at which he chose from custom to worship.[12] And it has been conceded that they may equip fully the Lord's households.[13]

Nevertheless, that our bounty may be even greater, we have deigned to legislate also this: that, if any houses and lands which formerly happened to belong to the Christians' legal right, pursuant to the order of our fathers, have fallen to the fisc's legal right or have been confiscated by any city, whether sale of these has occurred or they have been given to anyone for a gift, we have ordered these all to be restored to the Christians' former legal right, that in this also all may take knowledge of our Piety and Providence.

1. Nicephorus omits the caption.
2. Interchanged by Nicephorus.
3. The Greek means "has in himself" and is idiomatic.
4. Neither Lactantius nor Eusebius mentions this particular part of the so-called first edict against the Christians in 303, when they summarize its contents. See the Appendix on Persecutions.
5. Possibly "harassments", i.e. persecutions, another meaning for this word (σεισμός).
6. Eusebius transliterates the word from *officialis*, but Nicephorus turns it from *beneficiarius* (substituting *l* for *r*). While the former word designates a member of an office staff (*officium*), the latter word signifies a privileged soldier, who usually attended his commanding officer and through his favour (*beneficium*) was exempted from such menial duties as digging ditches and procuring provisions and was employed in special work, either military or administrative or clerical in character. Whichever reading is correct, a high-ranking administrator's (whether civil or military) aides are meant.
7. The epistle to Sabinus (no. 13) is meant.
8. Nicephorus substitutes "such".
9. Nothing as generous as this provision appears in Maximin's letter to Sabinus, who was instructed to use persuasion and exhortation in attempting to convert the Christians to an alteration of their attitude toward the pagan gods.
10. Nicephorus reads "every suspicion from fear and uncertainty".
11. See no. 7, n. 13.
12. The etymological figure is in the Greek: *worship* (θρησκεία) as a noun and *worship* (θρησκεύειν) as an infinitive.
13. Although τὰ οἰκεῖα means simply "household property", some interpreters think that the emperor authorizes the Christians to erect churches. But in view of the rest of the edict, which obviously has been modelled on the Edict of Milan (no. 12) in what follows, the translation in the text probably is the better, because the Milanese Edict is silent about new construction of churches. Doubtless there would have to be considerable renovation and redecoration of ecclesiastical property restored from pagan use to Christian service.

15. LETTER OF CONSTANTINE I ON STATE SUBSIDIES TO CHURCHES AND ON SEDUCERS OF CHRISTIANS, 313

(Eusebius, *HE* 10. 6)

This imperial constitution, which is the earliest evidence of the State's support of the Church's current expenses, Eusebius translates from Latin into Greek. Its importance lies not so much in its announcement of governmental subvention of the Christian clergy in north-west Africa—and, by inference, of the clergy in other provinces, for we know no reason why such support should have been denied to other districts—as in its authorization that Caecilian, who, as bishop of Carthage, was the principal prelate in those provinces, should attract the attention of the highest secular authorities therein to "certain persons of unsettled mind", who sought to seduce the people from the Church, that these authorities might proceed to correct this situation.

Nicephorus (*HE* 7. 42) also has this letter.

Copy of an imperial epistle, in which monies are granted to churches.[1]

Constantine Augustus[2] to Caecilian, bishop of Carthage.

Inasmuch as it has been my pleasure that through all provinces, namely, the African and the Numidian and the Mauretanian, something should be provided for expenses to certain specified persons of the ministers[3] of the legitimate and most holy Catholic religion, I have sent a letter to Ursus, the most illustrious[4] catholicus[5] of Africa,[6] and I have indicated to him that he should be careful to pay to your Constancy 3,000 folles.[7] Do you, therefore, when you will procure receipt of the aforesaid amount of money, direct that this money should be distributed among all the abovementioned persons according to the brief[8] sent to you by Hosius.[9] But if, then, you should observe that anything is lacking for the fulfilment of this my policy in regard to them all, you ought to demand unhesitatingly from Heraclides, the procurator of our estates,[10] whatever you should consider to be necessary, for I ordered him, when he was present, that if your Firmness should ask any money from him he should be careful to pay it without any uncertainty.

And since I have learned that certain persons[11] of unsettled mind desire to divert by some base seduction the people of the most holy and Catholic Church, know that I have given orders to Anuline, the proconsul, and also to Patricius, the vicar of the prefects,[12] when they were present, that they should pay proper attention in all other matters and particularly in this and that they should not permit themselves to overlook such an occurrence. Wherefore, if you should observe that any such persons continue in this madness, without any uncertainty go to the abovementioned governors and bring this very matter to them, that they may correct them, exactly as I ordered them when they were present.

May the Divinity of the Great God guard [13] you for many years.

1. Nicephorus omits the caption.
2. Nicephorus omits the rest of the superscription.
3. Who these were we know not, though they apparently were named by Constantine (cf. *infra* text at n. 8). The word for minister (ὑπηρέτης) has a variety of meanings in Greek, but generically it signifies a servant (*minister*); its use here seems to mean a person who serves the Christian cult in an official capacity, i.e. a clergyman.
4. Nicephorus omits the adjective.
5. See no. 64, n. 20.
6. The civil diocese of Africa, which included the aforenamed provinces, not the province of Africa itself.
7. φόλλις = *follis*. A follis originally was a bag containing 3,125 double denarii, which probably were sealed in it at a mint, and was used conveniently to make a large payment. Then the name was transferred from the bag to the coin, since the double denarius itself was called a follis. We know not what was worth this coin in Constantine's time, since Diocletian's Edict of Prices shows that a vicious spiral of inflation was in progress at its emission (301) and since evidence from Egypt confirms its continuance throughout the century. Doubtless not 3,000 coins, but 3,000 bags of these (9,375,000 coins) are meant, since in an inflationary period 3,000 coins of almost any ancient denomination would have been too picayune in both value and number to be worth while to distribute among the clergy in the diocese's three provinces. Even if we equate the follis with one United States cent, such a sum of 9,375,000 double denarii (nominally $93,750), is a lordly largess and probably too good to be true, if extended to other provinces in the Empire, especially in view of the next sentence, which allows Caecilian to ask, if necessary, and to get, after asking, additional amounts.
8. βρεούιον = *brevis* or *breve*: a schedule used in the Dominate's fiscal administration, particularly for official reports of payments received as taxes and of administrative expenditures.
9. Usually identified as the famous bishop of Córdoba, who at this time was Constantine's chief ecclesiastical adviser, who presided at the First General Council of the Church at Nicaea in 325, and who lived to be a centenarian. His life has been written at length and recently by V. C. de Clercq, *Ossius of Cordova: A Contribution to the History of the Constantinian Period* (Washington, 1954), who shows that the orthography of his name is Ossius (44–8).
10. Probably the *procurator rei privatae* for financial matters concerning Africa. The Greek is ἐπίτροπος τῶν ἡμετέρων κτημάτων.

16. CLERICAL EXEMPTION FROM PUBLIC DUTIES, 313   43

11. Since Constantine perhaps still was unaware of the Donatist disturbance, these are supposed to be pagans. If he knew about the schism, it was unfair for him to have directed measures against the Donatists, while their case against Caecilian was still *sub iudice*. It may be that he had heard about some disorders, in which the Donatists probably were involved, but that he had an unclear notion about the matter and that he merely ordered that steps to preserve peace should be taken. But it is possible that Constantine prejudged the case (see nos. 10, n. 1, and 16, n. 8) and it made quite a difference, when he instructed not only Ursus and Heraclides to pay Caecilian as representative of the Catholics, but also Anuline and Patricius to proceed against the seducers of the Catholics, before he had heard the Donatists' side.

12. This title οὐικάριος τῶν ἐπάρχων (= *vicarius praefectorum*) seems to preserve the earlier notion that the several imperial prefects in Rome were regarded as constituting a college. But at this time, though the municipal prefects in the two capitals (Milan and Nicomedia) perhaps considered themselves as colleagues, the four principal prefects—those directing the major divisions of the Empire in the prefectures of the East, Illyricum, Italy, the Gauls—were too distant from one another—in Nicomedia, Sirmium, Milan, Trèves—to count as associates. These latter prefects alone had vicars, of whom there were fourteen, one for each of the dioceses (of which Africa was one) into which the prefectures were subdivided. So Patricius as vicar of Africa is called anachronously a vicar of the prefects, when in reality he was subordinate to only one prefect, that of Italy, in Milan. See no. 20, n. 15.

13. Nicephorus has future optative.

16. LETTER OF CONSTANTINE I ON CLERICAL EXEMPTION FROM PUBLIC DUTIES, 313

(Eusebius, *HE* 10. 7)

This letter, translated from Latin into Greek by Eusebius and preserved by Nicephorus (*HE* 7. 42), while it confers a doubtlessly desired boon on Christian clergymen in a period when enforced holding of civil offices and compulsory performance of public duties for the ordinary subject in municipalities were not welcomed because of the burdensome expense entailed,[1] and while the immunity from such service authorized in it seems to have been granted to them for the first time,[2] yet had a different effect on the ecclesiastical establishment than Constantine perhaps had designed, especially insofar as Donatism was concerned.[3]

The subsequent stampede into the class of the clergy ("the unholy rush for holy orders") consequently caused limitations to be put on this privilege and repetitions of these limitations to be made. But it was not until 451 that the Fourth General Council at Chalcedon in its canon 7 made the holding of civil office by clergymen an offence against canon law, and it was not until 531 that Justinian I (no. 629) legislated that appointment of a civil official to clerical office was an offence against civil law.

Copy of an imperial epistle, in which he commands the churches' presidents to be released from every public service concerning civic affairs.[4]

Greeting, our most honoured Anuline.

Since from many circumstances it is evident that the setting at nought of religious worship, in which the chief reverence for the Holiest Heavenly Power is maintained, has brought great dangers upon public affairs and that its authorized reception and preservation have furnished the greatest good fortune to the Roman name and remarkable felicity to all the affairs of men, for divine favours provide this, it has seemed right that those men who give their services to the maintenance of divine worship, with due sanctity and with observance [5] of this law,[6] should reap the rewards of their own labours, most honoured Anuline.[7]

Wherefore I wish that those who, within the province entrusted to you, in the Catholic Church over which Caecilian presides,[8] furnish their service to this holy [9] worship—whom they are wont to call clergymen—should be kept once for all entirely exempted from all public services, that they may not be diverted from the worship due to the Deity by any error or sacrilegious lapse,[10] but rather without any hindrance may serve to the utmost their own law.[6] For, when these persons perform greatest service to the Divinity, it seems that the greatest possible advantage will accrue to public affairs.

Farewell, our most honoured and most cherished Anuline.

1. On this subject see *MARE* 84–116.

2. This grant, it appears, applied only to the province of Africa (of which Anuline, the addressee, was proconsul), since six years later (21 October 319) Constantine included Lucania and Bruttii (no. 29) and perhaps in the same year extended it through the entire Empire (no. 30).

Since in the North African commercial cities Christianity seems to have won converts from the wealthier classes at a comparatively earlier stage than in other areas and because the number of clergy liable to public services was therefore proportionately larger, it is in North Africa, then, that the antagonism against combining civil and clerical functions appears first to have arisen. Apparently the argument was not the inherent incompatibility of the two functions, but that the proper discharge of the duties of the one left insufficient leisure for the proper discharge of the duties of the other.

3. It is necessary as well as noteworthy to detect among the Donatists that the economic aspect loomed larger than the ecclesiastical animus. Recognition of orthodoxy would be rewarded by obtaining pecuniary privilege, and they were averse from forfeiting any financial advantage by being adjudged schismatics, if they could take steps to avoid such a sentence. Hence their complaint against Caecilian (see introd. to no. 17).

4. While the caption (omitted by Nicephorus) mentions only the presidents (προεστῶτες), who would be bishops (ἐπίσκοποι), for the Greek words usually are equated, yet it is evident from the epistle that whoever concocted the caption meant it to include clergymen of at least major orders. Just as Greek and Latin words (see no. 158, n. 1) for "priest" (G. ἱερεύς; L. *sacerdos*) serve for "bishop" (G. ἐπίσκοπος; L. *episcopus*), so we must conclude that an opposite process is operative here.

It is not apropos here that Tertullian asks (*De Exhort. Cast.* 7 *ad med.* = *CSEL* 70. 138) his celebrated question "Are not even we laymen priests [*sacerdotes*]?" and answers it by quoting Rev. 1. 6, where "priests" is ἱερεῖς in Greek and in Latin *sacerdotes*, since not only all Israelites (Ex. 19. 6) participate in a kingly priesthood (G. βασίλειον ἱεράτευμα) or a priestly kingdom (L. *regnum sacerdotale*), but also all Christians (1 Pet. 2. 9) constitute a royal priesthood (G. βασίλειον ἱεράτευμα; L. *regale sacerdotium*).

5. Nicephorus reads προεδρείᾳ for παρεδρίᾳ, but both nouns mean about the same.

6. Christianity.

7. Nicephorus omits the last three words.

8. If we believe that the emperor not yet had heard about the Donatists (but see no. 15, n. 11), this phrase must mean that the exemption embraced only those clerics subject to Caecilian, about whom Constantine could have learned through other channels than by the complaint of schismatics, since the name of the incumbent of so important a see as was Carthage, which had metropolitan jurisdiction, was not likely to have been unknown to the emperor in a period when the province of Africa was provisioning Italy—and indeed (no. 15) already was known to Constantine.

But the adjective *Catholic* may have been supplied by an episcopal adviser— perhaps Hosius of Córdoba, who probably was conversant with the situation (see no. 15, n. 9), since the Donatists declared that Hosius had influenced Constantine against them.

9. Nicephorus has "holiest" for *this holy* by converting ἁγίᾳ ταύτῃ into ἁγιωτάτῃ—an understandable confusion.

10. Constantine's concern for the clergy's abstention from secular affairs may have been inspired by clerical protests against the pagan atmosphere wherein some public duties had to be discharged, for otherwise it is hard to see how a confirmed Christian—and especially a clergyman in the early fourth century—easily could wander into theological error or could commit a sacrilegious fault through performance of public service.

Long before the toleration of Christianity pagan priests enjoyed such exemption.

17. LETTER OF CONSTANTINE I ON THE DONATIST SCHISM, 313

(Eusebius, *HE* 10. 5. 18–20)

Whether Constantine the Great—in whose reign the Empire began to assume Christianity and Christendom began to assume religious control of the Empire—sincerely professed Christianity or merely used it as part of the machinery of sovereignty,[1] this letter, translated from Latin into Greek by Eusebius and also reproduced faithfully by Nicephorus (*HE* 7. 43), is important for two reasons: (1) it appears to be the earliest extant document on imperial intervention in the internal affairs of the Christian Church;[2] (2) it seems to inaugurate imperial recognition of the competency of episcopal jurisdiction in civil causes of a distinctly clerical character.[3]

The epistle was evoked by a communication from Anuline, Constantine's proconsul of Africa, and by petitions from Christian schismatics in that province. The schism started after the archdeacon Caecilian had been consecrated bishop of Carthage either in late 311 or in early 312 by three bishops, of whom Felix of Aptunga (Henchir es Souar in Tunisia), was regarded (falsely, as the event proved) as a *traditor*[4] by some African Christians. Although he was the popular choice of the Carthaginians for the vacancy in the see, Caecilian seems to have been obnoxious to certain other Africans, who had their own opinions about his activities during the last persecution (303-11) recently ended by the Galerian Edict of Toleration (no. 7), and to some neighbouring bishops, who expected to be consulted about filling the see of Carthage lately vacant by the death of Mensurius, Caecilian's predecessor.[5] These joined forces to declare Caecilian's consecration invalid as having been celebrated by a traditor and to consecrate a rival bishop, Majorine by name, who became merely the nominal leader of the schism, which, rapidly spreading throughout North Africa, resulted in the consecration of anti-bishops to other sees in opposition to the Caecilianist party, produced martyrs on both sides, and persisted for a century.[6] The real leader, after whom was named the schism, was a certain Donatus, bishop first of Negrene (Casae Nigrae *al*. Nigrenses) and then of Carthage (in succession to Majorine [5] after 313).[7]

Early in 313 Constantine, whether or not aware of the African schism, sent Anuline a letter which conferred on the Christian clergy in Africa exemption from public duties (no. 16). Whatever the emperor might have intended by the phrase "the Catholic Church over which Caecilian presides", on whose

17. THE DONATIST SCHISM, 313

clergy this immunity was conferred, the Donatists decided that it excluded them from this exemption. Thereupon the schismatics sent through Anuline to Constantine petitions, which contained charges against Caecilian and a plea for a trial by impartial judges [8] from Gaul, where there had been no recent persecution and consequently were no traditors. While Constantine was too cautious to give Gallic bishops as judges of an African dispute and he referred the matter to Pope St Miltiades (*al.* Melchiades) as being above either party, yet he conceded so far to the Donatist request that he ordered three of the principal bishops in Gaul to assist at the trial in Rome.

While the emperor seemed to have considered the pope and his imperially chosen colleagues simply as a board of judicial arbiters, Miltiades, perhaps perceiving that important principles were involved, expanded the tribunal by summoning eighteen bishops (of whom fifteen had Italian sees) to transform the commission into a synod.

Copy of an imperial epistle, in which he orders a synod of bishops to be held at Rome about the churches' union and concord.[9]

Constantine Augustus to Miltiades, bishop of the Romans, and to Mark.[10]

Since to me by Anuline,[11] the most illustrious proconsul of Africa, have been sent many such documents in which it is entered that Caecilian, the bishop of the Carthaginians' city, is called to account on many matters by some of his colleagues established in Africa and since it seems to me a most serious matter that in these provinces, which Divine Providence has delivered voluntarily to my Majesty and where there is a great number of people, the multitude is found following the baser course, dividing—as it were—into factions, and the bishops have differences meanwhile, it has seemed good to me that Caecilian himself (with ten bishops, who appear to accuse him, and ten others, whom he may consider necessary to his case) should sail to Rome, that there in the presence of yourselves, but moreover of Rheticius and Maternus and Marinus,[12] your colleagues, whom for this purpose I have commanded to hasten to Rome, he can be heard as you may perceive to be consonant with the most reverend [13] law.[14]

Nevertheless, that you also can have the fullest knowledge about these matters, I have subjoined to my letter copies of the documents sent to me by Anuline and I have sent these to your abovementioned colleagues. And your Constancy, after reading these, shall consider in what way it is necessary to examine most carefully and to decide justly the abovementioned case.[15] For it does not escape your Diligence that I render such great reverence to the legitimate Catholic Church that I desire you to leave not at all schism or division in any place.

May the Divinity of the Great God guard you [16] for many years, most honoured one.[16]

1. On this problem consult the summary of various scholarly views collected by Coleman, 20-3.

2. For apparently the earliest, but non-documentary, instance (272) see no. 5, n. 1. See also no. 10, n. 2.

3. While we have considerable evidence about the seeds of the *ius canonicum* (starting with the *acta* of the so-called Council of Jerusalem *c.* 49 [Acts 15. 6-29] and excluding two earlier apostolic sessions [Acts 1. 15-26, 6. 1-6], which should not be elevated to the level of synods) before these blossomed into fuller flower at the First Ecumenical Council of Nicaea, called by Constantine I in 325 (no. 48), yet to suppose (as some have said) that the emperor's application of the epithet σεβασμιώτατος to νόμος (cf. *infra* n. 13) meant more than cheilotherapy to whatever local rules for decision on ecclesiastical litigation may have existed in the Roman Church and marked in effect the abdication of secular in favour of ecclesiastical law, in that the Donatist dispute was referred to the bishop of Rome for adjudication, is to anticipate too much too soon. Constantine probably believed that in preferring the Roman prelate as his deputy to decide the case he was simply appointing a person who with the aid of his episcopal assessors would act as an *arbiter*. However this may have been and despite the inconclusive issue of the decision, for the complainants refused to abide by the ruling (nos. 18 and 19), at a later date (318) Constantine authorized both Christian litigants in civil cases to resort to a bishop's court (no. 28) and still later (333) permitted either Christian party, even when the other party was opposed, to bring his case into a bishop's court (no. 65). But it is to these later constitutions rather than to this earlier epistle that we should turn for the true origin of the State's recognition of episcopal jurisdiction.

The prehistory of non-State courts in Roman Law may be reconstructed briefly, so far as it affects directly the Christian Church. The earliest Christians, who were Jews, were familiar with the Jewish system of courts, of which recognition by the Roman State can be traced documentarily as high as 47 B.C. in Syria (if Caesar's decision preserved by Josephus [*Ant. Iud.* 14. 10. 2. 190-5] is genuine and if it can be extended to confirm Jewish recourse to Jewish courts in litigation of private law) and certainly in Egypt at least as early as 25-19 B.C. on Strabo's evidence quoted by Josephus (op. cit., 14. 7. 2. 117) and examined by E. R. Goodenough (*The Jurisprudence of the Jewish Courts in Egypt* [New Haven, 1929], 16-22). But on the Christian side Jesus had delivered to his disciples the doctrine that disputes among his followers should be solved without aid from the secular arm (Matt. 18. 15-17) and St Paul, the only apostle learned in the law, counselled his converts to settle their suits among themselves, when he wrote that the saints were better judges than the unjust (1 Cor. 6. 1-8). And the anonymous *Didache* (our oldest source of ecclesiastical law), which usually is assigned to the first half of the second century and paints a picture of the Church's life in possibly the latter part of the previous century, contemplates congregational control over Christian disputants (14. 2; 15. 3).

The *Constitutiones Apostolorum*, which in its present form was edited probably toward the end of the fourth century (after Constantine's death), transports its reader into the midst of the Church's life during the third, if not the last half of the second, century—at any rate before Constantine's reign. In this document, which preserves most of the earlier *Didascalia* (midway between it and the *Didache*), is demonstrated a well-developed administration of justice by clerics (2. 37-56): deacons should hear minor matters, but bishops, attended by priests and by deacons, should adjudicate weightier cases; Monday is reserved for trials, that by the ensuing Sunday the litigants may be reconciled; procedure of the court is regulated; the bishop's verdict is final, for he has Christ to confirm his judgement; the punishment should fit the crime; for the more heinous crimes the penalty is excommunication. The tone of these regulations shows more affinity with the spirit of primitive Christianity than with that of contemporary Roman law.

It is not too much to believe that Constantine became acquainted with this Christian practice in due course and that, pursuant to his liberal attitude toward the Church in assisting the establishment of the "City of God" upon earth, the emperor enacted legislation (as we have seen) to accommodate it to the administration of the law.

4. In Christian parlance a *traditor* was a Christian who had surrendered to the secular authorities in a period of persecution either a copy of the Scriptures or a sacred vessel used in church or a fellow-Christian.

The other consecrators, Faustinus of Thuburbo Maius and Novellus of Tyzica, also were alleged *traditores*, but Felix bore the brunt of the charge.

5. Numidian jealousy of Carthaginian supremacy played a part in the non-theological factors present in the early stage of the schism. After St Cyprian's time (mid-third century) the primate of Numidia exercised the right to consecrate the bishop of Carthage, who was the African primate, although the Carthaginian clergy often opposed this custom. It appears that Caecilian's consecration was advanced to anticipate the arrival of Secundus, bishop of Tigisis, the Numidian primate, with his suffragans. They appeared after the ceremony—some seventy of them—and, linking themselves with what personal opposition against Caecilian existed, condemned in council (312) Caecilian's consecration and chose Majorine, one of Caecilian's readers, as a rival bishop of Carthage.

6. Caecilian's consecration was investigated five times in seven years (313-20)—so zealous was Constantine to serve the cause of justice, if he could, and to restore peace to the African Church. But the persistence of the Donatists proved too obstinate to be overcome by the emperor, who finally committed the case, as he said, to the judgement of God (no. 39).

That the Donatist schism was supported by a nationalist tendency is noted by E. L. Woodward in his *Christianity and Nationalism in the Later Roman Empire* (London, 1916), 28-40). And T. M. Parker professes in his essay "Feudal Episcopacy" in K. E. Kirk, ed., *The Apostolic Ministry* (London, 1946), 362, n. 1, that "Donatism, especially in its Circumcellion form [the Circumcellions formed the gangster group in Donatism], was largely an economic movement of the depressed classes against the possessing classes". Certainly the Catholic clergy in North Africa were largely landowners.

But the ecclesiastical and theological issues must not be minimized, for these were more prominent in the earlier period. The Donatists, whose schism—like Montanism and Novatianism—showed some puritanical and rigoristic colour, declared that bishops who had been traditors should be deposed and should not administer the sacraments, of which their ministers' guilt invalidated the validity and extinguished the efficacy. And they proceeded beyond this to the principle of infection: that those who should communicate with such traditors could not remain real communicants of the Church of Christ, whose sanctity is seen in the saintliness of its members and which must not retain within its ranks notorious sinners. So the Donatists rebaptized such converts and reordained such clergy as came to them from the Catholic Church.

A thorough treatment of this schism is by W. H. C. Frend, *The Donatist Church: A Movement of Protest in Roman North Africa* (Oxford, 1952).

7. In antiquity there was some confusion about the identity of the Donatus whose name was given to the schism. Some authors agreed on that Donatus who succeeded Majorine as schismatic bishop of Carthage and who sometimes was surnamed "the Great" to distinguish him from Donatus of Casae Nigrae. It seems rather strange that the latter, a comparative outsider, should have appeared as the leader of the schism, when the more likely candidate for eponymous honours would have been the former, for Majorine lived not long after his election (312) and was followed immediately by Donatus the Great, who enjoyed a long episcopate (313–55). But other authors accepted Donatus of Casae Nigrae ("Black Huts"), who was hostile to Caecilian, and asserted that the Donatists of the time when the schism was solved (411) were loath to admit that their famous protagonist, Donatus the Great, had been condemned and thus they procured a convenient substitute in Donatus of Black Huts. Most modern scholars suppose that these two Donati were one and support the view taken in the text (so Palanque, 1. 36; but Kidd keeps them separate, 1. 537 and 542).

8. An appeal invoking the intervention of imperial authority in the ecclesiastical establishment perhaps was unfortunate, but it was bound to be brought sooner or later to a Christian emperor who would take more than a passing interest in the Church's internal problems. And Constantine, who eventually believed himself to be a brother bishop (see Introd., n. 29), was not a sovereign likely to let slip the opportunity thus offered to him. Henceforth heresy and schism—the twin threats to any imperial effort to procure ecclesiastical peace—could be and were considered offences punishable by law.

9. Nicephorus omits the caption.

10. Mark is unknown, but some suppose that he was Merocles, bishop of Milan, and others think that he was the Roman archdeacon who became pope in 336 and later was canonized.

11. His report (*relatio*) to the emperor has been preserved by Augustine, *Ep.* 88. 2 (*CSEL* 34. 408). From this it appears that he transmitted two petitions (*libelli*) from the Donatists.

12. These three men were bishops in Gaul and respectively presided over the dioceses of Autun, Köln, Arles.

13. The adjective σεβάσμιος in its positive and superlative degrees frequently was applied to the emperor and is found in this connection as early as our second century.

14. The Christian religion perhaps is meant.

15. Since Constantine doubtless considered that in a dispute of this character he was not conversant with the Church's customs, he preferred to permit the pope to prescribe the procedure for the conduct of the case.

16. Eusebius has plural for *you* (Miltiades and Mark) and singular for *most honoured one* (Miltiades), but Nicephorus has plural for both words.

The emperor assigns to the pope the honorary position of proconsul in addressing the prelate as *most honoured one* (τιμιώτατε).

18. LETTER OF CONSTANTINE I ON THE DONATIST SCHISM, 313

(Eusebius, *HE* 10. 5. 21-4)

Eusebius translates from Latin into Greek this imperial letter, which must have been one of several similar letters, for there is one like it in Latin (no. 19). In it Constantine informs Chrestus, bishop of Syracuse, that, since the trial of the African Donatists before the Council of Rome under Miltiades, bishop of Rome (no. 17), resulted both in their condemnation and in their demand for a new hearing, he has convoked a larger council of bishops to assemble at Arles in Gaul and is commanding Chrestus to journey thither at governmental expense. As the event proved, the Donatists again were defeated and again appealed to the emperor, who himself heard their case in 316 at Milan, whence he issued a decree against them, banishing them and confiscating their churches. Later Constantine relented and rescinded his sentence of exile and left the case to the judgement of God (no. 39).

This letter is important for its additional testimony to the State's interference in ecclesiastical matters, for the emperor appoints an episcopal synod arbiter in a Christian controversy.

Nicephorus (*HE* 7. 43) also gives this letter.

Copy of an imperial epistle, in which he commands a second synod to be held for removing all dissension of bishops.[1]

18. THE DONATIST SCHISM, 313

Constantine Augustus to Chrestus, bishop of the Syracusans.

Already formerly, when basely and perversely some began to separate concerning the worship of the Holy and Heavenly Power and the Catholic religion,[2] I, having desired to curtail such dissensions among them, had ordered that—after certain bishops had been sent from Gaul,[3] but moreover, after there had been summoned from Africa those[4] contending obstinately and persistently together from the opposing parties, also in the presence of the bishop of Rome—this matter, which seemed to have been raised, might receive a successful settlement through their presence together with every attentive examination.[5]

But since, as it happens, certain persons, being unmindful both of their own salvation and of the reverence owed to their most sacred religion, still even now cease not to continue their private enmities, being unwilling to comply with the decision already delivered and declaring that, after all, some few persons pronounced their opinions and judgements or else that they hurried very swiftly and sharply to pass sentence, not even having previously examined precisely all the matters which ought to have been investigated;[6] and since, as a result of all these affairs, these following things happen to have transpired: that those very persons, who ought to maintain fraternal and concordant unanimity, shamefully, nay rather, abominably are at variance from one another and that to persons who have souls alien from this most sacred religion they give an excuse for mockery; wherefore it became necessary for me to provide that that which ought to have ended by a voluntary agreement,[7] after the decision had been delivered, even now at last might find a conclusion in the presence of many persons.

Therefore, since we have ordered very many bishops from divers and countless districts to assemble at the city of the Arlesians[8] by 1 August, we have done you the honour to write to you that you, having procured from the most illustrious Latronian, the corrector[9] of Sicily, public conveyance,[10] should join to yourself also two others of those of the second office,[11] whomever you yourself decide to select, and, moreover, having taken besides three servants, who will be able to serve you on the way, present yourself by that same day at the aforesaid place: so that, both by your Constancy and by unanimous and united decision of the rest assembled, this matter also, which hitherto has endured basely because of certain shameful quarrellings, after has been heard all which will be said by those—whom likewise we have ordered to be present—now at variance one from another, may be able to be restored, if only tardily, to the proper religion and faith and fraternal harmony.

May the Omnipotent God guard[12] you in good health for many years.

19. THE DONATIST SCHISM, 313   53

1. Nicephorus omits the caption.

2. The word is αἵρεσις, whence comes our "heresy", but the adjective καθολική attached to it shows that Eusebius understood that Constantine by the noun meant a choice of religious tenets not unorthodox. See no. 7, n. 13.

3. Nicephorus erroneously substitutes "Galatia" in Asia Minor.

4. Nicephorus substitutes the article for the demonstrative.

5. For the emperor's command see no. 17.

6. Constantine repeats this complaint in no. 19.

7. The emperor makes the point that, since they had concurred with his appointment of the court, which sat at Rome, the Donatists should have abided by the decision there delivered.

8. The advantages of Arles—a site so favoured by Constantine that he constructed across the Rhône River from it another community, which he called Constantina after his name—were acknowledged more than a hundred years afterward, for Honorius in 418 issued a constitution (H 238), which acclaims its abundant commercial activities (Bury, I. 208).

9. For governors of certain provinces (see no. 229, n. 2) appears a late title κουρήκτωρ in Greek (Nicephorus has the variant κεντίκτωρ) and *corrector* in Latin.

10. See no. 95, n. 41.

11. Of the three major clerical grades (bishop, priest, deacon) priests (the second) are meant. The word is θρόνος = *sedes*, on which see no. 311, n. 5.

12. Nicephorus changes the tense from aorist to future, but retains the optative mode.

19. LETTER OF CONSTANTINE I ON THE DONATIST SCHISM, 313

(*CSEL* 26. 204–6)

This Latin letter,[1] longer than the letter (preserved only in Greek) to Chrestus, bishop of Syracuse (no. 18), Constantine sent to Aelafius,[2] vicar of the diocese of Africa. Each touches the same subject: provision of transportation at public expense for the journey to Arles, where a second hearing of the Donatist charges against Caecilian, bishop of Carthage, was scheduled for 1 August 314. Whereas the letter to Chrestus was to a future participant in that council, the emperor writes to Aelafius more fully about his concern to procure the peace of the Church and about his vicar's part in providing transportation for the African clerics who are to attend the council at Arles.

This letter, like that to Chrestus, has a twofold importance in law: (1) the emperor recognizes the Donatist appeal from the Roman verdict (313) and convokes a second synod to consider their charges against Caecilian; (2) Constantine sets a precedent both for himself—for he conferred the same privilege of public conveyance to the 318 bishops who assisted at the First General Council of the Church in 325 at Nicaea—and for his successors, who conveyed bishops at public cost to conciliar gatherings.

Constantine Augustus to Aelafius.

Already indeed previously, since it had been brought to my knowledge that in our Africa many persons with mad fury and with fruitless charges against one another had begun to separate from one another over the observance of the most sacred Catholic law,[3] for the sake of composing this kind of quarrel it had been my pleasure that not only Caecilian, the Carthaginian bishop, against whom especially his opponents[4] often had addressed me, but also some of these who had believed that certain charges should be made against him should present themselves in the city of Rome. For I also had ordered certain bishops from the Gauls[5] to proceed to our aforesaid city of Rome, that not only these, in view of the integrity of their life and laudable mode of living, and also seven of the same communion,[6] but also the bishop of the city of Rome and others,[7] who should examine the case with the said persons, might be able to put a deserved end to the question which seems to have been raised. And indeed these also by the records produced have brought to my knowledge all that had been done in their presence, affirming also verbally that their verdict had been expressed in accord with the equity of the circumstances and saying that those who had arranged to adduce certain charges against Caecilian were rather the ones guilty in the case—to such a degree that, after judgement had been delivered, they forbade[8] those very persons to return thence[9] to Africa.

Wherefore, because of all these things, I had hoped by an acceptable appraisal of the facts[10] that a proper end had been put to all seditions and contentions of every kind which suddenly had been excited by these persons. But when I had read your Excellency's[11] letters,[12] which your Gravity had believed should be sent to Nicasius[13] and the rest about these same quarrels,[14] I clearly recognized that they are willing to place before their own eyes neither regard for their own salvation nor—what is more important—reverence for Almighty God,[15] if indeed they persist in such conduct, which not only conduces to their own shame and disgrace, but also offers an opportunity of disparagement to those persons who are known to avert their own minds far from the most sacred observance of this sort.[16] For it is also proper that you know this: that from these same persons have come those who assert that the said Caecilian should be regarded unworthy of the worship of the most holy religion, and that in response to my reply to the said persons—that they voiced this in vain, since indeed the case had been concluded in the city of Rome by bishops, capable and most excellent men—they thought fit that they should answer obstinately and pertinaciously that indeed the entire case had not been heard, but rather that the same bishops had secluded themselves somewhere and had passed sentence according as it had been suitable to themselves.[17]

Wherefore, since I perceived that these numerous and weighty matters were prolonging too obstinately the dissensions, so that in no wise an end seems possible to be given to the said dissensions,[18] unless both the said Caecilian and any three [19] of those who are at variance with him shall have agreed to come to the town of Arles [20] to a trial of those charges which they apprehend against Caecilian,[21] I have decided that upon your Ingenuity must be enjoined that, as soon as you shall have received this my letter, you should cause not only that the aforesaid Caecilian with some of those whom he himself shall have selected and also one each from the provinces of Byzacium, Tripolis, the Numidias, and the Mauretanias [22]—and these must bring some of their own, whom they themselves shall have decided ought to be chosen [23]—and also some of those who are at variance with the said Caecilian, after public conveyance [24] has been provided through Africa [25] and Mauretania,[26] should sail thence to the Spains [27] by the short crossing; and that nevertheless you should give to each bishop a single authorization for the journey [28] thence, that they themselves can arrive speedily at the aforesaid place by 1 August.[29] You shall announce to the said persons that, before they leave, they must arrange that in their absence both suitable discipline may be maintained and no sedition or altercation of any parties—which would tend to the greatest disgrace—perchance may arise.[30]

As for the rest: after a full investigation has been undertaken, let there be an end. For when they shall have appeared, let all those things, which now are known to be in dispute and which deservedly ought to have a timely termination, be concluded and settled as quickly as they can.[31] For I confess to your Gravity, since I am certain that you also are a worshipper of the Most High God, that I think it not at all right that contention and altercations of this kind should be concealed from us, as a result of which perhaps the Most High Divinity can be moved not only against the human race but also against me myself, to whose care by his own celestial command he has committed all earthly matters to be managed, and in his wrath may determine otherwise than hitherto. For then I shall be able to be truly and most fully free from anxiety and can hope ever for all most prosperous and excellent things from the most instant kindliness of the Most Powerful God, when I shall have perceived that all with harmonious maintenance of brotherliness reverence the Most Holy God in the duteous worship of the Catholic religion. Amen.

1. St Optatus, bishop of Milevis (*al.* Mileve, Mileu, Mileum) in Numidia during the late fourth century, the historian of the Donatist controversy, wrote a work of seven books on this schism and to it he appended at least ten documents, of which this letter is the third, to establish the accuracy of his statements. All this material has been edited by C. Ziwsa in *CSEL* 26.

2. Aelafius is not known elsewhere, nor is he counted in the received list of African vicars. Duchesne has suggested that Aelafius is a copyist's error for Aelius Paulinus, who is known to have been vicar of Africa 313-4.

3. Religion.

4. Reading *diversi* for *universi* (Turner). This and other conjectures C. H. Turner first published in his "Adversaria Critica" in *JTS* 27 (1925-6) 283-96, and most of these were incorporated in the apparatus criticus to the text of this letter which was printed in the posthumous portion of his *Ecclesiae Occidentalis Monumenta Iuris Antiquissima* (Oxford, 1939), 1. 2. 2. 376-8.

At times and without indication (only Turner's reading will be noted) conjectures from Ziwsa's apparatus will be translated.

5. See no. 203, n. 4.

6. From the emperor's earlier epistle to Miltiades and Mark (no. 17) it appears that Constantine commanded only three Gallic bishops to assist at the Roman Synod (the first body to hear the Donatist accusations), yet here *seven of the same communion* are added to their party. The place of this phrase has caused much discussion: it makes sense, but it does not tally with what is known elsewhere. Since this letter survives only in an eleventh century MS., "copied from a very much older MS., which was in parts already mutilated and illegible, there is greater excuse for courageous treatment of the text", believes N. H. Baynes ("Constantine the Great and the Christian Church", in *Proceedings of the British Academy*, 15 [1929] 414), who supports Turner's transposition of the Latin *sed et septem eiusdem communionis* to a higher position, where it can be associated with Caecilian, who, we know from Constantine's earlier letter, was authorized to take with him as many as ten whom he might consider as necessary to his defence. To assign these seven clerics (probably prelates) to Caecilian's contingent still curtails it by three, but perhaps some modification in numbers was made between the dates of the two documents. In Turner's proposed position the translation would read: ". . . had addressed me, but also seven of the same communion, as well as. . . "

7. Reading *alii* for *illi* (Turner).

8. Some would emend *prohiberent* (they forbade) to *prohiberem* (I forbade) on the ground that the Synod of Rome had no such power, which would have been reserved for the emperor. But, even if the synod had not juridical power to enforce its decrees, at least it could propose such a sentence in the hope that the emperor, who has sent the controversy to it (no. 17), would

consent to its execution. The summary of the judgement given by the Roman Synod (*CSEL* 26. 27) clearing Caecilian is silent on this subject. At any rate Donatus returned, apparently with impunity, to Carthage, whither he was followed by Caecilian (*CSEL* 26. 26), and then the Donatists appealed for a second trial, which was to be held at Arles, as this letter shows.

9. Reading *istinc* for *istud* (Turner).

10. Probably Constantine means that the episcopal estimate of the case as expressed in their findings earned his approval—with the added hint, perhaps, that all right-minded persons would concur with the conciliar verdict.

11. Reading *dicationis* for *dictationis* (Turner). Anuline, proconsul of Africa, calls himself *dicatio*, a title of address in late Latin, in his report to Constantine (Augustine, *Ep.* 88. 2 = *CSEL* 34. 408).

12. These, which evidently described the Donatist activities in Africa, are not extant.

13. Not identifiable, though he probably was a notary in the imperial secretariat, in whose charge was the correspondence with Africa.

14. Reading *simultatibus* for *simulationibus* (Turner).

15. This phrase *salvation . . . God* is reminiscent of Constantine's words to Chrestus (no. 18).

16. Such is the literal meaning. Doubtless Constantine means "the observance of this our most sacred Catholic law", as he writes at the opening of this letter. The thought *conduces . . . sort* has a parallel in the epistle to Chrestus (no. 18).

17. This charge reappears in the letter to Chrestus (no. 18).

18. In *prolonging . . . dissensions* is a loose parallel to the letter to Chrestus (no. 18).

19. Baynes (op. cit., 415) believes that *tres* (three) is clearly corrupt.

20. See no. 18, n. 8.

21. Turner's emendation of *quae . . . consensum dederint* is preferred to both Ziwsa's and Baynes': all three find difficulty with the text, which seems untranslatable, Baynes advancing much transposition in an effort "to restore common sense to the emperor's epistle" (op. cit., 415).

22. Besides the province of Africa, whence came Caecilian, the provinces here named belonged to the diocese of Africa.

There were two Mauretanian (Moroccan) provinces: Caesariensis and Tingitana—each adjective often and perhaps more properly preceded by the noun Mauretania. After Constantine's time and about the beginning of the fifth century Mauretania Caesariensis was divided into Mauretania Caesariensis and Mauretania Sitifensis, on the latter of which see no. 441, nn. 2 and 6.

Numidias is a loose geographical expression, for there appears to have been never more than one Numidia at any one time. Sometimes it is called Numidia Cirtensis (from its provincial capital, Cirta), which is additional testimony to the popular use of "Numidias" to cover more than the provincial borders, because the ancient kingdom was larger than the actual province (Sallust,

Bell. Iug. 5. 4) for over 150 years (201–46 B.C.) amd also at King Masinissa's death in 149 B.C. was divided among his three sons, until Jugurtha, his illegitimate grandson, through murder and by war reunited the districts in 112 B.C.
Therefore the provinces listed here in the letter total five.

23. So also Chrestus is commanded to choose certain of his clergy (no. 18).

24. As Aelafius is ordered to provide transport at governmental expense for this African contingent, so Chrestus is directed to demand from the governor of Sicily public conveyance (no. 18; see also no. 95, n. 41).

25. Here the province probably.

26. Loosely used geographically to include Numidia, which lay between the province of Africa and that of Mauretania Caesariensis (later Sitifensis), on which cf. *supra* n. 22, for it was impossible to proceed by post from Africa to Mauretania without passing through Numidia.

27. The civil diocese of Spain in Constantine's days contained seven provinces constructed from the two provinces (Hispania Citerior and Hispania Ulterior) organized *c.* 205 B.C.: Asturia et Gallaecia (sometimes shortened to Gallaecia), Baetica, Baleares (or Insulae Baleares), Carthaginiensis, Lusitania (modern Portugal), Tarraconensis, Tingitana. Of these Tingitana (more properly perhaps Mauretania Tingitana), since it was the Mauretanian (Moroccan) north-western part of Africa and geographically and popularly considered part of Mauretania, would not be included in *the Spains* in this instance, because from it—probably from Tingis (modern Tangier)—the bishops would sail for Baetica, the peninsula's southernmost province.

28. This authorization for the trip was called *tractoriae* (sc. *litterae*), an imperial (here vicarial) letter given to legates or others sent on official missions, that necessaries for the journey might be provided for them at public expense. It listed the places through which they should pass and what carriage and provision should be supplied. See no. 95, n. 41.

Some scholars have attacked the authenticity of this letter on the ground that the itinerary was circuitous and improbable and that it was simpler and cheaper and quicker for the bishops to sail from Carthage to Marseille. But these critics, if they have not forgotten that most ancient mariners coasted by landmarks (on the critics' route: Carthage to Sicily, thence along the Italian shoreline to Massilia), also do not know what circumstances caused Constantine to issue such instructions. If the letter had been forged, it was forged for circulation in the fourth century, when the forger would have been careful not to have inserted in it an impossible itinerary.

29. The same date is set for Chrestus (no. 18).

30. This word ends a sentence of nineteen lines in Ziwsa's text marked by several anacolutha.

31. Taking *ut* with *protinus* (Turner, who otherwise would excise *ut*) in imitation of the Greek idiom ὡς τάχιστα.

20. LETTER OF CONSTANTINE I ON A DONATIST APPEAL FROM CATHOLIC BISHOPS, 314

(CSEL 26. 208–10)

From this letter in St Optatus' *dossier du Donatisme* we learn of Constantine's deep concern over the Donatists' contumacious refusal to acquiesce in the decision of the Council of Arles (314). Its pious tone should produce no surprise, for the emperor's epistle to Chrestus (no. 18) is not far behind it in such expressions, and quite probably it was put into final form by one of his ecclesiastical scribes, of whom several are said to have served in his secretariat.

Its importance is seen in that Constantine, though scandalized at the stubbornness of the schismatics, evidently felt that he had not yet the legal right to enforce the appealed decisions of two ecclesiastical synods (Rome, 313; Arles, 314), to which he had referred successively the case against Caecilian, bishop of Carthage (nos. 17–19),[1] but that it was his duty to provide for trial of such cases as were appealed to his attention and to take at last personal cognizance of this case in his own *cour de cassation*, in the hope that he himself might end by his unappealable decision this schism, which was dividing Christians in Africa.

Constantine Augustus to the Catholic bishops, dearest brethren, greeting.

The eternal and conscientious incomprehensible compassion [2] of our God not at all allows human nature to wander in darkness for too long a time nor permits the odious wills of certain ones to become so over-powerful that it, by opening anew through its clearest lights a road of salvation, does not afford them conversion to the rule of righteousness. In fact I have learned this by many examples; of these same matters I judge from my own experience. For originally there were in me things which seemed to lack righteousness, nor did I think that the Supernal Power saw anything which I carried within the secrets of my heart. What fortune, as I have said, ought these things indeed to have brought? Surely one overflowing with all evils. But Almighty God, who sits in the watchtower of heaven, has bestowed what I did not deserve: truly indeed, those things which in his heavenly benevolence he has granted to me, his servant, can be neither named nor numbered.

Most holy bishops of Christ the Saviour, dearest brethren, I therefore rejoice, I specially rejoice that at last, after a most equitable judicial examination has been made,[3] you have recalled to a better hope and fortune those whom the wickedness of the Devil seemed to have diverted by his wretched persuasion from the clearest light of the Catholic law.[4] O truly triumphant providence of Christ the Saviour!

that it could have regard even for those who, already deviating from truth and in some way taking arms against itself, have joined themselves to the pagans;[5] because, if even now they shall have wished with pure faith to render obedience to the most sacred law,[4] they will be able to perceive what great provision has been made for them by God's command. And this indeed, most holy brethren, I hoped could be restored even in those in whom has been engendered the greatest hardness of heart. But with them right judgement has not been helpful nor into their dispositions has entered the Gracious Divinity; for truly, not undeservedly Christ's clemency must have departed far from these men, in whom it is clear with manifest light that they are of such a character that we see these persons even hated by Heavenly Providence.[6] What great madness persists in these very persons, when with incredible arrogance they persuade themselves of things which it is right neither to be said nor to be heard, departing from right judgement given,[7] on which by Heavenly Providence I have learned that they demand my decision![8] What power of wickedness perseveres in these same persons' hearts! How often [9] have they been overwhelmed already by me personally in a reply quite deserving of their own most shameful approaches! And, to be sure, if they had cared to keep this before their eyes, not at all would they have introduced this very appeal. They demand my judgement, but I myself await Christ's judgement.[10] For I declare, as is the truth, that the bishops'[11] judgement ought to be regarded just as if the Lord himself were sitting as judge. For it is not lawful for them to think other or to judge other, save that which they have been taught by Christ's instruction. Why, then, as I have said truly, are wicked persons influenced by the Devil's services? Abandoning heavenly things, they seek worldly things. O raving audacity of rage! Just as happens usually in lawsuits of pagans,[5] they have introduced an appeal. Indeed pagans,[5] sometimes fleeing lower courts, where justice quickly can be had, are wont rather to resort to the higher courts by interposition of authority and thus to an appeal. What about these recusants from the law, who, refusing the heavenly judgement, have thought that mine should be demanded?[12] To think thus of Christ the Saviour! Behold, they are already betrayers; behold, without any keener investigation they themselves of their own accord have betrayed their own wickednesses! What human feeling is felt by the very ones who savagely have sprung upon God himself?

Dearest brethren, although these things apparently are detected in these very men, nevertheless do you, who follow the way of the Lord the Saviour, exhibit patience by giving them still a choice as to what they think should be chosen. And if you shall have seen that these persist in the same courses, forthwith depart with those whom the Lord has judged worthy of his worship [13] and return to your own sees and remember me, that our Saviour ever may have mercy on me.

As for the rest: I have directed my men that they should bring these same abominable deceivers of religion straightway to my court, that they may live there and there may survey for themselves something worse than death.[14] I have sent also an authoritative letter to him who holds the vicariate of Africa,[15] that, as many as he shall discover like these madmen,[16] he should send them straightway to my court, lest any longer beneath so great a splendour of God such things should be done by them as can incite the greatest wrath of Heavenly Providence.

May Almighty God guard you, dearest brethren, safe through the ages by my and your prayers.

1. This forbearance was not so nicely observed by his successors, who often did not depend on conciliar sessions to decide who should be the ordinary of a disputed see (e.g. introd. to nos. 137 and 352).

Constantine's banishment of the Arian bishops, Secundus of Ptolemais and Theonas of Marmarica, and even of St Athanasius, patriarch of Alexandria, is not *ad rem*, though the former were condemned by the Council of Nicaea (325) and the latter, when haled before the emperor (336), was not allowed to plead his case. There was no question of who was rightful incumbent in these situations; rather security of peace in the Church was expected by these sentences of exile which debarred these men from their dioceses.

2. Some editors emend the Latin to read: "Eternal religion and the incomprehensible compassion" etc.

3. Constantine refers to the Council of Arles, where the Donatists pleaded their case.

4. Religion, as often in late Latin, when applied to Christianity.

5. By this word (*gentes*) the emperor means that the Donatists, who still were Christians, by persistence in their schism really were aligned with pagans, who would rejoice at the rift in the Christian Church. Since he writes to Christians, it is not out of character for Constantine, already kindly disposed to Christians, to put the name of pagans on his non-Christian subjects. See nos. 121, n. 3, and 148, n. 4.

6. This seems to be the literal meaning of *a caelesti provisione exosos*, when the sense demands some translation like "removed from heaven's care". Ziwsa's apparatus gives no variant for *exosos*, but a possible conjecture is *excisos*, for CI in a majuscule MS. can be converted easily into O. Then the alternative translation suits. But in any event the thought is not noted for its Christian charity.

7. That is, refusing to accept the episcopal sentence.

8. If the emperor ascribes to divine interposition the fact that the bishops at Arles had informed him of the Donatists' intention to appeal their verdict, such a notice is not extant. Not even their synodal letter to Pope St Silvester I includes such information about the Donatists' next move (*CSEL* 26. 206–8).

Perhaps *caelesti provisione* should be omitted as dittographical (cf. *supra* n. 6).

9. Probably no exaggeration. Constantine may have denounced the Donatists in answering their appeal from the Synod of Rome, but we have neither his reply nor any other letter from him to them before the second appeal from the Council of Arles.

Optatus, however, contributes an anachronistic answer (see also next note) of Constantine to the Donatists' appeal from the Synod of Rome; but this reply belongs to the present letter, which was written after the Donatists had appealed from the Council of Arles. The imperial answer assigned by Optatus is "O raving audacity of rage! Just as happens usually in lawsuits of pagans, a bishop [Donatus] has believed that an appeal should be made" (*CSEL* 26. 27). These words, slightly altered, appear, apparently in their proper place, in the text of the present letter below at the second occurrence of n. 5.

10. Words so famous that Optatus inserts these anachronistically (*CSEL* 26. 26), where in slightly different form Constantine wrote: "You seek a judgement from me in this world, when I myself await Christ's judgement" in his response to the Donatists, who had requested a trial by Gallic bishops (as being impartial) to consider their charges against Caecilian.

11. He uses *sacerdos* (priest), which was synonymous with *episcopus* (bishop) in Tertullian's time, a century earlier (see no. 16, n. 4 *ad fin.*).

This sentence's thought reappears in one of Constantine's speeches to the Council of Nicaea in 325 (see no. 49, n. 3).

12. Constantine by this comparison with the heathen means that, while the pagans appeal from lower to higher tribunals, the Donatists appeal from higher to lower courts, that is, from the judgement of heaven (in the bishops' persons) to the judgement on earth (in the emperor's person).

13. That is, the non-Donatists whether among or before the council.

14. What the emperor meant by this is unknown. The Latin reads *ibi sibi mortem peius pervideant*, but, even if *mortem* be changed to *morte*, it still is unclear.

15. Literally "the delegated prefectship throughout Africa" (*vicariam praefecturam per Africam*), which is another way of referring to the vicariate of Africa, a large division of the prefecture of Italy (see no. 15, n. 12).

16. Literally "like this madness" (*huius insaniae similes*).

21. RESCRIPT OF CONSTANTINE I, MAXIMIN II, AND LICINIUS ON A DONATIST FORGER, 315

(*CSEL* 34. 410–11; 52. 485–7)

This letter, though superscribed with the names of Constantine and Maximin and Licinius, from its text evidently pertains only to the first. It is part of the aftermath of the second investigation (Carthage, 15 February 314) into Donatism ordered by the emperor, after the Donatists had complained that the first investigation (Rome, 2 October 313; no. 17), which had pronounced against their claim that Caecilian was wrongfully bishop of Carthage, had not issued in a fair verdict. To appease the Donatist dissidents Constantine ordered a re-examination of the case of Felix, bishop of Aptunga, whose consecration of Caecilian as bishop of Carthage was considered invalid by the Donatists on the ground that Felix during the last persecution had betrayed the Church (no. 17). At the renewed hearing (which was the second investigation) of this case before Aelian, proconsul of Africa, it developed that a letter, on which the Donatists relied to convict Felix, had been forged (in 303) by a decurion, one Ingentius, and consequently Aelian cleared Felix and committed Ingentius to prison.

Apparently Constantine had not had time to review the acts of these proceedings (CSEL 26. 197–204), for he yielded to the Donatists' importunity and ordered a third investigation (Arles, 1 August 314; nos. 18 and 19); but, when he had read the report from Aelian, Constantine discovered that the case against Felix had collapsed through the confessed forgery of Ingentius and that this failure automatically had cleared Caecilian. So to conclude the case Constantine wrote to Probian, Aelian's successor, and commanded him to send Ingentius to the imperial court, that he might repeat in the presence of the Donatists, who had appealed from their condemnation at Arles, his confession of forgery.

Whether Ingentius was sent to Constantine, whether he readmitted his forgery, whether the emperor heard him in the presence of the Donatists—all this is not known. But if these three events ensued, they had no noticeable effect, since Constantine was constrained to hold a fourth investigation (Milan, 10 November 316; no. 27), at which he presided and which still failed to settle the furore, for a fifth inquiry (Thamugada, 13 December 320) was equally inconclusive and led Constantine to leave the case to the judgement of God (no. 39), in whose good time the schism was not terminated till early in the next century (30 January 412), when Honorius dealt the Donatists their death-blow by his constitution *Cassatis quae* (no. 329).

The legal importance of this imperial letter is twofold: (1) it shows that the emperor has been informed (through personal inspection) of the *acta* of a proconsular trial; (2) it presumes that the prince will preside in person at a review before which will appear appellants, who have refused to accept as closing their case the acquittal of a defendant by two ecclesiastical synods (Rome and Arles), and a confessed criminal, on whose recently acknowledged forgery the appellants have constructed their case—at least in part.

Augustine gives this letter twice (*Cont. Cresc.* 3. 70. 81; *Ep.* 88. 4). The textual differences are slight.

Emperors Caesars Flavians,[1] Constantine and Maximin[2] and Valerius Licinian Licinius, to Probian, proconsul of Africa.

When[3] the most excellent Verus, vicar of the prefects in our

Africa,[4] then was being restrained by ill health, your predecessor Aelian, in discharging the duties of the said person, deservedly among all other matters believed also that this business or rather the hatred which appears to have been aroused against [5] Caecilian, a bishop of [6] the Catholic Church, ought to be referred to his investigation and authority. For when he had caused Superius, a centurion, and Caecilian, a magistrate of the Aptungitans, and Saturnine, an ex-curator, and Calibius Junior, a curator of the same city, and Solon, a public slave of the abovementioned city, to be present, he provided a proper hearing:[7] so that, when it had been objected against Caecilian that the episcopate appeared to have been conferred on him by Felix, against whom it appeared that betrayal and burning of the Divine Scriptures had been charged, he decided that Felix had been innocent of this. Finally, when Maximus maintained that Ingentius, a decurion of the Ziquensians' city, had falsified a letter of Caecilian, an ex-duovir, we [8] have perceived from the *Acts*, which were submitted, that the said Ingentius himself was raised [9] and was not tortured for the reason that he had asserted that he was a decurion of the Ziquensians' city.

Wherefore we wish that you should send the said Ingentius himself under proper escort to my court of Constantine Augustus, that, in the hearing and the presence of those who at present make accusations and cease not to appeal day after day, it can be clear and be made known that in vain they have desired to prepare hatred against Bishop Caecilian and to bestir themselves violently against him. For thus it will come to pass that when altercations of this character have been abandoned, as is proper, the people without any dissension may serve their own [10] religion with due reverence.

1. Flavius was the *nomen* of Constantine and Licinius, but was not associated with either Maximian II (*ob.* 311) or Maximin II (*ob.* 314). This fact and the further fact that both Maximian and Maximin (most MSS. have the latter) had died before the composition of this letter have induced some editors to omit mention of their names.

2. The letter reads *Constantinus Maximus*, which can mean either "Constantinus the Greatest" or "Constantinus, Maximus"; in the latter case *Maximus* seems substituted for "Maximinus".

3. "While" (*dum* for *cum*) is the letter's variant.

4. See no. 20, n. 15.

5. The letter has "about".

6. The treatise reads "and" for *of*.

7. The surviving *acta* of the renewed trial mention only the ex-duovir Caecilian of the five men named by Constantine here.

8. The treatise inserts "also".

9. The Latin *suspensus* indicates that Ingentius was hoisted upon some

instrument of torture. Since *suspensus* can mean also "raised for flogging" (i.e. tied to a post) and then "flogged", some suppose that Ingentius was scourged short of actual torture. From the *acta* (*CSEL* 26. 202, 5–7 and 203, 20–3) it appears that Aelian said: *suspendatur . . . submittite illum*, which may mean merely "let him be raised . . . lower him".

10. That is, their true religion as uncontaminated by Donatist doctrine as to how Christians should consider Caecilian's claim to the Carthaginian see.

22. LETTER OF CONSTANTINE I ON PERSONAL COGNITION OF DONATIST BISHOPS' APPEAL, 315

(*CSEL* 26. 210–11)

Although Caecilian had been cleared by two episcopal synods, one in Rome (313; no. 17) and one at Arles (314; nos. 18 and 19), in this letter the emperor notifies the schismatic Donatist prelates that he himself will act as judge in their case against Caecilian, bishop of Carthage. The hearing was at Milan (316; no. 27), where Caecilian was vindicated for the third time.

This document is the earliest known evidence for an emperor's intention to preside at a trial in which Christians were combating Christians in court.

Constantine Augustus to the bishops.

A few days ago it had been my pleasure, according to your request, that you should return to Africa, that there the entire case, which to you appears to apply to Caecilian, should be tried by my friends, whom I have selected, and should receive a fit termination.

But this seemed the most preferable course for me, considering it at length and not improperly wishing it in my heart, that—since I know that certain quite factious and stubborn-minded ones of you pay the least regard to the correct judgement [1] and to the reasonableness of the complete truth, and that on account of this it perhaps may happen that, if the trial should be in that same place,[2] the case would not end as is fitting and as consideration of truth demands, and that because of your excessive obstinacy some such thing would result as both would displease the Heavenly Divinity and would embarrass very much my reputation, which I wish ever to maintain unimpaired—it has been my pleasure, as I have said, that Caecilian preferably should come hither in pursuance of the former arrangement. And I believe that he soon will arrive in consequence of my letter.[3]

Moreover I promise you that if in his presence you shall have proved through your very own selves anything about only one crime or evil deed of his, it will be with me as if all accusations, which you aim at him, appear to have been proved.

May Almighty God grant you perpetual security.

1. Perhaps is meant the verdict of the two episcopal synods.
2. It is not clear whether Constantine meant before a secular or a third clerical court, for the reference to his *friends* (above) is indecisive, though it is unlikely that the emperor would have appointed his enemies as judicial assessors. Perhaps Constantine was considering a laic court in view of the probability that a third ecclesiastical council would not succeed in satisfying the schismatics, when two previous ones had failed, and that the equation of "friends" to "bishops" would make it appear that he had prejudged the case. Apart from this, to try the case in Africa, where the tide of partisan passion ran high, seeing that the schism had started there, seemed impolitic.
3. This epistle to Caecilian is not extant.

23. MANDATE OF CONSTANTINE I ON JEWISH MOLESTATION OF CHRISTIANS, 315

(CT 16. 8. 1)

This ordinance seems to be the earliest imperial constitution protecting Christians from Jewish attack, inspired because certain Jews had become converts to Christianity.

Justinian re-enacted only the first sentence of it (*CI* 1. 9. 3).

Emperor Constantine Augustus to Evagrius.[1]

We will that it should be made known to Jews and their elders [2] and patriarchs [3] that if after this law anyone shall have dared to assail with rocks or with another kind of madness—which we have learned is being done now—anyone who has fled their deadly sect and has turned his attention to God's cult, he must be delivered immediately to the flames and with all his accomplices must be burned.

Moreover, if anyone from the people [4] shall have joined their nefarious sect and shall have attached himself to their assemblies, he shall sustain with them deserved punishments.

Given on 18 October at Murgillum,[5] Constantine Augustus and Licinius being consuls for the fourth time.

1. From Justinian's version we learn that Evagrius was a praetorian prefect, probably of Italy.

2. Though Jewish elders often are mentioned in the Bible, nowhere therein are defined clearly their position and functions. Even in Egypt the Israelites had a council of elders—called in Ex. 3. 16, 18 abstractly γερουσία (LXX) and concretely *seniores* (Vulg.)—composed apparently of heads of clans within the tribes and exercising local authority. After the Exodus seventy elders—now called πρεσβύτεροι and *senes* in Num. 11. 16, 24, 25—were appointed to assist Moses. Some scholars see in this senate the origin of the Sanhedrin—in Matt. 26. 29 συνέδριον and *concilium*—of 70 or 71 members with religious, civil, criminal jurisdiction. But while the Sanhedrin had elders in it, it also had priests and "rulers" and scribes (Acts 4. 5–15); so most scholars suppose that the Great Sanhedrin was organized in Maccabean times (*c.* 141 B.C.)—though Josephus (*Ant. Iud.* 12. 3. 3. 142) mentions it in Antiochus III the Great's reign (223–187 B.C.)—and was superseded in Roman times (A.D. 66 or 70) by the Palestinian patriarchate.

It seems rather that Constantine refers to the so-called elders of the city (γερουσία τῆς πόλεως, πρεσβύτεροι τῆς πόλεως; *seniores civitatis, maiores natu civitatis, seniores urbis*), who—first mentioned in Deut. 19. 12—had authority in civic affairs and continued into the Christian era as representatives of their co-religionists wherever Jews congregated in communities within the Empire. In 331 they seem to have been associated with synagogues under the titles also of *archisynagogi* and *patres synagogarum* (*CT* 16. 8. 4).

3. These seem to have been chiefs of Jewish communities in the provinces and subordinate to the Palestinian patriarch, whom the Romans recognized as the spiritual leader of Jewry after 66 or 70 and on whom see no. 341, n. 2 *ad init.*

4. Whether Christians or pagans is unclear, but it is of minor moment, since by this date—only nine days short of three years after Constantine's vision of the Cross—the emperor's Christian advisers had the time to have influenced him against allowing either Christians or pagans to join the Jews.

Perhaps the persistent animosity between Jews and Christians—ascending into the apostolic age (as the New Testament abundantly witnesses) and prominent throughout this sylloge—was assisted by the ancient astrological assumption that different religious professions are associated popularly with different regnant planets. Thus the Jews are under Saturn and their holy day is Saturday (Saturn's Day), while the Christians are under the Sun and their holy day is Sunday (the Sun's Day), on which see no. 34, n. 5.

Be that as it may, yet on the political plane the Jews, disliking Greek symmetry and perspective and despising Roman order and logic, were inimical toward the classical State, which conceived itself as something eternal and divine—no matter what its form. Their philosophy was not political, but was racial and individual. Having no State, they existed in, but apart from, western society and have been placed by some civilians among the stateless persons (*dediticii*) of Roman law.

5. Probably an error for Milan, where Constantine was one day later, according to another constitution (*FIRA* 2. 523).

24. LETTER OF CONSTANTINE I ON PERSONAL COGNITION OF THE DONATIST SCHISM, 315

(*CSEL* 26. 211-12)

The emperor's letter reveals not only considerable irritation toward the schismatic Donatists, but also his determination to decide their case against Caecilian, bishop of Carthage, in Africa, whither he did not proceed after all, for both Caecilian (after some delay) and the chief Donatists (already in Italy) were heard in Milan, where Constantine pronounced judgement in favour of Caecilian (no. 27).[1]

But this letter, while it merely reinforces, though in stronger terms, Constantine's decision to take personal cognizance as appellate judge in this case, as already he had signified in his letter to the Donatist bishops (no. 22), betrays a certain prejudice, unbecoming to the role of a judge: the emperor seems to have prejudged the matter when he writes to Celsus, his vicar of Africa, not only that he will make it quite clear to each party in a perfectly plain verdict what kind of worship must be given to God, but also that he will destroy those persons who cause the people to withhold from God the worship which is his due. Such sentiments stand midway between those of earlier emperors who persecuted their subjects for their Christianity and those of later emperors who punished Christians for their heterodoxy. It is this tone which gives this letter its additional importance as a legal document.[2]

To Celsus, vicar of Africa.

Your Gravity's latest dispatches—in which you, dearest brother, have related that you, adhering to our order about the punishment of their sedition and in the matter of that disturbance, which they were organizing, have been hindered[3]—have borne witness that that Menalius,[4] of whom madness long ago took hold, and the rest, who have departed from God's truth and have surrendered themselves to most perverse error, persevere. And as a result[5]—since it has been evident that they have been planning wicked deeds from this fact that, when I had decided to investigate very fully between them and Caecilian about the various accusations, they have striven to withdraw from my presence by taking to flight[6]—by this very disgraceful deed they admitted that they hasten to return to those things which they both previously had done and now persevere in doing. But since it is established that none ever at all converts his own misdeeds entirely to his own profit, even if punishment for these has been postponed for a little time, I have decided that your Gravity should be instructed that in the meantime you indeed should disregard these same persons and should know that no notice of them must be taken.[7]

But after you have read this epistle, you should make clear both to

24. PERSONAL COGNITION OF THE SCHISM, 315

Caecilian and to these same persons that when I shall have come to Africa with the favour of divine righteousness,[8] I shall make it quite clear to all, not only to Caecilian but also to these who appear to act against him, by reading a perfectly plain verdict, what and what kind of worship must be given to the Supreme Divinity and in what manner of service he seems to delight; that also, by exercising a careful examination, I shall discover quite fully and shall cause to come to light those matters which now some persons think they can conceal as a result of the snares of their mental ignorance; that these same persons, who excite matters of this sort and cause that the Supreme God is not worshipped with the veneration which he ought to have, I shall destroy and shall shatter. And since it is sufficiently clear that none can acquire a martyr's blessedness by this sort of martyrdom, which is seen to be foreign from the truth of religion and unsuitable, those persons, whom I shall have recognized as against the right and religion itself and whom I shall have detected as guilty of violence toward the legal worship, without any delay I shall cause to suffer the destruction rightly due to their madness and audacious obstinacy. And so I shall cause them [9] to know for certain what they are bound to hold, after they have invoked even salvation as witness to the fullest belief,[10] because most scrupulously I shall investigate not only concerning the laity but also concerning these clergymen, who are the leaders, and I shall give that judgement which is clear to be most true and most religious,[11] and I shall indicate also to these same persons what and what sort of worship must be paid to the Divinity. For I believe that by no means I can escape the greatest guilt otherwise than that I should think that I not at all must leave unnoticed that which is wicked. What ought to be done by me more in accord with my practice and the duty of a prince himself than that, after errors have been dissipated and all reckless opinions have been removed, I should cause all persons to exhibit true religion and harmonious simplicity and the worship due to Almighty God?

1. Augustine, *Ep.* 43. 20 (= *CSEL* 34. 101–02).
2. Since, save for this, it repeats what already is known from no. 20.
3. There is some difficulty here. First, Constantine's order is not extant. Second, the phrases *about ... punishment* and *in ... disturbance* may be construed either with *order* (as in translation) or with *hindered*, in which latter case *de* should be translated "from". Third, *inhibitum esse* seems to be passive (as in translation). If so, Constantine is lenient with Celsus, who evidently has failed in procuring peace in Africa. This leniency toward an official who confessed his failure may be due to Constantine's recognition of the contumacy of the Donatists, who had refused to submit to two ecclesiastical sentences already passed against them. On the other hand, if *inhibitum esse* should be taken as

middle (which is rare), then the thought would be that Celsus has been employing himself (for *inhibere* sometimes is used in the sense of *adhibere*) in the matter of the punishment and concerning the disturbance, but that little progress can be reported because of the persistent attitude of Menalius and the rest.

4. A Donatist and presumably a bishop of an unknown see. He may have been that Menalius who during the tenth persecution was a Christian turncoat (*CSEL* 26. 16).

5. The connection between the Donatists in Africa and those in Italy is expressed in *unde*, but the only real consequence is that in each place the Donatist deeds flow from the same persistence in defying synodal decisions.

6. So Augustine (loc. cit.) corroborates, but from his account they even effected their escape, since Constantine had the rest conveyed under guard to Milan, where he presided over the case.

The MS. gives *praesentia mea susceptam fugam subtrahere*. Even with Ziwsa's emendation of *praesentiae meae*, it still is difficult; but if Du Pin's conjecture of *suscepta fuga se subtrahere* be adopted, then the translation in the text results.

7. The word is *dissimulandum esse*, which can be translated also as "there must be dissemblance on our part". But this interpretation is pointless, for the emperor in the next sentence announces his intended journey to Africa, where he will settle the case. So Constantine is not disclosing to Celsus the colour of any deep diplomacy. He merely repeats the idea in *omittas* (you should disregard).

8. This phrase, *favente pietate divina*, is another form of our *Deo favente* or *Deo volente*.

9. The construction is not clear: *scire* (to know) depends on something, probably *faciam* (I shall cause) in the previous clause, and, if so, is in the same construction as *persolvere* (to suffer).

10. The meaning seems to be that the parties must call their hope of salvation into witness for the fullest faith in the truth of their testimony (cf. the later Christian formula "As I hope for salvation"). On the other hand, *to the fullest belief* may be construed with *bound to hold*, if Constantine means that he will make sure that all concerned will know for certain what is the completest measure of Christian belief that Christians ought to have.

11. "I shall judge according to that which obviously is in the interests of truth and of religion" is a possible paraphrase and may represent Constantine's intention.

25. LETTER OF ANNIAN AND JULIAN ON TRANSPORTATION FOR DONATIST CLERGY, 316
(CSEL 26. 212)

This letter from two praetorian prefects [1] to the vicar of the African diocese authorizes public transportation homeward for certain Donatist clerics, who were returning from the Council of Arles, whither the emperor had summoned them, to their homes in Africa.

Petronius Annian and Julian [2] to Domitius Celsus, vicar of Africa.

Since his Worthiness has commanded Lucian, Capito, Fidentius, and Nasutius, the bishops, and Mammarius, the priest [3]—who pursuant to the celestial command of the Lord Constantine, Greatest, Unconquered, Ever-August had come to the Gauls [4] with other persons of that law [5]—to come to their own homes, we have given, brother, pursuant to the order of his Eternity, the said most clement emperor, to these men public transportation [6] with suitable provisions [7] so far as the port of Arles, [8] by which they may sail thence to Africa—a fact which it is fitting for your Ingenuity to know from our letter.

We wish you, brother, to fare well very happily.

Hilary, chief of the office staff, [9] presented this.

On 28 April [10] at Trèves.

1. Mommsen has established that the senders were praetorian prefects, for whom exists epigraphical evidence (*CIL* 3. 13734).

2. His *nomen* Julius has disappeared from the text, but can be recovered from the abovementioned inscription. Mommsen conjectures that Julian was praetorian prefect of the East and that Annian was praetorian prefect of Gaul, whence the epistle—as the subscriptional evidence shows—emanated.

3. These men are identifiable only as Donatists.

4. See no. 203, n. 4.

5. That is, Donatism as opposed to Catholicism.

6. The word is *angarialis* (adjective), derived from *angaria* (noun), on which see no. 434, n. 2. See also nos. 18, n. 10; 19, nn. 24, 28; 95, n. 41.

7. Literally reversed, "suitability pertaining to provisions" (*annonaria conpetentia*). See no. 301, n. 7.

8. See no. 18, n. 8.

9. Instead of the usual phrase *princeps officii* simply *princeps* appears (as in *FIRA* 1. 331, a document dated about 45 years later). A *princeps* in an administrative capacity was the chief executive officer in a governmental department, whether civil or military. While it is unknown in which office this Hilary was, perhaps he served in the praetorian prefecture of Gaul, where he supervised the submission of this epistle at Trèves.

10. The true date seems to be 27 February.

26. MANDATE OF CONSTANTINE I ON MANUMISSION IN CHURCH, 316

(*CI* 1. 13. 1)

To the three traditional modes of formal manumission[1] the emperor adds a fourth method, whereby masters may free their slaves in church before the bishop and the congregation.

On bishops also Constantine confers the same privilege and apparently relaxes the rules by which they can manumit their slaves, provided that the evidence is clear.

Emperor Constantine Augustus to Protogenes,[2] bishop.

For some time[3] it has pleased us that in the Catholic Church masters can bestow freedom on their own slaves,[4] if they should do this in the sight of the people, the Christians' bishops being present, that on account of the reminder of the deed some sort of writing, in which they themselves should seal in the place of witnesses, may be introduced for the sake of the records.

Wherefore freedom by you yourselves also not undeservedly[5] must be given and must be bequeathed, in whatever way any of you shall have wished, provided that clear evidence of your wish should appear.[6]

Given on 8 June, Sabinus and Rufinus being consuls.

1. These ways were: (1) *censu*, when a master entered his slave's name on the censor's register at the quinquennial census (*census*)—but, since the censorship had been abolished in 22 B.C. and because the census thereafter occurred at irregular intervals, this mode attracted little use in the Empire; (2) *vindicta*, when before a magistrate possessing jurisdiction a master in a fictitious lawsuit with another freeman did not dispute the latter's claim that the former's slave had been free-born, and then struck lightly the slave with a rod (*vindicta*) in a symbolic ritual; (3) *testamento*, when a master in his will (*testamentum*) conferred freedom on his chattel.

Informal methods of manumission included: (1) declaration among friends that a master was freeing his slave; (2) master's epistolary announcement to his slave that he was liberating him; (3) master's invitation to his slave to dinner. Justinian I added (4) appointment of slave as master's heir; (5) nomination of slave in master's testament as guardian for master's child; (6) master's adoption of slave as his son.

2. Bishop of Sofia.

3. Although the adverb (*iam dudum*) indubitably indicates an earlier enactment, it is not known when it was emitted.

4. The introduction of this mode of manumission perhaps came from the

Greek custom of selling slaves to a temple of a deity. In such case the slaves were considered sacred and free from secular, though seemingly not from sacral, law.

This practice, associated with pagan religion, may have resulted, conversely, in the assignment of funds collected in Christian congregations to purchase freedom for slaves, who presumably were converts to Christianity (*CA* 4. 9).

5. The litotes is in the Latin.

6. Pitra prints (2. 634) a late Greek paraphrase of the law: "For some time it has pleased us that in the Catholic Church a master can bestow freedom on his own slaves, if they should do this in the eyes of the common people, the most Christian bishops being present, that an account of the records in respect to a complete reminder may be introduced in some sort of writing, in which these also should seal in the place of witnesses. Wherefore by us ourselves also not undeservedly freedom should be given and should be bequeathed, and clear evidence of persons wishing in agreement appears."

27. LETTER OF CONSTANTINE I ON CAECILIAN'S INNOCENCE, 316

(*CSEL* 52. 487)

Constantine, asserts St Augustine, relates to Eumalius, his vicar of Africa, how the Caecilianists and the Donatists appeared at Milan before him for judgement, after the verdicts of the episcopal councils at Rome (313; no. 17) and at Arles (314; nos. 18 and 19) had failed to satisfy the Donatists.[1]

The emperor's decision in favour of Caecilian, bishop of Carthage, probably was embodied in a decree, which may have been in or with the letter, for publication in Africa, where the Donatist schism flourished.

Augustine preserves only part of the epistle (*Cont. Cresc.* 3. 71. 82), which is one of our principal sources for the penultimate investigation into the schism.

And in this [2] I perceived that Caecilian was a man endowed with entire innocence and observing the due duties of his religion and serving it in such a way as he ought. And it had been clear also that no fault, such as had been invented against him in his absence by the insincerity of his adversaries,[3] could be found in him.

1. See also Augustine, *Ep.* 43. 20 (=*CSEL* 34. 101–2) and no. 22.
2. The context shows that "trial" is meant.
3. Augustine (*CSEL* 52. 488) accuses the Donatists of *calumnia* (calumny), on which see no. 334, n. 3, and it is known that Donatist calumniators were

active in Africa. However, nothing appears to have happened to those involved in Caecilian's trial before Constantine, but the mandate on defamatory writings (*CT* 9. 34. 1) sent to the vicar of Africa early in 319 may have been constructed to publish such calumniating pamphleteers.

28. EDICT OF CONSTANTINE I ON EPISCOPAL JURISDICTION, 318
(*CT* 1. 27. 1)

By this important instrument, whose authenticity often has been suspected, the first Christian emperor, who five years earlier authorized Christian bishops to judge ecclesiastical causes (no. 17), raises the Christian episcopate to the status of judges in such cases involving private law as litigants agree to plead before bishops. The law allows litigants to transfer suits from civil judges to bishops, whose verdicts are recognized as final.

The precedent thus created has continued as a legal custom in certain parts of the modern world.[1]

Emperor Constantine Augustus.
Pursuant to his own duty a judge shall be bound to observe that, if there should be an appeal to an episcopal court, silence should be applied [2] and that, if anyone shall have wished to transfer a matter to the Christian law and to observe that sort of court, he should be heard, even if the matter has been begun before the judge, and that whatever shall have been judged by them [3] should be held as sanctioned rulings: so that, however, there should not be a usurpation in this procedure—that one of the litigants should go to the aforesaid court and should announce his own choice.[4] For the judge ought to have the choice of jurisdiction of the pending case, that he may pronounce sentence after acceptance of all the facts presented.[5]

Given on 23 June at Constantinople,[6] . . . Augustus and Crispus Caesar [7] being consuls.[8]

1. Today almost entirely in the eastern area of the Mediterranean Sea episcopal jurisdiction survives, chiefly in nominally Mohammedan nations, where bishops are competent to judge suits of private law between Christians, e.g. the Coptic patriarch of Alexandria acts as the referee in matrimonial and testamentary causes of his Catholic communicants. But the best illustration is provided by the Ecumenical Patriarch, the archbishop of Constantinople, who, though Turkish by birth, was an American citizen until 1949, when he was recalled from New York City to Istanbul to preside over the Holy Orthodox

28. EPISCOPAL JURISDICTION, 318

Catholic Apostolic Church. In his ecclesiastical court, whose civil competency was sanctioned by the Turkish captors of Constantinople in 1453, the patriarch still applies the Roman law as developed in and received from the Byzantine Empire, when there come before it cases involving marriage, divorce, inheritance, guardianship, personal status of his followers in the Turkish Republic. So there, in that corner of this old household of the world, without a lapse for almost 1,900 years, from the time (77) when the Romans incorporated into their provincial system Byzantium (called Constantinople from 330, now known officially as Istanbul—a name derived from Constantinople—since 1929), Roman rules of civil conduct, some of which tradition places in the legendary period of the Roman Kingdom (753–509 B.C.), have served to control a part (once large but now small, because of the creation of autonomous and autocephalous churches in eastern Europe and in western Asia) of Christian mankind n their legal dealings. Such a condition of *continuous* development of law and of *permanency* of legal administrations perhaps never has been equalled outside the city of Rome itself.

A good example of the *audientia episcopalis* is preserved in a Greek papyrus of the fourth century. In it a bishop decides about the division of an estate between two Egyptian heirs, of whom one is a nun, and allows twelve days for the division to be effected. It is edited in *FIRA* 3. 574–6.

That episcopal courts were popular in the fifth century is clear from the evidence of Bishop Possidius, who (*c*. 432) composed a life of St Augustine, bishop of Hippo Regius. According to him—and he appears to have observed his subject's daily life continuously for at least a lustrum of their almost forty years' acquaintance—Augustine sometimes spent an entire day without food in trying cases brought to his court either by Christians or by persons of any religion (*Sancti Augustini Vita*, 19 *ad med.* =*PL* 32. 50). And Augustine himself has an interesting account of the many matters accepted for episcopal adjudication (*Ep*. 33. 5 = *CSEL* 34. 22).

2. That is, the judge must not object and must allow the appeal.

3. The bishops. As persons of presumably better education than other ecclesiastics and of proven administrative ability, they probably were able magistrates.

4. The idea seems to be that a litigant must appear first in a civil court and then appeal for a change of venue to an episcopal court. Another reading *renuntiet* (renounce) for *enuntiet* (announce) gives the meaning that the litigant rejects the civil court, where ordinarily he must plead, if *arbitrium*, translated *choice*, means "tribunal" here.

5. It is believed that this sentence is defective. No satisfactory attempt to improve it has achieved acceptance.

6. The subscription is partly suspect (cf. *infra* n. 8), for Byzantium was not renamed Constantinople ere 330 (see no. 62, n. 2).

7. The title *Caesar*, derived from the cognomen of Gaius Iulius Caesar (102?–44 B.C.), until Hadrian's reign (117–38) was used by members of the

imperial family, but thereafter its use by others than the regnant emperor was restricted (as here) to a sovereign's designated successor and/or co-regent performing administrative duties. See no. 146, n. 5, for a later variant.

8. Licinius, the colleague of Constantine the Great in the sovereignty (307-24), seems to be the missing consul's name. The only year known to fit is 318, since epigraphical evidence shows that of Crispus' (Caesar 316-26) three consulates (318, 321, 324) in only the first his name stands in second place and then it is preceded by that of Licinius (Augustus 308-24), who never was consul with Crispus in any other year. Moreover Crispus shared his other two consulates with his younger brother Constantine II (Caesar 316-37, Augustus 337-40).

29. MANDATE OF CONSTANTINE I ON CLERICAL EXEMPTION FROM PUBLIC DUTIES, 319

(*CT* 16. 2. 2)

Immunity from public services—already granted to African clerics (no. 16)—is extended to clergymen in southern Italy by this ordinance, which thus constitutes another step in the spread of this concession throughout the Empire.

The same Augustus to Octavian, corrector of Lucania and of Bruttii.

Whoever devote to divine worship the services of religion, that is, those who are called clergymen, should be excused entirely from all public services, lest through certain persons'[1] sacrilegious malice they should be diverted from divine services.

Given on 21 October, Constantine Augustus for the fifth time and Licinius Caesar[2] being consuls.

Interpretation: By special ordinance this law commands that no person whatsoever should presume by sacrilegious ordinance to make tax-collectors[3] and tax-receivers[3] of clergymen, whom, free from every public service, that is, from every office and every service, it orders to be devoted to the Church.

1. Probably Donatists.
2. The use of *Caesar* (on which see no. 28, n. 7) here indicates not the Licinius who was Constantine's brother-in-law and fellow-sovereign, but the Licinius who was the former's son and the latter's nephew. Born a bastard of a servile mother in 315, proclaimed Caesar in 317, degraded after his father's downfall in 324, Licinius Junior is reported to have been murdered with Crispus, Constantine's eldest son, in 326.
3. Collectors (*exactores* or *compulsores*) collected taxes when delinquent; receivers (*susceptores* or *allecti*) received taxes when due.

30. MANDATE OF CONSTANTINE I ON CLERICAL EXEMPTION FROM PUBLIC DUTIES, (?)319
(CT 16. 2. 1)

This statute, addressed to an unknown official, grants to clergymen immunity from public services (see also nos. 16 and 29).

While its received date is 313, editors suggest that the directive was issued in 319 and therefore emend the corrupt subscription to the form translated.

Emperor Constantine Augustus.

We have learned that clergymen of the Catholic Church are so harassed by a faction of heretics [1] that contrary to privileges granted to them they are overburdened by nominations to office [2] or by certain undertakings,[3] which public custom demands.

Wherefore it pleases us that, if your Gravity shall have found anyone thus harassed, another person should be substituted for the said person and that hereafter injustices of this type should be averted from persons of the aforesaid religion.

Given on 31 October, Constantine Augustus for the fifth time and Licinius Caesar [4] being consuls.

1. Perhaps Donatists.
2. This should be understood rather in the sense of appointments, for ordinarily a nomination (lacking confirmation, as we use the word) is not particularly, though it can be, vexatious.
3. These are either public services (*munera*) or perhaps receipts of taxes (*susceptiones*) as here (see no. 29, n. 3).
4. See no. 29, n. 2.

31. EDICT OF CONSTANTINE I ON RESCISSION OF PENALTIES FOR CELIBACY AND FOR CHILDLESSNESS, 320
(CT 8. 16. 1)

As the doctrine of the superiority of the celibate life over the marital state—a teaching which was chiefly Gnostic in origin—had gained ground among Christians by the time of the State's recognition of Christianity, it is not unreasonable to suspect that for Constantine's repeal of legal disabilities on celibates and childless persons the influence of his clerical counsellors was responsible. Eusebius (*VC* 4. 26) claims that the emperor considered it unjust to continue penalties inflicted on childless couples, who perhaps desired a numerous progeny, but were prevented by physical infirmity from obtaining their desire, and on persons, particularly women, who through consecration to God's service preserved a pure virginity. Whether the emperor arrived, as Eusebius implies, at his decision unaided or was impelled to it by his aides, certainly the removal of such restrictions as forfeiture of inheritance favoured the clergy and fostered the growth of monachism.

Justinian retains most of this statute (*CI* 8. 57. 1).

Emperor Constantine Augustus to the people.

Whoever were considered celibates by the old law [1] should be freed from the laws' threatening terrors and should live so as if in the number of married persons they were supported by the bond of matrimony; and for all persons should be the equal situation of taking that to which each one is entitled.[2] Nor indeed should anyone be considered childless; the penalties proposed for this name should not harm him.

And we consider that this provision should be applied to women and we release indiscriminately from all of them the law's commands, like some yokes, imposed on their necks.[3]

But the use of this benefit [2] shall not extend to husbands and to wives with respect to each other, because their generally deceptive blandishments are restrained scarcely even by the law's opposed rigour, but between such persons should continue the laws' ancient authority.[4]

Given on 31 January at Sofia. Posted on 1 April at Rome, Constantine Augustus for the sixth time and Constantine Caesar [5] being consuls.

1. The Augustan *Lex Iulia de maritandis ordinibus* (18 B.C.) was revised by the *Lex Iulia et Papia Poppaea* (A.D. 9), which made more comprehensive the provisions of the earlier statute and to which Constantine perhaps refers, for we know of no previous repeal of it—in fact certain senatusconsults, such as the Tiberian *Senatus Consultum Persicianum* (*c.* 34) added to its disabilities.

We are concerned here not with the Augustan legislation on marriage in all its aspects or with what provisions were in the one or the other statute (on which see *CAH* 10. 441-56), but rather about the privileges for persons with families and about the penalties for unmarried and/or childless persons. Among the benefits bestowed by the Augustan laws—neither their privileges nor their penalties conspired to increase the birth rate, which was the ostensible object— was the celebrated right of children (*ius liberorum*), which conferred on its holder (who had, in Rome, three children or, in Italy, four children or, in the provinces, five children) (1) preference in candidacy for office, (2) holding office either before the legal age or without observance of the legal interval between offices, (3) preference in assignment as provincial governor, (4) precedence before both equals in rank and colleagues in office, (5) exemption from both judge's and guardian's duties, (6) mitigation of punishment in certain cases, (7) partial remission of taxes. As for women: free-born women with three children and freedwomen with four children—whether alive or dead was immaterial—were exempted from the guardianship to which in widowhood they normally were subject and were given a right of succession to their children's inheritances. The laws' principal penalties were the opposite of the previously listed privileges: (1) inability of celibates to accept inheritances and legacies, if men over twenty-five and under sixty years of age and if women between twenty and fifty years old; (2) payment of a celibate's tax. As a special favour the *ius liberorum* was granted by emperors to childless couples.

2. He refers to the right to accept inheritances and legacies.

3. Here ends Justinian's excerpt.

4. This seems in accord with the old doctrine in Roman law that gifts between husband and wife were prohibited, if either was under paternal power (*patria potestas*). The rule appears as an imperial regulation as early as 222-7 (*CI* 5. 16. 4), but Ulpian, who was murdered in its author's presence (228), quotes Emperor Antoninus Pius (138-61) as regarding the rule as ancestral (*D* 24. 1. 3. pr.) and he himself ascribes it to custom (*D* 24. 1. 1). But the regulation perhaps did not ascend high into the republican period, since the *Lex Cincia de donis et muneribus* (204 B.C.), which prohibited gifts above a fixed (but unknown) amount except to certain relatives and other persons, such as wards and freedman, did not apply apparently to inter-marital donations.

Exceptions, however, permitted interchange of presents (1) on holidays and on certain festivals and at other times, if moderate in amount, (2) if gifts were not to become effective till after dissolution of marriage, (3) if presenters were not made poorer and receivers were not made richer.

5. See no. 28, n. 7.

32. EDICT OF CONSTANTINE I ON CLERICAL EXEMPTION FROM TAXATION, 320

(*CT* 16. 2. 10)

The emperor confers on the clergy and their dependants exemption from certain taxes as well as from public services of a menial nature.

Emperor Constantine Augustus [1] to all bishops throughout the various provinces.

That the churches' assemblies [2] may be crowded with a vast con-

80   32. CLERICAL EXEMPTION FROM TAXATION, 320

course of peoples,³ immunity should be provided for clergymen and youths⁴ and from these should be removed exaction of menial public services.⁵

They should be not at all subjected to tradesmen's expenses,⁶ since it is certain that the profits, which they collect from shopstalls and workshops, will benefit poor persons. We also decree that all expenses⁶ should be withdrawn from their men who engage in commercial activities.

Likewise equally exaction of extra transport provisions⁷ should cease.⁸ And this we grant to their wives and children and attendants (males and females alike), whom we also order to continue exempt from taxes.⁹

Given on 26 May at Constantinople, Constantine Augustus for the sixth time and Constantine Caesar¹⁰ being consuls.

1. Both superscription and subscription of this constitution are suspect. Editorial emendation, assigning the act to Constantine I instead of Constantius II, is accepted. Not only does most of the legislation of this type belong to Constantine's reign, but also the received date of 353 in the subscription does not agree with the emperors mentioned in the superscription, Constantius II and Constans I, of whom the latter died in 350.

2. Perhaps are meant not congregations as such, but parochial organizations of various kinds.

3. The Latin exhibits synesis, where the adjective, grammatically attached to one noun but belonging logically to the other, produces literally "a concourse of vast peoples".

4. Originally persons between twenty and forty years of age, but here probably acolytes.

5. Many of these are listed more appositely in no. 186, n. 5.

6. In the sense of taxation on the privilege to do business as well as on sales. From this it appears that certain congregations managed commercial enterprises and, as the emperor explains, devoted their profits to relief of their poor. See no. 107, n. 8.

7. Transliterated from παραγγαρεία. See also nos. 102, n. 7; 107, n. 13; 434, n. 3; 438, n. 5. This was an extraordinary public service, on which see no. 226, n. 3.

8. It seems from this provision that they still were held to the ordinary contributions for the maintenance of the public post. This was no more than fair, perhaps, because Constantine I had inaugurated the policy of permitting bishops the free use of the system of public transport (see no. 95, n. 41). Eventually, however, the clergy of the following century failed to conserve this exemption (nos. 325 and 438).

9. The anonymous author of the so-called *Syro-Roman Lawbook* (*Liber Iuris Syro-Romanus* or *Liber Graeco-Syriacus Iuris Romani* or simply *Leges Saeculares*)—

compiled perhaps in the fifth century in Latin originally, but later turned into Greek and extant now only in oriental (Arabic, Armenian, Syriac) versions—may refer to this constitution, when he writes (§117) that "the blessed [*beatus* in the modern Latin version of the Syriac translation for the usual *divus*, on which see no. 127, n. 7] King Constantine himself also honoured by degrees Christ's Church in his rather many ordinances [cf. e.g. nos. 10, 12, 15, 16, 23, 28–30, 33, 34, 36, 41, 45, 46, 48, 54–6, 59, 60, 63–5, 76] and liberated clerics from all tribute, that they should give neither silver for the head [i.e. capitation tax, on which see no. 67, n. 37] nor the *chrysargyron* [i.e. lustral tax, on which see no. 97, n. 1] nor anything of this kind" (*FIRA* 2. 794). But the author appears to be in error when in the next and final sentence of the section he states that "Moreover he liberated clerics also from their parents' power", for it seems that this freedom from paternal power (*patria potestas*) was postponed until 539, when Justinian I applied it only to bishops (*N* 81. 3), whom he calls spiritual fathers (πνευματικοὶ πατέρες; *spirituales patres*), perhaps because of the domestic power demanded for them by St Paul (1 Tim. 3. 4).

10. See no. 28, n. 7.

33. MANDATE OF CONSTANTINE I ON ADMISSION OF POOR PERSONS TO THE CLERICATE, 320

(*CT* 16. 2. 3)

Soon after the recognition of Christianity as a lawful religion (no. 12) the increase in members of the Church invited more candidates for ordination, particularly after Constantine had freed the clergy from the economic burden of public duties (nos. 16, 29, 30, 32). Because this rapid resort to privileged positions deprived the State of the services of a growing class of citizens, the emperor in this mandate debars decurions and their descendants as well as persons whose wealth entitled them to be drafted for public duties from entering ecclesiastical service, and orders the clergy to be chosen from the poorer citizens.

The same Augustus to Bassus, urban prefect.[1]

Since an issued constitution [2] commands that thereafter no decurion or a person begotten by a decurion or even a person provided with sufficient property and suitable for performing public services should have recourse to the name and the service of clergymen, but that thereafter into deceased clergymen's places should be substituted only those persons who, slender in fortune, are not bound to be obligated for civic services, we have learned that also are disturbed those persons who before the law's [2] promulgation have associated themselves with the society of clergymen.

And therefore we command that, when the latter have been freed from all annoyance, the former who, avoiding public duties, have had recourse to the number of the clergymen after the issuance of the law,[2] when they have been separated from that body, should be restored to their municipal senate and to their orders [3] and should devote themselves to their civic duties.

Posted on 18 July, Constantine Augustus for the sixth time and Constantine [4] Caesar [5] being consuls.

1. Septimus Bassus was prefect of the city of Rome at this time, but eleven years later he was praetorian prefect of an unknown prefecture. So Mommsen emends this constitution's superscription, which makes Bassus praetorian prefect in 320 rather than in 331.
2. This law is not extant.
3. See no. 325, n. 6.
4. Editorial emendation, proposing "Constantinus" for "Constantius", is accepted.
5. See no. 28, n. 7.

34. MANDATE OF CONSTANTINE I ON RECOGNITION OF SUNDAY, 321

(*CI* 3. 12. 2)

This is the earliest extant imperial legislation to recognize Sunday as a day of rest,[1] the only persons excepted being farmers, whose necessary duties need not be suspended on that day.

Emperor Constantine Augustus to Helpidius.[2]

All judges and urban peoples and artisans [3] of all crafts should rest on the venerable [4] day of the Sun.[5]

However, persons situated in the country may attend freely and unhinderedly to cultivation of the fields, since it frequently happens that not on another day more suitably are entrusted seeds of grain to furrows or vines to ditches, lest the opportunity granted by heavenly provision should be lost by the favourable moment of a short season.

Posted on 3 March, Crispus [6] and Constantine [6] being consuls for the second time.

1. As a day of rest Sunday seems to be mentioned expressly in Christian literature first by Tertullian, writing *c.* 202 (*De Orat.* 23 *ad med.*).
2. Helpidius probably acted for a praetorian prefect.
3. The word is *officia*, which usually means "office staffs", i.e. the abstract conception in late Latin for the concrete expression "magistrate's or official's apparitors or assistants", but here the context of *artium cunctarum* ("of all arts or crafts") demands a meaning like that taken in the translation. Since an *officina* is a workshop, perhaps an *officium* in relation to it is the body of workmen working in it. Both words stem from *opus* and *facere* ("to make a work", i.e. to do a service—whether freely or of necessity—for another).
4. This adjective, in which some scholars see simply a reference to pagan worship of the sun, may refer equally well to Christian worship on the first day of the week (Acts 20. 7).
5. While English *Sunday* is derived from Anglo-Saxon *sunnandaeg* (cf. German *Sonntag*), its Latin equivalent *dies solis* (here used) has fathered no such descent in the several Romance languages, which speak of "the Lord's Day" (*domenica, domingo, dimanche,* etc.).

Already in the apostolic age Sunday was known as the Lord's Day (Rev. 1. 10), which is the usual Christian term. St Justin Martyr, writing *c.* 153, appears to be the first Christian author to call the day Sunday (*Apol. pro Christ.* 1. 67. 3).

Vasiliev's statements that Constantine "never called Sunday anything but 'the day of the sun' (*dies solis*); and the 'invincible sun' (*sol invictus*) at that period usually meant the Persian god, Mithras"—this cult was Christianity's most serious competitor—and that "it is certain that Constantine was a supporter of the cult of the sun" (49) are true, but need qualification. Probably Constantine espoused such preference from paternal example, for had not his father Constantius I Chlorus—perhaps to satisfy his soldiers, who worshipped Mithras in this Caesar and who wanted a god to go before them (cf. Ex. 32. 1, 23; Acts 7. 40) in their battles against the barbarians of the northern night—in or soon after 296 caused a gold medallion to be minted at Trèves (the Empire's northernmost capital) with the motto REDDITOR LVCIS AETERNAE (Restorer of Eternal Light)? But Constantine's constitutions aiding the Church and its clergy compensate for his attitude towards the Sun's cult: an attitude which persisted, despite his Christian conversion, until his Christian baptism upon his death-bed in 337—witness his introduction of the gold headband (*nimbus*, which in art developed into the halo or circle of radiant light around the heads of deities, sovereigns, and saints) and his ordinary official title of Lord (*Dominus*, which was associated with the Sun-god, to whom was assigned as sacred the Lord's Day or Sunday) according to Bury's note in Gibbon, 2. app. 10.

Though the conception of Sunday as a day of rest reflects the Christian reception of the Jewish Sabbath, which also was reserved for rest (Gen. 2. 2–3; Ex. 20. 8–11, 31. 12–17, 35. 1–3; Lev. 19. 30, 23. 1–3, 26. 2; Deut. 5. 12–15), yet it is curious that Constantine, despite his desire to patronize Christians, departed from the Christian practice of calling it the Lord's Day and accepted the pagan dedication of Sunday to the Sun. Perhaps his indoctrination into Christian principles was still so imperfect that Constantine conjectured that the Christians also held this holy day as sacred to the Sun. Certainly for three more years coins continued to carry the legend SOLI INVICTO (To the Unconquered Sun): evidence, if we may conclude from his coinage, that the emperor showed special devotion to this deity during those days. But see also A. Alföldi, *The Conversion of Constantine and Pagan Rome* (Oxford, 1948), 48–9, 54–9.

Certainly the present document, which is preserved in Justinian's Code (534), must have been considered by the Code's compilers to refer to the Christian Sunday, for it is inconceivable—from what we know of Justinian's theological tenets—that Justinian could have favoured any pagan faith. Even earlier than Justinian—between the promulgation of Theodosius II's Code (438) and Alaric II's Breviary (506)—the interpreters of no. 37 (issued only four months after no. 34) decided that the *dies solis* was the *dies dominicus*.

Eusebius (*VC* 4. 23) associates with this constitution Constantine's statute (not extant) commanding provincial governors to respect martyrs' days and to honour ecclesiastical feasts.

6. The emperor's son with rank of Caesar, on which see no. 28, n. 7.

35. MANDATE OF CONSTANTINE I ON MANUMISSION IN CHURCH, 321

(*CT* 4. 7. 1)

This constitution (retained in *CI* 1. 13. 2) authorizes masters to manumit their slaves in church, thus adding a fourth method to the three traditional ways of freeing slaves,[1] and bestows on clergymen an additional privilege in their performance of manumission. The directive exceeds Constantine's earlier constitution (no. 26) in that it expressly confers Roman citizenship on the ex-slaves.

Pitra prints (2. 634) a later Greek version of the statute.

Emperor Constantine Augustus to Hosius,[2] bishop.

Whoso with devout mind shall have granted deserved freedom to his slaves[3] in the Church's bosom shall appear to have given the said freedom with the same legal right as that with which Roman citizenship has been wont to be given by completed formalities; but it has pleased us that this[4] should be relaxed only for those who shall have granted it in the sight of bishops.

Moreover we concede more to clergymen, that, when they bestow freedom on their slaves, they may be said to have granted complete enjoyment of freedom not only in the sight of the Church and of religious people, but also when they have given freedom by a last decision [5] or when they have ordered it to be given by any words whatsoever, so that direct freedom may be effective from the day of the publication of the will without any witness-at-law or negotiator.

Given on 18 April, Crispus and Constantine Caesars [6] being consuls for the second time.

Interpretation: Whoever shall have had the desire to manumit in the sacrosanct Church, it is only needed that he should wish to free his slaves in the bishops'[7] presence and should know that, when their freedom has been received, these become Roman citizens; for, if clerics shall have wished to give freedom to their own slaves, even if they shall have done it outside the bishops'[7] sight or shall have freed them without writing and by words, full and complete freedom shall remain for them as Roman citizens.

1. See no. 26, n. 1.
2. See no. 15, n. 9.
3. The diminutive, which can connote contempt or compassion or smallness of size or youthfulness or fondness, is used (*servulus* for *servus*). Probably the last notion is meant, on the theory that a master would be more likely to liberate a favourite slave than any other kind.
4. The customary formality of manumission according to the traditional ways, on which see no. 26, n. 1.
5. That is, in a will, which ordinarily represents one's last judgement about one's property, as is stated in no. 36.
6. See no. 28, n. 7.
7. The word is *sacerdotes*, on which see no. 16, n. 4.

36. EDICT OF CONSTANTINE I ON LEGACIES TO THE CHURCH, 321

(*CT* 16. 2. 4)

By this constitution (repeated in *CI* 1. 2. 1) the Church receives the same privilege of accepting testamentary benefactions as some pagan corporations enjoyed.[1] It is another early reference to the Church's corporate character [2] and the first law authorizing churches to accept legacies.

The same Augustus to the people.

Each and every one should have, when departing,[3] the freedom to leave what property he has wished to the most holy and venerable council [4] of the Catholic Church.

Decisions [5] should not be void.

There is nothing which is more due to persons than that the writing of their last will, after which they no longer can will anything, should be unrestricted and that their decisions, because it does not return again, should be free.

Posted on 3 July at Rome, Crispus and Constantine Caesars [6] being consuls for the second time.

1. The jurisconsult Paulus (*flor.* 200) is quoted in *D* 34. 5. 20 thus: "Since the Senate in the times of the deified [on this word see no. 127, n. 7] Marcus [Aurelius] has permitted persons to bequeath to guilds, there is no doubt that, if a bequest has been made to a corporation which is allowed to assemble, it is owed to it; but, if a bequest should be made to one which is not allowed, it shall not be valid, unless the bequest should be made to individuals [in it], for these, not as if a guild, but as if specific persons, shall be admitted to the bequest."

See *CI* 6. 48. 1 (dated 528/9) for later and more elaborate rules on such legacies, of which those regulations affecting the Church are translated in no. 585.

2. See no. 4, n. 4.

3. The word is *decedens,* euphemistic for *moriens* (dying).

4. *Concilium* seems to be used in the local sense of an individual unit or congregation of a church, which would be recognized in law as a religious corporation, for it would have been absurd to bequeath property to an ephemeral assembly of prelates, whose corporate existence ends with the conclusion of their conference on doctrinal and disciplinary affairs.

5. About dispositions of property expressed in a will.

6. See no. 28, n. 7.

37. MANDATE OF CONSTANTINE I ON EMANCIPATION AND MANUMISSION ON SUNDAY, 321

(*CT* 2. 8. 1)

Within four months from his first recognition of Sunday as a day of rest (no. 34) Constantine found it advisable to infringe upon the legal holiday, on which there was no litigation allowed, by authorizing on Sundays emancipation of children [1] and manumission of slaves,[2] which were juristic acts and ordinarily were performed in a magistrate's presence.

Justinian preserves part of this law in *CI* 3. 12. 7.

Emperor Constantine Augustus to Helpidius.[3]

Just as it seemed most unfitting that the day of the Sun,[4] celebrated by its own veneration,[5] should be occupied with wrangling lawsuits and noxious contentions of litigants, so it is pleasant and agreeable that acts which especially are desired should be accomplished on that day.

And,[6] therefore, all should have permission of emancipating and of manumitting on the festal day and transactions[7] concerning these matters should not be prohibited.

Posted on 3 July at Cagliari, Crispus and Constantine Caesars[8] being consuls for the second time.

Interpretation: Although we have commanded that on the holy Lord's day[4] all lawsuits and reclamations[9] should cease,[10] nevertheless we not at all forbid persons to emancipate and to manumit and by a corresponding order we permit acts concerning these matters to be accomplished.

1. Emancipation of children from paternal power was usually performed before witnesses, though not necessarily before a magistrate. But at least by 502 judges exercised jurisdiction over emancipation (*CI* 8. 48. 5).
2. On manumission of slaves see nos. 26, n. 1, and 35.
3. On Helpidius see no. 34, n. 2.
4. See no. 34, n. 5.
5. See no. 34, n. 4.
6. Justinian's excerpt begins here, for *And, therefore,* substituting "However, in these [days]", where "days" refers to the fifteen paschal days (no. 220), for he joins this sentence to the single sentence of no. 238.
7. This word (*acta*) perhaps carries the accessory notion of public registration. In that case attendance at least of magisterial attendants would be necessary.
8. See no. 28, n. 7.
9. The word (*repetitiones*) is not inappropriate, for most suits concerned litigants' claims for some sort of restitution.
10. So in no. 34.

38. EDICT OF CONSTANTINE I ON MILITARY PRAYER, (?)321

(Eusebius, *VC* 4. 20)

Apparently soon after he had recognized Sunday as a day of rest (no. 34), Constantine not only conceded to Christian soldiers leisure to attend divine services on Sunday (Eusebius, *VC* 4. 18), but also commanded his pagan soldiers to convene on every Sunday in an open plain near Constantinople and there to offer to God with one accord in Latin the following prayer,[1] which he himself had prescribed [2] for all his soldiers and which they then had memorized (Eusebius, *VC* 4. 19).

Eusebius gives the prayer in Greek.

We know thee as the only God, we recognize thee as king, we invoke thee as an ally, by thee we have gained victories, through thee we are superior to our enemies, to thee we declare thanks for past benefits and we hope for future favours; we all are thy suppliants, imploring thee to preserve to us for the longest time of life, safe and victorious, our emperor Constantine and his God-beloved sons.[3]

1. See no. 11 for a similar imperial prayer.
2. It is perhaps not a matter for marvel that Constantine himself composed a prayer. Eusebius in his *Vita Constantini* claims that the emperor prayed to God for a sign—the celebrated trophy of the Cross with the inscription ΤΟΥΤΩΙ ΝΙΚΑ (popularly Latinized as IN HOC SIGNO VINCES), used by him as a military standard (1. 29–31; cf. 2. 5, 2. 7, 2. 16, 4. 21) and by him ordered to be imposed on his soldiers' shields (4. 21; cf. Lactantius, *De Mort. Pers.* 44. 5–6)—before his victory over Maxentius, the imperial usurper, at the Milvian Bridge outside Rome in 312 (1.28); prayed in his tent before his defeat of Licinius, his imperial colleague, at Adrianople in 324 (2. 12, 14); zealously prayed for the Empire's peace (4. 14); caused his image with eyes uplifted as in prayer to God to be impressed on gold coins, and his full-length portrait with eyes upraised to heaven and with hands outspread as if in prayer to be placed over the gates of palaces in certain cities (4. 15); regularly prayed with all his courtiers (4. 17); in the innermost rooms of his palace at stated times daily in solitary converse with his God knelt in suppliant petition and entreated the blessings of which he was in need (4. 22); kept the Easter vigil with prayers (4. 57); prayed in church before his baptism in 337 (4. 61–2).
3. J. Burckhardt, *The Age of Constantine the Great* (New York, 1949), 298, remarks: "Christians would be content with this formula, and the pagans who might have taken offense at such outspoken monotheism were before all else soldiers.... How significant is this so-called prayer! Emperor, army, victory—and nothing else; not a word for moral man, not a syllable for the Romans."

39. LETTER OF CONSTANTINE I ON TOLERATION OF DONATISTS, 321 or 322
(*CSEL* 26. 212–3)

This document, which exhorts the African Christians of the Caecilianist party to tolerate the Donatist recalcitrants in their midst, expresses the hope that the abandonment of rigorous measures will result in eventual resolution of the schism.

39. TOLERATION OF DONATISTS, 321 OR 322

It is of legal interest, since Constantine in effect retreats from the enforcement of his own decision which in court at Milan (no. 27) he had given against Donatus and for Caecilian. And it is also of psychological and historical interest, for its tenor shows that Constantine, weary of the Donatist conflict and yearning for Christian peace, at last renounced imperial intervention in the matter, after episcopal arbitration (no. 17), magisterial examination (no. 21), conciliar decision (nos. 18–20), imperial cognition (nos. 21, 22, 24, 27), imperial legislation [1] had failed to solve the schism.

Constantine Augustus to all the bishops throughout Africa and to the people of the Catholic Church.

You know quite well that, as faith compelled, as far as prudence prevailed, according as sincerity [2] controlled, I have attempted by all duteous services of humane administration that the peace of the most holy brotherhood,[3] whose grace the Supreme God has instilled in his servants' hearts, should be maintained steadfast through complete concord pursuant to the precepts of our law.[4]

But because the reasonableness of our effort has been unable to subdue that stubbornly clinging power of crime infused into the minds of men, though few; since protection [5] for them still favours this wickedness, that they would not permit on any account to be wrested from them that in which they rejoiced to have sinned;[6] we must consider that, while all this evil is fixed in a few, by Almighty God's mercy it may be mitigated for the people. For we ought to hope for a remedy from that source whither all good desires and deeds are referred. But, until the heavenly medicine manifests itself, our plans must be regulated to this extent, that we cultivate patience and, whatever by their insolence they try or do in pursuance of their practice of insubordination, we should tolerate all this with the strength derived from tranquillity. Let not wrong be repaid for wrong: for it is the part of a fool to take into his hands vengeance, which we ought to reserve to God,[7] particularly since our faith ought to trust that whatever shall be suffered from the madness of men of this ilk will avail before God for the grace of martyrdom. For what else in this world is it to conquer in God's name than to endure with steadfast heart the rude onslaughts of persons who harass the people of the law of peace?

But, if your Sincerity will have heeded this, you shall see speedily, through the Supreme Divinity's grace, that all those who offer themselves as banner-bearers of this most miserable strife, when their practices or customs begin to weaken, may realize that through the persuasion of a few they ought not to surrender themselves to perish in eternal death, when by the grace of penitence, after their errors have been corrected, they always could be restored to everlasting life.

Farewell, dearest brethren, with common prayer, forever, by God's command.

1. No. 163 refers to a lost law believed to have been drafted against the Donatists in 316.
2. Perhaps "simplicity" or "singlemindedness of purpose".
3. The Christian (Catholic) Church.
4. Christianity, as often in late Latin.
5. This may mean either that the Devil defends the Donatists, as a patron protects his clients, or that these schismatics secure some sort of princely protection by virtue of the fact that the emperor has not resorted to extreme measures against them. The word is *patrocinium*.
6. The clause *that . . . sinned* is not clear. Some suppose that the Donatists refused to renounce their sin of scandalizing Christendom by continuing in schism, but others believe that the Donatists defied any attempt to oust them from the churches over which they had gained control and that for the sake of comparative peace Constantine preferred to refrain from proceeding to extrude them. The resigned tone of the letter makes the latter view more acceptable.
7. Possibly by this time in his life Constantine may have had his attention attracted to the text in Rom. 12. 19, of which this expression is an echo.

40. LETTER OF CONSTANTINE I ON TRANSFER OF HERETICS' ORATORIES TO THE CHURCH, 322 or 332

(Eusebius, *VC* 3. 64-5)

Constantine in his effort for harmonious thought on Christian doctrine bans heretics from congregating even in private and orders such ecclesiastical edifices as they occupy to be surrendered to the orthodox. The tone of the document displays no toleration and reflects the previous position of the State toward the Church in the periods of persecution.

Letter of the emperor to the ungodly heretics.
Victor Constantine, Greatest, Augustus to heretics.
Know now by this legislation, Novatians, Valentinians, Marcionites, Paulianists, and whoever are called Cataphrygians,[1] and—to speak simply—all who muster heresies by private assemblies,[2] with how many lies your vanity has been entangled and that your teaching is maintained by certain venomous poisons, so that through you the

healthy are driven to disease and the living to perpetual death. Haters of truth, enemies of life, and counsellors of destruction, all things among you are opposed to the truth, consonant with shameful villainies, useful for absurdities and fictions, through which you fabricate falsehoods, afflict the guiltless, deny the light to believers. Always offending under the costume of godliness, you pollute all things, you wound with death-dealing blows the guiltless and clean consciences, you snatch—I may almost say—the very daylight from human eyes. And what need is there to speak about each one, when at all events to say anything about your evil deeds according to their due depends upon neither a brief time nor our leisure? [3] For so great and immoderate are your offences, so odious and full of every atrocity, that not an entire day suffices for description of these. Especially it is fitting from such subjects to avert one's ears and to divert one's eyes, to prevent the pure and sincere zeal of our faith from being contaminated by the narration of each one. Why, then, shall we endure further such evils? But the long endurance causes even the healthy to be defiled by—so to speak—a pestilential disease. For what reason, then, do we not excise most quickly the roots—so to speak—of so great an evil by public severity?

Therefore, since it is no longer possible to bear this plague of your utter destructiveness, by this law we order publicly that none of you may dare to assemble hereafter. Wherefore we have commanded that all your houses, in which you muster these assemblies, should be taken from you—this care going so far that not in public only, but not even in a private house or in any private places the assemblies of your superstitious senselessness should meet. And, besides, this is better: as many as cultivate the true and pure religion, enter into the Catholic Church and share in its holiness, through which you will be able also to attain to the truth. Most certainly the deceit of your distorted doctrine—I mean the cursed and pernicious discord of heretics and schismatics—should be excluded from the good fortune of our times. For it is proper to our happiness, which we enjoy with God's blessing, to lead the persons living in good hopes from all disorderly error into the straight path, from darkness into light, from vanity into truth, from death to salvation.

And that there may be the necessary power for this treatment, we have ordained—as previously said—that all the meeting-places of your superstition—I mean all the heretics' houses used for prayer, if at least it is proper to name these houses used for prayer—after these have been withdrawn incontrovertibly from you, should be surrendered to the Catholic Church apart from any delay; that the remaining places should be adjudged to the State; and that no opportunity for assembling in the future should be left for you, in order that from the present day in no place either public or private your unlawful assemblies may dare to be mustered.

Let it be proclaimed.

1. Of these five the first and the last—the Cataphrygians are better known as Montanists—were more schismatical than heretical, but sometimes it is difficult to decide when persistent schism passes into heresy.

2. The terse Greek means those who fill by their presence the religious schools which meet privately or which have systems peculiar to themselves and at variance from the generally received principles.

3. That is, to assess adequately their misdeeds demands either more time or more leisure than the emperor can afford to devote to this task.

41. MANDATE OF CONSTANTINE I ON CLERICAL IMMUNITY FROM PAGAN SACRIFICES, 323

(*CT* 16. 2. 5)

In this ordinance Constantine confirms the principle of religious toleration, proclaimed by the Edict of Milan (no. 12), by establishing penalties for pagans who compel Christian clerics to participate in pagan ceremonies.

The same Augustus to Helpidius.[1]

Since we have learned that certain ecclesiastics and all others serving the Catholic sect are compelled by persons of various religions to celebrate the sacrifices of lustrations,[2] by this ordinance we order that, if anyone shall have believed that these persons who serve the most holy law[3] ought to be forced to an alien superstition's rite,[4] he should be beaten publicly with cudgels, if his status permits; but if regard for his rank should repel such harm from him, he should undergo the condemnation of a very heavy fine, which shall be claimed for the public administration.

Given on 25 May[5] at Sirmium, Severus and Rufinus being consuls.

1. On Helpidius see no. 34, n. 2.

2. Lustral rites used to be conducted in the Republic quinquennially after the completion of the census and consisted of the sacrifice of a pig and a sheep and a bull (Suovetaurilia) in a public service of solemn purification. Although the censorship as a magistracy had been abolished in 22 B.C. and although the census was conducted thereafter at irregular intervals either by the emperor alone or

by him with a kinsman as his colleague, yet pagans continued the lustral ceremony as a religious rite and thus the lustration was carried into the Christian Empire. Since one of the objects of such sacrifices was to prevent peril to the State, the pagans, who probably were avenging themselves on the Christians by compelling their clergy to sacrifice, could construe abstention from such rites as antagonistic to the national welfare.

Custom called the period between the republican celebrations a *lustrum*, whose meaning—a five-year period—is preserved in modern languages.

3. Christianity.

4. In exempting Christians from compulsory participation in pagan ceremonies the emperor may have considered St Paul's prohibition against "eating of those things that are offered in sacrifice unto idols" (1 Cor. 8. 4). A pagan sacrifice, after the sacrificial animal's appropriate parts had been consumed upon the altar, was followed frequently by a social meal, wherein the worshippers ate "in the idol's temple" (1 Cor. 8. 10) such portions of the victim as were not reserved for the priests and their attendants (1 Cor. 9. 13) or were not sent to be "sold in the shambles" (1 Cor. 10. 25). Although earlier "the apostles and elders and brethren" (Acts 15. 23) in an encyclical epistle, emitted from Jerusalem, had commanded Christians to "abstain from meats offered to idols" (Acts 15. 29), yet later again arose the question "touching things offered unto idols" (1 Cor. 8. 1), since some Corinthian Christians considered that consumption of such food conveyed spiritual contamination to those who fed on it. The apostle carefully distinguished between eating in private houses and eating in pagan temples. The first he allowed (1 Cor. 10. 25–7), but added that Christians should abstain, if their partaking would offend over-scrupulous brethren (1 Cor. 10. 28–33). The second he forbade (1 Cor. 8. 7–13) and, having declared that the pagan deities are devils (1 Cor. 10. 20), decided that he "would not that ye should have fellowship with devils . . . . ye cannot be partakers of the Lord's table and of the table of devils" (1 Cor. 10. 20–1).

5. Editors suspect the month, which does not allow for Constantine's presence at Sirmium in this year because of the civil war between him and Licinius, his colleague in the sovereignty.

42. RESCRIPT OF LICINIUS ON PUNISHMENT OF CHRISTIANS, c. 323

(*Ante-Nicene Christian Library* [Edinburgh, 1871], 20. 2. 92)

After 320 Licinius, who shared the government of the Empire with Constantine the Great, instituted repressive measures against the Christians,[1] despite the Edict of Milan (no. 12), either to secure pagan support in the West against his colleague [2] or because he believed the Christians in the East to be partisans of Constantine.[3]

The occasion of the present document, translated from Syriac,[4] was the delation of Habib, deacon of the village of Telzeha, to Lysanias, governor of Osrhoëne [5] in Mesopotamia, on the ground that in defiance of the imperial ordinances he was ministering secretly to the Christians in the vicinity. Lysanias wrote to Licinius, the eastern emperor, about Habib's activities and asked for instructions, since the imperial command that all should sacrifice to the pagan gods contained no direction about what should be done to those who did not sacrifice. After Lysanias had received the following rescript, he presided in Edessa,[5] the provincial capital, at the trial of Habib—who surrendered himself to free his family arrested in the search for himself—and, after having interrogated him with the usual tortures reserved for martyrs, had him burned to death.[6]

Whoever it is that has been so daring as to transgress our command, our Majesty has commanded that he shall be burned with fire; and that all others who do not consent to sacrifice shall be put to death by the sword.

1. In *HE* 10. 8. 10, 14–19, and *VC* 1. 51–4, 56; 2. 1–2, 5, Eusebius describes the Licinian persecution, which featured expulsion of Christians from his palace, demotion or discharge of Christian soldiers, demolition or closing of churches, torture and imprisonment and murder of bishops, restriction of bishops to their sees, abolition of synods, confiscation of Christians' property, prohibition of both sexes from attending church together, denial of episcopal instruction to women.

2. This theory is not regarded with enthusiasm in *CAH* 12. 6. 95.

3. So Eusebius, *HE* 10. 8. 8.

4. Entitled *Martyrdom of Habib the Deacon* and translated by B. P. Pratten from a collection of documents acquired by the British Museum (1841–7) from Egypt, but apparently part of the archives of Edessa mentioned by Eusebius, *HE* 1. 13. 5.

5. Pratten has "Lysanias, the governor who was in the town of Edessa", the metropolis of Syriac-speaking Christians, but the provincial governor normally resided in the provincial capital.

Edessa has the distinction of being the first ancient city to embrace Christianity as its official religion. In its municipal archives Eusebius found in Syriac an exchange of letters between Abgar V, king of Edessa, and Jesus (*HE* 1. 13. 6–10), wherein the former asks the Saviour to heal his sickness and the latter promises to dispatch a disciple for this purpose after his ascension. To these was appended an account of how St Thaddaeus was sent to Edessa, how he cured Abgar and other Edessans, how he preached to them and converted them to Christianity (*HE* 1. 13. 11–22, 2. 1. 6–7). The correspondence—it scarcely need be said—

is considered apocryphal and the conversion of the entire city is a pious attempt to antedate the foundation of the Church of Edessa to the apostolic age.

6. The conclusion of the document sets the date of the martyrdom just before what apparently is the Battle of Adrianople, 3 July 324, two months ere Constantine became sole emperor. The date given at the beginning of the document is far too early: August 295, which the ancient author gives as the 620th year of the era of Alexander the Great and as in a consulate of Licinius and Constantine, who are known to have shared the consulate in 309, 312, 313, 315.

43. LETTER AND RESCRIPT OF CONSTANTINE I, CONSTANTINE II, AND CONSTANTIUS II ON STATUS OF ORCISTUS, 323-31

(*MAMA* 7. no. 305)

An inscription on a pillar, found (1752) on the site of Orcistus (now Alikel), a town of Phrygia in Asia Minor, exhibits on three sides four documents, of which the second and the fourth are translated: (1) the last part of a covering letter of Ablabius, a praetorian prefect, to the Orcistans; (2) a letter of Constantine to Ablabius, who is informed that the Orcistans' petition for restoration of their town to the status of a city has been granted by the emperor for economic reasons and because all the inhabitants are Christians; (3) the Orcistans' petition to the emperor and three of his four sons [1] for such restoration;[2] (4) an imperial rescript [3] releasing the Orcistans from paying to the Nacolaenses [4] money previously contributed for pagan cults.

Taken with Eusebius' report (*VC* 4. 37-9) of special honour shown to the town of Maiuma, which, renamed Constantia, was elevated to the status of a city as a reward for its profession of Christianity,[5] and to another (unnamed) town in Phoenicia for the same reason, this inscription confirms Constantine's patronage of Christians.

I

Hail, Ablabius, most dear to us.

The inhabitants of Orcistus, already now a town [6] and a city,[7] have furnished a pleasant subject for our Munificence, dearest and most agreeable Ablabius.

For to those to whom there is a desire either to found new cities [8] or to perfect ancient cities [8] or to restore decayed cities [8] this, which was petitioned, has been most acceptable. For they have asserted that in a former age's times their village [9] had flourished with a town's [6] splendour, so that it both was adorned with magistrates' annual fasces [10] and was crowded with curials and was full with a populace of citizens. For so suitable in site and in character is said to be the place, that from four directions flow together thither just as many roads, by virtue of which for all public officials this may be said to be indeed an advantageous and convenient stopping-place.[11] There are an abundant affluence of water, also their public and private baths, a forum adorned with statues [12] of old-time leading men, so crowded a populace of inhabitants that the seats, which are in the said place, easily can be filled, besides a copious number of water-powered mills from the descents of waters [13] flowing past.

And since the said place is said to abound in all these things, they have asserted that it had happened that the Nacolaenses demanded before this time that they [14] should be joined to them.[15] But this is unworthy of our times, that so suitable a place should lose the title of a city,[7] and disadvantageous to the inhabitants, that by more powerful persons'[15] plundering they should lose all their own conveniences and advantages. And to all these matters a certain crown—as it were—is added, because in the said place all are said to live as followers of the most holy religion.

And since they prayed that our Clemency should grant to them their ancient right and title of city,[7] just as the copies subjoined with prayers [16] for our annotation [17] testify, we have given a decision of this sort. For these matters, which they have incorporated into the prayer,[16] require rightly that they obtain the restoration of both name and rank.

Hence, by your Gravity's intercession, we ordain that what had been cancelled should be restored to the integrity of the ancient honour, that both they themselves and the town,[6] defended by your Diligence, may enjoy fully the desired splendour of the laws and of the name. Therefore it is just that your Sincerity speedily should fulfil toward the petitioners that which we have granted very promptly in view of the grandeur of our time.

Farewell, Ablabius, most dear and most agreeable to us.

II

Written on 30 June at Constantinople.

Emperor Caesar Constantine, Greatest, Gothicus, Victor and Triumpher, Augustus and Flavius Claudius Constantine, Alamannicus and Flavius Julius Constantius,[18] Noblest Caesars [19] to the Senate of the Orcistans' city, [7] greeting.

It has been done by our Indulgence's gift to safeguard not only the right of city [7] granted to you in honour, but also the privilege of liberty.

Accordingly the Nacolaenses' wrongdoing, enduring beyond our Indulgence's benefits, we remove by the present rescript and to your petition's entreaties [20] we grant the following: That henceforth you do not at all pay the money which for cults you previously were wont to contribute.

This, therefore, our Leniency has written explicitly to the Asian diocese's most perfect treasurer, who, having followed the form of the indulgence conceded to you, henceforth will prevent money for the aforesaid pretext from being claimed and demanded from you.

We desire you to fare well.

Bassus and Ablabius being consuls.

1. Constans, who was only three years old at the issuance of the first document, is not named.

2. Why Orcistus had lost its status as a *civitas* (on which cf. n. 7 *infra*) is unknown; but it may have been caused by a decline in prosperity or in population (on which see Isidore, *Orig.* 15. 2. 11)—certainly the emperor's letter mentions their (improved) condition as a reason why Orcistus should regain its status, and the untranslated petition, of which only the initial part remains, attracts the imperial attention to the community's advantageous situation.

3. Dated 30 June 331, it confirms the earlier grant.

4. Nacolaea, a Phrygian city presumably near Orcistus, claimed Orcistus as an appendage and taxed the Orcistans.

5. But Julian II the Apostate about forty years later reduced it to the rank of a town and made it tributary to the city of Gaza (Sozomen, *HE* 5. 3).

6. The word is *oppidum*.

7. The word is *civitas*, the basic unit of Roman provincial administration. A *civitas* was originally a sovereign state, but under the Empire came to be any autonomous municipal unit—subject, of course, to imperial legislation—and often had a considerable territory of village communities assigned to it for administration.

In *MARE* 495 is cited this document as evidence that *civitas* by this time came to be the generic name for such a municipality.

8. The word is *urbs*.

9. The word is *vicus*.

10. On fasces see no. 439, n. 3.

11. Orcistus probably was a station in the postal system.

12. Two of their bases have been found and their inscriptions have been published; see *MAMA* 1, no. 416, and 7, no. 304.

13. The phrase is *decursus aquarum*, but *decursus* by itself in the concrete sense is sufficient to denote a descending aqueduct.

14. Orcistans.

15. Nacolaenses.
16. The petition.
17. See no. 317, n. 2.
18. In the eight years' interval between the two documents Crispus, Constantine's oldest son, was murdered at his father's command (326), but Constans was now old enough to have been included among the senders.
19. See no. 28, n. 7.
20. A hendiadys.

44. LETTER OF CONSTANTINE I ON CONDEMNATION OF IDOLATRY AND ON BEHALF OF PEACE, 324

(Eusebius, *VC* 2. 48–60)

Eusebius translates from Latin into Greek what he professes to be an autograph epistle of Constantine. The earlier part of this letter gives general remarks on virtue and vice, mentions the persecutions and the persecutors' fate, and glorifies God for divine aid in battle against the emperor's foes; the latter part may be considered an edict calling for peace among the emperor's eastern subjects, whether idolaters or Christians.

Scholarly opinion is divided over the authenticity of this document.

Letter of the emperor to all the provincials.

Victor Constantine, Greatest, Augustus to the eastern provincials.

All things which are embraced by Nature's most authoritative laws provide for all persons an adequate perception both of Providence and of consideration in relation to the divine order. Nor to those, to whom their thought is led along the straight road of knowledge to that goal, is there any uncertainty that the accurate apprehension of sound reasoning and of sight itself rises through the sole influence of true virtue to the knowledge of God. Wherefore every intelligent man never could be disquieted in seeing the masses influenced by opposite preferences. For virtue's charm would be unprofitable and unnoticed, unless vice should present in opposition a life of perverted folly. Hence a crown is proffered for virtue, but the Supreme God has full power over judgement.[1]

I shall try to make acknowledgement to you all—as quite clearly as it is possible—about my hopes.

I myself was wont to hold the former emperors[2] as austere on account of the savagery of their ways. Only my father practised deeds of gentleness, invoking with wonderful reverence the Saviour God in all his actions.³ But the rest,⁴ not sound in mind, cultivated savagery rather than mildness and nurtured this unrestrainedly, perverting the true doctrine during their own times. The severity of their wickedness attached itself to them to such a degree, that, when all divine and human interests were at peace together, civil wars were rekindled by them.⁵

At this time they say that Apollo pronounced ⁶ from a certain cave and dark recess and not with human voice ⁷ that indeed the righteous persons on earth were an obstacle to his speaking the truth and that for this reason the oracles of the tripods were reckoned fallacious.⁸ Therefore his priestess, letting down her dejected tresses and spurred by frenzy, bitterly lamented the evil among men. But let us see to what kind of result these matters were brought. I now invoke ⁹ you, the Supreme God: I, being then still quite a child, heard how he, who at that time among the Roman emperors held the premier place,¹⁰ wretched, truly wretched, deceived in his soul by error, curiously inquiring from those attending him as a bodyguard, asked who then were the righteous persons on earth, and how one of the sacrificing priests, having answered, said: "Christians, doubtless." And he, having gulped the reply like some honey, unsheathed the sword,¹¹ which was devised against crimes, against blameless holiness. Straightway, therefore, he ordained ordinances—so to speak—by swordpoints bloodstained with gore ¹² and ordered his judges to stretch their natural sagacity to invention of newer punishments.

It was possible, then, it was possible to see with what great abuse of authority that gravity of godliness was exposed daily to no chance outrages by the continuance of cruelty and how modesty of character, which none of our enemies ever had outraged, became a subordinate interest of the intoxicated behaviour of irascible citizens. What kind of fire, what kind of tortures, what kind of rather refined torments were not applied indiscriminately to everybody and to every age? Then the earth truly wept; the all-encompassing universe, polluted with gore, mourned; the very day hid its face in grief at the sight.

But what are these results? In contrast to those deeds the barbarians, who received those persons then fleeing from us and guarded them in philanthropic captivity, now boast that they arranged for them not only safety but also the possession of holiness in security.¹³ And now the Roman race bears this lasting stain, which the Christians, at that time driven from the Roman world and fleeing to the barbarians, have inflicted on it.

But why is it necessary for me to mention further those lamentations and the world's common grief? Those authors of abomination now are gone, having been delivered with an infamous end to Acheron's ¹⁴ gulfs for lasting punishment.[15] Having become involved in intestinal wars, they have bequeathed neither their name nor their race. And surely this would not have befallen them, unless that impious prophecy of the Pythian's [16] oracles had had deceitful power over them.

Now I beseech you, the Supreme God: may you be merciful and kind to your eastern peoples; to all your provincials, crushed by long-lasting misfortune, may you proffer healing through me, your servant. And these things indeed I ask not unreasonably, Lord of the universe, Holy God, for by your guidance I have initiated and completed salutary measures; advancing your sign [17] before me everywhere, I have led a victorious army; and, if anywhere any need of public affairs calls, I, following your Perfection's same symbols, advance against the enemy. On account of these things, then, I have dedicated to you my soul compounded purely with love and fear, for I genuinely love your name and I revere your power, which you have exhibited by many proofs, and by it you have caused my faith to be made firmer. I hasten, then, putting my shoulders under the task, to restore for you the most holy edifice,[18] which those impure and most profane persons have outraged by the offence of demolition.

That your people should live peaceably and abide free from faction I desire on behalf of the general interest of the world and the advantage of all persons. Let the ones in error rejoicingly receive the pleasure of both peace and tranquillity like those who believe. For this pleasantness of equal association will be powerful both to correct the former and to lead them to the straight road. Let none annoy another, let each maintain whatever his soul desires, let him make full use of it. But it is necessary for persons who think rightly to believe that these alone live holily and purely, whom you yourself call to rest upon your holy laws.[19] But let them who withdraw themselves have willingly their precincts of falsehood; we have the most splendid edifice of your truth. What you have given by nature,[20] this we pray also for those, that they too may recover the gladness of heart manifestly through the common unity. For our worship is neither new nor rather recent, but you have ordained this from when we have believed the orderly arrangement of the universe had been established firmly with reverence proper to yourself. The human race, misled by all sorts of errors, has been deceived, but, you, having upheld a pure light through your Son, that evil not further should prevail, have reminded all persons about yourself.

Your acts make these things trustworthy; your might makes us guiltless and faithful. Sun and moon have their legally ordained course; the stars have no irregular circuit round the world's sphere; the seasons' changes revolve conformably with law; the earth's firm position has been framed by your word; the wind makes its motion according to ordered rule; the waters' running course advances by measure of immense flood; the sea is surrounded by firm boundaries; and, whatever is coextensive with earth and ocean, all this is devised for certain wondrous and serviceable expenditures. And unless this was effected according to your will's decision, undoubtedly so great a diversity and the great separation of authority would have destroyed all life and its affairs. For those who have fought mutually thus would have injured far more grievously the human race—and this, though not seen, they practise.[21]

But greatest gratitude must be given to you, Lord of all, Mightiest God, for by how much human nature is made known by diverse pursuits, by that much the more to those thinking more correctly and cultivating genuine virtue the divine reason's lessons are confirmed. However, whoever prevents himself from being cured [22] should not account this to another person; for the medicine, which in plain sight is exposed for all persons, is superior to other remedies.[23] Only let not anyone injure this religion, which circumstances recommend to be immaculate.

Therefore let us—all persons—enjoy the joint portion of the good given,[24] that is, the virtue of peace, by clearly excluding our conscience from everything contrary to it. However, what each one has received after he has persuaded himself, let him not injure another by this belief; what one or another has understood and has known, let him aid his neighbour by this knowledge, if possible; but, if impossible, let him stop. For it is one thing to engage voluntarily in the struggle for immortality, but it is another thing to constrain others by means of retributive punishment.

These things I say, these things I have related in greater detail than the object of my Fairness requires, because I was unwilling to conceal my belief in the truth, particularly because certain persons—as I hear—say that the usages [25] of the heathen temples and the power of darkness [26] have been removed. And this I should have recommended to all persons, if the violent insurrection of fallacious error has not been fixed unceasingly in the souls of some to the detriment of the general salvation.

1. Perhaps the obscurity of this paragraph is due both to the emperor's own tortuous Latin—if we believe Eusebius' statement (in the previous chapter) that Constantine himself concocted the epistle in his own cheirography—and to the translator's still more tortuous Greek.

2. Probably Constantine ascends no higher than Diocletian and Maximian, the first joint-Augusti of the Dominate, who launched the last major persecution of the Church.

3. Constantius I Chlorus was renowned for his *humanitas*.

4. These included Galerius, Severus, Maximin II, Licinius, Alexander, Maxentius, who reigned as Augusti at varying times between 305 (when Diocletian and Maximian abdicated) and 324 (when Constantine I became sole emperor). Add also Maximian, who returned to power late in 306 and was relieved of it in 308.

5. A reference to the internecine conflicts of 306–13 and to the resumption of persecution in 311 (Maximin) and in 320 (Licinius).

6. Apollo among other functions was the god of prophecy.

7. Literally "from a human being". Under traditional stimulation of mephitic vapours emanating from cavernous crevices of oracular shrines, the voice of the interpreter (usually a female) of the divine foreknowledge well might appear to be unhuman. But apart from tradition, what was considered to be a divine timbre of voice could be imitated.

8. At Delphi, Apollo's most famous oracle, the priestess delivered her prophecies from a tripod.

9. Perhaps in the legal sense of summoning into court as a witness.

10. Constantine must mean Diocletian, because of his characterization of him here as being the chief emperor and because Lactantius confirms the incident concerning Diocletian's inquiry about to be related (*De Mort. Pers.* 10. 1–5).

As for Constantine calling himself a child ($παῖς$) when Diocletian inaugurated the final persecution in 303: none knows when Constantine was born, since ancient authors date his birth from 275 to 279. But the age of 24 to 28 seems too high a range for him to apply $παῖς$ (or *puer*, if he wrote this letter in Latin) to himself as of 303. Recently A. H. M. Jones has suggested convincingly that Constantine was about nineteen years old then; see his "Notes on the Genuineness of the Constantinian Documents in Eusebius' Life of Constantine" in *The Journal of Ecclesiastical History*, 5 (1954) 196–7.

11. Literally "stretched out the swords".

12. The idea seems to be that the edicts were written by bloody swordpoints rather than by ordinary penpoints.

13. Constantine seems to mean that thus some Christians both escaped persecution and practised their religion in peace.

14. In the classical myth Acheron is the principal river of the five rivers in the underworld. Among late authors Acheron usually designates the whole of the nether world.

15. The last days of the anti-Christian emperors, beginning with Diocletian, form the subject of most (chapters 7–52) of Lactantius' treatise *De Mortibus Persecutorum*.

16. *Pythian* is the epithet of Apollo, worshipped as the god of prophecy at Delphi, where he slew the serpent Python.

17. This was the *labarum* (described by Eusebius, *VC* 1. 31), the Christian standard borne by Constantine's bodyguard at the Battle of the Milvian Bridge on 28 October 312 and thereafter.

18. The Church is meant.
19. Perhaps a conscious reminiscence of Rom. 2. 17.
20. Or "naturally" (κατὰ φύσιν). Perhaps Constantine was influenced by the Pauline doctrine that men "by nature" (φύσει) possess the truth of God, but have changed it into a lie (Rom. 2. 14 with 1. 25; see 11. 21 and 24 for κατὰ φύσιν).
21. The idea appears to be that pagan deities or demonic powers could cause mankind's complete ruin, if not restrained by divine power, and that, as it is, they even continue to exercise themselves in this effort.
22. The sickness is of the mind: error.
23. This sentence may mean that the sovereign cure (belief in the Christian God) is available plainly to all persons.
24. The giver may be either God or Constantine.
25. That is, the customary rites.
26. Probably reminiscent of either Luke 22. 53 or Col. 1. 13.

45. LETTER OF CONSTANTINE I ON REPAIR AND CONSTRUCTION OF CHURCHES, 324

(Eusebius, *VC* 2. 46)

This letter, given also by Socrates (*HE* 1. 9), Theodoret (*HE* 1. 15. 1–2), Gelasius (*HE* 3. 3. 1–4), Nicephorus (*HE* 8. 27), was sent to other bishops besides Eusebius, bishop of Caesarea. By it the prelates are empowered to ask from the praetorian prefect and the provincial governors, who had received instructions to co-operate with the bishops, whatever aid may be needed in the project of repairing and building Christian churches,[1] made more easily practicable by Constantine's final victory over Licinius, his brother-in-law and colleague, whose persecution of Christians in the East perhaps came from the suspicion that they desired Constantine to enjoy alone the sovereignty—which indeed he did from this year.

Victor Constantine, Greatest, Augustus to Eusebius.[2]

Because until the present time the unholy will and tyranny have persecuted the Saviour God's servants,[3] I have believed and carefully have convinced myself, best beloved brother, that the edifices[4] of all the churches either by neglect have been ruined or through fear of the imposed injustice[5] have become less than their proper worth.[6] But now, since freedom has been recovered and that dragon[7] has been chased from the administration of public affairs by the providence of the Highest [8] God and by our effort, I believe both that the Divine Power has been made manifest to all and that those who through either fear or unbelief have fallen into some errors,[9] when they have learned to know [10] the True Being,[11] will come into the true and right [12] course of life.

Therefore, with respect to either whatever churches you yourself preside over or whatever other bishops and priests or deacons you know are presiding in the several places, do you suggest that they should be concerned about the buildings [13] of the churches: either to restore or to enlarge those in existence or, wherever need demands, to construct new ones. Both you yourself and the rest through you also shall ask the necessary things from both the provincial governors and the prefectural office.[14] For to these it has been commanded to assist to the utmost with all zeal [15] your Sanctity's words.

God shall guard [16] you, beloved brother.

1. For a competent account of Constantine's activity in constructing churches consult Coleman, 56–61. Nor should be neglected his long list of donations to churches in Rome and in Italy recorded in L. R. Loomis, *The Book of the Popes* (*Liber Pontificalis*) (New York, 1916), 42–71. See also nos. 54, 59, 63, 64 as well as *ILCV* 1. 1752 and 1753, where two Latin inscriptions commemorate the emperor's generosity in such matters.

The partial inscription in *ILCV* 1. 5 (fully printed by H. Dessau, *Inscriptiones Latinae Selectae* [Berlin, 1892], 1. 705), dated 333–7 and recording Constantine's and his three surviving sons' rescriptive permission to the citizens of Hispellum in Umbria to dedicate a temple to the Flavian family, on condition that "it should not be polluted by any contagious superstition's deceits", is considered commonly a Christian inscription. But it is not included in this sylloge, though this part and the rest of the document is of legal character, because it is unlikely that the emperor in permitting a pagan shrine to be erected in his family's honour would have called at that late date Christianity a superstition and it is more likely that he meant a debased form of pagan religion rather than Christianity at all, which Pliny two centuries earlier had stigmatized as a *superstitionis istius contagio* prevalent in cities and villages and rural districts of Bithynia (*Ep.* 10. 96. 9). For an English translation of this document see A. C. Johnson, P. R. Coleman-Norton, F. C. Bourne, *Ancient Roman Statutes* (Austin, 1961), no. 306.

2. Three captions are found before the superscription: (1) Socrates: "Another letter to Eusebius"; (2) Gelasius: "Emperor Constantine's letter to Eusebius of Pamphilus about the building of the churches"; (3) Nicephorus: "The great Constantine's letters about both the building of the churches and the restoration of the Holy Books".

Obviously Nicephorus' caption serves a dual purpose. The second letter introduced by it is no. 64.

45. REPAIR AND CONSTRUCTION OF CHURCHES, 324

3. Licinius began to persecute Christians intermittently from 320, when he emerged as the professed champion of paganism.
Gelasius reads "the servants of God and our Saviour".
4. Gelasius reads "the divine houses".
5. Socrates substitutes "activity".
6. A cumbersome way to express the idea that the buildings have received less than their due attention in maintenance, because of fear of reprisals from Licinius if the Christians in his parts of the Empire should have been active in repairing the churches.
7. The word is δράκων, which is the personification of wickedness (Rev. 12. 3-17 and esp. 20. 2).
Socrates adds "Licinius the persecutor".
8. Gelasius substitutes "all-creating" for this adjective.
9. All later versions read "through either fear or unbelief or some errors have fallen" (Nicephorus omitting "some").
10. Socrates and Gelasius insert "God".
11. Nicephorus omits this word.
12. Gelasius inserts "faith and".
13. Gelasius inserts "of the construction".
14. Most commentators conclude from this phrase, which is abstract for concrete, that the clergy are directed to ignore the vicars, who in the administrative chain of command were higher than governors and lower than prefects. Thus, to take Eusebius as an example, Eusebius would deal with the governor of Palaestina Prima on the provincial level, but would avoid the vicar of the Orient on the diocesan level, and, if necessary, would treat with the prefect of the Orient, who was directly responsible to the emperor. This arrangement seems almost incredible, unless Constantine considered that the programme should be accelerated by omitting one step, since at no other time were the Romans so tenacious of forms than in the generations of their decay (see no. 54, where in a similar situation the diocesan vicar is mentioned). However, the adjective translated *prefectural* (ἐπαρχικός) can mean just as well "provincial", though, when applied to the noun here (τιάξς = *officium*, on which see no. 325, n. 6 *ad fin.*), it usually refers to the praetorian prefect's office staff. If "provincial" is preferred, the difficulty disappears, for the clergy then would call upon the provincial governor and his aides for assistance. See no. 59, n. 10 *ad fin.*
15. All later versions substitute σπουδή for προθυμία. The words are synonymous.
16. Socrates and Nicephorus have future optative.

46. EDICT OF CONSTANTINE I ON BEHALF OF CHRISTIANS, 324

(Eusebius, *VC* 2. 24-42)

The last two-thirds of this long letter is an edict issued by Constantine, after he had become sole sovereign through his victory over Licinius in 324, treating a variety of topics touching Christians, such as restitution of confiscated property, restoration of exiles and of convicts and of free persons condemned into slavery, release from municipal services, resumption of military rank, nomination of the Church as heir to kinless decedents.

The genuineness of this constitution has been questioned by some scholars, but recently A. H. M. Jones has shown convincingly that a fragmentary papyrus (*P. Lond.* 878) contains part of this edict and thus "proves beyond all reasonable doubt" this document's authenticity.[1]

Letter of Constantine, son of Constantius, emperor of the Romans: the first edict sent to those in the eastern land after the victory over the tyrants.

Victor Constantine, Greatest, Augustus to the provincials of Palestine.

Among persons thinking correctly and soundly about the Almighty has been both from the beginning and for a long time quite manifest the distinction (repelling from afar even every uncertainty), in how great difference their careful observance of the most revered worship of Christianity has differed from that among persons who both have warred upon it and wish to treat it contemptuously. But now by even more evident acts and more manifest achievements has been demonstrated both the absurdity of the uncertainty and how large is the Great God's power, since to persons honouring faithfully his most holy law and not daring to transgress any of his commandments have been bounteous blessings and excellent strength occurring with good hopes for their undertakings, but to persons having unholy opinions have been consequences and results corresponding to their choices. For who can obtain any blessing, when he neither recognizes that God is the source of blessings nor wishes to honour things fitly pertaining to him? Even events give credence to what has been said.

If, then, anyone should recur in his mind to the times stretching from the beginning to the present and should contemplate by reflection the acts ever yet performed, he would find that all persons, who first have laid justice and goodness as a foundation for their acts, also have carried to a good accomplishment their undertakings and from a kind of sweet root—so to speak—have garnered sweet fruit, but that persons, who have engaged in unjust and reckless deeds or have raged senselessly against the Almighty or have taken no righteous reasoning in regard to the human race, but have ventured on exiles, disgraces, confiscations, murders, and many such acts and neither have repented ever of this nor have turned their mind to better activities, have received equal and retributive treatments. And these results can ensue not unnaturally nor apart from reason.

For as many as venture [2] upon any actions with just judgement and have continually the fear of the Almighty in mind, maintaining a firm faith about him, and do not hold present fears and dangers worth more than their future hopes, even if they should have experienced some distresses for a time, such persons have borne not weightily what has befallen them, because they believed that greater rewards are reserved for them, but they have acquired brighter renown in proportion to the weightier sufferings which they have experienced. But as many as either have disregarded dishonourably justice or have not recognized the Almighty and have dared to subject to cruel outrages and punishments persons faithfully following this [3] and have not considered themselves to be wretched among those whom they punish because of such motives [4] and those persons to be happy and blessed who preserve their piety toward the Almighty even as far as such sufferings, such persons' many armies have been vanquished, many armies have been turned to flight, entire arrangement for their wars has ended in infamous defeat.[5]

From such causes are produced grievous wars, from such causes all-destructive devastations; hence the deficiencies of necessities for needs and the multitude of impended ills; hence the originators of such great impiety either, having borne extreme sufferings, have been cursed with an utterly destructive death or, having lived a most infamous life, have acknowledged it as more grievous than death and—so to speak—have obtained their punishments of equal proportion to their offences.[6] For each found disaster, according as anyone had proceeded by senselessness to war against the divine law,[7] so that they awaited not only the burdens in life to press upon them, but also the bitterer fear of punishment beneath the earth.[8]

And so, when such oppressive impiety had encompassed human affairs and the State was in danger of being destroyed wholly—so to speak—by some pestilential disease and needed much salutary healing, what relief for, what riddance of ills did the Divinity design? (And that, at all events, must be considered Divinity which is alone and truly God and has competent power through all time. And at all events it is not boasting for one who acknowledges the Almighty's beneficence to use elegant phrases about it.) My service he both sought and chose as suited for his will. Having begun from the sea adjacent to the remote Britons [9] and from the regions where by a certain necessity it has been ordained that the sun sets, by the Almighty's power I banished and scattered all the prevailing ills, that at the same time the human race, educated by my service, might be recalled to the observance concerning the most holy law [7] and at the same time the blessed faith might increase under the Almighty's guidance, for never may I be insensate in respect to gratitude due.[10] Having believed that this excellent service was offered to me as a special gift,[11] I advanced as far as the eastern regions, which, encompassed by rather weightier disasters, called for greater treatment from us.[12] At all events, I believed firmly that wholly I owed both my entire soul and my every breath and, in short, whatever of my thoughts most secretly is involved—all this to the Greatest God.

Therefore I know accurately that they, who have pursued rightly heavenly hope and have established this both preferably and firmly in divine places, do not need good will from men, for they enjoy higher honours proportionately as they have sundered themselves from earthly inferiorities and ills. However, I think that it becomes us to repel as far as possible the sufferings inflicted upon them for a time and the unbefitting afflictions from groundless accusations and groundless liabilities; otherwise it would be most marvellous that their soul's endurance and perseverance should be recognized adequately by those who were quite eager to persecute such men because of their service to the Divinity, but that their glory should not be exalted to a brighter and more blessed appearance by God's servant.[13]

Therefore, let all, whether any have accepted foreign residence in exchange for their native country, because they did not discard their faith in the Divinity, to which with whole hearts they had dedicated themselves, having been subjected to harsh sentences of judges after the fashion of what times all and each severally happened to be tried, or any have been registered in senatorial rolls,[14] though not filling the number of these previously [15]—let all such, having been restored both to their ancestral estates and to their accustomed tranquillity, present thank-offerings to God, the liberator of all. And if any were deprived of their properties and, terrified by the loss of all their past possessions, were passing hitherto a most sorry life, when they have been restored to their original dwellings and families and resources, may they enjoy with rejoicing the Almighty's beneficence.

Moreover we command also that as many as against their will the islands detain [16] should enjoy this consideration, in order that they, who till now have been enclosed both by the rough terrain of mountains and by the encircling sea and have been liberated from a sullen and desert solitude, may restore themselves to their nearest and dearest, thus having fulfilled their desired yearning. And who passed a life for a long time in want amid ill-omened squalor, having regarded their restitution as some sort of a windfall and having been released from anxieties hereafter, may they live with us not in fear. For to live with fear under us, who both boast and believe that we are God's servants, would be one of the most extraordinary things even to come into one's hearing, let alone also to believe; and we have been born to correct others' errors.

And also as many as have been sentenced either to work in toilsome mines or to fulfil the services relative to the public works, after they have got sweet leisure in exchange for long-lasting hardships, let them live a life lighter and in accord with their own authority forthwith, when they have put an end to the unmeasured unpleasantnesses of toils in exchange for mild relaxation. And if any should have failed in obtaining the common freedom of action and should have been unfortunate in respect to deprivation of civic rights, with befitting good cheer let them hasten to their native communities, resuming their former rank, seeing that they have been divorced from it by some lengthy residence abroad.

Moreover as to those who once have been numbered in military offices,[17] but have been deprived of these because of both a cruel and an unjust excuse that they, acknowledging the Almighty, held this knowledge more to be preferred than the rank which they had, let it be according to their wish either to remain in what precise position they were, if they are content with military services,[17] or to live in free leisure after an honourable discharge. For it should be proper and consistent for him, who has exhibited such magnanimity and courage in respect to presented perils, to enjoy, if he should wish, the choice both of retirement and of rank.

And besides also, as many as, stripped perforce of their noble birth,[18] have submitted to some such sentence of judges, so that, when thrust into either women's apartments [19] or linen-factories, they endure strange and sorry toil or are used as slaves of the treasury, since their higher birth not at all has stood to their credit, let these, rejoicing in both the honours which they formerly enjoyed and the blessings of freedom, after they have been recalled to their wonted dignities, live hereafter with every gladness.

And also the person who has gotten slavery in exchange for liberty[20] by some illegality and inhumanity and even insanity and frequently has lamented bitterly his unaccustomed menial services and has discovered himself—as it were—a sudden slave instead of a free person, after he has received his former freedom in accordance with our ordinance, let him restore himself to his parents and let him pursue the labours proper to a free person, after he has discarded from memory what improper services he had performed previously.

Nor must we pretermit the matter of the estates of which all and each severally have been despoiled by divers pretexts. But if any, having undertaken the excellent and divine contest of martyrdom with fearless and bold will, have been despoiled of their properties, or if any have become confessors [21] and have procured eternal hope for themselves, and as many as themselves were deprived of their properties by having been constrained to emigrate, because they yielded not to the persecutors by discarding the faith, or if any, not sentenced to death, have been unfortunate in respect to the spoliation of their properties, we ordain that the inheritances of these should be assigned to persons in respect to relationship. At all events, inasmuch as the laws explicitly declare the nearer persons of the next of kin, it is easy to distinguish to whom the inheritances belong and that according to rule should come into the succession these persons who precisely were more closely related, if those deceased had experienced a natural end. But if of the next of kin none of any of the aforesaid persons should survive to become an heir according to rule (I speak of either the martyrs or the confessors or the settlers in another country who for such a cause have been banished), let the church in each and every place always be appointed to receive the inheritance. This will not be at any rate grievous to the departed, even if they should obtain as heir her for whose sake they have submitted to all sufferings. And also it is necessary that the following should be added: that, if any of the aforesaid persons have presented any of their properties to whom they wished, it is reasonable that to them the ownership should remain valid.

And that in the ordinance there should not appear any misleading point, but that it should be easy for all to know what is lawful, let all know that, if they should occupy a landed property or a house or a plantation or any other thing of the aforesaid persons, it is honourable and advantageous for them both to admit it and to restore it with all speed. For, although some of them should appear especially to have reaped many profits from the unjust ownership and we do not judge the demand for the return of these to be just, nevertheless they, acknowledging both how much and whence they gathered, should beg that there should be pardon from us for this error, in order that partly by such amendment the previous covetousness may be remedied and partly the Greatest God, accepting this—so to speak—as a kind of repentance, may be well-disposed toward those who have been in error. But perhaps they who have become owners of such properties—if indeed it is proper or possible to support this title in their case—alleging as a pretext in place of an apology, will say that it was not possible to refrain from the properties at a time when the spectacle of all the sufferings was manifold: persons ejected rudely, persons slain mercilessly, persons expelled remorselessly, constant confiscations of property of persons not at all guilty, incessant persecutions, auctions of properties. If any should rely on such reasons and should continue in insatiate policies, they shall learn such a course not to be with impunity for themselves—and especially when our business in such a matter is giving service to the Supreme God. As many things, at least then, as ruin-bringing necessity in the past compelled persons to seize, to withhold these now is dangerous; especially it is necessary in every way to reduce insatiate desires by reasonings and by examples.

Nor shall the treasury be allowed to possess securely whatever of the aforesaid things it may possess, but, not daring to speak—as it were—against the holy churches, it justly shall relinquish to the churches possession of these things which for a time it unjustly retained. . . .[22] We ordain that all things, as many as properly may appear to belong to the churches, whether houses or certain fields and plantations or any other things of whatever character happen to be the piece of property, are to be restored, with no right for ownership diminished but with all things remaining unreserved.

Moreover who can doubt or cannot ordain also that the very places, which have been honoured by the martyrs' bodies and are become memorials of their glorious departure, belong to the churches, at a time when neither a gift can be better nor another labour can be more pleasing and containing much profit than to be exerting oneself concerning such matters with the Divine Spirit guiding and then to preserve again to the holy churches the justly restored things, which with worthless pretexts have been taken by unjust and very knavish men?

And since it would not pertain to a complete provision to pretermit in silence these persons, as many as indeed have purchased by right of purchase anything from the treasury or have kept it when given by a gift, having extended their insatiate desires without reason even to such things, let them know that such persons, although, especially because they have dared to purchase these things, they have tried to make our Benevolence unfavourably disposed toward them, nevertheless they shall not be unfortunate in this as far as the possible and proper condition is concerned. To such an extent, then, let these things be restored.[23]

And since it has been revealed by clearest and plainest proofs and by the Omnipotent God's excellence and also advices and aids, which he through me deems worthy to administer many times, that the vexation formerly engaging all human affairs has now been removed from all the earth under the sun,[24] do you, both one and all together, with earnest thoughts observe how great has become that power and how great that grace, which both have destroyed and have annihilated the seed—so to speak—of most knavish and most rascally persons, extend to all lands ungrudgingly the re-established joy of good persons and again give complete authority both to honour, as is reasonable, the divine law [7] itself with all reverence and to reverence, as is proper, the persons who have dedicated themselves to it. They,[25] as if having ascended from some dark depth and having acquired a clarified knowledge of events, henceforth shall display both befitting attention to it and honour harmonious with it.

Let it be promulgated in our eastern regions.[26]

1. "Notes on the Genuineness of the Constantinian Documents in Eusebius' Life of Constantine" in *The Journal of Ecclesiastical History*, 5 (1954) 197-200. T. C. Skeat gives "a revised text of the papyrus, collated with that of Eusebius, together with notes on the palaeography and restoration of the text" on pp. 198-9. Cf. *infra* n. 26. The fragment represents *VC* 2. 26 *ad init.*—29 *ad init.*

2. The papyrus starts with part of this verb, which in Greek appears midway in the English version's first prepositional phrase, which itself is preceded in Greek by the English translation's second prepositional phrase.

3. Probably is meant a course of just action coupled with acknowledgement of God's supremacy expressed in their action and worship.

4. The idea seems to be that oppressors, who think that they are making other persons miserable by persecuting them, fail to realize that they make themselves miserable eventually.

5. An allusion to Constantine's conquest of the forces of Licinius, who is represented here as anti-Christian (as indeed he was).

6. This statement Lactantius supports in his treatise *De Mortibus Persecutorum*, which recounts the frightful fate of the principal persecutors of the Christians.

7. Christianity.

8. That is, in the future life, which in later classical mythology was passed underground in Hades, divided into departments of beautitude (Elysium) and chastisement (Tartarus).

9. Constantine was in Britain in 306, when he was appointed Caesar at his father's death. Acclaimed as Augustus in 307 and in 308, Constantine administered the West until 324, when he became sole sovereign.

For the Britons' remoteness from the Romans cf. e.g. the references in Catullus (*Carm.* 11. 11-12; 29. 4, 12), Horace (*Carm.* 1. 35. 29-30; 4. 14. 47-8), Vergil (*Ecl.* 1. 66), of which the last—happily turned by Tennyson in his ode *To Virgil* (9. 3-4)—is perhaps the best known. See no. 52, n. 47.

10. Probably Constantine means gratitude due to God for his guidance.

11. The papyrus ends with this word, though *having* ... *that* and *to me* follow *was offered as a special gift* in Greek.

12. Licinius, who governed in the East, favoured Christianity far less than Constantine. About 320 his indifference ripened into persecution, which was ended by his rival's victory.

13. The contrast is between Licinius the persecutor and Constantine the believer.

46. ON BEHALF OF CHRISTIANS, 324

14. Of the municipal senates in the province.

15. That is, having been exempted in the past from such service.

16. Insular exile dates from the principate of Augustus (27 B.C.–A.D. 14), who banished a grandson, Agrippa Postumus, to Planasia (now Pianosa) between Italy and Corsica, and Julia, his only legitimate child, to Pandataria (now Ventotene) off the Campanian coast.

The first noted Christian to endure exile on an island was St John the Divine, who traditionally under Domitian was relegated to Patmos, one of the Aegean Sporades (Rev. 1. 9). See no. 330, n. 9.

17. Although the Greek is στρατιωτικαὶ ἀξίαι ... τὰ στρατιωτικά, perhaps the phrases should be translated "governmental service", on which see no. 186, n.4.

18. That is, probably, the privileges consequent upon their nobility.

19. To perform tasks traditionally imposed upon females in a household, where normally women's and men's suites were separate—at any rate in Asia, whither this edict was directed.

20. Constantine refers to a freeman of lower birth than those just mentioned, one who laboured for a living but who thereby had not subjected himself into servitude.

21. *Confessor* in Christian terminology has three meanings: (1) the earliest signifies a person whose public confession of faith in periods of persecution is punished by imprisonment or torture or exile or work in the mines, but whose witness has not led to his martyrdom or death for the faith; (2) about a generation after this edict's date "confessor" is a title to designate a person of outstanding virtue and knowledge exemplified by his life and writings and preachings to such a degree that he has become an object of veneration; (3) in modern times a "confessor" is one who distinguishes himself by such heroic virtue that it has worked miracles recognized by ecclesiastical authorities, who thereupon adjudge him worthy of veneration by the faithful.

22. A lacuna is in the Greek text.

23. It is not certain that Constantine by this sentence does not mean "So far, then, my decision on this matter goes".

24. A reference to the removal of Licinius.

25. It is unclear whether are meant the clergy or all subjects.

26. This seems to be Constantine's authorizing subscription, to which Eusebius refers at the end of chapter 23, before he quotes the letter, in these words: "It [the document] has been taken from the authentic imperial law, kept in our possession, to which the inscribed signature of his right hand marks distinctly the proof of the credence of my words by—so to speak—a sort of seal". (Eusebius uses the letter as evidence for some earlier statements.)

There is nothing improbable in Eusebius' claim to have a copy (whether certified or not is immaterial) of this document, for we have evidence that for years he was a trusted consultant to Constantine.

47. LETTER OF CONSTANTINE I ON THE ARIAN CONTROVERSY, 324

(Eusebius, *VC* 2. 64–72)

This letter, by which the emperor seeks to reconcile Arius, the heresiarchic priest, and Alexander, the patriarch of Alexandria, to whom Arius owed canonical obedience, is presented only in part by Socrates (*HE* 1. 7), Gelasius (*HE* 2. 4. 1–13), Nicephorus (*HE* 8. 13), but is quoted entirely by Eusebius, whose text, being earlier and more complete, is translated. Cassiodorus (*HE* 1. 19) translates the Socratic excerpt into Latin.

Arianism—"the price paid for the early and fruitful alliance of Christianity with Greek philosophy" principally in Alexandrian dialectics, where it appeared as another ancient apple of discord—took its name from Arius, who so advertised the Antiochene doctrine of the relation of the Father and the Son, that what had started as "an academic controversy was carried into the streets", an ecclesiastical "dissension became a political, a national, one might almost say a racial, issue", because in general the Greek East favoured Arius and the Latin West fought Arianism.[1]

Though the epistle is quite hortatory in its endeavour to compose this religious controversy, which rapidly was eviscerating eastern Christendom and would divide presently the Roman world for two generations and would require two general councils [2] before its settlement, yet the letter can be considered as of some legal importance. It is true that it threatens little and that it prescribes no penalties, but it also is true that its chief concern is the pacific condition of Christendom, which is what Constantine's government unceasingly sought to attain and, as the event showed, despite the emperor's personal efforts and the earnest labours of bishops, failed to achieve. This letter, revealing the political purpose of his religious policy, is a statesmanlike document in its character of rising superior to dogmatic interests, which perhaps the emperor did not understand or of which it was to the purpose of some of his advisers that he should have imperfect knowledge. But Constantine could not be kept long indifferent to this important question, for, after he had found that this epistolary effort was futile, he convoked the First Ecumenical Council of the Christian Church to assemble at Nicaea in 325, when and where he saw to it that "the faith once delivered unto the saints" [3] was defined.

Victor Constantine, Greatest, Augustus to Alexander and Arius.[4]

That I had a twofold purpose for these things for the execution of which I undertook the duty, I make a witness God himself, as is reasonable, the helper of my undertakings and the saviour of all. For I have been eager, first, to unify the mental disposition of all peoples concerning the Deity into a single structure of a settled state and, second, to restore and to unite the body of the whole world, which had suffered like as if with some painful wound.[5] And taking provision for these objects, I was calculating the one with the secret eye of thought and I was endeavouring to correct the other by the power of military force,[6] knowing that, if I should establish according to my prayers a mental concord common to all God's servants, the intercourse of public affairs also would reap the change corresponding with the pious dispositions of all. For, to be sure, when an unbearable madness had seized all Africa through those who had dared to split by ill-advised folly the people's religion into diverse factions,[7] I, having desired to repress this disease, found no other remedy sufficient for the situation than if, after having removed the world's common enemy,[8] who had set his unlawful [9] decision against your holy synods,[10] I should send some of you as helpers for the concord of the persons differing in opinion one with another.[7]

For, since the power of light and the law of sacred worship, produced by the Almighty's benevolence—as it were—from the East's bosom,[11] have flashed with holy illumination upon the whole world at once, I, reasonably believing that you would take the initiative as leaders of the salvation of the nations, tried at the same time to seek for you with the approval of my spirit and with the activity of my eyes.[12] At all events, together with the great victory and the veritable triumph over enemies,[13] I chose first to inquire into this, which I considered to be primary and most important of all things for me.[14]

But, Fairest and Divine Providence, what a vital wound assailed my ears,[15] rather my very heart, namely, the indication that among you is a dissension far more grievous than those which continued there,[16] so that the factions among you, from whom I had hoped there would start the cure for the others,[7] are in need of a greater remedy! And yet, by me, when I consider the origin and the basis of these matters, the cause was observed as quite worthless and not at all worthy of such contentiousness.[17] Wherefore, since I have been urged to the necessity of this letter and since I am writing to your united Sagacities and since I have invoked Divine Providence as a helper in the matter, I suitably introduce myself as a sort of minister of peace in the midst of your controversy with each other. And the very fact that, with the Almighty aiding, if the occasion of the dissension were even greater, I might have been able with no difficulty, by entrusting my plea to the hearers' pious judgements, to change each one for the better, how shall this not promise me an easier and a far speedier settlement of the matter, when the occasion, which stands in the way of complete concord, is paltry and quite insignificant?[18]

I perceive, then,[19] that the foundation of the present dispute has arisen thence. For,[20] when you,[21] Alexander, asked [22] of the priests whatever each of them understood [23] about a certain passage of the things [24] written in the law [25] or rather about an inconsequential [26] part of some question,[27] you, Arius, improvidently opposed [28] this opinion, which it was proper [29] to have been conceived never at all or, if conceived, to have surrendered to silence. And from it,[30] when the dissension between you had been awakened, the synod was rejected [31] and the most holy laity, split into two sides, was separated from the harmony of the common body. Accordingly let each of you, exhibiting equally forbearance,[32] receive [33] whatever your fellow-servant [34] justly advises.[35] But what is this?[36] It was proper neither to ask about such affairs in the beginning [37] nor to answer that which is asked. For such questions, as many as [38] the compulsion of any law does not prescribe but the quarrelling of an unprofitable leisure advances,[39] although they may be for the purpose of some philosophical [40] exercise, nevertheless we ought to enclose [41] within our thought and not rashly to produce into popular meetings nor inconsiderately to entrust to the peoples' ears.[42] For how many individuals are there either to understand precisely or to interpret duly the meaning of matters so important and very difficult?[43] And, although someone should be considered [44] to do this easily,[45] how great a part of the people doubtless [46] will he persuade? Or who in the niceties of such inquiries [47] could emerge beyond the danger of [48] error? Surely then, one must be able to check [49] loquacity in such matters, lest, either if we ourselves have been able because of the weakness [50] of nature to interpret the matter proposed for examination or if the [51] hearers because of rather sluggish comprehension [52] have been incapable of advancing to an accurate apprehension of what has been said,[53] from either of these the populace should turn to the necessity either of blasphemy or of schism.[54]

Wherefore let both the unguarded query [55] and the unpremeditated reply [55] repay equal forbearance on each side by each other. For neither the cause of the contention [56] in your case has been dependent [57] on a chief point of the commands [58] in the law [25] nor any new heresy about God's religion has been introduced among you,[24] but you have one and the same reasoning, so that you are able to unite in respect to the symbol of communion.[59] For, when you are disputing with each other about petty and very infinitesimal matters, it is believed to be neither seemly nor at all allowable by the laws of God and of men for so many of God's people, for whom it is proper to be guided by your hands,[60] to differ in opinion.[61] That I may remind your Wisdoms by a little example:[62] you know, of course,[24] the philosophers themselves—that they all are agreed on one belief, but often,[63] whenever [47] they disagree in some part of their assertions,[58] even if they differ because of the quality of their knowledge, yet by the unity of their belief [64] again achieve unity with one another.[65] If this is so, how is it

47. THE ARIAN CONTROVERSY, 324

not [63] far more observant of duty for us,[66] the ordained [63] ministers of the Great God, to be of the same mind one with another in such [63] a profession of religion? But [67] let us investigate with greater reasoning and [68] with more wisdom what has been said,[69] if it is indeed right for brethren to oppose brethren [70] because of trifling and foolish contentions of words among you [24] and for the dignity of the synod to be split by profane discord through us,[71] who are contentious with one another about matters so small and not at all essential. These things are vulgar and appropriate to puerile ignorance [72] rather than suitable to the understanding of priests and of sensible men.

Let us willingly keep aloof from diabolical temptations. Our Great God, the Saviour of all,[73] extended the light common to all. And by his providence do you grant to me, the Almighty's [74] servant, to bring this effort to an end, that I may restore [75] his people themselves [63] to the [76] fellowship of the synod by my exhortation and service and interposition of admonition.[77] For, since, as I said, in us [66] is only one faith and one understanding about our [78] religion and since the command of the law [25] in its two [79] parts unites everything into a single spirit of statement,[80] this,[81] which indeed has aroused a slight [82] contention between you with each other,[83] especially since it involves not the validity of the whole law,[25] should not at all produce in you any division and dissent. And these things I say, not for the purpose of compelling you to agree entirely on an exceedingly simple [84] question, of whatever character that is. For the dignity of the synod can be preserved unimpairedly for [85] you and the one [86] and the same communion for all can be maintained, even if there should be between you [56] with each other any particularly partial disagreement on a very slight matter, since neither in all affairs we all desire the same thing nor in us [87] governs any one nature or judgement.[88] Therefore concerning Divine Providence let there be in you one belief, one understanding, one agreement respecting the Almighty;[89] but what concerning these very [63] insignificant inquiries you ponder [90] accurately [63] with each other, even if you agree [90] not on a single opinion,[91] it is proper to repose, guarded by the secrecy of thought, within one's reasoning power. However, let the [92] special privilege [93] of common friendship and the faith in the truth and the honour toward God and toward the law's [25] religion [94] remain unmoved among you; return, then, to friendship and good will toward each other, restore to all the laity their [95] familiar [63] embraces, and do you yourselves, just as if having cleansed your own souls, again recognize each other. For frequently friendship [55] becomes sweeter, when after the removal [96] of enmity [55] it [55] again has returned [97] to reconciliation.[98]

Restore, then, to me serene days and nights free from care, that to me also may be preserved henceforth a certain enjoyment of pure light and gladness of tranquil life; but if not, it is necessary for me to lament and wholly to be confounded with tears and not even to sustain peacefully the period of life. For, while God's people—of my fellow-servants I speak—have been divided among one another by [99] so unrighteous and injurious contention, how is it possible for me to be secure in mind for the future? That you may perceive the excess of grief on this matter,[100] listen.[101]. After I had halted lately in the Nicomedians' city,[102] I forthwith was intending to proceed to the East. For me, while hastening toward you and being more than half-way toward you,[103] the announcement of this matter turned the plan into reverse,[104] lest I should be forced to see with my eyes what I thought was impossible to perceive beforehand [105] with my ears. Open, then,[106] henceforth by the harmony between you the road to the East, which by the contentions [58] between each other you have obstructed,[107] and allow me rather [63] soon to see both you and all the other peoples rejoicing together and to express to the Almighty [89] by laudatory evidence of words due thanks for the general unity and the liberty of all.

1. So H. Grégoire in N. H. Baynes and H. St. L. B. Moss, eds., *Byzantium* (London, 1948), 90-1.

2. Nicaea in 325 and Constantinople in 381.

3. Jude 3.

4. For a caption Gelasius has "Emperor Constantine's letter, transmitted through Hosius, bishop of Córdoba, to Alexander and Arius"; Nicephorus has "The God-beloved emperor's letter, sent to Alexander and Arius".

In the superscription Cassiodorus substitutes "Pious" for *Augustus*.

5. The first object perhaps refers to the well-known desire of despots to channelize their subjects' thoughts—here, however, ostensibly from a pious motive. The second object probably looks to Constantine's successful effort to end the destructive dissension, which had ill effects upon the body politic, between him and Licinius.

6. Literally "hand".

7. Probably the Donatist controversy in Africa is meant (cf. *infra* nn. 14 and 16 and see nos. 17 and 39).

8. His former colleague, Licinius, whom Constantine conquered in this year.

9. That is, from Constantine's point of view, at least after he and Licinius had issued the Edict of Milan (no. 12), which legally sanctioned Christianity.

10. Eusebius earlier in this biography of Constantine mentions this prohibition of Christian synods (1. 51).

11. A reference to Christianity's origin in Palestine.

12. This figurative language seems to mean that the emperor employed mental and physical means (thinking and looking) to enlist eastern aid in his efforts to settle the Donatist schism.

47. THE ARIAN CONTROVERSY, 324   119

13. Again a reference to Constantine's defeat of Licinius in 324.

14. The emperor means that, having ended once and for all the Licinian opposition, he was ready to deal more effectively with the Donatists; but he seems not to have sent eastern bishops to Carthage—a procedure of which he was thinking at the end of the previous paragraph.

15. Literally "hearing" (abstract for concrete).

16. Among the Donatists, chiefly centred around Carthage in Africa (cf. *supra* nn. 7 and 14).

17. This is the first indication that Constantine either has misunderstood the dangerous errors of Arianism or has been misinformed purposely by Arian sympathizers among his Christian advisers. Probably the latter view is the better, though nowhere in this or in other letters the emperor gives evidence of a fine grasp of doctrinal niceties—probably because he had weightier matters with which to deal, because he seems to have relied much upon his theological advisers' explanations, which were not always orthodox, and because he was too ignorant of the things of the spirit. Nor must be excluded the possible explanation that Constantine, considering Arius as a priest and Alexander as his bishop, with an authoritarian attitude saw in Arius' conduct simply a subordinate's action subversive of his superior's authority.

18. After this paragraph begins the part preserved by the later historians.

19. Omitted by Socrates, Gelasius, Nicephorus.

20. Cassiodorus to this point reads "I have learned, then, that the origin of the present question was born".

21. Gelasius inserts "father".

22. Nicephorus inserts "to learn".

23. Socrates omits this word, for which Gelasius and Nicephorus each use a different synonym and in the present tense.

24. Cassiodorus omits the prepositional phrase.

25. Constantine seems to use this word (νόμος) in the sense of the collected Sacred Scriptures, whence Christians draw their law.

The *locus* probably is Prov. 8. 22ff.

26. This, of course, is Constantine's opinion or, at least, that of his advisers, of whom some showed sympathy with Arianism at that time.

27. Socrates and Nicephorus insert "you inquire" and Gelasius has "it is inquired"—an unneeded predicate for this part of the sentence. Cassiodorus reads "a part of some inconsequential question".

28. Socrates and Nicephorus substitute "inserted".

29. Gelasius substitutes "it was necessary" and Cassiodorus substitutes "it had been bound"; both read *it was proper* after *if conceived*.

30. Nicephorus omits the first three words.

31. A synod at Alexandria in 321 condemned Arianism and excommunicated Arius and his adherents. The refusal or the denial, which is the nominal notion of the verb, then probably refers to the Arians' rejection of the synodal rulings and to their persistence in their heretical position.

For *the synod was rejected* Cassiodorus unaccountably substitutes "the mysteries are contemned"—which was equally true. The rest of the sentence he reads independently thus: "But the holy laity has been divided into two sides; the common body's harmony is separated".

32. All later historians substitute "judgement" for this word.
33. Nicephorus turns *let receive* into the second person; Cassiodorus reads "let obey" for the verb.
34. Probably Constantine himself.
35. Gelasius and Cassiodorus add "you".
36. Cassiodorus omits the sentence.
37. Cassiodorus substitutes "accordingly" for the phrase.
38. Gelasius begins "For all such questions".
39. Cassiodorus has "For questions of this sort, which are not proposed by any law's compulsion, require time of unprofitable leisure".
40. All later historians read "natural" for this word.
41. Since Cassiodorus starts a new clause with *and although* at figure 39 in text, he supplies an object "these" here.
42. All later authors have "the ears of all persons".
43. Gelasius omits the next two sentences.
44. Cassiodorus alters to "able".
45. Cassiodorus substitutes "though difficult".
46. All later authors omit the adverb.
47. Nicephorus omits the word.
48. Cassiodorus inserts "his".
49. Gelasius reads "avoid".
50. Socrates and Nicephorus incorrectly make this word a nominative.
51. The later Greek historians insert "instructed".
52. The later Greek authors incorrectly convert this word into a nominative.
53. The later Greek versions insert "again".
54. This sentence Cassiodorus changes thus: "Therefore loquacities in such matters must be avoided, lest perchance, while what is proposed is not at all explained because of our nature's weakness, since the mind of learning hearers is not able because of rather sluggish intellect to attain complete perception of the question, the people should be led to the necessity of blasphemy or of schism".

Gelasius omits the next two sentences and most of the third.

55. Plural in Cassiodorus.
56. Socrates and Nicephorus omit the phrase.
57. Cassiodorus reads "inflamed".
58. Singular in Cassiodorus.
59. For the last clause Socrates and Nicephorus read "just as the symbol of communion"; Cassiodorus has "just as also one symbol of communion".
60. Socrates and Nicephorus substitute "wits".
61. Cassiodorus for the conclusion of the sentence substitutes "it is neither

seemly nor believed to be at all allowable by God's law for so many of God's people, for whom it is proper to be guided by your prayers and prudence, to differ in opinion."

62. Socrates and Nicephorus insert "I shall speak".
63. Cassiodorus omits this word.
64. Socrates, Cassiodorus, Nicephorus substitute "body".
65. This is a naïve belief, unless Constantine, writing in a Pickwickian sense, regards the essential unity of all philosophers as resident in their search for truth through separate roads.
66. Eusebius has *us*, but the unanimous later reading of "you" has its merits. Sometimes, it is true, Constantine associates himself with his correspondents.
67. Cassiodorus has "Accordingly".
68. All later authors insert "let us ponder".
69. Cassiodorus omits the clause.
70. Gelasius inserts "and children [to oppose] fathers".
71. Cf. *supra* n. 66. But here Socrates is wrong in reading "you", for he retains in the clause's verb the first person. Cassiodorus and Nicephorus alter the verb to the second person. Gelasius also shows "you", but omits the relative clause and the subsequent sentence. Cassiodorus converts the relative into a temporal clause.
72. Nicephorus substitutes "thoughts".
73. Nicephorus reads "The Great God and Saviour of us all".
74. Cassiodorus substitutes "God's".
75. Socrates, Gelasius, Cassiodorus insert "you", while Nicephorus reads "through you".
76. Gelasius inserts "holy".
77. Gelasius omits the three following sentences.
78. Socrates and Cassiodorus have "your".
79. The later writers omit the numeral, which refers to the Old and the New Testaments. Cf. *supra* n. 25.
80. Literally "a single statement of spirit". Cassiodorus for *unites ... statement* has "tends to the statement of a single spirit".
81. Cassiodorus inserts "therefore".
82. The later authors omit the adjective.
83. Cassiodorus turns the phrase into "amid other matters".
84. Cassiodorus conceives the adjective in its good sense and translates εὐήθης by *optimus* (excellent).
85. Cassiodorus reads "by".
86. Socrates and Nicephorus omit the connective and the numeral.
87. Nicephorus substitutes "you".
88. Cassiodorus reads "or one judgement is perceived".
89. "God" in Cassiodorus.
90. Cassiodorus alters this verb into the third person plural passive.
91. Cassiodorus inserts "yet".

92. Socrates and Nicephorus insert "secret and".
93. Cassiodorus has "bond".
94. Gelasius makes this word one of the subjects.
95. Cassiodorus substitutes "your".
96. Socrates and Cassiodorus agree in reading "cause" (though plural in the latter), since the shift from ἀπόθεσις to ὑπόθεσις is short.
97. Imperative in Socrates.
98. For the thought cf. Terence, *And.* 555.
99. Cassiodorus inserts "your" and for the following question reads "now it is the time to be united".
100. Cassiodorus associates the phrase with *grief*, which produces "such grief of mine".
101. All later writers insert the imperative.
102. Nicomedia in Bithynia at this time (before the transformation of Byzantium into Constantinople in 330) was in a sense the capital of the eastern part of the Empire.
103. Literally "being with you by the greater ["greatest" in Cassiodorus] part".
104. Cassiodorus reads "I was restrained by the announcement of this matter".
105. The later Greek writers read "to tolerate"; Cassiodorus has "to come to my ears' understanding".
106. Cassiodorus inserts "for me".
107. Gelasius adds "for me".

48. LETTERS OF CONSTANTINE I ON CONVOCATION OF THE NICENE COUNCIL, 324-5

(*PO* 23. 204-5; B. H. Cowper, *Syriac Miscellanies* [London, 1861], 1-2, 5-6; *PO* 7. 546-7)

After the defeat of Licinius in 324 had secured Constantine in the sole sovereignty of the Empire, the emperor considered another attempt at unity—this time of the Church, which was divided over the date for the celebration of Easter and was distracted by the Arian debate. To effect ecclesiastical concord, which thus would attest the close alliance of Church and State, Constantine, who, though not even a baptized Christian,[1] yet believed himself to be a God-appointed bishop of the Church in its relations with the world (Eusebius, *VC* 4. 24; cf. 1. 44), concluded that he should convoke at Nicaea in Bithynia a universal council of bishops, over whom he would preside and whose decision he could enforce by law. The convocation of this council appears to be the first attempt to have both Church and State convene in serene conference.

48. CONVOCATION OF THE NICENE COUNCIL, 324-5

While from various sources we know that Constantine convoked the First General Council of the Church by an epistle, the document seems to have survived only in Syriac and Arabic versions, which obviously were made from Greek instead of Latin, no matter in what language the original summons was composed.[2]

A Syriac version, translated by F. Nau into French (*PO* 23) and demanding the date 324 is translated into English first (I). This is followed by Cowper's English version of a Syriac translation (II), of which exist two versions: one from a manuscript in Paris *c*. 795 and one from a manuscript in London *c*. 501. The latter has been chosen on the grounds that it is earlier and that there is no significant difference between the two versions (but important variations will be noted), but some of the mechanical features of his translation have been changed to conform with more modern canons of style. An Arabic version, translated by A. A. Vasiliev into French (*PO* 7), is fairly close to Cowper's translations from Syriac and is Anglicized here (III).

In English the latest study of the Council of Nicaea appears to be A. E. Burn's *The Council of Nicaea* (London, 1925), an excellent account, but it should be supplemented by the chapter on the same subject in A. H. M. Jones' *Constantine and the Conversion of Europe* (New York, 1949), 152-71.

I

The pious priests,[3] victorious, to all the Church, which is under the skies, with (the priests) [4] submissive and not submissive, greeting in Christ, our emperor.

Do you all raise yourselves with alacrity and diligence to come to a council in the country of Bithynia, in the city of Nicaea, with a view to examine the true faith. Let those who are united among you, as those who are not united, then be not hindered from coming and let none bring his companion by force and let him not hinder him from riding to the council and from defending himself on the profession of faith in the council from all the bishops, in order that there may occur a single accord and bond and a single union without distinction, so that, by the faith without division, all the Church may subsist in a single body of perfect will (comprising)[4] the priesthood and the Empire.

We have given you also a time which will suffice for traversing the road (namely):[4] a year and two months.[5]

Let all the bishops meet on 1 October [6] at Nicaea, a city of Bithynia, which is in the vicinity of our loyal court.[7]

Farewell in our Lord.

II

Epistle of Constantine, the king,[8] summoning the bishops from Ancyra [9] to Nicaea.[10]

That there is nothing more honourable in my sight than the fear of God is, I believe, manifest to every man.

Now, because the synod of bishops at Ancyra [9] of Galatia consented formerly that it should be, it has seemed to us [11] on many accounts that it would be well for a synod to assemble at Nicaea, a city of Bithynia, both because of the bishops who from Italy and the rest of the countries of Europe are coming and because of the excellent temperature of the air [12] and because I shall be present as a spectator and participator of those things which are done.[13]

Wherefore I signify to you, my beloved brethren, that [14] all of you promptly assemble at the city which was named, that is, at Nicaea. Let every one of you, therefore, regarding that which is best, as I before said, be diligent, without delay in anything,[15] speedily to come, that he may be in his own person present as a spectator of those things which are done by the same.[16]

God keep you, my beloved brethren.[17]

III

From the Emperor Constantine to the bishops and to the monks who shall receive our present message, greeting.

You already know that I have expressed in an absolute manner that I have nothing more in my heart and that there is nothing more beautiful to my eyes than the fear of God and the veneration which is due to him, with which one approaches God.

The first synod already has met at Ancyra,[9] a city of Galatia. Now we have judged it good to convoke another synod in the city of Nicaea for several reasons: the first is the convenient situation (of that city) [4] for the bishops of Antioch and of the other cities;[18] the second, the uniformity and the sweetness of the climate;[12] the third, that I shall find myself in the vicinity of the synod and that I shall assist at the sessions which will take place there.[19]

Wherefore I make known to you, my brethren, and I order you to prepare yourselves and to decide to dispatch yourselves to the aforesaid city of Nicaea, that each of you should reflect upon my order and should consider it as his duty; decide to come quickly, without slowness and without negligence. Let each of you assist at the Council of Nicaea, as we have said.

May God guard you and may his grace be accomplished upon us. Farewell.

1. For his delay of this sacrament see Jones, op. cit., 239–47.
2. So Cowper, op. cit., 100, at least for his translated versions.

It is interesting to note that those advocates of papal privileges who assert that only the pope can call an ecumenical council reject conveniently the explicit Eusebian reference (*VC* 3. 6) that the emperor convoked an ecumenical synod by respectful epistles summoning bishops to hasten from every place and attack this document's authenticity, for which Cowper, loc. cit., advances a dozen convincing arguments. See also the same Cowper's earlier *Analecta Nicaena* (London, 1857), 1 (where he gives the Syriac text), 21 (where he translates it), 29 (where he comments on it).

More recently F. Dvornik, a Roman Catholic ecclesiastical historian, in his monograph "The Authority of the State in the Oecumenical Councils" in *The Christian East*, 14 (1933) 95-108, demonstrates the analogy between the Roman Senate and general councils in respect to imperial convocation, payment of expenses, transportation of members, presidency (emperors personally or their deputies), precedence (seating arrangements), procedure (voting and acclamation), confirmation of legislation (104-6), and decides that the institution of such synods coincided with the Christianization of the Empire, since in the fourth century "the very genius of the new religion forbade that the affairs of that religion should be submitted to the members of the Senate, the majority of whom were pagan" (104). Add now the same author's later article, "Emperors, Popes, and General Councils" in *Dumbarton Oaks Papers*, 6 (1951) 1-23.

And most recently V. C. de Clercq, a Roman Catholic religious, printing under ecclesiastical approbation his thesis, *Ossius of Cordova* (Washington, 1954), says: "It is now generally agreed that the first Ecumenical Council of Nicaea was formally convened by the emperor, Constantine, and by him alone" (211; see his nn. 11-14 thereon).

3. In his apparatus Nau emends this to "emperors", which looks backward to 324, when Constantine and Licinius were ruling jointly.

4. Parenthesized in French.

5. Another indication (cf. *supra* n. 3) that this letter supposedly was written in 324.

6. The accepted date for the opening of the synod's sessions is 20 May, though variant dates are reported in ancient documents. The council seems to have been concluded on 25 August.

7. Nau renders the received reading as *empire* in French and then after it inserts (*cour*), thus indicating by this parenthetical insertion that "empire" should be understood in the sense of *court*.

8. Probably βασιλεύς in Greek, regularly applied to the emperor; but see Vasiliev, 199, and esp. n. 23 thereon.

9. From these versions it appears that the fathers should assemble in Asia Minor at Ancyra (later Angora, now Ankara [the Turkish capital], where in 1555 was found the famous *Monumentum Ancyranum* [containing the *Res Gestae Divi Augusti*], which Mommsen called "the Queen of Inscriptions"]. Nothing about their doctrinal deliberations is known nor is it certain how comprehensive Constantine intended this council to be (consult Jones, op. cit., 149-51).

10. The superscription of the first version reads "Epistle of Constantine, the king, to the synod of 318 bishops".

On the number 318 see no. 53, n. 12.

11. For *it has seemed to us* Cowper's first translation reads simply "it now seems".

12. Writing at least three centuries earlier, Strabo states (*Geog.* 12. 4. 7) that the site was not at all salubrious in summer (cf. *supra* n. 6), but conceivably during that interval the climate had improved, because both Constantine and Marcian (no. 464; but see no. 468, n. 6) convened councils there, and thither was convoked the Seventh General Council in 787.

13. The last five words here are reduced to "what is done" in Cowper's first version.

14. Here are inserted "I earnestly wish" by Cowper in his first translation.

15. Cowper has "without any delay" in his first version.

16. The last eight words here are reduced to "what is done" in Cowper's first translation.

17. J. B. Pitra in his *Analecta Sacra Spicilegio Solesmensi Parata* (Paris, 1883), 4. 452, has a Latin translation of the later Syriac version, which in English reads in this fashion:

"Letter of Constantine, the emperor, to the 318 bishops.

"That nothing is so dear to me as piety toward God I think is known to all.

"Moreover, because it had pleased that the synod of bishops should be assembled previously in the city of Ancyra of Galatia, it now has seemed to be more satisfactory on many accounts that they should be assembled in the city of Nicaea of Bithynia, whether that the bishops from Italy and from the rest of Europe may hasten more easily to it or because in it the temperature of the air is more healthful or that I myself can be present and have part in the things which shall be done.

"Wherefore, beloved brethren, to you I make known that I wish all to be congregated as soon as possible at the aforesaid city, I mean Nicaea.

"Let everyone of you, attentive to the things which are of more moment, as before has been said, hasten to approach without delay speedily, that he being present may assist in those things which are done.

"May God guard you, most beloved brethren."

18. Cowper's versions are silent about Antioch and the other cities and substitute "Italy and the rest of the countries of Europe".

19. Another reason for its appositeness may have been in the emperor's mind, because in choosing this site Constantine presented the synod to the Saviour as a thank-offering for his victory over his enemies (Eusebius, *VC* 3. 7; cf. 4. 47), of whom the last was Licinius, his former fellow-sovereign. The point is that the town's name means Victory (Eusebius, *VC* 3. 6). Originally known as Ancore or Helicore, the site was rebuilt *c*. 315 B.C. by Antigonus I, who called it Antigoneia, and was renamed Nicaea by Lysimachus *c*. 300 B.C. to honour his wife of the same name.

49. DECREE AND ORATIONS OF CONSTANTINE I ON CONCILIAR PROCEDURE, 325

(Eusebius, *VC* 3. 12; Rufinus, *HE* 10. 2; Socrates, *HE* 1. 8; Sozomen, *HE* 1. 17, 19; Theodoret, *HE* 1. 7. 12; Gelasius, *HE* 2. 7. 39–41, 2. 8. 3; Cassiodorus, *HE* 2. 2. 2, 2. 5. 7; Barḥadbešabba Arbaïa, *History* [*PO* 23. 207]; Isidorus Mercator, *Decr. Coll.* 59 [*PL* 130. 254]; Gregorius Presbyter, *De Conc. Nic. Prim.* [*PG* 111. 429, 433]; Anon., *Nestorian History* [*PO* 4. 278]; Nicephorus, *HE* 8. 16)

After Constantine the Great had convoked (no. 48) what was to become the First General Council of the Christian Church in 325, the emperor declared his will to the assemblage on at least three occasions, on which the report of his words varies among the several writers who record these.[1]

The first occasion (I) was his decision about the disposition of documents submitted to him by those members of the synod who were preferring accusations against one another. The emperor, after he had spoken about these, ordered these, unread, to be burned.

The second occasion (II) was his desire that the conclavists would heal the division in the Church caused by the adherents of Arianism.

The third occasion (III) was his dismissal of the council with the reminder of his past co-operation in the propagation of the faith and with the hope of their future effort therein.

In each set of translations the versions are arranged chronologically, that the reader may discover the debt of a later to an earlier reporter.

I (Rufinus) [2]

God has appointed you as bishops and has given to you the power of judging also about us; and, therefore, we rightly are judged by you, but you cannot be judged by men. And on this account await the judgement of God alone among you and to that divine investigation let your quarrels, whatsoever they are, be reserved. For you also have been given to us by God as gods and it is not suitable that man should judge gods, but he alone, about whom it has been written: "God has stood in the congregation of the gods; moreover in the midst he judges among the gods".[3] And, therefore, after these matters have been dismissed, apart from any contention of spirits [4] decide those things which pertain to the faith of God.

I (Socrates)

Christ orders him eager to obtain forgiveness to forgive his brother.[5]

I (Sozomen)

These accusations have a proper time, the day of the great judgement,[6] and the Judge, who then is going to judge over all persons. But for me, being a man, it is not right to take such a hearing upon myself, when priests are accusers and accused, for such persons ought not at all to permit themselves to be judged by another. Come, then, having imitated the divine benevolence,[7] in pardon for one another, after the accusations have been cancelled, let us be persuaded and let us be earnest about matters concerning the faith, on account of which we have assembled hither.

I (Gelasius)

Since God has chosen you to be both priests and rulers both to judge, and to judge between, the masses and has ordained you to be gods, as if prominent above all men, according to the saying "I said, you are gods and all sons of the Highest"[8] and "God has stood in the congregation of gods",[3] it is proper to take small account of common matters and to make all haste concerning divine affairs.

I (Cassiodorus)

These accusations, indeed, will have a proper time, that is, the day of the great judgement, moreover that Judge, who then will judge over all persons. For me, therefore, being a man, it is not permitted to have a hearing about matters of this kind, obviously when priests are accusers and are accused, who it is not at all suitable that they ought to be shown such that they may be judged by others. Come, now, imitating the divine clemency in pardon of each other, let us efface each other's accusations and let us be earnest to deliberate about these matters which pertain to the faith, on account of which we have assembled here.

I (Barḥadbešabba Árbaïa)[9]

Here today has been given to you power over all the Church, over the priesthood and over the Empire, and over all the orders [10] which are subjected to the priesthood and to the Empire.

It is to you from whom the Lord will demand accounting for all the Church's lost and recovered children.

I (*Nestorian History*) [11]

God has given to you power over the priesthood and has given to me power over the Empire. But today God gives you power over the priesthood and over the Empire. I am subject to you and I shall follow your orders.

Judge according to the truth conformable to God's order and to his Christ's will. You are the cause of the life of those who live and that of the loss of those who are lost—and that for eternity. See also among those who are dissident and whom they style heretical, if there are not those who would have distorted the Divine Books in adding to these and in subtracting from these; make them come and discuss with them to open their eyes for them; perhaps they will return to the truth and to its partisans. As for those who are manifestly enemies of the truth, who would have distorted the Scriptures and would have altered the faith: shun them and do not involve them in your discussions, except those who would have returned from their errors and would have given reassuring tokens of their true repentance and of their sincere conversion.

I (Nicephorus)

These accusations have been left free for that great Judge—and the time for these is that of the last judgement [12]—for whom even the secret matters become manifest;[13] but for me, being a sinful man indeed, it is not right to receive and to arrange for a hearing accusations of priests, for by me at any rate it has been reckoned not sanctioned by divine law that such appointed ministers of God ought to permit themselves to be judged by others or by us. For, if the offences in the case of priests have become known to very many persons, a very great occasion for scandal emerges for those wishing to sin fearlessly.[14] Come, then, having imitated Christ, in pardon for one another let us heal our own affairs, for he says that the person yearning to obtain forgiveness ought to forgive debts.[15]

II (Eusebius)

The purpose of my prayer, friends, was to enjoy your presence [16] and, having obtained this, I admit that I acknowledge thanks to the King of all, because besides all other things he has granted me to see also this blessing surpassing every blessing—I mean, of course, to behold you all gathered together to take away [17] one all-shared, united judgement.

Therefore let not any malicious foe spoil our excellences nor, since the tyrants' hostility to God has been removed out of the way by the Saviour God's power,[18] in other ways let the evil-loving Demon encompass the divine law with blasphemies; for the intestinal discord of God's Church has been deemed by me even more troublesome than any war and dangerous strife and these disagreements appear more distressing than external dissensions. At all events, when I had won victories over my enemies [18] by the Almighty's will and co-operation, then I considered that nought remained but to give thanks to God and to rejoice with the persons freed by him through our efforts. But when I had learned of your disagreement contrary to every expectation, I did not rate the tidings in second place, but, having prayed to find even in this a remedy through my efforts, without delay I summoned you all to my service.[19] And I rejoice in seeing your assembly, but I judge that I shall achieve then the greatest success in accordance with my prayers, when I can see you all combined in spirit and one common, all-agreed, peaceful harmony, which it would be fitting for you, dedicated to God, to represent to others.

Delay not, then, beloved ministers of God and good servants of the common Lord and Saviour of us all, beginning in consequence forthwith to discuss [20] the causes of dissension among you and to dissolve by the principles of peace every constriction of controversy. For thus you shall have accomplished things pleasing to the God above all and you shall give a surpassing favour to me, your fellow-servant.[21]

II (Sozomen)

For all things I give thanks to God, not least in that I see your assembly, friends. And for me the result has been better than my prayers—that I have brought into the same place so many priests of Christ. Now I shall desire to see you united and sharers of a harmonious opinion, since I consider it more troublesome than every evil for God's Church to be in a state of discord. Therefore, when there had been announced what I ought not to have heard, I was grieved exceedingly in spirit in having learned that you, for whom it least was fitting, being ministers of God and arbiters of peace, differed in opinion.

And for this reason I have convoked your holy synod. Being both your emperor and fellow-servant, I ask to receive a favour pleasing both to God, the common Lord, and to me, and proper for you to grant. This is it: to discuss the causes of the controversy and to put a united and peaceful end to these, so that I with you may erect this trophy against the jealous Demon, who, after aliens and tyrants have been removed,[18] roused this intestinal discord by having begrudged us our blessings.

II (Theodoret)

For the evangelical and the apostolical books and the ancient prophets' oracular sayings plainly teach us what it is necessary to think about God. Banishing, therefore, hostile contention, from the God-inspired words let us take the solution of the questions.

II (Gelasius)

Therefore[22] let the most hallowed synod of your Holinesses receive me and do not suffer the most prudent Church and the doors of the chaste and common mother of us all to be set against me, although especially even now the reasoning of my soul, seeking the perfect purity of the Catholic faith, thinks it not worthy that this should be done by it,[23] nevertheless it urges and suggests it. And the forehead of proper modesty has exhibited the seal of all the fairest virtues and has begun to touch the gates of immortality and to knock upon these, so that even you straightway have deigned to pardon the good will of our Brotherhood, when you look favourably upon the peace of the Catholic faith.[24]

For this is proper to God and fitting to the faith of the Catholic Church and advantageous to the State: that for the most valued peace,[18] divinely granted to us, we all together should offer a worthy recompense to him who has bestowed this on us. For it would be truly marvellous and exceedingly marvellous, after our enemies have been destroyed [18] and after none still dares to resist, to fight among ourselves and to offer to our enemies pleasure and laughter, above all when disputing about divine matters and when we have the recorded teaching of the All-Holy Spirit. For the evangelical and the apostolical books and the ancient prophets' oracular sayings plainly teach us what it is necessary to think about God. Banishing, therefore, hostile contention, from the God-inspired words let us take the solution of the questions.

II (Cassiodorus)

For there are the evangelical and the apostolical books and the ancient prophets' ordinances, which teach us what we should know about the sacred law. Banishing, therefore, hostile contention, from divinely inspired words let us perceive by the mind the solution of the questions.

II (Gregorius Presbyter)

Act, holy fathers, that both with all zeal and with intense application we may make both the assessment and the apprehension of the truth [25] through the prophetic proclamations and the apostolic traditions, apart from all indecorous fraternal hatred and vainglory. For it is awful if, after polytheistic impiety has been destroyed and enemies have been subjected to us and civil wars have ceased,[18] we, the faithful, strike one another not with swords but with dogmas and we attempt by subtlety of doctrines and by variety of words to pervert the evangelical teaching, which is simple and artless and has its power not in words but in works.

Therefore, committing to God the Father and to the Only-Begotten Son of the Father and to the Vivifying Spirit the revelation of the things now being examined by us, let us cleave to the investigation. For we eagerly shall grant that we ourselves assist you and share with you the contests until the final revelation of the truth. For we believe also that the Vivifying Spirit's visitation will prosper, through which our saving faith, untouched by every heretical notion and free from wicked opinion toward the Divinity, will have its certainty.

II (Nicephorus)

I give thanks to God for all things, not less for the present assembly, beloved fathers and brethren, for so I call you, since our common Saviour has shown us favour, for even better than according to my prayer the matter has resulted: for at what value could anyone set the expectation to see so many of God's priests assembled in the same place? But at any rate I could wish you all to be minded to see the same things and by harmony of soul to take a stand on one opinion. For to see God's Church distracted in strife and separated into opposing opinions, I judge is, for me at any rate, worse than and beyond every evil of which anyone can speak. Therefore, when—would that it had not been—what had been announced to me was quite clear, how do you think that I have been stung in my soul, when I had learned that you were in a state of discord? And not at all was this befitting you, God's ministers and appointed arbiters of peace. For who can persuade others to be quiet, when thus you engage in battle and arm against one another?

Wherefore also I summoned your holy synod, being both your emperor and fellow-servant. And at least I ask one favour, which is assuredly right both for me to receive and for you to grant: to discuss the matters which have created the discord and, having dissolved the controversy in peacefulness, to bring all persons into peace according to the grace dwelling in you and to supply to doctrine freedom from faction, that together with such a great holy army I may erect a joint trophy against the jealous Demon, who, after abominable tyrants, who had done things dear to him, have been removed as speedily as possible,[18] then, having been at a loss, fanned this intestinal war, by being ever resentful and by attacking our blessings.

Wherefore I beg, as if God were present, let each one, discarding whatever pressing burden he has, approach the advantage of common concord. For let none suppose that public affairs go well, when matters thus have been disposed in discord and disagreements among you. For it also would be marvellous and too absurd, if, after our enemies thus have been destroyed [18] and none still dares to resist, you arm against one another, and this indeed becomes an ironical situation for the pleasure and the laughter of enemies, when you discuss these things about divine matters, you to whom the Spirit's teaching expressly instructs what ought to be done. For the writing of the holy evangels and the God-inspired words of the apostles and, in addition to these, the ancient oracular sayings of the prophets clearly teach us what it is necessary both to say and to think about God. Casting, therefore, as far as possible the contention which has excited this holy war, by the God-spoken lessons let us seek the solution of the disputed matters. And the discovery really will be easy, as I really think, if, indeed, we wish.

III (Gregorius Presbyter) [26]

You see my religious worship in respect to the Divinity by your instructions and that ardently I have worked at the destruction of idols [27] and zealously have caused the Christians' faith to be proclaimed everywhere, so that no heterodox kind of cult is left for us, except that only Christians both adore and embrace the Holy and Consubstantial Trinity. Today I transmit to you this [28] in its purity. May it be your prayer and care, with the Lord co-operating, in respect to its daily exaltation and increase.

1. In connection with these speeches exists a lengthy oration (printed usually as an appendix to Eusebius' *Life of Constantine* and often considered as its fifth book), which Eusebius says (*VC* 4. 32) is suppended to his biography. As in other cases, Constantine composed it in Latin for translators to turn into Greek (loc. cit.), and pronounced it on Good Friday of an unknown year before "the Assembly of the Saints" and dedicated it "to the Church of God".

The connection of the discourse, which displays not a little learning in philosophy and theology as well as some acquaintance with pagan and patristic and Hebraic literature, with these orations comes from some scholars' conjecture that, since Constantine addressed the fathers assembled at Nicaea, some Christian found in that fact a chance to fabricate this speech to add colour to that situation. But against such supposition it may be argued that (1) there is the witness of Eusebius that Constantine wrote it; (2) the date of the discourse differs from that of the synodal sessions (see no. 48, n. 6); (3) the speech's authenticity stands on the same basis as the rest of the imperial documents recorded by the emperor's biographer. In any event the oration, while it shows the sovereign's theological opinions, has no legislative significance.

For a recent appreciation of Constantine's attitude at the council consult A. H. M. Jones, *Constantine and the Conversion of Europe* (New York, 1949), 152-71.

2. Isidorus Mercator repeats this version, except that in the last sentence he has "other" for *those*. His place in the *catena* is after that of Cassiodorus.

3. Ps. 82. 1 with modification. See no. 20, n. 11.

4. He means "apart from any passionate controversy".

5. On this see Matt. 18. 15–35, esp. 21 and 35; Luke 17. 3–4.

6. Cf. Jude 6.

7. Cf. *supra* n. 5 and Matt. 6. 14; Mark 11. 24–6; Luke 6. 37.

8. Ps. 82. 6.

9. This brief admonition (translated from the French version of a Syriac history composed *c*. 590) seems to conform more with the subject of his first address than with those of his other speeches and, therefore, is assigned to this place; otherwise a fourth occasion must be invented, if the allocution is authentic and is not to be assumed as a paraphrase of his first pronouncement.

10. See no. 325, n. 6.

11. In n. 9 *supra* is discussed the allocation of the following words to this place. Here is more expansion as found in the French version of an anonymous work in Arabic apparently composed *c*. 1250.

12. Cf. John 12. 48.

13. Cf. Rom. 2. 16.

14. Cf. Rom. 14. 13.

15. Cf. *supra* n. 5 and Matt. 6. 12; Luke 11. 4.

16. Literally "dance", especially "choral dance with music". The idea seems to be that the sight of the prelates gathered in a group, which would be in harmony as a band of dancers in time with music, was the emperor's prayer, and that its fulfilment effects in him pleasure.

17. At the council's dissolution, when the members return to their sees.

18. A reference to his recent victories over Licinius in 324 at Adrianople, off the Dardanelles, at Scutari, which made Constantine sole emperor.

19. Literally "all the services" or "all classes of servants".

20. Literally "to bring into the middle", that is, to set for discussion.

21. Eusebius remarks that Constantine spoke in Latin, which an interpreter turned into Greek, but he fails to comment on the rather mechanical method adopted by the autocrat to promote the peace of Christendom—but then the prince was confronted by the new problem of how to concoct unity in truth as opposed to unity in form.

22. The first part—and that the greater—of this oration is omitted, because it is merely a lengthy confession of Constantine's acknowledgement of the mercies of God, together with a profession of God's omnipotent providence, and because it has no connection with the agenda of the council. The translated portion begins where the emperor turns to the necessity, as he sees it, for conciliar action to bring peace to the Church.

23. He means apparently that in an ideal situation there should be no need for the Church to provide for its own purity, but that conditions call for such action.

24. By this self-appraisal of his character under God's provident protection Constantine seems to mean that he has dared to approach the bishops with his plea for a united Church and that the result is that they in their desire for ecclesiastical peace have pardoned the emperor, who counts himself as their brother, for his suggestion that they set their house in order.

25. The idea seems to be that they first should calculate by balancing truth's various aspects and then should seize upon the solution, which would be the truth.

26. Eusebius (*VC* 3. 21) summarizes Constantine's final speech thus in *oratio obliqua*: That they should be diligent among one another to maintain peace and to avoid contentious arguments, not to be jealous, if any among the bishops should seem esteemed on account of wisdom, but to consider the excellence of an individual as a common blessing, nor the superior to be arrogant toward the inferior—for judgement of the really superior belongs to God—and through consideration of forgiveness to condescend to the weaker, because perfection by all means is rare. That, therefore, they also should accord forgiveness to one another failing in slight matters and should be indulgent and should pardon whatever are human failings, all highly honouring concordant harmony, lest a cause of mockery by their factions should be provided for persons prepared to blaspheme the divine law, for which persons—able to be saved, if our conduct should seem admirable to them—should be especially all their concern, and they should not be mistaken in this: that the profit from words is not productive for all persons. For some delight to be aided in the things pertaining to sustenance, others are wont to court personages, others cling to persons who greet them with salutations, and others love to be honoured with gifts, but few are the lovers of true words and rare indeed is the friend of truth. That, therefore, they should be adaptable to all persons, like a physician, administering to each the things advantageous to salvation, so that the salutary doctrine should be glorified fully by all persons. [Such things, says Eusebius, he recommended especially.] Finally, that they diligently should make supplications for him to God.

27. See no. 44 and (by anticipation) nos. 54 and 63.

28. Faith, not the Trinity, seems to be meant.

50. LETTER OF CONSTANTINE I ON EXILE OF EUSEBIUS, 325

(Gelasius, *HE* 3, Suppl. 1)

The emperor explains to the Nicomedians why he has exiled Eusebius, their bishop, who, as a persistent Arian at the First General Council of the Church at Nicaea in 325, had been one of the last to subscribe to the creed there composed. Constantine concludes his communication with the threat that whoever shall have presumed to speak in Eusebius' favour will be suppressed by the imperial authority. But Constantine did not persist long in this attitude, for by 329 Eusebius reappeared in high favour with the emperor (whom on the latter's death-bed he baptized in 337) and eventually served as bishop of Constantinople from 339 to 342.

The entire letter is given only by Gelasius. The earlier portion is a disquisition on the relation between God the Father and God the Son (doubtless drafted for the emperor by an ecclesiastical aide) and ends by attracting attention to one of the propagators of incorrect opinions about this relation. The latter portion, preserved by Theodoret (*HE* 1. 20. 1-10) and turned into Latin by Cassiodorus (*HE* 2. 22. 5-16), starts by stating that this exponent of errors is Eusebius.

Against Eusebius and Theognius.[1]

Constantine Augustus to the Catholic Church of the Nicomedians.

You all know accurately, beloved brethren, that the Lord God and Saviour Christ are obviously both Father and Son: the Father, I say, without beginning, without end, parent of the world itself; the Son, that is, the Father's will, which neither has been assumed through any thought nor has been accepted through any sought essence in respect to the perfection of its own works. And he who both perceives and shall perceive this shall have an unwearied endurance toward every kind of punishment.[2]

But the Son of God, Christ, the Demiurge [3] of all things and the supplier of immortality itself, was born (so far as it pertains to the faith, in which we have believed), was born, rather he himself proceeded, being even always in the Father, to the orderly arrangement of the things made by him, was born, therefore, by indivisible procession, for the will at the same time was implanted in its habitation and according to the quality of each it both manages and administers those things which need different care. What, then, is it? What is the difference between God the Father and the Son? Obviously nothing; for the completion of things has accepted by perception the order of the will, but, not divided from the Father's essence, it has separated the will.

But as for what follows these principles: who is there who, as a follower of Christ, the Son of my Lord, fears through reverence rather than through folly? Does the Divinity, therefore, suffer? After the soul, the habitation of the august body, hastens to the knowledge of its own holiness, does what has been separated from the body fall beneath a touch? Has not the Divinity separated this, the soul, which has been taken from the body's humility? Do we not live, even if the soul's glory shall summon the body to death?

50. EXILE OF EUSEBIUS, 325

What, then, here has both innocent and sincere faith found worthy of doubt? Do you [4] not see that God has chosen a most august body, through which he wanted to manifest the evidences of the faith and the indications of his own virtue and to dispel the perdition of the human race, already compounded by destructive error,[5] and to give a new doctrine of religion and by the indication of ignorance to purge the mind's unworthy actions, then to dissolve death's torture and to proclaim immortality's rewards?

But you, whom the communion of love reasonably causes to be addressed by me at last as brethren, are not ignorant that I am your fellow-servant, you are not ignorant of your salvation's stronghold, of which I nobly have taken upon myself the care and through which not only we have conquered the armed forces of our enemies, but also we have compelled persons still living to the revelation of humanity's true faith.[6] But I especially rejoiced in these blessings because of the restoration of the world.[7] For it truly also was worthy of wonder that so many peoples, who a short time ago were said not to know God, have come into harmony. But how would these peoples, who took upon themselves no care for emulous eagerness, know?

Why, then, do you, beloved brethren, think that I blame yourselves? We are Christians and we think dividedly with lamentable disposition. Is this, then, our faith? Is this the most holy law's teaching? But what is the reason on account of which the plague of the present evil has been excited? Oh, the absurdity! Oh, the excess of hatred, exceeding the magnitude of all vexation! What has appeared to be the terribleness of this bandit?[8] Does he deny that God's Son has proceeded from the Father's undivided essence? that God is everywhere (and yet we perceive that he always is with us)? that through this one's [9] power the orderliness of the universe has come into existence (and yet indeed he has been deprived of the cleavage of separation)?

Lest, then, anything should be done by us, beloved brethren, perceive now, I beg, the torments of the present grief. You proclaim yourselves to be confessors of him, whom you deny exists, when the abandoned teacher persuades you of this.

I ask, who is it who has taught the so innocent multitude these things?[10] Obviously Eusebius, the co-operator [11] with tyrannical cruelty.[12] For that he has been [13] a client of the tyrant everywhere it is possible to comprehend [14] from all [15] considerations. For the slaughters of the bishops—of those who were truly bishops [16]— testify to this;[17] the fiercest persecution of the Christians expressly proclaims this. Indeed I shall not speak now about the outrages perpetrated against me,[18] through which, when particularly the tumultuous concourses of the opposing factions exerted themselves,[19] this fellow both was sending spies [20] against me and all but was joining with the tyrant in recruiting armed forces.²¹ Let none imagine that I am unprepared in respect to the demonstration of these things. For there is precise proof, because it is well known that the priest and the deacons who attend upon Eusebius openly have been arrested by me. But I pretermit these matters,²² which ²³ have been advanced by me now not for the purpose of anger but for the shame of those persons.

Only this I dread, this I consider: that I see that you are summoned into the association with the accusation. For through Eusebius' guidance and perversion ²⁴ you have seized upon a knowledge divorced from the truth. But cure ²⁵ is not slow, if indeed, after you now at all events ²⁶ have received a bishop both faithful and sincere,²⁷ you look to God. And this for the present is in your power and previously it could have depended ²⁸ upon your decision, if the aforesaid Eusebius with a whirlwind of companions had not come hither ²⁹ for this purpose and had not assisted shamelessly in the correction of order.³⁰

But since it is meet to say a few words about Eusebius himself ³¹ to your Loves,³² your Patiences remember that at the city of the Nicaeans has been held a synod,³³ at which even I myself was present in a manner befitting the duty of my conscience,³⁴ having no other desire than to produce unanimity for all persons and above all both to refute and to dispel this trouble, which had taken beginning through the madness ³⁵ of Arius the Alexandrian, but was strengthened forthwith through the absurd ³⁶ and destructive zeal of Eusebius. But, most beloved ³⁷ and most honoured, with how great a tumultuous concourse (inasmuch as he was convicted by his own conscience), with how much shame do you think ³⁸ this very Eusebius remained firm in falsehood, which had been refuted from every side, both by sending secretly ³⁹ to me different persons petitioning on his behalf and by asking from me a sort of alliance,⁴⁰ lest he, though convicted of such great fault, might be deposed ⁴¹ from the dignity ⁴² belonging to him? A witness of this for me is God himself (who may remain benevolent toward both me and you), when that fellow ⁴³ both perverted and with impropriety deceived me ⁴⁴—and this you yourselves also ⁴⁵ will know. For all things were done then,⁴⁶ just as he himself, concealing every evil whatsoever ³⁹ in his thoughts, was wishing.

But very recently,³⁹ that I may pass by the rest of this fellow's mischief, hear, I beseech, what particularly he accomplished with Theognius,¹ whom he has as an associate of his folly.⁴⁷ Certain Alexandrians, who had withdrawn from our faith,⁴⁸ I ordered to be sent hither, since through their activities the torch of the discord had been raised.⁴⁹ But these honourable and good bishops,⁵⁰ whom once the truth of the synod preserved for penitence,⁵¹ not only received and safeguarded those persons among themselves, but also with them participated in the malignity of their characters.⁵² Therefore concerning these ungrateful [53] persons I decided to do this: for I ordered them to be arrested and to be banished as far away as possible.[54]

Now it is [55] your duty to look to God with that faith, with which it is well known that you always have existed and it is proper that you should exist, and so to act,[56] that we rejoice in having holy and orthodox and philanthropic bishops. But if anyone shall dare to cling imprudently to those corrupters in respect to mention or to praise, forthwith he shall be repressed from his own audacity by the activity of God's servant, that is, myself.[57]

God shall guard [58] you, beloved [59] brethren.

1. Otherwise Theogonius (so Theodoret), the contemporary bishop of Nicaea and exiled with Eusebius.

2. The idea seems to be that correct knowledge about the Father-Son relation of God brings to a person possessing such belief sufficient strength to sustain any sort of punishment inflicted by those of other opinions.

3. On him see no. 648, n. 6.

4. Constantine shifts from the plural to the singular, as if addressing the Nicomedians collectively as a congregation.

5. That is, error, already mixed by Satan for our destruction, causes mankind's perdition.

6. Constantine refers to his protection of the Church, his attainment of sole rule after the recent defeat of Licinius (his fellow-Augustus), and his attempt to enforce orthodoxy. Possibly the last phrase should read "of a real belief in humaneness".

7. The fact that in the previous year Constantine succeeded in grasping complete control of the Empire lends colour to what he here calls the restoration of the world: at any rate after civil conflict he now was free to reorganize the Roman world without a colleague's interference.

Among the panegyrists Constantine is hailed as *restitutor*.

8. Eusebius is meant.

9. Christ is meant.

10. With this sentence Theodoret and Cassiodorus start their extracts. Gelasius also inserts the rest of this letter earlier into his history (1. 11. 22–31). Cassiodorus omits *I ask* and *these things*.

11. The noun (συμμύστης) literally indicates a person who has been initiated with another into a religious cult. Cassiodorus has *excultor* (cultivator).

12. This and the next three sentences refer to Eusebius' activity in behalf of Licinius, Constantine's lately conquered colleague.

13. Cassiodorus reads "is known to be".

14. Cassiodorus reduces *is . . . comprehend* to "appears".

15. Gelasius earlier and Theodoret and Cassiodorus substitute "many".

16. This aside perhaps was inspired by Constantine's latest contact with Arianizing prelates at the council just concluded.

17. Cassiodorus reads "For the destruction of true bishops testifies to this".
18. Gelasius earlier reads "the things perpetrated by him against me".
19. Cassiodorus substitutes ". . . the plots . . . were running about".
20. Literally "spying eyes"—a reference to several clergymen sent by Eusebius to observe Constantine's activities at the start of the struggle between the two emperors and to report these to Licinius.
21. This seems to be the meaning, but the Greek literally gives "and all but was joining with the tyrant in paying the war tax in respect to armed services rendered". Gelasius earlier adds "himself" after *tyrant*. Cassiodorus has "and this only failed him—that he has not offered also armed service boldly to the tyrant".
22. An instance of the old classical device of professing not to descant on certain details and yet of attracting attention to these by the very disclaimer.

Gelasius earlier reads "But these matters have been advanced by us now" etc.

23. Cassiodorus inserts "are known to".
24. Cassiodorus substitutes "seduction and subversion".
25. Cassiodorus inserts "of this matter".
26. Cassiodorus omits the phrase.
27. A certain Amphion succeeded Eusebius in the see.
28. Cassiodorus reads "And what interest at any rate for the present is in you, that also ought previously to have depended".
29. To the council, whose agenda included restoration of Christian peace.
30. Cassiodorus has "with a very bad protecting escort of his companions had not come here and most shamelessly had confounded the order of rectitude".
31. Cassiodorus gives "the mentioned Eusebius" for *Eusebius himself*.
32. Gelasius earlier inserts "hear patiently" and Cassiodorus has "hear".
33. Gelasius earlier adds "of bishops".
34. Cassiodorus reads "at which even I myself befittingly exhibited the cultivation of my conscience".
35. Cassiodorus has "pride".
36. Cassiodorus has "depraved".
37. Cassiodorus has the positive degree.
38. Cassiodorus omits these three words.
39. Omitted by Cassiodorus.
40. Cassiodorus has "comfort".
41. Earlier Gelasius reads "might fall".
42. That is, his episcopal office.
43. Gelasius earlier gives "Eusebius".
44. Gelasius earlier inserts a parenthesis "but Divine Providence has brought me back into its truest way".
45. Gelasius earlier inserts "knew and"; Cassiodorus has simply the perfect tense.

46. Gelasius earlier adds "by him, I speak of the unholy Eusebius".
47. Gelasius earlier has "of his unholy purpose". For the clause Cassiodorus has simply "the sharer of his wickedness".
48. Probably Arians, because Arianism flourished there and because Arianism was the principal problem confronting the Nicene Council.
49. Cassiodorus reads "since through their service the flame of the mind was surging".
50. Eusebius and Theognius. The adjectives, of which Cassiodorus makes the second superlative, are ironical.
51. They were about the last of those members who reluctantly subscribed to the conciliar formula, which expounded what then was believed to be the Christian truth.
52. Cassiodorus reads "but also decided to participate in their evil wills".
53. Ungrateful, in the emperor's estimation, because the council had exempted them from deposition for their persistent opposition and scantily disguised submission.
54. Cassiodorus gives "that they, when arrested, should be deported far away into exile" for the last half of the sentence.
55. Cassiodorus inserts "accordingly".
56. Cassiodorus makes the rest of the sentence independent instead of a dependent clause.
57. For this sentence Cassiodorus reads "But if anyone perhaps imprudently dares to be excited to mention or to praise of those pestilential persons, forthwith he shall be repressed in his own daring by the activity of God's servant, that is, my own."
Perhaps such a threat as this, when coupled with the emperor's words as reported at the Council of Nicaea in 325 (see no. 49, I), explains "why Constantine called the first great council . . . why he placed himself as super-pope to formulate the faith of the Christian world and then to resume his sceptre of super-kaiser in order to see that all his subjects obeyed, not only the policeman, but the priest as well. . . . The great Constantine had spoken. . . . The orthodox alone were deemed fit to become saints and all who favored another creed were officially branded as criminals condemned to suffer, not merely the wrath of God on earth, but eternal damnation in a world of which neither party could speak with historical precision" (P. Bigelow, *Genseric: King of the Vandals and First Prussian Kaiser* [New York, 1918], 86–7, 91).
58. Cassiodorus uses the subjunctive mode.
59. Cassiodorus has the superlative adjective.

51. LETTER OF CONSTANTINE I ON CONFORMITY WITH ORTHODOXY, 325

(Gelasius, *HE* 3, Suppl. 2)

The emperor in this epistle to Theodotus, bishop of Laodicea in Syria, an Arian sympathizer at the Council of Nicaea in 325, admonishes his addressee that he will do well to learn the lesson of the fate which has overtaken two other Arian adherents, whom the emperor has exiled for their recalcitrance (no. 50). Apparently Theodotus heeded the warning, since it seems that no action was taken against him.

Victor Constantine Augustus to Theodotus.

How great has waxed the strength of the divine wrath it is easy for even you to learn from what both Eusebius [1] and Theognius [2] have suffered, who, having cast abuse upon the most holy religion by the troop of their own band of bandits and after they had gained pardon, have sullied the Saviour God's name. For, when especially after the synod's [3] consentient harmony it was necessary that they should have corrected their earlier error, then they were caught cleaving to their absurdities. Therefore, then, Divine Providence has expelled them from its own people, since it did not endure to see guileless souls corrupted by a few persons' senselessness and now has demanded proper punishment from them and will exact even greater thereafter through all time.

Wherefore I have thought that it ought to be made manifest to your Sagacity that, if any evil advice of such persons—as I myself do not suppose—should settle in your course of life, you, after having removed this from your mind, should be zealous to show pure thought—as is proper—and sincere consecration and undefiled faith in the Saviour God. For this is proper to be done by that one who would desire to be deemed worthy of the eternal life's inviolate rewards.

May God guard you, beloved brother.

1. Bishop of Nicomedia (see introd. to no. 50).
2. Or Theogonius, bishop of Nicaea.
3. The Council of Nicaea is meant.

52. LETTER OF CONSTANTINE I ON THE PASCHAL QUESTION, 325

(Eusebius, *VC* 3. 17–20)

This letter, Eusebius says, was written in the emperor's own handwriting and of it a faithful (or authoritative) copy was posted to every province. It is preserved also by Socrates (*HE* 1. 9), Theodoret (*HE* 1. 10), Gelasius (*HE* 2. 37. 10–22), Nicephorus (*HE* 8. 25).

The emperor announces the settlement of the long-standing controversy over the proper time for the celebration of Easter, effected, as he hoped,[1] by the First General Council at Nicaea in 325, and bids the churches both to accept the conciliar arrangement and to establish it, but neglects to proclaim any penalty for non-observance beyond the hint that the council's decision is referable to the divine will.

This letter marks the second of the three phrases through which this vexatious question passed. The third may be dismissed because it began and ended about three centuries after the Nicene ruling.[2] The first, concerned chiefly with the legality of celebrating Easter on a weekday, had been dissipated about two generations before the council met.[3] The second, solved at Nicaea, involved the determination of which Sunday was to serve as Easter, since several systems had their defenders.[4]

The emperor's letter, which he wrote to the churches, after the synod had been assembled in Nicaea, about the salutary festival.[5]

Constantine, Victor, Greatest, Augustus to the churches.[6]

Having experience from the prosperity of public affairs as to how great has been the grace of the Divine Power, I judged this to be above all things: that I concern myself with the object that among the most blessed multitudes of the Catholic Church one faith and sincere love and harmonious piety toward Almighty God should be preserved. But since this could not possibly obtain both a steadfast and a constant establishment[7] unless, when all or at least the majority of the bishops has assembled together in the same place, there would be an examination of each of the points pertaining to the most sacred religion; because of this, when as very many as possible[8] had been convened (I myself, as one of you, was present—for I should not deny that I have been your fellow-servant, wherein particularly I rejoice), all matters received a competent investigation to such a degree until a decision, satisfactory to God,[9] the overseer of all, was brought into the light for the harmony of unity, so that nothing still remains for dissension or dispute over faith.

There also, when inquiry concerning the most holy day of Easter had been made, it was resolved by common opinion that it would be well for all [10] everywhere to celebrate it [11] on one day. For what will be able to be for us more seasonable, what more sacred, than that this festival, whence we have taken the hope of immortality,[12] should be kept unerringly among all in one order and by clear regulation?

And first, it seemed to be inappropriate to observe that most holy day by following the custom of the Jews, who, having besmeared their hands by unlawful crime,[13] defiled in respect to their souls, deservedly are blind. For, since their nation [14] has been discarded, it is possible for the celebration of this observance to be prolonged [15] even to future ages in the truer order, which we have maintained from the first day of the Passion [16] until the present. Therefore let us [17] have nothing in common [18] with the most hateful mob of the Jews. For [19] from the Saviour we have received another way;[20] before our most holy religion lies a legitimate and proper course.[21] Unanimously laying claim to this, let us, most honoured brethren, detach ourselves from that disgraceful [22] complicity. For how [23] truly very absurd is it for those persons to boast [24] that we are not competent indeed to observe these matters except for their instruction! How will those be able to consider correctly, who, after that murder of the Lord and patricide,[25] having lost their wits, are led, not by any reasoning power, but by an uncontrollable impulse, whithersoever their [26] innate madness may impel them? Thence, therefore, even in this particular they see not the truth, so that they,[27] erring for the most part,[28] in place of proper correction celebrate the Passover twice in the same year.[29] Why, then, do we follow these persons, who are acknowledged to be sick with fearful error?[30] For [31] never surely shall we endure to keep Easter twice in one year![29] But though these matters were not proposed, it was necessary that your Sagacities maintain both by diligence and by prayer [32] always that on no common point the purity of your [33] soul should seem to accord with [34] usages [35] of utterly depraved men.

Moreover it is obvious to comprehend also this: that in such a matter and in a festival of such [36] a worship for a disagreement to exist is unlawful. For our Saviour has transmitted to us the one day of our deliverance, that is the day of the most holy Passion; he has wished his Catholic Church to be one,[37] of which the members, although certainly they have been distributed [38] into both many and diverse places, nevertheless by one spirit, that is, the divine will, are cherished. Let your Sanctities' sagacity consider how both grievous and unsuitable it is that on the same days some should observe fasts, but others should celebrate feasts, and after the days of Easter some should appear at feasts and at amusements, but others should devote themselves to appointed fasts.[39] On this account, then, Divine Provi-

52. THE PASCHAL QUESTION, 325

dence desires to obtain appropriate correction and to bring this to a single regulation—as I indeed think that all understand.[40]

Since, then, it was fitting that this should be corrected in such a way that there should be nothing in common [41] with the nation of [42] those patricides [13] and slayers of the Lord and since the arrangement is quite proper, which all the churches of the western and the southern and the northern sections of the world—and some of the eastern parts [43]— observe carefully, all, therefore, at the present time have considered it to be well. And I myself undertook that it would please your Sagacities that whatever is observed by one and harmonious opinion in the Romans' city, both Italy and all [44] Africa, Egypt, the Spains,[45] the Gauls,[46] the Britains,[47] the Libyas,[48] all Greece,[49] the Asian and the Pontic and the Cilician dioceses, your Wisdoms unrestrainedly would accept also this, when they consider not only that the number of churches in the abovementioned regions is rather large, but also that this particularly is a most sacred matter for all in common to wish [50] whatever strict reason appears to require and to have no communion with the perjury of the Jews.[51]

That I may state briefly the chiefest point, by the common decision of all it was resolved that the most holy feast of Easter should be celebrated on one and the same day. For in such holiness it is not seemly that there should be any difference and it is more meritorious to follow this opinion, wherein will be no combination of alien error and mistake.

Since these matters, therefore, are thus arranged,[52] receive unrestrainedly God's grace [53] and truly divine command, for, whatever may be [54] done in sacred sessions of the bishops, all this has reference to the divine will.

Wherefore, when you have indicated to all our beloved brethren the matters publicly proclaimed, you are obliged forthwith both to accept the aforesaid arrangement [55] and to establish the observance of the most holy day,[56] that, whenever I have come into the presence of your Dispositions, long desired by me, I can celebrate with you the holy festival on one and the same day and I may rejoice with you for all things, when I see diabolic savagery destroyed by the Divine Power through our endeavours, while your [57] faith and peace and harmony flourish everywhere.[58]

God shall guard [59] you, beloved brethren.

1. The most opposition, though temporary, arose among the Syrian Christians, although their bishops seem to have co-operated loyally with the sentence of their Nicene colleagues.

2. When Pope St Gregory I the Great's representatives reached Britain in 597, they discovered that the few Christians in southern England were keeping

Easter according to a computation perhaps originally imported from Asia Minor, but certainly long obsolete in the rest of Christendom. It was not until the Synod of Whitby (Streoneshalh) in 663/4 that the Roman system was substituted (Bede, *HE* 3. 25). Even then in some sections there was the lapse of several generations ere the adoption of the Catholic Easter became general in Britain.

3. The controversy, which caused considerable acrimony, was primarily whether Easter should be observed on a Sunday or on the Jewish holy day of Nisan 14, which could occur on a weekday. Those who followed the Jewish practice consequently were called Fourteenthers (Quartodecimans, Tessarescaedecatitans, Tetraditans). After Pope St Victor I (189-99) had excommunicated them (Eusebius, *HE* 5. 23-5), such nonconformists, who were strongest in Asia Minor, gradually disappeared. Consult F. E. Brightman, "The Quartodeciman Question" in *JTS* 25 (1924) 254-70; Jalland, 115-22.

That the dispute should be about the date of a festival of the Church is characteristic of the age, but imposes no discredit on its intelligence; again and again deep differences, whether national or religious, have wrought external expression in equally insignificant ways. Modern industrial disputes have developed from capital's refusal to raise labour's rate of pay by a few pennies.

4. Syrian and Mesopotamian Christians kept their Easter festival on the Sunday after the Jews had held their Passover. But Egyptian Christians particularly (and probably others) calculated the Sunday for Easter without reference to the Jewish calendar. Among the latter there was considerable variation because of different lunar cycles as well as divergent equinoctial dates. Although we have not the text of the individual Nicene canon to indicate the solution reached in the council, from scattered, but contemporary, notices it appears that the fathers ordained: (1) Easter should be observed by all and everywhere on the same Sunday; (2) this Sunday should succeed the fourteenth day of the paschal moon; (3) that moon should be the paschal moon whose fourteenth day followed the vernal equinox; (4) the Church of Alexandria, since the most competent astronomers were in that city, should decide the date and then should announce it annually to the world.

Pursuant to the last decision—which was natural, for after the foundation of Alexandria (see no. 98, n. 1) all ancient astronomers of note either taught there or were trained there—the Alexandrian Church accepted the commission and continued such announcement at least into the latter half of the next century. From the earlier period are preserved (mostly in Syriac, partly in Greek) parts of 27 of the 45 *Festal Letters* known to have been written by St Athanasius while patriarch of Alexandria (328-73). Athanasius usually concludes the more complete epistles by giving the dates for the commencement of Lent and of Holy Week as well as for Easter and for Pentecost. Translated into Latin (*PG* 26. 1360-1444) and into English (*A Select Library of Nicene and Post-Nicene Fathers of the Christian Church* [New York, 1892], 2. 4. 506-53), the letters' interest, apart from chronology, is chiefly practical, for the use and the abuse of fast and of feast maintain a prominent place.

The Roman reception of the tables of Dionysius Exiguus *c.* 525 led to the current system of calculating Easter Day as the first Sunday occurring after the first fourteenth day of the fictitious calendar moon following the vernal equinox, which usually is reckoned to be 21 March. In simpler style, as a result, Easter falls earliest on 22 March and latest on 25 April.

5. Several captions exist: Socrates has simply "Another letter"; Gelasius gives "The Emperor Constantine's letter, which from the Nicenes' city he sent to the bishops who had been absent from the synod"; Nicephorus reads "The great Emperor Constantine's letter to the churches everywhere about the accomplishments in the holy synod".

6. Socrates and Theodoret have "Constantine Augustus to the churches", but Gelasius reads "Constantine Augustus to churches and bishops, who have been absent from the holy and great synod in Nicaea, greeting". Nicephorus has no superscription.

7. All later writers insert "otherwise".

8. Gelasius inserts "of the most God-beloved bishops in this city of the Nicenes".

9. Socrates omits this word.

10. Gelasius inserts "Christians".

11. Gelasius substitutes "the salutary festival of the most holy Easter".

12. Gelasius substitutes "truth".

13. Apparently an allusion to their action in the conviction of Jesus. Consult Toynbee, 8. 283.

It was rather ironical for Constantine to hold up holy hands in horror at the Jews, whom he later in this letter accused of patricide (cf. *infra* the text at nn. 25 and 42), when he himself soon was to be guilty of filicide, nepoticide, uxoricide (see no. 63, n. 2). But the murder of a god in human guise and the murder of a son and of a nephew and of a wife doubtless are different.

14. An old emendation of ἔθους (usage), which Gelasius' editor adopts, for ἔθνους (nation) may be valid, though Constantine in this letter has shown and will show anti-Semitism.

15. All later writers substitute "to appear".

16. The crucifixion of Jesus is meant.

17. Nicephorus reads "you".

18. There is an obvious lacuna in Gelasius' text here, for all the others have the phrase.

19. Socrates and Gelasius omit the word.

20. Socrates and Nicephorus insert "for".

21. Gelasius reads "a course and a proper law", misreading νόμιμος (legitimate) as νόμος (law); Nicephorus has "a course and a legal (νομικός) and proper standard (κανών)".

22. Socrates has "hateful".

23. Gelasius omits this adverb.
24. Gelasius inserts "against us".
25. Eusebius alone exhibits *and patricide*. Cf. *supra* n. 13.
26. Nicephorus omits the pronoun.
27. All later writers insert "ever".
28. For the phrase Nicephorus substitutes "according to experience".
29. Both St Ambrose (*Ep.* 23. 15) and St Epiphanius (*Haer.* 3. 1. 70. 11) testify that the Jewish Passover can come ere the equinox (21 March), which starts the solar year. Therefore, if the Jews calculated from one to another vernal equinox, it occasionally happened that in a twelve-month span two Passovers were celebrated, though, since their religious year was lunar, this seems not to have troubled them, who from their point of view, of course, never celebrated the Passover twice in the same year. But the same charge still can be made against Christians, for the most recent instance, Easter falling in 1958 on 6 April and in 1959 on 29 March, provides two Easters in different months within one year of twelve months. It may be interesting to note the rare conjunction of Passover and Easter on 18 April 1954—a coincidence which the fathers at Nicaea aimed to avoid.
30. Gelasius reads "who acknowledgedly have fearful error?"
31. Socrates substitutes "at least".
32. Gelasius has a gap, wherein *maintain . . . prayer* has disappeared.
33. Socrates and Nicephorus read "our".
34. Nicephorus inserts "or to follow".
35. Gelasius substitutes "perception".
36. Socrates takes *such* with *festival* and later with Nicephorus substitutes "most ungodly" for *unlawful*.
37. This desire is expressed exegetically from Jesus' words in John 10. 16, 17. 20–3.
38. Gelasius reads "collected".
39. That is, it is indecorous for Christians, by calculating Easter at different dates, to present to pagan (as well as to Christian) sight the varied spectacle of some fasting in Holy Week and of others feasting in Easter week.
40. Nicephorus substitutes "as I indeed understand dispassionately".
41. Gelasius inserts "to us".
42. Theodoret, Gelasius, Nicephorus omit *the nation of* and the last writer also omits the next three words.
43. Cf. *supra* n. 4 *ad init*. Gelasius adds "do not accept".
44. Socrates' editor so punctuates that *all* belongs with *Egypt*.
45. See no. 19, n. 27.
46. See no. 203, n. 4.
47. Britain—the term *British Isles* (*Insulae Britannicae*) antedates that of Britain (*Britannia*)—by this time had evolved from the single province of Britannia (created after part of England had been conquered in 43) and from the two provinces of Britannia Superior and Britannia Inferior (formed from

the original province in 197) into the four provinces of Maxima Caesariensis, Flavia Caesariensis, Britannia Prima, Britannia Secunda. To these was added Valentia as a fifth province in 369. While the general position of these five divisions is known, their precise limits are unknown. The Roman-held part of Great Britain constituted a civil diocese, whose vicar usually resided at Eboracum (York).

48. While the term *Libya* is a very loose geographical expression—ancient geographers sometimes applied it to Africa as a whole and sometimes regarded it as part of Asia or even of Europe—early in the Dominate the combined province of Cyrenaica and Crete (created in 67 B.C. after the conquest of the former in 74 B.C. and of the latter in 67 B.C.) was divided into the two provinces of Libya Superior and Libya Inferior, of which the latter was the larger, and whose division lay close to the 40th degree of east longitude. Each province was attached to the civil diocese of the East, while Crete became a separate province and fell to the diocese of Moesia in the Balkans. The Libyan provinces included then that portion of North Africa west of Egypt, east of Tripoli, north of the Sahara Desert, and roughly corresponded with the ancient district of Cyrenaica in its widest sense.

49. Gelasius' order after *Africa* and before *Asia* is "and Spain and Gaul, the Britains and Egypt and the Libyas and all Greece and".

50. Gelasius substitutes "to plan".

51. Probably a reference to their conduct in accepting God as their king and then denying Jesus, when they professed to Pilate that they had no king but Caesar (John 19. 15).

Most of this sentence Socrates requotes (*HE* 5. 22).

52. Gelasius adds "by divine decision through so many and such holy bishops".

53. Socrates and Nicephorus substitute "celestial" for *God's grace*, while Theodoret and Gelasius read "celestial" for *God's*.

54. Gelasius reads "has been".

55. Gelasius adds "of the Catholic faith".

56. Gelasius adds "of Easter".

57. Theodoret and Gelasius have "our".

58. Gelasius adds "I shall send with you thankful hymns up to God, the All-Benefactor and Saviour."

59. Socrates and Nicephorus convert the indicative into the optative.

53. LETTER OF CONSTANTINE I ON CONFORMITY WITH ORTHODOXY, 325

(Socrates, *HE* 1. 9)

Since some of the chief supporters of the Arian heresy, which was condemned at the First Ecumenical Council of Nicaea in 325, were of Egyptian provenance,[1] Constantine, who had convoked the council to compose this controversy, considered that more effect would be given to the restoration of peace, if he should exhort the Christians of Alexandria, whose Christian community was traditionally the oldest in Egypt [2] and whose church was the seat of one of the five patriarchates of the early Church,[3] to accept the synod's decision, which the emperor termed the judgement of God.

Gelasius also has this letter (*HE* 2. 37. 1–9).

Emperor Constantine's letter.[4]
Constantine Augustus to the Catholic Church of the Alexandrians.[5]
Greeting, beloved brethren.

From Divine Providence we have received the perfect favour that we, having been removed from all error, may recognize one and the same faith. Not at all, then, is power over us permitted to the Devil; if he, having used base devices, had made any attack, everything has been destroyed entirely.[6] The brilliance of truth, pursuant to God's command, has conquered the dissensions, the schisms, those tumults, and—that I may say so—the deadly poisons of the discords. One, therefore, we all and by the name [7] worship and that he exists we believe.

But that this might happen, by God's suggestion I convoked to the Nicaeans' city most of the bishops, with whom I,[8] one of you, rejoicing exceedingly to be your fellow-servant, also myself undertook the investigation of the truth. Accordingly all matters, as many as seemed to engender ambiguity or a pretext for disagreement,[9] have been canvassed and accurately have been scrutinized. And let the Divine Majesty pardon as many terribly great blasphemies about our Saviour [10] and about our hope and life as certain persons unbecomingly uttered, both declaiming and confessing that they believe things contrary to the God-inspired Scriptures and the holy faith. At all events,[11] when three hundred and more bishops,[12] admired for both prudence and sagacity, were confirming one and the same faith, which by the truths and the precisions of God's law has been begotten to be *the* faith,[13] Arius alone, yielding to the Devil's activity, was observed as having disseminated by unholy intention this evil, first among you and then among the rest.

Therefore let us accept the verdict [14] which the Almighty [15] has provided; let us return to our beloved brethren, from whom a certain irreverent servitor of the Devil has separated us; let us go with all zeal to the common body and our legitimate members.[16] For this befits your wisdom and faith and holiness, that, since the error of that man, who has been proved to be an enemy of the truth, has been refuted, you should return to the divine favour. For what has pleased the three hundred[17] bishops is not at all other than God's[18] judgement, particularly whereas the Holy Spirit, resident in the thinking faculties of such and so great men, has illuminated the divine will.

Wherefore let none doubt, let none defer; but all eagerly return into the truest road, in order that, whenever I come to you presently, I may avow with you due thanks to the All-Overseeing God, because he, having indicated the pure faith, has restored the love invoked for you.[19]

May God guard[20] you, beloved brethren.

1. Theonas, bishop of Marmarica, and Secundus, bishop of Ptolemaïs, were condemned along with the heresiarch himself, Arius, priest of Alexandria. Besides these three, Meletius, bishop of Lycopolis, who eventually led about thirty Egyptian bishops into schism (see no. 68, n. 2), was permitted to retain his episcopal rank, but was deprived of his jurisdiction and was sentenced not to depart from his own city in the Thebaïd.

2. St Mark, the evangelist and St Peter's disciple (1 Pet. 5. 13; Eusebius, HE 2. 15, 3. 39. 15), was its reputed founder (Eusebius, HE 2. 16, 24).

3. The other four were Antioch, Rome, Constantinople, Jerusalem (see nos. 284, n. 4, 375, n. 7, 470, n. 44).

The theory of the patriarchs' pentarchy was prevalent in the East after the Fourth Ecumenical Council at Chalcedon in 451 had added Jerusalem as the fifth patriarchal see. But Peter III, patriarch of Antioch (1052-6), asserted (PG 120. 757) that *stricto sensu* only the ordinary of the see of Antioch is a patriarch, for he regarded the bishops of Constantinople and of Jerusalem as archbishops and the bishop of Rome (who by most eastern prelates was esteemed as *primus inter pares*) and the bishop of Alexandria as popes (see no. 68, n. 1). Peter's attitude well attests the animus evinced in the Church of the fourth and the fifth centuries, when patriarchs sometimes possessed more pride of place than passion for piety and in their emulation occasionally endangered the faith of a few even of the faithful.

See S. H. Scott, *The Eastern Churches and the Papacy* (London, 1928), 250-6, for the title "patriarch".

4. Gelasius adds "to the Alexandrians against Arius and to all the orthodox".

5. Gelasius adds "and of all the orthodox".

6. Literally "from the foundations"; our idiom is "from the roots".

7. This curious expression *and by the name* (καὶ τῷ ὀνόματι) is susceptible of several interpretations: (1) "nominally", which, though true, weakens the emperor's position; (2) "even (*or* also) one in name", which, while it ignores the

nice distinction of the two persons in Christ and the doctrine of the Trinity, yet is a strong appeal for the unity which Constantine craves; (3) "and by the name", which in periphrasis may mean: "we all worship one God and we know whom we worship by the name which is his", i.e. the one true God.

8. Gelasius inserts "myself, just as".

9. The reading is uncertain. Later in this chapter, when he comments on this letter, Socrates writes "a pretext for either ambiguity or disagreement". Possibly the received reading should be retained: "through ambiguity a pretext of disagreement". A conjecture is "through ambiguity or disagreement a pretext for dissension". Gelasius reads "ambiguities and pretexts for disagreements".

10. A variant reading, which makes better sense than the received text, is translated.

11. Gelasius prefixes "therefore" to this phrase.

12. The traditional number of bishops assisting at the Church's first council is 318, a figure symbolically explained in Christian antiquity as derived from Abraham's circumcision of 318 men of his household (Gen. 14. 14, 17. 23). Doubtless the explanation was aided by the so-called *Epistle of Barnabas*, 9. 7-9 (dated between 70 and 135), where Abraham's act is interpreted as mystically indicating the name and the crucifixion of Jesus. In Greek, which expresses its numerals by alphabetic letters, 318 is TIH in capitals: T = 300, I = 10, H = 8. IH are the first two letters of the word Jesus (IHΣOΥΣ) and T, of course, represents the Cross, on which Jesus was crucified and which in Christian art is the well-known Tau cross.

While the tradition of 318 is ascribed to St Athanasius (PG 26. 1032), yet this eyewitness elsewhere estimates about 300 (PG 25. 772) and Constantine, the convocator of the council, calculates here more than 300; but Eusebius, another participant, puts the number at more than 250 (VC 3. 8) and St Eustathius, another conclavist, reports as many as 270 (Theodoret, HE 1. 8. 1). The truth is that the several surviving lists, which are not in agreement and quite likely are incomplete, indicate about 220 (see Kidd, 2. 23).

13. Gelasius reads "which also by the truths has been begotten to be the divine law's precise faith".

14. Gelasius reads "faith".

15. Gelasius adds "God".

16. Gelasius reads "let us return to the common body and our legitimate members; let us go with all zeal".

The figure of Christians being members of one church, which is Christ's mystical body, is as old as St Paul: Rom. 12. 4-5; 1 Cor. 6. 15, 12. 12-27; Eph. 4. 25, 5. 30.

17. Gelasius reads "holy" for this numeral.

18. Gelasius inserts "only Son's".

19. Gelasius has "us".

20. Gelasius has future indicative for future optative.

54. LETTER OF CONSTANTINE I ON ERECTION OF THE CHURCH OF THE HOLY SEPULCHRE, 326

(Eusebius, *VC* 3. 30-2)

This letter, preserved also by Socrates (*HE* 1. 9), Theodoret (*HE* 1. 17), Gelasius (*HE* 3. 5), Nicephorus (*HE* 8. 28), authorizes Macarius, bishop of Jerusalem, to construct a church over the Holy Sepulchre in Jerusalem and promises the co-operation of the diocesan vicar and the provincial governor, whom the emperor has commanded to assist.

In obedience to Constantine's order Macarius erected a magnificent edifice,[1] whose details Eusebius describes (*VC* 3. 33-40) and which was dedicated in 335.

Letter of the emperor to Macarius, bishop of the Church in Jerusalem, about the construction of the martyry.[2]

Victor Constantine, Greatest, Augustus to Macarius.[3]

So great is our Saviour's grace that no supply of words seems to be sufficient[4] for the present miracle.[5] For that the mark[6] of that most holy Passion,[7] buried beneath the earth long ago, should have escaped detection for so many periods of years, until[8] it was destined to shine forth to his servants, who have been liberated through the removal of the common enemy of all,[9] truly exceeds all wonder. For, if all who throughout the whole world are reputed to be wise, when collected into one and the same place,[10] should wish to say something worthy of the[11] event, they could not achieve the slightest part of it, since[12] the belief in this miracle surpasses every nature capable of human reasoning by as much as celestial matters are[13] mightier than human affairs. Hence, therefore, this ever is my first and sole object: that, as the belief in the truth daily[14] shows itself by newer miracles, so the souls of us all may become more eager toward the sacred law[15] with all[16] prudence and harmonious zeal.

What,[17] therefore, I think is evident to everyone, that I wish you especially to believe: namely, that I care more than all things that with beauty of buildings we may adorn[18] that hallowed place, which by God's command I have[19] lightened of a most shameful appendage[20] of an idol, as of some imposed weight—a spot considered sacred from the beginning by God's decision, but declared more sacred, since it has brought to light the guarantee of the Saviour's Passion.

Therefore it is proper for your Sagacity both to make arrangements and to make provision for each of the necessary things in such a way that not only the basilica[21] may be better than those everywhere, but also the rest [22] may be [23] such that all the most beautiful buildings in every city may be surpassed by [24] this building.

And know that attention concerning both erection [25] and enhancement of the walls has been entrusted by us to our friend Dracilian, who manages the [26] prefects' [27] matters,[28] and to the province's governor.[29] For by my Piety it has been ordered that immediately through their care should be dispatched artificers and artisans and all things, as many as [30] they may know from your Sagacity happen to be necessary for the construction. Concerning pillars or marbles, after an estimate has been made, whatever you should have considered as both most worthy [31] and most useful,[31] hasten to write to us, that, of what quantity and of what quality we may learn through your letter there is need, these can be transported from every side,[32] for it is just for the most miraculous [31] place in the world to be made deservedly splendid. With respect to the ceiling of the basilica [33] I wish to know from you whether that it be panelling [34] or that it be made of some other sort of [35] work seems good to you, for if it is going to be panelling,[34] it will be possible for it to be adorned also with gold.

For the rest:[36] your Sanctity should make [37] it known to the aforesaid governors as speedily as possible of how many artisans and artificers and of what expenses there is need and immediately should hasten [38] to report to me not only about both marbles and pillars but also about panellings,[34] if really this you should decide is more beautiful.[39]

God shall guard [40] you, beloved brother.

1. Consult G. Jeffery, *A Brief Description of the Holy Sepulchre*, etc. (Cambridge, 1919), 53–62 (esp. figs. 11, 12, 14–16); and H. T. F. Duckworth, *The Church of the Holy Sepulchre* (London, 1922), 93–135. Add now K. J. Conant and G. Downey, "The Original Buildings at the Holy Sepulchre in Jerusalem" in *Speculum*, 31 (1956) 1–48, and A. Parrot, *Golgotha and the Church of the Holy Sepulchre* (New York, 1957), 49–59, 66–76.

2. Socrates' caption is "Another letter to Macarius" and Gelasius supplies "Letter of Constantine, the pious emperor, to the bishop of Jerusalem about the Saviour's tomb". The other versions are captionless.

It seems rather odd, perhaps, to call the church a martyr's chapel, but, of course, the Crucifixion properly can be considered a martyrdom.

3. Socrates adds "of Jerusalem" and Gelasius adds "bishop of Jerusalem".

4. Gelasius inserts a parenthetical "I suppose".

5. Socrates substitutes "event" ($\pi\rho\tilde{\alpha}\gamma\mu\alpha$ for $\theta\alpha\tilde{\upsilon}\mu\alpha$).

6. By this word the emperor means either the Cross, whereon Jesus was crucified and which, tradition tells, St Helena (on whom see no. 525, n. 1), Constantine's mother, discovered, or the sepulchre, wherein Jesus was buried

54. CHURCH OF THE HOLY SEPULCHRE, 326

and which St Helena also revealed by excavation and resolved to restore as part of a Christian church. Although the site is still controverted (see Parrot *supra* in n. 1), according to Eusebius (*VC* 3. 26–7) the sepulchre was covered with dirt and rubbish as a foundation for a temple of Venus, all of which Constantine ordered to be removed. St Jerome (*Ep.* 58. 3. 5) says that from Hadrian's time [doubtless after 130, when the emperor resettled Jerusalem as Colonia Aelia Capitolina, on which see no. 483, n. 15] statues to Jupiter and to Venus marked the spot.

7. Gelasius substitutes "tomb".

8. Gelasius reads "until through our Saviour God's grace the tyranny of the common enemy of us all was removed; and Christ, the absolute monarch, granting freedom from this tyranny to his servants, shed light upon the knowledge of this most holy place, so that truly it exceeds all wonder".

9. By defeating in battle Licinius, his colleague in rule, Constantine became sole emperor in 324.

10. Or possibly "when united for one and the same project".

11. Gelasius substitutes "this".

12. Socrates, Theodoret, Nicephorus omit the conjunction.

13. All later authors insert "to be" as an infinitive.

14. Nicephorus omits the adverb.

15. Christianity. Nicephorus omits the phrase.

16. All later authors omit this word.

17. All later authors prefix this paragraph with "since".

18. The Greek style closes the paragraph with *we may adorn* and, since these words are thus rather removed from the object *that hallowed place,* Gelasius feels that he must give some indication of the superior object; so he inserts "this" with reference to *that hallowed place.* Besides he changes the construction *that . . . we may adorn* to "to adorn".

19. Gelasius inserts "ordered to be".

20. Gelasius substitutes "error".

21. Gelasius inserts "of the said most holy site".

22. Constantine may refer to other buildings to be built in connection with the church or may contrast the church as a whole with the church in its particular details.

23. Gelasius inserts "shown".

24. Gelasius inserts "the splendour of".

25. Socrates and Nicephorus read "work" (ἐργασία for ἔγερσις).

26. All later authors insert "the most distinguished".

27. Gelasius reads "provinces", probably through a typographical error, for the apparatus criticus shows no variant.

28. This Greek circumlocution appears to denote the function of the diocesan vicar, who, as in no. 15, n. 12, appears as the assistant to the praetorian prefects. The prefecture is that of the East, the diocese is that of the East, the province is Palaestina Prima.

29. See no. 59, n. 10 *ad fin*.
30. Gelasius and Nicephorus insert "which" and "if" respectively.
31. All later authors have the comparative degree.
32. Gelasius inserts "for the said building's splendour".
33. Gelasius inserts "of the said building".
34. Transliterated from Latin *lacunarium*, but made feminine in Greek.
35. Gelasius inserts "most brilliant".
36. Theodoret's and Gelasius' editors make this phrase the subject of the preceding infinitive. Gelasius starts the new sentence with "And about these matters".
37. Gelasius reads future indicative for aorist subjunctive.
38. All later authors have aorist imperative for aorist subjunctive.
39. Eusebius later announces (*VC* 3. 36) that the church had a gold-panelled ceiling.
40. Socrates and Nicephorus have future optative.

55. MANDATE OF CONSTANTINE I ON EXCLUSION OF RICH PERSONS FROM THE CLERICATE, 326

(*CT* 16. 2. 6)

When he has learned that his earlier law (no. 33) on debarment of wealthier classes from the clerical ranks, whither they had fled to escape the burden of public services, was not producing the anticipated results, since municipal senators continued to enter the clerical calling, Constantine repeats his statute that the clergy should be selected only from the poorer citizens.

The same Augustus to Ablavius,[1] praetorian prefect.

Exemption from public services should be conferred neither by popular consent nor on any persons at all petitioning under pretext of being clergymen;[2] and great numbers should not be added to the clergymen heedlessly and beyond measure; but, when a clergyman shall have died, to the deceased person's place should be selected another who shall have had no familial connection with municipal senators [3] and who has not the wealth of resources, which can endure very easily public functions: so that, if there is a doubt between the community and the clergy over anyone's name, if equity ascribes him to public services and if he is known to be suitable as a municipal senator [3] because of family or patrimony, he should be excluded from the clergy and should be assigned to the community. For it is proper that the rich should sustain the necessary expenses of the present world, but that the poor should be supported by the churches' wealth.[4]

Posted on 1 June, Constantine Augustus for the seventh time and Constantius Caesar [5] being consuls.

1. Otherwise and more frequently Ablabius.
2. In *CT* 1. 6. 4 (dated 365) Valentinian I and Valens regulate petitions from a sacred and venerable people (*sacer ac venerabilis populus*) by refusing to accede to requests before they have been consulted. The phrase is obscure and need not refer to the clergy, but may be a periphrasis for the people of either capital city. At any rate the emperors are courteous, though they promise nothing.
3. Here *municeps* for the more usual *curialis* or *decurio*.
4. See no. 515, n. 3.
5. See no. 28, n. 7.

56. MANDATE OF CONSTANTINE I ON CLERICAL PRIVILEGES, 326

(*CT* 16. 5. 1)

This directive (repeated in *CI* 1. 5. 1) debars heretics and schismatics from exemptions enjoyed by the orthodox clergy.

Emperor Constantine August to Dracilian.[1]

Privileges which have been bestowed in consideration of religion ought to benefit only observers of Catholic law.[2]

Moreover we wish heretics and schismatics not only to be alien from these privileges, but also to be bound and to be subjected to various public services.

Posted on 1 September at Gerastus, Constantine Augustus for the seventh time and Constantius Caesar [3] being consuls.

1. He was vicar of the diocese of the Orient.
2. The Catholic religion.
3. See no. 28, n. 7.

57. MANDATE OF CONSTANTINE I ON PRIVILEGES FOR NOVATIANS, 326

(CT 16. 5. 2)

Constantine the Great by this constitution recognizes the Novatians only as schismatics, though they also were heretics, and exempts them from his programme of enforcing the canons of the Nicene Council.[1]

The same Augustus to Bassus.[2]

We have not discovered that Novatians were pre-condemned to such an extent that we should consider that on them ought not to be bestowed what they have requested.

Accordingly we order that they firmly should possess without disquietude their own church's buildings and sites suitable for burial: namely, those properties which for a long time they either have had through purchase or have acquired in any way whatsoever.

Of course, there shall be made provision that they should not try to appropriate unlawfully to themselves any of those properties which clearly had belonged before the schism [3] to the churches of perpetual sanctity.

Given on 25 September at Spoleto, Constantine Augustus for the seventh time and Constantius Caesar [4] being consuls.

1. See especially canon 8, where the Novatians are called Cathari ("the Clean"). The council met in 325.
2. See no. 33, n. 1.
3. It began in the spring of 251, when Novatian, after whom these primitive Puritans took their name, became anti-pope in Rome.
4. See no. 28, n. 7.

58. LETTER OF CONSTANTINE I ON RECALL OF ARIUS, 327–34

(Socrates, HE 1. 25)

Through the intrigues of Eusebius, bishop of Nicomedia, and of others, an Arian priest, whom Constantia, the sister of Constantine, maintained in her household and whom at her death she commended to her brother's attention, persuaded the emperor that the heresiarch Arius, whom he had exiled, had been misrepresented and really was in agreement with the decisions of the Nicene Council (325) and, if received at court, would assent publicly to its canons and its creed. Whereupon, though professing amazement, Constantine recalled

Arius in the following letter, which Nicephorus also preserves (*HE* 8. 47) and on whose date see introd. to no. 71.

To what can be attributed the changed attitude of Constantine toward Catholicism? Beyond the explanation above advanced—and it accounts only for Arius' recall—must exist something stronger to explain the emperor's demand that Arians should be readmitted into the Church (nos. 71 and 72) and his exile of St Athanasius (see introd. to no. 75) and of other orthodox prelates (related by the ecclesiastical historians) and his baptism at the hands of an Arian bishop (see introd. to no. 50). Probably Constantine eventually discovered that the Nicene Council's decision against Arianism was disapproved by most Christians in the East, where this heresy had its headquarters, and gradually and in the interest of pacification—an ideal evinced in his earlier epistles against Arianism (nos. 47, 48, 50, 51, 53)—the sovereign changed sides and championed the majority's cause.[1] Fortunately, however, he had not long to live to lend his name's prestige to a perverted phase of Christianity.

Victor Constantine, Greatest, Augustus to Arius.

Some time ago it was disclosed to your Constancy that you might come to my court, that you could enjoy our sight. We are greatly surprised that you have not done this immediately.

Wherefore now, having mounted a public conveyance,[2] hasten to come to our[3] court, that, having experienced our kindness[4] and attention, you can return to your native community.

May God guard you, beloved.

Given on 27 November.

1. Vasiliev, 56–7, supports this suggestion, which is not devoid of difficulties.
2. See no. 95, n. 41.
3. The number of the possessive pronoun shifts here to the plural.
4. Nicephorus reads εὐνοίας for εὐμενείας, but, since the words seem synonymous, the difference is negligible.

59. LETTER OF CONSTANTINE I ON CLERICAL EXEMPTION FROM PUBLIC DUTIES AND ON CONSTRUCTION OF A BASILICA IN NUMIDIA, 330

(*CSEL* 26. 213–6)

In this imperial constitution about the Donatist schism Constantine grants to the clergy in the province of Numidia the freedom from all public obligations which he had conferred on those in the province of Africa some seventeen years previously (no. 16) and orders the construction of a basilica at the imperial treasury's expense. One paragraph in this epistle shows not a little verbal accord with Constantine's letter, which the emperor mentions here, to the consular of Numidia (no. 60).

Constantine, Victor, Greatest and Triumpher, Ever-August to Zeuzius, Gallicus, Victorine, Sperantius, Januarius, Felix, Crescentius, Pantius, Victor, Babbutius, Donatus, bishops.

Since it is certain that this is the will of the Supreme God, who is the author and the father of this world, through whose beneficence we enjoy life, look up to heaven, even rejoice in human fellowship, that the whole human race should be in common accord and should be cemented in a certain affection of association—as it were—by mutual embraces, it is not doubtful that heresies and schism have proceeded from the Devil, who is the source of wickedness. And so no doubt exists that whatever is done by heretics is done by the instigation of him who has possessed their senses, minds, and thoughts, for, when he has reduced persons of this character under his power, he controls these same ones in everything.[1] Moreover what good can be done by one who is insane, faithless, irreligious, profane, opposed to God, inimical to the Holy Church, who in departing from the Holy, True, Just, Supreme God and Lord of all—who has created us and has reared us in this world,[2] who has given breath for the life which we enjoy and who has wanted us to have that which is his own [3] and has perfected all things by his will—descends by a downward detour to the Devil's side? But, because a soul once possessed by the Evil One— for it must be busy in the business of its teacher—performs those things which appear contrary to equity and to justice, therefore those who have been possessed by the Devil submit to his falsity and wickedness. Moreover it is not marvellous that the bad depart from the good, for thus rightly it has been signified by the proverb, "Like with like foregather".[4] Those who have been infected with the evil of an impious mind necessarily should withdraw from our fellowship. "A man, if indeed wicked," as the Scripture says, "from a wicked treasure produces wicked things, but a good man from good produces good."[5]

But since, as has been said, heretics and schismatics, who, forsaking good and following evil, do those things which displease God, are proved to cling to the Devil, who is their father, your Gravities have done very correctly and wisely and pursuant to the holy precept of the faith by abstaining from their perverse altercations and by conceding to these same persons that which, though not due to them and not their property, they claim to enjoy,[6] lest, as their perversity is malicious and treacherous, they even might burst forth into riots and amid tumultuous meetings might incite others like themselves, and thus might arise something which could not be stayed. Their wicked design, to be sure, ever demands that they do the Devil's works. And so, when they with their own father [7] are in the ascendancy through the patience shown by God's priests,[8] let these who worship the Supreme God get glory for themselves, but let those obtain damnation and condign punishments. Surely the judgement of the Supreme God may appear greater and juster from this, because with equanimity he tolerates them and with longsuffering he condemns all the acts which have proceeded from these persons by enduring them, since indeed God has promised that he will be the avenger of all.[9] And so, when vengeance is committed to God, severer punishment is inflicted on the enemies. And now I have learned that you, God's servants and priests,[8] have done this willingly and I have rejoiced greatly because on the impious and the wicked, the sacrilegious and the profane, the faithless and the irreligious and the unacceptable to God and the enemies of the Church, you demand no punishment and because you request that these same persons rather should receive pardon. This is to know God truly and thoroughly, this is to follow his precepts, this is to believe happily, this is to think truly, this is to know that, when in this life these same persons are spared, greater punishment is occasioned hereafter for the opponents of the Church.

Thereupon, on receipt of a letter of your Sapiences and Gravities, I discovered that the heretics or the schismatics had decided to seize with customary wickedness that basilica of the Catholic Church, which I had ordered to be constructed in the city of Constantine,[10] and, though often warned both by us and by our governors at our orders, had been unwilling to relinquish what was not theirs; but that you, however, imitators of the patience of the Supreme God, with calm mind relinquishing to their wickedness those things which are yours, beg rather for yourselves another place in exchange, namely, the treasury building. And this petition in pursuance of my custom I gladly accepted and I immediately sent a suitable letter to the treasurer, that he should cause the building of our properties [11] to be transferred with all its legal authority to the ownership of the Catholic Church.[12] And this I have given with ready liberality and I have commanded it to be delivered to you straightway.

And, moreover, in that place I have directed a basilica to be built at the fiscal expense and also I have ordered a letter to be written to the consular of Numidia, that he himself should assist your Holinesses in all matters concerning the construction of the said church.[12]

I have directed also, according to the statute of my law,[13] that the lectors and the subdeacons of the Catholic Church and also the rest, who by the instigation of the abovementioned [14] have been summoned to public services or to the decurionate in view of certain characteristics of fitness for service therein, should be summoned to no public service; but also those who have been drafted at the heretics' instigation we have ordered to be freed forthwith from burdensome performances of public duties.

Moreover I also have commanded that my law promulgated concerning Catholic clergymen should be observed.[15] And all these matters, that they may become known to your Patiences, have been written in full by the attestation of this letter.[16]

And, indeed, would that the heretics or the schismatics at length were providing for their own salvation and that, after they had wiped away their darkness, they were opening their eyes to a vision of the true light and that they were departing from the Devil and that, even late, they were fleeing to God, who is one and true, who is the judge of all![5] But, because it is certain that they remain in their wickedness and desire to die in their crimes, our admonition and previous earnest exhortation is enough for these same persons. For, if they had desired to obey our orders, they would be delivered from all evil.

Let us, brethren, however, follow the things which are ours, let us follow eagerly the commandments, let us by good acts keep the divine precepts, let us, defending our life from errors, with God's mercy favouring us, direct it along the right path!

Given on 5 February at Sofia.

1. *Usquequaque* can denote also a temporal ("always") or a spatial ("everywhere") notion.

2. Literally "in this light" (*in hac luce*), a common Christian phrase.

3. This makes the best sense of a corrupt clause, which is *qui nos id quod suum esse voluit*. Probably *est habere* should be read for *esse*.

4. *Pares cum paribus congregari*. Apparently in Latin as old as Cicero, who in his *Cato Maior*, 3. 7 (written 44 B.C.) has Cato the Censor quote it at the supposed date of the dialogue (150 B.C.) and characterize it then as an ancient adage. But the idea is in Greek as old as the *Odyssey*, where it occurs in 17. 218.

5. The closest Biblical reference to this is Matt. 12. 35 (cf. Luke 6. 45).

6. The reference perhaps is to ecclesiastical establishments (churches and other properties) occupied by the Donatists, who refused to surrender these.

7. The Devil is meant.

8. See no. 16, n. 4.

9. A reminiscence of Rom. 12. 19 or of several Old Testament texts.

10. Formerly Cirta, a Phoenician foundation in Numidia, restored by Constantine, who called it Constantina (now Constantine in Algeria) after himself.

Since Constantine renamed Cirta as Constantina and ordered the building of a basilica there, it is interesting to note that two generations later (in 394) an imperial constitution (*CT* 15. 1. 31 = *CI* 8. 11. 10) considered it high treason for any provincial governor to inscribe his own name rather than that of the emperor on any completed public work. For gubernatorial assistance in such work see nos. 45 and 54.

11. The phrase *domus bonorum nostrorum* probably means the local headquarters of the emperor's private properties (*res privatae*) in Numidia.

12. This letter has not survived.

13. No. 60.

14. The schismatics are meant.

15. It is not certain of which statute Constantine thinks. Of those extant the likeliest is no. 30, but nos. 16, 32, 41, 56 cannot be excluded.

16. That is, this epistle serves to certify and to confirm all these privileges.

60. MANDATE OF CONSTANTINE I ON CLERICAL EXEMPTION FROM SENATORIAL SERVICE, 330

(*CT* 16. 2. 7)

Confirmation of this statute comes from this emperor's epistle of the same date to the Numidian bishops (no. 59). In the present directive Constantine directs that the minor clergy should not be drafted for duty in local senates.

The same Augustus to Valentine, consular of Numidia.

Lectors of the Divine Scriptures and subdeacons and all other clergymen, who through heretics'[1] injustice have been summoned to a municipal senate,[2] should be released and for the future (according to the similar case of the East) should not be at all summoned to municipal senates, but should possess fullest immunity.

Given on 5 February at Sofia, Gallican and Symmachus being consuls.

1. Probably Donatists, who were prevalent in Africa.

2. That is, to serve as members. Since such membership meant also that the senators were obliged to perform public services, their immunity is instructed in consonance with Constantine's policy to free the clergy from the burdens of public duties.

61. LETTERS OF CONSTANTINE I ON EPISCOPAL ELECTION, 330

(Eusebius, *VC* 3. 60–2)

Eusebius preserves three letters from Constantine on the subject of his translation from the bishopric of Caesarea in Palestine to that of Antioch. In these letters the emperor opposes the promotion designed for the "Father of Ecclesiastical History" and expresses his desire that Eusebius should remain at Caesarea and that the choice should fall upon another to succeed Eustathius, whose deposition on sundry charges had created a vacancy at Antioch and led to a schism lasting almost a century (330–414).

These documents afford early evidence for imperial interference in episcopal elections.

I

Letter of the emperor to the Antiochenes on the unity of the people and concerning the lack of need to desire a foreign bishop.

Victor Constantine, Greatest, Augustus to the people of the Antiochenes.

How acceptable to the intelligence and the wisdom of the world is the concord among you! And I myself, brethren, have determined to love you with an undying love, challenged both by the law [1] and by your life and zeal.[2] Therefore it is by the use of both right and sound understanding that we really and rightly enjoy blessings. For what can be so becoming to you? Surely, then, I should wonder that I should say that the truth is the reason of your security rather than of hatred for you.[3] Among brethren, then, whom both one and the same disposition to walk in the upright and the righteous way promises, under God, to enrol into his pure and holy household, what can be more honourable than with good fortune to acquiesce in all persons' blessings? Especially since the teaching of the law [1] directs your intention into a better amendment and we desire our judgement to be fortified by good decisions.

Perhaps this appears surprising to you—whatever the introduction of this my address means. I shall not refuse or decline to state the reason. For I admit that I have read the records, in which—by clear panegyrics and testimonies, which you have applied to Eusebius, now bishop of the Caesareans, whom I myself for a long time indeed have known well for his learning and goodness—I perceived that you pressingly attempt to appropriate him. What, then, do you think that I, eager for a strict search for the right course, have considered? What anxiety do you think that I have acquired from your eagerness? O holy faith, which through our Saviour's discourse and judgement

61. EPISCOPAL ELECTION, 330

gives to us—as it were—a model of life, how hardly would you yourself resist sins, unless you should have refused service for gain! And to me, at least, he who exerts himself rather for peace seems to be superior to victory itself; and where the proper course is possible for anyone at all, none surely could be found who would not delight in it. I ask, then, brethren, why do we so determine to inflict injury on others through the things which we choose? Why do we welcome those things which will condemn the credit of our reputation?

I myself praise the man who is approved by you as worthy of both honour and affection. Nevertheless it is not proper to have weakened that which ought to abide both authoritative and steadfast for each and every one, so that each should not be satisfied with his own opinions and that all should not enjoy their proper privileges and that in the conflicting examination [4] not only one but also many appear not worthy in comparison with this particular person. Wherefore nothing either of consternation or of harshness will cause trouble, if it should happen that the dignities of the Church should be on an equal basis and should be accepted equally by all. For it is not reasonable that for the advantage over others should be made an examination about this one,[5] since the judgement of all churches—whether they seem greater or less—equally receives and maintains the divine ordinances, so that in no respect one is inferior to another in regard to the common law.

If then we expressly declare the well-known truth, one should say that not the retention, but the removal, of this man will result and that the event will be a work of violence, not of justice:[6] whatever people generally may think otherwise, I, at least, declare expressly and boldly that this measure, provocative of a disturbance of no ordinary faction, is an occasion of an accusation against you—at all events, even sheep show both the nature and the power of their teeth, whenever, because their shepherd's customary care has slipped slightly, they have been bereft of his former guidance to their disadvantage.

If then this is so and if we are not mistaken, consider, brethren, this first of all—for many and weighty matters will present themselves to you from the first—whether your sincerity and affection for one another will not be seen to have declined from what it is. Next consider that he who came to you for the sake of correct counsel enjoys the reward due to him in accordance with divine judgement, since he has received no ordinary reward in respect to the important decision which you had cast concerning his fairness.[7] Then, pursuant to what is your custom, with good judgement display a becoming earnestness in the selection of the man whom you need,[8] excluding all factious and disorderly clamour, for such clamour is always wrong and from the collision of disagreeing elements both sparks and flames will arise.

Therefore may I so please God and you and may I so live in accordance with your wishes, that I love you and the haven of your gentleness, since you, having repelled that filth,[9] have introduced in its place by good morality concord, having taken on board the sure standard and having run a course toward the heavenly light—as one may say—by iron rudders. Wherefore you have chosen the incorruptible cargo, for everything harmful to the ship has been removed—as it were—from the ship's hold. Wherefore now it is needful that we take thought so to have the enjoyment of all these things, that later we may not seem either to have fastened generally on any course by unconsidered or unprofitable zeal or to have attempted at the outset an inexpedient course.

May God preserve you, beloved brethren.

II

Letter of the emperor to us [10] on the refusal of the bishopric of the Antiochenes.

Victor Constantine, Greatest, Augustus to Eusebius.

I have read with greatest pleasure the letter which your Wisdom has composed and I have perceived that the canon of ecclesiastical discipline [11] has been observed with precision; at all events, you abide by these principles which appear both pleasing to God and consonant with apostolic tradition.

Consider yourself happy also in this matter: that in the testimony of the whole world—so to speak—you have been judged worthy to be the bishop of any church, for, if all desire you to be among them, they indisputably assist in increasing true happiness for you in this respect.

But your Wisdom, which has determined to observe both God's commandments [12] and the apostolic canon [13] and the Church's canon,[13] has done excellently in declining the bishopric of the church in Antioch and in desiring to continue in that church, for which it [14] first received the bishopric by God's will.

Concerning this matter I have composed a letter to the people and to your other fellow-ministers,[15] who themselves had happened to write to me about these matters. And on reading these your Purity easily will discern that, since justice speaks against them, I have written to them at the Divinity's direction. And at their council it will be necessary that your Wisdom should be present, that in the Antiochenes' Church should be decreed that which should be decided as most proper both for God himself and for the Church.

May God guard you, beloved brother.

III

Letter of the emperor to the synod of the Antiochenes.

Victor Constantine, Greatest, Augustus to Theodotus, Theodore,

Narcissus, Aetius, Alpheus, and the rest of the bishops who are in Antioch.[16]

Having read the letters from your Wisdoms, I have approved the prudent preference of Eusebius, who is consecrated along with you.[17] Having discovered also all which has been done, partly by your letters and partly by those of Acacius and of Strategius, the most distinguished counts,[18] to the people of the Antiochenes I have written that which both is pleasing to God and is suitable for the Church and I have ordered a copy of the letter to be suppended to this letter, that you yourselves may know whatever I, summoned to the cause of justice, have chosen to write to the people, since this proposition was contained in your letters: that, pursuant to the wisdom and the desire of both the people and your choice, Eusebius, the most holy bishop of the Church of the Caesareans, should preside over that of the Antiochenes and should accept the charge over it.

Now Eusebius' letters, which appear to observe particularly the Church's ordinance, advanced the opposite opinion: that not at all he should abandon the church entrusted to him by God. Therefore it has seemed best that this preference, so proper and worthy to be observed by you all, should be made rather authoritative and that he should not be detached from his own church.

And it was necessary that also my opinion should be made clear to your Wisdoms. For it has come to me that Euphronius,[19] the priest, who is a citizen of Caesarea in Cappadocia, and George the Arethusian,[20] likewise a priest, whom Alexander[21] in Alexandria had ordained in this order, are most approved in respect to the faith. It was well, therefore, to signify to your Wisdoms that in respect to these men proposed and any others, whom you have considered worthy for the dignity of the episcopate, you should determine these matters as would be concordant with the tradition of the apostles. For, when such measures have been prepared, your Wisdoms will be able, according to the Church's canon and the apostolic tradition,[22] to arrange the appointment in such wise as the consideration of ecclesiastical discipline should direct.

May God guard you, beloved brethren.

1. Perhaps of God.
2. Constantine may mean their esteem for himself.
3. The emperor probably means that the Antiochene devotion to truth is the reason why the Antiochenes have secured security for themselves rather than have incurred the enmity of others.
4. That is, when considering rival candidates' claims to succeed the recently removed patriarch of Antioch.
5. A reading, rejected by the editor of VC, is received by the present

translator in the interest of clarity. The general tortuosity of the Greek translation of Constantine's Latin is a strong argument against the Eusebian authorship of constitutions ascribed to the emperor.

6. Constantine puts it rather strongly, when he charges the Antiochenes with "retaining" Eusebius, who was refusing consideration for their bishopric, but the implication is not unclear. To remove Eusebius from Caesarea Constantine considers the real injustice and akin to force, rather than the Antiochene desire to secure and then to retain Eusebius for themselves.

7. It was Eusebius, bishop of Nicomedia, who led the opposition against the Nicene decisions (after his recall from exile, on which see nos. 50 and 51) and who opened the attack against the Nicene leaders by contriving the deposition of Eustathius. The reference is to his presence at the Synod of Antioch (330), which deposed Eustathius, and to the vote of that council in support of the Eusebian-inspired charges, which were sustained only after the Eustathians had separated themselves from its sessions. That vote seems to have been the reward mentioned, for not until nine years later did he receive a higher recompense— his translation from Nicomedia to Constantinople, where he died as bishop (342). Cf. *infra* n. 11 *ad fin*.

8. That is, the successor to Eustathius, who, as the event proved, was a certain Euphronius of Caesarea in Cappadocia.

9. This must refer to the deposition of Eustathius.

10. Eusebius.

11. Canon 15 of the Nicene Council (325) prohibits the translation of any clergyman from one city to another, probably in the desire to deter clerical ambition to move from smaller to larger places. This rule, oftener honoured in its breach by the East than by the West, was patterned on an earlier canon of the *Constitutiones Apostolorum*, where it stands as 8. 47. 14 in that document, which purports to be the work of the apostles (whose instructions were supposed to have been compiled by Pope St Clement I [88–97]) and which served as the basis for much ecclesiastical legislation in the early Church. But the apostolic canon expressly recognizes an exception when "a bishop . . . can contribute much greater profit to the people of the new parish by the word of piety; but this is not to be settled by himself, but by many bishops' judgement and by very great supplication". See no. 270, n. 3.

Eustathius himself had moved from the see of Beroea to that of Antioch (*c.* 323) and Eusebius, the notorious courtier-prelate and Eustathius' enemy, held three bishoprics in succession: Beirut (before 319), Nicomedia (319–25, 329–39), Constantinople (339–42). The latter apparently had no anchylosis of the articulations to prevent his promotion from see to see.

12. There is nothing in Holy Writ against episcopal translation, but Constantine may have been thinking of the Pauline qualifications for bishops (1 Tim. 3. 1–7).

13. Cf. *supra* n. 11.

14. Constantine construes *Wisdom* as the understood subject.

15. The letters preceding and succeeding the present epistle.
16. These were the chief electors of the successor to Eustathius.
17. Constantine's periphrasis for "fellow-minister".
18. Both men became praetorian prefects of the East.
19. Cf. *supra* n. 8.
20. This Syrian, who was tainted with Arianism (of which Constantine probably was unaware), later became bishop of Laodicea in Syria. He seems to have been very able and quite learned.
21. Patriarch of Alexandria and immediate predecessor of St Athanasius in that see.
22. Cf. *supra* n. 11.

62. LAW OF UNKNOWN EMPEROR ON CLERICAL DEFENDANTS IN LAWSUITS, 330–534

(CI 2. 2. 4)

While from its position in Justinian's Code this law, which appears to be an interpretation of an ordinance, can be dated any time after 287, it probably approaches a time closer to 534 than to 330, when Constantine I on the still-occupied site of Byzantium created the eastern capital of the Empire and endowed the city called after him with the epithet "eternal" [1] in conformity with a celestial command,[2] since reference to Constantinople seems to be made in this statute.

It directs that an action begun against a person who later becomes a clergyman must be defended in the court of first instance to which the clergyman as a layman has been cited, since the alteration in status cannot entitle the cleric to a change of venue.

He who once has summoned [3] anyone in the royal city [4] or in the provinces, after summons [5] has been presented to him, no longer shall summon [3] the said defendant [6] either in writing or not in writing, that is, he shall not make against him an action [7] not in writing, but he shall wait by the first judge.[8]

Moreover he who has accepted the summons,[5] although he should have transferred to another order,[9] since perhaps he has performed governmental service [10] or he has become a clergyman, shall answer absolutely in the first court (which has been considered competent to his former order [9]), not having any prescription of forum.[11]

But he who once has summoned,[3] if, after the summons [5] has been presented to the person summoned,[3] he should have called him into another court on the same charges, both shall effect immunity for the person summoned [3] and shall be cast in his lawsuit, although he had a just action.[7]

1. For "eternal" applied earlier to Rome see no. 140, n. 1.
2. So he claimed in CT 13. 5. 7 (dated 334). See no. 617. n. 10.

After five years of converting Byzantium into a city suitable to be the seat of empire, Constantine renamed it Constantinople (Constantine's City) and dedicated it on 11 May 330—a date celebrated as its official birthday until its capture in 1453 by the Turks, who eventually called it Istanbul (derived from Constantinople), the designation which became official in 1929 and was deplored by Churchill in 1945, when he wrote that "Constantinople should never be abandoned, though for stupid people Istanbul may be written in brackets after it" (W. S. Churchill, *Triumph and Tragedy* [Boston, 1953], 752). It had been called Byzantium for almost a thousand years before its transformation, and the word "Byzantine" persisted as a label for its culture.

When Constantine transferred the Empire's centre to Constantinople, the emperor in this eastern move emulated Alexander the Great in moving his capital eastward, though it is true that in this transference Constantine translated into action what perhaps might have been attempted three centuries previously by Augustus (whom he resembled: for Constantine, like Augustus, was simultaneously of the past and of the future—which circumstance perhaps explains why for so long a period [31 years] he could dominate the present and could develop the despotic programme of his predecessor Diocletian). Augustus had toyed with the thought of removing the capital from Rome to Troy (Horace, *Carm.* 3. 3. 57–72). Already Caesar, whose trip to Troy is learned from Lucan (*Phar.* 3. 950–1001) and who was influenced by the same *Ruinensehnsucht* which a view of the site inspired in other tourists (R. Macaulay, *Pleasure of Ruins* [London, 1953], 41–8), had been supposed to conceive, probably for a geopolitical purpose, a shift from Rome to Troy or to Alexandria (Suetonius, *Iul.* 79. 3; Nicolaus Damascenus, *Aug.* 20. 68). Augustus, however, rejected the proposal to the relief of the Romans, perhaps on account of Antony's abortive attempt at Alexandria to establish his seat of empire and because Caesar's alleged intention was an added impetus to his assassination.

Probably Constantine's vision of the possibilities of the site—unsurpassed anywhere on earth for the location of a capital, where two continents and two seas combine to crown Constantinople the queen of cities, and competing with Rome in majesty among classical antiquity's chiefest cities—has been of richer value to the world than his reported vision of the Cross, which led to his constructive championship of Christianity (see Introd., n. 14), for eventually another Caesar would have patronized the Church. Gibbon's major description of the city seems still to be the *locus classicus* in English (2. 141–58; cf. 6. 409–12 and 7. 132–4, 200–2). While Constantine's motives in constructing a second Rome are still mooted (consult F. Lot, *The End of the Ancient World and the*

62. CLERICAL DEFENDANTS IN LAWSUITS, 330-534   171

Beginnings of the Middle Ages [New York, 1931], 35–9), yet the natural genius of Constantine's ecumenical emperorship is attested by the construction of Constantinople, which, though patterned on Latin and pagan Rome administratively, yet was quite Christian and Greek in character; which decided the subsequent history of the State, determining in two generations (330–95) the Empire's division into eastern and western halves; which demonstrated soon thereafter the eastern half's predominance; and to which penetrated and in which was preserved the best of classical culture. Consult Bury, 1. 67–88; A. Alföldi, "On the Foundation of Constantinople" in *JRS* 37 (1947) 10–16, and *The Conversion of Constantine and Pagan Rome* (Oxford, 1948), 110–16; A. H. M. Jones, *Constantine and the Conversion of Europe* (New York, 1949), 232–8.

"New Rome", the second capital, became the cultural, economic, political, and (to some degree: see no. 375, n. 7) religious centre of the civilized world for a millennium and eventually the doomed and devoted cushion between Europe and its eastern enemies, until its guardianship of the products of Greek Christianity was sacrificed to savage Turks (1453) by the thoughtless selfishness of Latin Christendom.

As for "Old Rome": it ceased to be the invariable western capital during the last century of the Western Empire's existence. Valentinian I ruled from Trèves (Trier); Valentinian II resided at Vienne; Theodosius I reigned from Milan; Honorius retired to Ravenna, where succeeding sovereigns usually remained, trying to redeem the time (Eph. 5. 16; Col. 4. 5), which proved too troubled to be restored.

3. The verb (ἀπαιτεῖν) means simply "to demand", but in a legal context is widened to signify "to summon into court".

4. Probably Constantinople, for the Greek text has no subscription.

5. Literally "notice".

6. Literally "the person liable or answerable".

7. Literally "approach".

8. That is, the complainant must not seek action before another judge in the event of the defendant's delay.

9. See no. 325, n. 6.

10. See no. 186, n. 4.

11. The meaning is that his new status does not entitle him to a change of venue in defending the old suit. See no. 334, n. 5.

Although within this sylloge's scope the clergy won the right to have their cases heard in episcopal courts (see e.g. no. 96), yet here the emperor objects to the transfer of a taboo from the object of a cult to its conductors. But prescription of forum (*praescriptio fori*) and benefit of clergy (*beneficium cleri*) persisted for centuries and in some countries still are practised, where Roman Catholic canon law is received. This regards (*Codex Iuris Canonici*, 2. 1. 1. 2. 120) privilege of forum (*privilegium fori*)—remotely sanctioned by 1 Cor. 6. 1—as a right for its clergy, who consider the Church an authority separate from as well as superior to the State and who are reminded not to render unto Caesar the things that are God's (cf. Matt. 22. 21; Mark, 12. 17; Luke 20. 25). See also no. 528, n. 7.

63. LETTER OF CONSTANTINE I ON SUPPRESSION OF IDOLATRY AND ON ERECTION OF A BASILICA AT MAMBRE, 332

(Eusebius, *VC* 3. 52-3)

This letter attracts the attention of Palestinian bishops to idolatrous worship at Mambre and threatens condign punishment for anyone who shall commit any act of impiety there after the destruction of the heathen apparatus and the construction of a church in its stead.

Letter of the emperor concerning the place at the oak tree called Mambre.

Victor Constantine, Greatest, Augustus to Macarius [1] and the rest of the bishops of Palestine.

One—and this the greatest—service of my most devout mother-in-law [2] has befallen us: through letters to us she has made known cursed men's madness, which until now has escaped notice among you, so that the overlooked sin receives through us fitting correction and cure, although late, but still necessary. For truly it is also a very great act of impiety that hallowed places should be polluted by impious impurities. What is it, then, most beloved brethren, which, when it eluded your Sagacities, the aforesaid person through her piety toward the Divinity was not able to leave unmentioned?

The place which is called after the oak tree of Mambre, where we learn that Abraham had his hearth,[3] she says is defiled in all kinds of ways by certain superstitious persons; she disclosed that idols,[4] worthy of utter demolition, have been erected beside it and that an altar stands nearby and that impure sacrifices continually are performed. And for this reason, since it is plain that it is both alien from our times and unworthy of the site's sanctity, I desire your Reverences to know that it has been made clear to us in a letter to Acacius, the most distinguished count [5] and our friend, that without any delay as many idols as can be found at the aforesaid place should be consigned to fire, and that the altar should be overturned from the foundations, and that—to speak simply—after all such things thence have been destroyed wholly, he should be earnest with every power and way to purify the entire environment and afterward, as you yourselves should arrange, he should cause to be constructed in the same spot a basilica worthy of the Catholic and Apostolic Church.[6]

It shall remain the duty of your Wisdoms and Devoutnesses, whenever you have learned that all the abominations have been removed entirely thence, to assemble thither with the bishops of Phoenicia, whom you shall be empowered to summon by this letter's authority, and to design a basilica worthy of my Munificence, that, in conformity with the commands given, the splendour of the work in accord with the merit both of the antiquity and of the sanctity of the site can be brought to completion with all speed by our aforesaid count's care.

I desire you to observe also the following point above all: that none of those cursed and abominable persons should dare to approach the place in the future, for it is truly to us unendurable, and deserving of punishment to all those who so dare, that after our command anything unholy should be performed in such a place, which we have ordained to be adorned by the pure structure of a basilica, that a meeting-place worthy of holy persons may be created.

But if anything should happen to occur contrary to the command given, it is fitting that through your letters it should be made known clearly to our Clemency apart from any delay, that we may command that the person detected should submit to punishment to the utmost limit as one who has transgressed the law.

For you are not unaware that there first God, the lord of all things, both appeared to and conversed with Abraham. There, then, first the observance of the holy law [7] took its beginning; there first the Saviour himself with the two angels freely bestowed upon Abraham the manifestation of himself; there God made a beginning of appearing to human persons; there to Abraham he spoke about his future seed and immediately fulfilled the promise; there he foretold that he would be the father of the greatest number of nations possible.[8]

And since these things are so, it is meet—as it appears to me, at least—that through our care this place both should be kept pure from every pollution and to its pristine sanctity should be restored, so that nothing other should be done in it except that there should be performed the religious service befitting the Almighty God and our Saviour and lord of all things. And this it belongs to you to safeguard with needful care, if your Reverences desire to fulfil—as I indeed believe—the things in my mind, which have been fixed specially upon God's service.

May God guard you, beloved brethren.

1. Bishop of Jerusalem.
2. Eutropia, mother of Fausta, who was both Constantine's second wife and

half-sister of his stepmother Theodora and whom he is said to have suffocated in her bath six years ere he wrote this letter. Since the ancient accounts vary between Fausta's attempted seduction of his eldest son Crispus (whom he earlier had executed either on her charge that Crispus had tried to tempt her or because Crispus had abducted a maiden and had made her his concubine) and her adultery with one of the emperor's entourage, it is not clear on which count Constantine condemned her. But at any rate the relations between the murderer and his mother-in-law, who lived in Palestine, seem not to have been severed by the death of her daughter (see no. 52, n. 13). Consult A. H. M. Jones, *Constantine and the Conversion of Europe* (New York, 1949), 243–6.

3. See Gen. 13. 18, 14. 13.
4. The older commentators have conjectured that these were images of the angels who had appeared to Abraham at Mambre (Gen. 18. 1–22), but whom these idols represented is unknown.
5. Perhaps the count of the East, who was vicar of the diocese of the East.
6. See A. E. Mader's excellent monograph on the excavations at Mambre near Hebron revealing the Constantinian church there in *Rivista di archeologia cristiana*, 6 (1929) 249–312.
7. Religion, as often.
8. All this is derived from Gen. 18. 1–19.

64. LETTER OF CONSTANTINE I ON PREPARATION OF COPIES OF THE BIBLE, 333

(Eusebius, *VC* 4. 36)

This celebrated letter, sent to Eusebius, bishop of Caesarea, is also of bibliothecal interest, because the *Codex Sinaiticus* (now in the British Museum) generally is believed to be the sole surviving specimen of this imperial command for fifty copies of the Sacred Scriptures.

The letter is preserved also by Socrates (*HE* 1. 9), Theodoret (*HE* 1. 16. 1–4), Gelasius (*HE* 3. 4. 1–5), Nicephorus (*HE* 8. 27). Cassiodorus (*HE* 2. 16. 1–5) translates it into Latin.

The emperor's letter about the restoration of the Sacred Scriptures.[1]
Victor Constantine, Greatest, Augustus to Eusebius.[2]
In the city named for us,[3] through the co-operating providence of the Saviour[4] God, a very great multitude of persons have entrusted themselves to the most holy Church,[5] so that, since all things there are taking a great advance, it appears very fitting[6] that also more churches in it should be built.[7] Therefore receive very readily the resolution in respect to our policy. For[8] it has appeared fitting[9] to

64. PREPARATION OF COPIES OF THE BIBLE, 333

make this known to your Wisdom,[10] that you should order fifty volumes, obviously,[11] of the Sacred [12] Scriptures,[11] whose restoration [13] and use you know to be most necessary for the instruction of the Church,[14] in well-prepared [15] parchments, easy for reading aloud and portable [16] for the hands,[17] to be written by copyists competent and accurately conversant with their art.[18]

Letters have been sent from our Clemency [19] to the catholicus of the diocese,[20] that he should be careful to provide all things requisite for their restoration.[13] For this shall be the task of your Diligence: that the written volumes should be completed as quickly as possible.[21]

Also [22] from the warrant of this [23] our letter [24] it is proper for you to have authority [25] for two public conveyances for transportation.[26] For thus very easily also the very satisfactorily written [27] volumes will be transported [28] for our eyes [29]—one of the deacons of your church, of course, performing this service, who, when he has come to us, will experience our benevolence.[30]

God shall guard [31] you, beloved [32] brother.

1. Socrates and Theodoret omit the caption; Gelasius has "Emperor Constantine's letter about the preparation of the Holy Books"; Cassiodorus reads "Written to Eusebius of Palestine about the production of the Sacred Books"; Nicephorus has "The great Constantine's letters about both the building of the churches and the restoration of the Holy Books"—a caption serving a dual purpose, for the first letter is no. 45.

2. Socrates adds "of Caesarea"; Gelasius adds "the bishop"; Cassiodorus substitutes "Pious" for *Augustus*.

3. See no. 62, n. 2.

4. Gelasius omits *the Saviour*. To this point Cassiodorus reads "As we know in the city of our name, through the provident aid of our Saviour God".

5. Gelasius reads "Christ has entrusted a very great multitude of persons to his most holy Church".

6. Cassiodorus uses the positive and Gelasius inserts "to us".

7. Socrates makes an independent sentence of the result clause.

8. Socrates and Gelasius omit this word.

9. Gelasius inserts "to us".

10. Cassiodorus, starting with the previous sentence, reads thus far "Therefore it has been fitting for us to make known to your Wisdom what has seemed best to our will".

11. Gelasius omits the word.

12. Cassiodorus substitutes "Divine".

13. Cassiodorus prefers "production".

14. Cassiodorus: "you have known to be necessary for the churches".

15. Probably what we should call de luxe editions. The *Codex Sinaiticus* is written on beautiful vellum. Cassiodorus reads "well-produced".

176   64. PREPARATION OF COPIES OF THE BIBLE, 333

16. The later Greek versions alter the preposition in the compounded (in Greek) adjective and thus give the meaning "easy to steer".

17. Cassiodorus for *easy . . . hands* has "handy for use".

18. The characters in the *Codex Sinaiticus* are well-formed capitals and are assigned to the style of the fourth century. Tischendorf, who discovered the manuscript in a monastery on Mount Sinai in 1844, distinguished four hands at work in it as well as five later stages of correction, of which the earliest is contemporary with its composition.

19. Cassiodorus substitutes "Tranquillity" and starts the sentence with "For".

20. The supervisor of accounts (καθολικός [Lat. *catholicus*] = *rationalis* or *rationalis summarum*) in the diocese of the Orient, in which Caesarea was the capital of the province of Palaestina Prima. Cassiodorus, however, has "the province's governor" for this official.

21. Cassiodorus says simply "rather quickly" and prefers "produced" as the verb.

The speed demanded may account for the work of four distinct transcribers observed by Tischendorf (cf. *supra* n. 18).

This paragraph also finds an echo almost thirteen centuries afterward in the preface of the Authorized Version of the Bible, where the translators record that King James I of England urged and excited "those to whom it was commended, that the work might be hastened, and that the business might be expedited in so decent a manner, as a matter of such importance might justly require".

22. Cassiodorus starts the sentence with "For".

23. Gelasius and Cassiodorus omit the word.

24. Cassiodorus calls it a rescript here.

25. For *to have authority for* Cassiodorus reads "to take".

26. Cassiodorus expands the phrase to "for bringing these". See no. 95, n. 41.

27. Cassiodorus reduces the modified participle to "well-written".

28. All later Greek versions alter the future indicative, attested by Cassiodorus, to the aorist optative.

29. Constantine uses the plural of an abstract noun (ὄψις); Cassiodorus has a singular abstract noun (*aspectus*).

30. Cassiodorus has "our Piety's munificence".

31. Socrates and Nicephorus have the future optative; Cassiodorus has the present subjunctive.

32. Cassiodorus reads "dearest".

65. RESCRIPT OF CONSTANTINE I ON CONFIRMATION OF EPISCOPAL JURISDICTION, 333

(CS 1)

By this constitution Constantine the Great confirms in the Empire's legal system the already introduced episcopal court (nos. 17 and 28), which had been an institution characteristic of the life of the nascent Church.[1] The emperor not only sanctions the expression of a bishop's opinion as an interpretation of law, but also commands the execution of an episcopal sentence to be effected through the secular courts. And when we consider that a bishop's administration of justice—more often than not—was actuated by his peculiar conception of right and wrong as developed in Christian ethics and also that no appeal lay from an episcopal verdict, we can conclude justly that his arbitral authority transcended that of a civil judge.

Emperor Constantine Augustus to Ablabius, praetorian prefect.

We have been surprised sufficiently, Ablabius, dearest and fondest cousin, that your Gravity, which is full of justice and of sound religion, has wished to ask our Clemency what either our Guidance previously has determined [2] or we now desire to be maintained about bishops' verdicts. Accordingly, because you have wished to be instructed by us, again we create by a wholesome command the arrangement of the formerly promulgated law.[2]

For we have ordained, just as the plan of our edict declares,[3] that bishops' verdicts of any kind whatever, when issued, should be preserved and always inviolate and incorrupt without any distinction of age,[4] obviously that whatever shall have been ended by a verdict of bishops should be held always as sanctioned and venerable sentences.

Accordingly, whether between minors or between adults shall have been a judgement by bishops, we wish that to you, who hold the highest post of the courts, and to all other judges should be made reference for execution.[5]

Accordingly, whosoever having a lawsuit—whether defendant or plaintiff, whether amid the beginnings of the lawsuit or after courses of time have been traversed,[6] whether when the matter is concluded or when the verdict is begun to be pronounced—shall have chosen the court of a bishop of the sacrosanct law,[7] immediately without any hesitation, even if the other party resists, the persons of the litigants should be directed to the bishop.[8] For the sacrosanct religion's authority investigates and publishes many matters, which, if deceptive in a trial, the fetters of prescription do not permit to be expressed.[9]

Accordingly all cases which are administered by either praetorian or civil law,[10] when terminated by bishops' verdicts, should be confirmed by the perpetual law of stability [11] nor should it be permitted that a matter, which a verdict of bishops shall have decided, should be reexamined.[12]

Also it is permitted that every judge should accept unhesitatingly evidence presented by one bishop, nor another witness should be heard when a bishop's evidence shall have been produced from any party's side.[13] For that is confirmed by the authority of the truth, that is incorrupt, which the conscience of a pure mind shall have produced from a sacrosanct person.

Finally we have decreed this by wholesome edict,[2] we confirm this by perpetual law, in repressing the malicious seeds of lawsuits, that unfortunate persons, involved in the long and almost perpetual toils of lawsuits, may depart by an early end from wicked claims or from unseasonable greed.

Accordingly whatever concerning bishops' verdicts our Clemency had decreed and we now have embraced by this law is fitting for your Gravity and for all others to observe as a verdict issued in perpetuity for all persons' advantage.

Given on 5 May at Constantinople, Dalmatius and Zenofilus [14] being consuls.

1. See no. 17, n. 3 *ad med.*
2. No. 28.
3. In his edict of 318 (no. 28) Constantine says more briefly what he is about to write here: the chief resemblance is that in each document whatever shall have been decided by a bishop shall be held as sanctioned.
4. Of the litigants.
5. Obviously there then is no appeal from the bishops.
6. By *courses of times* (*temporum curricula*) is meant the statutory amount of time allowed either for starting a suit or for conducting a case. Each period varies from time to time throughout the long history of Roman law, and for each period we have only isolated information true for certain areas and ages. Connected with the calculation of these periods are such factors as (1) the duration of a court day; (2) the computation of days on which a court could sit, since days devoted to legislative or electoral activities (in the Republic and in the early part of the Principate), holy days (in the Christianized Empire), holidays and unlucky days (in any era) created a year of court days (*annus utilis* or *tempus utile*) well in excess of a calendar year (*annus continuus* or *tempus continuum*)—and these, of course, varied; (3) the reckoning of when such periods should start, for circumstances altered cases then as now—and the reckoning was not always constant; (4) the regulation of adjournments and of appeals—both in number and in length and whether discretionary or statutory—in calculating the time allotted for hearing a case; (5) the operation of public

65. EPISCOPAL JURISDICTION, 333

opinion, juristic doctrine, administrative attitude, economic conditions, and (in the Empire) imperial interest or indifference in accepting or in altering previous practices—particularly in arranging a statute of limitations.

Here, however, our primary concern is with the regulation of these periods in the reign of Constantine, from whom the document under discussion comes and who seems to have been the first emperor to enact systematic legislation on the subject.

As for the conduct of a case: Speed is desired in both original (*CT* 1. 12. 3; ? 313) and appellate (*CT* 11. 30. 3; 315) jurisdiction. A mandate directing completion of causes—whether civil or criminal—within three to five days (*CT* 1. 12. 1; 313–15) is modified by two others granting extension of four months in certain circumstances (*CT* 2. 6. 1; 316 and 2. 7. 2; 327) and by one giving an unspecified postponement because of a litigant's death (*CT* 2. 6. 3; 317–19 or 321). To actions for forgery (*CT* 9. 19. 2; 320 or 326) as well as (perhaps) where the fisc is involved in a suit (*CT* 10. 1. 4; 320) is allotted one year (apparently a "court" year). Two calendar years for cases of fraud (*dolus malus*) are allowed (*CT* 2. 15. 1; 319). In the matter of appeals a provincial governor has fifteen continuous days in civil cases (*CT* 11. 30. 1; 313) and later in both private and fiscal suits twenty days (*CT* 11. 30. 8; 319) to submit an appeal to the emperor. Four months to complete a cause are accorded to the heirs of a litigant who has died during trial of an appeal (*CT* 11. 35. 1; 317 or 319 or 321). The last decision on length of cases belongs to Justinian, who in 530 ordained three years for all suits save those involving the fisc and taxes (*CI* 3. 1. 13. 1).

As for starting a suit: Speed again is desirable, at least from the viewpoint of a judge who is penalized for his indolence and negligence in causing a complainant to be debarred from litigation, because a statute of limitations can prevent the timely presentation of his plea (*CT* 2. 6. 2; 319); but no prescription of time exists in actions against forgers (*CT* 9. 19. 2; 320 or 326) or against adulterers (*CT* 9. 7. 2; 326) or for a person asserting his freedom—no matter how long he has been in servitude—(*CI* 7. 22. 3; 314) or for a person on return seeking recovery of his property illegally possessed in his absence (*CT* 4. 22. 1; 326). Two months are allowed for prominent personages to exclude the fisc's claim for confiscation of such property as they have given not only to specified socially and legally inferior women who had borne children to them, but also to such children (*CT* 4. 6. 3; 336). One year suffices for owners of property to bring pleas for recovery of fisc-confiscated property (*CT* 10. 1. 1; 315) and for persons between 25 and 26 years of age to start suit for vindication of real estate or of rustic slaves alienated without a decree (*CT* 3. 32. 1; 322 or 325). Two years are granted to sue on an action for fraud (*CT* 2. 15. 1; 319). Three or four or five years are allowed for ex-minors (those below 25 years of age) on attaining their majority to institute an action for restoration to their original condition (*restitutio in integrum propter aetatem*) on account of the mismanagement of their affairs, depending (respectively) whether they live in a province or in Italy or within a hundred miles of Rome (*CT* 2. 16. 2; 315 or 319). Constantine perhaps refers to one of his earlier laws, when he interprets the law that an ex-slave cannot be reduced to slavery after his claim to freedom has remained unchallenged for sixteen years (*CT* 4. 8. 7; 331). Whatever once fisc-owned property anyone for any time and by any means has possessed continuously until 315 without another's claim upon it belongs to the possessor (*CT* 4. 11. 1; 316). But the most important law on institution of a suit is Constantine's rule that those who can prove possession of property for forty years need no title to offset a suit for recovery, while those who have possessed by legal title can counter successfully claimants from the same province (*inter praesentes*) after ten years and from another province (*inter abstentes*) after twenty years (*FIRA* 1. 464; 326-33)—the ten-twenty years' prescription (παραγραφή; *praescriptio*) instituted by Septimus Severus and Caracalla (*FIRA* 1. 437; 199) being confirmed by Constantine. (The latter document seems to be our oldest evidence extant for an institution older than it.) This forty-year rule outlawing claims against ownership, to which reference is made in 365 (*CI* 7. 39. 2), inspired various and later enactments, of which only the most noted need mention. While in 349 Constantius II and Constans I forbade the application of Constantine I's regulation to personal actions (*CT* 4. 11. 2), it remained for Theodosius II in 424 to bar the institution of almost all actions after thirty years (*CT* 4. 14. 1). In 491 Anastasius I raised to forty years prescription for cases excluded by Theodosius (*CI* 7. 39. 4) and also banned from prescriptive rules claims for taxes (*CI* 7. 39. 6). In 530 Justinian I reduced the term to thirty years for all actions apart from those on mortgage, which he retained at forty years (*CI* 7. 40. 1; see also no. 627 of the next year), but in the same year extended the limit to a hundred years for ecclesiastical and pious foundations in certain cases (no. 604), for which in 541 he restored the forty-year rule (*N* 111).

Perhaps it should be added that for a prescription of very long time (*praescriptio longissimi temporis*) to operate as a divestitive fact (1) it must run from the day when the right of action exists and is not exercised; (2) it must not be interrupted by the interposition of a claim, that is, the non-claim to action must be continuous on the plaintiff's part—otherwise the prescription starts to be re-counted from such claim, provided that the plaintiff has taken no action on the claim; (3) it must adhere to what rules exist for the time required to institute action.

7. Religion, as often in imperial constitutions.

8. This concession was cancelled two generations later (no. 271).

9. Apparently bishops are allowed more time than lay judges for the conduct of a trial, and their sacred character better enables them to arrive at the truth of the matter, when litigants through respect for their episcopal judges would not resort so readily to tricky devices; but even if they did there would be more time to find the truth. At least, such may have been the emperor's pious hope, but his experience with ecclesiastical eccentricities (e.g. Donatism first

65. EPISCOPAL JURISDICTION, 333

and then Arianism) ere this rescript's emission should have shown him that laymen were not likely to fall far short of their clerical leaders in legal chicanery.

By prescription (*praescriptio*) the emperor probably means exception (*exceptio*), a general term in the legal terminology of this period for any legal technicality presented by a defendant. Originally and in the earlier part of the formulary period of civil procedure—sometime in the second century B.C. and apparently linked with the *Lex Aebutia*, which, of quite uncertain date (300–100 B.C.), reformed civil procedure—there were prescriptions favouring the plaintiff (*praescriptiones pro actore*) and prescriptions in favour of the defendant (*praescriptiones pro reo*). But by the late second century A.D. only the former retained its old name and the latter was called an exception (*GI* 4. 130, 133). However, the post-classical jurists, to whom—so loath is the law to advance—antiquarianism appealed, reintroduced *praescriptio* for *exceptio* and applied it to any equitable defence which a defendant could excogitate.

10. The *ius civile*, which is primarily statute law binding on the citizens (*cives*), according to the classical definition (*D* 1. 1. 7), was aided or corrected or supplemented by the *ius praetorium* (more commonly called *ius honorarium*), which is the law created chiefly by magisterial edict and corresponds to what we call judge-made law or case-law.

11. Probably what is meant is "by the law [i.e. right] of perpetual stability"—a case of transferred epithet (antiptosis).

12. This clause reinforces the comment in n. 5 *supra*.

13. This curious concession, which human frailty must have conspired at times to convert into a miscarriage of justice, runs counter to both Mosaic and Christian law (Deut. 17. 6, 19. 15; Matt. 18. 16), which required two or three witnesses to establish a matter, and to Roman law, wherein the oratorical doctrine was that "the uncorroborated testimony of one witness should not be sufficient to secure a conviction" (A. H. J. Greenidge, *The Legal Procedure of Cicero's Time* [Oxford, 1901], 481f), not even when the "sea-green incorruptible" Marcus Porcius Cato Minor Uticensis (95–46 B.C.) was concerned, for Plutarch preserves the anecdote that, when a counsel for the defence had attracted the jurors' attention to the fact that the prosecution could provide only one witness against his client, the lawyer told them that they ought not to rely on a single witness, not even though he were Cato himself (*Cato Minor*, 19. 4). Generally speaking, while it seems that at least two witnesses were required to prove any fact (*D* 22. 5. 12), we have no direct information, as the Catonian anecdote shows, that necessarily this rule was observed.

It is interesting to note that three years later Constantine reversed himself, when he ruled that in no case proof of a fact should be adduced from the testimony of one witness, however eminent he might be (*CI* 4. 20. 9). Cf. the maxim *testis unus, testis nullus*.

14. This is apparently a Latin variant for Xenophilus.

66. LETTER OF CONSTANTINE I ON ARIANISM, c. 333

(Socrates HE 1. 9)

In an attempt to annihilate Arianism, the emperor in this universal epistle, addressed to clergy and to laity, decrees death for whoever shall be detected in concealing any book composed by Arius and shall not produce it for destruction by fire.

Gelasius (*HE* 2. 36. 1-2) and Nicephorus (*HE* 8. 25) preserve this letter in Greek and Cassiodorus (*HE* 2. 15) translates it into Latin. Two Arabic paraphrases also survive, but these are so loose that they show resemblance only to the last half of the document: the first is from the *Nestorian History* (PO 4. 279-80);[1] the second is from Agapius' (Mahboub's) *Universal History* (PO 7. 550-1).[2] A Syriac version is translated by B. H. Cowper, *Syriac Miscellanies* (London, 1861), 6-7.[3]

Another letter of Constantine.[4]

Victor Constantine, Greatest, Augustus to bishops and to laymen.[5]

Since Arius has imitated wicked and impious persons, he is bound to undergo the same disgrace awarded to those.[6]

Therefore, just as Porphyry,[7] the enemy of godliness,[8] because he had concocted[9] unlawful compositions against[10] religion, gained for himself[11] a deserved recompense and such that for the future time he has become most disgraced and has been filled with the greatest ill-repute[12] and his impious compositions have been destroyed, so also now it has seemed best that both Arius and the likeminded with Arius[13] should be called Porphyrians, that they may assume[14] even the appellation of those whose ways they have imitated.

And, in addition to these,[15] if any treatise[16] composed by Arius should be discovered, it has seemed best to surrender this to fire,[17] that not only the depravities of his doctrine should be destroyed, but not even a memorial of him at all should be left.[18]

Also I proclaim publicly[19] the following: that, if anyone should be detected in hiding a treatise[16] composed by Arius[20] and should not consume it by bringing it forward immediately to the fire,[21] for this person the penalty shall be death;[22] for immediately after he has been condemned on this charge, he shall submit to capital punishment.

May God guard you.[23]

1. The French version yields the following English translation:

"From Emperor Constantine to all those who shall receive our present letter —bishops, archbishops, priests, officials—and to all our subjects, greeting.

"Arius, the impostor, making himself the tool of the very wicked Satan, has violated the faith, has separated himself from the faithful, and has invented an inconceivable heresy. Behold! That is why he has drawn upon himself misfortunes and frightful calamities.

"It is necessary then, to burn all his books, writings, and maxims—to allow no trace of these to exist.

"Whoever after our present edict should have kept in his dwelling or in his possession a writing of Arius shall expose himself to the punishments of the civil and religious authorities. Let none give a pretext for these punishments.

"Fare you well."

2. The French version gives the following English translation:

"From Emperor Constantine to the bishops, to the metropolitans, to the priests, to the governors, and to all persons who shall receive our letter, greeting.

"Arius, the liar, resembles the Devil, accursed and wicked, and he has separated himself from the faith. That is why he has contradicted the people and has become the author of an unprecedented heresy. Thus misfortune has seized him and trial has come for him.

"It is necessary to burn his books, so that no record of him nor of his words may remain.

"And I order those persons who have any of them to burn and to destroy all that; if not, they shall be smitten with the misfortune which has come to Arius and none among them shall find for his soul the way of salvation, if God wishes it!"

3. Cowper's English version (with stylistic adaptation) follows:

"Letter of the same Constantine against the Arians.

"Constantine, the king, to the bishops and to the nations everywhere.

"Inasmuch as Arius imitates the evil and the wicked, it is right that like them he should be rebuked and rejected. As, therefore, Porphyry, who was an enemy of the fear of God and wrote wicked and unlawful writings against the religion of Christians, found the reward which befitted him, that he might be a reproach to all later generations, because he fully and insatiably used base fame, so that on this account his writings were destroyed righteously: thus also now it seems good that Arius and the holders of his opinion all should be called Porphyrians, that he may be named by the name of those whose evil ways he imitates.

"And not only this, but also that all the writings of Arius, wherever they may be found, shall be delivered to be burned with fire, in order that not only his wicked and evil doctrine may be destroyed, but also the memory of himself and of his doctrine may be obliterated, that not by any means there may remain to him remembrance in the world.

"Now this also I ordain: that, if anyone shall be found concealing any writing composed by Arius and forthwith shall not surrender and burn it with fire, his punishment shall be death; for, as soon as he is caught in this, he shall suffer capital punishment by beheading without delay."

4. Gelasius and Nicephorus omit the caption, but Cassiodorus has "About Arius and his writings".

5. Nicephorus omits the superscription, in which Cassiodorus has "people" for the last word.

6. For the main part of the sentence Cassiodorus has "it is proper that he should undergo also their punishment".

7. Porphyry of Tyre (233–304), probably the most lucid of the followers of Plotinus (c. 203–62), who founded Neoplatonism (in which welter of ideas Greek philosophy may be said to have committed suicide), was distinguished also by the bitterness of his opposition to Christianity, which he assailed in a special diatribe known now by only a few fragments preserved by Christian apologists.

The name Porphyrians, proposed by Constantine later in this letter for the adherents to Arius, never acquired much acceptance.

8. Cassiodorus substitutes "divine piety".

9. Gelasius inserts "certain".

10. Nicephorus reads "about".

11. For *because . . . himself* Cassiodorus has "by producing unfair volumes against religion, has deserved to discover".

12. Cassiodorus omits the ensuing eight words and starts a new sentence with "And also now" etc.

13. For *the . . . Arius* Cassiodorus has "his fellow-followers".

14. Cassiodorus has "enjoy".

15. Gelasius has the singular.

16. Nicephorus produces *figura etymologica* by substituting σύνταγμα for σύγγραμμα (σύνταγμα . . . συντεταγμένον).

17. Cassiodorus simplifies the apodosis to "it should be surrendered to fire" and has in the protasis the indicative mode.

18. Cassiodorus changes the clause to "that not only his depraved doctrine should be destroyed, but not even any fictions of his should be able to remain".

Constantine, who had only several years of life left to him, lived long enough to ascertain that a bonfire of books did not destroy Arianism, which was destined to have a long history of hatching many more heresies, especially in the East, and to produce in the West political developments rather than doctrinal battles among the barbarian successor-states in and after the fifth century. *Habent sua fata libelli.* See no. 382, n. 1.

19. Cassiodorus reads simply "command" for the verb and the adverb.

20. Cassiodorus has "if anyone is found to have hidden Arius' treatises".

21. Gelasius reads "and in not bringing it forward immediately and in not consuming it by fire"; Cassiodorus has "and, not producing these immediately, shall not have consumed these by fire".

22. Cassiodorus substitutes "he shall underlie the punishment of death".

23. Gelasius adds "beloved brethren" and changes the present optative to the future indicative; Nicephorus omits the sentence.

67. RESCRIPT OF CONSTANTINE I ON ARIANISM, c. 333

(Gelasius, *HE* 3. 19)

This long diatribe against Arius and his adherents contains much acerb abuse of Arius and controverts in some points the Arian position as propounded in a letter sent by Arius to Constantine. It is valuable not so much for its repertoire of imperial invective, as for its evidence of the emperor's interest in securing uniformity of theological belief among his subjects. Toward the end of this exercise in declamation Constantine proposes penalties for failure to follow the Nicene faith.

M 2. 930–9 has a Latin version of this letter.

Letter of the most God-beloved Emperor Constantine to Arius and Arians.

Constantine Augustus to Arius and to Arians.[1]

A wicked interpreter really is an image and a statue of the Devil.[2] For as skilled sculptors mould him for an incitement to deception, as if cunningly contriving a goodly appearance of beauty for him, who by nature is absolutely most base, that he may destroy miserable persons by offering error to them, in the same way, I think, must act this fellow, to whom only this appears to be worthy of zeal: namely, to proffer profusely the poisons of his own effrontery. Therefore he introduces a belief of unbelief—new and never yet at any time seen since men have been born. Wherefore truly that does not seem at variance from the truth, which long ago was described distinctly by the divine saying: "They are trusty for evil."[3]

For why can anyone say this: that he who no longer desires to find any aid for alleviation has lost the grace of taking advice? Why, then, do I say: "Christ, Christ; Lord, Lord!"?[4] Why in the world do bandits injure us daily? A certain harsh and violent audacity stands before[5] us; it roars, gnashing its teeth, deformed by dishonour, and wounded by manifold accusations. Of course, it, just as if scattered by certain storms and waves of evils,[6] in the law and the proclamation about you[7] vomits pernicious words and in writing produces these,[8] which you, who do not at all coexist with the Eternal Father[9] of your origin, have defined by cognition about yourself. In short, it collects and gathers certain terrible and lawless impieties, now indeed agitating tongues, now again uplifted by enthusiasm for miserable persons, whom, when present for security, it deceives and destroys.

But now I wish to examine the character of its chief proponent. For what says he? He says: "Either let us hold that, of which already we have been made possessors, or let it be done, just as we ourselves desire." He has fallen and in these matters he has fallen dead; he says: "By treachery or cleverness of knavery"—it makes no difference. He considers holy only what has crept into him through base thought. He says: "We have the masses."[10] Indeed, I myself shall advance a little farther, that I may become a spectator of the wars of insanity. I myself, I said, shall advance, I who have been accustomed to end wars of senseless men. Come now, Ares Arius,[11] there is need for shields. Do not do this, we beg; at least, then, let Aphrodite's intercourse detain you.[12] But really, would that, as you seem to fashion the finest things for the masses, so it would be your part to abound in piety toward Christ! Look, I come again as a suppliant and, though powerful in weapons in respect to the whole populace, I do not wish to fight; but fortified by Christ's faith, I desire you both to be cured and to heal others.

Why, therefore, do you say that you do these things, which befit not your character? But with what peace, tell me, or encompassed with what abundance, but, rather, advanced with what rashness? Oh, audacity worthy to be destroyed by thunderbolts! For hear what he, writing with a pen distilling poison, recently has explained to me. He says: "Thus we believe." Then, I suppose, having added I know not what certain things somehow swaggeringly and quite accurately elaborated, he, going farther, left unsaid nothing at all of bitterness, but he opened the whole—as someone may say—treasury of madness. He says: "We are expelled and they take from us permission to be admitted."[13] But this is not at all apposite to the matter; turn your mind to what follows, for I shall use his words.

He says: "We ask that, if the bishop of Alexandria[14] remains in the same opinion, hereafter it be granted to us—according to the law's arrangement—to celebrate the lawful and indispensable services to God." Oh, terrible shamelessness, which ought to be refuted thoroughly by the zeal for truth! For what has happened to please him, this has been marked by conciseness of expression. What do you say, foolish one? Do you prepare to construct the disease of your savage thought against me as a discord, which is specious in our sight? And do you hasten to destroy the persons involved with you in evil? "What, then," you say, "shall I do, if none deems me worthy to be admitted?" For this you often shout from a profane throat. But I shall speak against you: Where have you shown a clear mark and proof of your intelligence? And this you ought to have disclosed and to have established clearly for gods and men[15]—and especially when poisonous serpents even then are by nature more savage, when they know that they themselves are found in recesses of dens. But that is indeed quite urbane of him: that quite eagerly, just as if under a certain mask of modesty, he pretends silence. You indeed show yourself tame and submissive by the artifice of pretence; you escape the notice of many, when you within are full of countless evils and plots. But, oh, wretchedness! As the Devil has desired, so he had made Arius a manufactory of iniquity for us.

Advancing now, tell me the mark of your faith and indeed not at all be silent. Oh, you possessor of a mouth perverted and a nature quickly roused to wickedness! "Do you talk of one God?" You have me of the same opinion; think so. Do you say that "the Word [16] of his essence is the Word without beginning and without end"? I acquiesce in this; believe so. If you add anything further, this I abrogate. If you join anything to an impious separation,[17] I confess that I neither see nor perceive this. If you accept "the body's lodging in respect to the administration of divine operations", I do not reject it. If you say that "the spirit of eternity was born in the pre-eminent Word", I receive it. Who has known the Father, unless he who comes from the Father? Whom has the Father known, unless him whom he has begotten from himself eternally and without beginning?[18] You think that you ought to substitute a "foreign hypostasis", [19] believing doubtless badly; I know that the plenitude [20] of the Father's and the Son's pre-eminent and all-pervading power is one substance.[21] If, therefore, you detract from him, from whom not yet ever anything has been able to be separated even by idle talkers' process of thinking, you pave the way for the marks of addition and, in short, you determine the signs of inquiries for him, to whom he has given entire eternity for himself and uncorrupted intelligence and has assigned belief in immortality through both himself and the Church.[22]

Discard, then, discard this silly transgression of the law, you witty and sweet-voiced [23] fellow, singing evil songs for the unbelief of senseless persons.[24] Quite fittingly the Devil has subverted you by his own wickedness; and perhaps this seems pleasant to certain persons (for thus you have persuaded yourself). But it is in every way a destructive evil. Come now, having departed from your occupation with absurdities, listen, good [25] Arius, for I discourse with you. Do you not understand that you have been barred publicly from God's Church? You are lost (be well assured), unless, having regard for yourself, you condemn your present folly. But you will say that the masses act with you and dispel your anxieties. Lend your ears and listen a little, impious Arius, and understand your folly. O God, protector of all, may you be well-disposed to what is being said, if it should admit of faith! For I, your man, holding to your propitious providence, from the very ancient Greek and Roman writing shall demonstrate clearly Arius' madness, which has been prophesied and predicted three thousand years ago [26] by the Erythraean sibyl.[27] For she indeed says: "Woe to you, Libya,[28] situated in maritime regions, for there shall come to you a time, in which with the people and your daughters you must be compelled to undergo a terrible and cruel and very difficult crisis, from which a judgement both of faith and of piety in respect to all persons will be given, but you will decline to extreme ruin, for you have dared to engulf the receptacle of celestial flowers and to mangle it with a bite and you have polluted it with iron teeth."[29] What, then, knave? Where in the world do you admit that you are now? There, obviously; for I have your letters, which you have scraped with the pen of madness toward me, in which you say that all the Libyan populace is of the same opinion with you—doubtless in regard to salvation.[30] But if you shall deny that this is so, I now call God to witness that truly I send to Alexandria—that you may perish more quickly—the Erythraean Sibyl's very ancient tablet, composed in the Greek tongue.[31]

Are you, then, really blameless,[32] gallows rogue?[33] Have you not, then, really perished, sorry fellow, surrounded by such great horror? We know, we know your undertaking; what kind of anxiety, what kind of fear troubles you, wretched and miserable person, has not escaped our notice. Oh, the dullness of your wits, you profane person, who do not restrain your soul's sickness and helplessness, who undermine the truth by varied discourses. And, since you are such, you are not ashamed to disparage us, now refuting (as you indeed suppose), now again admonishing (as if superior in faith and in discourses), a person from whom, of course, wretched persons are eager to procure aid for themselves, although they ought neither to associate with such a person nor, in short, to address him, unless anyone thinks that in this one's rotten words and metres [34] is stored the hope of living uprightly. But this is not so; indeed, in very truth it is far from it. Oh, your folly, as many of you as associate with this person! What madness, then, has compelled you to endure this one's bitter tongue and sight?

Well; but now I shall proceed by my discourse against you yourself, you fool in respect to your soul, you wordy one in respect to your tongue, you infidel in respect to your wits. Grant to me a field for discussion (I do not say one wide-spreading and fit for horsemanship, but indeed a circle easy to trace, not one decayed, but firm and solid by nature), you truly profane and basest and dissembling person. For I am excited to say these things; but rather, having fastened a noose around you and having entangled you by discussion, I shall set you in the midst, that all the people may observe well your worthlessness. But I shall proceed now to the matter itself.

Certainly my hands have been cleansed.[35] Let us proceed, then, to invoke God with prayers: rather, wait a little while. Tell me, you very hasty one, what God will you invoke for aid? For I cannot keep myself quiet. O Lord, you who have the supreme authority over all things, O Father of singular power, because of this profane person your Church receives both reproaches and griefs and also both wounds and pains. Arius now adapts for you a place (and very cleverly indeed), in which, constituting—as I think—a synod for himself, by the law of adoption he procures and preserves your Son Christ, born from you, the bringer of our aid. Hear, I entreat you, this marvellous faith. He thinks that you, Lord, the principle of motion, are demoted from your place. He dares to circumscribe you by a circle of a defined seat. For where is not your presence? Or where do all persons not perceive your activity from your all-pervading laws? For you yourself encompass all things and it is not right to think of either a place or anything else outside you. Thus your power with activity is infinite. Do you, God, then, hear; do you, all the people, pay attention.

For this fellow is shameless and useless, who, having progressed to the height both of wickedness and likewise of lawlessness, pretends piety. He says: "Away! I do not wish God to appear to be subject to suffering of outrages, and on this account I suggest and fabricate wondrous things indeed in respect to faith: that God, when he had made the newly born and the newly created essence of Christ, prepared aid for himself, as it seems indeed to me. For what you have taken from him, this you have made less."

Is this, then, your faith, spoiler and destroyer? According to hypothesis do you accept as a figment him who has condemned the figments of the heathen? Do you call foreign and—as it were—a servant of duties him who without reflection and reasoning, in that he coexists with the Father's eternity, perfected all things? Now adapt, if indeed you dare, adapt, I say, to God both precaution and hope of what will happen, also reflection, reasoning, declaration and articulation of considered judgement, and, in short, delight, laughter, grief. What, then, do you say, one more wretched than the wretched, oh, truly an adviser of evil? Understand, if you can, that in your very knavery you are destroyed as a villain.

He says: "Christ has suffered for us." But I already have said that he was sent in the form of a body. He says: "Truly; but it is necessary that we seem not to make him less in any respect." Then, mediator of wild beasts, when you say these things, are you not mad and clearly raving? For, look, the world itself is a form or at any rate is a figure; and the stars indeed have produced their images; and, in short, the spirit of this spheroidal circle is an appearance of existing things and—as it were—a figuration. And, nevertheless, God is present everywhere. Where, therefore, in God are outrages? Or in what respect is God made less? Oh, you patricide of equity! Consider, then, conjecturing from yourself, and conclude, if this seems to be a sin, that God is present in Christ. That fellow, then, has known well the disgracefulness of his talk and not slowly he brought punishment on himself. Moreover doubtless daily sins are committed in the world—and, nevertheless, God is present and punishments are not delayed. In this respect, then, what diminution is made in his power's magnitude, if punishments are perceived everywhere? Nothing, I think. For the mind of the world is through God; through him is all stability; through him is all justice; the faith of Christ is without beginning from him. In short, God's law is Christ, having through him boundlessness and also endlessness.

But you appear to take thought from your own self. Oh, excessive madness! Turn now to your own destruction the Devil's sword. See, then, all see how he, when pierced by the viper's bite, now produces lamentable sounds; how his veins and muscles, when attacked next by the venom, evoke terrible pangs; how his whole emaciated body has wasted away, is full of squalor and filth and lamentations and pallor and horror and myriad ills, and has withered frightfully; how odious and dirty in his thicket of hair; how wholly half-dead and already exhausted in his glance; how bloodless in his face and wasted under anxiety; how all things converging at the same time upon him—frenzy and madness and vanity—through the long time of the calamity have made him both boorish and bestial. For example, he does not perceive in what bad state he is. He says: "I am exalted with delight and I jump, leaping with joy, and I soar."[36] And again quite youthfully he says: "Well, we have perished." And this indeed is true, for to you alone wickedness bountifully has supplied its own enthusiasms; and what had been bought for a great price, this has been given very easily to you. Come now, tell, where are your august counsels? Wash yourself, then, in the Nile, if possible, you fellow full of absurd insensibility; and indeed you have hastened to disturb the whole world by your impieties.

Do you understand that I, the man of God, already know all things? But I am in doubt whether I ought to remain or to depart, for I no longer am able to look upon this person and I am ashamed at sin, Arius. You have brought us into the light; you have hurled yourself, wretched one, into darkness. This has appeared the end of your labours.

But again I return thither. You say that there is a multitude of persons wandering about you. That is likely, I think; and take them, then, I say, take them, for they have given themselves to be eaten by wolves and by lions. However, each one of these, oppressed by additional payment of ten capitation taxes [37] and by the expenses of these, immediately will sweat,[38] unless, running as speedily as possible to the salvation-bringing Church, he has chosen the peace of love through affection for harmony.[39] For no longer will they, condemned for wicked complicity, be deceived by you nor will they, entangled in your abominable investigations, continue to perish absolutely. Your sophisms are clear and known to all persons, at all events for the future. Nor indeed will you yourself be able to accomplish anything, but in vain will you contrive, counterfeiting both fairness and gentleness of discourses and donning externally—so to speak—a mask of simplicity. In vain will be all your artifice, for straightway the truth will circumvent you, straightway the rain of divine power—so to speak—will quench your flames. And, of course, the functions of the public services will overtake your associates and likeminded persons,[40] who have become liable to the senate,[41] unless indeed they, fleeing as speedily as possible association with you, accept in exchange the uncorrupted faith.

But do you, iron-hearted man, give to me an evidence of your purpose, if you have faith in yourself, and be strong in the strength of faith, and you absolutely will have a pure conscience. Come to me, come, I say, to a man of God; believe that by my interrogations I shall search your heart's secrets; and, if any madness shall seem to be in you, I, after having invoked divine grace, shall heal you fairer than a model. But if you shall appear to be healthy in respect to spiritual matters, I, after I have recognized the light of the truth in you, shall give thanks to God and I shall rejoice with myself for the sake of piety.

And by another hand: May God guard you, beloved.

And this was executed [42] by Syncletius and Gaudentius, magistrians,[43] when Paterius was prefect of Egypt,[44] and was read in the palace.

1. St Epiphanius inserts "Greatest" after *Augustus* and has nominatives for datives (*Haer.* 2. 2. 69. 9).

2. St Epiphanius quotes this sentence (*Haer.* 2. 2. 69. 9).

3. The quotation is adapted from Jer. 4. 22, which reads "They are wise to do evil".

4. Cf. Matt. 7. 21-2, 25. 11; Luke 6. 46, 13. 25.

5. The Greek preposition (ἐξεναντίας) is reported elsewhere only in the Septuagint.

6. The metaphor is as old as Aeschylus, *Prom.* 1015.

7. The sentence is sufficiently obscure both in the original Greek and in M's Latin version without the addition of this compound prepositional phrase. Apparently, however, there had been a law promulgated against Arius; his audacity (which *it* represents) in being buffeted by the law spews abominable words under this pressure (as a ship emits noises in a storm) and even inspires written pamphlets (in his defence); his words he has concocted by taking thought about himself in pondering his source, but the result is sorry, since, not being coexistent with God the Father (as is God the Son, about whom he has inadequate views), he has not the correct solution on theological matters.

8. Perhaps a reference to his *Thalia*, composed partly in verse, and to his letters, of which St Epiphanius knew a collection amounting to about seventy (*Haer.* 2. 2. 69. 4). We have fragments of the *Thalia* and only two letters.

9. Another shaft from the sovereign's arsenal: Arius denied the eternal coexistence of the Son with the Father.

10. Arius' claim that he has the multitude on his side sets Constantine on the tangent of military reminiscence.

11. A poor, though imperial, pun; Ares (Mars) being the god of war. Cf. Homer, *Il.* 5. 31. Hence, later, the shields, for in art Ares often has a shield.

St Epiphanius quotes this sentence (*Haer.* 2. 2. 69. 9).

12. An allusion in doubtful taste, for Arius' personal life was pure (despite what Constantine writes in this letter), whereas Ares, having committed adultery with Aphrodite (Venus), the goddess of love, in heaven, is detained long enough for her husband Hephaestus (Vulcan), the god of fire, to find them asleep in his bed (Homer, *Od.* 8. 266-366).

St Epiphanius quotes this sentence (*Haer.* 2. 2. 69. 9).

13. Arius was exiled to Illyricum in 325, but was restored *c.* 330 and by the Council of Jerusalem in 335 was received into communion on the basis of a formula submitted to Constantine on the occasion of his recall.

14. He was Alexander, patriarch from 313, who had excommunicated Arius in 321 and whom Athanasius succeeded in 328.

15. This simply is a commonplace: Constantine has not relapsed into polytheism by his mention of gods.

16. This is the Logos (λόγος).

17. That is, in respect to the essence of the Father and of the Son—the problem of their relation being the chief question to wreck the Church's peace in this century. Arius denied that the Son is of one essence (οὐσία; *essentia*) or substance (ὑπόστασις; *substantia*) or nature (φύσις; *natura*) with the Father. Hence *separation*.

In the original Nicene use ὑπόστασις seems equivalent to οὐσία. Specifically is meant the Godhead's unique essence and substance and also, as such, that of the three persons of the Trinity. But since essence and substance mean exactly what later theologians did not wish to say, they substituted person (πρόσωπον; *persona*) and thus, though ὑπόστασις bears the same relation to the individual as does οὐσία to the class, πρόσωπον became more or less interchangeable with these and produced interminable discussion. Thus, as in no. 645, n. 17, ὑπόστασις denotes one of the persons of the Godhead and also Christ's whole personality as distinguished from his two natures (divine and human).

One of the latest, clearest, fairest statements of the significance of these technical terms is in E. J. Bicknell, *A Theological Introduction to the Thirty-nine Articles of the Church of England*[3] (London, 1955), 47-50.

18. Cf. Matt. 11. 27; Luke 10. 22.

19. Cf. *supra* n. 17 (ὑπόστασις).

20. The pleroma (πλήρωμα) or the aggregate of properties constituting the complete nature of a thing. So St Paul says (Col. 2. 9) that "in him [Christ] dwelleth all the fulness of the Godhead [τὸ πλήρωμα τῆς θεότητος] bodily".

21. Cf. *supra* n. 17 (οὐσία).

67. ARIANISM, C. 333

22. This passage is corrupt, nor does M's Latin version do much to clarify the thought.

23. Ironical adjectives.

24. Another reference to the *Thalia* (cf. *supra* n. 8), whose metrical portion were designed to be sung. Arius also composed other songs for popular usage by tradesmen and travellers.

25. Probably ironical, as often in Greek comedy.

26. Obviously a round number.

27. The following prophecy is a loose prosaic paraphrase of part of a metrical oracle on Libya, preserved in the *Oracula Sibyllina*, 3. 323–33, but there is nothing in the context to show that this emanated from the Erythraean Sibyl in Ionia rather than from another Sibyl.

28. Libya is mentioned also in a prophecy recorded in Ezek. 30. 5 and 38. 5; cf. Dan. 11. 43.

29. The expression "iron teeth" occurs in Dan. 7. 7.

30. The only bishops among Arius' first adherents were Libyan: Secundus of Ptolemaïs and Theonas of Marmarica, who stood with Arius throughout the controversy and accompanied him into exile.

31. The Erythraean Sibyl, since she was a Greek dwelling in Greek-speaking Ionia, normally delivered her responses in Greek. The threat to send this oracle in Greek has a triple significance: (1) the reply would lose nothing by translation into Latin; but (2) Arius, whose Latin was probably meagre, thus would understand it better; and (3) the Alexandrians, with whom Greek was more prevalent than Latin, also would understand it better, if any publicity should be given to it.

32. Or "sinless", if a theological overtone is wanted.

33. This epithet of vituperation, δικρανοφόρος, corresponds precisely with and obviously is a translation of *furcifer* (yokebearer), a common term of verbal abuse in Roman comedy. If the emperor personally dictated this letter, he probably used Latin. At any rate he addressed the overwhelmingly Greek-speaking Council of Nicaea in Latin (Eusebius, *VC* 3. 13).

34. Another allusion to Arius' poetic dress for his doctrine. Cf. *supra* nn. 8 and 24.

35. A reminiscence of ritual still observed in some religions, where worshippers wash their hands (at least) before approaching the Deity in prayer. Such is the lavabo (based on Ps. 25. 6–12) in the Roman Catholic Mass, where the celebrant washes his hands after the Offertory and before the Consecration. Add also Islamic lustration before prayer, when in the desert sand is a lawful substitute for water. But perhaps the allusion is simply to Pilate's hand-washing (Matt. 27. 24).

36. Literally "I am furnished with feathers"; metaphorically "I am excited".

37. The idea seems to be that a confirmed Arian will have to pay in addition to his ordinary tax a tenfold poll-tax (κεφαλή here, more usually ἐπικεφάλιον; *caput* or *capitatio*). As early as 51 B.C. the poll-tax (*exactio capitum*) levied on

Cilician provincials was characterized as very harsh (Cicero, *Ad Fam.* 3. 8. 5). In the Empire, at least from Hadrian's reign, this assessment was one per cent of each man's property (Appian, *Bell. Syr.* 8. 50) and appears to have been levied upon citizens as well as upon provincials. Lactantius describes the horrible scenes which attended the collection of the capitation tax under Galerius just before the recognition of Christianity as a lawful religion (*De Mort. Pers.* 23). See no. 107, n. 3.

38. Apparently a colloquial expression like our "pay through the nose"; certainly a picturesque phrase at any rate.

39. Literally "by a charm to promote concord".

40. By this the emperor means that he revokes from Arian clergymen the immunity from public service hitherto granted to Christian priests.

41. Since it is not clear why the Roman Senate should have jurisdiction here, probably the local senate in any community is meant. On the other hand, the words may mean that Arian sympathizers will be drafted for service in local senates, a service which entailed financial outlays—often burdensome—for senators. Another interpretation is that the Arians were liable to penalties imposed by the imperial privy council.

42. That is "drafted" or "processed".

43. The *magistriani* were members of the staff of a high official.

44. See no. 489, n. 12.

68. LETTER OF CONSTANTINE I ON ACCUSATIONS AGAINST ATHANASIUS AND ON PUNISHMENT OF RIOTERS, 334

(PG 25. 369–72)

The chief legal interests in this document, preserved by St Athanasius (*Apol. adv. Ar.* 67–8), are three: (1) Constantine's description of charges levied against Athanasius, patriarch of Alexandria; (2) Constantine's authorization for Athanasius to read frequently this letter in public, that all may know his innocence of these accusations and that his opponents may cease from faction; (3) Constantine's promise to take personal cognizance of future disturbances engineered by the enemies of Athanasius.

Victor Constantine, Greatest, Augustus to Athanasius, pope.[1]

Having read the letters from your Wisdom, I myself was of this opinion that, writing in return to your Constancy, I should urge you that you would be eager to lead God's people to orderly behaviour and compassion. For in my own soul I hold these things to be of primary importance: that we should cultivate truth and ever maintain righteousness in thought and rejoice particularly in these persons who walk in the right road of life.

But concerning those persons who are deserving of every execration, obviously the most mischievous and lawless Meletians,[2] who at last have become stupefied by their stupidity [3] and only by envy and storm and uproar set absurdities in motion, by displaying their lawless intention—these things I shall say. For you see that the men, who those persons were saying had been slain by a sword, are now in our midst and enjoy life.[4] Now in respect to these matters what could be a severer prejudgement, so clearly and plainly directed toward the punishment of those persons, than that these persons, who they were saying had been slain, both live and enjoy life, who obviously will be able also to speak for themselves? But this also was added by those Meletians:[2] for they were maintaining strongly that you, entering with a lawless assault and seizing a chalice deposited in the most holy place, had broken it,[5] than which matter there truly could not be a greater charge nor so great an offence,[6] if this deed happened to have been done thus and this sin to have been committed. But what is this accusation? What are the reversal and variation and difference in the circumstance, so that now they shift to another person the accusation of this complaint?[7] And this circumstance obviously is more luminous than light itself—so to speak—in that they were eager to plot against your Wisdom. After this who could be willing to follow those persons, who have invented such things for injury, since they especially are driving themselves to destruction and are able to see that they are accusers of feigned and false matters? As I said, therefore, who could follow those persons and could depart downward into the way of destruction—into that, obviously, in which they alone suppose that they have the hope of salvation and of succour? For if they should be willing to proceed toward [8] a clean conscience and to be reminded by the best judgement and to proceed toward [8] a sound mind, they easily will perceive that they have no succour from Providence, inasmuch as they are admirers of such things and tempt their own destruction. This, then, I should not call any harshness of judgement on them,[9] but justly the truth.

Finally also I add this: that indeed we wish these things to be read publicly often by your Wisdom, in order that thence it can come to the knowledge of all and particularly can come to that of those persons, whosoever thus act and thus create disturbances, that these things, which are said by us according to direct reason, have been said according to the actual truth.[10]

Therefore, since in this affair is so great an offence,[11] let them know that thus I have judged and that I am of this resolution: that, if they should cause any such excitement, no longer then according to the ecclesiastical but according to the public laws I myself in person shall hear the matter and then I shall discover in them that they appear to be some sort of bandits not only against the human race but also against the divine doctrine itself.

May God guard you, beloved brother.

1. This was a title (πάπας; *papa*) assumed by the patriarchs of Alexandria and generally recognized in Christian antiquity as one of their prerogatives. It dates at least from the period 257–9, when St Dionysius the Great, who was patriarch of Alexandria (*c.* 247–*c.* 265), applied it to his immediate predecessor St Heraclas (Eusebius, *HE* 7. 7. 4). But its use for any bishop seems to have occurred as early as 202, when it was used of the bishop of Carthage (*Passio Sanctarum Martyrum Perpetuae et Felicitatis*, 4. 3 [= *PL* 3. 46]). And while Tertullian may have referred it to the bishop of Rome *c.* 220 (*De Pud.* 13 *ad med.*), yet the title's first recorded application in Rome for the Roman bishop appears to be *c.* 303 in an inscription mentioning Pope St Marcelline (296–308) and published in *ILCV* 2. 3458.

See S. H. Scott, *The Eastern Churches and the Papacy* (London, 1928), 249, n. 65.

2. The last pagan persecution (303–13), begun by Diocletian, saw the birth of Meletianism, a schism which took its name from Meletius (properly Melitius), bishop of Lycopolis in the Thebaïd, who violated ecclesiastical discipline by ordaining priests in other bishops' dioceses. Meletius appears to have acted in the absence of fugitive bishops and for the purpose of providing pastors for vacancies caused by the persecution, lest the faithful laity should be left shepherdless. Even after Meletius' excommunication and death, his adherents continued in schism and, after they had allied themselves with the Arians in ecclesiastical politics, they eventually passed into heresy. When Athanasius became patriarch of Alexandria (328), the Meletians counted in their number over thirty bishops in Egypt alone. Meletians are mentioned as existing as late as the mid-eighth century.

H. I. Bell, *Jews and Christians in Egypt* (London, 1924), 38–99, publishes with translation ten papyri (seven Greek and three Coptic) illuminating the Meletian schism. While none of these documents is legislative in character, yet the information which they all afford is not without historical interest, particularly since they support the Meletian side (hitherto known almost entirely from its enemies' statements). They are dated 330–40 and may be cited papyrologically as *P. Lond.* 1913–22 in continuation of the series *Greek Papyri in the British Museum* (5 vols., London, 1893–1917), to which Bell's book stands as a supplement. Two additional papyri (Coptic) relative to the schism appear with translation in W. E. Crum's article "Some Further Meletian Documents" in *The Journal of Egyptian Archaeology*, 13 (1927) 19–25.

3. Since the rest of the sentence shows that they were far from being torpid

68. ATHANASIUS: PUNISHMENT OF RIOTERS, 334

(as the Greek verb indicates), we must interpret the stupefaction as a kind of moral insensibility, which made them numb to or unaffected by the claims of ecclesiastical discipline.

4. The Meletians claimed that Athanasius had murdered a certain bishop named Arsenius. But they had concealed him, that he might seem to have been slain when he no longer was seen, and exhibited as evidence of his murder a hand which they said was his. Arsenius later was discovered and Athanasius confronted him at the Synod of Tyre in 335. On this charge see Athanasius, op. cit., 5, 8, 14, 17, 27, 38, 42, 46, 63, 65–7, 69, 72, 85, 87.

Fragmentation of cadavers for magical purposes in antiquity is well attested. The tale of the treasure of King Rhampsinitus (? Rameses III) in Herodotus (*Hist*. 2. 121) is familiar (see J. G. Frazer, *Pausanias's Description of Greece* [London, 1898], 5. 176–9, for almost thirty versions of it). Doubtless the severed hand had magical implications, since, next to the skull, the most highly prized part of a corpse was the right hand. And centuries later, and again in Egypt, the amputated hand of Arsenius was said to have been used for magical arts by Athanasius. That such an accusation could be made against such an eminent ecclesiastic as was Athanasius and at a Christian council provides excellent evidence for the extent of the delusion and for the frequency of the practice.

5. The Meletians accused Athanasius of having broken a communion-cup in the sanctuary of a church. Athanasius assembles evidence to show the falsity of this charge in op. cit., 8, 11–14, 17, 28, 46, 60, 63–5, 72, 74, 76, 85, 87.

Other charges against Athanasius were (1) that he had taxed Egyptians with a tribute of linen vestments, apparently for ecclesiastical use; (2) that he had given a large sum of gold to a certain Philomenus, who was suspected of rebellion against the emperor; (3) that he had interrupted forcibly the celebration of Mass by one Ischyras (on whom see no. 78) and, besides breaking the aforesaid chalice (cf. *infra* n. 7), had demolished an altar and had burned liturgical books.

On the refutation of these additional accusations see op. cit., 46, 60, 74, 83.

6. Literally "strange sight", "untoward occurrence".

7. Later the charge was transferred from Athanasius to Macarius, one of his priests, whom the patriarch had sent to investigate the report that Ischyras (cf. *supra* n. 5 and no. 78), a layman, was masquerading as a priest (op. cit., 11–13, 28, 46, 60, 63, 65, 68, 72, 74, 76, 83, 85). It was this Ischyras whom the Meletians had suborned to calumniate Athanasius.

8. Perhaps the prepositions express relation rather than place; if so, for *toward* we should translate "regarding" or "in respect to".

9. The translator has added these two prepositional phrases.

10. This seems to be the sense of the relative clause, which reads literally "which are said by us by the reasoning of a direct line, are said by the action of the truth". There evidently is a contrast between "reason" (λόγος) and "action" (πρᾶξις), which may be expanded into "theory" and "practice".

Constantine perhaps means that his theoretical deduction is confirmed by the actuality of the case; in that situation, then, the veritable acts of the Meletians serve as the basis for his dismal view of their future doom.

11. Cf. *supra* n. 6.

69. LETTER OF CONSTANTINE I ON ADHERENCE TO ATHANASIUS, 334

(*PG* 25. 360-1)

Soon after St Athanasius had been consecrated patriarch of Alexandria in 328, the schismatic Meletians [1] in Egypt, inspired by unreconstructed Arians, began intrigues against Athanasius both in the patriarchate, which they disturbed, and at the imperial court, where they accused Athanasius of several unlawful acts.[2] Imperial investigation acquitted Athanasius, who returned to Alexandria with the following letter addressed to the Alexandrians by Constantine, who in it castigated them as disturbers of public peace and admonished them to accept Athanasius as their bishop.

Athanasius preserves this letter (*Apol. adv. Ar.* 61-2). Theodoret (*HE* 1. 27) and Gelasius (*HE* 3. 16. 1-3) quote a small part of it.

Constantine, Greatest, Augustus to the people of the Catholic Church in Alexandria.[3]

Beloved brethren, I address you, invoking God, the greatest witness of my will, and the Only-Begotten, the author of our law,[4] who presides over the life of all and hates dissensions. But what should I say? That we are in good health? But it would be possible for me to enjoy better strength, if you loved yourselves mutually by having discarded from yourselves the hatreds, through which by the waves of quarrellers we have left the haven of love. Alas, this absurdity! How many calamities every day are provoked by the envy producing disorder among you! Thus evil reports have come upon God's people. Whither, then, has departed the faith of righteousness, since we have been encompassed by the mist of darkness, not only through manifold error but also through ungrateful persons' faults, to such an extent that we endure those who champion folly and that we disregard, though we are aware of, those who repel equity and truth? What strangeness of our perversity is this? We do not convict enemies, but we follow their banditry, through which the guile of destruction, since none is opposed to it, easily has made for itself—that I may say so—a certain road. Is there no understanding, not even for the credit of the common nature of all persons, if indeed we have neglected the law's [4] commands?

But someone will say: Love is discovered through nature. How, then, is it that we, who have God's law in addition to natural goodness, endure the disturbance and the disorder of enemies, who are inflamed—as it seems—by certain firebrands? And, though having eyes, we do not see [5] nor do we understand, though fortified by the law's [4] intelligence? How great a terror has seized our life, when we thus neglect ourselves, although God recalls these things to us! Is it then not an intolerable evil? Is it not proper to consider these persons, but not the household and the people of God, as enemies? They act offensively toward us and they, utterly abandoned persons, bring charges and they attack us hostilely.

I ask you yourselves to consider with how great madness they do this. For the fools have wickedness situated on their tongues. These fellows, in truth, carry around with themselves a kind of leaden wrath, so that they smite themselves reciprocally and drive us with them to the increase of their own punishment. He who teaches well is judged an enemy; but he who guards himself with the vice of envy lays hold upon the people's gentleness improperly, ravages, consumes, and makes himself malevolent, adorns and arranges himself with praise, subverts the truth, and corrupts the faith, until he discovers a hole and a hiding-place for his own conscience. Thus their very stupidity makes them wretched, whenever they recklessly approve themselves, though they are unworthy, by saying: "Ah, the mischief! That person is too old; and that person is a boy. The office belongs to me; it is due to me; it was taken from him. When I have won all persons to my interest, I shall try to ruin him with my power." This proclamation of madness is plain: to see companies and assemblies or—that I may say so—election of their wicked coalitions. Oh—that I may say so—our absurdity! Is the exhibition of folly in God's Church? Are they, then, not ashamed? Do they not blame themselves? Are they not stung in their souls, that now at least they may seem to have a proper sense in opposition to guile and quarrelling? The sole force of envy is supported by its own venoms.

But [6] the wretches cannot prevail against your bishop. Believe me, brethren, they pursued zealously nothing else than that, after they have exhausted our times, they [7] have no place of repentance in this life. Therefore aid yourselves, I beseech you, cherish our [8] love and with all might [9] prosecute those desiring to destroy the grace of our concord and, looking toward God, love yourselves.[10]

For I eagerly have accepted Bishop Athanasius and so I have addressed him in the persuasion that he is a man of God.[11] It is your function to observe, not mine to judge, these matters.[12] For I have considered it necessary that the most reverend Athanasius himself should present my salutation to you,[13] for I note the diligence of his goodness, which, not unworthily of my peaceful faith, ever is occupied for the good of salutary opinion and will have reason to direct it.

May God guard you, beloved brethren.[14]

1. See no. 68, n. 2.
2. See no. 68, nn. 4 and 5.
3. Both Theodoret and Gelasius omit the superscription, but the latter supplies as a caption "End of Emperor Constantine's letter written about Athanasius to the Alexandrians' Church".
4. Religion, as usual.
5. Perhaps a reminiscence of Ps. 115. 5 and 135. 16, where the same words occur, though applied to idols, rather than to Jer. 5. 21 or to Ezek. 12. 2 or to Mark 8. 18, where the application is to human beings with a different verb for *see*.
6. Theodoret's and Gelasius' quotations start here.
7. Gelasius inserts "can".
8. Theodoret and Gelasius have "your" and the latter inserts "holy".
9. Gelasius inserts "love yourselves and receive Athanasius, your bishop, with insatiate festivity, beloved, although I well know especially that his separation has not produced in you so much grief as you have an excess of joy for his return to you".
10. That is, the Alexandrians are to discard their discord and to love one another with a love derived from Godward duty.

Gelasius adds "I beseech you".

11. Theodoret and Gelasius end their quotations here.
12. This is an unexpected admission from Constantine, who apparently did not intend to intrude himself further into the controversy between the patriarch and his schismatics.
13. Literally "render as a service to you the salutation from me". Either the epistle or the imperial greetings is the *salutation*.
14. Gelasius has this subscription, but changes the future optative into the future indicative, which probably is more correct.

70. RESCRIPT OF CONSTANTINE I ON JOHN ARCHAPH'S CONFORMITY WITH ORTHODOXY, 334

(PG 25. 373)

John Archaph, a leader of the Meletian schism [1] in Egypt, having joined forces with the Arian opponents of St Athanasius, patriarch of Alexandria, was involved in a baseless cabal to discredit Athanasius, the chief eastern champion of orthodoxy. But when John's particular part in the plot had been exposed at Tyre, he confessed his crime in a letter to Constantine, who rejoiced at his contrition and commanded him to present himself at court.

Athanasius preserves this letter (*Apol. adv. Ar.* 70).

Constantine, Greatest, Augustus to John.

The letter from your Prudence was very welcome to me, for from it I know what I very greatly desired to know: that you had discarded all smallness of spirit, had communicated with the Church, as was fitting, and came in the highest degree into concord with Athanasius, the most reverend bishop. Know well, therefore, that with respect to these circumstances I have exceeding praises for you, because, having surrendered all altercation, you have done what is pleasing to God in acquiring instead for yourself unity in regard to the Church.

Therefore, that you may appear to have obtained also what you desire, I have thought that I ought to permit you to mount a public conveyance [2] and to hasten to our Clemency's court. Let it then be yours not to delay at all, but, with this letter supplying to you authority for a public conveyance,[2] to come immediately to us, that you also may fulfil your desire and in seeing us you may enjoy suitable pleasure.

May God guard you, beloved brother.

1. See no. 68, n. 2.
2. See no. 95, n. 41.

71. LETTER OF CONSTANTINE I ON READMISSION OF HERETICS, 334 or 335

(Gelasius, *HE* 3. 15. 1-5)

Gelasius gives Alexander, patriarch of Alexandria, as the recipient of this imperial order to receive into communion the heresiarch Arius and his associate Euzoius, whom he had excommunicated in 321, but who had been recalled between 327 and 334 (but nearer the latter date) from exile (no. 58) and had recanted in an evasive confession submitted to the emperor. However, some scholars suppose that on chronological considerations such ascription is impossible, because Alexander died in 328, and conjecture that the letter was addressed to the Alexander who was bishop of Constantinople from 320 to 336.

Although the chronology of Arius is uncertain in some points and even if Alexander of Alexandria was the person addressed, the letter's order apparently was not obeyed, for in 335 Constantine the Great wrote to St Athanasius, who had succeeded Alexander as patriarch of Alexandria, and commanded him to admit Arius into communion (no. 72)—an order likewise disobeyed. The problem, however, soon was settled, for Arius died a dreadful (but natural) death c. 336, while Euzoius survived to become patriarch of Antioch in 361.

Victor Constantine, Greatest, Augustus to father Alexander, bishop.

And now indeed the all-abominable jealousy will bay in answer with ungodly sophisms of excess.[1] What, then, has this to do with the present situation? Most honoured brother, do we decree other things beyond the decisions made by the Holy Spirit through you?

Arius, I say, that Arius, has come to me, the Augustus, in accordance with the exhortation of very many persons,[2] announcing that he thinks about our Catholic faith those things which in the synod at Nicaea[3] have been defined and confirmed through you, when also I was present and marked as your fellow-servant.

Forthwith, then, this person along with Euzoius, having recognized, of course, the will of the imperial mandate,[4] has come to us. Therefore I conversed with them in the presence of rather many persons about the Word of Life. I am that man, who have dedicated to God my mind with pure faith; I am your fellow-servant, who all the . . .[5] and I have taken upon myself the care for concord. (And after other matters:)[6]

Therefore I have sent an order, not only reminding, but also asking the suppliant man to be received. If indeed, then, you have found them claiming the right and ever-living apostolic faith established at Nicaea[3] (for even in our presence they have maintained strongly that they think this), provide for all things,[7] I beg. For if you should make provision for these things,[7] you would conquer hatreds by concord. I beg, therefore, aid concord; co-operate in the beauties of friendship toward the persons who do not doubt the matters of faith; make me to hear those things which I wish and desire: the peace and the concord of you all.

May God guard you, most honoured father.

1. This may mean the outcries of the orthodox, who are outraged at the restoration of Arius.

2. Among these the chief was Eusebius, bishop of Nicomedia, an Arian sympathizer, also lately recalled from exile to an advisory post at court. On him see introd. to nos. 50 and 58 as well as no. 61, nn. 7 and 11 *ad fin*.

3. In 325 at the First General Council.

4. Recalling Arius from exile (no. 58).

5. Editors mark a defective text here.

6. Gelasius apparently abbreviates the letter.

7. It is not clear whether Arius and Euzoius (and others) are meant or something impersonal is intended.

72. LETTER OF CONSTANTINE I ON READMISSION OF HERETICS, 335

(PG 25. 357)

After the heresiarch Arius had secured imperial permission to return to Alexandria less than a decade after his condemnation at Nicaea (no. 58), St Athanasius, patriarch of Alexandria, refused to receive him into communion (see introd. to no. 71). When Constantine had heard this, he ordered Athanasius either to admit Arius or to suffer deposition. But the patriarch persisted in his refusal and after a command audience with the emperor was absolved.

Part of the imperial order is preserved by Athanasius (*Apol. adv. Ar.* 59), Socrates (*HE* 1. 27), Sozomen (*HE* 2. 22), Gelasius (*HE* 3. 14), Nicephorus (*HE* 8. 48). The later historians regard this letter as a rescript in reply to an earlier epistle from the patriarch to the emperor, but from Athanasius' own account it appears that he had written not to Constantine but to Eusebius, bishop of Nicomedia, one of the imperial advisers, and that Eusebius induced the emperor to take the initiative.

The Athanasian version, being the earliest text, is translated.

Part of Emperor Constantine's letter.[1]

Having, therefore, knowledge of my will, afford unhindered entrance to all wishing to enter into the Church. For, if I know that you have prevented any of them[2] laying claim[3] to the Church[4] or have debarred them[5] from entrance, I shall send forthwith one who in accordance with my command both will depose you and will banish you from the place.

1. Socrates' caption is "Part of the emperor's letter", to which Gelasius adds "to Athanasius". Sozomen and Nicephorus omit the caption.

2. Gelasius omits the phrase.

3. Nicephorus omits *laying claim*.

4. Gelasius substitutes "to the ecclesiastical faith".

5. Gelasius reads "such persons".

73. LETTER OF CONSTANTINE I ON CONCILIAR UNITY, 335

(Eusebius, *VC* 4. 42)

As part of the celebration of the thirty years of his reign (Tricennalia) Constantine decided in 335 to dedicate the Church of the Holy Sepulchre, which in 326 he had ordered to be built in Jerusalem (no. 54), and to summon a synod at Tyre, whither he commands bishops to convene for consideration of the agenda in the following document.

Theodoret (*HE* 1. 29. 1-6) and Gelasius (*HE* 3. 17. 1-7) also have this letter.

Letter of the emperor to the synod at Tyre.[1]

Victor [2] Constantine, Greatest,[2] Augustus to the holy synod [3] at Tyre.

It would be equally consistent with and particularly becoming to the prosperity of the times that the Catholic Church should be free from faction and Christ's servants at the present time should be free from every reproach. But since some, driven by the vehement passion of unwholesome contention (for I should not speak [4] of persons living worthily [5] of themselves),[6] try to confuse everything (and this to me seems to have advanced beyond all misfortune),[7] I urge you, who are running for the sake of this, that is, the reason,[8] to assemble into one place apart from any delay, to muster a synod,[9] to defend those who need aid, to heal the brethren who are in peril, to restore the divisions of the members to oneness of mind, to correct erroneous matters, by assembling, that is to say, with all sincerity and faith,[13] vinces the proper harmony, which—alas the anomaly!—the arrogance of very few persons has destroyed. That this is pleasing to God, the lord of all things,[10] and to us and to you yourselves, above all [11] prayer, if really you should restore peace (a result productive of no ordinary honour), I think that all persons agree. Therefore do not then delay, but, by therefore expediting the objects of your zeal already manifested, be eager to put the proper end to the prescribed matters, by assembling, that is to say, with all sincerity and faith,[12] which, when he almost speaks aloud, that Saviour whom we serve particularly asks from you on every occasion.

Nothing of what relates to my Devoutness shall be lacking to you.[13] As many matters as you have indicated in writing, all these have been performed by me. I have sent orders to those of the bishops whom you have desired, that they, being present, may participate with you in the deliberations;[14] I have sent Dionysius, of consular rank,[15] who will remind the persons who are bound to come to the synod with you [16] and will be present as a supervisor of the proceedings and especially of orderly behaviour.[17] Indeed, if anyone (as I do not suppose), attempting to evade even now our command, should not be willing to be present,[18] forthwith from us shall be sent one who, banishing him by virtue of an imperial edict, shall teach him that it is not proper to act against an emperor's decisions published in defence of truth.

For the rest: it shall be the labour of your Sanctities by a unanimous decision neither in respect to enmity nor in respect to favour,[19] but in accordance with ecclesiastical and apostolical rule, to contrive the fitting cure for errors which have been done or really have happened accidentally through mistake, that you may liberate the Church from all defamation and may lighten my cares and, by restoring to those now divided the grace of peace, may procure for yourselves the greatest glory.[20]

May God guard you, beloved brethren.

1. Theodoret omits the caption, into which Gelasius inserts "Constantine" after *emperor* and "assembled" after *at*.
2. Theodoret omits this epithet.
3. Gelasius inserts "assembled".
4. Gelasius inserts "anything otherwise".
5. Theodoret and Gelasius read "unworthily".
6. The idea seems that the emperor excludes those Christians who—as we say—"live up to" their profession of Christians, in that they follow the Christian ideal of living peaceably with all persons (cf. Rom. 12. 18).
7. That is, that the situation of doctrinal confusion worse confounded has outstripped any ordinary bad fortune of a temporary character.

Constantine certainly was plagued with ecclesiastical exacerbations, of which Donatism and the varied varieties of Arianism were the worst. But he was partly to blame, since his release of Christians from pagan persecution automatically set Christians free to persecute one another and in the process to keep his subjects in a sad state of disunity on theological matters.

8. Constantine in the words *who . . . reason* seems to indicate that the bishops are advancing to their assembly for the purpose of settling such controversial matters as have arisen, chiefly the discord in the Church which has caused so much confusion. Doubtless some of the more earnest bishops, concerned about the state of affairs, had entreated the emperor to summon a synod. For that reason they were running. The words *that . . . reason* explain the phrase *for . . . this*.
9. Gelasius adds "of spiritual assembly".
10. Gelasius omits the phrase.
11. Gelasius attaches to *us* this adjective.
12. Gelasius adds "and provide that that peace be obtained in all matters both for you and for all persons", omitting the rest of the sentence and the two succeeding sentences.

13. Theodoret omits the phrase.
14. About 150 prelates assisted at the synod.
15. Athanasius (no. 74) calls him a count (κόμης).
16. There were cited for appearance at the synod certain persons, among whom was St Athanasius, patriarch of Alexandria. Presumably, then, Dionysius was charged with seeing that the summoned persons would attend.
17. Good order not seldom was conspicuously absent from conciliar sessions, especially in the East, where councils during the Church's early era frequently were uproarious and unruly gatherings, to which spectators and auditors contributed often their own share to control an assembly's action. To assist at the sessions clerical factions even enlisted laymen, who, though voteless, yet by their excitement contrived to exert some influence on conciliar deliberations and at least to add their contribution to the acrimony of debate by applause and by deprecation. See nos. 401, n. 2, and 404, n. 1.

The councils, of course, were the last refuge of freedom of speech in a realm where control of thought was enforced increasingly as time progressed and in a sense were reminiscent of the disorderly assemblies so characteristic of some Hellenic city-states (notably Athens). But the riot (one of the most resonant in religious records) by pagans who, protesting against the new religion preached by St Paul, persisted in their racket for two hours at Ephesus in the theatre (Acts 19. 23–41; see also W. Keller, *The Bible as History* [New York, 1956], 382–4) was an anaemic affair compared with later Christian action, advancing at times to bloodshed, concerning ecclesiastical questions in eastern cities.

18. Gelasius adds "at the synod".
19. Cf. Tacitus, *Ann.* 1. 1. 6: *sine ira et studio.* See no. 75, n. 8.
20. Gelasius substitutes "good fortune".

74. LETTER OF DIONYSIUS ON CONCILIAR PROCEDURE, 335

(*PG* 25. 393–6)

Constantine I sent Count Flavius Dionysius, an official at the imperial court, to represent him at the Council of Tyre, which met in 335 to consider allegations against St Athanasius, patriarch of Alexandria. After he had received from several orthodox and pro-Athanasian bishops letters protesting about the anti-Athanasian conspiracies and manoeuvres occurring in the sessions, especially about a so-called fact-finding commission of six Arians, who were sent from Tyre into Egypt to collect evidence about Athanasius, Dionysius wrote the following letter to caution the commissioners about their procedure.

As the event proved, the commissioners scorned the count's admonitions

74. CONCILIAR PROCEDURE, 335

and Dionysius failed to take appropriate action. Athanasius was deposed by the council and after an appeal to the emperor, who was persuaded by the patriarch's enemies, he departed into his first exile (336–7).

Athanasius has this letter (*Apol. adv. Ar.* 81).

Dionysius, count,[1] to those associated with Eusebius.[2]

These matters are what already I have discussed with my lords associated with Flacillus,[3] that Athanasius, having appeared, made accusations, saying that these persons, whom I[4] deprecated, are sent and crying that he is wronged and is circumvented; these matters also Alexander,[5] the lord of my soul,[6] has dispatched. And that you may know that what has been written to me by his Excellency is agreeable to reason, I have suppended it[7] to be read by you.

Remember also what has been written previously by me.[8] For I wrote to your Excellencies, my lords, that those who are sent ought to have been sent by general decision and decree.[9] See, therefore, lest what has been done should succumb to reproach and lest we should give an occasion for just complaint to those who desire to accuse us. For as it is not proper that the accusers' side should be oppressed, so not even that of the defendants.

But I think that no little occasion for blame against us exists, when my lord Alexander[5] obviously is not in agreement with what is done.

1. The ecclesiastical historians describe him merely as of consular rank (no. 73, n. 15).
2. This Arianizing courtier-prelate (on whom see no. 71, n. 2) and inveterate enemy of Athanasius was a leader, if not the president (cf. *infra* n. 3), of the Council of Tyre (335).
3. Patriarch of Antioch and an Arian sympathizer. Some scholars suppose that he presided at the synod's sessions.
4. If the Greek is correct, Dionysius objected to the commission's personnel as being biased against Athanasius. The Latin translation in *PG* takes as the understood subject Athanasius.
5. Bishop of Thessalonica and an orthodox prelate.
6. This curious phrase seems to mean "my beloved lord".
7. Athanasius reproduces this in the preceding section (80).
8. This letter is not extant.
9. From our information about the anti-Athanasian animus of the council it appears that the Arian faction named the commissioners.

75. LETTER OF CONSTANTINE I ON TRANSFER OF THE TYRIAN COUNCIL TO CONSTANTINOPLE, 335

(PG 25. 401-6)

After St Athanasius, patriarch of Alexandria, had been deposed at Tyre through the effort of influential Arians among the assembled bishops, he journeyed to Constantinople, where he intercepted Constantine returning to the city and so successfully interceded with him that the emperor condescended to judge his case in person. To hear this appeal from the synod's decision, Constantine sent the following letter, which commanded the bishops to come to Constantinople.

As the event proved, Athanasius lost his case, when his enemies among the bishops—most of the prelates of Tyre, alarmed by the imperial summons, disobeyed it and departed to their dioceses—discarded their old charges and advanced another: that Athanasius had threatened to prevent the annual exportation of grain from Alexandria to Constantinople. At this Constantine took alarm and, without hearing the appellant's defence, exiled Athanasius to Trèves in Gaul, where he remained for two years, until Constantine II, who succeeded his father in 337, restored him to his see (no. 77).

This letter, found in Athanasius (*Apol. adv. Ar.* 86), is preserved also by Socrates (*HE* 1. 34), Sozomen (*HE* 2. 28), Gelasius (*HE* 3. 18. 1–13), Nicephorus (*HE* 8. 50). Cassiodorus translates it into Latin (*HE* 3. 7. 2–13).

Victor Constantine, Greatest,[1] Augustus to the bishops [2] convened in Tyre.[3]

I know not what are the matters decided by your synod amid [4] clamour and storm, but somehow the truth seems to have been perverted by [5] a certain disorderly confusion, in that you obviously through mutual quarrelling, which you wish to be prevailing, consider not the things which please God.[6] But it will be the work of Divine Providence both to scatter the evils of this contentiousness,[7] when openly detected, and to show expressly to us if you, when assembled there, have had any concern for the truth and have decided apart from any favour and enmity [8] the matters which have been decided.[9] Therefore I desire [10] that you all assemble speedily [11] before my Piety,[12] in order that you in your own person [13] may render the precise account of the matters transacted by you.

For what reason I have deemed it right to write [14] these things to you and why I summon you before me by letter, you will discover from the following. Well then, to me, when entering our eponymous and all-blessed city of Constantinople [15] (it happened that at that time I was riding on horseback),[16] suddenly Athanasius, the bishop,[17] in the middle of the highway with certain others,[18] whom he had with him,[19] so unexpectedly approached [20] that he even produced [21] an occasion of consternation. For God, the overseer of all things, bears witness for me that I was not able at first sight even to [22] recognize [23] who he was, unless some of our attendants [24] had reported to us [25] when learning by inquiry the details (as was natural):[26] both who he was and what injustice he has suffered.[27] Then I neither conversed with him at that time nor shared communications. But when he petitioned to be heard [28] and I was refusing and was little far from ordering him to be removed,[29] with more outspokenness he petitioned for himself nothing else from us than your arrival, that in your presence he might be able to complain bitterly about what he perforce has suffered. And since this appeared [30] to me [31] to be reasonable and suitable to the times, I eagerly [32] ordered these things to be written to you, in order that you all, as many as have composed the synod held in Tyre, immediately might hasten to my Clemency's [33] court for the purpose of proving by the facts themselves your decision's honesty and integrity, obviously, before me, who not even you can deny am a genuine servant of God.[34]

Therefore through my religious services toward God everywhere there is peace and God's name truly is praised by the barbarians themselves,[35] who till now were ignorant of the truth. And it is evident that he who is ignorant of the truth knows not [36] God. Nevertheless—as has been said previously—even the barbarians now [37] through me, God's genuine servant, have learned to know God and have learned to reverence him,[38] who they have perceived by very deeds everywhere shields and provides for me;[39] and hence chiefly they also know God, whom those reverence because of their dread toward us. But we,[40] who are supposed to propose—for I cannot say to protect—his Benignity's [41] holy mysteries [42] (we, I say),[43] do nothing else than things which tend [44] to dissension and hatred and—to speak simply—which [45] have reference to the human race's destruction.

But hasten—as has been said previously—and all hurry [46] to us with speed, having been persuaded that I [47] shall try with all strength to bring to a successful issue that in God's law may be guarded especially inviolate these matters,[48] whereon neither blame nor dishonour [49] will be able to be attached, when the enemies of the law,[50] whosoever behind [51] the appearance of the holy name produce manifold and varied blasphemies,[52] certainly have been scattered and utterly have been shattered and entirely have been suppressed.[53]

1. Cassiodorus omits this word and substitutes "Pious" for the next; for *in Tyre* he reads "in the Tyrians' city".

2. Gelasius inserts "again", for the bishops had adjourned to Jerusalem in the interim.

3. Before this superscription (which is missing in Sozomen and Nicephorus) captions appear in two authors: Socrates has "How the emperor summoned the synod to him by letter, that in his presence the matters against Athanasius might be examined accurately"; Gelasius has "Letter of the God-beloved Emperor Constantine to the bishops withdrawn from Aelia [Capitolina, i.e. Jerusalem] to Tyre".

4. Gelasius inserts "so much"; Cassiodorus reads for this and the next three words "clamorously and with storm" in inconcinnity.

5. Cassiodorus reads "for it appears that the truth has been overwhelmed by" etc.

6. Cassiodorus reads "in that you obviously consider not the things which please God, because of quarrels which you have against the persons nearest to you, and you want your wishes to be invincible".

7. Gelasius reads "to scatter the dreadful things of contentiousness or rather of your bad fighting" and Cassiodorus reads "that this contentiousness should be able to be ousted".

8. See no. 73, n. 19.

9. For *have had . . . decided* Cassiodorus substitutes "have done anything without any favour or because of enmities".

10. Socrates substitutes "it is necessary" for *I desire*.

11. Cassiodorus has "with all speed".

12. Sozomen and Gelasius read "Devoutness"; Cassiodorus has "Reverence".

13. Sozomen inserts "before us" and Gelasius inserts "before me".

14. For *have . . . write* Cassiodorus has "have written" and the next verb is "have summoned". Gelasius also shows a past tense for the second verb, thus making with Cassiodorus both dependent verbs uniform in time, Cassiodorus prefixes "But" to the sentence.

15. Cassiodorus has "the city of our name of the most happy fatherland".

16. For the parenthesis Cassiodorus reads "while I was about to mount onto a horse".

17. To this point Gelasius reads "Since in my presence is Athanasius, the bishop of the Church in Alexandria, the pupil of the divine law, who came to me when entering from a progress our eponymous and all-blessed Constantinople".

18. Socrates and Cassiodorus substitute "priests".

19. Gelasius inserts "bewailing and lamenting".

20. Gelasius reads "and made a sudden advance so"; Cassiodorus adds "us".

21. Gelasius inserts "for us"; Cassiodorus reads "that suddenly a cause for some fear was given to us".

22. Nicephorus for *was . . . to* has only "did not".

23. Proleptic "him"—familiar from the evangelical dialogue (Mark 1. 24; Luke 4. 34)—is omitted from the translation.

24. For *unless . . . attendants* Sozomen has "unless some", while Nicephorus omits all five words and begins a new sentence with *had reported*, for which

an indefinite subject must be supplied. In Cassiodorus *some* is singular in number.

25. Gelasius and Cassiodorus omit the phrase.

26. Gelasius and Cassiodorus omit the parenthesis and the latter also omits the preceding six words.

27. Cassiodorus has the pluperfect tense for this verb.

Gelasius, after adding "from you", then appends material not recorded by the others: "We saw the man so humble and dejected that we fell into unspeakable pity for him, when we knew him to be Athanasius, whose sacred sight is sufficient to draw even the heathen to reverence for the God of all things, whom formerly certain wicked men and aliens to peace and concord encompassed with no chance slanders, so that even I myself, caught by their much-skilled guile, was about to sin against the man, unless, moved by divine judgement, I had ordered him then to come with all speed from Alexandria to our Clemency's court. And so, when he had been examined before my Devoutness concerning the things falsely dramatized against him, the man, standing his ground before us, proved the falsity of the accusations against himself and, having appeared blameless in all those matters, was returned to his native city by us with the most honour that was possible, having been restored to the orthodox people, who are guided by him. But now again he cries with more outspokenness that a second round of things—worse than the first—has been ventured against him, demanding from us nothing else than your arrival before us, which he has petitioned should be allowed to him, that in your presence he might be able to complain bitterly about what he perforce has suffered."

On the basis of this long addition with some other alterations N. H. Baynes believes that Athanasius abbreviated and "edited" the original letter which appears more fully in the Gelasian version (*Byzantine Essays and Other Studies* [London, 1955], 282–7).

28. Sozomen omits the passive infinitive.

29. Gelasius rejoins the others here.

30. Socrates and Cassiodorus have the present tense and the former reads the verb before *suitable* again.

31. Plural in Gelasius.

32. Gelasius omits the adverb.

33. "Piety's" is in Socrates and "Gentleness' " is in Cassiodorus; Gelasius substitutes "our" (ἡμέτερον) for "Clemency's" (ἡμερότητος), as if by error.

34. Gelasius adds "when you defend the decisions made by you".

35. Gelasius reads "and most tribes of the barbarians themselves reverence truly God's name".

36. Cassiodorus has "cannot know".

37. Socrates and Cassiodorus omit the adverb.

38. For *God's . . . him* Cassiodorus reads "a loyal servant, have known and have learned to fear God".

39. Cassiodorus reads "who has been shown by very deeds everywhere as a any rate my protector and provider".
40. Cassiodorus has the second person.
41. Socrates has "the Church's"; Cassiodorus has "his Clemency's".
42. This phrase τὰ ἅγια μυστήρια (*sancta mysteria*) usually refers to the central act of Christian worship (see no. 139, n. 5), which has been characterized by many titles, beginning with *the Lord's Supper* (1 Cor. 11. 20), which St Paul derives (1 Cor. 11. 23-9) from the last supper shared by Jesus and his disciples on the eve of the Crucifixion (Matt. 26. 17-29; Mark 14. 12-25; Luke 22. 7-20). St Ignatius, traditionally third bishop of Antioch (*ob. c.* 108), seems to have been the first to call it the *Eucharist* (*Ad Smyrn.* 7. 1), although his earlier contemporary Pope St Clement I (*ob. c.* 100) apparently applies the verbal form to the rite (1 Cor. 38. 4). But despite the precedence of *Eucharist* in theologians' technical terminology, popular usage devised other descriptions, of which (Divine) Liturgy, (Holy) Mass, (Holy) Communion have the most venerable history respectively for Orthodox, Roman Catholics, Protestants. The literal translation *holy mysteries* survives twice in the Exhortation in the "Order of the Administration of the Lord's Supper, or Holy Communion" in the Anglican and Episcopalian Book of Common Prayer.

But here as elsewhere occasionally in this sylloge—the context must be consulted—the phrase may mean the religious doctrines which were guarded carefully from the knowledge of profane (in its primary meaning) persons in the early days of Christianity. In this sense it is the secret and esoteric truth obtained by revelation and transmitted through teachers, for in all ancient religions every mystery required a mystagogue by whose instruction an initiate was led, ordinarily *orally*, to its logical explanation. So far as concerns Christianity, the principal proof text is the testimony of St Paul, the self-called "steward of the mysteries of God" (1 Cor. 4. 1), in 1 Cor. 2; an excellent example is his *written* explanation of the resurrection of the dead in 1 Cor. 15 (note well v. 51: "Behold, I show you a mystery").

For the meaning of μυστήριον see A. D. Nock, "Mysterion", in *Harvard Studies in Classical Philology*, 60 (1951) 201-4. On the range of the word see H. G. Liddell and R. Scott, *A Greek-English Lexicon*[9] (Oxford 1925-40), s.v. 1156 and 2091. For the interconnection of early Christianity and pagan mysteries consult B. M. Metzger's recent summary in his authoritative article "Considerations of Methodology in the Study of the Mystery Religions and Early Christianity" in *HTR* 48 (1955) 1-20.

Now most mysteries may be said to be of two sorts: (1) such as never would have been known without revelation, but, when revealed, are mostly explainable and usually understandable—e.g. Christ's Atonement, Resurrection, and Ascension; forgiveness of sins; eternal life in the future world; (2) such as, when revealed, are known, but the manner and the mode of their existence cannot be comprehended—e.g. the Trinity and the incarnation of the Word (Logos) as Jesus Christ. (The calling of the Gentiles [Rom. 16. 25; Col. 1.

26–7], Christ's spiritual union with the Church [Eph. 5. 32], the kingdom of God [Matt. 13. 11; Mark 4. 11; Luke 8. 10] also are mysteries, but are minor when compared with the others.) Patristic tradition presents many testimonies to support this teaching. Obviously, of course, the original explanation of some of the Christian mysteries was lost at an early date, otherwise Tertullian would not have confessed (*c.* 210) that the death of God's Son must be believed, because it is absurd, and that his resurrection is certain, because it is impossible (*De Carn. Chr.* 5 *ad med.*), and St Augustine would not have considered (*c.* 400) the Trinity a riddle, and that only a rare soul knows of what it speaks when it speaks of it (*Conf.* 13. 5 and 11).

43. Gelasius omits the parenthesis.

44. Cassiodorus reads "are known to tend".

45. Cassiodorus inserts "are seen to" and renders the previous parenthesis as "that I may speak clearly".

46. Socrates and Gelasius omit *and* and *hurry*.

47. Plural in Socrates.

48. Thus far Cassiodorus reads "But hasten—as I have said—to come to us straightway, knowing that I shall try with all strength to effect that those things which are in God's law may be guarded especially without any wavering".

49. Cassiodorus prefers "evil superstition" (*mala superstitio*) for κακοδοξία which is a possible interpretation, especially when applied to heresy.

50. Gelasius adds "of God" and Cassiodorus characterizes it as "most sacred". By *law* is meant Christianity, as often.

51. Cassiodorus substitutes "under".

52. Gelasius adds "for beguilement of rather simple persons".

53. Gelasius concludes "since we yearn for, as much as possible, the purity of the Catholic Church, which our Saviour preserves spotless and holy and faultless, having bought it by his salutary and precious blood, just as his divine and unbroken laws declare".

Some of this addition shows a similarity to St Paul's words in Eph. 5. 25–7.

76. LETTER OF CONSTANTINE I ON JEWISH MOLESTATION OF CHRISTIANS, 335–6

(CS 4)

This law, of which the Theodosian Code has extracts (*CT* 16. 8. 5 and 16. 9. 1), orders manumission for Christian slaves circumcised by Jewish masters and forbids Jewish attacks upon Christian converts from Judaism. In the latter case it reiterates a twenty-year old ordinance (no. 23) issued by Constantine, who apparently is compelled by circumstances to re-enact the constitution and to add to it.

Emperor Constantine to Felix, praetorian prefect.[1]

Long ago, indeed, has been promulgated the most salutary sanction of our constitution,[2] which we reiterate with respect for our repeated law, and we desire that if[3] anyone of the Jews, having bought a Christian slave or one of any other sect whatsoever, shall have not had great horror to circumcise him,[4] the circumcised one indeed, made possessive of freedom by this statute's measure, shall obtain the privileges of the said freedom: it should not be lawful for a Jew who shall have circumcised a slave of the mentioned class to retain him for the obedience of slavery.

And indeed by this same sanction we command the following: that if anyone of the Jews, unlocking for himself the door of everlasting life, shall have delivered himself to the holy cults and shall have chosen to be a Christian, he should not suffer from Jews any disquietude or molestation. But if anyone of the Jews shall have thought that he who from a Jew has become a Christian can be assailed with injury, we desire that the contriver of contumely of such kind should be subjugated to avenging punishments according to the character of the crime committed, dearest cousin Felix.[5]

Whereore by the Divinity's compassion we trust that in all the Roman world this person will be safe through the maintenance of due respect for us.

And we desire that your excellent Sublimity by your letters sent throughout the diocese[6] entrusted to you should caution the governors most earnestly that due reverence of this character should be maintained.

Given on 21 October. Posted on 9 March at Carthage, Nepotian and Facundus being consuls.[7]

1. Cf. *infra* n. 6.
2. No. 23.
3. Here begins *CT* 16. 9. 1.
4. For the predicate of the protasis *CT* 16. 9. 1 reads simply "shall have circumcised him" and then has as the apodosis "he should not at all retain in slavery the circumcised person, but he who shall have endured this should obtain the privileges of freedom".

There follows this interpretation: "If anyone of the Jews shall have purchased and shall have circumcised a Christian slave or one of any other sect whatsoever, he, taken from the power of the Jew himself, should remain in freedom".

The subscription is "Given on 21 October at Constantinople. Posted on 8 May at Carthage, Nepotian and Facundus being consuls". Since these men were consuls in 336, the law was issued in 335.

77. RECALL OF ATHANASIUS, 337

The Jewish religious rite of circumcision ascends into the patriarchal period, when it was ordained by God not only for Abraham and his male descendants, but also for his male servants and/or slaves and all males born of them in his household (Gen. 17. 9–14). Closer to Christian times the compulsory aspect of this practice reappeared in the reigns of (John) Hycranus I, king of Judaea (134–104 B.C.), and of his son and successor (Judah) Aristobulus I Philhellen (104–103 B.C.), who compelled respectively the Idumaean and the Ituraean victims of their conquests, if they wished to remain in their countries, to be circumcised (Josephus, *Ant. Iud.* 13. 9. 1. 257–8, 13. 11. 3. 318).

Hadrian is said to have forbidden the Jews in 131 to practise circumcision (Scriptores Historiae Augustae: *Had.* 14. 2); but this order apparently was rescinded after 138 by rescript of Antoninus, who allowed Jews to circumcise only their own sons and ordered castration for non-Jews who used circumcision (*D* 48. 8. 11. pr.).

5. For this sentence *CT* 16. 8. 5 reads "It should not be permitted that Jews disturb or assail with any injury him who from a Jew has become a Christian—contumely of such kind being punished according to the character of the committed act".

The subscription is "Given on 22 October at Constantinople. Posted on 8 May, Nepotian and Facundus being consuls". The place of posting—Carthage cf. *supra* n. 4 *ad med.*)—is not named.

An addendum reads "This law does not need interpretation".

6. Since he was a praetorian prefect, Felix was not actually the governor of a diocese, which was governed by a vicar, but, while both his prefecture and the diocese are unknown, yet in a loose sense it is possible to consider Felix as controlling a diocese (for its vicar was subordinate to him), because Felix' prefecture comprised several dioceses.

7. Cf. *supra* nn. 4 and 5 for variations in the Theodosian subscriptions.

77. LETTER OF CONSTANTINE II ON RECALL OF ATHANASIUS, 337

(PG 25. 405–8)

This letter to the Alexandrian Church announces the return of St Athanasius, patriarch of Alexandria, to his see from his first exile, a restoration which—so the writer claims—was intended by his father, Constantine the Great,[1] who had banished the bishop in 336.

This document is preserved by Athanasius (*Apol. adv. Ar.* 87), Socrates (*HE* 2. 3), Sozomen (*HE* 3. 2), Theodoret (*HE* 2. 2), Nicephorus (*HE* 9. 3), and by Cassiodorus is translated into Latin (*HE* 4. 2. 2–6).

77. RECALL OF ATHANASIUS, 337

Constantine Caesar [2] to the people of the Catholic Church of the city of Alexandria.[3]

I think that it has not escaped your sacred thought's knowledge [4] that Athanasius, the expounder of the adorable law,[5] had been sent for a time into the Gauls [6] for this reason, lest perhaps, since indeed his bloodthirsty and hostile [7] enemies' savagery was persisting [8] to the hazard of his sacred life, he should sustain fatalities [9] through evil persons' perversion.[10] Therefore to escape [11] this, after he had been snatched from the throats of the men who were attacking him,[12] he has been ordered to live under my control [13] in such a way that in this city,[14] wherein he was living, he has abounded in all the necessities of life,[15] although certainly his celebrated virtue, having trusted in divine aids, lightens the burdens of rather harsh fortune.[16]

Therefore, although indeed in regard for your most beloved godliness [17] our Lord Constantine Augustus,[18] my father, had purposed to restore the said bishop to his own place, nevertheless, since indeed, when he had been anticipated by human lot, he has rested [19] before he had fulfilled his wish,[20] I, having been appointed his successor,[21] have considered it consistent to fulfil the purpose of the emperor of divine memory.

And whenever he may gain your presence, you will know how much respect he has obtained.[22] For it is not wonderful if I [23] have done anything [24] on his behalf, for both the representation of your longing for him and the character of so great a man moved and impelled my soul to this.

May Divine Providence preserve [25] you, beloved [26] brethren.

Given on 17 July at Trèves.[27]

---

1. In 335 Constantine I, dreading the proximity of death (which for a biennium was postponed), with the folly of fondness and unable to secure the peaceable succession of a sole heir, divided the Empire among his surviving sons, Constantine, Constantius, Constans, of whom the second outlived his siblings. Many have declared this division a mistake. But his predicament was the price of monarchy. Perhaps he surmised that they, emulating his example, would struggle with one another for sole supremacy; yet he may have been convinced that they would contest the succession even more certainly, if he should have selected one of them or another as his heir. Nor was he in error, for Constantine, the eldest, succumbed in 340 to the swords of the soldiers of Constans, the youngest, whose share of the spoil he had tried to take.

2. See no. 28, n. 7.

3. Several captions before the superscription are found: Socrates' "How Athanasius, relying on Constantine the Younger's letter, controlled Alexandria"; Sozomen's "About Athanasius the Great's return from Gaul and the letter of Constantine Caesar, the son of Constantine the Great"; Nicephorus'

77. RECALL OF ATHANASIUS, 337

"How Athanasius with Caesar Constantine's letter returned from the Gauls".

In the superscription variants also occur: after *Church* Socrates and Nicephorus have "of the Alexandrians"; Theodoret has "of the Alexandrians' city"; Cassiodorus has "established in Alexandria". Only Sozomen agrees with Athanasius and even he reverses the last two nouns.

4. Cassiodorus reads "I do not think that your most sacred mind is ignorant"; Nicephorus adds "for what reason it has happened" and omits later *for this reason*.

5. Christianity.

6. See no. 203, n. 4.

7. For these adjectives Cassiodorus gives simply "cruel".

8. Cassiodorus reads "threatening".

9. Cassiodorus has "something unsuitable".

10. Cassiodorus gives "cunning".

11. All the Greek versions have a verb meaning "to laugh at", "to make light of"; Cassiodorus preserves the extended meaning "to avoid", "to escape".

12. Cassiodorus weakens the clause by reading "he was removed from the hardships threatening him".

13. Cassiodorus substitutes "command".

14. Trèves, as the subscription shows.

15. Cassiodorus reads "the necessary good things were not lacking to him".

16. The concessive clause makes the following independent sentence in Cassiodorus: "For such is his venerable virtue, relying on divine aids, that it even despises a rather worse fortune's miseries."

17. Cassiodorus has "reverence".

18. "Pious" is substituted by Cassiodorus. All later authors insert "of blessed memory".

19. Euphemistic for "died".

20. Plural in Cassiodorus, who has imperfect for pluperfect tense.

21. Cassiodorus omits these five words in participial construction.

22. All later writers add "from me".

23. Plural in Cassiodorus.

24. Cassiodorus inserts a qualifying clause "which may be praised".

25. Theodoret has the future indicative for the other Greeks' optative and Cassiodorus' subjunctive.

26. Cassiodorus has the superlative degree.

27. All later authors omit the subscription.

78. LETTER OF HEMERIUS ON ERECTION OF A CHURCH IN EGYPT, c. 337

(*PG* 25. 401)

The Meletian opponents [1] of St Athanasius, patriarch of Alexandria, to ensure the loyalty of a certain Ischyras, who had accused Athanasius falsely, to their conspiracy against Athanasius, persuaded the emperor to write to Flavius Hemerius, the chief financial officer (*catholicus*) in Egypt, the authorization that a church should be built for Ischryas.[2] The present document (preserved by Athanasius in *Apol. adv. Ar.* 85), which originally was suppended to the imperial instructions (now lost), transmits the ordinance and entrusts its execution to an anonymous collector of taxes in the district wherein Ischyras was domiciled.[3]

Flavius Hemerius to the tax-collector of Mareotis, greeting.

Since Ischyras, the priest, has petitioned the Piety of our lords, the Augusti[4] and the Caesars,[4] that a church should be built in the district of Irene Secontarurus, their Divinity has ordained that this should be done as speedily as possible.

Therefore take care, when you have obtained both the copy of the sacred letter, which with proper reverence has been placed above it,[5] and the notes, which have been processed in my Devotion's presence, that, after you have made the epitome speedily, you should transfer it to the register, in order that the divinely made orders may be able to be brought to a consummation.

1. See no. 68, n. 2.
2. That Ischyras was not a priest (see no. 68, n. 7) was not mentioned in the petition. The construction of a church for him was conceived to add more colour to the charge that either Athanasius or Macarius, his agent, had burst into Ischyras' church during a celebration of the communion and had committed sacrilege there (see no. 68, n. 5). To bind Ischyras more closely to the Meletian party it appears that his nomination to a bishopric was secured (*Apol. adv. Ar.* 12, 46, 85).
3. The village where Ischyras lived was so small that it was operationally impracticable to support a church, and so its Christians worshipped in the church of an adjacent village. The district was directly dependent upon the see of Alexandria, whose ordinary administered its ecclesiastical affairs without the aid of a suffragan (*Apol. adv. Ar.* 85).
4. Constantine II, Constantius II, Constans I.
5. The petition.

79. MANDATE OF CONSTANTIUS II ON JEWISH OWNERSHIP OF CHRISTIAN SLAVES, 339

(*CT* 16. 9. 2)

This directive (enlarged in *CI* 1. 10. 1) orders immediate liberation of such Christian slaves as have been bought by Jews and penalizes Jews who have circumcised their slaves.

Emperor Constantius Augustus to Evagrius.[1]

If anyone of the Jews shall have believed that a slave of another sect or people can be bought, the slave straightway should be claimed for the fisc.

But if he shall have circumcised a bought slave,[2] not only he should be penalized by the loss of the slave, but also he should be punished by a capital sentence.[3]

But if a Jew should not hesitate to buy slaves adhering to the venerable faith, all slaves who are found in his power straightway should be removed and not any delay from depriving him of possession of those persons who are Christians should be interposed.

And the rest.

Given on 13 August, Constantius Augustus for the second time and Constans Augustus being consuls.

1. What magistracy Evagrius held is unknown, but probably he was a praetorian prefect.

2. From the beginning to this point Justinian, who adapts the first paragraph from the first sentence of no. 348, reads: "A Jew neither must buy a Christian slave nor should acquire one by gifts or by another title whatsoever. But if anyone of the Jews either shall have had a Christian slave or shall have believed that one of another sect or people can be possessed for any reason whatsoever and shall have circumcised him".

3. Justinian concludes by adding "the slave himself being presented with freedom for a reward".

80. MANDATE OF CONSTANTIUS II ON JEWISH PROSELYTISM AMONG CHRISTIAN WOMEN, 339

(CT 16. 8. 6)

The emperor seeks to combat Jewish missionary efforts directed toward former employees of the imperial weaving establishment and orders the return of such apostates.

Emperor Constantius Augustus to Evagrius.[1]
After other matters.
As far as concerns the women whom, when formerly engaged in our weaving establishment,[2] Jews have led into the association of their turpitude, it is our pleasure that the said persons should be restored to the weaving establishment and that this should be observed for the future: they should not attach Christian women to their disgraceful acts or, if they shall have done this, they should be subjected to capital peril.
Given on 13 August, Constantius Augustus being consul for the second time.[3]

1. On Evagrius see no. 79, n. 1.
2. The weaving establishment among its workers employed reformed prostitutes, who worked therein as penitents until the law let them marry.
3. From no. 79 (issued on the same day) it is clear that Constans was associated with Constantius in the consulship of 339 and that his name should be added to this subscription.
Some manuscripts add "This law does not need interpretation".

81. MANDATE OF CONSTANTIUS II AND CONSTANS I ON EXEMPTION OF CLERGYMEN'S SONS FROM CIVIC DUTIES, (?) 342

(CT 16. 2. 11)

This ordinance frees clergymen's minor and dependent sons from senatorial services.

The same Augusti to Longinian, prefect of Egypt.
Formerly we have ordained[1] that the Catholic law's[2] bishops and clergymen, who possess nothing at all and are useless in respect to patrimony, should not at all be summoned to curial public services.[3]

82. REDEMPTION OF CHRISTIAN PROSTITUTES, 343

But we learn that they in their perfection [4] are being disturbed for no public advantage.

And therefore we command that their sons, whosoever are found to be less wealthy and below the legal age,[5] should endure no molestation.

Given on 26 February, Constantius Augustus for the third time and Constans Augustus for the second time being consuls.[6]

1. The reference is possibly to no. 89, but cf. *infra* n. 6.
2. By *law* is meant religion, as often.
3. They were *useless* because a poor man had not enough property to permit his eligibility for service in a local senate. See no. 60, n. 2.
4. That is, their life of perfection, as dedicated to God, is being disturbed by the prefect's apparitors.
5. Presumably 25 years (*FIRA* I. 211); but perhaps thirty years, if a decurion had not held a magistracy.
6. Since the prefect of Egypt (on whom see no. 489, n. 12) during 341-3 was Longinian, to whom was sent this document, the editors have suspected that this document's original date of 354, when Sebastian Thrax was Egyptian prefect, and its probable reference to no. 89 (dated 349) are incorrect and have suggested the subscription as above translated.

82. MANDATE OF CONSTANTIUS II ON REDEMPTION OF CHRISTIAN PROSTITUTES, 343
(*CT* 15. 8. 1)

This constitution authorizes only Christian clergymen or laymen to purchase Christian women exposed for sale as slaves after service as prostitutes.

Emperor Constantius Augustus to Severus, urban prefect.[1]

If anyone shall have desired to subject to certain abuses women who are known to have dedicated themselves to the veneration of the most holy Christian law[2] and if one should cause them, when sold to brothels, to fulfil the vile service of prostituted shame, no other one should have the opportunity of buying the said women, except those who either are known to be ecclesiastics or are demonstrated to be Christian persons, after the proper price has been paid.

Given on 4 July at Hierapolis, Placidus and Romulus being consuls.

1. Severus' name is not on the official list of persons who were prefects of the city of Rome or of Constantinople.
2. Religion.

83. LETTER OF CONSTANTIUS II ON CLERICAL EXEMPTION FROM TAXATION, 343

(*CT* 16. 2. 8)

This document, partly re-enacted by Justinian (*CI* 1. 3. 1), besides confirming to clergy immunity from new taxation, adds that they may conduct tax-free businesses and releases them from the requirement to house persons quartered on citizens by the State.

Emperor Constantius Augustus gives greeting to clergymen.
According to the sanction,[1] which you are said to [2] have obtained long ago, no one shall obligate both you and your slaves [3] to new taxes,[4] but you shall enjoy exemption.
Moreover you shall not receive guests.[5]
And if any of you for the sake of a livelihood desire to conduct a business,[6] they shall possess immunity.
Given on 27 August, Placidus and Romulus being consuls.

1. Not extant, unless no. 32 is meant.
2. Justinian omits the Latin for *are said to*.
3. At least in the provinces during the Empire slaves were taxable property. On the various taxes assessed against such chattels consult W. W. Buckland, *The Roman Law of Slavery* (Cambridge, 1908), 38, n. 10.
4. Literally "contributions", especially gifts collected for the emperor on special occasions.
5. These would be soldiers principally, but sometimes imperial officials travelling through the provinces. We have several complaints from provincial municipalities about the burden of this practice (see e.g. *MARE* nos. 139 and 141), an age-old custom, against which Amendment III to the United States Constitution legislated in 1791.
Justinian ends his excerpt here.
6. See nos. 32, n. 6, and 107, n. 8.

84. LETTERS OF CONSTANTIUS II ON RECALL OF ATHANASIUS, 345-6

(*PG* 25. 340-4)

St Athanasius preserves three letters from Constantius II, the eastern emperor, recalling him from his second exile (339-46) after his vindication, which was initiated at the Council of Rome (340) and was completed at the Council of

84. RECALL OF ATHANASIUS, 345-6

Sardica (343).[1] Constans I, the western emperor, was the prime mover in persuading his brother Constantius to reinstate Athanasius, for he threatened to effect personally the restoration, unless Constantius would act. Under the circumstances Constantius had no choice but to consent. After Arian intrigue at Antioch had impeded Constantius' action for at least a year, Athanasius' hesitation to trust the eastern emperor accounted for the repetition of the restoratory epistles.

Socrates (*HE* 2. 23) and Nicephorus (*HE* 9. 21) have all these letters, but Theodoret (*HE* 2. 11) gives only the second. Cassiodorus (*HE* 4. 26-27. 6) translates the three letters into Latin. They are found first in Athanasius (*Apol. adv. Ar.* 51), whose text is translated.

I

Constantius, Victor, Augustus to Athanasius.[2]

Our Clemency's benevolence[3] has not permitted you for a long time[4] to be buffeted and[5] to be tempest-tossed by the sea's wild waves; our untiring Piety has not overlooked you, deprived of your paternal home[6] and stripped of your possessions and wandering in pathless places infested with[7] wild beasts.[8]

And although[9] for a long time I have delayed especially[10] to write the purpose of my thought, expecting you voluntarily to come to us and to ask a cure for your sufferings,[11] yet, since perhaps fear has checked the course of your purpose,[12] to your Constancy,[13] therefore,[10] we have sent a letter, most full of bounty, that fearlessly you may hasten to present your speedy[14] presence to our sight, whereby, having obtained enjoyment of your desire[15] and having experienced our benevolence,[16] you may be restored to your possessions.

For this purpose I have besought for you my lord and brother, Constans Victor Augustus, that he should give to you authority to come,[17] that with us both assenting you may be restored[18] to your native community, taking this[19] pledge of our favour.

II

Second letter.[20]

Although by a previous letter we have shown particularly[10] that you should[21] come unconcernedly to our court,[22] because we particularly desired[23] to send you to your possessions, yet even now also[24] we have given[25] to your Constancy[26] this letter, by which we urge you without any mistrust and fear to mount the public conveyances[27] and to hasten[28] to us, that you can obtain enjoyment of the things which you desire.

III

Third letter.[29]

When we were residing in Edessa, while your priests were present, it pleased us that, when a priest [30] had been sent to you, you should [21] hasten to come [10] to our court,[22] that you, after seeing our sight, might travel immediately to Alexandria.

But since very much time has passed after you, having received letters from us, have not come to meet us, we, therefore, also now have hastened to remind you that even now you may hasten to make your speedy [14] presence before us, and so you can be restored to your native community and can attain [31] your prayer.

For a fuller [32] statement [33] we have dispatched the deacon Achitas,[34] from whom you can know the purpose [35] of our spirit, and that you can attain those things for which you pray.

1. On the Council of Sardica (perhaps more properly "Serdica") in Dacia (now Sofia, capital of Bulgaria) see H. Hess, *The Canons of the Council of Sardica, A.D. 343* (Oxford, 1958), esp. 1–18, 140–4.

2. Two captions are found: Socrates' "Constantius' letter to Athanasius"; Cassiodorus' "Copy of Emperor Constantius' [letter] to Athanasius, bishop".
To the superscription all later authors append "bishop".

3. Cassiodorus reads "Our Gentleness' clemency".

4. Cassiodorus has the superlative degree here. The time was only six years.

5. Socrates and Nicephorus insert "likewise".

6. Cassiodorus reads "land".

7. Cassiodorus substitutes "of" for *infested with*.

8. The last clause contains more rhetoric than truth, for he resided in six cities (Rome, Milan, Trèves, Sofia, Nish, Aquileia) during his relegation.

9. Socrates and Nicephorus omit *And*; Cassiodorus alters *although* to "therefore".

10. Omitted by Cassiodorus.

11. Cassiodorus reads "to demand from us satisfaction of your hardships".

12. Cassiodorus reads "the purpose of your thought". All later writers express *your* as a pronoun, which is understood in the Athanasian text.

13. "Beautitude" in Cassiodorus.

14. Cassiodorus transforms the adjective into the adverb.

15. Nicephorus probably mistakenly substitutes "dignity" (ἐπιτιμία) for *desire* (ἐπιθυμία); the confusion is understandable.

16. Cassiodorus substitutes "clemency" and, while retaining the preceding and succeeding verbs as given here, changes the former into a finite verb and the latter into a participle.

17. Cassiodorus inserts "to us".

18. Cassiodorus reads this verb as a participle and the next verb as finite.

19. Cassiodorus substitutes "a very great".

20. For this Athanasian caption Socrates gives "Another letter to Athanasius" and Cassiodorus reads "Copy of the second letter of Emperor Constantius to Athanasius". Theodoret and Nicephorus have no caption.

All later authors supply a superscription reading "Constantius, Victor, Augustus to Athanasius, bishop" save Theodoret, who omits the last word.

21. Cassiodorus substitutes "ought to".
22. The Greek κομιτᾶτος is transliterated from the Latin *comitatus*, which Cassiodorus has.
23. Socrates alone reads "planned" by expanding βούλεσθαι to βουλεύεσθαι.
24. Omitted by all later authors.
25. Socrates and Nicephorus read "shown" by mistaking δεδώκαμεν for δεδηλώκαμεν.
26. Cassiodorus substitutes "Sanctity".
27. Constantine I inaugurated for Christian prelates free passage by state-controlled transportation (see no. 95, n. 41).
28. Cassiodorus inserts "to come".
29. Socrates' caption is "Another letter to the same" and Cassiodorus' is "Copy of the third letter of Emperor Constantius to Athanasius".

All three later authors agree in the superscription "Constantius, Victor, Augustus to Athanasius, bishop".

30. Plural in Cassiodorus.
31. Cassiodorus reads "enjoy securely".
32. Positive degree in Cassiodorus.
33. Cassiodorus substitutes "knowledge".
34. "Achetas" in Socrates and Nicephorus; Cassiodorus has "Achitus".
35. Cassiodorus substitutes "thought".

85. LETTER OF CONSTANTIUS II ON RECALL OF ATHANASIUS, 346

(*PG* 25. 348)

This letter, preserved by Athanasius (*Apol. adv. Ar.* 54) and Socrates (*HE* 2. 23) and Nicephorus (*HE* 9. 25) and translated into Latin by Cassiodorus (*HE* 4. 30), is an encyclical epistle to announce the restoration of St Athanasius, patriarch of Alexandria, from his second exile and the rescission of penalties against his adherents, who with him have suffered from Arian machinations.

Victor Constantius, Greatest, Augustus to bishops and to priests of the Catholic Church.[1]

The most reverend [2] Athanasius has not been abandoned by God's grace, but,[3] although for a short season [4] he had been subjected to trial according to human beings, yet from the All-Seeing Providence he has obtained [5] the due decision, in that by the will of the Almighty [6] and by our judgement he has regained his native community and at the same time his church, of which by divine favour he happened to be [7] the regent.

The matters consistent with this required it to belong to our Gentleness that all the ordinances before this [8] against the persons who have been in communion with him should be committed to oblivion,[9] that all suspicion against them should cease henceforth,[10] that the immunity, which the clergymen with him formerly have obtained, should be confirmed to these duly.[11]

Moreover we have thought it just to add this to our favour toward him: that all of the sacred catalogue [12] should know that freedom from fear has been granted to all who have been associated with him, whether bishops or clergymen. A sufficient token of each one's correct intention shall be union with this person.[13] For as many as should choose [14] his communion, in that they are at the same time [15] of both more honourable judgement and lot, all these we have ordered,[14] in accordance with the imitation of the previous Providence, to enjoy also now the favour furnished from us by the Almighty's will.[16]

May God guard you.[17]

1. Socrates' caption preceding the superscription is "Constantius' letter about Athanasius", to which Nicephorus adds "to Alexandrians"; Cassiodorus' caption reads "Constantius' letter, written on behalf of Athanasius, to bishops and to the people in Alexandria and in Egypt".

To the superscription Nicephorus adds "of Alexandria", while Cassiodorus substitutes "Pious" for *Augustus*.

2. Socrates and Cassiodorus insert "bishop", to which Nicephorus adds "of you".

3. Cassiodorus substitutes "for".

4. His second exile extended from 339 to 346.

5. Cassiodorus reads "is known to have received".

6. "God" is substituted by Cassiodorus.

7. Cassiodorus condenses the verbal forms to "was".

8. Cassiodorus omits the phrase and for the following phrase and clause has "against him and his communicants".

9. From this word ἀμνηστία comes our "amnesty".

10. Cassiodorus reads "and all suspicion and deceit enacted against them should be null and void henceforth".

11. For the predicate Cassiodorus has "should remain duly firm".

12. That is, the sacerdotal register: simply, the clergy. Cassiodorus reads "order", on which see no. 325, n. 6.

13. In Cassiodorus this sentence is "For union suffices in the case of anyone of correct thought about him".

14. Present indicative in Cassiodorus.

15. Cassiodorus omits the phrase.

16. Cassiodorus reads "to obtain also now by God's will our Grace's bounties".

The thought seems to be that Constantius is copying God's forethought, demonstrated in the past, for mankind by offering imperial favour to Athanasius' associates and by claiming that this proffer is made by God's will.

17. All later authors omit the wish.

86. LETTER OF CONSTANTIUS II ON RECALL OF ATHANASIUS AND ON ENFORCEMENT OF LAWS AGAINST RIOT, 346

(PG 25. 348-9)

Athanasius (*Apol. adv. Ar.* 54-5), Socrates (*HE* 2. 23), Nicephorus (*HE* 9. 25) have in Greek, while Cassiodorus (*HE* 4. 31) has in Latin, this letter proclaiming the return of St Athanasius to his see of Alexandria from his second exile, admonishing the Alexandrians to observe the laws against rioting, exhorting them to honour their restored patriarch.

Second letter.[1]

Victor Constantius, Greatest, Augustus to the laity of the Catholic Church in Alexandria.[2]

Making our aim your good order in all matters [3] and knowing that for a long time [4] you have been deprived of the bishop's superintendence,[5] we have deemed it just [6] to send again to you Athanasius, the bishop, a man well known to all both for his innate righteousness and for the good disposition of his personal character.[7] After [8] you have received this person in your usual way and in due manner and after you have constituted him an assistant in prayers to [9] God, be zealous to maintain the best [10] concord and peace, pursuant to the Church's canon,[11] both becoming to you and most advantageous [12] for us. For it is not reasonable that any dissension or faction should be excited among you in opposition to the felicity [13] of our times. On the one hand, we wish this to be foreign from you entirely; on the other hand, we exhort you to be steadfast habitually in employing him—as has been said previously—as a champion and an ally constantly in prayers to the Divinity,[14] so that, beloved,[15] when this your [16] resolution has affected the prayers of all persons, even those of the heathen, still even now devoted to the error of idols, they may hasten most eagerly [17] to the knowledge of the holy religion.[18]

And again, therefore, we exhort you to abide in the aforesaid matters: gladly [19] receive and with all soul and [20] mind [21] hold welcome the bishop, sent by the Almighty's [22] judgement and by our decision, for this both befits you and is [23] proper to our Gentleness.

Concerning the removal of every pretext for disturbance and faction from the persons wilfully employing evil measures:[24] we have commanded [25] by [26] letters the governors among you to subject to the laws' [27] vengeance all whom they should discover factious.

Therefore, considering both matters (our decision in accord with the Almighty's decision and the consideration for you and for concord and for the punishment against factious persons),[28] maintaining the things which are becoming to and befitting to the right [29] of the holy religion,[30] treating the aforesaid person [31] with all respect and honour, be zealous to offer [32] to God, the Father of all things,[33] prayers along with him[34] for both yourselves and the good ordering of all life.[35]

1. Socrates reads "Another letter sent to the Alexandrians", but Cassiodorus has "Another letter of the same Emperor Constantius on behalf of Athanasius". Nicephorus omits the caption.

2. After *Greatest* Cassiodorus has "Pious to the Alexandrian laity of the Catholic Church".

3. Cassiodorus substitutes "Extending the aim of our fairness in all matters".

4. Only seven years, 339-46.

5. Cassiodorus substitutes "of your guardian's foresight" and then adds "that is, the pontiff Athanasius", substituting "him" for the later *Athanasius, the bishop*.

6. Cassiodorus has "we have decided".

7. Socrates and Nicephorus condense the last two phrases into "for his personal good disposition".

8. Cassiodorus begins this sentence with "accordingly".

9. Cassiodorus inserts "the kindly".

10. Cassiodorus reads "sufficiently".

11. Cassiodorus has "sanction everywhere approved".

12. For the superlative Cassiodorus reads "pleasing" as a positive.

13. Cassiodorus reads "discipline".

14. Cassiodorus reads " . . . we exhort you solemnly to pursue prayers sufficiently to God, with him, obviously, as champion and assistant".

15. Socrates and Nicephorus substitute "dearest Alexandrians"; Cassiodorus has "Alexandrians, dearest to us".

16. Cassiodorus reads "such" for *this your*.

17. Nicephorus omits the adverb and Cassiodorus reads "even the heathen, still serving the error of idols, may hasten under speed".

18. Nicephorus reads "sacrifice".
19. Cassiodorus inserts "and dutifully all".
20. Cassiodorus inserts "all".
21. Nicephorus reads "with all soulful mind".
22. Cassiodorus substitutes "supernal".
23. Cassiodorus inserts "known to be".
24. Cassiodorus has more simply "Moreover, that every occasion for disturbance and faction may be destroyed".
25. Present tense in Cassiodorus.
26. Cassiodorus inserts "our".
27. Cassiodorus substitutes "lawful".
28. Cassiodorus more simply reads the parenthesis as "both our decision with God and the consideration for your declaration and also the punishment proclaimed against factious persons".
29. Cassiodorus reads "maintain becomingly and fittingly the rights".
30. Socrates and Cassiodorus insert "and".
31. Cassiodorus has "treat the aforesaid man, beloved of God".
32. Cassiodorus for *be . . . offer* has "and offer gladly".
33. Cassiodorus substitutes "the Saviour of all men".
34. The pronoun is omitted in Nicephorus, probably through a printer's error.
35. For *and . . . life* Cassiodorus substitutes "the favour of our life".

If the Greek reading is correct, the prayers under Athanasius' guidance are to be made for all living creatures, not only for the Alexandrians and Constantius; but in their constitutions the emperors often direct prayers for themselves.

87. MANDATE OF CONSTANTIUS II ON RESCISSION OF STATUTES AGAINST ATHANASIUS AND ON CLERICAL EXEMPTION FROM PUBLIC DUTIES, 346

(*PG* 25. 349–52)

This instruction in epistolary form is addressed to Nestorius, prefect of Egypt,[1] primarily, and secondarily to three other provincial governors. It authorizes the cassation of all enactments against St Athanasius, patriarch of Alexandria, now restored from his second exile, and the confirmation of all immunities previously enjoyed by his adherents (see no. 85).

Athanasius has this order (*Apol. adv. Ar.* 56) and it is preserved also by Socrates (*HE* 2. 23) and Nicephorus (*HE* 9. 25) and Cassiodorus (*HE* 4. 32), who has a Latin version of it, which possibly may have been the original, for a note in the manuscript of the Socratic version claims that Socrates translates the letter from Latin into Greek.

Victor Constantius Augustus to Nestorius.[2]

In the same form also to the governors of Augustamnica[3] and of the Thebaïd and of Libya.[4]

If any ordinance [5] ever heretofore is found to the harm and the injury of the persons in communion with Athanasius the bishop, these [6] we desire [7] now to be erased. For we wish also them [8] to have again the same exemption from public service which his clergymen had.[9] We will [10] this our ordinance to be observed, so that, after Athanasius the bishop has been restored to his church, the persons having communion with him should have the exemption from public service [11] which they always have had and which [12] the rest of the clergymen [13] have, that they also, having it thus, may rejoice.[14]

1. On this official see no. 489, n. 12.

2. Socrates prefixes the superscription, which Nicephorus omits, with the caption "Letter about the acts against Athanasius to be destroyed", while Cassiodorus' caption reads "Emperor Constantius' letter on behalf of Athanasius the bishop, ordering what things have been enacted against him to be erased".

3. The Athanasian spelling of this Egyptian province seems correct. Socrates has it as Augustomnica. It appears also as Augustamnichus.

4. Cassiodorus ends the note with "it was written", but Nicephorus starts the note with "He wrote the same form" etc. and after *Libya* adds "in which were also these things".

5. Socrates reads "an act"; Cassiodorus begins "Whatever act"; Nicephorus has "any act".

6. The later authors use the singular number.

7. Cassiodorus has "command".

8. Socrates omits the word; Cassiodorus reads "the same ones".

9. Cassiodorus reads "For we wish also the same ones to have again the service of which his clergymen had been deprived". There seems to be a misunderstanding here: either Athanasius misinterprets *ministerium* (service, functions, ministry), if the Cassiodoran version is the original and is correct, or Cassiodorus, in translating the Socratic version which he seems to have used, misinterprets ἀλειτουργησία (exemption from public service).

10. Cassiodorus reads "We accordingly decree".

11. Again Cassiodorus has *ministerium* for ἀλειτουργησία (cf. *supra* n. 9).

12. Cassiodorus inserts "also".

13. Cassiodorus inserts "are known to".

14. Cassiodorus reads the clause as "that they also may obtain joy", while Nicephorus reads "that they also thus may rejoice".

88. MANDATE OF CONSTANTIUS II ON DISPATCH OF DOCUMENTS ABOUT ATHANASIUS, 346

(*PG* 25. 720)

This imperial order, preserved by Athanasius (*Hist. Ar. ad Mon.* 23), apparently implements a previous directive (no. 87) addressed also to Nestorius, prefect of Egypt.[1] The present instruction commands the prefect to remit to the imperial court whatever documents concerning St Athanasius are in the prefect's files.

Victor Constantius Augustus to Nestorius, prefect of Egypt.[1]

It is known that ere this has been issued our ordinance to the effect that certain documents against the reputation of Athanasius, the most reverend bishop, should be found. And these exist in your Devotion's register.

Therefore we wish that your Sobriety, approved after scrutiny by us as fit, should send to our court, pursuant to this our command, all the letters, as many as concern the name of the aforesaid person, present in the register under your charge.

1. On this official see no. 489, n. 12.

89. MANDATE OF CONSTANTIUS II ON CLERICAL EXEMPTION FROM CIVIC DUTIES, 349

(*CT* 16. 2. 9)

While Constantius continues Constantine I's policy of conferring upon clerics immunity from service in municipal senates (no. 60), yet he commands their sons ordinarily to remain in the Church—another instance of the imperial tendency in that century to have sons succeed to their fathers' professions or vocations.

The same Augustus to Severian, proconsul of Achaea.

It is proper for all clergymen to be exempt from curial public services[1] and from all annoyance of civic duties, but for their sons, however, to continue in the Church, if they are not held subject to the municipal senates.

Given on 11 April, Limenius and Catulline being consuls.

1. See nos. 60, n. 2, and 81, n. 3.

90. LETTER OF CONSTANTIUS II ON EPISCOPAL DUTIES, 350

(PG 25. 624, 720-1)

St Athanasius preserves two Greek versions of this letter's Latin original, each of which is translated here (that from *Apol. ad Const.* 23 first, then that from *Hist. Ar. ad Mon.* 24).

The emperor exhorts the patriarch to continue in teaching the orthodox religion and in prayer, because such instruction and supplication suit the imperial will.

I

Constantius, Victor, Augustus to Athanasius.

That I always prayed that all affairs should succeed favourably for my late brother Constans has not passed over your Wisdom.[1] And your Prudence easily will be able to judge with how great gloom I have been encompassed, when I learned that he had been removed as a result of the treachery of very wicked persons.[2]

And since there are certain ones who at the present time try to frighten you in respect to so tearful a tragedy,[3] for this reason I have decided to send this present letter to your Dignity, urging you that, as befits a bishop, you should teach the people to concur with the acknowledged[4] religion and with them you should devote your time to prayers according to custom, for to us this is agreeable. And according to our desire we desire you in every season to be a bishop in your own place.

And by another hand: May the Divinity guard you, dearest father, for many years.

II

Victor Constantius Augustus to Athanasius.

That I always had this prayer, that all affairs should succeed for my late brother Constans according to his intentions, has not escaped your Wisdom. And your Prudence is able again to conjecture with how great grief I have been disposed, when I learned that he had been removed by certain very profane persons.[2]

Therefore, since there are certain ones trying to frighten you at the present time, which is so mournful,[3] for this reason I have decided that this letter should be delivered to your Constancy, urging you that, as befits a bishop, you should teach the people the things bound to be rendered to the divine religion and with them you should devote your time habitually to prayers and you should not believe in vain murmurs,[5] whatever they may be. For this has been fixed in our mind, to wish, pursuant to our purpose, you to be a bishop always in your own place.

May the Divine Providence maintain you, dearest father, for many years.

1. Constantius, who knew how staunch a supporter of Athanasius had been Constans, wants Athanasius to believe that all along the emperor had been agreeable to Constans' efforts in behalf of Athanasius and professes that this knowledge was not unknown to Athanasius.

2. He was murdered in February 350 by cavalrymen of Magnentius, who had raised a revolt in the West.

3. Probably by representing to the patriarch that he no longer can count on protection against Constantius, who had exiled him in 339 and was to banish him again in 356.

4. Literally "obligated" or "owed as a debt".

5. Probably rumours about Constantius' attitude toward Athanasius.

91. MANDATE OF CONSTANTIUS II AND JULIAN II ON CHRISTIAN CONVERTS TO JUDAISM, 352 or 357

(CT 16. 8. 7)

Apostasy from Christianity to Judaism is penalized in the following constitution, which with slight change is repeated in CI 1. 7. 1.

The same Augustus and Julian Caesar [1] to Thalassius, praetorian prefect.[2]

We[3] have ordered by the established venerable law [4] that if anyone, having become a Jew from a Christian, should join their sacrilegious assemblies, when the accusation shall have been proved, his [5] property shall be claimed for the ownership of the fisc.

Given on 3 July at Milan, Constantius Augustus for the eighth time and Julian Caesar [1] for the second time being consuls.[6]

This law does not need interpretation.

1. See no. 28, n. 7.
2. Of the Orient.
3. For *We . . . anyone* Justinian reads "We order that if anyone, as established by the venerable law".
4. No. 23.
5. Justinian reads *eiusdem* (of the said person) for *eius* (his).

6. The editors consider the subscription corrupt, because Thalassius is supposed to have died in 353 and because no other evidence that Constantius was at Milan in 357 exists. They propose as consuls Constantius Augustus for the fifth time and Constantius Caesar and date the document in 352.

This Constantius Caesar, whose full name was Flavius Claudius (Julius) Constantius Gallus and who was known also as Gallus and as Constans, was the first cousin of Constantius II. He and his younger brother, Flavius Claudius Julianus, who later became Julian II the Apostate, were the only men spared from the general slaughter (c. 338), arranged by or agreeable to Constantine I's three sons, of the surviving male scions of Constantius I Chlorus by his second wife, Flavia Maximiana Theodora. Constantius II caused Constantius, whom he had named Caesar in 351, to be beheaded in 354.

92. MANDATE OF CONSTANTIUS II ON RAPE OF RELIGIOUS WOMEN, 354

(CT 9. 25. 1)

The emperor here rules that rapists of holy virgins or of holy widows (who constituted recognized classes in the Church as early as the apostolic era)[1] shall not escape punishment.[2]

Emperor Constantius Augustus to Orfitus.[3]

The same severity should strike each rapist[4] nor any distinction should be between those who are discovered to ruin by rape's wicked violence the honour of sacrosanct virgins and the chastity of widows. And no one should be able to delude himself[5] as a result of the raped woman's later consent.

Given on 22 August, Constantius Augustus for the seventh time and Constans Caesar[6] being consuls.

Interpretation: If anyone perhaps shall have raped a woman—virgin or widow—consecrated to God and if later an agreement about marriage shall have been between them, they should be punished equally.

1. For virgins see 1 Cor. 7. 8, 9, 25, 34; for widows see Acts 6. 1, 9. 39; 1 Cor. 7. 8, 9; 1 Tim. 5. 3-16. While virgins evolved into nuns and widows became deaconesses, the latter, as an order, ceased to exist in the Roman Church in the tenth century and in the Greek Church in the twelfth century. Deaconesses, not necessarily widows in civil status, were revived in the nineteenth century among certain Protestant churches, particularly the Lutheran, the Methodist, the Presbyterian.

Consult M. R. Nugent, *Portrait of the Consecrated Woman in Greek Christian Literature of the First Four Centuries* (Washington, 1941).

2. According to *CT* 9. 24. 2 (of 349) the crime of rape was capital, which might mean either death or loss of citizenship. Earlier (320) by *CT* 9. 24. 1 (to which apparently *CT* 9. 24. 2 refers) a rapist's accomplices and assistants were punished by drinking molten lead (if free) or by being burned (if servile) —but nothing in that law is said about the punishment of the ravisher himself.

3. He was urban prefect of Rome.

4. As the sequel shows, a rapist whether of a virgin or of a widow is meant.

5. That is, he should not deceive himself that he could escape the penalty of his crime.

6. See nos. 28, n. 7, and 91, n. 6 *ad fin.*

93. LETTER OF CONSTANTIUS II ON ECCLESIASTICAL UNITY, 355

(*PL* 13. 564–5)

This imperial letter summons St Eusebius, bishop of Vercelli in Italy, a notable champion of the Nicene Creed, to the Council of Milan (355), which Pope Liberius requested Constantius to convoke in the hope of ending the dissensions between the orthodox and the Arians.

Since he anticipated that Arianism would triumph in the council, Eusebius refused to attend it, but eventually appeared after the pope had pressed him and the emperor had ordered him. By withholding his signature from the document which exiled St Athanasius, Eusebius, in effect, signed his own order for exile, whither he was sent and where he stayed until Julian II's accession (361) allowed exiled bishops to resume their sees.[1]

Constantius, Victor and Triumpher, Ever-August to Eusebius, bishop.

I trust that your Gravity can judge easily, since the importance of the situation puts it in mind, that, though all matters pertain to my care, with reference to the heavenly religion I prefer what is superior and that in my heart it has pre-eminence; yet I trust that by also often-delivered proofs this is known to your Prudence, when you clearly see that I do by night and by day that which I trust can be of advantage to the venerable religion. For what is more gratifying to me or more advantageous than to have devoted the heart to God—to so great an extent that I feel that every effort is subordinate to such exertion?[2] Accordingly I always look upon the venerable churches with the deepest affection of the heart and I desire to recover and to maintain firmly their unity, which is salutary for all.

Wherefore it has pleased me that an assembly of holy bishops is being held in the city of Milan—even those especially who can uncover [3] easily things done elsewhere;[4] certainly in various provinces have been convened councils of bishops, but in the Council of Milan quite clearly has been shown what the most learned bishops with harmonious unanimity have decided one by one.

Then a few,[5] coming from separate provinces, have shown themselves in accord with a common will and in like manner have fortified the veneration due to the law.[6] Therefore what had been proper for religion[7] has been strengthened by the same persons'[5] opinion: that they voted that four men from their group should be sent to your Sanctity,[8] likewise impressing upon your Gravity to follow them in respect to that which is not inconsistent with the Church's advantage. Certainly we, who boast that we are God's servants, urge likewise and admonish that you do not delay to adhere to your brethren's unanimity. We trust, to be sure, when this shall have been accomplished, to be able to congratulate the churches on their firmest unity.

May God always guard you for many years, dearest and most loved brother.

1. See introd. to no. 112.
2. Or perhaps "every instability is obnoxious to such interest".
3. An alternative reading is "extirpate" (*revellere* for *revelare*).
4. That is, the activities of the orthodox bishops in the East, where theological questions and quarrels generally arose, in the opinion of the Arian-sympathizing emperor.
5. The *few* appear to have been eastern bishops, who were mostly Arians, but they controlled the council. Their number was small, since most of the eastern bishops excused themselves because of the length of the journey (Socrates, HE 2. 36; Sozomen, HE 4. 9; Cassiodorus, HE, 5. 15. 2) or old age (Socrates and Cassiodorus, loc. cit.) or illness (Sozomen, loc. cit.).
6. Religion.
7. An alternative reading is "religious persons" (*religiosis* for *religioni*).
8. If four had been selected, only two were sent. (*M* 3. 236).

94. EDICT OF CONSTANTIUS II ON EPISCOPAL OBEDIENCE, 355

(PG 25. 732)

In preparation for the imperially planned third exile of St Athanasius, patriarch of Alexandria, who from the pro-Arian Constantius' viewpoint was obstructing the Church's unity, the emperor summoned about three hundred bishops, mostly western, to meet at Milan in an effort to compel them to sever communion with Athanasius. When the orthodox laity, who were present in the principal church, where the prelates met in conclave, had protested against the intrigues of the Arianizing cabal, the council was transferred to the imperial palace, where the emperor himself assisted at the sessions, though concealed behind a curtain, by sending instructions.

When in reply to the emperor's verbal accusation of Athanasius the pro-Athanasian party objected that Constantius had no personal knowledge to qualify him as an accuser, that the accused was not present, and that the imperial command to condemn Athanasius had no ecclesiastical canon to justify its issuance, Constantius pronounced *in propria persona* the following edict, which Athanasius reports (*Hist. Ar. ad Mon.* 33).

But whatever I will, let this be considered a canon;[1] for the so-called [2] bishops of Syria let me speak thus. Therefore either you obey or you also will be exiled.[3]

1. "It was the voice of Caesarism undisguised" (Kidd, 2. 125) and an egregious example of the egomaniac effrontery characteristic of Constantius. But Constantius was merely anticipating the assertion to absolute authority, which, although it had been adumbrated some 175 years earlier in the statement "A constitution of the emperor is what the emperor by decree or by edict or by epistle has constituted. Nor has it ever been doubted that this obtains the force of statute, since the emperor himself by statute acquires supreme power" (*GI* 1. 5), yet awaited preciser pronouncement almost 180 years later in the principle "What has pleased the emperor has the force of statute" (*II* 1. 2. 6). So Constantius simply stood mid-way between Gaius and Justinian. But this maxim of the civil law met constant and constitutional opposition from St Athanasius and Pope St Julius I in his generation and later in the century from SS. Ambrose of Milan and Basil of Caesarea and Chrysostom of Constantinople.

This pronouncement by Constantius II provides extra evidence—if any more still should be necessary, since Constantine I's arbitrary attitude in readmitting to communion and in rewarding Arians condemned at Nicaea is noticed in introd. to nos. 50 and 58 and in nos. 71 and 72—that the Church not yet had established (despite an ecumenical council [Nicaea in 325], whose rulings on some subjects were reversed by succeeding synods [e.g. Jerusalem in 335]) the theory that ecumenical councils are intrinsically infallible, or its own ecumenical authority, and therefore was submissive to the sole ecumenical power then evident in the Empire: the personal supremacy of the sovereign.

2. The participle reflects imperial irony intended to characterize the Syrian prelates completely under Constantius' control. Its significance emphasizes the eastern situation, whether the emperor actually employed the epithet or Athanasius added it through his animosity toward Constantius.

3. A few bishops refused to subscribe to the condemnation of Athanasius, even after Constantius actually had drawn his sword from its scabbard against them and ordered them to be led to execution—an order which, however, he rescinded.

95. COLLOQUY BETWEEN CONSTANTIUS II AND POPE LIBERIUS ON ADHERENCE TO THE MILANESE COUNCIL, 355
(Theodoret, *HE* 2. 16)

This document, given in Greek by Theodoret and turned into Latin by Cassiodorus (*HE* 5. 17. 2–26), purports to be a verbatim account of a colloquy between Emperor Constantius II and Pope Liberius.[1] It contains several principles of law, the expression of the imperial will and the papal objection to it, and the choice, offered to the pope, between compliance and exile.

The background briefly is this: In his efforts to press western bishops to sever communion with St Athanasius, patriarch of Alexandria, whom he was about to send into a third exile, Constantius convoked a council of some three hundred bishops at Milan in 355 and by threat of resort to force compelled most of the prelates to subscribe to a condemnation of Athanasius (see no. 94). After Constantius (through Eusebius, his castrated chamberlain, as envoy to Liberius, who had not attended the conclave) had failed to secure the pope's adherence to the synodal *acta*, Liberius was haled to the imperial court, where occurred this dialogue both of argument and of admonition on the part of each participant.

The result was that the bishop of Rome was banished to Beroea in Thrace and stayed there until late in 357, when by subscription to heretical doctrine[1] he secured his release and returned to Rome, where an archdeacon had reigned meanwhile as Felix II, who, as the third anti-pope, remained in nominal schism until he died in 365 (one year before the death of Liberius).

Dialogue of Emperor Constantius and Liberius, bishop of Rome.[2]

Emperor Constantius said: "Because you are a Christian and bishop of our city,[3] we have judged it right[4] and, having summoned you, we admonish you to renounce communion with the unspeakable senselessness of the impious Athanasius. For the world has approved that this is good [5] and by the synod's [6] decree has judged him alienated from ecclesiastical communion."

Bishop Liberius said: "Emperor, ecclesiastical verdicts ought to be accomplished with much [7] righteous judgement. Wherefore, if it pleases your Piety, command a court to be convened; and, if Athanasius has appeared deserving of condemnation, then according to the form of ecclesiastical procedure the [8] vote against him will be produced. For it is not possible to condemn a man whom we have not judged."[9]

Emperor Constantius said: "The whole world has condemned his impiety and [10] he, as from the beginning, laughs at the time."[11]

Bishop Liberius said: "Whoever have subscribed had not been eyewitnesses, but because of glory and fear and disgrace from you."[12]

The emperor:[13] "What is meant by glory and fear and disgrace?"

Liberius: "Whoever love not God's glory, preferring [14] rather your gifts, have condemned him whom they, not examining, saw not with their eyes—a thing which is foreign from Christians."[15]

The emperor: "And yet he has been examined in person at the synod held [16] in Tyre and in the synod all the bishops of the [17] world [18] have condemned him."[19]

Liberius: "Never in his presence has the man been sentenced, for whoever then assembling condemned him, after Athanasius had withdrawn from the trial, condemned him."[20]

Eusebius, the eunuch, said: "In the synod at Nicaea [6] he was proved alien from the Catholic faith."[21]

Liberius: "From the persons who sailed with him to Mareotis, whom they had sent against the accused to compose memorials against him, only five have delivered judgement.[22] Of these who accordingly had been sent two have died, Theogonius [23] and Theodore, but the remaining three are living, namely Maris and Valens and Ursacius. From these who had been sent, a vote at Sofia for this action was held.[24] And they presented a petition in the synod, asking pardon, because in Mareotis they had composed memorials against Athanasius in the manner of dishonest accusation and from only one side; and their petition we now have in our hand.[25] With which of these, Emperor, ought we to have agreement and to have communion: these who formerly condemned him and later asked pardon or those who now have condemned these?"[26]

Bishop Epictetus [27] said: "Emperor, today Liberius [28] makes his explanation not on behalf of the faith or in defending [29] ecclesiastical judgements, but that he may boast before the senators in Rome [30] that he has out-reasoned the emperor."

The emperor said to Liberius: "What portion of the [17] world are you, that you alone support an [31] impious fellow and destroy the peace of the earth [32] and of the whole world?"

Liberius: "Not because I am alone is the argument of the faith weakened, for in antiquity only three men are found resisting an [33] ordinance." [34]

Eusebius, the eunuch, said: "You have made our emperor a Nebuchadnezzar." [35]

Liberius: "No, but you unreasonably condemn a person whom we have not tried.[36] But I ask first to produce a universal subscription, confirming the faith expounded at Nicaea, that thus, after our brethren have been recalled from exile and have been restored in their own places, if they who now cause confusions in the churches should be seen assenting to the apostolic faith, then all assembling at Alexandria,[37] where will be [38] the accused and the accusers and their defender,[39] after we have examined these matters, we may carry together these matters to a conclusion." [40]

Bishop Epictetus said: "But the public post system will not support[38] the need for the bishops' transit." [41]

Liberius: "Ecclesiastical affairs have not need of the public post system, for the churches are able to transport their own bishops as far as the sea." [42]

The emperor: "It is not possible for matters which already have taken form to be annulled,[43] for the vote of the majority of bishops ought to prevail. You alone are the defender of the friendship with that impious person."

Liberius said: "Emperor, we never have heard of a judge proclaiming his impiety, when the accused is not present, by employing his own enmity against the person." [44]

The emperor: "He has wronged all in common,[45] but none so much as me. And he, not content with the destruction of my elder brother,[46] ceased not to provoke [47] the blessed [48] Constans [49] into enmity of me, except that we with more clemency submitted to the decisive influence of the provoker and of the provoked.[50] No success, not even that against Magnentius and Silvanus,[51] means so much to me as that abominable person being removed from ecclesiastical affairs." [52]

Liberius: "Do not aid your enmity, Emperor, by means of bishops, for the hands of ecclesiastics ought to have time only [53] for sanctification. Wherefore, if it pleases you, order the bishops to be recalled to their own places. And, if they should appear consonant with him who today defends the orthodox faith expounded at Nicaea,[54] then, having assembled together, they should see to the peace of the world, lest a man who has not transgressed should be proved to be stigmatized." [55]

The emperor: "There is one thing to be required. For I desire to

95. ADHERENCE TO THE MILANESE COUNCIL, 355

send you, after welcoming communion with the churches,[56] back to Rome. Therefore be persuaded [57] to peace and, after subscribing, return to Rome."

Liberius: "Already I have said adieu to the brethren in Rome. For the ecclesiastical ordinances are more important than residence in Rome."[58]

The emperor: "Very well, you have an interval of three days for consideration. If you wish, after subscribing,[59] return to Rome or [60] consider to what place you wish to be transferred."

Liberius: "The interval of three days alters not [61] my reasoning. Wherefore send me where you wish." [62]

1. In the opinion of Denny, 386, "the conversation of Liberius with the Emperor . . . is probably not more authentic than the speeches in Livy [the Roman historian]".

Liberius is remarkable for two reasons: (1) to him is credited in 352—through a legend which apparently ascends no further than the thirteenth century—the construction of the Basilica Liberiana (see no. 138, n. 3), which he reared in response to a dream that the Blessed Virgin Mary had directed him to construct a church to her in Rome on the spot where he should see snow on the next morning (5 August), and which stood on the site of the modern Santa Maria Maggiore, one of the seven patriarchal basilicas of Rome, built by Pope St Sixtus III (432-40), of whose building the nave with its marble columns and mosaics still survives; (2) it is said and is denied that he was the first pope who endorsed heresy—with serious consequences to the dogma of Papal Infallibility voted by the Vatican Council of 1869-70; see Chapman, s.v. "Liberius" in *The Catholic Encyclopedia*, in contradiction; Kidd, 2. 155-7, for a middle position; Denny, op. cit., 384-90, in affirmation. Roman Catholics are not concordant about his canonization and consequently in some lists (published with ecclesiastical approbation) of popes the style of saint is taken from Liberius, who thus appears to be the only one among the first 49 popes (to Pope St Gelasius I [492-6]), left without this title. We may justify, however, its being conferred upon him on the sophistic ground that, even if he endorsed heresy, he never taught heresy either *motu proprio* or *in propria persona*. But the matter is of minor moment, when we consider that Hippolytus, the first anti-pope (217-35), retains his sainthood and receives the honours of the altar annually on 13 August. While of each then it may be said *eius modi homines vix singuli singulis saeculis nascuntur*, yet in each case it also may be said *suo iudicio cuique utendum est*.

2. In Cassiodorus the caption is "Disputation of Emperor Constantius and Liberius, Roman pontiff".

3. Rome is meant, though Constantius was at Milan.

4. Cassiodorus reads from here "that we, summoning you, admonish that you should not delay to renounce the communion of the most wicked Athanasius and of [one] held fast by unspeakable pride".

5. Cassiodorus has "is well done".
6. Cassiodorus uses the adjectival form. The council was in 355.
7. Cassiodorus has "most".
8. Cassiodorus inserts "proper".
9. Cassiodorus alters the clause to "about whom nothing has been examined".
10. Cassiodorus has "wickednesses; but".
11. This probably means that Athanasius derides the danger threatening him.
12. Cassiodorus' Latin is more expansive and clearer: "Whoever have subscribed have themselves not seen what things have been done, but they have acquiesced because of glory and fear and lest they should endure disgraces from you".
13. Here and later Cassiodorus always supplies "said", which Theodoret omits usually from this point onward.
14. Cassiodorus converts the participle into a finite verb.
15. Cassiodorus after *gifts* makes another sentence: "And therefore they, not examining him whom they have not seen, have adjudged what is alien from Christianity".
16. Cassiodorus omits the participle and for *examined* has "condemned".
17. Cassiodorus inserts "whole".
18. Cassiodorus reads "likewise have decreed against him".
19. This was in 335, when about 150 prelates, chiefly eastern, met at Tyre. Athanasius left the council before the sentence (which was not unanimous) of deposition had been passed. It was the prelude to his first exile (336–7).
20. Cassiodorus reads "produced sentence".
21. This statement, of course, is untrue. One manuscript reads a Greek adverb meaning "foolishly", which applies to the eunuch's remark. Other suggestions are that "Arles" (in 353 an Arianizing council condemned Athanasius) or "Tyre" (cf. *supra* n. 19) or "Mareotis" (see next note) should be substituted for *Nicaea,* where in 325 Athanasius stood *contra mundum* for orthodoxy.
22. Six Arian commissioners were sent by the Council of Tyre to investigate alleged misconduct of Athanasius in the Alexandrian suburban lake district of Mareotis. The sixth commissioner, Macedonius, bishop of Mopsuestia in Cilicia Secunda, is not named (below) by Liberius.
23. Otherwise Theognis (so also Cassiodorus).
24. Both Theodoret's Greek and Cassiodorus' Latin ("From these who have been sent a synod at Sofia for this cause was held") are obscure. However, it is known that about 170 bishops at the Council of Sofia (343) acquitted Athanasius.
25. It was sent to Pope St Julius I, Liberius' predecessor, and so would have been in the papal archives. Cassiodorus pluralizes *petition* in this sentence.
26. Cassiodorus reads "hasten to make these accusations".
27. Bishop of Centumcellae (now Civitavecchia in central Italy), this prelate

95. ADHERENCE TO THE MILANESE COUNCIL, 355   243

was a rabid Arian adviser to the emperor and was instrumental in installing the archdeacon Felix in Liberius' see.

28. Cassiodorus does not express the subject.
29. Cassiodorus omits the phrase.
30. Cassiodorus reads "senators established in the Roman city".
31. Cassiodorus has the superlative degree.
32. Perhaps "of the Roman world" as distinct from the next phrase, for which Cassiodorus substitutes "of the Church".
33. Cassiodorus inserts "king's".
34. If Liberius was thinking of Old Testament heroes, he may have had in mind Shadrach, Meshach, and Abednego, who disobeyed Nebuchadnezzar's edict (the following interruption by Eusebius perhaps confirms this) to worship the golden image (Dan. 3. 1-18), or he may have alluded to three separate cases, such as Daniel's disobedience of Darius' statute not to ask a petition (Dan. 6. 4-17), Mordecai's contempt of Ahasuerus' command to reverence Haman (Esther 3. 1-6), Azariah's expostulation with Uzziah's attempt to burn incense (2 Chron. 26. 16-21).

Add also the scene where seven unnamed brothers disobeyed Antiochus IV Epiphanes' personal command to eat pork and were tortured to death (2 Macc. 7). St Augustine asserts that the Church accepted the Maccabean books, where this episode exists, on account of the mighty and marvellous passions of certain martyrs (*De Civ. Dei*, 18. 36 *ad fin.*).

35. This is an interrogative sentence in Cassiodorus.
36. Cassiodorus turns this interrogatively: "But must a person who has not been examined be adjudged so unreasonably?"
37. Probably there because most of the antagonism against Athanasius arose in the East, especially in Egypt.
38. Present tense in Cassiodorus.
39. It is not clear who is meant by *their defender*; perhaps this person is the emperor himself.
40. Cassiodorus reads "after the case has been examined, we can produce sentence".
41. Constantine I first permitted prelates summoned to synods to use the public vehicles, which ordinarily were reserved for officials on business of the State (see nos. 18, 19, 25).

Ammianus Marcellinus (*Res Gestae*, 21. 16. 18) remarks that in Constantius II's reign such troops of bishops rushed hither and thither to synods in carriages provided by the public post system, while the emperor tried to reduce the whole religion to his own will, that he cut the sinews of the courier system. Although Constantius attempted to restrict the abuses of the public post (*CT* 8. 5. 5-10 [all dated between 354 and 358], whereof 8. 5. 8 reappears with alterations in *CI* 12. 50. 3), yet in none of his laws he expressly refused permission to bishops to travel at public expense.

But Julian II, his successor, in his zealous supervision of this system (*CT*

8. 5. 12-15 [all dated in 362], whereof 8. 5. 14 and 15 with abbreviations appear also in *CI* 12. 50. 4 and 8. 10. 7) permitted only his praetorian prefect to write post warrants at will and authorized him to allocate to each provincial governor annually two such warrants for their apparitors' administrative use, while he himself in his own hand wrote about a dozen warrants for each diocesan vicar (annually?)—doubtless for their discretionary dispensation—and gave one warrant (annually?) to each provincial governor for use in reference of matters to the emperor himself (*CT* 8. 5. 12). Such acute restriction would leave little room for accommodation of Christian clerics—a situation which would cause scant concern to this sovereign.

42. After reaching the coast, presumably they would proceed by ship at the State's expense.

43. But at that time, as history and some documents (see e.g. introd. to no. 246) in this sylloge show, neither imperial constitutions were like "the law of the Medes and Persians, which altereth not" (Dan. 6. 8, 12, cf. 15) nor ecclesiastical canons were irreformable of their own nature (*ex sese irreformabiles*), despite what claim about the latter has been advanced both before and in and after 1870, when the dogma of the Papacy's Infallibility (cf. *supra* n. 1 *ad med.* and no. 350, n. 13) was substituted for that of the Infallibility of the Church.

44. Cassiodorus omits the phrase and pluralizes both *impiety* and *enmity*.

45. Cassiodorus misinterprets the Greek adverb (κοινῶς), which he turns into the Latin noun *communio* (as if he were translating κοινωνία), meaning "communion".

46. Athanasius appears not to have had a hand in the death of Constantine II, who had befriended the patriarch in his first exile (336–7) and from it had recalled him (no. 77). Constantine fell in battle against Constans I, his youngest brother, from whom he had tried to wrest part of Africa and the co-administration of Italy.

47. Cassiodorus inserts "often".

48. Cassiodorus has "of blessed memory".

49. Constans was instrumental in compelling Constantius to restore Athanasius from his second exile (339–46), but there is no evidence that Athanasius incited Constans against Constantius.

50. Cassiodorus reads the clause thus: "except that we, restrained by greater gentleness, moderated the provoker's decisive influences".

51. Constantius avenged Constans' murder (350) by the troops of the usurping Magnentius, when Magnentius after defeat in battle committed suicide (353).

Silvanus rebelled in Gaul, assumed the purple, was assassinated in a church at Koln (355).

52. For this sentence Cassiodorus reads "And so to me is no victory, not even against Magnentius or Silvanus, unless I shall have removed that wicked person from ecclesiastical affairs".

53. Omitted by Cassiodorus.

54. For the relative clause Cassiodorus has "whom at present we defend according to the orthodox faith established in the Nicene Synod".
55. Cassiodorus ends "should be reproved unjustly".
56. Cassiodorus substitutes "ecclesiastical" for *with the churches*.
57. Cassiodorus has "And therefore agree".
58. Cassiodorus has "the Roman city".
59. Cassiodorus reads "If you wish to subscribe".
60. Cassiodorus inserts "certainly".
61. Cassiodorus reads "never can alter".
62. Both Theodoret and Cassiodorus record that thereupon the emperor and empress each sent to the pope five hundred denarii to defray the expenses of his journey into exile and that Liberius declined the gift, saying that Constantius needed the money to pay his soldiers.

Thus Liberius, a pope too powerful to be a puppet and too important to be ignored, elected exile, as did his medieval successor St Gregory VII (1073-85), whose last words were "I have loved righteousness and I have hated wickedness [cf. Ps. 45. 7 and Heb. 1. 9], therefore I die in exile"; but Liberius, as has been noted in introd. *ad fin.*, eventually won his release from relegation and returned to Rome.

96. LETTER OF CONSTANTIUS II AND CONSTANS I ON EPISCOPAL DEFENDANTS IN LAWSUITS, 355

(*CT* 16. 2. 12)

This ordinance reserves to a bench of bishops the first instance in cases where bishops are accused. It seems that only after they have found such a defendant guilty can a bishop be tried in a secular court. Probably—as the letter hints—among the rival Christian sects was sufficient partisan activity to bring bishops into court on theological grounds not always well understood by lay judges. If so, it appeared advisable to have brother-bishops first find a true bill of indictment before transmitting the cause to a lay court. Herein we see operative a species of benefit of clergy (*privilegium clericale*), which later created a precedent for ecclesiastical examination of clerics charged with crimes.

The same Augusti to their own Severus,[1] greeting.

By a law of our Gentleness we forbid bishops to be accused in the courts,[2] lest, while impunity is calculated to be a protection because of their kindness, an opportunity for accusing them should be unrestricted for fanatical spirits. Therefore, if there is any complaint which anyone brings, it is fitting for it to be examined first of all before other bishops, that an opportune and appropriate hearing for the investigations of all [3] may be arranged.

Given as a letter on 23 September. Accepted on 7 October, Arbitio and Lollian being consuls.

Interpretation: It specifically is forbidden lest anyone should dare to accuse bishops before secular judges, but he should not delay to bring to a hearing of bishops whatever he thinks can be due to him in view of the character of the case, that whatever he asserts against a bishop may be determined duly in a court of other bishops.

1. His position, whether clerical or lay, is not known.
2. Of a secular character.
3. It is not clear whether persons or charges is meant.

97. MANDATE OF CONSTANTIUS II AND JULIAN II ON CLERICAL EXEMPTION FROM TAXATION, 356

(CT 13. 1. 1)

Constantius frees Christian gravediggers from payment of the lustral tax.[1]

Emperor Constantius Augustus and Julian Caesar [2] to Taurus, praetorian prefect.[3]

It is proper for all tradesman to pay immediately gold and silver, but for only the clerics who are called gravediggers [4] to be exempted and for anyone else not to be immune from the duty of this contribution.

Given on 2 December. Accepted at Rome on 6 February, Constantius Augustus for the ninth time and Julian Caesar [2] for the second time being consuls.

1. Called the *collatio lustralis*, because officially the levy was collected every *lustrum* (on which see no. 41, n. 2), though the government not seldom exacted it in less than quinquennial periods; this tax was called also the *chrysargyron*, because it was paid in gold (χρυσός) and/or silver (ἄργυρος).

While its principal payers were persons engaged in professions and trades, there were liable also mendicants, procurers, prostitutes, servants. Some scholars enlarge its scope to include taxation of livestock and of tools of trade (Vasiliev, 112), while others think of it as a tax on receipts from business (Bury, 1. 441). Although the pagan Zosimus, who was hostile to Constantine I's memory, because Constantine was the first Christian emperor, ascribes the *chrysargyron's* institution to him (*Hist.* 2. 38), yet Evagrius clears Constantine of this charge (*HE* 3. 40). It appears that the *chrysargyron* was not assessed before 356, for this law is the earliest on this tax in *CT*, and that the levy was abolished by Anastasius in 498 (*CI* 11. 1. 1; Evagrius, *HE* 3. 39) amid much popular elation, because its erratic incidence and its iniquitous administration had continued to evoke much indignation from the persons who were subject to it (Libanius, *Cont. Flor.* 46. 22; Zosimus, loc. cit.).

2. See no. 28, n. 7.
3. Of Italy.
4. The same word *copiata* (transliterated from κοπιάτης) reappears in no. 107, where—four years later—it is said to be of recent application to this group among the minor clergy. The more usual word for gravedigger is *fossor* or *fossarius*. The oldest fresco of fossors dates from the late second century and is in the Catacomb of San Callisto outside Rome. The earliest literary reference to gravediggers appears to antedate 235, about when died the anti-pope St Hippolytus, who in his *Apostolica Traditio*, 34, refers to the wages for their work. The oldest inscription relating to fossors is dated between 336 and 352 and comes from the Cemetery of Santi Mareo, Marcelliano, e Damaso in Rome. In time the Christian gravediggers became veritable controllers of cemeteries and catacombs, showed scandalous partiality in allotment of graves, and extorted exorbitant prices to place a corpse next to the remains of martyrs, who seemed to the faithful to have a higher seat than ordinary saints in the heavenly hierarchy. They disappeared from notice early in the fifth century.

98. LETTER OF CONSTANTIUS II ON DISPARAGEMENT OF ATHANASIUS, 357

(PG 25. 632–6)

This imperial letter extols the Alexandrians, excoriates St Athanasius, then in his third exile (356–62), threatens death for the banished prelate's followers, unless they shall renounce their adherence to Athanasius and shall shift their spiritual allegiance to George, the new patriarch of Alexandria.

Athanasius gives this letter (*Apol. ad. Const.* 30).

Victor Constantius, Greatest, Augustus to the Alexandrians.

The city, guarding its native character and remembering its colonizers' excellence, habitually and now shows itself submissive; we, unless we shall have obscured even Alexander [1] in favour toward your city, shall be conscious that we err in respect to necessary matters.[2] For as it is proper for self-control to apply orderliness to itself in all affairs, so it is for royalty to welcome—allow me to say—your excellence above all others: you, the first ones established as teachers of wisdom,[3] the first ones knowing God,[4] who also have chosen the best teachers[5] and willingly have acquiesced in our judgement, justly turning from the cheat and the impostor[6] and dutifully adhering even to holy men who are beyond all marvel. And yet who even of those inhabiting the remotest regions does not know the rivalry in the events that have occurred? And we know not anything of events that have happened worthy to be compared with these.[7]

For most of those in the city were blind; and a man won power, rushing from the lowest depths, beguiling into falsehood, as in darkness, persons desirous of truth, never furnishing fruitful discourse, defiling souls also with useless quibblings. Flatterers shouted and applauded; they were amazed[8] and they still, it is likely, mutter secretly;[9] the majority of the simpler persons lived for their signal.[10] And thus affairs were carried downstream, as in a flood, all matters being neglected utterly. A man of the crowd was in command (how can I say it more truly?), differing from the vulgar in nothing, performing for the city only this service: not to push the people in it down into the depths. But the noble and splendid[11] person waited not for judgement against himself, after he had passed sentence of exile on himself rightly; so indeed it is for the barbarians' interest to remove him, lest he seduce some of them into impiety,[12] just as in a play one entreats with tears and lamentations the first persons met. To this one, then, shall be said a long adieu.[13]

But you I ought to class with few, rather to magnify alone above others you, in whom abounds so much of excellence and of intellect as your actions, praised almost through all the world, proclaim. Well done, self-control! Would that I should hear so many messengers both recounting again and magnifying your deeds, O you who have eclipsed your ancestors in distinction and will be an honourable example to both contemporaries and descendants,[14] you alone who have selected the most perfect of mortals as director for your conduct both in words and in works[15] and have not hesitated for a moment, but courageously have altered your opinions and have allied yourselves with the others,[16] having turned from these ground-lying and earth-bound persons toward heavenly matters, with the most reverend George[17] guiding toward the same matters, a man who above all has investigated thoroughly such matters and because of whom also you will continue with fair hope through the future life and you will live with tranquillity that in the present! Would that all those in the city together cling to this one's discourse, as a sacred anchor, lest we need cuttings or cauteries for those damaged in their souls!

And them we most strongly recommend to renounce their zeal for Athanasius and not even to remember that excessive garrulity, else

98. DISPARAGEMENT OF ATHANASIUS, 357

unawares they will be liable to extreme dangers, whence we know not if anyone of the very capable will rescue the factious persons. For it is also absurd, on the one hand, that the pest Athanasius, having been convicted of the worst crimes, should have been driven to land after land,[18] so that that one ever should pay the deserved penalty in full, even if anyone should take away his life ten times besides, but, on the other hand, that we overlook that one's flatterers and attendants, certain mountebanks and such fellows, whom it is a shame to name, who struggle against us, whom long ago it has been declared plainly to the judges to put to death. And perhaps not yet they shall die, if they, having refrained from their earlier errors, at length should have retracted. And them the most villainous Athanasius used to lead, corrupting the entire commonwealth and putting his impious and cursed hands on the most sacred things.

1. In 332 B.C. Alexander the Great founded Alexandria in Egypt.
2. Literally "things not happening accidentally".
3. This claim seems confirmed specifically in the sphere of science, since Alexandria appears as the hive wherein the sweetest honey of Hellenistic science was stored, for every superior Hellenistic scientist who flourished after the city's foundation either was trained or taught there. However, if the emperor is equating Alexandria with Egypt, the ancients generally accepted that the Egyptians even before Solon's generation (?638–?559 B.C.) were the first professors of philosophy in the western world to impress their influence on the Greeks, who in turn taught the Romans.
4. Again, if Alexandria stands for Egypt, Egyptian theology—even though turned toward pagan subjects originally—preceded chronologically (so the ancients assumed) theological investigation elsewhere. Certainly among Jews and Christians other cities antedated Alexandria in theology.

If by *first* he means "foremost" (πρῶτος can mean either), the emperor has authority on his side, for Alexandria's catechetical school or theological seminary (on which see no. 189, n. 2) was unequalled in Christian antiquity.

5. For pure speculation in all departments Alexandria probably feared no rivalry from teachers elsewhere for centuries. Without doubt the supreme facilities of its libraries and laboratories attracted superior savants and instructors. See no. 189, n. 2.

Consult H. T. Davis, *Alexandria, The Golden City* (2 vols., Evanston, Ill., 1957).

6. Athanasius is meant.
7. If only Christian riots are meant, Constantius is correct. But in racial riots pre-Christian Alexandria and in political tumults pre-Christian Athens and Rome far surpassed Christian Alexandria's theological bloodshed.
8. Doubtless in a good sense, at Athanasius' mental powers.
9. Literally "under tooth", that is, not daring to protest openly at his exile.

10. That is, took their cue from Athanasius' chief adherents.

11. Adjectives applied ironically to Athanasius.

12. Athanasius spent his third exile (356–62) among the monks in the Egyptian desert, who, while uncouth in appearance, were not barbarians. Their tenacious fervour for orthodoxy offered scant hope for anyone's success in introducing impiety among them.

13. This was true, so far as Constantius was concerned, for Athanasius did not return from exile until after the emperor's death, which occurred at least four years after this letter's date.

14. It was an Alexandrian mob (activated by monks), whose maddened shouts swelled into a raucous roar as of beasts hungry for human blood and which brutally butchered the most beautiful and the most famous female philosopher in history, Hypatia, in 415 (a short two generations later: see introd. to no. 347)—which proves how poor a prophet was the prince.

15. This complimentary allusion is to the patriarch after Athanasius, George of Cappadocia, whose library Julian the Apostate admired and acquired (no. 113) after the Alexandrian mob had murdered him, but who had commenced his career in Constantinople as a purveyor of pork to the army and by speculation had amassed a fair fortune.

Gibbon (2. 470–2) graphically sketches George's life and death and suggests that in time the Cappadocian George was transformed into St George, the patron saint of England. This suggestion is not supported by E. O. Gordon, *Saint George: Champion of Christendom and Patron Saint of England* (London, 1907), 8–9. But whether Gibbon's theory is true or false and whether or not Gentile deification of heroes developed into generous Christian canonization of dubious saints, there are known to be other cases where Arians have been admitted to the honours of the Church's altars (see Bury's note in Gibbon, 2. 568).

16. The Arians are meant.

17. Cf. *supra* n. 15.

18. On the untruth of this migration in his third and current exile cf. *supra* n. 12.

99. LETTER OF CONSTANTIUS II ON RETURN OF FRUMENTIUS, 357

(PG 25. 656–7)

South of Egypt, but within the Roman orbit, if not politically as a client kingdom, yet commercially, lay the Ethiopian (Abyssinian) kingdom of the Auxumites, whose capital was Auxume or Auxumis (the modern Aksum, Axum, Axoum). Thither had gone St Frumentius,[1] consecrated earlier by St

99. RETURN OF FRUMENTIUS, 357

Athanasius, patriarch of Alexandria, to be its (missionary) bishop and, as the event proved, the founder of the national Church of Ethiopia,[2] whose Ethiopic liturgy is allied to the Coptic rite. But the departure of Athanasius into his third exile and the installation of George into his see served as the occasion for the Roman emperor to write to the two equal and joint rulers of the Auxumites, by name Aezanes and Sazanes,[3] that Frumentius should be sent to Alexandria to receive fresh instructions from George, for with the patriarch of Alexandria reposed the prerogatives of appointment to and decision about the churches in the southern kingdom.[4]

The result of the letter, preserved by Athanasius (*Apol. ad Const.* 31), is not known.[5]

Victor Constantius, Greatest, Augustus to Aezanes and Sazanes.

Knowledge of the Almighty is very much the greatest concern and care to us, for, I think, it is necessary that the common race of men should claim equal solicitude in such matters,[6] that they, knowing such things about God and not differing concerning the investigation of righteousness and of truth, should pass their life in hope.[7]

Therefore, thinking you worthy of the same provident attention and giving you a share of equal regards with Romans, we order that the same doctrine as theirs should prevail in the churches. Send then Frumentius, the bishop, as speedily as possible into Egypt to the most reverend George, the bishop, and the others in Egypt, who have particular authority to appoint to office and to decide such matters. For of course you know and remember—unless you alone feign not to know what are acknowledged surely by all persons—that this Frumentius has been brought to this rank of his life by Athanasius, a person guilty of myriad evils, who has not been able rightly to free himself from any of the accusations brought against him, but immediately has been banished from his see and, having failed utterly to obtain any settled life anywhere, is a wanderer, migrating from one to another land,[8] as if thus he could escape the fact of being wicked.

If, therefore, Frumentius should obey readily by being about to submit to an investigation about the entire appointment, it will be clear to all that in no point he is in disagreement with the Church's law and the prevailing faith. And having been brought to trial and having given proof of his entire life and having provided an account of it in the presence of those who judge such matters, he also shall be appointed by them, if he shall agree to be really and rightly a bishop. But if he should delay and avoid the trial, it doubtless will be quite clear that, guided by the reasonings of the most wicked Athanasius, he is impious toward God, since he thus has preferred to be wicked as that one has been shown to be. And there is fear lest he, having crossed into Aksum, corrupt those among you by advancing polluted and impious statements, not only by confounding and disturbing the churches and blaspheming against the Almighty, but also by effecting from these means complete overturn and ruin to the persons in nation after nation. But we know that he, having learned also something and having obtained a great and general profit from the association with the most venerable George and the rest, as many as know very well how to teach such things, will return home,[9] after having understood thoroughly to the highest degree all matters of an ecclesiastical nature.

May God guard you, most honoured brethren.

1. Frumentius was canonized by Romans and Greeks and Copts. He was called Abuna (Father) or Abba Salama (Father of Peace), titles still applied to the head of the Ethiopian Church.

2. This establishment is remarkable, for its calendar contains a saint not recognized elsewhere: Pontius Pilate, whom the Ethiopians have canonized because he had washed his hands and had said: "I am innocent of the blood of this just person" (Matt. 27. 24). See also no. 159, n. 27.

3. These may be not so much personal as official appellations.

4. Until 1950 the catholicus or metran (metropolitan of the national Church) was consecrated by the Coptic patriarch of Alexandria. For the close ecclesiastical relation of Ethiopia with Egypt in the period of this sylloge see A. H. M. Jones and E. Monroe, *A History of Ethiopia* (Oxford, 1955), 35-8.

5. If Frumentius returned to Alexandria, he apparently was allowed to return to Aksum, although the imperial attempt to secure Frumentius' acceptance of Arianism seemingly had not success.

6. That is, a proper knowledge about God.

7. Literally "as far as hope". The idea is that people should live in hope until at death their hope of salvation would be realized.

8. But see no. 98, nn. 12 and 18.

9. Literally "to the same [place]".

100. LETTER OF CONSTANTIUS II ON CONDEMNATION OF ATHANASIUS, 357

(PG 25. 744)

St Athanasius preserves (*Hist. Ar. ad Mon.* 43) two sentences of a letter from Constantius II to Hosius, bishop of Córdoba and the most prominent champion of orthodoxy in the West (as was Athanasius in the East), during the early conflict against the Arians. The tone of the letter seems to be that of command, for the Arian-sympathizing sovereign strove to secure the support of Hosius to the second and heterodox creed concocted by the Council of Sirmium in

357. It appears that the centenarian prelate, probably weakened in his mental faculties and subjected undoubtedly to great pressure, signed this declaration, which was published as the Hosian formula, but that, however, he refused to renounce Athanasius. There is a tradition that Hosius on his death-bed recanted his signature.

Do you happen to be still the only one opposed to the heresy?[1] Be persuaded and sign against Athanasius, for he who signs against that person will be absolutely with us on the side of the Arians.

1. Constantius, who composed confessions of faith and yet lived contrary to the faith, apparently was not ashamed to call Arianism *heresy*.

101. MANDATE OF CONSTANTIUS II AND JULIAN II ON PRIVILEGES OF THE ROMAN CHURCH, 357

(*CT* 16. 2. 13)

The occasion for this order to an unidentified magistrate is unknown, but it may have been connected with the recall of Pope Liberius from exile (see no. 95) in 357.

The same Augustus and Julian Caesar[1] to Leontius.
The privileges granted to the Church of the city of Rome and to its clergymen we order to be guarded firmly.
Given on 10 November at Milan, Constantius Augustus for the ninth time and Julian Caesar[1] for the second time being consuls.

1. See no. 28, n. 7.

102. LETTER OF CONSTANTIUS II AND JULIAN II ON CLERICAL EXEMPTION FROM TAXATION AND PUBLIC DUTIES, 357
(CT 16. 2. 14)

This ordinance, sent probably to Pope Felix II,[1] repeats previous legislation freeing clergymen from certain kinds of taxation.
Justinian adopts this constitution in *CI* 1. 3. 2.

The same Augustus and Julian Caesar [2] to Felix,[1] bishop.

From clergymen should be withheld every injustice of an undue indictment and every improbity of an unjust exaction and against them should be no indictment for menial public services.[3]

And though tradesman are summoned to some legally obligatory payment, from all these persons [4] a disturbance of this nature should be stopped; for if they shall have accumulated anything by either thrift or foresight or trading, but yet honestly, it ought to be administered for use of the poor and of the needy, that what has been able to be acquired and collected from the said persons' [4] workshops or shopstalls, this they may consider as collected for the profit of religion.

Moreover for the said persons' men, who have their work in commercial activities, the statutes of the deified [5] prince, that is, of our sire,[6] have provided with manifold care, that the said clergymen may abound with numerous privileges.

Accordingly from the aforesaid the compulsion of extraordinary demands and all molestation should be stopped.

Also to the obligatory payment of extra transport provisions [7] should not be called the said persons' resources and substance.

A prerogative of this kind should aid all clergymen: that clergymen's wives and children also and attendants (that is, males and females alike) and also their children [8] should continue always exempt from taxes and free [9] from public services [3] of this character.

Given on 6 December at Milan. Read into the records on 28 December, Constantius Augustus for the ninth time and Julian Caesar [2] for the second time being consuls.

1. This prelate, originally an archdeacon, became bishop of Rome in 355, after Pope Liberius had been exiled, and by some scholars is counted as an anti-pope. Felix was exiled in 358 and died in 365, ten months before the death of Liberius, who seems to have regained his see in 358.
2. See no. 28, n. 7.
3. See no. 186, n. 5.
4. That is, clergymen.

5. See no. 127, n. 7.
6. For this legislation see no. 32.
7. See no. 32, n. 7.
8. That is, those of the attendants.
9. Justinian omits the Latin for *from taxes and free*.

103. LETTER OF CONSTANTIUS II ON EXPULSION OF ANOMOEANS FROM ANTIOCH, 358

(Sozomen, HE 4. 14)

After the Anomoeans, who formed the ultra-Arian fringe in the East, under the leadership of Eudoxius [1] captured ecclesiastical power in Antioch without the emperor's authorization, this letter (given also by Nicephorus, HE 9. 36) disavows Constantius' acquiescence with their intrusion into that city—where the followers of Christ first were called Christians [2]—and rallies the orthodox to extrude the heterodox, for whom he promises punishment if they persist in their heresy.

Emperor Constantius' letter exiling Eudoxius and the ones with him.[3]

Victor Constantius, Greatest, Augustus to the holy Church in Antioch.

Eudoxius had not come from us; let none think thus. We are far from showing favour to such persons. But if along with other matters they craftily devise also this, doubtless they quite clearly are inventing a subtlety against the Almighty. For from what can they desist willingly who enter into cities for the sake of domination, leap from one to another like some vagrants, pry into every nook through passion for gain? The report is that with them are certain vagabonds and sophists, whom it is not right even to name—a wicked and most impious crew. You yourselves, I suppose, are quite aware of the gang. At all events, from the reports [4] you are acquainted with Aetius [5] and the ones devoted to this heresy. And for them exists only this single task: to corrupt the masses. But these men, subtle and audacious in all affairs, already have made some such insolent boast that we rejoice in their [6] ordination, by which they have ordained themselves. These things indeed are chanted by those wont to babble such things. But it is not at all so, not even near it.

Now recall, I pray, the first discussions, when we were considering about the faith:[7] and in these our Saviour was shown as the Son of God and in essence similar to the Father. But these noble persons, when also they recklessly make off-hand statements about the Almighty, have come to such a pitch of godlessness that they think also certain things other than the true things and they try to teach other persons. And we fully believe that it will recoil on their own heads. In the meantime it suffices that they should be debarred from synods and public assembly. For I should not [6] be brought to say at the present how many things those shall suffer a little later, unless they should abstain from this frenzy.

Indeed they—for what do they not add also to their evil?—enrol into the clergy the basest persons, as if collecting them pursuant to an ordinance, I mean these very chieftains of heresies, thus adulterating the reverend rank, just as if it is permitted them to manage all things.[8] And yet who of mortals [9] can endure these persons, who fill the cities with impiety and cover the countryside [10] with corruptions, prizing only this single task: that they hate unceasingly the good? Let that wicked gang cease to sit in the sacred seats! [11]

Now is the time for the truth's disciples to come into the light and the centre, as many as, having fled from their abodes, were detained by fear not long ago.[12] For the subtleties of these persons have been refuted and there will be no vain way of contrivance which will deliver these persons from impiety. It is the duty of good men to dwell in their fathers' faith and—as had been said—to increase it,[13] but not to be busy in inquiring beyond.[14]

Moreover I should admonish them who late at length have returned from the pit [15] to set themselves in accord with the decision which the bishops, wise in respect to divine matters, dutifully have decided concerning the Almighty.

1. Eudoxius trimmed the sails of his public profession of faith to catch the breeze of favour: first an Arian, then a semi-Arian, next an Anomoean, finally an Arian, Eudoxius exercised episcopal functions for thirty years in three cities, successively becoming bishop of Germanicia in Armenia (340-57), patriarch of Antioch (357-60), bishop of Constantinople (360-70).

2. So Acts 11. 26.

3. Nicephorus omits the caption.

4. Or possibly "from my words"; though the possessive pronoun is absent, Constantius may mean that he has said sufficient for the Antiochenes to guess whom he has in mind.

5. Aetius, more a logician than a theologian, was a deacon who reduced Anomoeanism into a system and was the brainiest member of the movement. Nicephorus transforms the proper noun Ἀήτιον into the common noun αἴτιον (defendant, culprit)!

6. Nicephorus omits the word.

7. Probably a reference to the First General Council at Nicaea in 325.

8. The phrase is literally "to drive [animate beings] and to carry [inanimate things]" (ἄγειν καὶ φέρειν = *agere et ferre*) and is as old as Homer, *Il.* 5. 484, where it first occurs in Greek to describe the plundering of a predatory party. But sometimes it means simply to gather things into one's control.

9. Literally "being born into living beings".

10. Literally "the country beyond one's own borders". But it is not clear that Constantius was so convinced of the Christian message that he was concerned about the effect of the Anomoeans' propaganda of the gospel in foreign parts outside the Empire.

11. That is, the ecclesiastical places of dignity in Antioch.

12. When the State's persecution of Christians had ended in Constantine's reign (no. 7), Christians were free to persecute fellow-Christians. Factional strife in eastern cities rose so high and drew so much blood that not seldom discretion in fleeing was the better part of valour in remaining, after one party had captured the churches in a city.

13. The reference is unknown, unless Constantius or his secretary is thinking of a combination of Luke 17. 5 with Col. 1. 10; in the latter passage the simple form of this verb is used. Loose quotations from memory and conflations of two texts never have been uncommon either in literature or in speech.

14. Nicephorus uses the comparative adverb for Sozomen's positive form.

15. The pit of heresy is meant.

104. LETTER OF CONSTANTIUS II ON CONCILIAR FAITH AND UNITY, 359

(*CSEL* 65. 93–4)

When the Emperor Constantius II, who was hoping to restore peace between the orthodox and the semi-Arians, had failed in his plan to convene a general council of the Church, he convoked two synods: one for the East at Seleucia in Cilicia and one at Rimini (Ariminum) in Italy for the West—a solution justified by the growing separation of the East and the West in language. More than four hundred bishops assembled at Rimini, whither Constantius sent an imperial letter (preserved by St Hilary, bishop of Poitiers, among the fragments of his historical writings) to guide their deliberations.

Here begins a copy of Emperor Constantius' letter to the Italian bishops, who assembled in the Council of Rimini.

Victor Constantius, Greatest, Triumpher, Ever-August to the bishops.

Previous ordinances, venerable men, preserve the notion that the sacredness of the law rests upon ecclesiastical matters. Enough and too much we have observed by letters sent to your Prudences that you ought to give attention to these same matters, since surely both this befits the office of bishops and the salvation of all peoples far and wide is strengthened by this foundation. But the situation has reminded us that the ordinances still exist. For someone will not judge it superfluous for the statutes to be repeated, when frequent reminder will have been wont to augment the addition of diligence. Since present affairs are such, your Sincerities should know that there ought to be discussion on faith and unity and that attention ought to be given that suitable order should be provided for ecclesiastical matters. For the prosperity of all peoples everywhere will spread here and there and steadfast harmony will be preserved, when the utter removal of all questions on matters of this character shall have impressed upon us what principles ought to be followed.[1]

Your affairs ought not thus to extend too long the industry of your attention, for the business does not allow anything to be determined in your council about eastern bishops.[2] Accordingly you ought to discuss only about those matters which your Gravities know pertain to yourselves and, after all matters have been completed, to send with unanimous consent ten men to my court,[3] as we have made known to your Prudences by previous letters. For the aforesaid men can reply to all points which the Easterners shall have proposed or discuss about the faith, that by a suitable conclusion every question may be ended and uncertainty may be laid to rest. Since this is the situation, it is proper for you to decide nothing concerning the Easterners; or, if you shall have wished to determine anything against these same persons in the absence of the aforesaid, that which shall have been adopted unlawfully will vanish with vain effect.[4] For that decision, to which our statutes witness that strength and power already now is denied, will not be able to have any validity. Since this is the situation, by restraint agreeable to the venerable bishops of religion you ought to perfect principles worthy of respect,[5] that that which religion demands may be explained and that that which reason forbids to be heard none may assume.

May the Divinity preserve you, fathers, for many years.

Given on 28 May in the consulate of Eusebius and Hypatius.[6]

1. A free translation of an editorial conjecture for a corrupt clause. The idea seems to be that once the council shall have decided on credal matters, it will then establish what points of order in ecclesiastical affairs must demand adherence.

2. These were meeting a little later, but in the same year, at Seleucia, where the great majority were semi-Arians.

3. They would confer with an equal deputation from Seleucia, whither similar instructions had been sent.

4. This is an egregious and early example of Caesaropapism.
5. A possible variant is "by restraint of religion agreeable to the venerable bishops".
6. These consuls were the emperor's brothers-in-law.

105. RESCRIPT OF CONSTANTIUS II ON DETENTION OF THE RIMINESE COUNCIL, 359

(PG 26. 792)

This imperial letter answers an epistle sent to this Arian-sympathizing emperor by some four hundred bishops assembled at Rimini (Ariminum). The bishops, who were from the West, wrote to acquaint Constantius with their resolve to preserve the orthodox position in the Arian controversy, to ask his permission to disband,[1] to request that nothing either should be added to or should be subtracted from the faith. It appears that Constantius through anger reserved his reply for some time, but at last responded in the following rescript, bidding them to mark time until he could send them his proposal, on which they should act favourably for the Church's welfare.[2]

Athanasius (*De Syn.* 55) and Socrates (*HE* 2. 37) have this letter in Greek and Cassiodorus (*HE* 5. 22. 1-3) has it in Latin.

Translation of the letter.[3]

Constantius, Victor and Triumpher, Augustus to all the bishops assembled at Rimini.

That we have ever especial[4] thought relative to the divine[5] and adorable law[6] not even[7] your Excellencies[8] are ignorant, but now the twenty bishops, sent from your Wisdoms, who have undertaken the embassy from you,[9] we have not been able to see hitherto. For a certain[10] necessary expedition in respect to the barbarians[11] was pressing upon us[12] and, as you know, it is fitting that the soul, being free from all thought, should study the matters relative to[13] the divine law.[6]

Therefore we have ordered the bishops to await in Adrianople our return, that, when all public affairs have been settled well, then at length[14] we may be able to hear and to assay[15] whatever they may have produced.[16] However,[17] let it not appear grievous to your Constancies[18] that you should await their return, that, when they return, carrying to you our answers,[19] you may be able to bring to an end the matters appertaining to the advantage of[20] the Catholic Church.

1. Since Constantius had convoked the synod, it was discourteous, if not hazardous, for the bishops to depart without permission.

2. In their reply to the rescript the bishops reaffirmed their stand and again asked that they might be dismissed. When no answer had come from Constantius, many orthodox bishops left for their sees, an act which the emperor interpreted as contumelious. Constantius thereupon ordered that the rest should remain and should sign an Arian type of creed and that all who would not subscribe to it should be expelled from their sees. The order for detention and the threat of expulsion so aided the Arian minority at the council to extort concessions from the orthodox majority that eventually all the prelates subscribed with modifications to an essentially Arian profession of faith. The news of this imperial triumph evoked from St Jerome his bitter and famous characterization of the council: "The whole world groaned and marvelled to find itself Arian" (*Ingemuit totus orbis et Arianum se esse miratus est.* PL 23. 181).

3. Socrates has no caption; Cassiodorus reads "Emperor Constantius' letter to the Riminese Council".

4. Cassiodorus has "and above all things".

5. Cassiodorus reads "sacred".

6. Christianity.

7. Omitted by Cassiodorus.

8. "Benignities" in Cassiodorus.

9. Cassiodorus for *sent* . . . *you* reads "whom your Wisdoms have sent for the sake of your embassy".

10. Socrates and Cassiodorus omit the word.

11. The emperor was in Illyricum, where he was superintending his generals in their campaign against the invading Quadians and Sarmatians.

12. Socrates and Cassiodorus alter the sentence to read "the expedition . . . was necessary to us".

13. Cassiodorus has "usefulness of" for *matters . . . to.*

14. Cassiodorus omits the phrase.

15. Cassiodorus omits the connective and the infinitive.

16. Socrates has the present indicative; Cassiodorus has the perfect indicative.

17. "Therefore" in Cassiodorus.

18. "Sanctities" in Cassiodorus.

19. Singular in Cassiodorus.

20. For *appertaining* . . . *of* Cassiodorus has "which are known to be advantageous to".

106. MANDATE OF CONSTANTIUS II ON ECCLESIASTICAL EXEMPTION FROM TAXATION, (?)360
(CT 11. 1. 1)

This order, part of which Justinian preserves (*CI* 10. 16. 4), commands that none except for imperial private property and Catholic churches (as corporations and as juristic persons) and the households of two specified persons shall be assisted by special advantages for his personal property in the matter of taxation. Since Justinian omits these exceptions, it seems that such exemption was granted only temporarily and for a reason now unknown.[1]

Both superscription and subscription are faulty, for these assign the document to Constantine I and to 315. But the persons mentioned in it as well as the official addressed are known to have been active in the reign of Constantius II, to whom the editors—whose emendations here are accepted—have ascribed it.

Emperor Constantius Augustus to Proclian.[2]

Except for our private property and the Catholic churches and the households of Eusebius[3] of most distinguished memory, ex-consul and ex-master of the cavalry and of the infantry,[4] and of Arsaces,[5] king of the Armenians,[6] none in accordance with our order should be aided by particular benefits for his domestic property.

For the most distinguished Datian,[7] a patrician,[8] who previously had secured this favour, has requested that this should be withdrawn from him—with as much earnestness as others have been wont to request it.

And therefore all[9] persons shall be obligated to pay what shall be allotted by our hand to tax assignments, but nothing more of exaction. For if any vicar or governor of a province shall have believed that anything now can be remitted to anyone, he shall be compelled to give from his own resources what he shall have remitted to others.

Given on 18 January at Constantinople, Constantius Augustus for the tenth time and Julian Caesar[10] for the third time being consuls.

1. It may have been that, since property might be held which contributed nothing to national expense, if the property were held by an untaxed clergy, and since property could not be held without responsibility, even if held by the clergy, the emperor here reverses previous practice and rules that the clerical holders of property—as distinct from the churches which they served—should participate in bearing the public burden (see no. 107, esp. n. 13). On this subject imperial legislation shifted from time to time, as the financial situation improved or worsened.

2. Proconsul of Africa in 356 or 360 (*CT* 4. 13. 4).

3. Probably second father-in-law to the emperor and consul in 349.

4. *Magister equitum et peditum.* The title seems to be synonymous with "master of each soldiery" (*magister utriusque militiae*, as in nos. 442 and 500), with "master of the soldiery" (*magister militiae*, as in no. 415, at n. 1), and with "master of the soldiers" (*magister militum*, as in nos. 415, at n. 10, and 512), for in the third and the fourth phrases the commander commands both the cavalry and the infantry. When there was a master of the infantry (*magister peditum*), he took precedence of the master of the cavalry (*magister equitum*), his colleague in command.

The office dates from Constantine I's reign and in the military establishment was analogous to the praetorian prefecture in civil administration. Its occupant was the emperor's generalissimo and ordinarily he had the additional title of patrician (*patricius*, on which cf. *infra* n. 8). The number of masters increased with the Empire's division into prefectures (Gaul, Italy, Illyricum, the East or the Orient), so that normally, when the Empire was divided permanently in 395 upon Theodosius I's death, there were two masters in the West and five masters in the East. The eastern enlargement was peculiar in that while in Constantinople resided two masters of the cavalry and of the infantry "in the presence" (*in praesenti*), i.e. in immediate attendance upon the emperor, the other three masters had independent commands in three administrative areas—the East, Illyricum, and Thrace—and were subordinate to the *magistri militum in praesenti*. Thus we find the "master of each soldiery throughout the East" (*magister utriusque militiae per Orientem*, as in no. 244) and its synonym "master of the soldiers throughout the East" (*magister militum per Orientem*, as in no. 646, 11; see no. 512, n. 1).

5. As exemption of Eusebius' relatives may be explained by reason of relationship, so also Arsaces, the third Armenian king of this name, was excused. With Roman approval Arsaces married Olympias, daughter of Constantine I's praetorian prefect Ablabius, who was a close kinsman of Constantine's half-sister Constantia, whom Constantine had given in marriage to his fellow-sovereign Licinius.

From 297, after Galerius had defeated Narses, the Sassanid king of Persia, Rome exercised a protectorate over Armenia and received an annual tribute. But the relief of Arsaces' property from taxation, we conjecture, would affect only what property he held within the Empire and would not be effective in Armenia itself, where native norms—under Roman regulation perhaps—would be used to collect the tribute due to Rome. Whether or not Arsaces taxed his Armenian holdings was no particular concern of Constantius, provided that the tribute was paid.

6. The "ambiguous" Armenians—to employ the noted Tacitean epithet (*Ann.* 2. 56. 1)—both geographically and politically brought more bane than blessing to the Empire, because their land lay as a bone of contention and a buffer state between the eastern frontier proper and Parthia (later Persia) and the people themselves—or rather their rulers—played each power against the

other in the oft-empty but omnipresent hope of being masters of their own house. But in Christian history Armenians hold a conspicuous advantage. Their King Tiridates III antedated Constantine in accepting Christianity *c.* 276 and they were the first people as a nation to be converted to the Christian faith. The chief agent in the conversion of the Armenians to Christianity was St Gregory the Illuminator, patriarch of Armenia, whose indefatigable genius is commemorated in the Christian calendar, especially among the eastern communions.

7. Consul in 358.

8. The word *patricius* refers not to the ancient upper class among the Romans, but is an imperially bestowed title, which, while not associated with any office, was instituted by Constantine the Great and sparingly—at first—was conferred upon men who had distinguished themselves in the State's service.

9. Justinian's excerpt begins here.

10. See no. 28, n. 7.

107. LETTER OF CONSTANTIUS II AND JULIAN II ON CLERICAL EXEMPTION FROM TAXATION AND PUBLIC DUTIES, 360

(*CT* 16. 2. 15)

This statute, of which Justinian preserves a small part (*CI* 1. 3. 3), draws a distinction between property owned corporately by the Church and property privately owned by clergymen and it ordains that for the purposes of imperial taxation and public duties the latter, when it consists of real estate in the provinces, shall not be immune.

The same Augustus and Caesar to Taurus, praetorian prefect.[1]

In the Synod of Rimini, when a discussion about privileges of churches and clergymen was held,[2] a settlement proceeded to this effect: that tax units [3] which appear to belong to the Church, should have relief from public taxation, with a cessation of disturbance about this [4]—a condition which our sanction seems to have rejected previously.[5]

But clergymen or those whom recent usage has begun to call gravediggers [6] ought to be made immune from menial public services [7] and from contribution of taxes thus, if by very small commercial activities they shall seek for themselves meagre food and vesture;[8] but the rest, whose names the tradesmen's register has included at that time when the collection of taxes has been made, should acknowledge the public services and the payments of taxes, since they later have joined themselves to the societies of clergymen.

Concerning those clergymen who possess landed estates, however,[9] your sublime Authority shall order not only that they not at all should exempt other persons' tax units,[3] but also that the said men should be pressed to make payments to the fisc for the landed estates which they themselves possess. For indeed we order all clergymen—in so far as they are possessors of provincial estates— to acknowledge payments of fiscal taxes,[10] particularly since in our Tranquillity's court [11] other bishops,[12] who have come from the districts of Italy and also those who have travelled from Spain and Africa, have approved this rule to be very just and suitable—that, besides these tax units [3] and the public declaration of property which belongs to the Church, all clergymen should be obligated to be held for undertaking all public services and for fulfilling the provisions for transportation.[13]

Given as a letter on 30 June at Milan,[14] Constantius Augustus for the tenth time and Julian Caesar [15] for the third time being consuls.

1. Of Italy.
2. In 359; but the reports of its *acta* are silent on this subject.
3. The tax unit (*iugum*) was used to collect dues from imperial estates originally and then was extended to subjects' real estate. The *iugum*, which was the amount of land (arable or plantable) ploughable by a yoke (*iugum*) of oxen on one day, often is supposed to represent a juger (*iugerum*) of land 28,800 square feet in area (the Anglo-American acre has 43,560 square feet). But the size of a *iugum* varied at various times and in various places, for such factors as situation (plain or hillside), produce (grain or grapes or olives), and fertility normally were considered. Thus a juger of vineyard could be equated with several jugers of cropland or of orchard—according to site and condition of soil. Moreover, since a *iugum* presupposes a *caput* (head), i.e. a person who cultivates it, and therefore presents a close connection between the land and the labourer, some scholars see the land-tax (*iugatio*) and the poll-tax (*capitatio*) as two different methods of denoting one and the same tax for farmers and farms (Pharr), but other investigators insist that these were different taxes (Berger). Although perhaps the problem still awaits more discussion before a solution can be achieved (see no. 67, n. 37), there is no doubt that the government forced the free farmers (and their heirs) to stay on their farms and forbade landlords to alienate their lands without the serfs (on whom see no. 528, n. 2) and the slaves who cultivated the soil. On this there was much legislation, of which may be noticed especially *CT* 13. 10. 3 = *CI* 11. 48. 2 (dated 357), *CI* 11. 48. 7 (dated 367-75), 11. 48. 15 (dated 408-23), 11. 48. 23 (dated 531-4).
4. It seems that the Arian clergy complained that their churches' property was assessed for public services, but that the property of the orthodox Church was exempt.
5. This apparently has not survived.
6. See no. 97, n. 4.

7. See nos. 32, n. 5, and 186, n. 5.

8. According to E. Hatch, *The Organization of the Early Christian Churches* [3] (London, 1888), 151, "there is no early trace of the later idea that buying and selling, handicraft and farming, were in themselves inconsistent with the office of a Christian minister. The bishops and presbyters of those early days kept banks, practised medicine, wrought as silversmiths, tended sheep, or sold their goods in open market." In a long note on this passage Hatch assembles examples of clergymen engaged in various crafts.

St Basil the Great (?330–?379), in whose life this document is dated, testifies to clerical business when he writes (*Ep.* 198 *ad med.*) in 375 that the clergy do not deal in commerce or follow the out-of-doors life, since they generally practise sedentary crafts, deriving therefrom their daily livelihood. Thus this seems to be true of Asia Minor (as it was of Illyricum, Italy, and the Gauls, on which see no. 165), where St Basil was bishop of Cappadocian Caesarea and where the Apostle Paul, "a Jew of Tarsus, a city in Cilicia, a citizen of no mean city" (Acts 21. 39), previously pursued the trade of tentmaking (Acts 18. 3).

9. Justinian starts his excerpt with this paragraph, but omits this word.

10. Here Justinian's statute ends, but by adding "and for fulfilling the provisions for transportation" from what follows.

11. In Constantinople, whither Constantius had gone in 359 because of the Persian invasion into Mesopotamia.

12. These appear to have been Arian or semi-Arian prelates, whose influence on Constantius was marked.

13. There are apparently two views as to what *translatio* means here. Some suppose that it is "transportation of the taxes" to the receiver of tax; others think that it is equivalent to παραγγαρεία (on which see no. 32, n. 7). If the latter view is correct, then some eighty years before the date of no. 434 (q.v.) the emperor revoked the earlier exemption (no. 32) of the clergy from providing extra transport provisions.

14. Editors suppose that the subscription should be emended to read ". . . letter. Accepted on 30 June at Milan . . ." (cf. *supra* n. 11).

15. See no. 28, n. 7.

108. EDICT OF CONSTANTIUS II AND JULIAN II ON CLERICAL EXEMPTION FROM PUBLIC DUTIES, 361

(*CT* 16. 2. 16)

Constantius in this edict to the citizens of Antioch in Syria announces that those who have taken vows of the Christian faith, that is, the clergy, should acquire perpetual security, which commentators consider to be freedom from compulsory public duties.

The same Augusti to the Antiochenes.

In any city, in any town, village, fortress, municipality,[1] whoever by a vow of the Christian law [2] shall have shown to all persons the merit of extraordinary and unparalleled virtue should acquire perpetual security. For we wish always to rejoice and to glory as a result of faith,[3] because we know that our State is preserved more by religion than by duties and by the body's toil or sweat.

Given on 14 February at Antioch, Taurus and Florentius being consuls.

1. The names for these units are in order: *civitas, oppidum, vicus, castellum, municipium*. All save the first appear at least as early as the latest date (42 B.C.) assigned to the promulgation of the *Lex Rubria de Gallia Cisalpina* (in *FIRA* 1. 169-75), which has a longer list of settlements in a similar series. Thus it is not without interest to note the continuity of tradition in Roman law, when over four centuries later an imperial constitution reproduces in part such an arrangement.

2. Religion.

3. Perhaps the person who has taken the vow should be understood as the subject of the infinitives, which lack in Latin a subject.

109. MANDATE OF CONSTANTIUS II ON CLERGYMEN'S PROPERTY, 361

(*CT* 12. 1. 49)

This lengthy constitution permits bishops to retain what property they possess, but commands that the lower clergy shall surrender theirs, unless they are extraordinarily virtuous and the municipal senates and their fellow-citizens permit them to keep their property. Those, however, who enter the clerical life clandestinely or through devious ways, that they may escape their due civic obligations, must cede to their children or relatives or, if none exist, the municipal senates all but a third of their property.

The same Augustus to Taurus, praetorian prefect.[1]

None should compel only a bishop to transfer his property to a municipal senate, just as previously had been established,[2] but he should remain a bishop and should not make a surrender of his substance.

However, if any persons shall have attained to the rank of priests or also of deacons or of subdeacons and of all the others,[3] the municipal senate being present and expressing its consent under the governor's supervision, when it shall have been established that the life of these persons is distinguished and innocent in every goodness, he ought to have the heritage of an approved way of life, that he may retain his own property, particularly if it is requested by the voices of the whole people.

But if perchance any persons by clandestine devices should aspire to or by endeavour of a fraudulent device should have crept into those ranks which we have mentioned, when the curials do not give evidence before the governor and, finally, when the people do not request, they should surrender their patrimony to their children, who have been elected as substitutes in respect to curial services. But if offspring shall have been lacking, he should surrender two-thirds of his own property to his relatives, provided that they could enter the grades of lawful succession, keeping one-third for himself, obviously that by his relatives, if they are curials or even if they never previously have performed service for a municipal senate, after they have received his property, the services may be performed. But if these persons, who shall have thought that by abandoning the municipal senate they can pass into the service of divine worship, shall not have had children or relatives, the municipal senate, thus abandoned, shall be bound to take two-thirds, one-third having been left with him who—we have said previously—has aspired to the society of ecclesiastical persons by insidious devices.

Moreover those properties, which shall have passed to the municipal senate from these persons' ownership, ought to belong to the municipal senate and ought not to be transferred from its ownership. But since it must be feared that, after such properties have been alienated or conveyed previously to other persons' ownership, it can be provided in no respect for the municipal senate's interests, it ought to be observed that, if fraudulent plans shall have been exposed, a person who has been joined by any relation whatever, when he shall have been able to prove this, should receive the said properties for the purpose of performing the services for the municipal senate's public services; or, if search for relatives should be void, to the municipal senate should be transferred all the properties, which shall be proved to have been alienated under any title whatever, after that time from which he, who enters upon the way of divine worship, shall have started to decline the municipal senate's public services.

If provosts of granaries and those persons who are about to undertake a magistracy, also provosts of the peace or receivers of various taxes in kind shall have believed that they can aspire to the Church, after they have entered upon the posts of care or of honour imposed upon them, it shall be proper that the celestial law's [4] bishops themselves first should oppose this, they themselves first striving that the said persons should be recalled to their proper services; or, if they [5] shall have neglected this, they [6] must be withdrawn by the curials with the support of the governor's office staff.

And the rest.

Given on 29 August, Taurus and Florentius being consuls.

1. Of Italy.
2. This law is not extant.
3. That is, those included in the so-called minor orders, such as acolytes, cantors, catechists, exorcists, gravediggers, lectors, notaries, porters, stewards. In the course of time the Roman Church reduced the minor orders to four classes: acolyte, exorcist, lector, porter.
4. Religion's.
5. The bishops.
6. The officials named at the beginning of the paragraph.

110. MANDATE OF CONSTANTIUS II ON ADMISSION OF IMPERIAL OFFICIALS TO THE CLERICATE, 361

(*CT* 8. 4. 7)

The emperor here legislates about certain imperial officials who try to evade public services by becoming clergymen.

Justinian preserves part of this ordinance (*CI* 1. 3. 4).

The same Augustus to Taurus, praetorian prefect.[1]

Beneficiarians [2] or [3] officials of the treasury,[4] if, after they have neglected the maintenance of the public post or the compulsory service of commissary [5] and also after they have falsified a fiscal account,[6] they shall have thought that they can transfer to the churches,[7] should be recalled by the precedent of curials.[8]

But if they are not obligated with respect to their accounts or compulsory services,[9] after an examination by the governors and with their office staffs consenting, if desire for a laudable life [10] shall have demanded this, they should be transferred and they should not fear the surrender of their property.[11]

But if they shall have thought that by clandestine devices they can

110. ADMISSION OF OFFICIALS TO CLERICATE, 361

creep in,[12] according to the analogy of curials [13] they should surrender two-thirds from their own property to their children or, if offspring shall have been lacking, to their relatives, retaining for themselves one-third; but if the bond of relatives shall have been lacking, two-thirds should be left to the office staffs, wherein they serve—a third portion only having been retained for themselves.

Given on 29 August, Taurus and Florentius being consuls.

1. Of Italy.
2. On these see no. 14, n. 6.
3. Justinian starts his version after this word.
4. Literally "treasurer" (*rationalis*), the whole phrase denoting members of the office staff of the imperial receiver of revenues.
5. A *primipilus* was the chief centurion of the *triarii* or soldiers stationed in the third rank of a battle-line. On retirement from service he was called *primipilarius* and was granted certain privileges, but was obligated to the duty of supervision of military supplies. See nos. 383, n. 6, and 502, n. 3.
6. The reason for this ordinance was probably the attraction of the emperor's attention to some scandal in the administration of the imperial posting system, and this explains the combination of these classes of officials: the beneficiarians (in time apparently advanced to some of the commissary's duties) failing in provision of and supervision of the equipment, and the treasury officials falsifying the records either to protect the beneficiarians or for their own peculation. Such conditions not seldom are seen in any bureaucracy.
7. That is, to become clergymen and thus to shirk public service.
8. These (*curiales*) frequently were forbidden to evade their civic duties by entering the priesthood (nos. 32 and 55).

For *churches* . . . *curials* Justinian reads "honour of the clericate, should be recalled to their previous status".

9. Under what circumstances this would be the case is not clear, but there may have been some exemption on the grounds of seniority or of public duties previously discharged.
10. As a priest.
11. On this requirement see no. 109.
12. To the clerical class.
13. Justinian omits the phrase.

III. LETTER OF JULIAN II ON PAGAN RIOTS IN ALEXANDRIA, 362

(Julian, *Ep.* 378C–80D)

Late in December 361 an Alexandrian mob murdered George, Arian patriarch of Alexandria, instead of preferring charges against him in court. It appears that the archbishop's attempts to extirpate paganism in Alexandria resulted in the more intractable pagans of that city taking the law into their own hands in defence of the Egyptian deity, Serapis, whose shrine George with the aid of the secular arm had despoiled. While Julian as an apostate was not displeased with the pagan enthusiasm, as an emperor he deplored the lawlessness displayed by his fellow-idolaters and, loathing the murderers but loving the murder, as a bibliophile he demanded with indecent haste the deceased's library, with which he was familiar (no. 113).

This constitution, quoted *in toto* by Socrates (*HE* 3. 3) and Nicephorus (*HE* 10. 7), who call it a letter, is cited by Sozomen (*HE* 5. 7), who preserves a few phrases from it and also calls it a letter, and is mentioned by Ammianus Marcellinus (*Res Gestae*, 22. 11. 11), who calls it an edict, a characterization perhaps confirmed by the document's last sentence.

Emperor Caesar Julian, Greatest,[1] Augustus to the people of the Alexandrians.[2]

If you revere not Alexander, your founder,[3] and above him the great god, the most sacred Serapis,[4] how has no thought at least for the community, for humanity, for propriety [5] entered into you? And I shall add, also [6] for us, whom all the gods, especially the great Serapis, have deemed it right that we should rule the world and for whom it was fitting that you kept the decision about those who have transgressed. But perchance wrath and passion, which indeed is wont "to do terrible things, after it has expelled the wits",[7] seduced you, who,[8] after you had checked your impulse, afterward applied lawlessness to what at the moment had been planned [9] well and, as a people, were not ashamed to have the same effrontery as that for which you justly hated those persons.

For tell me, by Serapis, for what wrongs were you angry with George? Doubtless you will say that he provoked against you the blessed [10] Constantius,[11] then he brought an army into your sacred city, and the military governor [12] of Egypt seized the god's most holy shrine,[13] after having taken thence statues and votive offerings and the decoration in the temples. And when you reasonably were displeased and attempted to aid the god, rather the god's possessions, he [14] dared to dispatch soldiers against you unjustly and unlawfully and sacrilegiously, probably having feared George more than Constantius, who [15] was observing him [14] narrowly, to see if he should behave too moderately and too civilly toward you, but not rather too tyrannically.

Accordingly, therefore, angered at George, the enemy of the gods, you again dishonoured your sacred city, when it was possible to subject him to the judges' votes. For thus the matter would not have become murder or lawlessness, but a proper lawsuit, keeping you quite guiltless, but punishing the man who committed impiously unatonable deeds and restraining all others whosoever heed not the gods and besides hold in no regard such cities and flourishing communities, but consider that savagery toward these is an addition to their own power.

And so compare this my letter with that [16] which I sent a little earlier [17] and observe well the difference. How many praises of you wrote I then? But now, by the gods, though desiring,[18] I cannot praise you because of your lawlessness. The populace dares to rend a person, just as dogs a wolf,[19] then it is not ashamed to bring to the gods hands flowing with blood.[20] But, you will plead, George deserved to suffer such. And I might say perhaps that he deserved to suffer worse and harsher things than these. And "for your sake",[21] you will say. And I assent; but if you should say "by you", this I no longer admit.[22] For you have laws, which above all must be honoured and be cherished by all individually; but when it happens that some persons transgress an individual law, at all events the Commonwealth ought to have good laws and you ought to obey the laws and not to transgress whatsoever from the beginning have been enacted well.

It has been a piece of good luck for you, Alexandrians, that you have committed such an offence as this under me,[23] who through reverence toward the god and because of my uncle [24] and namesake, who governed both Egypt itself and your city, preserve fraternal favour for you. For the quality of power not to be despised and the quality of government to be rather severe and sound never would overlook a people's shameless act without purging it thoroughly by a rather bitter drug, just as if a dangerous disease. But I apply to you, on account of the reasons which I just now stated, the mildest medicine— exhortation and words—by which I know well that you will be more persuaded, if indeed you are, as I hear, anciently Greeks and [25] now still [19] in you survives in the process of thinking and the ways of living a noteworthy and high-minded mark of that nobility of birth.

Let this be published to my citizens, the Alexandrians.

1. If ἀρχιερεύς has disappeared before μέγιστος (Greatest), as some scholars suppose, for Julian calls himself elsewhere ἀρχιερεὺς μέγιστος (*Frag. Ep.*

298c), then the phrase in Latin would have been *pontifex maximus*, on which see Introd., n. 26.

2. Before the superscription, in which he omits *Augustus*, Nicephorus prefixes the caption "Julian's letter, sent because of George's murder, to the people of the Alexandrians".

3. See no. 98, n. 1.

4. Serapis (*al.* Sarapis) was the new divinity created by the Macedonian masters of Egypt to supplant the Egyptian Osiris in the cult of Isis, when they reformed the native religion to provide a common religious meeting-ground for Greek rulers and Egyptian subjects.

5. Socrates and Nicephorus omit the simple negative οὐκ used here by Julian. This suppression, however, does not alter the sense, since in Greek a compound negative such as οὐδείς (agreeing with λόγος, "thought") and translated *no*, following another negative in the same clause, simply strengthens the negation.

6. An editorial conjecture (ἔτι for ὅτι) is translated, although all authors agree on "that" for *also*.

7. An oft-quoted line from the tragic poet Melanthius of Athens, of whose dramas only this fragment survives. Cf. Plutarch, *Mor.* 453F and 551A.

8. An editorial conjecture (οἱ τά for εἶτα) is translated, though all versions read "then" for *who*. This is necessitated by Julian's use of *applied* in the second person plural, whereas Socrates and Nicephorus have it in the third person singular.

9. Socrates casts this (a participle in Greek) into the genitive singular, while the others prefer the dative plural.

10. All authors have the superlative for the positive, to which Julian's editors generally emend.

The word μακαρίτης means *blessed*, i.e. dead, especially one "lately dead" and hence "late" in our usage. It recurs in nos. 112 at n. 2 and in 115 at n. 3. See also no. 127, n. 7.

11. Constantius II, joint-emperor with his brothers (see no. 77, n. 1) 337–50, sole emperor 350–61. This last survivor of Constantine I's sons was Julian's cousin, for their fathers were half-brothers, as well as his brother-in-law, for Julian married Constantius II's younger sister Helena.

12. Artemius, military governor of Egypt in 361 and executed later by Julian in Antioch, was a zealous suppressor of paganism under Constantius II and a supporter of George. Socrates calls him king (βασιλεύς), but his proper title is general (στρατηγός = *dux*), as given by the others. See no. 8, n. 3.

13. The Serapaeum in Alexandria was to the Isiac cult what the Temple was to the religion of Israel.

14. Artemius.

15. George. Socrates and Nicephorus omit the word.

16. Not extant.

17. Nicephorus has πρόσθεν for πρώην, each synonymous.

18. Socrates and Nicephorus read "obligated", the one as a participle (as Julian's usage) and the other as a finite verb.

19. Socrates and Nicephorus omit the word.

20. Socrates and Nicephorus agree in reading "then is not ashamed to keep pure hands so as to bring these flowing with blood to the gods".

21. Julian's.

22. Socrates and Nicephorus have "And I assent; but 'by you', if this should be said, I no longer admit".

23. Because of his anti-Christian views Julian was averse from assessing a harsh penalty for the murder of a Christian (albeit a heretical) bishop.

24. His maternal uncle, Julian, count of the East (*comes Orientis*). But some manuscripts and Socrates give the Greek word for grandfather; Ammianus (op. cit., 23. 1. 4) calls him *avunculus* (maternal uncle).

25. Nicephorus repeats "if".

112. LETTER OF JULIAN II ON RECALL OF AETIUS, 362

(Julian, *Ep.* 404B–C)

In this letter the emperor recalls from exile (see no. 103) Aetius, who, surnamed the Atheist, was the celebrated founder of the Anomoean form of Arianism. But the law had a wider application—as is seen in its first paragraph and as its promulgator may have foreseen—in that the recall of heretic (no. 112) and schismatic (no. 120) and orthodox clergy (introd. to no. 115) proved their inability to live peaceably together and by their faction fostered the ruler's programme for the revival of paganism, against which a strife-ridden Christendom could offer consequently scant opposition. Indeed, both Ammianus Marcellinus (*Res Gestae*, 22. 5. 3-4) for the pagans and Sozomen (*HE* 5. 5) for the Christians assert that Julian announced this amnesty to set the several Christian sects in conflict against one another; but Socrates (*HE* 3. 1), Theodoret (*HE* 3. 4. 1), Rufinus (*HE* 10. 28), Cassiodorus (*HE* 6. 1. 32, 7. 1), and Nicephorus (*HE* 10. 5) mention no such motive for the restoration of the religious exiles, although Socrates, Sozomen, Cassiodorus, and Nicephorus also record the return of what resources had been confiscated from such Christians.

Julian to Aetius, bishop.[1]

In general, I have remitted their banishment for all who had been banished in any way whatever by the blessed [2] Constantius [3] on account of the Galileans' [4] madness.

Not only I recall you, but also, mindful of old acquaintance and intimacy,[5] I urge you to come to us. You should use a public conveyance [6] and one extra horse [7] as far as my court.

1. It generally is believed that Aetius was not a bishop at the time of his restoration and that, though later consecrated bishop in Constantinople, he never presided over a see.
2. See no. 111, n. 10.
3. Constantius II, Julian's cousin and predecessor as emperor.
4. Julian's constant and contemptuous name for the Christians, derived, doubtless, from Matt. 21. 11 (cf. John 7. 41, 52) and Acts 2. 7 (cf. Mark 14. 70 and Luke 22. 59). According to St Gregory Nazianzen (*Orat.* 4 = *Adv. Iul.* 1. 76 = *PG* 35. 601) the emperor by legislation ordered the use of this name.

The first of nine canons ascribed to an alleged apostolic Council of Antioch in Syria asserts that the apostles convened there and ordained that Galileans should be called Christians first of all, i.e. as their principal name, and a holy people, a royal priesthood, by the grace of holy baptism, as a surname. (The canons are in A. P. de Lagarde, *Reliquiae Iuris Ecclesiastici Antiquissimae* [Leipzig, 1856], no. 3, pp. 18–20.) Doubtless this canon was derived from the statement in Acts 11. 26. Though it seems to protest at Julian's epithet of "Galileans" for Christians, yet it appears that this collection of canons was known to Origen (*Cont. Celsum,* 8. 29 = *PG* 11. 1560) about a century anterior to Julian and it may have been concocted even a century earlier than Origen's reference.

An excellent and reasoned explanation of the Apostate's attitude toward Christianity and of his propagation of paganism may be read in W. Durant's *The Age of Faith* (New York, 1950), 10–19.

5. Gallus, Julian's older brother, had sent Aetius to Julian as his preceptor in Christianity, but Constantius exiled Aetius soon after Gallus' death in 354.
6. See no. 95, n. 41.
7. See no. 426, n. 8.

113. MANDATE OF JULIAN II ON CHRISTIAN WRITINGS, 362

(Julian, *Ep.* 377D–8C)

In a directive addressed to his prefect of Egypt [1] the emperor bids him supervise the collection of the library of George,[2] late Arian patriarch of Alexandria, that these books may become imperial property. Julian writes that among the volumes are many on Christian doctrine and that while he would wish that these should not be preserved, yet he wants them to be saved, lest in their destruction other more useful works may be destroyed.

114. RECALL OF DECURIONS FROM CLERICATE, 362

To Ecdicius, prefect of Egypt.[1]

Some have love for horses, others for birds, others for wild beasts; but in me from a child has penetrated a wondrous longing for acquisition of books. Therefore it is absurd if I should allow persons, for whom gold alone does not suffice to satisfy their great love for wealth, to appropriate these for themselves and also lightly intend to filch these.

Grant to me, therefore, this personal favour: that all of George's[2] books should be found. For in his possession were many on philosophy, many on rhetoric, and many on the impious Galileans'[3] doctrine. And these I should wish to be destroyed altogether, except that with these may be taken more useful books. And all these also shall be sought with minute care.

The leader of this search shall be for you George's[2] notary,[4] who, if he has traced them with fidelity, shall know that he will obtain his freedom as a reward, but that if he should have been knavish in some way or other about the matter, he will come to the test of tortures.

And I know George's books, even if not all, many at least, for he gave to me when I was in Cappadocia[5] some for transcription, and these he again received.

1. On this official see no. 489, n. 12.
2. On him see no. 98, n. 15.
3. See no. 112, n. 4.
4. The secretary (νοτάριος) may be that Porphyry to whom Julian wrote later in the year (*Ep.* 411C-D) and threatened a most severe penalty if he failed to employ all diligence (including torture) in tracing treatises stolen from George's library and in sending books to Antioch, where the emperor was.
5. Julian was interned by his cousin Constantius II at Macellum for six years in the 340s, during which period George, then a layman and a procurer of military provisions (see no. 98, n. 15), was at Caesarea near Julian's residence.

114. MANDATE OF JULIAN II ON RECALL OF DECURIONS FROM THE CLERICATE, 362

(*CT* 12. 1. 50)

Julian's attitude toward Christians may have been partly responsible for this statute (repeated in *CT* 13. 1. 4), whereby Christian municipal senators must not plead Christianity as a pretext for failure to perform the public duties compulsory upon them.[1]

Since the rest of this law is not concerned with Christian decurions, that part is omitted from the translation.[2]

Emperor Julian Augustus to Secundus, praetorian prefect.[3]
After other matters.
Decurions who as Christians avoid public services should be recalled. . . .
Posted on 13 March at Constantinople, Mamertin and Nevitta being consuls.

1. Commentators consider that the decurions had become clergymen and then secured exemption. Christian laymen could not plead successfully immunity from compulsory public services at any time, and especially over a generation after Christianity had been recognized finally as a lawful religion (313) and had been received by thousands of subjects as their religion.

2. The present translator has precedent for this procedure, to which Theodosius II and Justinian I themselves resorted in constructing their Codes: for the one see *Gesta Senatus Romani de <Codice> Theodosiano Publicando*, 4 *ad med.*, and in it also the use of *et cetera*, 4 *in fin* (dated 429), usually prefaced to editions of *CT*; for the other see the constitutions: *Haec*, 2 *in init.* (dated 528), *Summa*, pr. (dated 529), *Cordi*, 1 *in fin.* and 3 *in init.* (dated 534), usually prefixed to editions of *CI*.

3. Of the East.

115. EDICT OF JULIAN II ON EXILE OF ATHANASIUS, 362

(Julian, *Ep.* 398C–9A)

St Athanasius, champion of orthodoxy and patriarch of Alexandria, was exiled no less than five times during his intermittent incumbency of his patriarchate. Early in 362 Athanasius returned from his third exile, after Julian had authorized an amnesty for those ecclesiastics who had been persecuted by his heretical predecessor, Constantius II (no. 112). But the activities of Athanasius in the exercise of his episcopal duties apparently soon angered Julian, who in this constitution ordered his fourth suspension from his see.

Edict to the Alexandrians.
He who had been expelled by very many royal ordinances of also many emperors [1] ought to have awaited at least one royal command and then to have returned accordingly to his own native community, but not, having employed daring and folly, to have mocked the laws as though these were non-existent, since surely even now to the

116. CHRISTIAN TEACHERS, 362

Galileans[2] banished by the blessed[3] Constantius we have granted a return not to their churches, but to their native communities.[4]

But I learned that the very daring Athanasius, excited by his habitual insolence, has seized the throne[5] which is called episcopal by them,[6] and that this is not moderately odious to the God-fearing people[7] of the Alexandrians.

Wherefore we proclaim publicly to him to leave the city[8] immediately on the day on which he shall receive our Clemency's letter; and we proclaim publicly for him, if remaining within the city,[8] much greater and harsher punishments.

1. This is an exaggeration: Athanasius was banished only thrice ere this edict—once by Constantine I (336) and twice by Constantius II (340, 356).
2. See no. 112, n. 4.
3. See no. 111, n. 10.
4. No. 112.
5. The word is θρόνος = *sedes*, on which see no. 311, n. 5.
6. Christians.
7. Pagans.
8. Alexandria.

116. LETTER OF JULIAN II ON CHRISTIAN TEACHERS, 362

(Julian, *Ep.* 422A–4A)

This famous constitution, apparently incomplete in the manuscripts, forbids Christian teachers to teach pagan literature to their pupils and in effect excludes such instructors from schools, since the common curriculum comprised principally the reading of pagan authors.

This letter probably followed the edict (*CT* 13. 3. 5; dated 17 June 362), whereby Julian ordered the municipal authorities to approve teachers only after investigation of their merits and then to refer such appointments to him for review. Not a few notices to this attempt at suppression of Christian teachers appear in the ecclesiastical writers[1] and even a pagan historian deplores the emperor's action[2]—eloquent evidence of the Christians' entrenchment in the educational camp. It is uncertain to what extent the edict was enforced, but any enforcement was not over-long, since Julian survived for only a few months and either Jovian or Valentinian I and Valens soon rescinded the edict (*CT* 13. 3. 6; dated 11 January 364).

We consider that a proper education is not the costly [3] cadence in phrases and language,[4] but a condition of the intellect having sound sense [5] and true opinions about matters good and bad, noble and base. Whoever, therefore, thinks one thing, but teaches pupils another thing, this person seems to have fallen short of educating by as much as he has failed to be an honest man. And if in unimportant matters should be a difference of thought in relation to talk, somehow it, though wrong, is tolerable; but if in most important matters one should think one thing, but should teach the opposite of what one thinks, how is this not the practice of hucksters, not of honest, but of utterly depraved, persons, who commend most extravagantly whatsoever they consider most paltry, beguiling and seducing by praises those persons to whom they wish to transfer their—in my opinion—sorry stuff?

Now all who offer to teach anything at all must needs be good in respect to character and not carry in the soul opinions warring with what they put into practice publicly; and far more than all this I consider that it is necessary that as many as associate with the young for literary matters should be such, since they are interpreters of ancient writings, whether rhetoricians or grammarians and, still more, sophists. For besides other subjects they desire to be teachers not only of diction and style, but also of ethics, and they say that political philosophy is their peculiar province.

Whether or not this is true, let it be by-passed for the present. But in praising them striving for such good professions, I should praise still more, if they would not lie and convict themselves of thinking one thing but teaching pupils another thing. What then? Yet in all learning the gods led [6] Homer and Hesiod and Demosthenes and Herodotus and Thucydides and Isocrates and Lysias.[7] Did not they consider themselves dedicated: some to Hermes,[8] others to the Muses? [9] I consider it paradoxical for those who interpret the works of these writers to dishonour the gods who have been honoured by them. Nor yet, since I consider this paradoxical, I say that they, after they have changed their minds, ought to associate with the young; but I grant the choice: either not to teach what they do not consider excellent or, desiring to teach, to persuade first in actuality the pupils that neither Homer nor Hesiod nor any of these writers, whom they interpret and whom they have charged with impiety and folly and error in respect to the gods . . .[10] Since they, taking their fees, are supported from what those men have written, they admit that they are most sordidly greedy of gain and for the sake of a few drachmae endure everything.

Until now, indeed, there were many reasons for not going to the temples and the terror impending from all quarters gave excuse to hide the truest beliefs about the gods.[11] But because the gods have given liberty to us, it appears to me to be paradoxical for persons to teach those things which they do not think to be true. But if they think them wise, of whom they are interpreters and for whom they sit as prophets, let the memulate first their piety toward the gods; but if they suppose that they have been misled in regard to the most honoured gods, let them go to the Galileans' [12] churches for the purpose of interpreting Matthew and Luke . . . obeying whom,[13] you ordain by your law that men should abstain from sacrifices. I myself wish your ears and tongue to be born again, as you yourselves would say,[14] . . . concerning those matters [15] in which I myself and whoever thinks and does things pleasing to me ever may participate.

For directors [16] and teachers is ordained a general ordinance as follows: Any of the youth desiring to go to school is not debarred. Nor indeed is it reasonable to debar from the best path children still ignorant whither they should turn and to lead by fear them, when unwillingly, to the ancestral customs;[17] and yet it would be proper to heal these even so against their will, as the mentally deranged, except that to all belongs forbearance for such a sickness.[18] For it is necessary, I believe, to teach, but not to punish, the senseless.

1. E.g. Socrates, *HE* 3. 16; Sozomen, *HE* 5. 18; Theodoret, *HE* 3. 8; Jerome, *Chron. anno* 363; Rufinus, *HE* 1. 32; Augustine, *Conf.* 8. 5, and *De Civ. Dei*, 18. 52. See R. R. Bolgar, *The Classical Heritage and Its Beneficiaries* (Cambridge, 1954), 47.

Sozomen (ibid.) says that, after Julian had banned Christian instruction in pagan classics, a clever Apollinaris quickly converted parts of the Bible into an epic, comedies, tragedies, odes of an excellence equal to his classical Greek models, for the purpose of substituting these. When Julian had heard about this *tour de force*, he read enough of the concoctions—which are not extant—to write to the bishops in the style of Caesar's famous dispatch (Plutarch, *Caes.* 50. 2; Suetonius, *Iul.* 37. 2; Appian, *Bell. Civ.* 2. 91) these words: "I read, I recognized, I condemned." To which the bishops replied: "You have read, but you have not recognized; for if you had recognized, you would not have condemned."

2. Ammianus Marcellinus (*Res Gestae*, 22. 10. 7, 25. 4. 20) calls the law inhuman and says that it should be buried in eternal silence.

3. So the manuscriptal reading, but editors have suggested Greek emendations which mean "laboriously won" and "regulated" or "customary".

4. That is, a purely literary discipline inculcating a nice regard for style.

5. Or possibly "but a sound condition of the intellect which directs one's mind and true opinions," etc.

6. That is, perhaps, the gods divinely instructed, or by divine inspiration the authors to be named wrote their works.

7. It is not to be argued from this array of names that these authors only were in the ordinary curriculum, although doubtless they constituted its core

in Julian's time. The omission of philosophers and of dramatic poets, particularly the former, is noteworthy.

The men named are in chronological order save for Lysias, who should have preceded Isocrates, and for Demosthenes, who should have succeeded Isocrates. Of the seven men the first and the second are poets, the fourth and fifth are historians, the rest are orators.

8. Hermes as herald of the gods was also god of eloquence.

9. The normal number of Muses was nine, though originally they were three and though some lists show ten. As goddesses they presided over various types of literary and musical art, the exception being Urania, who was the muse of a science—astronomy.

10. Probably the conclusion was "is such as they state".

11. This must refer to the danger of open profession of paganism by frequenting heathen shrines, after the Christianization of the Empire had started under Constantine. It was not, however, till 380 in the reign of Theodosius I the Great that Christianity became the religion of the State (no. 167).

12. See no. 112, n. 4.

13. The relative pronoun may refer to what Julian might have thought were evangelistic injunctions to refrain from worship in pagan temples, where sacrifices were made. But there is nothing in either Matthew's or Luke's gospel on this subject—nor was there need for such prohibition to Jesus' followers, who, as Jews, were well-conditioned against such worship. However, if Julian believed that Luke had written Acts, in that book there are at least two prohibitions about abstaining from idolatry (15. 20 and 29), each of which exhibits the same verb as here.

14. A probable reference to baptismal regeneration: cf. Titus 3. 5.

15. An early conjecture to complete the sense in the lacuna. Julian must mean pagan authors' belief in pagan gods.

16. The Greek word (καθηγεμών) among its several connotations means earlier a scholarch of a philosophical sect, and later a bishop who presides over a church and an abbot who governs a monastery. Since Julian uses it in another letter (to a pagan priest) to characterize a priest who has initiated him into the Mithraic cult (452A), here he may mean "religious" as opposed to "laic" teachers.

17. Which implied, of course, belief in pagan deities.

18. Christianity, as often in Julian's works.

117. EDICT OF JULIAN II ON CHRISTIAN RIOTS IN BOSTRA, 362

(Julian, *Ep.* 435D–8C)

The emperor chides the citizens of Bostra in Arabia for their participation in riots between Christian factions and commands them all to preserve peace with one another.

Some scholars have erected into a separate edict of toleration the sovereign's express statement in this edict that he allows no Christian to be haled unwillingly to the altars (confirmed as late as the time of Nicephorus, *HE* 10. 5)—a concession earlier enunciated by Constantine I (no. 41). It also is possible that in this constitution Julian's cancellation of judicial functions conferred upon bishops by Constantine I (nos. 17, 28, 65) may have been the subject of a separate statute. In either case no such legislation seems to have survived.

To the Bostrans.

I supposed that the leaders [1] of the Galileans [2] would have for me greater good will than for him [3] who came before me to administer the government. For it happened under him that many of them had been exiled and prosecuted and imprisoned [4] and, moreover, many masses of those called heretics had been slain,[5] as at Samosata and Cyzicus and in Paphlagonia and Bithynia and Galatia,[6] and in many other provinces villages, having been plundered, had been ruined utterly: but under me the opposite occurs. For those who had been banished have been released and those who had undergone confiscation of property [7] have obtained leave from us by law to recover all their property.

But to such a paroxysm of madness and folly they have come that they, provoked because it is permitted to them neither to act like tyrants nor to do what once they committed against one another and then practised against us, who fear the gods, move every stone and dare to throw the populace into confusion and discord, both being impious toward the gods and disobedient to our edicts, although these are so humane. At least we permit none of them unwillingly to be haled to the altars, but expressly we proclaim to them that if anyone voluntarily chooses to participate with us in lustrations and libations, he first should offer purificatory offerings and should supplicate the gods, who avert evil (so far we happen to be ever from desiring or designing that anyone of the impious persons should share in the sacrifices lawful among us), before he has purified his soul by litanies to the gods and his body by customary purifications.

At least it is manifest that the populace, beguiled by those called clergymen, are in a state of discord because this licence has been cancelled. For those who till this time have acted like tyrants are not contented that they do not pay a penalty for what evil acts they have committed, but, yearning for their previous power, because it is not permitted to them to act as judges and to write wills [8] and to appropriate for themselves others' inheritances and to assign everything to themselves,[9] "they pull all of the ropes" of disorder and, according to the saying, "they conduct fire to fire by a conduit" [10] and are emboldened to impose still more on their earlier evils by leading the populace into dissension.

Therefore it seemed best to me to publish to all peoples through this edict and to make known that they neither may participate with clergymen in riots nor may be seduced by them to take up stones for street-fighting nor may disobey magistrates, but that they may assemble so long as they may desire and may pray what prayers they customarily use for themselves, but that if they should seduce them [11] to form a faction on their behalf, they no longer may be in accord with them in this, lest they should suffer punishment.

These circumstances have prompted me to make public proclamation in particular to the city of the Bostrans,[12] because their bishop Titus [13] and their clergymen, from the petitions which they have presented, have preferred charges against their own people, because they themselves exhort the people not to riot when the people are rushing into disorderliness. At least, the very sentence which he dared to inscribe in the petitions I have suppended to this my edict: "Although the Christians are equal to the mass of the pagan Greeks, since they are restrained by our exhortations, no one anywhere raises a riot." For these are the bishop's words about you. Do you see how he says that your good order is not a result of your inclination, because—so he says at any rate—you are restrained against your will by his exhortations? Therefore of your own will drive him as your accuser from the city, but do you, the people, live in accord with one another.[14]

And let none behave in the opposite way or do wrong; neither do you,[15] who have been misled, inflict outrages upon those who worship the gods properly and justly pursuant to what has been transmitted to us from the olden time, nor do you,[16] worshippers of the gods, inflict damage upon or despoil the houses of persons deceived by ignorance rather than by intention. By reason it is necessary to persuade and to teach persons, not by blows or by injuries or by outrage to the body. Again and frequently I exhort those who are eager for the true service of God [17] neither to maltreat the peoples of the Galileans [2] nor to assault them nor to commit outrage upon them. It is necessary to pity rather than to hate those who fare badly in most important matters: for how truly the greatest of goods is reverence for the gods and, on the other hand, the greatest of evils is irreverence toward the gods! It results that those who have turned themselves from the gods to corpses and to relics[18] have paid this penalty[19] . . . as with those seized by some sickness we show sympathy, but with those released and delivered by the gods we rejoice.

Given on 1 August at Antioch.

1. That is, the bishops, here called προστάται.
2. See no. 112, n. 4.
3. Constantius II.
4. Literally "fettered".
5. These activities, conducted by Constantius, were aimed almost entirely at the Athanasian or orthodox Christians, for he favoured the Arians, although his personal belief found a middle ground between the views of theology advanced by each party. Here *heretics* means the non-Arians, for the Arians were just as free in their use of the term as were the Athanasians.
6. The first and the second are cities; the others are provinces; all are in Asia Minor save Samosata, which is in Syria.
7. The Greek literally means "having been confiscated", but we do not confiscate a person. From the rest of the sentence it seems clear that their possessions only, not their persons, were seized by the State (see introd. to no. 112). Conversely, Sozomen (*HE* 5. 5) and Cassiodorus (*HE* 6. 7. 2) and Nicephorus (*HE* 10. 5) say that Julian compelled Christian virgins and widows, who were under the clergy's protection, to refund what money they had received from the fisc.
8. For other persons, who would be induced to leave legacies to the Church. Such bequests Julian banned.
9. The civil functions listed here had been acquired especially by bishops from earlier emperors and were rescinded by Julian.
10. There are here really two proverbial sayings, each probably derived from Julian's reading of Plato's dialogues. But the first, used with various verbs to indicate full speed ahead, is older than its appearance in the philosopher's *Protagoras* (338A), which is declared to be an early dialogue, but which defies exact dating. Euripides already employed it in 431 B.C. (*Med.* 278) and Aristophanes applied it in 424 B.C. (*Eq.* 756). The second, which Julian consciously calls a saying and which is like our "to add fuel to fire", seems to occur only in Plato's *Leges*, 666B.
11. Subject and object appear to be the clergymen and the populace.
12. This indication may point to an addendum to the edict—which so far has been general in its character—for what follows appears to be addressed principally to the Bostrans.
13. This ecclesiastic's polemic against the Manichaeans is our most valuable source for information about this synthetic religion, which was rising rapidly to great influence in the East during this century.
14. Sozomen reports (*HE* 5. 15) that Julian had written to Titus that the

emperor would hold the bishop responsible for any riot in the re-establishment of paganism at Bostra. Whereupon Titus replied in the words quoted by Julian.

The Bostrans apparently failed to adopt Julian's advice to expel Titus, for he survived in his see till *c.* 371, almost a decade after this devilish attempt to dislodge him.

15. Christians.

16. Pagans.

17. The *service of God* is in Greek θεοσέβεια, which can mean also "piety", "religiousness", "godliness".

Without delving too deeply into Julian's religious system—which may be collected from the works cited in no. 119, n. 5 *ad fin.*—it seems that in his public position he professed Graeco-Roman paganism and in his private life he combined Neoplatonism with Mithraism. He believed, briefly, that (1) God is absolutely ONE, the unity lying beyond multiplicity, the ultimate creative source, the primal cause, the supreme principle, the ruler of the intelligible world (κόσμος νοητός); (2) below the intelligible world is the intellectual world (κόσμος νοερός), wherein are the pagan deities, among whom he places the Persian Mithras, god of light, as the immediate source of intelligence and of creation and by emanation the counterpart of the ultimate creative source; (3) below the intellectual world is the perceptible world (κόσμος αἰσθητός), wherein Mithras is manifested by the Greek Helios, god of the sun, the common parent of all and the author of blessings for mankind (see no. 122). To promote his programme for the revival of paganism, Julian, however, was compelled to accept the popular anthropomorphic and polytheistic conceptions about the personality of God, because he realized that the common people could not ascend to the abstractions of the philosopher. Hence he could write, as he wrote in this edict, *God* and *gods*.

18. Evidently a reference to Jesus, who was crucified and buried, and to the Christian martyrs, whose relics were reverenced.

19. That is, the Christians fare badly as a penalty. The lacuna is in the Greek.

118. EDICT OF JULIAN II ON CLERICAL EXEMPTION FROM PUBLIC DUTIES, 362

(Julian, *Ep.* 380D–1A)

One of Julian's reforms was to fill municipal senates in the provinces with wealthy men, who then were expected to use their wealth in the public interest. This edict is aimed against those Byzacenes who entered the priesthood to take advantage of earlier emperors' legislation releasing Christian clergymen from public duties.

To the Byzacenes.¹

We have restored to you all senators and hereditary senators,² except those who have performed public services in the metropolis,³ whether they have given themselves to the Galileans'⁴ superstition or may have busied themselves somehow or other to avoid the municipal senate.

1. The Greek MSS. read "To the Byzantines", but, since Julian never writes of Constantinople as Byzantium, the superscription is suspected. Cumont proposes the reading here translated, for Valentinian I in 364 restored immunities to the curials of Byzacium on entrance into the priesthood (no. 130).

2. Various emendations have been made for πατρόβουλοι (*hereditary senators*), for its significance is not certain, although there were some hereditary seats even in the Roman Senate.

3. It is not clear whether Julian means the provincial capital, Hadrumetum, or the imperial capital, Rome (or Constantinople), but it seems that those Byzacenes who have served as senators in the imperial capital are exempted from additional senatorial obligations in the provincial towns of their residence.

4. See no. 112, n. 4.

119. LETTER OF JULIAN II ON PREFERENCE OF PAGANS OVER CHRISTIANS, 362

(Julian, *Ep.* 376C–D)

In this letter, apparently one of Julian's few autographic epistles, the emperor's anti-Christian bias appears quite clearly when he orders pagans to be preferred to Christians.¹ The letter may have formed part of a rescript in reply to a question on treatment of Christians in the province of the Euphrates, governed by Atarbius, to whom it is addressed.

Julian to Atarbius.
An autograph.²
By the gods I desire the Galileans ³ neither to be killed nor to be beaten unjustly nor to suffer any other harm; however, I declare absolutely that the god-fearing ⁴ must be preferred over them. For because of the Galileans' ³ folly almost everything has been upturned, but because of the gods' favour we all are saved. Wherefore it is necessary to honour the gods and the god-fearing,⁴ both men and cities.⁵

1. With this letter may be linked perhaps the same emperor's edict of 363

(Greek: *Hermes*, 8 [1874] 167-72; Latin: *CT* 9. 17. 5, *CI* 9. 19. 5), which, employing the excuse of pagan purification, condemns diurnal funerals and commands that burials should be conducted nocturnally. But it is not clear whether this change in custom meant that in his animus against Christianity Julian was aiming another arrow from his arsenal, since the command may be interpreted as a serious impediment to the Christian celebration of religious rites in respect to interment, or, since the Christians are not named in it, he was considering them at all, when both pagans and Christians at that time generally buried their dead by day.

A closer parallel is seen in another letter (*Ep.* 450B-1D), where Julian takes to task an unknown official (perhaps a governor of Caria—as Bidez and Cumont think), who has maltreated a pagan priest in his court. Julian suggests that the official's secret intercourse with Christian bishops and priests is the cause of his disrespect displayed toward the pagan priest, and the emperor by virtue of his position as pontifex maximus (so he says) prohibits the peccant official from being involved in any matter concerning priests for a period of three months.

2. The word is ἰδιόγραφον, which, from two late manuscripts Bidez and Cumont, without explanation, insert into their text.

3. See no. 112, n. 4.

4. Pagans.

5. One of the Apostate's crowning acts against Christians (according to Sozomen, *HE* 5. 5; Cassiodorus, *HE* 6. 7. 4; Nicephorus, *HE* 10. 4, 5) was his confiscation of ecclesiastical property, votive offerings, and sacred vessels as well as his condemnation of those who had demolished pagan temples during Constantine I's and Constantius II's reigns either to rebuild these or to pay the cost of their reconstruction. Many bishops, priests, and laics were tortured in the search for sacred money and were imprisoned for inability or refusal to pay for re-erection. Perhaps *CT* 10. 3. 1 (dated 362), though it is silent about religion, refers to this situation, since it starts the title "On Lease of Estates of Emphyteutic Law [see no. 537, n. 6] and of the State and of Temples". And we read (Sozomen, *HE* 5. 10; Theodoret, *HE* 3. 7. 6-10; Cassiodorus, *HE* 6. 12. 7-13; Nicephorus, *HE* 10. 9) that pagans of Arethusa in Syria almost martyred Mark, the city's bishop, when he had refused from piety as well as from poverty to pay even a token payment toward re-erecting a temple which he had razed. Julian is said also to have fined and to have penalized otherwise the Cappadocian Caesareans for their demolition of the last pagan shrine remaining in their city (Sozomen, *HE* 5. 4; Cassiodorus, *HE* 6. 4. 8-12; Nicephorus, *HE* 10. 4). This last severity stands in sharp contrast to the sovereign's attitude toward the Alexandrians after their murder of the Arian archbishop of that city (no. 111), as well as toward the popular persecutions of Christian clerics, e.g. in Syria (Sozomen, *HE* 5. 9, 10; Theodoret, *HE* 3. 7. 1, 3; Cassiodorus, *HE* 6. 11. 1-4; Nicephorus, *HE* 10. 8, 9), and coincides with his apparent condonation of provincial magistrates' activity in maltreating Christians as

destroyers of pagan shrines, e.g. in Phrygia (Socrates, *HE* 3. 15; Sozomen, *HE* 5. 11; Cassiodorus, *HE* 6. 13. 1-3; Nicephorus, *HE* 10. 10, 24).

Among other anti-Christian acts of the Apostate may be counted: (1) removal of Christ's monogram from the *labarum* (Sozomen, *HE* 5. 17; Cassiodorus, *HE* 6. 30. 2; Nicephorus, *HE* 10. 23), whereon Constantine I had placed it (Eusebius, *VC* 1. 31; cf. Lactantius, *De Mort. Pers.* 44. 5); (2) dismissal of Christians from the army (Sozomen, *HE* 5. 17, 6. 6; Theodoret, *HE* 3. 8. 2, 16. 2-3, 17. 8; Cassiodorus, *HE* 6. 17, 30. 15, 32. 1-3; Nicephorus, *HE* 10. 23); (3) exclusion of Christians from governmental office (Socrates, *HE* 3. 13; Sozomen, *HE* 5. 8; Rufinus, *HE* 10. 33; Nicephorus, *HE* 10. 24); (4) taxation of Christians who would not worship pagan deities (Socrates, *HE* 3. 13; Nicephorus, *HE* 10. 24); (5) closing of the cathedral of Antioch in Syria and connivance in the removal of its sacred vessels (Ammianus Marcellinus, *Res Gestae*, 22. 13. 2; Sozomen, *HE* 5. 8; Theodoret, *HE* 3. 12; Cassiodorus, *HE* 6. 10. 1, 32. 1-4; Nicephorus, *HE* 10. 7, 29); (6) his attack against Christianity, not only in his *Epistles* and *Orations* but chiefly in his diatribe *Contra Christianos*, of whose seven books there survive three books in St Cyril's *Contra Iulianum* (*PG* 76. 503-1064), a counterblast composed in 433 (seventy years afterward) by the archbishop of Alexandria; (7) his restriction of use of the public post, thus, in effect, directly affecting Christian prelates (no. 95, n. 41 *ad fin.*); (8) his statute that Christians should be called Galileans (no. 112, n. 4); (9) his legislation presented in nos. 115, 116, 119-23.

For this emperor, whose philosophy both finally exalted and further exhausted paganism, consult A. Gardner, *Julian, Philosopher and Emperor, and the Last Struggle of Paganism against Christianity* (New York, 1895); E. J. Martin, *The Emperor Julian: An Essay on His Relations with the Christian Religion* (London, 1919); W. D. Simpson, *Julian the Apostate* (Aberdeen, 1930); F. A. Ridley, *Julian the Apostate and the Rise of Christianity* (London, 1937); G. Ricciotti, *Julian the Apostate* (Milwaukee, 1960).

120. RESCRIPT OF JULIAN II ON RECALL OF DONATISTS, 362

(*CSEL* 52. 142)

St Augustine (*Cont. Litt. Pet.* 2. 97. 224) preserves in Latin a rescript of Julian,[1] in reply to a petition from three Donatist bishops, permitting Donatist exiles not only to return to Africa but also to regain the churches whence they had been extruded fifteen years earlier.[2] Their restoration was succeeded by scenes of sacrilege and of excess, including murder (see introd. to no. 112).

To Rogatian, Pontius, Cassian,[3] and all the other bishops and also clergymen, petitioning also this,⁴ it is added as an addition that after what had been done wrongly against them without a rescript has been annulled, all matters should be restored to their ancient status.⁵

1. Honorius ordered (405) the posting of this rescript in the most frequented places to publicize the discomfiture of the Donatists (no. 293).
2. An imperial constitution proclaiming unity between Catholics and Donatists and published by the proconsul of Africa in 347 has not survived (*PL* 8. 768).
3. The sees of these prelates are unknown.
4. That is, as the Augustinian context shows, restoration of their churches.
5. It was characteristic of Julian to show more conciliation to schismatic Christians than to Christianity, and certainly more charity than the Catholics and the Donatists showed toward each other. Thus we are informed by Socrates (*HE* 3. 11), Sozomen (*HE* 5. 5), Cassiodorus (*HE* 6. 27), Nicephorus (*HE* 10. 5, 20) that the sovereign commanded that at Cyzicus on the Mysian Peninsula in the Sea of Marmara a Novatians' church, which Arians had demolished utterly, should be rebuilt at the semi-Arian bishop's expense within two months. Julian, so Socrates says (*HE* 2. 38), also ordered another Novatians' church in the Constantinopolitan sector of Ceras (i.e. Chrysoceras, the Golden Horn), which, after condemnation by Arians, had been razed stone by stone and had been reconstructed across the Golden Horn in the suburb of Sycae, to be rebuilt on its former site.

121. MANDATE OF JULIAN II ON EXILE OF ATHANASIUS, 362

(Julian, *Ep.* 376A–C)

Julian in this mandate, couched in epistolary form, rebukes Ecdicius, his prefect of Egypt, for allowing St Athanasius, patriarch of Alexandria, to remain in Egypt contrary to the emperor's order of exile for him (no. 115). The last half of the mandate apparently is written by the emperor's own hand.

To Ecdicius, prefect of Egypt.
Even if you do not write to us as far as regards other matters, yet it was necessary that you write at least about Athanasius, the enemy of the gods, since you have known already for a long time what has been decreed justly by us. I swear by the great Serapis that, unless by 1 December Athanasius, the enemy of the gods, departs from that city,¹ rather from even all Egypt, the company commanded by you I shall fine a hundred pounds of gold.² You know that while I am slow

to pass sentence, yet I am still far slower, when once I have passed sentence, to let someone go unpunished.

And by his own hand: For my orders to be set at nought greatly grieves me. By all the gods I should see, rather should hear, gladly nothing done by you so much as that Athanasius has been deported from Egypt's districts, the blackguard who has dared in my rule to baptize pagan [3] wives of distinguished men. Let him be banished.

1. Alexandria.
2. The Greek word means literally "I shall assess an additional fine", but we know nothing about a previous fine in this case.

It seems strange that the prefect's soldiers should be charged with paying the fine. Such a penalty would not work for the prefect's popularity with his soldiers. Perhaps Julian means that their pay would be withheld to that amount, thereby forcing Ecdicius to compensate his soldiers from his own purse. But a clever prefect could reimburse himself by collection of additional taxes from the provincials.

3. In late Greek, especially among Christian writers and in the laws of Christian emperors, Ἑλληνισμός (Hellenism) and the several proper nouns and adjectives connected with this abstract noun stand for "paganism" and "pagan", on which see nos. 20, n. 5, and 148, n. 4. On "Hellene" consult Toynbee, 8. 570, n. 1 *ad fin*.

In the East " 'Hellenism', applied by Christians to their opponents, reveals the conscious, though unsuccessful, attempt to muster the traditions of classical culture in defence of the old religion. 'Paganism', its Latin counterpart in the West, points to the sporadic survival of primitive village rites." H. St L. B. Moss, *The Birth of the Middle Ages, 395–814* (London, 1935), II, n. 1.

122. RESCRIPT OF JULIAN II ON RECALL OF ATHANASIUS, 362

(Julian, *Ep.* 432C–5D)

After Julian had ordered St Athanasius, patriarch of Alexandria, to go into exile (no. 115) and had rebuked Ecdicius, prefect of Egypt, for not enforcing the emperor's command (no. 121), some Alexandrians petitioned Julian to permit Athanasius to remain in Alexandria. This rescript replies unfavourably to that petition.

To the Alexandrians.

If your founder [1] was one of the others [2] who, having transgressed their own law,[3] have paid what kind of penalties it was proper to pay, because they have chosen to live in transgression of the law and have introduced novel preaching and teaching, not even it would have been reasonable that Athanasius should be demanded by you to be allowed to return. But now, although Alexander was the founder of the city [1] and the lord Serapis is the guardian god for you along with his co-adjutrix, the lady and the queen of all Egypt, Isis,[4] . . . not emulating the sound but the sickly section of the city, dares to apply to itself the name of the whole city.[5]

I am exceedingly ashamed, by the gods, Alexandrian men, if any of the Alexandrians actually admits that he is a Galilean.[6] The fathers of the real Hebrews were anciently slaves to the Egyptians, but now you, Alexandrian men, conquerors of the Egyptians—for your founder [1] conquered Egypt—in opposition to your ancient ordinances submit yourselves in voluntary servitude to those who utterly have neglected the ancestral doctrines. And there enters not into you the memory of that ancient happy state, when for all Egypt there was communion with the gods and we had the advantage of many benefits therefrom. But they who now have brought you to this novel preaching: explain to me for what good to the city they have been responsible. Your founder [1] was a god-fearing man, Alexander the Macedonian, in no wise, by Zeus, being after the fashion of these [7] nor even like all the Hebrews, who are much better than they.[7] And really Ptolemy,[8] the son of Lagus, was superior to these [9] and Alexander, if he had gone into a contest for superiority with the Romans, would have granted a struggle for victory. What then? After the founder the Ptolemies,[10] having reared your city as if a legitimate daughter, increased its power—not at all by the words of Jesus nor by the teaching of the Galileans [6] most hateful to the gods they perfected for it this administration, under which it now is happy. Thirdly, when we Romans became its rulers, after we had dispossessed the Ptolemies,[10] who were ruling badly, Augustus, after he had visited your city and conversed with your citizens, said: "Alexandrian men, I free the city from all culpability [11] because of reverence for the great god Serapis and for the sake of both the people themselves and the city's greatness. A third reason I have for my good will—even my companion Areius." This Areius was not only your citizen, but also a confidant of Caesar Augustus and a man who was a philosopher.[12]

Such, then, are the advantages which accrued particularly to your city from the Olympian gods—to state these in short, but I keep silent about many others because of the length of time to list these. But how do you not know the advantages conferred by the visible gods in common, daily, not to few persons nor to one people nor to one city, but to the whole world at the same time? Are you alone insensible to the sunlight descending from Helios? Do you alone not know that summer and winter are from him? Are you alone ignorant that all living and growing things are from him? Do you not perceive for how many benefits to the city Selene, who from him and by him is the creator of all the universe, is responsible? [13] And dare you worship none of these gods, but do you think that Jesus, whom neither you nor your fathers have seen, ought to be God the Word? [14] But whom from olden time every race of men sees and beholds and worships, and, because it worships, prospers, I mean the great Helios, his intelligible [15] father's image, having life and having soul and having mind and doing good ... if you obey me, when I exhort even in trifling matters, you return yourselves to the truth. For you will not err from the right road, provided that you obey one who traversed that road of yours for twenty years and is traversing this road with the gods now for the twelfth year.[16]

Therefore, if it is pleasing to you to obey, you will gladden me rather greatly; but even if you wish to abide in the superstition and the instruction of wicked men, agree one with another and yearn not for Athanasius. At all events there are many of his disciples able to soothe sufficiently your itching ears, which stand in need of ungodly words. Would that to Athanasius alone had been confined the depravity of his ungodly school! But now you have a not low-born body of them and there is no trouble to find teachers. For anyone whom you would have chosen from the crowd of Christians will be not at all inferior to him desired by you—so far as it relates to the teaching of the Scriptures. But if you have made these requests through being in love with the different subtlety [17] of Athanasius—for I learn that the man is clever—know that because of this very reason he has been expelled from the city, for a meddlesome man is by nature unsuitable to be a leader of the people; but if he is not even a man, but a mean mannikin, like this great one who supposes that he hazards his head, this indeed gives a source for disturbance. Wherefore, lest such a thing should happen concerning you, long ago we have declared publicly to him to leave the city, but now also all Egypt.

Let this be published to our Alexandrian citizens.

1. See no. 98, n. 1.

2. The manuscriptal reading is obscure. Translated emendations for *others* are "wretched persons" and "Galileans" (i.e. Christians).

3. What law would be this is uncertain in view of the obscurity noted in the preceding note. If Christians are meant, it must mean that—as the rest of the sentence shows—the early Christians, who were Jews, had transgressed the Mosaic law by substituting the Christian dispensation for it. Cf. Julian, *Adv. Galil.* 43A, 238B-D, 305D-6A.

4. Isis was more than coadjutrix to Serapis: she was his wife.

5. The sound and the sick sections are respectively in Julian's regard the pagan and the Christian elements. Some such phrase as "the Christian element" may have been the lost subject.

6. See no. 112, n. 4.

7. The Christians are meant.

8. After Alexander's death in 323 B.C. Ptolemy, a prominent marshal of Alexander, received Egypt as his portion of Alexander's empire and as Ptolemy I Soter founded the Ptolemaic dynasty, which ruled Egypt till its incorporation in the Roman Empire by Augustus in 30 B.C.

9. He is said to have conducted a successful siege of Jerusalem in 305 B.C. and to have transported thence many captured Jews into Egypt.

10. Egypt was ruled by fourteen kings of the Ptolemaic name. The fourteenth, Ptolemy XIV Philopator Philometor Caesar (Caesarion), who was Gaius Julius Caesar's bastard by the celebrated Cleopatra VII Thea Philopator, who was the daughter of Ptolemy XI Neos Dionysos (popularly known as Auletes—Flutist—and a bastard both by birth and by instinct), succeeded his mother on her suicide and surrendered soon to Augustus.

11. Apparently for assisting with men and materials Antony and Cleopatra in their civil war with Augustus (32–31 B.C.).

12. He tutored Augustus in philosophy (Suetonius, *Aug.* 89. 1). Julian says that Areius declined the governorship of Egypt (*Ep. ad Them.* 265C).

13. Selene (moon) as the Demiurge of the world appears in Julian's fourth oration, *Ad Reg. Hel.* 150A, 154D. On the Demiurge see no. 648, n. 6.

According to a late account she was the daughter, not the sister, of Helios (sun).

14. Julian assails the doctrine of Jesus being God and God being the Word in his diatribe *Adv. Galil.* 327B–C, 333B–D.

15. That is, perceptible by the mind, not by the senses.

16. This *datum* helps to establish Julian's year of birth: he was born in 331 and his 32nd year ended in 363.

17. That is, his skill in argument is different from that of others in respect to its superiority.

123. EDICT OF JULIAN II ON CHRISTIAN RIOTS IN EDESSA, 362 or 363

(Julian, *Ep.* 424B–5A)

In this edict the emperor not only confiscates the ecclesiastical possessions of the Christian community in Edessa, which was the metropolis of Syriac-speaking Christians, but also bids the Edessans to refrain from their feuds, which stem from rival Christian factions.

123. CHRISTIAN RIOTS IN EDESSA, 362 OR 363

Julian to the Edessans.[1]

I have treated all the Galileans[2] so kindly and so benevolently that none submits to violence anywhere or is dragged into a temple or is threatened into anything else of this kind against his own intention.[3] But the adherents of the Arian congregation, spoiled by wealth,[4] have attacked the followers of Valentine[5] and have committed throughout Edessa such cruel deeds as never in a law-abiding city could happen.

Therefore, since by their most admirable[6] law[7] it has been ordered previously that they sell their property and give to the poor,[8] that more easily they may enter into the kingdom of heaven,[9] we, sharing with these persons in a contest for this end, have commanded that all the monies of the Church of the Edessans should be confiscated for the purpose of being given to the soldiers and that their properties should be added to our private property, in order that they, having become poor, may show self-control and may not be deprived of the heavenly kingdom,[9] for which they still hope.

To those inhabiting Edessa we proclaim publicly that they restrain themselves from all civil strife and contentiousness, lest you, having incited our Benevolence against yourselves, may pay the penalty for the disorder of the community by having been punished by the sword and by exile and by fire.

1. The superscription is defective. The manuscripts show τῷ αὐτῷ ἐκηβολῷ, which editors have emended to τῷ αὐτῷ Ἐκηβολίῳ on the assumption that the person addressed, Hecebolius, was one of Julian's already-known correspondents. But the present Hecebolius hardly can have been the latter; rather this Hecebolius must have been some official in Edessa. But the edict, as is later clear from its last sentence, is addressed to the Edessans and so Bidez and Cumont have supplied Ἐδεσσηνοῖς in the title.

2. See no. 112, n. 4.

3. While Julian sponsored no persecutions in a bloody sense, his conduct toward the Christians was not impartial (see nos. 114, 116, 119). He makes the same claim in his edict to Bostra (no. 117).

4. The Arian heretics in Edessa had been granted by Constantius II, Julian's predecessor, possession of the rich basilica of St Thomas the Apostle.

5. This man was the best known and the most influential of the Gnostic heretics in our second century, although by the time of this edict Valentinianism found few professed followers, for the movement had spent its force.

6. Ironical in this context.

7. Religion, as usual.

8. The manuscripts are defective here and editors generally emend from Matt. 19. 21.

9. Cf. Matt. 19. 23-4.

124. PETITIONS OF ARIANS TO JOVIAN AND JOVIAN'S ANSWERS, 363

(PG 26. 820–4)

Although the plan of this sylloge excludes documents and petitions presented to emperors, the following account, which appears to be authentic, of four brief colloquies between Arian deputations opposed to St Athanasius, patriarch of Alexandria, and Emperor Jovian is so interesting that it has been decided that the observance of the rule really is honoured by the breach in including this report, for it shows how an emperor can make law orally.[1] An added interest appears in that both heretics and orthodox accept with equanimity the fact that an emperor makes appointments to the episcopate, for the former petition for another bishop in place of Athanasius, whom Jovian has given (by restoration) to the latter.

Athanasius preserves this document (in an appendix to his *Ep. ad Iov.*).

Petition made in Antioch to Emperor Jovian by Lucius[2] and Bernician[3] and certain other Arians against Bishop Athanasius of Alexandria.

I

First petition, which they made, when the emperor was departing for camp, at the Roman Gate.

"We beg your Mightiness and your Majesty and your Piety: hear us."

The emperor said: "Who and whence are you?"

The Arians said: "Sire, Christians."

The emperor said: "Whence and from what city?"

The Arians said: "Of Alexandria."

The emperor said: "What wish you?"

The Arians said: "We beg your Mightiness and your Majesty: give to us a bishop."

The emperor said: "I ordered the former one, the very one whom you had formerly, Athanasius, to sit on the throne."[4]

The Arians said: "We beg your Mightiness: both in exile and under accusation he has been for many years."

A soldier, suddenly excited,[5] answered: "I beg your Majesty: do you yourself inquire who and whence they are. For these are the remnants and refuse[6] of Cappadocia, the residue of the unholy George who desolated the city and the world."[7]

Having heard this, the emperor spurred his horse and departed to the camp.

II

Second petition of the Arians.

"We have charges and proofs against Athanasius, who ten and twenty years ago was deprived by the ever-memorable Constantine and Constantius[8] and sustained exile in the time of the most God-beloved [9] and most philosophical and most blessed Julian."

The emperor said: "The charges ten and twenty and thirty years ago have passed now.[10] Do not speak to me about Athanasius, for I know why he was accused and how he was exiled."

III

Third petition of the Arians.

"And now again we have certain other charges against Athanasius."

The emperor said: "Not from the crowd and from the vociferations will appear the rights; but select two from yourselves and two others from those of the majority, for I cannot declare my opinion to each one of you."

They from the majority said: "These are the remnants from the unholy George,[7] who has desolated our province and who did not permit a senator [11] to dwell in the cities."

The Arians said: "We beg you: anyone you may wish except Athanasius."

The emperor said: "I said to you that the affair about Athanasius already had its settlement." [12] And, made angry, he said: "Strike, strike." [13]

The Arians said: "We beg you: if you send Athanasius, our city is ruined and none meets with him."

The emperor said: "And yet, when I had investigated thoroughly, I discovered that he thinks rightly and is orthodox and teaches rightly."

The Arians said: "With his mouth he speaks rightly, but in his soul he thinks deceitfully."

The emperor said: "This is enough, because you have witnessed about him that he speaks rightly and teaches rightly. But if he teaches and speaks rightly with his tongue and in his soul thinks wrongly, it concerns God. For, being human, we hear the word; but the things in the heart God knows."

The Arians said: "Command us to meet in a religious service." [14]

The emperor said: "Why, who prevents you?"

The Arians said: "We beg you: he describes us as heretics and dogmatists."

The emperor said: "It is his duty and that of the persons teaching rightly."

The Arians said: "We beg your Mightiness: we cannot endure this person and he has taken away the churches' lands." [15]

The emperor said: "You have come hither then on account of property and not on account of faith?" And he said again: "Depart and live peaceably." Besides he added and said to the Arians: "Depart into the church. Tomorrow you have a religious service.[16] And after the dismissal there are bishops here and Nemesinus [17] is here; each of you shall sign as he believes. And Athanasius is here; let him who does not know the word of faith learn from Athanasius. You have tomorrow and the next day, for I am departing for camp."

And a certain lawyer of the Cynics petitioned the emperor: "I beg your Majesty: at the instance of Athanasius the catholicus[18] has seized my houses."

The emperor said: "If the catholicus [18] has seized your houses, what connection has that with Athanasius?"

A certain other lawyer, Patalas, said: "I have a charge against Athanasius."

The emperor said: "And what connection have you with Christians, being a pagan?" [19]

But certain of the majority of the Antiochenes seized Lucius and brought him to the emperor, saying: "We beg your Mightiness and your Majesty: see whom they wished to make bishop."

IV

Another petition made by Lucius at the gate of the palace.

"I beg your Mightiness, hear me."

The emperor stopped and said: "I say to you yourself, Lucius, how came you hither, by sailing or by land?"

Lucius said: "I beg you: by sailing."

The emperor said: "To you, Lucius, I say: may God of the world and comet, sun, and moon [20] be angry with those very persons who sailed with you, because they have not cast you into the sea, and may that ship not have swift breezes for all time or, when tempest-tossed, attain a haven with persons sailing in it."

And through Euzoius[21] they requested those about Probatius, the successors of Eusebius and of Bardio, the eunuchs,[22] that the unbelieving Arians might obtain an audience. And the emperor, when he had known this and after he had tortured the eunuchs, said: "If anyone wishes to petition against the Christians,[23] let him suffer such treatment." And so the emperor dismissed them.

1. Precedent for the document's inclusion as a law may be seen in *CT* 7. 20. 2 = *CI* 12. 46. 1 (dated 320 or 326), which contains Constantine I's con-

versation with veterans at the imperial headquarters of his army and his proclamation which concluded the conversation.

2. He was the Arian patriarch of Alexandria officially from 373 to 378, but for some time previously Lucius was the leader of the Arian opposition to Athanasius in Alexandria.

3. This person is otherwise unknown.

4. Concrete for abstract; that is, "to occupy the bishopric".

5. Apparently one of the emperor's escort and of a combative character—for the word translated *excited* can mean "emulative" or, in a bad sense, "envious"—who knew more than the emperor about the petitioners.

6. The word is παραβολή, which gives us "parabola" in geometry, "conjunction" in astronomy, "division" in mathematics, and survives as "parable" in New Testament usage. In a bad sense it seems to mean "the thing thrown beside", "a byword".

7. The reference is to George of Cappadocia, the intrusive patriarch of Alexandria, who succeeded Athanasius when the saint entered into his third exile. See no. 98, n. 15.

8. These must be round numbers, because they are inaccurate. The first exile was 336–7 under Constantine I, the second exile was under Constantius II 339–46, the third exile also under Constantius was 356–61, the fourth exile was under Julian II 362–4. The time of the petition was late 363, for Jovian's reign was short: 27 June 363—16 February 364, and he was in Antioch from 23 October till sometime in December. Ten and twenty years then would be 353 and 343: 353 was not a year of exile and 343 fell under Constantius, and thus no account is taken of the earliest exile under Constantine.

9. The hollowness of honorary epithets attached to emperors (as well as to officials and prelates) is observed well in this case, where the Arians, who, while heretics, yet were Christians, call Julian the Apostate by this appellation. Even if they meant it in its active and less common sense "most God-loving", it still was inappropriate in a Christian mouth, inasmuch as Julian loved only the pagan gods—a circumstance known to both petitioners and emperor.

On this episode see K. M. Setton's doctoral dissertation, *Christian Attitude Towards the Emperor in the Fourth Century* (New York, 1941), 83–4, and consult his list on pp. 237–9.

In English the *loci classici* for titles of address (whether ecclesiastical or laic) are the doctoral dissertations of L. Dinneen, *Titles of Address in Christian Greek Epistolography to 527 A.D.* (Washington, 1929) and of M. B. O'Brien, *Titles of Address in Christian Latin Epistolography to 543 A.D.* (Washington, 1930). See also M. P. Charlesworth's excellent article, "The Virtues of a Roman Emperor: Propaganda and the Creation of Belief" in *Proceedings of the British Academy*, 23 (1937) 105–33. See Index of Titles of Address.

See no. 127, n. 7.

10. That is, are obsolete.

11. Members of municipal senates in Egypt are meant, but it is not at all

298   125. RECALL OF ATHANASIUS, 363 OR 364

clear how the spirituality thus could interfere with the temporality or why the emperor entered no objection to this information and apparently accepted it.

12. Literally "housekeeping", generally "internal administration"; that is, the problem had been settled.

13. The Greek words are transliterations of Latin imperatives: φέρι, φέρι = *feri, feri*. These seem to be orders to his guards to silence the petitioners.

14. Possibly with the extended meaning "for communion".

15. The word τέμενος means a plot of land restricted from common use and dedicated to a deity.

16. Cf. *supra* n. 14.

17. He probably was an imperial registrar or notary.

18. See no. 64, n. 20.

19. See no. 121, n. 3.

20. The verb has four subjects: *God, comet, sun, moon*, if the text is correct. The difficulty lies with the word translated "comet" (κομήτης), a noun originally meaning "a long-haired person" or simply "a person with hair on the head". Since such a condition is not characteristic of either sun or moon, "comet" is preferred as an independent noun. One manuscript reads κοσμητής, which means "director" or "orderer" or even "polisher" (of temple statues) or "sweeper" (of a monastery), but the editors reject this variation. It is tempting to twist the Greek in such a way as to read "the God and director of the world, the sun, and the moon". But the entire expression, when considered in its context, may be merely Jovian's customary method of invoking celestial ire. That certain celestial phenomena could portend calamity in antiquity is perhaps too well known to need proof beyond the evangelical evidence presented in no. 313, n. 1 *ad med*.

21. He was Arian patriarch of Antioch after having been a deacon in Alexandria.

22. The Greek shows that these are *those about Probatius*, but presumably their predecessors also were eunuchs, if the Eusebius named here is identical with the eunuch Eusebius at Constantius' court mentioned by Athanasius (*Hist. Ar. ad Mon.* 35) and appearing as an interlocutor in no. 95.

23. The emperor apparently recognized only the orthodox as Christians.

125. LETTER OF JOVIAN ON RECALL OF ATHANASIUS, 363 or 364

(PG. 26. 813)

The following imperial authorization for the return of St Athanasius to his patriarchal see of Alexandria from his fourth exile (362-4) is prefaced to a long letter sent to Jovian by Athanasius in response to the former's request [1] for the latter's statement on doctrinal matters before the emperor decided to revoke the saint's sentence of exile passed by Julian the Apostate, his predecessor.[2]

Copy of Emperor Jovian's letter sent to Athanasius, the most holy archbishop of Alexandria.

Jovian to the most God-beloved and friend of God, Athanasius.

Exceedingly admiring the virtuous acts of your very proper life and your resemblance to the God of all and your disposition toward Christ our Saviour, we accept you, most honoured bishop, also because you have not cowered from every toil and the fear of persecutors, in that you have regarded perils and threats of sword as excrement and are holding fast the helm of the orthodox faith, which to you is dear, and since you fight even until now for the truth and continue to present yourself as a pattern to all the people of the faithful and a model of virtue.

Therefore our Majesty reinstates you and wishes you to return to the instruction of salvation. Return, therefore, to the holy churches and shepherd the people of God and raise zealously to God your prayers for our Gentleness. For we know that by your supplications both we and they who with us hold Christian opinions shall have great succour from the Supreme God.

1. This letter is not extant.

2. It is supposed that Athanasius returned secretly to Alexandria in August 363, after he had heard about Julian's death in June of that year, and that he was in Antioch from September 363 to February 364, after which he formally resumed his episcopal duties in Alexandria; but it is not certain that the formal letter of his recall was written before the beginning of 364.

126. MANDATE OF JOVIAN ON PROPOSALS TO RELIGIOUS WOMEN, 364

(*CT* 9. 25. 2)

Ten years after a constitution against ravishing holy virgins and holy widows (no. 92), this mandate penalizes even advances against such with a view to marriage.

Justinian adapts it in *CI* 1. 3. 5, of which Pitra prints a late Greek version (2. 565).

Emperor Jovian [1] Augustus to Secundus, praetorian prefect.[2]

300   127. TAXATION OF CHRISTIAN MERCHANTS, 364

If anyone shall have dared, I shall not say to rape, but even[3] to solicit, sacred virgins or[4] widows[4] with a view to matrimony, he shall be smitten by a capital sentence.[5]

Given on 19 February[1] at Antioch, Jovian[1] Augustus and Varronian being consuls.

This law does not need explanation.[6]

1. Ten days elapsed in 364 between Jovian's death on 16 February and Valentinian I's accession on 26 February. Thus technically the Empire had no emperor, but the draft of the constitution may have been ready for publication and—the reaction after Julian's death on 27 June 363 still remaining—the ecclesiastically minded members of the emperor's entourage may have manipulated its emission without waiting to see who would be the succeeding sovereign.

2. Of the East.

3. *CI* substitutes "only" for the adverb.

4. *CI* omits this word.

5. *CI* alters *sentence* (*sententia*) to "penalty" (*poena*).

6. Though an explanation may not be needed, it may be excusable to note that affairs appear to have been in a sorry state to require the repetition (see no. 92) of such a regulation concerning virgins consecrated to God's service in a Christianized civilization, when in a pre-Christian culture pagan Romans respected the virtue of the Vestal virgins, who—it is only fair to note—were far fewer in number than the former.

127. MANDATE OF VALENTINIAN I AND VALENS ON TAXATION OF CHRISTIAN MERCHANTS, 364

(*CT* 13. 1. 5)

When the emperors readjusted ecclesiastical affairs after the death of Julian the Apostate, they did not revive the exemption from taxes granted by Constantius II to clergymen engaged in commercial activities (no. 102).

Justinian modelled two constitutions on this ordinance (*CI* 1. 4. 1, 4. 63. 1).[1]

Emperors Valentinian and Valens Augusti to Secundus, praetorian prefect.[2]

You should summon to the necessity of payment[3] tradesmen, if any belong to our household, provided that they appear to employ the expertness of trading, and Christians,[4] who, if their religion is true, wish to aid paupers and persons situated in need,[5] also persons dependent upon more powerful persons[6] and the more powerful

127. TAXATION OF CHRISTIAN MERCHANTS, 364

persons themselves, if, however, their concern is trading, particularly since anyone of the more powerful persons either ought not to participate in trade or ought to be the first to acknowledge payment,[3] as honour demands.

Given on 17 April at Constantinople, the deified [7] Jovian and Varronian being consuls.[8]

1. In the first adaptation Justinian so alters the statute's interpretation that it falls into a different category and is reproduced separately (no. 128). In the second adaptation Justinian adheres fairly closely to the statute's sense, but since he omits mention of Christians it is neither compared nor translated.

2. Of the East. Justinian assigns Julian, count of the East, as addressee.

3. Apparently of the lustral tax (on which see no. 97, n. 1), under whose title is set this statute.

4. Commentators think that only the clergy are meant.

5. The Christian conscience early proclaimed that property should be used freely to aid the needy (e.g. Matt. 19. 16-26 = Mark 10. 17-27 = Luke 18. 18-27; 2 Cor. 9. 6-7; 1 John 3. 17), particularly those persons "who are of the household of faith" (Gal. 6. 10). And in the apostolic age funds were collected in the churches on Sundays (1 Cor. 16. 2) for "the redemption of the saints, for the deliverance of slaves and of captives and of prisoners" *et al.* and "to maintain and to clothe from the righteous labour of the faithful those who are in want" (*CA* 4. 9). See also no. 515, n. 3.

Earlier Cicero had encouraged such charity when he wrote: "to ransom prisoners from servitude and to relieve the poor [*tenuiores*, on which word see next note] is a kindness serviceable to the State" (*De Off.* 2. 18. 63).

6. The relation of patron and client probably is meant.

The word is *potiores*, which has as its synonym *potentiores* and as its antonym *tenuiores* (slighter, poorer, less powerful). By this document's date, though there still persists some confusion both in literary and in juridical texts, this pair of opposites usually has superseded the earlier distinction between *honestiores* (more honourable) and *humiliores* (lowlier, meaner, poorer). *Honestiores* and *potentiores* were citizens whose origin or position (official or otherwise) or wealth put them in the higher social classes and won for them lighter penalties in criminal law; among such persons were Roman and Constantinopolitan senators and their families, soldiers and veterans and their children, municipal officials (outside the two capitals) and their descendants. *Humiliores* and *tenuiores* were all others, lower-class citizens, the masses, and were subjected to corporal and/or capital punishment on conviction of crime. Consult A. Berger, *Encyclopedic Dictionary of Roman Law* (Philadelphia, 1953), s.vv.

7. The adjective *divus* (deified *or* divine) defies satisfactory translation when applied to Roman emperors who, beginning with Constantine I and excepting Julian II, were nominally Christian. Its use in titles of such sovereigns does not attest to Christian subscription to the pagan belief in or practice of

deification of rulers—a belief and a practice particularly prevalent in the Hellenistic East (including Egypt, where Alexander the Great accepted it in 332 B.C.), where *post hominum memoriam* divinity not only hedged but also incarnated itself in kings and whence the belief and the practice took the road to Rome ere the reign of Augustus, the first Roman emperor, to whom divine honours began to be paid soon after his victory at Actium (31 B.C.) had made him master of the Mediterranean world. And the fact that from 40 B.C. Octavian (Augustus) was called *divi filius* (son of the deified [Julius Caesar, whom the Senate had deified in 42 B.C.—a biennium after his assassination]) gave the initial impulse to the creation of the imperial cult, which in adoring the autocrat also exalted the emperor. The Romans' yearning for a saviour-god who would deliver them from the century-old civil strife intermittent in the dying days of the Republic and who would terminate their "time of troubles" seemed to find fulfilment in Augustus, who established the *pax Augusta*. In his lifetime, therefore, began the belief that he was an incarnate deity. His immediate successors developed this sovereign idea into a religious dogma, which they in turn related to themselves and made it the principal part of a new cult, which rivalled and perhaps overshadowed the old religion and provided a pretext for persecution of Christians (see no. 1, n. 4 *ad init.*).

Originally and in the paganized Empire *divus* was added to an emperor's title *post mortem*, provided that popular (or at least senatorial) opinion considered him to have been a "good" emperor. A "bad" emperor suffered senatorial censure in having his memory execrated (*damnatio memoriae*) and in being denied the posthumous epithet of *divus*.

Though Pliny (*Nat. Hist.* 2. 5. 18) says that "It is god for mortal to aid mortal and this is the path to eternal glory"—a noble sentiment whereby the scientist sought to justify the deification of those Roman emperors who had done so much for mankind—yet retention of the title *divus* seems simply a terminological survival from the pre-Christianized Empire (without theological significance, so far as Christians are concerned) and indicates that the emperor to whom is attached the epithet has died.

In time, of course, the theory of the divine right to rule was substituted by the Christians for the pagan deification of emperors and far surpassed it in sincerity. Thus, about this document's date, Vegetius wrote: "When the emperor has accepted the name of Augustus, loyal devotion must be offered and ceaseless service must be applied to him as to a present and incarnate God. For either in peace or in war one serves God when one loyally loves him who rules under God's authority" (*Epit. Rei Mil.* 2. 5).

It may be added also that the pagan practice of raising men to the rank of gods or demigods crept into the Church in the honours of the altar paid to angels, apostles, confessors, martyrs, and saints.

Consult L. R. Taylor, *The Divinity of the Roman Emperor* (Middletown, Conn., 1931), esp. 69 and 241; M. P. Charlesworth, "Some Observations on Ruler-Cult Especially in Rome" in *HTR* 28 (1935) 5-44, esp. 26-42; id.,

"Providentia and Aeternitas" in *HTR* 29 (1936) 107-32; id., "The Virtues of a Roman Emperor" in *Proceedings of the British Academy*, 23 (1937) 105-33; C. Lattey, "The New Testament and the Pagan Emperors" in *Church and State: Papers Read at the Summer School of Catholic Studies, Held at Cambridge [England], July 27th to August 6th, 1935* (London, 1936), 1-28, esp. 1-10, 14-15; J. L. Tondriau, "Comparisons and Identifications of Rulers with Deities in the Hellenistic Period" in *The Review of Religion*, 13 (1948) 24-47, esp. 30-3; A. D. Nock, "Deification and Julian" in *JRS* 47 (1957) 115-23; J. Ferguson, "The Virtues of a Roman Emperor" in his *Moral Values in the Ancient World* (London, 1958), 179-207.

8. Although Jovian had died on 16 February, no suffect consul apparently was named as Varronian's colleague and the style of dating remained unaltered.

128. MANDATE OF VALENTINIAN I AND VALENS ON MERCHANTS' CHARITY TO CHRISTIAN PAUPERS, 364

(*CI* 1. 4. 1)

Justinian's version of this statute not only is shorter than that preserved in the Theodosian Code (no. 127), but also is so altered in meaning that it calls for separate translation. Whereas the Theodosian version directs Christian merchants (presumably clergymen conducting businesses for extra-ecclesiastical income) to pay taxes, the Justinianian version commands profit-making tradesmen (whose religion is not specified) to assist Christian paupers.

Emperors Valentinian and Valens Augusti to Julian, count of the East.[1]

Tradesmen, if any belong to our household, lest they should appear to exceed the profit of trading, should take care to aid Christians,[2] whose religion is true, paupers, and persons situated in need.[3]

Given on 17 April at Constantinople, the deified[4] Jovian and Varronian being consuls.[5]

1. The Theodosian version is addressed to Secundus, praetorian prefect of the East.
2. The Theodosian version regards the Christians as aiding the poor, but Justinian's interpretation is that the poor Christians should be objects of charity.
3. See no. 127, n. 5.
4. See no. 127, n. 7.
5. See no. 127, n. 8.

129. EDICT OF VALENTINIAN I AND VALENS ON EXCLUSION OF RICH PLEBEIANS FROM THE CLERICATE, 364

(CT 16. 2. 17)

This edict is designed to prevent wealthy citizens—of the lower classes at least—from shirking their financial obligations to the State by entering the priesthood.

Emperors Valentinian and Valens Augusti to the Byzacenes.
We absolutely debar the reception of rich plebeians by the Church.[1]
Given on 10 September at Aquileia, the deified [2] Jovian and Varronian being consuls.[3]

1. This must mean that they cannot become clergymen and thus gain immunity from public services, for it is almost inconceivable that nominally Christian sovereigns would forbid any orthodox subject—no matter what was his wealth—to have the status of a layman in the Church.
2. See no. 127, n. 7.
3. See no. 127, n. 8.

130. EDICT OF VALENTINIAN I AND VALENS ON ADMISSION OF CURIALS TO THE CLERICATE, 364

(CT 12. 1. 59)

By this statute the emperors not only annul one of Julian's constitutions (no. 118), but also decree that a propertied person desiring to become a clergyman should surrender his estate either to a relative or to his local senate, because the State was loath to lose the taxes assessable against such property in a period when ordinarily the clergy was exempt from most types of taxation.

The same Augusti to the Byzacenes.
Whoever selects the Church's service either should make a kinsman a curial in his stead by bestowing his own property on him or should cede his property to the municipal senate which he has left—a person who has done neither being recalled necessarily,[1] when he had begun to be a clergyman.
And the rest.

Given on 12 September at Aquileia, the deified [2] Jovian and Varronian being consuls.[3]

1. To service in the municipal senate.
2. See no. 127, n. 7.
3. See no. 127, n. 8.

131. SUBSCRIPTION OF VALENTINIAN I ON LAIC INTERFERENCE WITH CLERICAL CONCERNS, 364

(Sozomen, *HE* 6. 7)

When Hellespontine and Bithynian bishops and others, who were concerned about the Son's consubstantiality with the Father, had chosen Hypatian, bishop of Heraclea Perinthus in Thrace, to petition Valentinian, en route to Rome, that they might be permitted to meet for the purpose of correcting the teaching about the faith, the emperor replied orally and characteristically—for he believed that a sovereign ought not to occupy himself with theological controversies [1]—that the prelates should meet wherever it would please them. Accordingly the bishops convened at Lampsacus, where they, for two months discussing subjects relating to faith and order, issued some semi-Arian decrees.

For me, who have been ranked with the laity, it is not right to interfere in such matters; but the priests, to whom this is a concern, should convene by themselves wherever they wish.

1. To take only one—and that the most egregious—example hitherto, Valentinian certainly did not conform with the precedent set by Constantine the Great, on whom in such matters see Introd., n. 29, and nos. 15, 17-22, 24, 25, 27, 39, 40, 44, 46-53, 57-9, 63, 66-73, 75, 77. See also no. 136, n. 1 *ad fin*.

132. MANDATE OF VALENTINIAN I AND VALENS ON CONDEMNATION OF CHRISTIANS TO THE ARENA, 365

(*CT* 9. 40. 8)

The emperors here legislate against condemnation of a guilty Christian to the arena.

The same Augusti to Symmachus, urban prefect.¹

Whatever Christians should have been caught in any crime whatsoever should not be sentenced to a public game.²

If any of the judges shall have done this, both he himself shall be censured severely and his office staff shall submit to a very great fine.³

Given on 15 January, Valentinian and Valens Augusti being consuls.

1. Of Rome.
2. The word is *ludus* and in this connection connotes (according to most commentators) the gladiatorial combats staged in the amphitheatre, where men were "butcher'd to make a Roman holiday" (Byron).
On gladiatorial shows see L. Friedländer, *Roman Life and Manners in the Early Empire* (London, 1913), 2. 41–62 and his notes thereon in 4. 511–21.
3. The linguistic variety of the Latin language is illustrated by this law: in the first paragraph the verbs are perfect subjunctive and present subjunctive; in the second paragraph the first verb is future perfect indicative and the other verbs are future indicative. One would expect the scribe to have kept to one mode throughout this draft.

133. MANDATE OF VALENTINIAN I AND VALENS ON EXCLUSION OF BAKERS FROM THE CLERICATE, 365

(CT 14. 3. 11)

Consonant with the imperial policy in the Dominate to retain sufficient personnel in various guilds¹ considered vital to the public economy, the emperors here bar bakers from entering the Church as clerics.

The same Augusti to Symmachus, urban prefect.²

By this sanction generally we proclaim that permission to enter the churches³ should be extended to none at all for the purposes of avoiding baking.⁴

But if anyone should have entered,³ he should know that, since the privilege of Christianity⁵ has been abolished, he can and must be recalled at any time to the bakers' association.⁶

Given on 27 September at Aquileia, Valentinian and Valens Augusti being consuls.

1. The Roman guilds or corporations, save for a few of great antiquity, wer

133. EXCLUSION OF BAKERS FROM CLERICATE, 365

suppressed in the last days of the free Republic as a source of political disaffection and of public disorder.

Originally brotherhoods (*sodalitates*) based on kinship within the clan (*gens*)—though later in the concept of kinship reality was conquered by fiction—and organized to maintain religious rites and to provide social intercourse, these groups forged so close a bond that their unity eventually found an outlet in politics. When such bodies were bribed to surrender their suffrages to politicians in a period wherein partisan politics prevailed, the public peace was endangered by the violence which ensued in the elections. Thus the Senate in 64 B.C. dissolved the corporations which were considered dangerous (Asconius, *In Pis.* 6 and *In Cor.* 67). And after Publius Clodius Pulcher (the stormy petrel and the political gangster of the moribund Commonwealth) had revived these and had received power to create new corporations by his *Lex Clodia de collegiis* (so Cicero, *Ad Att.* 3. 15. 4) or *de collegiis restituendis novisque instituendis* (so Asconius, *In Pis.* 8) in 58 B.C. (Cicero, *Pro Sest.* 25. 55, *In Pis.* 4. 9; Dio Cassius, *Hist. Rom.* 38. 13. 2), again the Senate took action in 56 B.C. (Cicero, *Ad Q. Fr.* 2. 3. 5).

But despite the *Lex Licinia de sodaliciis* of 55 B.C. (Cicero, *Pro Planc.* 15. 36), which, while not a corporation law in our sense, attacked the organization of associations masquerading as corporations and procuring votes by intrigue and by intimidation, guilds were resuscitated and remained—almost all of them—to be outlawed by Gaius Julius Caesar *c.* 45 B.C. (Suetonius, *Iul.* 42. 3; Josephus, *Ant. Iud.* 14. 10. 8. 215). This act during his dictatorship need cause no surprise, though no evidence of electoral rioting in Rome exists for those years (49–44 B.C.). M. Radin in his *The Legislation of the Greeks and Romans on Corporations* (New York, ?1909), 90, remarks "Nobody knew better than the master-politician of Rome what an instrument the local collegia [guilds] could become for subversive purposes ... we must suppose this law to have been the ordinary attempt of the successful revolutionist to render impossible a repetition of his own act", for Caesar had not been unfamiliar with Catiline's machinations and with Clodius' operations.

It used to be believed that in the Principate the Caesarian policy was pursued generally throughout the Empire on the basis of the literary evidence supplied by Suetonius (*Aug.* 32. 1) for Italy and by Pliny (*Ep.* 10. 34, 93, 96. 7) for Bithynia and Pontus. If any exception was allowed, it was in Egypt, the imperial preserve (so to speak), where the emperors discovered that the corporative system (inherited from the Ptolemies) was a convenient organization to collect taxes on trades and to supply governmental requisitions. But the inscriptions edited in *FIRA* 1. 291–4 and 3. 91–121 and those mentioned by Radin, op. cit., 128–30 and 135–7, and S. Dill's detailed discussion in his *Roman Society from Nero to Marcus Aurelius*[2] (London, 1905), 251–86, esp. 264–8, attest the activity of associations in this period elsewhere than in Egypt and qualify the Suetonian and Plinian reports. Moreover the jurisconsults are not silent. In *D* 3. 4. 1 pr., Gaius, writing in the principate of Antoninus Pius

(138–61), mentions the corporations (*corpora*) of those who assist the government in farming the revenues and in operating gold and silver and salt mines, the guilds (*collegia*) of bakers and of some others (*quorundam aliorum*) in the city and of shipowners in the provinces. He says that societies and guilds and corporations (*societas . . . collegium . . . corpus*) are not allowed to all persons, but are controlled by laws and senatusconsults and imperial constitutions, which favour their formation in very few cases. Curiously he omits funeral associations (*collegia funeraticia*), which epigraphical evidence witnesses (e.g. *FIRA* 1. 291). A little later (197–211) in *D* 50. 6. 6. 12-13, Callistratus lists guilds or corporations (*collegia vel corpora*) of shipowners and of artisans, such as workers in wood or stone or metal, who perform work necessary for the public interest.

Finally, we find in the reign of Alexander Severus (222–35) what we may call a general corporation statute for the first time in Roman law, since he revived the artisan guilds on a wide scale, regulated their organization, and—by the same token—refused governmental recognition to such corporations as resisted the State's control (Scriptores Historiae Augustae: *Sev. Alex.* 33. 2). Thereafter a corporation's right to exist rested on the State's consent. Eventually, since the few privileges enjoyed by the guilds ceased to compensate the guildsmen for their responsibilities to the State, later emperors employed severe measures to keep the craftsmen in their colleges and so regimented the guilds that the guildsmen became practically governmental slaves—bound by birth to their trades, whence the law let none escape, even though in other occupations there might be better opportunities to lead more lucrative livelihoods.

For what crushing burdens befell the bread-makers, with whom the present document deals, see *CT* 6. 38. 1; 7. 5. 1; 9. 40. 3, 5–7, 9; 11. 16. 15, 18; 13. 5. 2; 14. 3. 1–8, 10–17, 19–20; 14. 17. 3, 4, 6 for the fourth century and *CT* 7. 4. 28; 7. 5. 2; 14. 3. 21, 22; 14. 4. 9; *LNV* 34. 1; *CI* 11. 16. 1 for the fifth century.

It was these guilds which—in so far as they had charitable aims—functioned as corporate charities before the State recognized the Church as a corporation capable of administering relief to the aged, the mendicant, the orphan, the sick, the wayfarer—though, of course, charity dispensed by individuals never was unknown (e.g. nos. 32, 102, 127, 128; see also introd. to no. 515).

2. Of Rome.

3. That is, of course, as a clergyman.

4. Literally "bakeries", that is, by extension, the baker's vocation.

5. This means that one cannot plead his clerical status as privileged to prevent his enforced return to his former occupation. See introd. to no. 96 *ad fin.*

6. The word is *consortium*, whereas the commoner terms for a corporation are *collegium* and *corpus*, of which the former is older and more widespread. But *consortium*—nor *societas* nor *universitas*, which also are frequent—does not appear in the otherwise adequate assembly of designations for associations discussed by Radin, op. cit., 13–32.

134. MANDATE OF VALENTINIAN I AND VALENS ON CHRISTIAN CUSTODIANS FOR PAGAN TEMPLES, 365

(CT 16. 1. 1)

This statute, which inflicts confiscation of property and death on officials who appoint Christians to tend pagan temples, strikes at the pagan tendency to annoy Christians, particularly those subordinate to them in administration.

Emperors Valentinian and Valens Augusti to Symmachus, urban prefect.[1]

Whoever, whether judge[2] or apparitor,[3] shall have appointed persons of the Christian religion to the care of temples should know that neither his life nor his property must be spared.

Given on 17 November[4] at Milan, Valentinian and Valens Augusti being consuls.

1. Of Rome.
2. While the word (*iudex*) usually means the judge ordinary or provincial governor, it often denotes any high administrator.
3. While from this document it appears that administrative aides made at least janitorial appointments, probably they also could influence nomination to other minor posts (as do their modern successors).
4. It is doubted that Symmachus was urban prefect at this time.

135. MANDATE OF VALENTINIAN I, VALENS, AND GRATIAN ON AMNESTY FOR PRISONERS AT EASTERTIDE, 367

(CT 9. 38. 3)

This ordinance releases from prison certain classes of persons because of the emperors' reverence for Easter.

Emperors Valentinian, Valens, and Gratian Augusti to Viventius, urban prefect.[1]

Because of the day of Easter, which in our innermost heart we celebrate, we dissolve the bonds for all persons whom accusation constrains and prison confines.

But nevertheless the traitor,[2] the necromancer,[3] the poisoner[4] or the magician,⁵ the adulterer, the rapist, the homicide should be barred from share in this boon.

Given on 5 May at Rome,⁶ Lupicinus and Jovinus being consuls.

1. Of Rome.
2. Literally "the committer of sacrilege in treason" (*sacrilegus in maiestate*), that is, one who in some way acts against the emperor's sacred person.
3. Literally "the person accused (*or* guilty) toward the dead" (*reus in mortuos*). If necrophilism had been meant, probably another phrase would have been used. However it may mean simply one who is a violator of tombs.
4. Or "sorcerer"—the word is *veneficus* from *venenum*, which originally, like φάρμακον in Greek, meant anything, especially any liquid substance, capable of affecting powerfully or changing the condition of the body. *Venenum* comes then to mean "noxious drug", "poison", "magical potion", "charm", and often combines the ideas of drug and of magic, with the conception of magic or sorcery being uppermost. Though sometimes the notion of poison is quite clear (as in no. 180), yet at other times it is difficult to detect the difference between poison and sorcery (as in nos. 145, 198, 201, 207). Cf. *infra* n. 5 *ad fin*.

As early as the time of the *Twelve Tables* (451–449 B.C.) the Romans legislated against sorcery by imposing a capital penalty for conviction (*FIRA* I. 52, 55; *TT* 8. 1a–b, 8a–b), while among the Greeks Plato (?427–347 B.C.) appears to have been the first person to advocate such legislation (*Leges*, 11. 933 B–E).

5. Here is seen a closer connection of poison with magic than in no. 145. Traditionally—as in the case of the mythological Medea (e.g. Euripides, *Med*. 384–5, 784–9, 1125–6, 1159–1221; Seneca, *Med*. 570–7, 670–738, 740–842)—a magician could prepare poison and a poisoner could manipulate magic. See Clyde Pharr, "The Interdiction of Magic in Roman Law" in *Transactions and Proceedings of the American Philological Association*, 63 (1932) 269–95.

Perhaps the chief reason for Christian condemnation of magicians was the belief that much of magic was performed by demons' assistance and involved their worship or other forms of idolatry. The boundary between pagan incantation and Christian exorcism, however, is too delicate to be trodden deftly.

Consult L. Thorndike, *A History of Magic and Experimental Science* (New York, 1923), 1. 1–547, for an account of ancient magic (esp. 1. 337–547 for magic in Christian thought and the special studies therein cited).

6. Mommsen suggests Reims as the place.

136. RESCRIPT OF VALENTINIAN I ON LAIC JUDGEMENT IN CLERICAL CASES, 367

(*PL* 16. 1045)

When St Ambrose, bishop of Milan, was cited to come before the imperial consistory in 386 to dispute with Auxentius, bishop of Silistria, then an Arian refugee in Milan, about possession of the Portian Basilica in Milan, he wrote a letter (*Ep.* 21) to Emperor Valentinian II, who had proposed himself as arbiter of the issue, and in it—in addition to alleging that the orthodox clergy and laity advised against his attendance and |that therefore he would not appear—he quoted to the son from his father's rescript to the effect that only bishops should judge about bishops (§2).[1]

In case of faith or of any ecclesiastical rank he who is neither unequal in office nor dissimilar in legal right ought to judge.

1. Ambrose asserts that Valentinian by this rescript (which is not extant) meant not only this, but also that if a bishop should have been accused also of other matters and his character should require investigation, even such examination pertained to episcopal scrutiny.

Later in the letter (§4) Ambrose asks "For who is there who would deny that in a matter of faith, in a matter, I say, of faith, bishops are wont to judge concerning Christian emperors, but not emperors concerning bishops?" and avers (§5) that Valentinian also was wont to say: "It is not my business to judge between bishops." This position, of course, is in strong contrast to Constantine I's precedent, on which see no. 131, n. 1.

137. LETTER OF VALENTINIAN I, VALENS, AND GRATIAN ON RECALL OF URSINIANS, 367

(*CSEL* 35. 48)

On the death of Pope Liberius in 366 the Papacy was contested by Damasus and by Ursinus so bitterly that contemporary reports record the slaughter of several hundred persons within a month in that year.[1] It appears that of the Roman clergy and laity the great majority elected Damasus, who—the Ursinians said—bought his election, and a smaller number selected Ursinus, who—the Damasines declared—was consecrated irregularly. To prevent further rioting Valentinian in 366 recognized Damasus and deported Ursinus with some of his supporters.

While personal hostility may have accounted for the violent scenes, the schism appears to have been the aftermath of the Felician schism of 357-65 (see introd. to no. 95 *ad fin.*), because Damasus had supported Felix II during the latter's pontificate of 355-65 and then had adhered to Liberius. The Ursinians probably urged that such a record demanded the repudiation of Damasus.

Though the present document, addressed to Vettius Agorius Praetextatus, the urban prefect of Rome and "probably the truest representative of the last generation of paganism",[2] rescinds conditionally the deportation of the Ursinians, the emperors later exiled again both the anti-pope Ursinus and his associates for their renewed opposition to Pope St Damasus I.[3]

Wherein Ursinus and those who are with him are released from exile.

Hail, Praetextatus, most dear to us.

Although the punishment seems to have been just, which has settled by chastisement the faction riotously undertaken there,[4] where harmony ought to be greatest, namely in either the seat or the state of the Church, each of which situations demands both moderation and reverence, nevertheless for all who recently have been condemned to deportation because of that disturbance we have compassion, most dear and most agreeable Praetextatus, both because of our nature's leniency and on account of consideration for religion itself and for the law.

Therefore all who are of that condition and guilt your lofty Sublimity shall release by the authority of our decision. Moreover you shall maintain this form [5] for the future, that if they, restored to their former status, shall have committed again anything similar in a restless spirit, whereby the re-established peace is disturbed, the severest sentence should be pronounced against them. For they who cease not to sin after pardon can deserve no pardon.

1. See no. 138, n. 3, for the scene of the slaughter, which is related by an anonymous author (*CSEL* 35. 2-4) and by Ammianus Marcellinus (*Res Gestae*, 27. 3. 12-13) and is reminiscent of what Thucydides (*Hist.* 4. 46-8) tells about Corcyra in 425 B.C., when the insular populace instituted a bloody butchery of its political prisoners.

2. So S. Dill, *Roman Society in the Last Century of the Western Empire* [2] (London, 1899), 17. Dill gives a good delineation of Praetextatus' personality (17-19).

3. See nos. 138, n. 1, for Ursinus (late in 367) and 140 for his associates (early in 368).

4. Rome.

5. Either the document itself or "pattern" or "precedent".

138. LETTER OF VALENTINIAN I, VALENS, AND GRATIAN ON RESTORATION OF A ROMAN BASILICA, 367

(CSEL 35. 49)

After he has exiled to Gaul the anti-pope Ursinus, who still was disturbing the peace of the Roman Church, Valentinian writes to Praetextatus, the urban prefect, that the single church still in the control of the Ursinian faction should be restored to Pope St Damasus I, whose supporters apparently have petitioned the emperor for this restitution.

Wherein the Basilica of Sicininus is returned.

Valentinian, Valens, and Gratian to Praetextatus, urban prefect.

By the removal of the author of dissension[1] all cause for discord ought to be settled, lest, if any fuel remains, it should be no advantage to have removed from the midst the touchwood of quarrels, dearest and fondest cousin Praetextatus.

Wherefore, since the petition of the defenders of the church of the city of Rome or of Damasus, the bishop of the sacred law,[2] has been perused, wherein only one of the churches of the Catholic religion is said still to be retained for worship by the dissenters,[3] inasmuch as there should be fear for the public security, lest from this circumstance some tumult again may arise (since not trifling is the image of schism, if thus something should be thought debarred),[4] your lofty Sublimity shall order this church to be opened to Damasus, that each and all may know with what zeal unity must be cultivated, with what peace all must live, since the congregation, everywhere permitted to assemble, when the churches have been restored, demands the fullest harmony.

1. The anti-pope Ursinus, who was banished to Gaul in November 367, is meant.
2. Religion.
3. In the two comparatively contemporary accounts the one places the massacre of the Ursinian party (see introd. to no. 137) in the Basilica of Sicininus and the other puts it in the Basilica of Liberius. Since it seems clear that the party of Ursinus was in control of a basilica and since Sicininus is not identifiable, the difficulty may be resolved either by conjecturing a manuscriptal corruption of *Ursicinius* (as Ursinus also was known) into *Sicininus* or by believing that the walls of the Liberian Basilica (now commonly known as Santa Maria Maggiore, one of the seven patriarchal churches of Rome) belonged to an earlier hall, a Sicininian Basilica, which perhaps formed part of a private palace (see no. 95, n. 1). The third hypothesis has the support of most scholars, who accept L. Duchesne's opinion that the Basilica Liberiana was the

scene of the slaughter (*Liber Pontificalis* [Paris, 1886], 1. 209). See also S. B. Platner and T. Ashby, *A Topographical Dictionary of Ancient Rome* (Oxford, 1929), 488–9 (s.v. Sicininum).

4. The thought seems to be that the separation in the Roman Church would continue, unless all the churches in Rome were under the control of its bishop Damasus. To end this internal division the emperor authorizes the urban prefect to return the dissenters' church to the pope's authority.

139. LETTER OF VALENTINIAN I, VALENS, AND GRATIAN ON PROTECTION OF GRAVES, (?)367–75

(*ILCV* 1. 14)

This restored [1] inscription, found in Rome (1607) in the pavement of a chapel in the old Basilica of San Pietro in Vaticano, apparently applies equally to both Christian and pagan sepulchres and particularly to those which, situated in privately owned plots, are subject to the whim of purchasers after a change in ownership of the ground.[2]

Emperors Caesars Flavians, Valentinian, Valens, and Gratian, Pious, Fortunate, Ever-August to their Flavius Eutherius,[3] greeting.

The eternal protection of graves, which clearly must be maintained for the particular benefit of all persons, is sought by us in accordance with the general opinion of the human race; and we consider it not religiously right for divine religious usage or for religious ceremonies that any prerogative should be lost.

Wherefore, lest it should be allowed to mock and to insult the relics of the dead, it is determined that a person giving a plot of ground for burial has so intended it by performing sacred services [4] in that place and by religiously celebrating rites,[5] that there may arise enclosures of boundaries to keep at a distance the plough, but also that poor persons' bodies may be received into it everywhere.

Wherefore, since continually and commonly divine and human laws require this,[2] lest, if the possession established in the said plot should find later any purchasers,[6] . . . any interpretation should confuse eternity of ownership and perpetual full right [7] contrary to the venerable cults, moreover that by protecting the monuments' boundaries perennial faith and reverence should remain . . .[6] defended by the perpetual dignity of the rites, it is determined that the venerable cult must be maintained and also the protection of the boundaries.

Given on 30 April . . . the most distinguished . . . being consuls. Favourably.[8]

1. Since the imperial names are restored, some scholars prefer the dates 375–83 and varying combinations of Valens, Gratian, Valentinian II, Theodosius I for the legislators.
2. For various sepulchral rights see also *ILCV* 1. 808–51, 2. 3823–83. See no. 641, nn. 14–22.
3. More properly Eucherius, who may have been urban prefect of Rome sometime in this period.
4. The word is *ministeria*, which looks to pagan rites.
5. The word is *mysteria*, which connotes Christian services (see no. 75, n. 42).
6. The lacuna is in the Latin.
7. Or perhaps "condition", if *causa* (the word here) is not equal—as it often is—to *iusta causa*.
8. This is intended to represent the letters PROSB, which may stand for *prospiter*, which in turn appears to be a syncopated form of *prosperiter*, which itself is reported only once and then from Ennius (239–169 B.C.). On the other hand and more probably the letters may represent *pro salute bona* (for good salvation) or *pro salute pia* (for pious salvation) or *pro salute principis* (for the emperor's safety), if B stands for P (as sometimes it does).

140. MANDATE OF VALENTINIAN I, VALENS, AND GRATIAN ON EXPULSION OF URSINIANS FROM ROME, 368

(*CSEL* 35. 49)

These imperial instructions to Praetextatus, urban prefect of Rome, order the expulsion of the Ursinian faction from Rome under rather liberal conditions.

On expelling Ursinus' associates outside Rome.
The same Augusti to Praetextatus, urban prefect.
Such innate restraint have we that we wish to protect the public discipline without disaster to anyone. Accordingly, since we do not favour occasions of punishments, Praetextatus, dearest and fondest cousin, it may be permitted to Ursinus' associates and accomplices, whom your very lofty Sublimity has thought ought to be removed for the sake of the eternal city's [1] quiet life, to live wherever they shall have preferred—Rome, whose tranquillity is desired, only excepted—without any harm to religion, under their own rights,[2] in such a way that they may seem to be sojourners rather than exiles. For it is indifferent to us what place of habitation they may choose, provided that, after the inciting discords have been removed, concord again may be established in the populace.

Given on 12 January at Trèves in the consulate of the Augusti.[3]

1. The epithet *eternal* was applied to Rome as early as the Augustan age, when the poet Tibullus (*c.* 48–19 B.C.) appears to have been the first who used it (*Eleg.* 2. 5. 23).

Many writers after Tibullus and into modern times have written tributes to the Romans' proud profession of faith in *Roma Aeterna* and have shown that not even the barbarians ever said of her *delenda est*, as once the Romans had cried about their rival Carthage (Plutarch, *Cato Maior*, 27. 1). Most recently D. A. Malcolm has traced this theme of Rome's *aeternitas* from the first century B.C. to the fifth century A.D. in "Urbs Aeterna" in *The University of Birmingham Historical Journal*, 3 (1951) 1–15.

But as the record reveals, neither Romulus, Rome's first king, nor Augustus, Rome's first emperor, was the real establisher of Rome's eternity. Rather after the vicissitudes of the fourth and the fifth centuries, during which Rome surrendered her universal status as a political capital to Constantinople in the East (see no. 62, n. 2) and in the West survived as the religious capital of Latin Christendom, it appears that the real authors of Rome's *aeternitas* were SS. Peter and Paul, the apostles who died martyrs' deaths in Rome over 250 years before a rival creation arose in Constantinople. That tradition and particularly the Petrine association (see no. 442, n. 7) aided the Papacy to retain Rome's prestige, despite the "Babylonian Captivity" at Avignon (1305–72) and despite the losses to Islam, Eastern Orthodoxy, and Protestantism.

2. That is, the Ursinian faction could live their life according to their own ecclesiastical pattern, provided that they would present no affront to the religious life of the locality wherein they should settle themselves. It is not clear how they could do this, but at least Rome would be spared their seditious presence.

3. Valentinian I and Valens were consuls in this year.

141. RESCRIPT OF VALENTINIAN I, VALENS, AND GRATIAN ON ECCLESIASTICAL DISTURBANCES, 368

(CSEL 35. 51–2)

This constitution is too general to point to a particular instance so far as the Christian population of Rome is concerned, unless it may be connected with the Ursinian commotion (nos. 137, 138, 140, 142, 143), but it may have been sent to Olybrius, the urban prefect of Rome, because the Christians had been disturbing the public peace on account of the apparently inadequate distribution of grain by the civic authorities. On the other hand, there may not have been any correlation of these circumstances.

The same Augusti to Olybrius, urban prefect.
Since nothing can be pleasanter than either prosperity or peace and since there is the highest happiness, as often as these two are combined, your Sublimity without doubt perceives how pleasing your letter has been to us, when it testifies both that these persons, who had disturbed the most sacred law [1] by riot and sedition, have been restrained and that the supply of grain for the common fatherland of all [2] gradually has begun to return to its former condition.[3] But we are not nearly surprised at these matters, after we have known of these,[4] for we presumed that you would be such a person, when we conferred the prefecture upon your merits, as we found you immediately in the beginnings of your administration.
Finally, we do not advise that your illustrious Authority, dearest and fondest cousin Olybrius, maintaining the same efficiency and devotion, should enhance completely the populace's condition either by transformation of the old discipline or by provisions of needful conveniences in respect to both the glory of propriety and the blessings of security.[5] Be solicitous for your own natural disposition. It is sufficient that future methods correspond with past methods. And you should not measure the sources of crime in such a way that you should think that our Clemency must be consulted about the corrections of individuals, since you should anticipate on your own responsibility and should repress so carefully and becomingly all matters from which can be any disturbance, that to us should remain not so much the need to incitement as the pleasure of approval.

1. That is, the Christian religion, as often.
2. This periphrasis merely means Rome, the centre of the Empire and in a historical sense the common parent of all the provinces.
3. Occasional public and private largess of grain to citizens can be traced well into the republican period, but the system of doles of cheap or free grain at public expense (*frumentationes*) was started by the tribune Gaius Sempronius Gracchus in 123 B.C. It is reported that after two generations 320,000 (later 150,000) citizens were registered as receiving grain gratis (Suetonius, *Iul.* 41. 3). The dole of grain was so popular that the imperial government never discontinued the practice. In the early Empire Augustus raised the number of recipients to a little over 200,000 (*Res Gestae Divi Augusti*, 3. 15; Dio Cassius, *Hist. Rom.* 55. 10. 1). And as early as Constantine I's reign the poorer citizens of the new capital of Constantinople shared with those of Old Rome the gratuitous supply of grain (Socrates, *HE* 2. 13)—a gift continued at least as late as Justinian I's times (*CI* 7. 37. 3. 1d).

Originally the republican aediles were charged with supervision of the sources (Italian or provincial) of grain, its transportation to Rome, its storage, and its distribution to the needy in the urban populace. But in A.D. 6 Augustus relieved the aediles of this responsibility (*cura annonae*) and appointed an imperial official, the prefect of the grain-supply (*praefectus annonae*), in their place and responsible to the emperor. By the Dominate, however, this officer became subordinate to the urban prefect, as appears in this document.

Almost everyone has heard of Juvenal's phrase *panem et circenses* (bread and games [*Sat.* 4. 10. 81]), by which, as the Emperor Trajan (his contemporary) knew, the Roman populace was controlled (Fronto, *Prin. Hist.* 17). The right to be fed and to be amused at the State's expense became before the end of the first century of the Christian era practically the only remaining privilege of Rome's proletariat, which by then had been relieved of almost all its political rights.

4. This clause is an expansion of the rare phrase *in noto*.

5. That is, the civic authorities must not relax their judicial and administrative control over the urban populace.

It seems somewhat severe for the sovereigns to advise against amelioration of the citizens' condition, particularly in respect to *provisions of needful conveniences*; but probably they considered that the imposition of some austerity in the gratuitous distribution of grain—which distribution apparently had been maladministered—was a punishment (additional to whatever the prefect already had inflicted) necessary to prevent future disturbances.

142. RESCRIPT OF VALENTINIAN I, VALENS, AND GRATIAN ON SCHISMATICAL ASSEMBLIES, 368

(*CSEL* 35. 50)

This is another imperial directive in the series of documents dealing with the Ursinian faction, which from this evidence persisted in meeting for worship near Rome and thus caused disturbances of the peace.

The same Augusti to Olybrius, urban prefect.[1]

Just as you have indicated by your last letter, you indeed have wished to guarantee by most earnest exertion that there can be no discord in the city of Rome and that the people of the Christians can enjoy profound security in peace. But, dearest and fondest cousin Olybrius, as the writings of the most distinguished Aginatius, the deputy-prefect,[2] have witnessed, to disturb peaceful affairs still delights some persons and repeated uproar is incited at meetings outside the city's walls.

Wherefore your excellent Sublimity by this order's authority should guarantee to the city and to the law that for dissenting people there can be neither a religious service nor an opportunity for congregating for such within the twentieth milestone, that the mad group may depart, as has been ordered, if it does not desire to be peaceful. For thus at last, after all disturbances have been removed to a great distance, settled peace will be granted to the people for all time.

1. Of Rome.
2. Literally "of the vicariate of the prefecture". Aginatius was urban vicar, the deputy of the prefect of Rome (see no. 143, n. 1).

143. RESCRIPT OF VALENTINIAN I, VALENS, AND GRATIAN ON SCHISMATICAL ASSEMBLIES, 368

(*CSEL* 35. 50–1)

This document, addressed to Aginatius, vicar of Rome, is quite similar to that sent to Olybrius, prefect of Rome (no. 142). It too calls for action against the Ursinian party, which held disturbing services in the environs of Rome.

The same Augusti to Aginatius, vicar.[1]

Desiring to remove every reason for these discords, which, as your Prudence has written, confuse the most sacred city [2] by the people of the Christians being driven hither and thither, we command by this letter that no meeting may be held within the twentieth milestone [3] by these persons whom factious disunion delights, most dear and most agreeable Aginatius.

Accordingly the command, salutary in a high degree and which should leave no room for interpretations as a result of ambiguity, your esteemed Sincerity should execute in this spirit, which both a judge [4] and a citizen owes to the restoration of peace and of tranquillity. In this also you have the aid of the urban prefecture, for your Serenity has addressed also the most distinguished and illustrious Olybrius [5] with equal authority against impious gatherings of factious persons, that he should ban these by the boundary [6] which is clearly determined, that not even in the neighbourhood may arise this commotion, which does not exist in the city. And you two easily will perform what you individually are able to perform.[7]

1. His full title is vicar of the city of Rome (*vicarius urbis Romae*). See the superscription to no. 153.

2. Rome.
3. From Rome in any direction.
4. While the vicar of Rome had civil jurisdiction as well as administrative functions, see no. 134, n. 2.
5. The urban prefect—superior to Aginatius, the urban vicar (his deputy).
6. That is, of the urban limits.
7. The idea seems to be that their joint action will be performed more easily than their separate action in suppressing the partisan strife.

144. MANDATE OF VALENTINIAN I AND VALENS ON JUDICIAL PROCESS AGAINST CHRISTIANS ON SUNDAY, 368-73

(*CT* 8. 8. 1)

In this administrative order (repeated in *CT* 11. 7. 10) the emperors forbid collectors of delinquent taxes from proceeding against Christians on Sunday.

Emperors Valentinian and Valens Augusti to Florian, consular [1] of Venetia.

We wish that on the Sun's day,[2] which long has been held auspicious, no Christian should be summoned into court by collectors of taxes, for by this our statute's interdict we ordain peril [3] against those who should have dared to do this.

Given on 21 April at Trèves, Valentinian and Valens Augusti being consuls.

1. For this title see no. 234, n. 3.
2. See no. 34, n. 5.
3. That is, peril of severe punishment.

145. MANDATE OF VALENTINIAN I, VALENS, AND GRATIAN ON AMNESTY FOR PRISONERS AT EASTERTIDE, 368

(*CT* 9. 38. 4)

This ordinance differs chiefly from the similar directive of the previous year (no. 135) in that necromancers are not included among the amnestied persons.

The same Augusti to Olybrius, urban prefect.[1]

The celebration of Easter demands that we absolve whomsoever the sorrowful [2] expectation of trial and the dread of punishment now worry.

Nevertheless compliance with the ancestors' decrees must be made, lest rashly we allow them to evade the crime of homicide, the filth of adultery, the wrong of treason, the wickedness of magic, the plots of poison,[3] and the violence of rape.

Read on 6 June, Valentinian Augustus and Valens Augustus for the second time being consuls.

1. Of Rome.
2. Probably a causative epithet: expectation which causes sorrow.
3. Or "sorcery", on which see no. 135, n. 4.

146. MANDATE OF VALENTINIAN I, VALENS, AND GRATIAN ON ECCLESIASTICAL APPEALS, 369

(*CT* 11. 36. 20)

This ordinance, on which Justinian models a statute repeated twice (*CI* 1. 4. 2 and 7. 65. 4a), authorizes Claudius, prefect of Rome, to fine a certain Chronopius, erstwhile bishop of an unknown diocese,[1] for having delayed by an appeal the execution of an unknown sentence which apparently was unappealable.

The same Augusti to Claudius, urban prefect.

Since Chronopius, the ex-bishop, has been in your court—the same person who previously had been in that of the seventy bishops [2]—and has suspended by an appeal a sentence from which there was no right to appeal, he should be compelled to pay a fine in silver, which a general sanction imposes on an act of this character.[3]

Moreover we wish this not to come to our fisc, but to be expended faithfully upon those who are indigent.[4]

And this should be done in this case and in all other ecclesiastical cases.

Given on 8 July, the most noble boy [5] Valentinian and the most distinguished [6] Victor being consuls.

Interpretation: Bishop Chronopius had been condemned by many bishops and before the court he had sought by an appeal to suspend the sentence which was issued; but from that sentence, because it had been issued justly, he ought not at all to have appealed.

322   147. ADMISSION TO ASCETIC LIFE, 370 OR 373

And in this case it [7] says that he had been sentenced by a heavy fine, that is, fifty pounds of silver, and, however, the sum of this fine was ordered not to benefit the fisc, but to be expended on paupers.

1. Probably an Italian see, however, because of his appearance before Claudius.
2. We are ignorant of what synod this was, but it may have met in support of Pope St Damasus I, whose early pontificate was troubled by the activities of the anti-pope Ursinus. Perhaps this council had deposed Chronopius, who then appealed, irregularly, against its verdict to Claudius and who now was appealing from the prefect's decision.
3. For this sentence Justinian substitutes "If a clergyman shall have flown to the aid of an appeal for the purpose of deceitful postponement before a definitive sentence, he should be compelled to pay a fine of fifty pounds of silver, which a general sanction imposes against appellants of this character".
The general sanction is *CT* 11. 36. 15 or 16. Each law (dated 364) specifies fifty pounds of silver as the penalty.
4. Here *CI* ends after reading "paupers" for the relative clause. Pitra prints (2. 537) a late Greek version of the Justinianian statute.
5. *Nobilissimus puer* is the phrase. Since Valentinian (later Valentinian II) was about one year old at this time, it can be estimated how empty was such an honour as the consulate in the eyes of adults in the moribund West. *Nobilissimus* is the adjective customarily applied to an emperor-designate too young to perform administrative duties. See also no. 28, n. 7.
6. Justinian omits the superlative adjective.
7. There is no subject in the Latin, but "law" must be understood.

147. MANDATE OF VALENTINIAN I AND VALENS ON ADMISSION TO ASCETIC LIFE, 370 or 373

(*CT* 12. 1. 63)

This directive, adapted by Justinian (*CI* 10. 32. 26), orders either the return of such men as have entered the monastic life for avoidance of public services owed to their municipalities, in which they probably had belonged to the curial class, or the transfer of their absently owned properties to those who will bear such burdens, in the event that such monks cannot be caught.

The same Augusti to Modestus, praetorian prefect.[1]
Certain adherents of inaction, by having deserted their communities' public services, strive to seize solitudes and secret places and under religion's pretext associate with bands of monks.[2]

148. PRO-CHRISTIAN LEGISLATION, 370

Therefore we have commanded [3] by a considered precept that these and others of this ilk, when caught within Egypt by the count of the East,[4] should be plucked from their hiding-places and should be recalled to undergo their native municipalities' public services; or pursuant to our sanction's tenor should be deprived of the allurements of their familial properties, which we have decided must be claimed by those persons who would be about to undergo the public services of public duties.[5]

Given at Beirut on 1 January, Valentinian and Valens Augusti being consuls.

1. Of the East.
2. This word *monazon* (transliterated from Greek) connotes not cenobitical but eremitical monks.
   See Aristotle, *Pol.* 7. 2. 2–4 (1324A), on the question of the active versus the contemplative life for the individual, that is the life of a citizen and participation in politics or the life of an alien and detachment from political activity. This he answers by asserting that it is erroneous to praise inaction above action, because happiness is an activity and the actions of just and temperate [*or* wise] persons contain the realization of much that is noble (7.3.3 = 1325A).
3. Justinian alters the tense to the present.
4. Justinian omits *within . . . East* to widen the statute's application, probably because by his time Egypt no longer maintained what was almost a monopoly in monachism at the date of the original document.
5. The ecclesiastical historians record that under this law Lucius, the Arian patriarch of Alexandria, assailed Egyptian monks in the desert, deposed their superiors, and banished most of the orthodox professors of monasticism (Socrates, *HE* 4. 24; Sozomen, *HE* 6. 19–20; Theodoret, *HE* 4. 22. 27, 35; Cassiodorus, *HE* 7. 39. 1–2, 30, 35).

148. MANDATE OF VALENTINIAN I AND VALENS ON CONFIRMATION OF CONSTANTIUS II'S PRO-CHRISTIAN LEGISLATION, 370

(*CT* 16. 2. 18)

If the date of this document is correct, Valentinian I and Valens waited almost seven years to annul at least some of the anti-Christian acts of Julian II,[1] who in turn had rescinded certain pro-Christian legislation of Constantius II. No reason for such delay can be assigned.

The same Augusti to Claudius, proconsul of Africa.

The decision [2] which, it has become clear, had existed in the deified [3] Constantius' last days should be valid and those things which then were decreed or done, when pagans' [4] minds were excited against the most holy law [5] by certain depravities,[6] should not gain validity on any pretext.

Given on 17 February at Trèves, Valentinian and Valens Augusti being consuls.

1. Soon after Jovian's death (16 February 364), however, they claimed for their privy purse such real estate, which must have included Christian property, as Julian had restored to pagan temples (*CT* 10. 1. 8; dated erroneously 4 February 364).

2. It is not certain to which decision (*sententia*) reference is made, but it apparently was suspended, if not outlawed, under Julian. Perhaps nos. 108 and 109 are meant.

3. See no. 127, n. 7.

4. This seems to be the earliest extant law in which the word *paganus* appears with the connotation of "heathen". On the word's etymology and history see E. Partridge, *Slang To-day and Yesterday* [3] (London, 1950), 40. See nos. 20, n. 5, and 121, n. 3.

The transformation of the State from an urban to an agrarian economy especially in the West, whence this constitution emanated, was not unmarked on the Church, for, although in the East Christianity successfully penetrated the countryside, in the West Christianity was essentially an urban religion in this sylloge's period (and later) and made no profound mark upon peasants, despite its evangelical imagery of agricultural allusions, until the missionary activities of western monks, whose monasteries in the rural districts were the centres of Christian doctrine, converted eventually the peasant population. The meaning of *paganus* (derived from *pagus*, properly a place with fixed boundaries, hence "canton", "district", "province", as opposed to *urbs* [city], *municipium* [municipality], *oppidum* [town], *civitas* [city]) retains in late Latin its classical significance of one who lives in the country rather than in a city, although it acquires the added meaning of a heathen as opposed to a Jew or a Christian.

Probably the Church of this period in its contest with paganism, which contained "gods many" (1 Cor. 8. 5) and many devils (cf. e.g. Matt. 8. 28–34; Mark 5. 1–17; Luke 8. 26–37), was not confronted with the difficulty which ministers of modern Christianity discover in persuading the majority of the laity to believe in even one God and one Devil, or at least to recognize their existence by regular attendance at ecclesiastical assembly (Heb. 10. 25). Probably, also, the only present-day pagans among professing Christians are those whose belief and behaviour contain or by custom retain certain primitive principles and practices of the converts from paganism in the so-called age of faith. Even so, although early Christianity pilfered from paganism more elements than the casual Christian commonly suspects, yet it is a form of religion far superior to that which it replaced by suppression. Moreover Wordsworth's wistful wish in his sonnet *The World*:

> Great God! I'd rather be
> A Pagan suckled in a creed outworn;
> So might I, standing on this pleasant lea,
> Have glimpses that would make me less forlorn;
> Have sight of Proteus rising from the sea;
> Or hear old Triton blow his wreathed horn.

forfeits most of its force nowadays, since most moderns, because of the low estate of classical learning, neither know nor, in the event that they know, evince any particular interest in either Proteus or Triton, whom ancient authors accounted inferior immortals.

5. Religion.
6. Probably an allusion to the Donatist wiles exercised upon Julian's mind.

149. MANDATE OF VALENTINIAN I, VALENS, AND GRATIAN ON EXEMPTION FROM CAPITATION, 370

(CT 13. 10. 6)

This constitution exempts nuns as well as widows and wards from the capitation tax.[1]

The same Augusti and Gratian Augustus to Viventius, praetorian prefect.[2]

No widow, no ward of either sex, until he enters those years[3] which no longer need public[4] tutors or curators, should acknowledge the tax of the people.[5]

Moreover, if any women have dedicated themselves to the perpetual service of the sacred law,[6] they should be considered immune from similar tribute.

Given on 30 March at Trèves, Valentinian Augustus and Valens Augustus for the third time being consuls.

1. *CT* 13. 10. 4 (dated ?368) also exempts widows, wards, spinsters, and women living in perpetual virginity (not necessarily nuns) from the same tax.
2. Of the Gauls, on which see no. 203, n. 4.
3. See no. 255, n. 2.

4. The Latin position of the adjective indicates that it may apply to either noun. The word's significance looks to appointment of guardians by the State in the absence of tutors and curators appointed by testament or by statute.

5. The *exactio plebis*, usually assumed to be the poll or capitation tax (*capitatio*), on which see no. 67, n. 37.

6. Christianity.

150. LETTER OF VALENTINIAN I, VALENS, AND GRATIAN ON DONATIONS AND LEGACIES TO CLERGYMEN AT THEIR SOLICITATION, 370

(*CT* 16. 2. 20)

In time Constantine I's grant that the Church could receive legacies (no. 36) became abused, for even from Christian sources we learn that the Roman clergy visited wealthy women to solicit gifts from them for the Church.[1] This letter of Valentinian to Pope St Damasus I seeks to stop such practices, especially where widows and wards are the persons wheedled.

Emperors Valentinian, Valens, and Gratian Augusti to Damasus, bishop of the city of Rome.

Ecclesiastics or sons of ecclesiastics or those who wish themselves to be called by the name of Continents[2] should not enter the houses of widows and of wards, but they should be banished by the public courts, if henceforth these women's kindred by marriage or by blood shall have thought that these persons ought to be accused.

We also decree that the aforesaid men should be able to obtain nothing from any generosity or by a final decision of that woman to whom they shall have attached themselves privately under the pretext of religion, and that everything which shall have been left to anyone of these men by these women should be invalid to such an extent that not even through an intermediate person they should be able to take anything either by gift or by will. On the contrary, if perchance after our law's warning these women shall have thought that anything ought to be left to the said men either by gift or by final decision, the fisc should seize this. But if they should accept anything by will of these women, to whose succession or property they are aided by civil law or by an edict's[3] benefits, they should take it as blood-relatives.

Read in the churches at Rome on 30 July, Valentinian Augustus and Valens Augustus for the third time being consuls.

1. St Jerome (*Ep.* 52. 6 = *PL* 22. 532) apparently refers to this law, of which

he does not complain, but of whose harshness he grieves that priests and monks were deserving, when he says that its provisions are violated by ecclesiastical rapacity, which continues unchecked and by a fiction of trusteeship defies the statute.

St Ambrose (*Ep.* 18. 13 = *PL* 16. 1017) notices this legislation more briefly, but believes that the Church has no cause for complaint.

St Paul earlier condemned men "which creep into houses and lead captive silly women" (2 Tim. 3. 6).

Legacy-hunting, of course, antedates the Christianized Empire; indeed, Horace pretends that it is as old as Homer, for he invents an imaginary colloquy between Teiresias, the blind Theban seer, and Odysseus, the king of Ithaca, in Hades. Horace commences the conversation (Homer, *Od.* 11. 92–149), where Teiresias has terminated it, by having Odysseus ask Teiresias how he can repair his fortunes, since one requires riches to be respected, after he has heard that, when he shall have returned to Ithaca, he will discover that his property has been squandered by his wife's suitors. Thereupon Teiresias describes the details of the art (Horace, *Serm.* 2. 5). Equally egregious is Pliny's portrait of Regulus, the infamous informer, who increased his income derived through delation of rich Romans by his additional accomplishment as a hunter of legacies from those whom he had not denounced as traitors (*Ep.* 2. 20; cf. M. Pellison, *Roman Life in Pliny's Time* [Philadelphia, 1897], 131–5).

2. That is, monks, who were vowed to chastity, in contrast to the secular clergy, of whom some at this time had wives and children.

3. Perhaps is meant the praetor's edict, which served to aid, to supplement, to correct the civil law (*D* 1. 1. 7. 1). Emperor Hadrian consolidated (*c.* 129) the extant praetorian edicts into an imperial perpetual edict.

151. MANDATE OF VALENTINIAN I AND VALENS ON RECALL OF CURIALS FROM THE CLERICATE, 370

(*CT* 16. 2. 19)

The emperors establish a statute of limitations, whereby from the clerical life can be recalled such persons as are entitled by birth to serve as curials.

The same Augusti to Modestus, praetorian prefect.[1]

Whosoever born of the class of curials shall have entered the clergy and shall have begun to be demanded [2] because of prejudice of birth should be defended by the limit of a definite period of time, that, if he shall have fulfilled a decade of quiet life in the company of the clergy, he with his patrimony should be considered exempt in perpetuity; but if he shall have been recalled within the prescribed years by the municipal senate, he with his substance should be subject to the services of his municipality: this rule being observed, that those persons whom a decade protects should not at all be vexed by an unnecessary claim.

Given on 17 October at Hierapolis, Valentinian and Valens Augusti being consuls.

1. Of the East.
2. By his municipal senate for return to service therein.

152. LETTER OF VALENTINIAN I, VALENS, AND GRATIAN ON MEASURES AGAINST URSINIANS, 370-2

(CSEL 35. 52-3)

This order to Ampelius, urban prefect of Rome, extends the ban against Ursinus, the anti-pope, to eight of his associates and forbids them to live in or near Rome.

The same Augusti to Ampelius, urban prefect.

Rightly it has been granted to our Gentleness' feelings either by Divine Providence or by Nature's serenity that, since we contend with delinquents' wickedness by the severity of the laws and with the hope of future amendment, we should not wish the punishment of correction to be milder than the desert of the offences demands,[1] dearest and fondest cousin Ampelius.

Provoked recently by the disturbance of Ursinus,[2] favouring the harmony of the Christian people, providing also for the peace of the most sacred city,[3] we had ordained that meanwhile in one place within the Gauls,[4] so far as this matter is concerned, the disturber of the public tranquillity should be confined by law, obviously lest by the application of his precepts [5] the disturbance of discord should be scattered widely. But overcome [6] by the kindness of our nature, we have given to the aforementioned person an opportunity of withdrawing,[7] so that he should not attempt to enter the city of Rome or at least its suburban districts or to instil the infection of his own wickedness.

And this also we ordain concerning all the other associates of this error, namely Gaudentius, Ursus, Rufus, Auxano, Auxanius, Adiectus, Leontius, and Rufinus, that the same condition of correction should bind them, whom the imitation of wickedness embraces. But if anyone of the aforesaid with sacrilegious intention shall have thought that our Gentleness' ordinance can be transgressed, no longer as a Christian, but as a person debarred from consideration of laws and of religion, let him know the severity of public punishment.

Moreover we wish to notify your Severity also that to the most distinguished Maximin, vicar of the city of Rome, we have given an expedient order about this same observance, in order that the judicial prosecution, more disposed by ordinances toward the persons of the aforesaid men,[8] may be ended by those who preside over our Commonwealth[9] and that greater may be the moderation of the said persons, who should have perceived that the quality of their character and acts pertains to the imitation of many.[10]

And by the emperor's hand: Farewell, dearest and fondest Ampelius.

1. Cf. Cicero, *De Off.* 1. 25. 89.
2. The anti-pope was banished to Gaul before October 368.
3. Rome.
4. See no. 203, n. 4.
5. Or perhaps "the close conjunction of his character" (*applicatio morum*) with his followers in Rome, through his presence there in a centre, whence his views could be exported rather easily.
6. Literally "having been made smooth".
7. That is, instead of taking harsher measures against him Valentinian has sent Ursinus into exile.
8. As Christian clergymen they had been entitled to an early form of benefit of clergy, but their commanded withdrawal from Rome would end such exemption by the urban prefect, since they would be beyond his jurisdiction and in effect would be outlawed.
9. That is, in the capacity of judges. Possibly also their cases, if they should violate the imperial instruction, would not be heard by ordinary judges, but would be referred to the prefect and/or to the vicar.
10. The idea seems to be that they should have been both in character and in action an example for the laity.

153. LETTER OF VALENTINIAN I, VALENS, AND GRATIAN ON MEASURES AGAINST URSINIANS, 370-2

(*CSEL* 35. 53-4)

In large measure this mandate, addressed to Maximin, vicar of Rome, repeats the substance of the order sent to the prefect of Rome (no. 152).

153. MEASURES AGAINST URSINIANS, 370-2

The same Augusti to Maximin, vicar of the city of Rome.

By Divine Providence such appointment has been made for our Gentleness, that, even if the amendment of conduct may suffice in the life of men, nevertheless we should withdraw from the eagerness and the wish of being indulgent and never should desire the punishment of correction to be milder than delinquents' deserts demand.[1]

And from this it happens that on Ursinus,[2] whom we have ordered to dwell meanwhile in one place within the Gauls [3] for the sake of the Christian people's peace and the obedience owed to religion and to the laws, we gave judgement under this condition of movement, that he should not dare to travel to the city of Rome or to its suburban districts. And if he through unpleasant obstinacy shall have thought that our Gentleness' ordinance can be overstepped, most dear and most agreeable Maximin, the law's severity should pursue the said person, no longer as a Christian, since indeed his spirit's restlessness separates him from religion's fellowship, but as a factious person and a disturber of public peace and an enemy of laws and of religion.

Therefore your Sincerity, after the context of our command has been posted with due respect, should assemble the chief men [4] and the inhabitants of each and every city and quarter [4] over which you temporarily preside, by your own written order, that they may know thus that the limits of egression [5] have been prescribed by law for the aforesaid person along with the associates of his restlessness and error, Gaudentius, Ursus, Rufus, Auxano, Auxanius, Adiectus, Leontius, and Rufinus, and that authorization[6] has been approved, that they may understand that entrance from the forbidden places must be withheld. For thus we regulate our Gentleness' indulgence, lest, when an occasion has been presented by the nearness of the disturbers, we should challenge the religious people's zeal to perhaps some outburst.

1. Despite editorial emendation the Latin is tortuous. This translation provides a meaning in agreement with the thought in the preceding document (no. 152) before n. 1 in the text.
2. See no. 152, n. 2.
3. See no. 203, n. 4.
4. See no. 356, n. 5.
5. From Gaul toward Rome.
6. By this and the preceding letter (no. 152).

154. MANDATE OF VALENTINIAN I, VALENS, AND GRATIAN ON RELEASE OF CHRISTIAN PLAYERS FROM THE THEATRE, 371

(*CT* 15. 7. 1)

From this legislation and later allied documents it is clear that the law, as the Empire became more and more Christianized, did not countenance Christian actors and actresses, whom it encouraged to abandon the prosperities of vice [1] and in exchange to accept what to some must have seemed the misfortunes of virtue.[1] Indeed, the writings of the Church fathers, long before this mandate's date, are replete with denunciations of the theatre's immorality and urge Christians not only not to follow the theatrical profession,[2] but also not to assist by their presence at representations in either the theatre or the amphitheatre.[3]

Emperors Valentinian, Valens, and Gratian Augusti to Viventius, urban prefect.[4]

If actors and actresses, who in the extremity of life and under the compelling necessity of imminent death have hastened to the Highest God's sacraments, perchance shall have escaped death, they should not be recalled hereafter on any indictment to a theatrical spectacle.

Before all, however, we order by a diligent ordinance that attention and consideration should be exercised, so that only those really situated in extreme danger and demanding this [5] for their salvation should secure this benefit, if, however, the bishops approve.

And that this may be done faithfully,[6] their desire should be made known to the governors, if they are present, or to the curators of the several cities, that by inspectors who have been sent it may be investigated with careful inquiry whether or not necessity requires that extreme aid should be bestowed as a favour on these persons.

Given on 11 February at Trèves, Gratian Augustus for the second time and the most distinguished Probus being consuls.

1. The subtitle of one of the two best-known works of the Marquis de Sade 1740-1814): *Juliette ou les prospérités du vice* and *Justine ou les malheurs de la vertu*.

2. St Cyprian, writing to Eucratius, a brother bishop, about an actor, forbids the latter, if he continues in his vicious vocation, from communion. The saint allows the actor the excuses neither that he has retired from the stage, so long as he teaches the histrionic art to others, nor that he gives instruction because he needs money, so long as congregational funds can supply his necessities (*Ep.* 2 = *CSEL* 3. 2. 467-9).

3. Tertullian's treatise *De Spectaculis* is the earliest extant essay on this subject and is a mine whence much ore may be extracted.

4. Viventius rather was praetorian prefect of the Gauls (on which see no. 203, n. 4) at this time (see no. 149), when Ampelius was urban prefect of Rome (see no. 152).

5. That is, admission to the sacraments, of which, of course, baptism is the first.

6. That is, that this legislation should be enforced with due care.

155. MANDATE OF VALENTINIAN I, VALENS, AND GRATIAN ON CLERICAL EXEMPTION FROM SENATORIAL SERVICE, 371

(*CT* 16. 2. 21)

Herein the emperors exempt from service in municipal senates such persons as have entered the priesthood before their reign.[1]

The same Augusti to Ampelius, urban prefect.[2]
Those persons who continuously have allotted service to the Church should be considered exempt from municipal senates, if, however, it shall have been established that they have devoted themselves to the cult of our law[3] prior to the beginning of our reign.[2]

But all others who have associated themselves with ecclesiastics after this time should be recalled.

Given on 17 May, Gratian Augustus for the second time and Probus being consuls.

1. Since these emperors' reigns began at different times (Valentinian, 26 February 364; Valens, 28 March 364; Gratian, 25 August 367), it is not certain whether the retroactive force of this ordinance ascends as high as Valentinian's accession. Because it is addressed to the Roman prefect, it may have been operative only in the West, where Valentinian and Gratian ruled.

2. Of Rome.

3. *Lex* often denotes the Christian religion, a connotation developed from its use in late Latin for God's commandments.

156. MANDATE OF VALENTINIAN I AND VALENS ON MANICHAEISM, 372

(CT 16. 5. 3)

This ordinance prohibits assemblies of Manichaeans.[1]

Emperors Valentinian and Valens Augusti to Ampelius, urban prefect.[2]

Wherever an assembly of Manichaeans[1] or a crowd of this kind is found, after their teachers have been penalized by a severe punishment and also those persons who assemble have been segregated from the company of men as infamous and ignominious, their houses and habitations, in which the profane instruction is taught, should be appropriated undoubtedly to the fisc's resources.

Given on 2 March at Trèves, Modestus and Arinthaeus being consuls.

1. Although some scholars maintain that Manichaeism (so known from the name of its Persian prophet Mani, who commenced to preach it at Ctesiphon in 242) was not a heresy, but rather was a heathen and syncretistic system of dualistic character and was really a rival religion to Christianity, yet its characteristic doctrines had infiltrated into Christian theology to such a degree that early in the fourth century it could be considered a Christian heresy. Certainly at times its followers claimed that it was the only true Christianity. Thus it is said that Mani asserted either that the Comforter or Paraclete promised by Jesus (John 14. 16-17, 26, 15. 26, 16. 7-11) spoke through him or that he himself was that Comforter. And also Mani, it is reported, superscribed his epistles thus: "Mani, Apostle of Jesus Christ" (Augustine, *Cont. Faust. Man.* 13. 4 = *CSEL* 25. 381). On the other hand, Arius, the heresiarch, attempted to affix the tag of Manichaean taint upon his orthodox opponents by saying that he and his adherents, unlike Mani, did not conceive of the Son as of the same substance (ὁμοουσιότης) with the Father (*PG* 26. 709). That the compilers of *CT* located all but two imperial laws (of which this document is the earliest example extant) on Manichaeans under the fifth title "On Heretics" in the sixteenth book of the Code shows that the emperors held Manichaeism to be a heresy.

Diocletian (with his three imperial colleagues) denounced Manichaeism in a rescript to Julian, proconsul of Africa. Since this law obviously was not intended by its author, who initiated the last major persecution of the Church by the State (303-11), to affect the Church, it is not included in this collection, but it may be found in *Coll.* 15, 3, where it is said to have been extracted from *CG* 7 under the title on "Sorcerers and Manichaeans". The constitution well illustrates the typically conservative attitude of the Romans, particularly in the domain of law.

The rescript, dated 31 March, was sent from Alexandria, where Diocletian is known to have been in 297 and in 302, either of which years may have been the date. Most recently (1941) it has been edited in *FIRA* 2. 580–1, which dates it as ?320, an erroneous date borrowed from P. Krüger's edition, which in the apparatus prefers 302 to 297 but in the margin transposes 302 to 320 (*Collectio Librorum Juris Antejustiniani* [Berlin, 1890], 3. 188–9). Other editors generally favour 302 or 297: e.g. M. Hyamson, *Mosaicarum et Romanarum Legum Collectio* (Oxford, 1913), 132; B. Kübler, *Iurisprudentiae Anteiustinianae Reliquiae* [6] (Leipzig, 1927), 2. 2. 383. Some scholars suggest also 296 or 308: e.g. Kidd, 1. 505, n. 1.

2. Of Rome.

157. MANDATE OF VALENTINIAN I, VALENS, AND GRATIAN ON DONATIONS AND LEGACIES TO BISHOPS AND VIRGINS AT THEIR SOLICITATION, 372

(*CT* 16. 2. 22)

In the Theodosian Code this law stands next to no. 155 and, when judged from its opening and closing words, should supplement it. But, since it cannot be shown that women served as municipal senators, editors have conjectured that this statute must refer to no. 150, which in the Code is separated from no. 157 only by no. 155, on the grounds that in no. 150 bishops and virgins, as such, are not specified and that by no. 157 their inclusion is intended.

The same Augusti to Paulinus, governor of New Epirus.

The regulation of the preceding resolution [1] also should be valid and should be extended with respect to the persons of bishops and of virgins and with respect to other women whose inclusion has been made in the preceding statute.

Given on 1 December at Trèves, Modestus and Arinthaeus being consuls.

1. Either no. 150 or no. 155.

158. MANDATE OF VALENTINIAN I AND VALENS ON REBAPTISM, 373
(CT 16. 6. 1)

Various interpretations of this law, part of which is repeated in *CI* 1. 6. 1, may be made. It may show simply the influence of ecclesiastical advisers upon Emperor Valentinian and may call for the deposition of bishops who permit rebaptism or—more likely—it may rescind in effect Julian's rescript favouring Donatists (no. 122), for it is addressed to Africa, where Donatism was still rampant, and may deprive Donatist bishops of the civil advantages associated with the episcopate. At any rate the law seems not to have achieved strict application, since later emperors enacted severer regulations against rebaptism.

Emperors Valentinian and Valens Augusti to Julian, proconsul of Africa.

We believe to be unworthy of the priesthood [1] a bishop who shall have repeated the sanctity of baptism by illicit use [2] and contrary to the ordinances of all shall have defiled this grace [3] by repetition.[4]

Given on 20 February at Trèves, Valentinian Augustus and Valens Augustus for the fourth time being consuls.

1. Or possibly the "episcopate", for *sacerdotium* (ἱερωσύνη) may be either. So in modern Roman canon law (*Corpus Iuris Canonici*) "the term *priesthood* includes the episcopate as well as the simple priesthood" (T. L. Bouscaren and A. C. Ellis, *Canon Law: A Text and Commentary* [2] [Milwaukee, 1953], 415). See no. 16, n. 4, for the concrete usage. A bishop, of course, possesses the plenitude of the priesthood.

2. Justinian ends his quotation here and then adds to it the first sentence of no. 163, which see for a late Greek paraphrase of each.

3. Theologically speaking, baptism is a sacrament of grace.

4. The *Constitutiones Apostolorum* command (8. 47. 47) deposition of bishops or presbyters either baptizing those who have had true baptism or not baptizing those who have been polluted by the ungodly. Presumably in the first case the Trinitarian formula (Matt. 28. 19) is used, while in the second case it is not employed by heretics or schismatics. It also is ordered (8. 47. 46) for bishops or presbyters or deacons who receive heretical baptism and is confirmed by reference to 2 Cor. 6. 15.

159. LETTER OF VALENTINIAN I, VALENS, AND GRATIAN ON CONSUBSTANTIALITY, 375

(Theodoret, *HE* 4. 8)

Valentinian I in the name of his two colleagues addresses to bishops in Asia Minor a letter to which he suppends his summary of the profession of faith as adopted by an episcopal synod of western Illyricum. He orders this doctrine to be preached as an antidote to the Arianism in Asia Minor and he forbids persecution of orthodox Christians.

This letter is almost unique among imperial constitutions concerning religion, for it reveals not only divergence between divine and imperial interests but also internal discord between Valentinian, a Catholic and tolerant ruler, and Valens, an Arian and intolerant sovereign. Valentinian's allusions to God's kingship suggest an appeal from Valens, the earthly king, to the celestial court and invite the eastern Arians to eschew Valens' Arianizing attitude. Valentinian's death in this year perhaps prevented a religious conflict with Valens or an alteration in his toleration toward Arianism.

Cassiodorus (*HE* 7. 9. 1–6, 8–11) in Latin and Nicephorus (*HE* 11. 30) in Greek preserve this letter.

Emperors, Greatest, Ever-August, Victors, Augusti Valentinian and Valens and Gratian to bishops of the dioceses of Asia, Phrygia, Carophrygia, Pactiana, greeting in the Lord.[1]

When so large a synod had been convened in Illyricum and much [2] investigation concerning the saving Word [3] had been made, the thrice most blessed [4] bishops declared the Trinity of Father and of Son and of Holy Spirit to be consubstantial. And, in not at all avoiding the public duties imposed on them by law, they worship the Great King's [5] religion.[6] Our Mightiness [7] has ordained that this religion should be preached, in such a way, however, that persons may not say: "We have come [8] to the religion of the emperor who rules this earth,[9] yet not being constant to him who has given us commands concerning salvation." For, as [10] the Gospel of our Christ,[11] which indeed has this judgement, says, "Render unto Caesar the things which are Caesar's and unto God the things which are God's".[12]

What [13] say you, bishops and protectors of the saving Word? [3] If your profession is thus, do you thus, of course,[14] loving one another,[15] cease from abusing the emperor's authority and do not persecute those who serve God faithfully,[16] by whose prayers both wars are ended on earth and attacks of apostate angels [17] are averted.[18] Through prayerful supplication they curb [19] all destructive demons and they are accustomed [20] to pay the taxes according to the laws and they gainsay not the ruler's power,[21] but they sincerely observe the commandment [22] of God,[23] the King above, and they submit to our laws. But you have been proved [24] to be disobedient. We have been subject to him who is the First and the Last,[25] but you have rendered account to yourselves. We, however, wishing [26] ourselves to be free from your guilt—even as Pilate [27] in the examination of Christ who lives in us,[28] when he did not wish to kill him and when he was exhorted about his punishment,[29] after having turned toward the quarters of the East [30] and after demanding water for the hands,[31] washed his hands, saying, "I am innocent of the blood of this just person" [32]—so also our Majesty continually has commanded that persons neither should persecute nor should overwhelm nor should envy the ones working in Christ's [33] field nor should expel the Great King's [5] stewards, lest in our reign you should seem to increase in power today and afterward to suffer the things of the covenant of him who had been summoned, as in the case of the blood of Zacharias.[34] But they with him after the advent of our King from above,[35] Jesus Christ, have been destroyed, having been delivered to the penalty of death [36] along with the destructive demon who co-operated with them.[37]

This we have ordained in the presence of Amigetius and Ciceronius and Damasus and Lampon and Brentesius,[38] who were auditors.[39] And we have sent to you the very enactments, that you may know the matters enacted in the virtuous [40] synod.[41]

We confess, following the great and orthodox synod, that the Son is consubstantial with the Father. And we do not thus understand the consubstantiality as certain ones formerly expounded, when they subscribed not truly,[42] and as other ones now, who call those persons fathers,[43] when they reject the force of the word and follow the persons who have written that similarity is signified by consubstantiality, because the Son is like to none of the rest of the creatures made by him, but is made like to the Father alone. For they who expound these things dogmatize impiously that God's Son is a special creature.[44]

But [45] we think, like also the synods recently both in Rome and in Gaul,[46] that the Father's and the Son's and the Holy Spirit's substance [47] is one and the same, in three Persons, that is, in three perfect hypostases.[47]

We confess [48] according to the exposition at Nicaea [49] that God's consubstantial Son was incarnate from the Holy Virgin Mary and dwelt among men [50] and completed all the dispensation concerning us (in birth and suffering and resurrection and ascension into the heavens) and that he shall come again, giving to us the divine similarity from himself,[51] being flesh-bearing God and God-bearing man.

And [45] we anathematize the persons thinking things contrary to the aforesaid things [52] and the persons who do not anathematize truly him [53] who said that, before he had been begotten, the Son was not, but wrote that, before he had been begotten in actuality, he was in potentiality in the Father.[54] For this is also so in the case of all creatures which not always are with God;[55] but the Son is always with the Father, since he has been begotten by an eternal begetting.[56]

1. In this superscription, to which Cassiodorus alone prefixes a caption ("Valentinian's and Valens' edict about the consubstantial Trinity"), Cassiodorus substitutes "Pious" for *Ever-August* and Nicephorus omits *and Valens*.
2. Cassiodorus turns this into "subtly".
3. That is, Christ who saves man. In patristic Greek the Logos (the Word) is identified often with the person of Christ.

Arianism in its attempt to rationalize the Trinity turned its attention principally to the nature of the Son and to the relation between the Father and the Son.

4. Cassiodorus uses the positive degree.
5. A reminiscence of Matt. 5. 35.
6. Literally "they worship the worship"—an instance of *figura etymologica*. But Cassiodorus thus translates this sentence: "And not all avoiding this, they employ themselves according to the services of the Great King's religion".
7. Cassiodorus inserts "therefore also".
8. Cassiodorus has "We follow".
9. Cassiodorus substitutes "fatherland".
10. Cassiodorus omits the word and the relative clause next following.
11. Nicephorus substitutes "God".
12. Matt. 22. 21; Mark 12. 17; Luke 20. 25.
13. Cassiodorus inserts "therefore".
14. Cassiodorus omits *thus, of course*.
15. Probably based on Rom 13. 8 and 1 Thess. 4. 9. Cf. also John 13. 34, 15. 12, 17; 1 John 3. 11-24, 4. 7-21, 5. 1-3.
16. That is, the Arians should not oppress the orthodox adherents of the Nicene Creed.

Themistius Euphrades, the distinguished pagan philosopher, rhetorician, and urban prefect of Constantinople in 384, earlier addressed Valens at Antioch on behalf of religious liberty, when Valens as an Arian was persecuting orthodox Christians. The philosopher told the emperor that difference in doctrine among Christians was no matter for marvel and was quite inconsiderable in comparison with the confused plethora of pagan religious opinions, amounting to more than three hundred, forasmuch as the Deity desires to be glorified in diverse modes and is the more respected the less anyone knows about him. This appeal disposed Valens to become more humane and to inflict the milder punishment of exile for the severer penalty of death (Socrates, *HE* 4. 32; Sozomen, *HE* 6. 36 *ad fin.*; Cassiodorus, *HE* 8. 12).

17. Cassiodorus has "of angels retreating from God".
18. Cf. Eph. 6. 11-18, esp. 11, 12, 18.
19. Cassiodorus has "confound"; Nicephorus has "avert eagerly".
20. Cassiodorus has a litotes: "refuse not".
21. Cf. Rom. 13. 1-7; Titus 3. 1; 1 Pet. 2. 13, 17.

This may be, but the New Testament also contains St John's Apocalypse, which evinces (chapters 17-18) uncompromising hostility toward the Roman Empire. The reconciliation of these two apostolic attitudes is referred rather to the theologians' than to the historians' province.

22. Plural in Cassiodorus.
23. Nicephorus omits this word; Cassiodorus reads "of the supernal God" and omits the appositional words.
24. Present tense in Cassiodorus.
25. Literally "to the Alpha as far as the Omega"—a reminiscence of the characterization of God in Rev. 1. 8, 11; 21. 6; 22. 13. Cassiodorus has *primus et novissimus*.
26. Cassiodorus reads "And so we wish".
27. Procurator of Judaea, a minor province. As its governor (*praeses*), Pontius Pilate was invested with power to inflict capital punishment (*ius gladii*) during his tenure (26-36). The Ethiopian Church has canonized both him and his wife, probably because the former had declared his innocence of Jesus' death (Matt. 27. 24) and the latter had demanded vainly from her husband the Saviour's life (Matt. 27. 19).
28. With the accessory idea of participating in the government—a circumlocutory way of claiming that the Empire is conducted on Christian principles. But the clause, in which Cassiodorus inserts "our" before *Christ*, may be merely reminiscent of Gal. 2. 20.
29. The text is corrupt and the clause is not given by Cassiodorus. The best emendation gives approximately this translation. The unemended Greek seems to mean "and when he [Christ] had been summoned to court for suffering".
30. This detail is recorded in the apocryphal *Gospel of Nicodemus* or *Acts of Pilate*, 9. 4, translated by M. R. James, *The Apocryphal New Testament* (Oxford, 1924), 103.
31. Cassiodorus omits the phrase.
32. Matt. 27. 24. For the whole interposition see Matt. 27. 11-25; Mark 15. 1-15; Luke 23. 1-7, 12-25; John 18. 28-19. 16. But only Matthew mentions the hand-washing.
33. Cassiodorus has "the Lord's" adjectivally for this noun.
34. The phrasing from *afterward* to *summoned* has troubled the Latin translator of Nicephorus and Cassiodorus' Latin ("to subject the testament to the Lord's passion") also is of little aid. Probably the passage is corrupt. *Covenant* appears to mean New Testament and *him . . . summoned* seems to signify Christ.

Since it is not quite clear who is this Zacharias, various theories have been proposed. (1) Some suppose that Zechariah the prophet, son of Berechiah and grandson of Iddo (Zech. 1. 1; cf. Ezra 6. 14) is meant. But there is no tradition about his death. (2) Others identify him with the Zacharias who was the father of St John the Baptist (Luke 1. 5–25, 39–45, 57–66), supposing him to be the Zacharias slain "between the temple [i.e. shrine] and the altar" (Matt. 23. 35, where he is called the son of Barachias, and Luke 11. 51, where his paternity is not mentioned). R. Graves appears to be the most recent to accept this identification in a remarkable reconstruction of Zacharias' murder in his *King Jesus* (New York, 1946), 107–26, which pages constitute a chapter called "The Blood of Zacharias" (the evangelists' and the emperors' phrase) and are concocted from St Epiphanius' report of the contents of a heretical book (*The Descent of Mary*), although that egregious heresy-hunter explains that the heretics erred both in asserting that Zacharias was killed and in antedating his death before the Baptist's birth (*Haer*. 26. 12). (3) But it seems likely that Jesus in linking Zacharias with Abel ("from the blood of righteous [St Luke omits the adjective] Abel unto the blood of Zacharias") includes all the righteous recorded as slain in the Old Testament, wherein Abel (Gen. 4. 1–8) and Zacharias (2 Chron. 24. 20–2) represent the beginning and the ending of the Hebrew Scriptures, of which Genesis and 2 Chronicles usually are the first and the last books. That the Zacharias of 2 Chronicles is the son of Jehoiada and the Zacharias of Matthew is the son of Barachias need create no special difficulty. Either Jesus or St Matthew or an editor of Matthew may have confused the priest of 2 Chronicles with the prophet of Zechariah, or Jehoiada may have had the surname of Barachias, or Jehoiada may have been his grandfather and Barachias (not otherwise mentioned) may have been his father, just as Zechariah the prophet is "Zechariah, the son of Berechiah, the son of Iddo" (Zech. 1. 1) and "Zechariah, the son of Iddo" (Ezra 6. 14). (4) Still others offer the Zacharias, son of Baris (*al*. Baruch and Bariscaeus), whom Zealots murdered in the Temple in Jerusalem after he had been acquitted on a false accusation of treasonable communications with Vespasian, then commanding the Romans in the Jewish War in 68 (Josephus, *Bell. Iud*. 4. 5. 4. 334–44). But this theory rests on a rather remote resemblance of names, since Baris and Baruch and Bariscaeus are quite different from Barachias and Berechiah, and, moreover, it is an anachronism for Jesus to antedate, as an accomplished fact and not as a prophecy, an event which occurred about forty years after his mention of it.

The reference appears to come from an apocryphal book, which probably was entitled the *Wisdom of God* (the words which introduce Luke 11. 49), on which consult C. C. Torrey, *The Apocryphal Literature* (New Haven, 1945), 18.

The idea seems to be that the emperors ban persecution to prevent their subjects from becoming blood-guilty and from suffering God's wrath, which will require punishment for such blood-guilt (according to the evangelists).

35. Cassiodorus reads "of our Supernal King".
36. Cassiodorus has briefly "to death".
37. *They* and *them* must refer to the persecutors; but who is *him*, if not Valens, is unclear. This sentence may be an interpolation inserted by a scribe

who knew that Valens had been a cruelly persecuting Arian and who here foreshadowed Valens' fate. The demon may have been Asmodeus, who was noted for his destructiveness (Tobit 3. 8, 17) and whom some scholars have identified with Abaddon (Rev. 9. 11). For the idea see 2 Thess. 2. 3–12.

38. In Cassiodorus the variants for these names are "Megetius", "Damascus", "Brintisius"; Nicephorus gives "Amegetius" and "Dialampon".

39. That is, they heard the document read before signature.

40. Cassiodorus has "most excellent" for this adjective.

41. The brief interpolations between the imperial letter and the imperial summary are:

(1) Theodoret: "With this letter he, having shown these in summary, conjoined also the synod's dogmas."

(2) Cassiodorus: "To this letter, therefore, he subjoined also the council's dogmas, having these summarily."

(3) Nicephorus: "And to the letter he also joined them, decreeing in summary these dogmas."

Theodoret (*HE* 4. 9), Cassiodorus (*HE* 7. 10), Nicephorus (*HE* 11. 30) preserve the synodal letter.

42. It is not known to what council the emperor refers, perhaps Antioch (341), Ancyra (358), Sirmium (358), Rimini (359), Seleucia (359), Lampsacus (364), Antioch in Caria (367), where semi-Arian formularies were adopted.

43. That is, the semi-Arian party so called its earlier exponents, such as Basil, bishop of Ancyra (336–63), their chief theologian.

44. The speciality seems to consist in his superiority over other creatures.

45. Cassiodorus reads "Therefore".

46. Late in 371 a council of Italian and Gallic bishops assembled in Rome under the presidency of Pope St Damasus I (usually called the Second Damasine Synod) and addressed a synodical letter to the Illyrian bishops against Arianism, which had active adherents in that area (Theodoret, *HE* 2. 22).

47. Here again are οὐσία and ὑπόστασις, on which see no. 67, n. 17.

48. Cassiodorus inserts "moreover".

49. At the First General Council in 325. Cassiodorus uses the adjective for the phrase.

50. The expression is reminiscent of John 1. 14.

51. Here Nicephorus has an anti-Nestorian interpolation "according to each one's life in the day of judgement, being seen in flesh and manifesting his divine power".

52. Nicephorus omits the phrase.

53. Any Arian is meant.

54. The distinction between actuality (ἐνέργεια) and potentiality (δύναμις) is as old as Aristotle (*Metaph.* 8. 1–9 = 1045B–51A).

55. For *with God* Cassiodorus has "just as God [exists]".

56. The etymological figure is in the Greek.

160. MANDATE OF VALENS, GRATIAN, AND VALENTINIAN II ON CONFISCATION OF HERETICS' CHURCHES, 376 or 380

(CT 16. 5. 4)

By this statute [1] are confiscated all sites used for heretical worship.

Emperors Valens, Gratian, Valentinian Augusti to Hesperius, praetorian prefect.[2]

Some time ago on behalf of the religion of Catholic sanctity, that unlawful use of heretical assembly might cease, we ordered [3] to be confiscated all places in which altars under the false cover of religion were located, whether the meetings were conducted in towns or in rural districts outside the churches, where our peace prevails.

And whether through governors' dissimulation or through profane persons' depravity this shall have occurred, the same destruction shall be in each case.

Given on 22 April at Trèves, Valens Augustus for the fifth time and Valentinian Augustus being consuls.

1. In Palanque, 1. 361, n. 1, it is contended that this law, enacted (like that in no. 166) supposedly under the influence of St Ambrose, bishop of Milan, should be postdated to 380.
2. Of Italy; but Mommsen suggests that he was proconsul of Africa.
3. This ordinance is not extant.

161. LETTER OF VALENS, GRATIAN, AND VALENTINIAN II ON EPISCOPAL JURISDICTION IN ECCLESIASTICAL INTERESTS, 376

(CT 16. 2. 23)

Since it naturally happened that the introduction of the episcopal court with final jurisdiction in civil cases and the exemption of bishops from regular criminal procedure caused some confusion and perhaps even abuse in the administration of justice, Gratian, the real author of this ordinance, here recognizes the right of ecclesiastical courts to try cases pertaining to the Church's internal interests, but reserves for secular tribunals cases of a criminal character.

162. CLERICAL EXEMPTION FROM PUBLIC DUTIES, 377

Emperors Valens, Gratian, and Valentinian Augusti to Artemius, Eurydicus, Appius, Gerasimus, and all other bishops.[1]

The same custom which exists in civil cases must be observed in ecclesiastical suits: so that, if there are any matters pertaining to observance of religion from certain dissensions and minor delicts,[2] these should be heard in their own places and by their own diocese's synods—those excepted which criminal action determines must be heard by ordinary and extraordinary judges[3] or by illustrious authorities.[4]

Given on 17 May at Trèves, Valens Augustus for the fifth time and Valentinian Augustus for the first time being consuls.

Interpretation: As often as among clergymen shall have arisen contention from any matter pertaining to religion, let this be observed particularly: that, when the diocesan priests have been convoked by a bishop, the matters which shall have come into contention should be terminated by a trial. To be sure, if anything criminal is alleged, let it be brought to the notice of a judge in the community in which the action is pleaded, that what is proved to have been committed criminally should be punished by his sentence.

1. Of the bishops named only the identification of Artemius is probable. He seems to have been bishop of Embrun. Perhaps the others were Gallican—or at least western—prelates, inasmuch as Gratian (with Valentinian) ruled the West.

2. Some commentators believe that this ordinance was directed against Priscillians, who fostered in Gaul a Gnostic heresy.

3. An ordinary judge (*iudex ordinarius*) usually was a provincial governor, while an extraordinary judge (*iudex extraordinarius*) was usually either a municipal magistrate or an official who had jurisdiction in military and/or fiscal matters.

4. The phrase is *inlustres potestates* and probably refers to praetorian prefects and urban prefects, who had both original and appellate jurisdiction.

162. MANDATE OF VALENS, GRATIAN, AND VALENTINIAN II ON CLERICAL EXEMPTION FROM PUBLIC DUTIES, 377

(*CT* 16. 2. 24)

By this ordinance (adapted in *CI* 1. 3. 6) various orders of the clergy are exempted from public services of a personal character.

The same Augusti to Catafronius.[1]

We order priests, deacons, subdeacons, and exorcists and lectors, also porters, and likewise all who are first in rank [2] to be exempt from public services of a personal character.

Given on 5 March, Gratian Augustus for the fourth time and the most distinguished[3] Merobaudes being consuls.

1. Perhaps he was vicar of Italy. Justinian spells his name as Cataphronius.
2. The word for *first in rank* is *primi* and should include bishops, who—as one would expect—should have been written first. Justinian omits *and likewise . . . rank* and thereby excludes bishops.
3. Justinian omits the superlative adjective.

163. MANDATE OF VALENS, GRATIAN, AND VALENTINIAN II ON REBAPTISM, 377

(CT 16. 6. 2)

This constitution, forbidding iteration of baptism, is more stringent than that issued four years earlier (no. 158), because it includes penalties for violation.

Justinian uses its first sentence as the last sentence in his repetition of this law (*CI* 1. 6. 1).

Emperors Valens, Gratian, and Valentinian Augusti to Florian, vicar of Asia.[1]

We condemn the error of those who, trampling upon the apostles' precepts, do not purify but defile by another baptism again persons who have received the sacraments of the Christian name, thus polluting them in the name of baptism.[2]

Therefore your Authority shall order them to desist from miserable errors, when the churches which they retain against the faith [3] have been restored to the Catholic Church.

Surely must be followed the instructions of those who have approved the apostolic faith without baptism's repetition.[4] For we wish that nought else be taught than what the Gospels' [5] and the apostles' faith and tradition have preserved uncorrupted, just as have been decreed by the divine law [6] of our progenitors, Constantine, Constantius, Valentinian.

But very many persons, expelled from churches, nevertheless rage with hidden fury, frequenting illicitly the places of great houses or of estates; and these places the fiscal confiscation shall seize, if they shall have provided secret places for sinful doctrine, that our sanction may abate nothing from that constitution which had been established in a command [6] given some time ago to Nitentius.[7] But if they love their error, let them—alone, however—cherish the virus of an impious doctrine to their hurt and in domestic secrecy.

Given on 17 October at Constantinople, Gratian Augustus for the fourth time and Merobaudes being consuls.

1. The manuscripts of *CT* read "Flavian, vicar of Africa"; those of *CI* have what is translated in the text. The former lection could be correct if the order did not emanate from Constantinople, for at that time Africa was administered from the West and epigraphical evidence shows that Flavian then was vicar of Africa.

2. This sentence and that of no. 158 are combined by Justinian to make *CI* 1. 6. 1, which he dates then in the latter year.

Pitra gives (2. 513) a late Greek paraphrase for no. 158 and this much of no. 163: "If any bishop rebaptizes a second time a person already baptized, he should be unworthy of the priesthood and should be expelled from it, for they should be condemned, whoever trampling upon the holy apostles' teachings lay claim to the Christians' name." See no. 158, n. 4.

3. Perhaps not the Catholic faith, but good faith, is meant.

4. Literally "change" or "intermutation".

5. "Gospellers' " or "evangelists' " is more symmetrical—and the omission of one Latin letter would give such a translation.

6. Not extant, but probably aimed primarily at Donatists.

7. He perhaps is identical with a tribune and notary known to have flourished *c*. 380. Otherwise he is unknown.

164. RESCRIPT OF GRATIAN AND VALENTINIAN II ON PAPAL JURISDICTION, 378 or 379

(*CSEL* 35. 54–8)

This constitution, though addressed to Aquiline, vicar of Rome, really is a reply to a petition forwarded by him from a council held in Rome under Pope St Damasus I in 378. The petition[1] falls into two parts: (1) that the bishop of Rome, if summoned before secular courts,[2] should be permitted to plead either before his own council or in the emperor's presence; (2) that the bishop of Rome should have his ecclesiastical jurisdiction over recalcitrant bishops confirmed[3]—so that secular judges might not try bishops—by being allowed to compel the appearance of such prelates, if living in Italy, in Rome or, if extra-peninsular, before their local metropolitans; that, if metropolitans themselves, they should appear either in Rome or before judges named by the Roman bishop; and that any bishop who had been condemned and then complained of judicial prejudice should appeal his case either to the bishop of Rome or to a synod of at least fifteen neighbouring bishops.

Gratian refused the first request by ignoring it—if the rescript is complete—though he tempered his rejection by ruling that the evidence of persons known to be of dubious morality or to be merely calumniators of the pope should be inadmissible. By granting the second request Gratian made the pope the normal court of first instance for western metropolitans and a court of appeal, apparently final, for western bishops subject to such metropolitans. Also, in effect, by not defining the law which the pope was to administer, Gratian gave to the pope the power to make his own law—a power quickly recognized by the Papacy, which soon regarded its papal decretals as having a force equivalent to that of conciliar canons in matters of judicial process. Herein lies the significance of this document, for thus Gratian assisted the growth of papal authority, although his acquiescence should not be interpreted as the State's recognition of inherent spiritual rights resident in the Papacy.

On rebaptizers.
Gratian and Valentinian Augusti to Aquiline, vicar.
Either the limit of time or the declaration of obstinate disobedience to a judicial order or the examination held in the presence of litigants confirms the verdicts of the customary judges and this well-balanced authority [4] does not become very frightened that it may be overthrown and eradicated either by the rather powerful or by the shameless: what patience, pray, could be able to endure that our commands have been disregarded by your negligence? And indeed, while you disdain, you excite it, so that it assumes the desperate tones of long forbearance and by fear it compels duty to be recognized.

Is what the madness of Ursinus [5] has imprinted still more vivid than what our Serenity has persuaded by mild edicts, namely that all who by polluted religion should try to hold impious gatherings should be expelled even to the hundredth milestone from the city,[6] where the obstinate madness, deprived of followers, might descend into only disaster for him who alone was in error and that they, when condemned by the judgement of rightly judging bishops, either should not have a return to the churches which they had defiled or in vain with shameless stubbornness should petition from us a renewal of the trial? Let your praiseworthy and respected Sincerity review such letters [7] as our Clemency has sent to the most distinguished Simplicius, formerly vicar, and cease to expect a repetition of the mandate, because our Clemency's propriety should disdain to repeat an instruction.

Gaul, indeed, confines Ursinus and, lest he may carry some disturbing movements into effect, his retreat at Köln [8] restrains him; but, nevertheless, we have heard that he himself is annoying through his attackers more often than that he is sorrowing at this—namely, that

164. PAPAL JURISDICTION, 378 OR 379

more frequently he is rebuffed.[9] A remote corner of Spain by the trench [10] of condemnation encloses Hisac,[11] who will not have good regard for his head [12] if in his madness he shall have excited any disorders. The bishop of Parma,[13] more pernicious on this account, because nearest to the celebrated city,[14] both, as a neighbour, rouses a multitude of inexperienced persons and disturbs the church, whence he has been removed by the sentence of the holy heads, obviously awaiting the vapid glory of a severer verdict; and if your predecessor [15] had had any devoted energy, he would have been bound to banish this person far beyond the boundaries. And Florentius of Pozzuoli, after he accepted condemnation, when convicted by a correct verdict, and received a reply worthy of his shameful offence, after he tried to disturb our Grace, again attempts to corrupt the church, from which he had been extruded fifteen years ago, strives to form illegal congregations, and by the persuasion of an abandoned mind depraves a multitude lacking sense, obviously relying on the carelessness of our governors, who surrender imperial instructions to private popularity and patiently permit religion, which we rightly reverence, to be disturbed, because perhaps they themselves neglect it. Also Claudian,[16] summoned by these persons, who contrary to divine commands repeat the initiations of religion,[17] by these persons, I say, whom we have ordered to be expelled, just as if he had undertaken too little wickedness if he should have remained in Africa, is said to have brought himself to Rome and, as a false teacher, strives either to defile by an erroneous religious rite [18] persons hitherto having no connection with it or to recorrupt by greater outrage persons already initiated in it, since its repetition does not enhance but subverts the teaching of the most holy religion.[17] And we, pursuing this Claudian [16] with a punishment different from that which he has deserved, have ordered him, with a severity aroused no further than this, only to return to his fatherland. But even now he is said to stay and, soliciting the inexperienced and seeking names with vain recompense, he damns the souls of redeemed bodies.

As a result, those persecutors of the most holy see,[19] having feared not to disturb by vilest calumnies Damasus the bishop, a man proved of saintliest mind, not only by God's divine will but also by judges' examination—as also was acknowledged by our deified [20] father Valentinian [21]—after they have had no expectation of being able to be punished,[22] disturb the populace, for whom he is a surety to the Divinity.[23]

But thus far shall have existed the lazy carelessness of the magistrates. Nor is it necessary to warn to what extent a despised ordinance can proceed.[24] Thus far, I say, shall have existed the supine sloth of the apparitors:[25] henceforth, unless all, as the totality of our ordinance embraces name by name, even those persons whom the consensus of the holy council of bishops [26] has shown as causing disturbances of this character, you shall have driven beyond the hundredth milestone from the city and shall have ordered them to be banished from those communities whose people or churches they vex either by themselves or by a rabble like themselves, you shall incur besides the damage to your reputation, of which the loss is not light among good persons, the punishment for having disregarded an ordinance.

Moreover we will that whoever shall have been condemned by Damasus' judgement—which he shall have given with a council [27] of five or seven bishops, or by the judgement and the council [27] of those [28] who are Catholics—if he shall have wished unjustly to retain his church or through contumacy not to attend, when summoned, an episcopal trial, either should be remitted by the illustrious praetorian prefects of Gaul and of Italy, by the application of authority, to the episcopal judgement or, when summoned by the proconsuls or the vicars, should come under prosecution to the city of Rome; or, if in more distant districts [29] such insubordination of anyone shall have arisen, the whole pleading of the said case should be brought to the investigation of the metropolitan [30] in the same province of the bishop,[31] or, if he himself is a metropolitan, he necessarily should hasten without delay [32] to Rome or to those judges whom the Roman bishop shall have appointed, so that, however, whoever have been deposed should be kept only from the territory of that city in which they have been bishops. For we restrain more mildly those who have deserved serious penalties and we punish sacrilegious pertinacity more lightly than they deserve. But if the unfairness or the favour either of a metropolitan bishop or of any other bishop should be suspected, it may be lawful for the arraigned to appeal to the Roman bishop or to a council of fifteen neighbouring bishops, provided that, after the investigation has been held, what has been determined should not be recanvassed.[33] But now this following practice, which natural justice has implanted in our hearts both in affairs of minor matters and in pleading of unimportant cases,[34] we wish much more earnestly to gain validity in cases involving the highest justice: that it may not be easy for anyone soever, corrupted by notorious depravity of morals or branded by infamous conviction for malicious prosecution,[35] to assume the role of accuser or to proffer evidence of testimony for accusation against a bishop.[36]

1. Preserved in *PL* 13. 575–84.
2. Both Ursinus (*c.* 370) and Isaac (*c.* 375) had instituted suits in secular courts against Damasus, who was acquitted; hence the purpose of this part of the petition. Cf. *infra* nn. 5 and 15.

164. PAPAL JURISDICTION, 378 OR 379   349

3. Valentinian I's confirmatory constitution (367–72) is not extant.

The recalcitrance in this instance consisted in the persistence of some bishops in requiring rebaptism during the Donatist schism (cf. *infra* nn. 20–2).

4. That is, judicial authority does not fear that it can be overturned.

5. The exiled anti-pope.

6. Rome is meant. Earlier mandates set the ban at twenty miles (nos. 142 and 143), but the limit, which is repeated lower in the script, may have been increased.

7. Perhaps *CT* 9. 29. 1 (23 March 374) refers to this.

8. Agrippina, more fully Colonia Agrippina, originally Oppidum Ubiorum, but renamed in 51 to honour the birth there of Agrippina the Younger (15–59), who was the great-granddaughter of Augustus (27 B.C.–A.D. 14), the granddaughter of the second wife of Tiberius (14–37), the sister of Caligula (37–41), the niece and the fourth wife of Claudius (41–54), and the mother of Nero (54–68).

9. Various conjectures have been made for what obviously is a corruption in the text here. The idea seems to be that Ursinus takes more pleasure in continuing his attacks on Damasus at long distance than finds grief in his being counter-attacked and remaining in exile.

10. In view of the subject and the predicate perhaps *titulo* is from *titulum* (protective trench before a gate of a camp) rather than from *titulus* (formal notice).

11. Or Isaac, a converted Jew who, instigated by Ursinus, preferred against Damasus charges of which the pope was cleared and for which Isaac was exiled into Spain. Some scholars suppose that Isaac was Ambrosiaster, the name given to the author of the earliest extant commentary on all the Pauline epistles and in several critics' opinion the best work on this subject written before the sixteenth century.

12. Probably literally here (*caput*) and not referring to his status, which *caput* can mean, for, as an exile, he had nothing more than his life to lose.

13. Apparently a certain Urban, who is the first bishop of Parma known to us.

14. Rome. The Latin is *magis proximus* (more nearest). The bishop of Parma was nearer to Rome than either Ursinus in Gaul or Isaac in Spain.

15. Simplicius is meant.

16. The Donatist bishop at Rome—though of African origin—whose adherents, called Claudians, were a sect within the larger body of schismatic Donatists.

17. Save in isolated instances in Christian history baptism has been a sacrament universally recognized as administered only once, unless there has been an obvious invalidity in its matter and/or form, no matter whether it has been performed by heretics or schismatics or orthodox. But in the Donatist schism rebaptism generally was required by both sides.

18. Literally "mystery" (see no. 75, n. 42); here, however, the sacrament of baptism.

19. Rome is thus characterized.
20. See no. 127, n. 7.
21. At least evident in this emperor's exiling of Ursinus early in the pontificate of Damasus.
22. The idea seems to be that the recalcitrant bishops, not having been punished by civil authorities, took courage from this laxity and continued their opposition.
23. That is, Damasus—in a sense—stands before God as the people's representative.
24. Gratian implies as an addition "without imperial punishment of those who neglect to enforce it".
25. *Apparitores* is the generic name for judicial assistants; but here it may mean more than these: officialdom generally, unless Gratian is thinking of the more mechanical aspects of justice and hits at the lower-echelon group, which should show some activity in setting in motion the machinery of justice.
26. Under Damasus a local synod of bishops had condemned various bishops for schismatic activities.
27. *Concilium* in concrete sense is, of course, a council, but *consilium* in abstract sense is the counsel given by a *concilium*. But manuscripts and editions often confuse these words, whose meanings also not seldom are interchanged. While *concilium* is the textual reading here, *consilium* (which one manuscript shows) is not impossible.
28. Presumably bishops also.
29. It is uncertain whether Gratian's rescript really enlarged the papal jurisdiction beyond what Valentinian I had conferred or merely defined in clearer terms its boundaries. The result, however, seems to have been the same.
30. The chief bishop in a civil province was the prelate who presided over the church in the capital (metropolis) of that province (hence "metropolitan") and who early acquired ecclesiastical jurisdiction over that province.
31. That is, the bishop of a diocese in the province of a metropolitan should be tried by his metropolitan.
32. Reading *dilatione* for *relatione*, which seems to be an error. *PL* has the former and the apparatus in *CSEL* shows no variant.
33. Literally "renewed". That is, the old evidence leading to the verdict should not be reheard, but it would be in order to present such evidence as supports the claim against judicial unfairness or partiality and, perhaps, new evidence bearing on the previous conviction.
34. Interpreting *levibus causae dictionibus* as an illustration of a transferred epithet and as equivalent to *levium causarum dictionibus*.
35. On calumny see no. 334, n. 3.
36. That the emperor, so propitious toward the pope, should be silent about the first part of the petition has led commentators to suspect that the rescript is incomplete.

165. MANDATE OF GRATIAN, VALENTINIAN II, AND THEODOSIUS I ON CLERICAL EXEMPTION FROM TAXATION, 379

(CT 13. 1. 11)

This constitution allows clergymen engaged in business in certain districts of the West exemption from the lustral tax.[1]

Emperors Gratian, Valentinian, and Theodosius Augusti to Hesperius, praetorian prefect.[2]

Although the paying of the lustral gold has in view all merchants, nevertheless clergymen within Illyricum and Italy should practise the exercise of their manner of life immune in ten solidi [3] each, within the Gauls [4] in fifteen each.[5] But whatever of business will be engaged above this limit [6] ought to be brought to the payment of the tax in gold.

Given on 5 July [7] at Aquileia, Auxonius [8] and Olybrius being consuls.

1. See no. 97, n. 1.
2. Of Italy.
3. On the value of a solidus see no. 433, n. 7.
4. See no. 203, n. 4.
5. No accepted reason for the disparity is known.
6. Perhaps, if not capital is meant, whatever profits are made beyond these amounts are assessed for tax.
7. An alternative date is 2 July.
8. More properly Ausonius, the Gallo-Roman poet and public official.

166. MANDATE OF GRATIAN, VALENTINIAN II, AND THEODOSIUS I ON PROHIBITION OF HERESIES, 379

(CT 16. 5. 5)

It is supposed that Gratian, the real author of this statute, possibly was influenced by St Ambrose, bishop of Milan, to issue this ordinance, which repeals a recent rescript [1] allowing some measure of toleration of heresy.

The first ten Latin words of this statute are repeated by CI 1. 5. 2, which combines these with part of CT 16. 5. 24 (no. 248).

166. PROHIBITION OF HERESIES, 379

Emperors Gratian, Valentinian, and Theodosius Augusti to Hesperius, praetorian prefect.[2]

All heresies, prohibited by both divine and imperial laws, should cease forever.

Whatever profane person by a punishable attempt impairs belief in God [3] should know such noxious matters only for himself, but should not disclose such matters harmful to others.

Whatever person by a renewed death corrupts bodies redeemed by venerable baptism, by destroying that which he repeats,[4] alone should know such things for himself, but should not ruin others by nefarious instruction.

Both all teachers and likewise ministers of this perverse superstition—whether they disgrace the name of bishops by assuming the episcopate or (what is the next step) they counterfeit religion by the designation of priests or they also call themselves deacons, although, indeed, they should not be considered Christians—these persons should abstain from the meeting-places of a doctrine already condemned.

Finally, since the rescript,[1] which at Sirmium recently was issued, has been annulled, only those statutes concerning Catholic observance, which our father [5] of eternal memory and we [6] ourselves by an equally manifold ordinance have commanded shall endure forever, should continue.[7]

Given on 3 August at Milan. Accepted on 20 August, Auxonius[8] and Olybrius being consuls.

1. Not extant, but perhaps Sozomen (*HE* 7. 1) refers to it when he says that Gratian enacted a law permitting all save Manichaeans and Photinians and Eunomians the exercise of their own religion and the right of assembly for worship. Cf. also Socrates, *HE* 5. 2.
2. Of Italy.
3. Or perhaps "the opinion or the concept about God".
4. The *renewed death* is the result of heretical teaching, which kills the soul's chance for salvation, that rebaptism—traditionally a never-repeated sacrament—is necessary under certain conditions. Some heretical (e.g. Eunomian in the East) and schismatical (e.g. Donatist in the West) sects insisted on rebaptizing their converts from the orthodox ranks. The association of baptism with death also ascends to the Pauline doctrine that converts "baptized into Christ Jesus were baptized into his death . . . that like as Christ was raised from the dead . . . so we also might walk in newness of life" (Rom. 6. 3–4).
5. Valentinian I. Probably nos. 137, 138, 140–3, 152, 153, 156, 158 are meant.
6. Reference may be to nos. 160 and 163.
7. Pitra prints (2. 600) a late Greek paraphrase of the law: "All heresies, prohibited by laws and by constitutions, should cease forever and none should teach or should learn profanities.

"Neither a bishop of heretics nor a minister, not having ordination, should ordain—not even pursuant to the magistrates' judgement.

"Everyone is a heretic who even by a little indication has appeared to have been turned against the Catholic Church's or reason's dogma."

8. See no. 165, n. 8.

167. EDICT OF GRATIAN, VALENTINIAN II, AND THEODOSIUS I ON ESTABLISHMENT OF THE CATHOLIC RELIGION, 380

(*CT* 16. 1. 2)

This famous edict (*Cunctos populos*), addressed to Constantinopolitans and published by Theodosius the Great soon after his baptism, in ancient Christian history stands second only to the Edict of Milan (no. 12), for, while the latter recognizes Christianity, the former makes Catholic Christianity the religion of the State. By this constitution (repeated in *CI* 1. 1. 1, where it significantly starts Justinian's Code, and given also by Cassiodorus, *HE* 9. 7. 2-5, and summarized by Sozomen, *HE* 7. 4 *ad fin.*) the Church in the Empire legally became the Church of the Empire.

Another of this edict's effects also became evident as time elapsed. Henceforth revolt against the Church, which regulates the relation between God and man, caused heretics and schismatics to be considered both as a menace to the Empire and as rebels against the State. Subsequently such sectaries saw themselves increasingly subject to civil disabilities in respect to status and rights of property, of testation, of assembly and liable to fines and exile and even death. The motive to such action against heretical and schismatical sects and their propaganda should be sought not so much in the emperors' efforts to conserve a Catholic Christian conscience in their subjects as in the sovereigns' profession that their sovereignty depends for divine protection upon their close connection with a divinely constituted Church and that therefore revolt from "the household of faith" (Gal. 6. 10) should be regarded and must be handled as a form of rebellion against the State. Thus the Church became a beneficiary of the Empire, when the equation of ecclesiastical allegiance and imperial citizenship was established by this epoch-making edict.

On the other hand, it may be held that Theodosius' interest in theological uniformity may have been inspired merely by his imperial passion for political unity. For the East, whence this edict was issued and whither it was intended, was "carried about with every wind of doctrine" (Eph. 4. 14) into far more disunion than was the West, into which heresies might enter from elsewhere, even as "long ago the Syrian Orontes flowed into the Tiber" (Juvenal, *Sat.* 1. 3. 62), but from which heresies hardly, if ever, emanated. What simpler solution could the emperor have sought than to discover in St Damasus—the episcopal successor of St Peter, to whom the Saviour had said "But I have prayed for thee, that thy faith fail not: and when thou art converted, strengthen thy brethren" (Luke 22. 32; cf. John 21. 15-17), and commonly considered the most eminent exponent of "the faith which was once delivered unto the saints" (Jude 3)—that contemporary centre wherein Christians could compose their differences of doctrine and thus should perfect their Saviour's prayer "that they may be one" (John 17. 20-2, cf. 10. 11-16)? Two centuries of precedent may have persuaded Theodosius, for it was two hundred years previously that, perhaps for the first time, St Irenaeus, an Asiatic bishop of a Gallic see, had insisted that "with this church because of its more powerful authority it is necessary for the entire Church, that is, those who are the faithful everywhere, to agree; wherein that tradition, which is from the apostles, has been preserved always by these [faithful persons] who are everywhere" (*Adv. Haer.* 3. 3. 2 *ad fin.*). Adherence to the truth as attested by "the church of God sojourning in Rome" (Clement, *1 Cor.* pr.) was the most practicable test to avoid the twin pitfalls of heresy and schism and the most hopeful sign for peace in an empire still divided by ecclesiastical disputes.

Emperors Gratian, Valentinian, and Theodosius Augusti.
Edict [1] to the people of the Constantinopolitan city.
All peoples, whom the moderation of our Clemency rules, we wish to be engaged in that religion, which the divine Peter,[2] the apostle, is declared—by the religion which has descended even to the present from him—to have transmitted to the Romans and which, it is clear the pontiff Damasus [3] and Peter,[4] bishop of Alexandria, a man of apostolic sanctity, follow: this is, that according to apostolic discipline and evangelic doctrine [5] we should believe the sole Deity of the Father and of the Son and of the Holy Spirit under an equal Majesty [6] and under a pious Trinity.[7]

We order those following this law [8] to assume the name of Catholic Christians,[9] but the rest, since we judge them demented and insane, to sustain the infamy of heretical dogma [10] and their conventicles not to take the name of churches,[10] to be smitten first by divine vengeance, then also by the punishment of our authority,[11] which we have claimed in accordance with the celestial will.

Given on 28 February at Thessalonica, Gratian Augustus for the fifth time and Theodosius Augustus for the first time being consuls.

1. Cassiodorus omits this word and earlier calls it a law (*lex*).
2. Traditionally bishop of Rome for 25 years (?42–?67) after having been bishop of Antioch in Syria, though the New Testament, admitting Peter's appearance in Antioch (Gal. 2. 11), nowhere tells that Peter ever resided in

167. ESTABLISHMENT OF CATHOLIC RELIGION, 380

Rome and never creates him the bishop of either city. The written tradition of Peter's episcopate in Antioch and in Rome ascends respectively to the second and the third centuries.

On the recent search for his sepulchre in Rome consult J. M. C. Toynbee and J. W. Perkins, *The Shrine of St. Peter and the Vatican Excavations* (London, 1957); M. Guarducci, *The Tomb of St. Peter* (New York, 1960). See also nos. 140, n. 1 *ad fin.*, and 442, n. 7.

On the other hand, we have true testimony (Acts 28. 16–31) to St Paul's residence in Rome and teaching there for at least two years (?60–?62), we have his Epistle to the Romans and his Galatians, Ephesians, Philippians, Colossians, 2 Timothy, Philemon purportedly written from Rome, and we have the common opinion that he was martyred in Rome on the same day and in the same year as St Peter suffered and that he too was buried there. These and other considerations—such as, e.g., his claim to be "the apostle of the Gentiles" (Rom. 11. 13; cf. Acts 9. 15, 21. 19, 22. 21; Rom. 15. 16; Gal. 2. 2; Eph. 3. 8; 1 Tim. 2. 7; 2 Tim. 1. 11)—might have tempted Theodosius to put St Paul's name beside that of St Peter here as a joint-founder of the Church in Rome, for the memory of these two apostles had been celebrated annually on 29 June in Rome from 258 onward.

3. Pope St Damasus I, bishop of Rome (366–84). It may be a tribute to the pope that the emperor has no need to characterize him to the Constantinopolitans, as he apparently must do immediately in the case of the Alexandrian patriarch.

4. Peter II, patriarch of Alexandria (373–81).

5. Tertullian teaches that such discipline (*disciplina*) and doctrine (*doctrina*) are apostolic only when these descend from the apostles, who received the faith from God through Christ and/or the Holy Spirit, and through apostolic churches, which they established (*De Praes. Haer.* 6, 8, 20-2, 32, 36 in *CSEL* 70).

The Church's apostolicity is attested by the circumstance that it is built upon the foundation of the apostles (Matt. 16. 18; Eph. 2. 19–22; Rev. 21. 14), from whose preaching is derived its faith (e.g. John 17. 6–26, esp. 20).

6. The notion of equality perhaps is derived from John 5. 18 and Phil. 2. 6 (cf. John 1. 1–2, 10. 33; Heb. 1. 1–5).

7. In making communion with the bishops of these cities the test of orthodoxy Theodosius recognized the fact that, though all bishops equally were successors of the apostles and belonged to the same order and shared the same power (as St Jerome, his contemporary, so eloquently expressed it [*Ep.* 146, 1. 7 = *CSEL* 56. 310–11]), yet bishops of the more important cities held privileged positions within the hierarchy (see also no. 182).

8. Christianity.

9. The earlier use of the word *Catholic* meant simply "universal", as first used by St Ignatius early in the second century (*Ad Smyrn.* 8. 2). But by Theodosius' time St Cyril of Jerusalem, his contemporary, not only insisted on the Ignatian conception of calling the Church Catholic because of its extension

throughout all the world, but also considered it Catholic because, among other functions, "it teaches universally and unfailingly all the doctrines which ought to come to men's knowledge" (*Cat.* 18. 23 = *PG* 33. 1043). In the later sense, then, Theodosius could deny the appellation "Catholic" to heretics, who in the emperor's estimation of their dementia and insanity inculcated theological tenets not consonant with the Cyrillic test of suitability for inclusion in the corpus of instruction.

10. *CI* and Cassiodorus omit the words between these numbers and Sozomen does not reproduce their sense.

11. Protection of the Church by imposition of her unity upon its subjects thus becomes the mission of the State, though Theodosius conveniently forgets that Tertullian taught that "it is not the function of religion to compel religion" (*Ad Scap.* 2 *ad init.* = *PL* 1. 777)—a thought to which later Lactantius perhaps looked in pronouncing that "religion cannot be compelled" (*Inst. Div.* 5. 19. 11 = *CSEL* 19. 463). See no. 173, n. 11 for imperial implementation.

To divine vengeance and imperial punishment is added ecclesiastical censure, which is expressed in *CA* 8. 47. 45, 46, 62, 64.

168. EDICT OF GRATIAN, VALENTINIAN II, AND THEODOSIUS I ON SACRILEGE, 380

(*CT* 16. 2. 25)

In this constitution (repeated in *CI* 9. 29. 1) the emperors enact that violation of divine law is tantamount to sacrilege, thus showing that in their general programme to establish religious unity in the Empire political expediency was outweighed by their religious conviction.

Emperors Gratian, Valentinian, and Theodosius Augusti.

Whoever either by ignorance confuse or by negligence violate and offend the divine law's [1] sanctity commit sacrilege.

Given on 28 February at Thessalonica, Gratian Augustus for the fifth time and Theodosius Augustus for the first time being consuls.

1. While this phrase (*divina lex*) is considered usually to refer to the Christian religion, while it is interpreted thus here, and while the conception of sacrilege properly should pertain to things sacred or religious or sanctioned (on which see no. 641, nn. 2 and 3), yet the use of the phrase here may be simply an example of the Dominate's extension of the idea of sacrilege to include violation of imperial constitutions, for everything associated with the emperor was considered divine and sacred and an act against his person was classed as sacrilege (no. 145).

168. SACRILEGE, 380

Thus, earlier than this edict it was sacrilegious for a judge to disregard regulations about appeal to the emperor (*CT* 11. 30. 6 = *CI* 1. 21. 2 [dated 316] and *CT* 11. 29. 5 [dated 374]) as well as for anyone to disregard statutes conferring privileges upon painters (*CT* 13. 4. 4; dated 374). And later than this edict the violation of a general decree entailed sacrilege (*CT* 6. 35. 13 = *CI* 12. 28. 4; dated 386). Akin to this statute are no. 308 (dated 408), which calls it sacrilege to resist imperial legislation; *CT* 7. 4. 30 = *CI* 12. 37. 13 (dated 409), which declares disobedience to divine statutes sacrilegious; no. 344 (dated 415), which punishes violators of imperial regulations as though guilty of sacrilege; no. 433 (dated 439), which condemns as sacrilegious a contemner of that constitution; constitution *Quantum* (issued by Valentinian III in 443 and usually prefixed to *CT*), which imposes the penalty of sacrilege on persons not obeying imperial laws; *LNV* 27 (dated 449), which accuses of sacrilegious audacity any violator of its provisions.

But the notion of sacrilege was extended beyond the above examples to embrace administrative matters. From the Codes may be chosen the following illustrations. Since coinage was under imperial control, in 348 or 352 or 356 a law (*CT* 9. 23. 1)—descending from the responses of the jurisconsult Papinian (on whom see no. 641, n. 13 *ad init.*)—sentenced for sacrilege and to capital punishment a melter of money and a transporter of money to different regions for the purpose of selling; so also in 381 a counterfeiter was sacrilegious (no. 180). In 382 it was the greatest sacrilege to petition for possessions of such value and of such extent as were more suitable for palaces than for landed estates (*CT* 10. 10. 16). In 383 it was sacrilegious for announcers and messengers of imperial announcements to accept fees (*CT* 8. 11. 4 = *CI* 12. 63. 1). In 384 usurpation of undue rank was sacrilege, because the usurper had ignored the divine commands (*CT* 6. 5. 2 = *CI* 12. 8. 1). In 385 it was a kind of sacrilege (*sacrilegii instar*) to dispute an emperor's delegation of authority (*CT* 1. 6. 9 = *CI* 9. 29. 2) and two years later it was almost like sacrilege (*paene sacrilegii simile*) not to honour a praetorian prefect's vicars (*CT* 6. 24. 4 = *CI* 12. 17. 1), who, of course, were imperial appointees. Associated with the last two laws is the declaration of 385 that unauthorized administration in a province is sacrilegious (*CI* 9. 29. 3). In 390 it was considered a sacrilege to erect a public work in Rome at public expense without the emperor's knowledge (*CT* 15. 1. 27). In 405 it was sacrilegious to petition the emperor for landholdings (*CT* 10. 10. 24). In 412 provosts of the public post who had violated discipline were guilty of sacrilege (*CT* 6. 29. 9). In 413 quartering officers who had tried to prepare quarters on public or private estates in Africa were sacrilegious (*CT* 7. 8. 10 = *CI* 12. 40. 5). In 415 it was sacrilege for municipal senates to exact taxes from provincials whose taxes had been remitted (*CT* 11. 28. 10). In 439 it was sacrilegious for a judge to waive prescription of time for petition to acquire ownerless property (*LNT* 17. 1). In 440 it was sacrilege for palatines (see no. 186, n. 3) to concoct fictitious tax accounts (*LNV* 7. 1).

Among miscellaneous matters it may be noted that in 339 adulterers were declared sacrilegious and were condemned to death (CT 11. 36. 4 = CI 9. 9. 29) and that in 439 it was sacrilegious for one to prostitute one's own or another's slaves or one's free-born employees (LNT 18. 1).

But as may be expected, the crime of sacrilege chiefly concerns religion: for example, in this sylloge several sects of heretics and of schismatics are assailed as sacrilegious (e.g. nos. 29, 173, 176, 179, 190, 232, 283, 289, 298, 299, 329, 330, 389, 440). Apostasy from Christianity (e.g. nos. 209 and 391), paganism (e.g. nos. 190 and 301), Judaism (e.g. nos. 91, 190, 303) are sacrilegious. To rout refugees from sanctuaries is sacrilegious (e.g. nos. 370 and 400). To violate tombs is sacrilege (e.g. no. 443; see also nos. 119, n. 1 *ad init.* [for CT 9. 17. 5 = CI 9. 19. 5 (dated 363), which, issued by Julian the Apostate, perhaps concerned Christians not more closely than it pertained to pagans], 139, 641, n. 17). Amnesty is withheld from sacrilegious persons (e.g. nos. 198 and 201). To commit outrage against the Church's buildings or ministers is as sacrilegious (e.g. no. 310) as to impugn the Church's privileges (e.g. nos. 318 and 387). A sacrilegious person is one who indulges in forbidden sacrifices with a view to foretelling the future (CT 16. 10. 7; dated 381). A judge (or perhaps a provincial governor: see no. 161, n. 3) is a sacrilegious violator of law if he enters polluted pagan temples (CT 16. 10. 11; dated 391).

From the Digest's doctrine—originally applicable to paganism—on sacrilege may be selected the following statements originating *c.* 130–*c.* 228. Heirs may not divide whatever will have been acquired from sacrilege (10. 2. 4. 2). A stipulation to commit sacrilege is invalid and on such an obligation no action at law is allowed (45. 1. 27). Treason is a crime nearest to sacrilege (48. 4. 1. pr.). A provincial governor should search for sacrilegious persons (1. 18. 13. pr. and 48. 13. 4. 2) and will be bound to decide the punishment for sacrilege more severely or more leniently in view of the person's quality and in view of the condition of the circumstance and of the time and of the age and of the sex (48. 13. 7). Sacrilegious persons are those who have plundered public sacred property, but persons who have made attempts on private sacred property or unguarded shrines are punished more than thieves and less than sacrilegious persons (48. 13. 11. 1). Punishments for sacrilege include condemnation to animals at amphitheatrical spectacles, cremation alive, hanging. The first penalty concerns persons who have broken into temples and have taken a god's gifts at night; but if a theft from a temple has been trifling, the penalty is condemnation to mines or, if the person is of noble birth, insular deportation (48. 13. 7). Another penalty is capital (48. 13. 11. 1).

The Digest reports a rather clever case of sacrilege and gives the penalty of insular deportation for the convicted criminal (48. 13. 12. 1): between 198 and 211 a certain most distinguished youth had put a man into a small chest (*arcula*) and then placed it in a temple; after the temple had been shut [presumably at eventide], the man emerged from the chest (*arca*), removed many objects from the temple, and re-entered the small chest (*arcula*). [It does not appear when the loss was discovered: whether the chest was searched in the

169. SUSPENSION OF CRIMINAL CASES, 380   359

temple or was withdrawn from the precincts before confession of the crime.]

Perhaps the subject of sacrilege can be summarized philosophically by Seneca's statement that "sacrilegious persons suffer penalties, although no one's hands actually can reach the deities" (*De Ben.* 5. 14. 2).

Theologians customarily consider three sorts of sacrilege: personal, local, real. Personal sacrilege includes imposition of violent hands upon a cleric, violation of ecclesiastical immunity, sin against the vow of chastity by persons consecrated to God. Local sacrilege is the violation of a sacred place, such as theft of something from it, infringement of the place's immunity, commission of some sinful act in it, perpetration of certain things (whether or not sins) particularly incompatible with the conduct expected proper in it. Real sacrilege is irreverent treatment of sacred things as distinguished from persons and places.

169. MANDATE OF GRATIAN, VALENTINIAN II, AND THEODOSIUS I ON SUSPENSION OF CRIMINAL CASES DURING LENT, 380

(*CT* 9. 35. 4)

By this ordinance, which Justinian also preserves (*CI* 3. 12. 5), trial of criminal cases is suspended during Lent.

Emperors Gratian, Valentinian, and Theodosius Augusti to Albucian, vicar of Macedonia.

During the forty days which anticipate the paschal time by the beginning of ceremonies,[1] all trial of criminal inquisitions should be prevented.[2]

Given on 27 March at Thessalonica, Gratian Augustus for the fifth time and Theodosius Augustus for the first time being consuls.

Interpretation: During the days of Quadragesima[3] in view of reverence for religion all criminal action should cease.

1. By this is meant penitential rites introducing continence and fasting for the Lenten season.

2. Probably because torture often was applied in such cases to extort what was believed to be the truth. If so, the emperors apparently were averse from making the penitential season of Lent more doleful by its use, on which see no. 204, n. 3.

3. In late Latin this may mean either the forty days of Lent (as in the law above), which is in English an obsolete usage, or Quadragesima Sunday, which is the first Sunday in Lent.

360   170. EXEMPTION OF CHRISTIAN ACTRESSES, 380

By the time (325) of the Council of Nicaea (canon 5) most of Christendom had adopted a Lenten fast (a disciplined preparation for Easter) of six weeks—roughly forty days—commemorating Jesus' forty-day withdrawal into the wilderness (Matt. 4. 1-2; Mark 1. 12-13; Luke 4. 1-2). But since Sundays are never fast days, a six-week Lent allows only 36 days of fasting. So eventually—but not before the seventh century, it seems—an exact 40-day period was perfected by prefixing to the season four days starting with Ash Wednesday (*Dies Cinerum*) before the first Sunday of Lent (*Quadragesima*).

170. MANDATE OF GRATIAN, VALENTINIAN II, AND THEODOSIUS I ON EXEMPTION OF CHRISTIAN ACTRESSES FROM THE THEATRE, 380

(*CT* 15. 7. 4)

In a series of legislative acts about the stage this law frees actresses from compulsory return to their theatrical vocation, if they have become Christians.

This statute is repeated almost verbatim as no. 183.

Emperors Gratian, Valentinian, and Theodosius Augusti to Paulinus, urban prefect.[1]

If women who, born from the lower class, are obligated to the services of the spectacles shall have shunned their theatrical duties, they should be assigned to dramatic services, if not yet, however, contemplation of the most sacred religion and reverence for the Christian law [2] have bound them to its faith, for we forbid these women, whom a better way of living has extricated from the bond of their natural condition, to be recalled.

We also command that those women, who have deserved by our Gentleness' favour to be free from a rather base public service, should remain free from the association [3] of prejudice connected with the theatre.

Given on 24 April at Milan, Gratian Augustus for the fifth time and Theodosius Augustus for the first time being consuls.

1. Of Rome.
2. Religion.
3. The word is *contubernium*, which means either a marital union between slaves or a master's habitual cohabitation with his female slave. Neither con-

nection was legal, but each was both tolerated and not uncommon. The emperors seem to envisage the abovementioned *bond of their natural condition* in the light of such a servile situation.

171. LETTER OF VALENTINIAN II, THEODOSIUS I, AND ARCADIUS ON AMNESTY FOR PRISONERS AT EASTERTIDE, 380 or 381

(CS 7)

The season of Easter occasions the following grant of imperial clemency for such incarcerated criminals as have not committed any of five capital crimes.[1]

Emperors Valentinian, Theodosius, and Arcadius Augusti to Eutropius, praetorian prefect.[2]

Moved by Almighty God's will, in view of the happiness of the age we proclaim placid benefits of leniency, that the favour of unhoped compassion may lead those persons whom terror of imminent punishment disturbs, after they have been restored to lasting security, to the joys of common life (which had been removed by the severity of their crimes), that they, when flooded by the light of new restoration, may possess the newness of a better life.

Finally, therefore, in view of the paschal feast, which we venerate with general and very high profession, we release criminals, that those whom our Gentleness' indulgence shall have liberated, when following the precepts of a better mode of life, may not dare to perpetuate anything dangerous, dearest and fondest cousin Eutropius.

Wherefore your Sublimity[3] should restore, with the exception of those whom the heinousness of five crimes[1] does not at all allow to be loosed, all others, freed from the custody of jail, to their former status, that they, delivered to common freedom, may enjoy the grace of granted security.

1. As early as 353 Constantius II created a category of five crimes entailing capital punishment, but neither proclaimed what crimes it contained nor prefaced it with a Christian colour (*CT* 9. 38. 2). Six later laws (nos. 135, 145, 180, 198, 201, 207) give *in toto* as many as thirteen crimes not subject to imperial pardon: treason, crimes against the dead, sorcery (poison), magic, astrology, sacrilege, seduction, incest, rape, adultery, counterfeiting, homicide, parricide. Of these crimes four appear in six constitutions: treason, sorcery (poison), adultery, homicide. The fifth may be either magic or rape, each of which occurs in five constitutions. The dates of the laws range from 367 (369) to 386.

2. Since the constitutions sent to Eutropius while praetorian prefect of the East belong to 380-1, the superscription should be emended by prefixing Gratian's name and by omitting that of Arcadius, for the former was still sovereign and the latter had not yet been created Augustus.

3. Editors supply this sentence's first three words, which seem to have fallen from the text.

172. MANDATE OF GRATIAN ON CONVOCATION OF THE AQUILEIAN COUNCIL, 380 or 381

(PL 16. 916-7)

In this mandate Gratian summons Italian and Illyrian bishops to assemble at Aquileia to decide whether two Arian bishops, Palladius of Ratiara (now Aržer Palanka in Bulgaria) and Secundian of Singidunum (now Belgrade in Yugoslavia), should retain their sees, from which their orthodox opponents were trying to oust them.

As early as 378 the emperor had granted these Danubian bishops' petition for a general council, wherein they were confident of eastern support to keep them in their sees. But St Ambrose, bishop of Milan, whose influence upon Gratian was immense, persuaded the emperor—who meanwhile had postponed convocation of the council—late in 380 or early in 381, that the issue was not sufficiently important for bishops to be summoned from the entire Empire and that the decision about the petitioners' right to remain in their bishoprics could be delegated to a smaller synod attended by prelates from the Italian prefecture. Accordingly 32 bishops, mostly from Italy, in 381 appeared at Aquileia under the presidency of St Valerian, that city's bishop, heard Palladius' and Tecundian's defence, and condemned them.

This council, cementing the conquest of Catholicism over Arianism in the West,[1] was dominated by St Ambrose, among whose *Epistulae* is preserved the imperial summons, apparently addressed to the praetorian prefect of Italy.[2]

Desiring[3] to try as soon as possible lest bishops[4] should dissent on account of ambiguous reverence for dogmas, we had ordered[5] bishops to convene in the Aquileians' city from the diocese entrusted to your Excellency's merits.[6] For controversies of dubious meaning could not be disentangled[7] more properly than if we had constituted the bishops themselves interpreters[8] of the arisen altercation, that obviously by the same persons, from whom proceed instructions of doctrine, discordant teaching's contradiction might be solved.[9]

Nor, to be sure, we now order otherwise than we have ordered,[5] not inverting the command's tenor, but considering the conveners' superfluous number. For because Ambrose, bishop of the city of the Milanese, conspicuous both for merit of life and for God's favour, suggests that there is not need for a multitude there where truth would not suffer in more persons, if it should have been placed in few persons,[10] and suggests that he and bishops [4] from the neighbouring cities of Italy can suffice satisfactorily and abundantly for the assertions of those who stand on the opposite side, we [11] have decided that we must refrain from wearying venerable men,[12] lest anyone either burdened by advanced age or weakened by bodily debility or slenderly circumstanced by laudable poverty should seek strange lands.[13]

And the rest.[14]

1. For an account of the council consult F. H. Dudden, *The Life and Times of St Ambrose* (Oxford, 1935), 1. 199–206.

2. The mandate lacks superscription (but cf. *infra* n. 3) and subscription, but probably was sent to this prefect, who implemented the imperial summons by issuing invitatory letters to bishops (*PL* 16. 918).

3. Migne reports that the earlier Roman edition prefaces "Gratian, Valentinian, and Theodosius . . . Emperors . . ." to the constitution, which he calls a rescript.

4. The word is *sacerdos*, on which see no. 16, n. 4.

5. This previous mandate has not survived. If issued, it probably was cancelled by Ambrose's intervention.

6. While a vicar headed a civil diocese, yet several dioceses composed a prefecture. Therefore a praetorian prefect could be considered as having a diocese under his care. Cf. *supra* n. 2 and see no. 76, n. 5.

7. A variant "manifested" is reported.

8. The Roman edition has the phrase "for the judgement" for this word.

9. The Latin's triple chiasmus is kept in the English translation.

10. The sense is that a small synod would suffice to decide the dispute without prejudice to the truth more conveniently than a large council.

11. The Roman edition inserts "therefore".

12. A variant reading is "that venerable men must refrain from weariness of journey". The bishops, of course, are meant.

13. Thus Gratian neatly excludes eastern prelates.

14. Ambrose omits the rest of the mandate.

173. MANDATE OF GRATIAN, VALENTINIAN II, AND THEODOSIUS I ON HERETICAL ASSEMBLIES AND ON ADHERENCE TO THE NICENE CREED, 381

(*CT* 16. 5. 6)

In this ordinance (republished in *CI* 1. 1. 2) Theodosius the Great forbids meetings of heretics and requires adherence to the faith as defined at the Council of Nicaea (325). This directive is important for three reasons: (1) it contains the phrase, *deum de deo, lumen ex lumine*,[1] made famous later in the year by the Second Ecumenical Council's version of the Nicene Creed; (2) it no longer sets the faith of the bishops of Rome and of Alexandria as the standard of conformity (no. 167), but substitutes the Nicene Creed of eastern origin, probably because the emperor, now in the East, observed that the re-establishment of orthodoxy there could be consummated only by action from the East's own orthodox ranks, whose resentment against Italian and Egyptian interference was intermittent; (3) it marks the virtual extinction of Arianism within the Empire, whence it migrated beyond the boundaries to burgeon among the barbarians.

The same Augusti to Eutropius, praetorian prefect.[2]

To heretics let no place for their mysteries,[3] no opportunity for exercising their rather obstinate mind's madness be allowed. Let all persons also know that it is not valid, if anything by this kind of men has been obtained by means of any special rescript whatever elicited through fraud.

Let crowds be kept at a distance from all heretics' illicit congregations.[4]

Let the name of the One and Highest God be celebrated everywhere; let be maintained the observance, which shall endure forever, of the Nicene faith, transmitted long ago by our ancestors and confirmed by the divine religion's testimony and declaration;[5] let even from our very hearing be abolished the Photinian pest's contamination, the Arian sacrilege's poison, the Eunomian perfidy's crime, and the sects' wicked marvels,[6] unspeakable on account of their authors' monstrous names.

Moreover that man must be accepted as an advocate of the Nicene faith,[7] a true worshipper of the Catholic religion, who confesses Almighty God and Christ, God's Son, under one name, God of God, Light from Light;[1] who does not violate by denial the Holy Spirit, which we expect and accept from the Supreme Author of things; in whom by the perception of undefiled faith is honoured the Uncorrupted Trinity's undivided substance,[8] which by the declaration of [9] a

Greek word is called *ousia* [8] on the part of right believers. These beliefs surely are more acceptable to us; these must be venerated.

But let whoever are not devoted to the said beliefs cease to assume by studied deceits the alien name of true religion and let them be punished for their obvious crimes.[10] Let them be removed and absolutely be debarred from the threshold of all churches, since we forbid all heretics to conduct unlawful gatherings within towns and since, if a factious outburst shall have attempted anything, we command them, when their madness has been exterminated, to be driven from the very walls of cities, that Catholic churches in the whole world may be returned to all orthodox bishops, who hold the Nicene faith.[11]

Given on 10 January at Constantinople, Eucherius and Syagrius being consuls.

1. See no. 569, n. 5.
2. Of the East.
3. See no. 75, n. 42.
4. The idea is either that crowds must be restrained from attending heretical assemblies or even that large numbers of heretics must be prevented from meeting; probably the latter, for in view of the first sentence the emperor does not countenance any heretical gathering at all and it appears absurd then to allow such assemblies but to keep away curiosity-seekers or searchers after novel doctrines.
5. *CI* omits the rest of the paragraph.
6. Literally "prodigies" (*prodigia,* used usually in a bad sense).
7. *CI* inserts "and".
8. *Substantia* . . . οὐσία, on which see no. 67, n. 17.
9. *CI* omits *the . . . of.*
10. Or perhaps "let them be stigmatized, when their crimes have been disclosed". It is not certain that the verb *denotare* cannot mean to make a physical mark, i.e. a brand, upon these unorthodox, for in classical Latin it carries the idea of making a mark with chalk or paint, but even in that period of the language such usage is less common than its figurative sense.
11. Thus, after the imperial establishment of Catholic Christianity as the State's religion (no. 167), appears the earliest in a long list of civil penalties ordained against heretics: extrusion from cities. Presumably, then, the secular power would proceed against persons whom the Church should have pronounced heretical and excommunicated, for hitherto only spiritual penalties attended ecclesiastical excommunication, which had been practised as early as the apostolic age (1 Cor. 5. 1–7; 2 Cor. 2. 5–11; 1 Tim. 1. 19–20 with 2 Tim. 2. 17–18; Titus 3. 10; 2 John 10–11; 3 John 9–10; cf. 1 Cor. 16. 22 and Gal. 1. 8–9, where anathema implies ecclesiastical censure). Exclusion from the congregation ascended at least into Ezra's time (458 B.C.), according to Ezra's

witness (Ezra 10. 8), and was familiar to the evangelists (Matt. 16. 19, 18. 15-18; Luke 6. 22; John 9. 22, 34, 12. 42, 16. 2).

174. MANDATE OF GRATIAN, VALENTINIAN II, AND THEODOSIUS I ON CLERICAL EXEMPTION FROM CAPITATION, 381
(CT 16. 2. 26)

This directive, directed to the count of the Orient, concerns especially clerics in charge of the holy places in Palestine, which was in his jurisdiction, and it releases such persons from liability to pay the capitation tax.

The same Augusti to Tuscian, count of the East.

We ordain that all persons who shall have been proved to be guardians of churches or of holy places and to be devoted to religious services should not undergo the annoyance of any attempt.[1] For who should allow these persons, whom he knows to have been assigned to the aforesaid necessary[2] service, to be bound as assessed on the capitation-tax list?[3]

Given on 31 March at Constantinople, Eucherius and Syagrius being consuls.

1. The Latin word *adtemptatio* (or *attentatio*) is very rare and usually means "attack", "assault", "trial". Here it probably means (in view of what follows) an attempt to compel such persons to pay poll-tax.
2. This adjective is indistinguishable from the adverb and from its position may be read perhaps with the clause's verb.
3. The last ten words are an expansion of *capite censos esse devinctos*, where *capite censi* (rated by the head) is a phrase ascending into republican times and originally denotes propertyless persons entered on the censors' list only as regarding their person (*caput*). See no. 67, n. 37.

175. MANDATE OF GRATIAN, VALENTINIAN II, AND THEODOSIUS I ON APOSTATE CHRISTIANS' WILLS, 381

(*CT* 16. 7. 1)

By this ordinance testamentary rights are taken from Christians who have apostatized.

Emperors Gratian, Valentinian, and Theodosius Augusti to Eutropius, praetorian prefect.[1]

From those who from Christians have become pagans should be taken the power and the right of making a will and every will of such a deceased person, if there is a will, should be rescinded unconditionally.[2]

Given on 2 May at Constantinople, Syagrius and Eucherius being consuls.

1. Of the East.
2. The English adverb represents the Latin phrase *submota conditione* or *summota condicione* (condition having been withdrawn).

176. MANDATE OF GRATIAN, VALENTINIAN II, AND THEODOSIUS I ON TESTAMENTARY RESTRICTIONS FOR MANICHAEANS, 381

(*CT* 16. 5. 7)

The power of taking and of bequeathing legacies is denied to Manichaeans by this directive, which goes so far as to make this denial retroactive.

The same Augusti to Eutropius, praetorian prefect.[1]

If any Manichaean—man or woman—from the day of the law enacted long ago and originally by our parents [2] has transmitted his own property to any person whatsoever by having made a will or under title of any liberality whatsoever or by form of donation, or if anyone of these persons has been enriched by grant of an inheritance entered through any form whatsoever (since immediately from the said persons, under branded [3] infamy's perpetual stigma, we withdraw all capability of making a will and of living under Roman law, and since we do not permit them to have the power either of leaving or of taking any inheritance), the whole[4] by an immediate investigation on the part of our fisc, should be joined to its resources. Whether by illicit liberality this property shall have come to a husband or to a relative or to anyone whatsoever who well has deserved it or even to children, whom indeed the villainies of the same criminal life [5] shall unite, or even if through any intermediate person whatsoever it shall profit the said person who is found to be of such a class and a company of persons,[6] it [4] should be claimed under the title of vacancy.[7]

The rule of this law issued by our Gentleness should prevail not only for the future but also for the past;[8] whatever either such persons as owners [9] have bequeathed or as heirs [9] have held, the fisc's acquisition of the advantage should ensue. For, although the orderly arrangement of celestial [10] statutes indicates observance of a sacred [10] constitution in respect to matters about to follow afterward and has not been wont to be prejudicial to completed matters, nevertheless in this ordinance only, which we wish to be specially vigorous, by a sense of just instigation we recognize what a habit of obstinacy and a persistent nature deserve [11] and we regard as guilty of sacrilege on the ground of violation of this described law [12] those persons who, even after the law originally had been issued, have not at all been able to be restrained at least by divine [10] admonishment from illicit and profane assemblies. We sanction the present statutes' severity not so much as an example of a law to be established but as of a law to be vindicated, so that a defence of time cannot also profit them.[13]

The inheritance of paternal or maternal property should be conferred only on those children who, though born from Manichaeans, yet shall have withdrawn themselves from associations of the said life and profession, because they have been admonished by a sense of and a desire for their own salvation, have dedicated themselves in respect to pure religion, and are immune from such a crime.

To this ordinance we add also the following: that they should establish neither in conventicles of towns [14] nor in famous cities their wonted sepulchres of funereal mysteries;[15] they should be restrained completely from sight in a crowded community.

Nor with malignant fraud they should defend themselves under pretence of those fallacious [16] names, by which many, as we have discovered, desire to be called and to be designated as of approved faith and of rather chaste course of life; especially since some of these persons desire themselves to be denominated Encratitans, Apotactitans, Hydroparastatans, or Saccophorians and by a variety of diverse names falsify—as it were—the services of their religious profession. For it is proper that all these persons should not be protected by a profession of names, but should be held notorious and execrable by the criminality of their sects.

176. RESTRICTIONS FOR MANICHAEANS, 381

Given on 8 May at Constantinople, Eucherius and Syagrius being consuls.

1. Of the East.
2. Apparently this is the law issued only nine years earlier (2 March 372), for that seems to be the oldest law on Manichaeans in the Code (no. 156).
3. It is not believed that any physical brand is to be imposed on the violator; rather it seems to be an emphatic synonym for "deserved".
4. The property.
5. A hendiadys: "of the same life and crime" as the owner who has bequeathed or has bestowed the property.
6. Manichaeans.
7. In Roman law, as elsewhere, heirless property (*caducum*—the word here) passed to the State.
8. An example of a retroactive law, foreign to the general spirit of Roman jurisprudence and quite contrary to *CT* 1. 1. 3 (dated 393), which forbids any prosecution for past deeds and declares that all constitutions establish regulations for the future. But *CT* exhibits at least eight other examples of violation of this principle, of which one (no. 218) affects Christian heretics.
9. The Latin has abstract for concrete, "ownership . . . heirship", with verbs in the singular number—an instance of antimeria.
10. In this case pertaining not to God, but to the emperor.
11. Here he refers, of course, to the contumacious Manichaeans, who persist in their beliefs.
12. Cf. *supra* n. 2.
13. That is, Manichaean defendants cannot plead that the enactment is not retrospective or that the lapse of time has barred legal action. See no. 65, n. 6.
14. The phrase *conventicula oppidorum* is uncommon and what is meant is unclear. Perhaps merely meeting-places are meant.
15. While the language sounds as if the emperors are banning Manichaean cemeteries, it is believed that they merely mean that the sacraments (see no. 75, n. 42) which the Manichaeans celebrate have a deadly effect upon the partakers and transform the places of such celebration into what usually can be called tombs. Evidently the emperors have strong opinions on the subject or else the orthodox secretaries who drafted the directive are touched with *odium theologicum*, as often may be observed in the laws legislating about heretics.
16. This seems to be a transferred epithet (*antiptosis proleptica*): grammatically it goes with *pretence*, where it is unnecessary, for the pretence is always deceptive, but logically it belongs with *names*, for the names deceive the ignorant.

177. MANDATE OF GRATIAN, VALENTINIAN II, AND THEODOSIUS I ON RETURN OF APOSTATE ACTRESSES TO THE THEATRE, 381

(CT 15. 7. 8)

The emperors, while permitting a Christian actress release from her profession on religious reasons, yet require her return on proof of her continued unchastity and of her betrayal of religion.

This law's cold and cruel language shows contempt for a class which society plunged into vice and punished for being vicious.[1]

The same Augusti to Valerian, urban prefect.[2]

If a woman of the stage shall have requested release in religion's name, the favour indeed should not be denied to her on proffer of petition.

But if, involved in shameful embraces afterward, she is discovered both to have betrayed the religion which she shall have sought and to continue in the vocation which she had abandoned, by being, however, an actress in spirit, she, when retracted to the stage, should remain there continuously without any hope of absolution, until a ridiculous old woman, ugly through old age, she not even then can acquire absolution, although she cannot be anything else than chaste.[3]

Given on 8 May at Aquileia, Syagrius and Eucherius being consuls.

1. In contrast to this contempt is the concern exhibited thirteen years later by the emperors, who then displayed more interest in actresses' dresses than in their morals (no. 247).
2. Of Rome.
3. Whoever wrote this concessive clause appears to have been unaware that late chastity not always coincides with anility or even with senility. When he assumes that so-called normal sexual activity can afford neither rejoicing nor revenue for the aged and that persons of advanced age perforce must be passionately abstinent, the sovereign or his scribe indicates his ignorance of *psychopathia sexualis*, which even in antiquity—as evidence evinces—attracted elderly practitioners, who scarcely even in a Pickwickian sense could be called chaste.